Dictionary of Literary Biography

Dictionary of Literary Biography Documentary Series

Dictionary of Literary Biography Yearbooks

1980 edited by Karen L. Rood, Jean W. Ross, and Richard Ziegfeld (1981)

1981 edited by Karen L. Rood, Jean W. Ross, and Richard Ziegfeld (1982)

1982 edited by Richard Ziegfeld; associate editors: Jean W. Ross and Lynne C. Zeigler (1983)

1983 edited by Mary Bruccoli and Jean W. Ross; associate editor Richard Ziegfeld (1984)

1984 edited by Jean W. Ross (1985)

1985 edited by Jean W. Ross (1986)

1986 edited by J. M. Brook (1987)

1987 edited by J. M. Brook (1988)

1988 edited by J. M. Brook (1989)

1989 edited by J. M. Brook (1990)

1990 edited by James W. Hipp (1991)

1991 edited by James W. Hipp (1992)

1992 edited by James W. Hipp (1993)

1993 edited by James W. Hipp, contributing editor George Garrett (1994)

1994 edited by James W. Hipp, contributing editor George Garrett (1995)

1995 edited by James W. Hipp, contributing editor George Garrett (1996)

1996 edited by Samuel W. Bruce and L. Kay Webster, contributing editor George Garrett (1997)

1997 edited by Matthew J. Bruccoli and George Garrett, with the assistance of L. Kay Webster (1998)

1998 edited by Matthew J. Bruccoli, contributing editor George Garrett, with the assistance of D. W. Thomas (1999)

1999 edited by Matthew J. Bruccoli, contributing editor George Garrett, with the assistance of D. W. Thomas (2000)

2000 edited by Matthew J. Bruccoli, contributing editor George Garrett, with the assistance of George Parker Anderson (2001)

Concise Series

Concise Dictionary of American Literary Biography, 7 volumes (1988-1999): *The New Consciousness, 1941-1968; Colonization to the American Renaissance, 1640-1865; Realism, Naturalism, and Local Color, 1865-1917; The Twenties, 1917-1929; The Age of Maturity, 1929-1941; Broadening Views, 1968-1988; Supplement: Modern Writers, 1900-1998.*

Concise Dictionary of British Literary Biography, 8 volumes (1991-1992): *Writers of the Middle Ages and Renaissance Before 1660; Writers of the Restoration and Eighteenth Century, 1660-1789; Writers of the Romantic Period, 1789-1832; Victorian Writers, 1832-1890; Late-Victorian and Edwardian Writers, 1890-1914; Modern Writers, 1914-1945; Writers After World War II, 1945-1960; Contemporary Writers, 1960 to Present.*

Concise Dictionary of World Literary Biography, 10 volumes projected (1999-   ): *Ancient Greek and Roman Writers; German Writers; African, Caribbean, and Latin American Writers; South Slavic and Eastern European Writers.*

British Philosophers, 1500–1799

Dictionary of Literary Biography® • Volume Two Hundred Fifty-Two

British Philosophers, 1500–1799

Edited by
Philip B. Dematteis
Saint Leo University

and

Peter S. Fosl
Transylvania University

A Bruccoli Clark Layman Book
The Gale Group
Detroit • San Francisco • London • Boston • Woodbridge, Conn.

Library of Congress Cataloging-in-Publication Data

British philosophers, 1500–1799 / edited by Philip B. Dematteis and Peter S. Fosl.
  p. cm.–(Dictionary of literary biography; v. 252)
"A Bruccoli Clark Layman book."
Includes bibliographical references and index.
ISBN 0-7876-4669-5 (alk. paper)
1. Philosophy, British–History–Bio-bibliography–Dictionaries. I. Fosl, Peter S. II. Series.

B1111 .B75 2002
192'.03–dc21   2001051274
[B]

10 9 8 7 6 5 4 3 2 1

For our wives, Mary Dematteis and Cate Fosl

Contents

Plan of the Series

. . . Almost the most prodigious asset of a country, and perhaps its most precious possession, is its native literary product—when that product is fine and noble and enduring.

Mark Twain*

The advisory board, the editors, and the publisher of the *Dictionary of Literary Biography* are joined in endorsing Mark Twain's declaration. The literature of a nation provides an inexhaustible resource of permanent worth. Our purpose is to make literature and its creators better understood and more accessible to students and the reading public, while satisfying the needs of teachers and researchers.

To meet these requirements, *literary biography* has been construed in terms of the author's achievement. The most important thing about a writer is his writing. Accordingly, the entries in *DLB* are career biographies, tracing the development of the author's canon and the evolution of his reputation.

The purpose of *DLB* is not only to provide reliable information in a usable format but also to place the figures in the larger perspective of literary history and to offer appraisals of their accomplishments by qualified scholars.

The publication plan for *DLB* resulted from two years of preparation. The project was proposed to Bruccoli Clark by Frederick G. Ruffner, president of the Gale Research Company, in November 1975. After specimen entries were prepared and typeset, an advisory board was formed to refine the entry format and develop the series rationale. In meetings held during 1976, the publisher, series editors, and advisory board approved the scheme for a comprehensive biographical dictionary of persons who contributed to literature. Editorial work on the first volume began in January 1977, and it was published in 1978. In order to make *DLB* more than a dictionary and to compile volumes that individually have claim to status as literary history, it was decided to organize volumes by topic, period, or

From an unpublished section of Mark Twain's autobiography, copyright by the Mark Twain Company

genre. Each of these freestanding volumes provides a biographical-bibliographical guide and overview for a particular area of literature. We are convinced that this organization—as opposed to a single alphabet method—constitutes a valuable innovation in the presentation of reference material. The volume plan necessarily requires many decisions for the placement and treatment of authors. Certain figures will be included in separate volumes, but with different entries emphasizing the aspect of his career appropriate to each volume. Ernest Hemingway, for example, is represented in *American Writers in Paris, 1920–1939* by an entry focusing on his expatriate apprenticeship; he is also in *American Novelists, 1910–1945* with an entry surveying his entire career, as well as in *American Short-Story Writers, 1910–1945, Second Series* with an entry concentrating on his short fiction. Each volume includes a cumulative index of the subject authors and articles.

Since 1981 the series has been further augmented by the *DLB Yearbooks,* which update published entries, add new entries to keep the *DLB* current with contemporary activity, and provide articles on literary history. There have also been nineteen *DLB Documentary Series* volumes which provide illustrations, facsimiles, and biographical and critical source materials for figures, works, or groups judged to have particular interest for students. In 1999 the *Documentary Series* was incorporated into the *DLB* volume numbering system beginning with *DLB 210: Ernest Hemingway.*

We define literature as the *intellectual commerce of a nation:* not merely as belles lettres but as that ample and complex process by which ideas are generated, shaped, and transmitted. *DLB* entries are not limited to "creative writers" but extend to other figures who in their time and in their way influenced the mind of a people. Thus the series encompasses historians, journalists, publishers, book collectors, and screenwriters. By this means readers of *DLB* may be aided to perceive literature not as cult scripture in the keeping of intellectual high priests but firmly positioned at the center of a nation's life.

DLB includes the major writers appropriate to each volume and those standing in the ranks behind them. Scholarly and critical counsel has been sought in deciding which minor figures to include and how full their entries should be. Wherever possible, useful references are made to figures who do not warrant separate entries.

Each *DLB* volume has an expert volume editor responsible for planning the volume, selecting the figures for inclusion, and assigning the entries. Volume editors are also responsible for preparing, where appropriate, appendices surveying the major periodicals and literary and intellectual movements for their volumes, as well as lists of further readings. Work on the series as a whole is coordinated at the Bruccoli Clark Layman editorial center in Columbia, South Carolina, where the editorial staff is responsible for accuracy and utility of the published volumes.

One feature that distinguishes *DLB* is the illustration policy–its concern with the iconography of literature. Just as an author is influenced by his surroundings, so is the reader's understanding of the author enhanced by a knowledge of his environment. Therefore *DLB* volumes include not only drawings, paintings, and photographs of authors, often depicting them at various stages in their careers, but also illustrations of their families and places where they lived. Title pages are regularly reproduced in facsimile along with dust jackets for modern authors. The dust jackets are a special feature of *DLB* because they often document better than anything else the way in which an author's work was perceived in its own time. Specimens of the writers' manuscripts and letters are included when feasible.

Samuel Johnson rightly decreed that "The chief glory of every people arises from its authors." The purpose of the *Dictionary of Literary Biography* is to compile literary history in the surest way available to us–by accurate and comprehensive treatment of the lives and work of those who contributed to it.

The *DLB* Advisory Board

Introduction

Philosophers have generally drawn their influences across national boundaries and have made assertions that claim universal validity. Yet, it would be a mistake to say that no characteristic features can be discerned among the works of philosophers of a particular nationality. British philosophy is most often characterized as more "empirical" than that produced in other nations. Drawn from the Greek *empeiria*, for "experience," the term was not widely used until well into the nineteenth century. But it is not improper to apply it retrospectively to earlier periods because British philosophers since at least the thirteenth century have tended to be more guarded than French or German thinkers about the capacity of the human mind to penetrate into the hidden recesses of reality; instead, they have characteristically sought to restrict their analytical endeavors to the realm of common, lived human experience. Suspicious of comprehensive philosophical system-building, they have preferred to take a piecemeal approach, focusing on particular issues. British philosophers have also been less critical than those on the Continent of the importance of natural science and have undertaken greater efforts to refine its methods and to establish the legitimacy of its findings. With a few notable exceptions—including, among the philosophers treated in this volume, George Berkeley (1685-1753) and David Hume (1711-1776)—its principal figures have shied away from the idealism (the claim that reality is fundamentally mental or spiritual in nature) and skepticism (doubt that knowledge of reality is possible) more commonly found across the English Channel in favor of what is known as perceptual realism (the belief that material objects exist independently of perception of them). Correspondingly, in political theory British philosophers—again, with exceptions such as Thomas Hobbes (1588-1679)—have tended to take a moderate stance, advocating limited government and individual liberty rather than placing all political authority in a ruler or set of rulers who are thought to possess exclusive insight into human nature or the principles of morality. And even Hobbes attempted to justify the dictatorial powers of what he called the "sovereign" on the consent of the governed—although that consent, given once in a hypothetical "social compact," could never legitimately be revoked.

The British emphasis on common experience is evident as early as the Middle Ages, a period that precedes the time span covered in this volume. (British philosophers are included, along with those of other national backgrounds, in *DLB 115: Medieval Philosophers.*) Roger Bacon (circa 1214-1292) advocated the use of observation to increase human knowledge and did experimental work of his own in optics; legend has it that he died of a fever after stuffing a dead chicken with snow to test the preservative properties of cold. John Duns Scotus (1266-1308) shifted the center of philosophical gravity toward the world of ordinary experience by holding that terms, such as *being* and *wisdom,* are univocal—that is, have the same meaning—when applied to God as they do when applied to creatures. William of Ockham (1290-1349) developed a "nominalist" theory of universals, according to which applying the same word (such as *dog* or *tree*) to a group of similar things does not, as some ancient and medieval philosophers thought, imply that a "universal" or "substantial form" exists in each member of the group. Only words are universal; all existing things are individual. Ockham also put forth the methodological principle that has come to be known as "Ockham's Razor," which says that entities should not be multiplied beyond what is necessary. This principle did away, at one fell swoop, with the many unperceived "occult qualities," "species," and "essences" that cluttered up medieval metaphysics (theories about the nature of reality). John Wyclyf (circa 1320-1384) produced a vernacular translation of the Bible, thereby disclosing Scripture to all who could read, and advanced the revolutionary notion that priests and, therefore, the church hierarchy could be wrong—that their pronouncements and actions can be open to scrutiny by laypeople.

The literary and visual arts underwent development in Britain during the politically turbulent fifteenth and early sixteenth centuries around norms of Renaissance humanism, principally through the influence of Humphrey, Duke of Gloucester (1391-1477). But the period yielded relatively little of philosophical significance. The dissolution of the monasteries under Henry VIII (1491-1547; reigned 1509-1547) diminished the vitality of English universities. Without secure sources of able students or finance, the universities were unable to educate any but those who were wealthy enough to sustain them. Philosophy in the universities stagnated around arcane elaborations of Aristotelian logic. What remained vital in British philosophy was found in the work of individuals working outside of the academy; British universities did not reclaim the mantle of philosophy until well into the nineteenth century.

DLB 252: British Philosophers, 1500–1799 begins chronologically (though not alphabetically) with Francis Bacon (1561–1626). Bacon not only represents British philosophy's decisive break at this time with the universities; he also launched the era's most influential British attack on the traditional theories and practices of philosophy itself. His work, however, was not simply critical but offered an alternative vision of a profoundly different and more powerful form of philosophy. It is, indeed, not an exaggeration to say that modern British philosophy begins with Bacon. In *The Advancement of Learning* (1605) and the *Novum organum* (1620) Bacon launches trenchant assaults on the tangled, empirically ungrounded, theologically constrained, and excessively abstract investigations of the Scholastic (medieval school) traditions. He insists on a strict separation of philosophy from theology; he criticizes what he calls the "Idols of the mind," by which he means intellectual habits that hindered the proper use of reason; and he calls for a practical science based on inductive reasoning from concrete facts rather than deduction from assumed principles, a science that will give humanity technological power over the natural world and relief from earthly suffering.

Just as Bacon was cleaving philosophy from theology, Baron Herbert of Cherbury (1583–1648) was elaborating a method of establishing truths about God through the natural capacities of the human intellect, independently of revelation, and thereby became the founder of the influential movement known as "deism." Much as the ancient Stoics had appealed to "cataleptic," or self-verifying perceptions, and as later British thinkers such as Thomas Reid (1710–1796) and Richard Price (1723–1791) appealed to indubitable thoughts and experiences, Herbert of Cherbury held that the mind possesses certain "common notions" on which the truths of perception and religion irrefutably rest. The task of rational science and religion is to make use of those common notions, together with reason and experience, to advance knowledge of the world and its supernatural creator. Following the general line of thought laid down by Herbert of Cherbury, John Toland (1670–1722) became, at the age of twenty-five, one of deism's most influential advocates and definitive figures with his *Christianity Not Mysterious: Or, A Treatise Shewing That there is nothing in the Gospel Contrary to Reason, Nor above it: And that no Christian Doctrine can be properly call'd a Mystery* (1696).

Hobbes, by contrast, produced in works such as *De Corpore* (1655) a complete and systematic theory of the nature of the universe resting entirely on the new materialistic and geometrical physics of the Italian Galileo Galilei (1564–1642), whom Hobbes had visited in 1635. Eliminating spiritual substances, such as God and the soul, from his concept of reality; articulating a purely egoistic theory of motivation and action; and developing a sensuous theory of cognition, Hobbes reduced humans to material bodies actuated by selfish desires. In his *Leviathan* (1651) Hobbes formulates a completely secular political philosophy that makes the legitimacy of the state the result of a prudential contract entered into by individuals to provide themselves protection from each other.

The absolute power of Hobbes's sovereign to declare some actions morally right and others morally wrong was opposed by Benjamin Whichcote (1609–1683) of Emmanuel College, Cambridge University, who held that the rightness or wrongness of an action is intrinsic to that action and not the product of the will of a higher authority—not even that of God. Active during the conflict-ridden period of the Scottish National Covenant (1638), the English Civil Wars (1642–1651), and the Commonwealth and Protectorate (1649–1660), Whichcote advanced what came to be known as religious liberalism, stressing the virtues of reason, tolerance, and good acts rather than adherence to dogma and creed. The poet and literary and social critic Matthew Arnold (1822–1888) found inspiration in Whichcote's sermon as late as the Victorian period. Whichcote and some of his Cambridge colleagues, including Henry More (1614–1687), John Smith (1618–1652), Ralph Cudworth (1617–1688), and Nathanael Culverwel (1619?–1651?) developed a metaphysics (theory of the nature of reality) that emphasized the importance of "spirit" in opposition to the materialism of Hobbes and the Frenchman Pierre Gassendi (1592–1655). Influenced by the philosophy of Plato (428–348 or 347 B.C.) and the Neoplatonism of Plotinus (204–270), they became known as the Cambridge Platonists.

An Anglican preacher and ardent supporter of the Royal Society (established in 1662), Joseph Glanvill (1636–1680) was influenced by More and sympathetic to the ideas of the Cambridge Platonists. His philosophical treatises, however, exhibit rudimentary elements of a more empiricist strain of thought, together with skepticism in regard to what he considered the misguided and pseudoscientific doctrines of Scholasticism. Glanvill's *The Vanity of Dogmatizing* (1661) and *Scepsis Scientifica* (1665) argue that skeptical scrutiny of the possibility of knowledge is necessary if genuine science is to progress. Glanvill's criticisms of the cause-effect relationship prefigure those of Hume, although Glanvill's motivation—quite different from Hume's—was to show that only God is a true cause.

Among More's informal pupils was Anne, Vicountess Conway (1631–1679). Drawing on More's theory of the "spirit of nature," the cabalistic instruction of Francis Mercury van Helmont–the son of Jan Baptista van Helmont (1577–1644), the "father of biochemistry"–and Quaker teachings concerning the divine within human beings, Conway wrote *The Principles of the Most Ancient and Modern Philosophy,* which was published posthumously in 1690. The volume presents an extensive critique of Hobbesian mechanistic materialism and advances a vitalistic conception of matter according to which matter is animate and the source of its own motion. A similar challenge had already been developed by another independent female thinker, Margaret Cavendish, Duchess of Newcastle (1623–1673), among whose many publications *The Philosophical and Physical Opinions* (1655) and *Philosophical Letters* (1664) indicate her concurrence with materialistic atomism but also describe a hierarchy of matter, the higher orders of which, she claims, possess both sensation and the capacity to initiate motion.

The poet Alexander Pope (1688–1744) wrote that "Nature and nature's laws lay hid in night. / God said, 'Let Newton be,' and all was light." In the late seventeenth and eighteenth centuries, most concurred with that assessment. After studying mathematics and physics without distinction at Trinity College, Cambridge, Isaac Newton (1642–1727) fled to his country home in Woolsthorpe for eighteen months in 1665 to avoid an outbreak of the plague in the university town. During that brief period he calculated the law of gravity and the laws of thermodynamics, invented differential calculus, discovered the composition of light, and set the foundation for modern optics. A quiet, ruminating, and often morose man, Newton seemed not to appreciate the magnitude of his accomplishment; he kept his work from publication until 1687, when he brought out his grand *Philosophiæ Naturalis Principia Mathematica.* The formulation of a mathematical, relatively simple, and comprehensive theory of the natural world–a theory that could as readily predict the motion of planets as of billiard balls–validated for many thinkers the new naturalistic and quantitative physics and provided a model for philosophy. Through the power of his work and the efforts of popularizers such as Voltaire (1694–1778), Newton helped to engender a period of Anglomania among the French.

Newton's description of a regular, law-governed cosmos open to rational explanation inspired visions of a rational creator who had constructed a clocklike universe. But by showing that the operation of that universe could be understood without appeal to divine intervention, Newton's work also invigorated attempts to argue that God does not exist. Newton's retort to criticism that he had failed to explain the ultimate cause of gravity, "*Hypotheses non fingo*" (I feign no hypotheses), became a rallying cry for those who were opposed to theological speculation. Yet, Newton was himself extremely devout (though not orthodox in his beliefs), writing much more on religious topics and ancient history, especially prophecy and the Book of Daniel, than on physics or mathematics. He also devoted a large amount of energy to alchemical investigations.

While the impact of Newton's physics was vast, his friend John Locke (1632–1704) was the most influential British philosopher of the seventeenth century outside the realm of natural science. The first of the three great British Empiricists–the others being Berkeley and Hume–Locke adopted what he called the "Way of Ideas" developed by the French philosopher and mathematician René Descartes (1596–1650), along with Galileo's distinction between primary and secondary qualities, and asserted that experience consists of mental "ideas" and that only the quantitative aspects of those ideas, such as size, shape, number, and motion, are copies of objects in the world outside the mind (primary qualities), while those that cannot be put in mathematical terms, such as color, taste, and odor, are subjective (secondary qualities). Locke rejected Descartes's contention that some ideas, such as that of God and certain logical principles, are innate in the mind; instead, he said, the mind at birth is a "*tabula rasa*" (blank sheet of paper), and all of the ideas it ever acquires come from experience. Locke abandoned the attempt to provide an account of the true nature of the universe, maintaining that primary qualities indicate merely the existence of external "powers" whose actual essence cannot be known.

In articulating this position in *An Essay concerning Humane Understanding* (1690), Locke described himself as "an under-labourer to the incomparable Mr. Newton"; and his empiricist standpoint provided the philosophical underpinnings for Newtonian science as it increasingly eclipsed the rationalistic (deductive) metaphysics of Descartes. Locke's book quickly became one of the central texts of British philosophical instruction, and it framed debates about epistemology (the theory of knowledge) for nearly a century.

Locke engaged in a correspondence with Cudworth's daughter, Damaris Cudworth, Lady Masham (1659–1708), who also took up an epistolary philosophical conversation with the German rationalist philosopher Gottfried Wilhelm von Leibniz (1646–1716). Locke's *An Essay concerning Humane Understanding* gained support through another important early modern female thinker, Catherine Trotter Cockburn (1679–1749), who wrote *A Defense of Mr. Locke's Essay of Human Understanding* (1702) in reply to an anonymous attack on Locke by one of Ralph Cudworth's students.

In spite of his empiricism, however, Locke remained sympathetic with ethical rationalism, holding, like Samuel Clarke (1675–1729), that moral truths could be demonstrated in a manner similar to those of geometry. A friend and supporter of the liberal Anglican clergy, Locke was also an advocate of natural theology, maintaining in *The Reasonableness of Christianity* (1695) that revelation is rational and that its claims can be tested by natural human reason. Though he distanced himself from Toland's work, many deists found inspiration in Locke.

In reply to Hobbes's absolutism, Locke–a strong supporter of the Glorious Revolution of 1688–constructed in his *Two Treatises of Civil Government* (1689) a liberal version of the social contract and a natural-rights theory that placed the sovereignty with the citizens, limited the powers of government, and upheld the right of rebellion against a government that infringes on the rights it was set up to protect. Locke's principles had a profound influence on the founding documents of the United States.

While criticisms of Locke's empiricism were lodged by John Norris (1657–1711), generally considered the last of the Cambridge Platonists, the most powerful attack on Locke's theory of perception and causation was made by the bishop of Cloyne, George Berkeley. What made Berkeley's attack so devastating was that it radicalized Locke's own empiricist principles, turning them back on him. Berkeley developed an idealistic metaphysics (that is, a theory of reality according to which only mental entities exist) that was intended to defend common sense from what he regarded as the confusions advanced by Locke and the physicists. Berkeley was not, however, an opponent of Newtonian science; he claimed that his theory was designed "in opposition to sceptics and atheists . . . to open a method for rendering the sciences more easy, useful, and compendious." One of the first philosophers to argue that certain philosophical claims are not simply false but literally meaningless (a mode of philosophical argumentation that became extremely widespread in British philosophy in the twentieth century), Berkeley maintained that the concept of a material substance existing independently of perception is nonsense because, as Locke had shown, the meanings of all concepts derive from experience; and all that is perceived are mental entities–that is, ideas. Material substance is not a mental entity; thus, there is no idea of it–it is just a word without meaning. Locke had admitted as much, calling material substance a "something I know not what" that underlies and somehow supports the qualities that are perceived; but Locke was too wedded to common sense to draw the conclusion that, on empiricist grounds, belief in the existence of matter could not be justified. Berkeley had no such compunctions. Science, according to Berkeley, is nothing more than an account of the order to be found among ideas–and that order, and the ideas themselves, are produced in the human mind directly by God.

The work of Mary Astell (1666–1731) not only prefigures later feminist philosophies but also exhibits the way in which, in the wake of the Glorious Revolution, Whig concerns with liberty and equality were beginning to take shape and to pervade intellectual culture. Astell's two-part *A Serious Proposal to the Ladies* (1694, 1697) argues for female advancement. She explored the implications of her claims in correspondence with the Cambridge Platonist Norris, published as *Letters Concerning the Love of God* (1695), before launching a pointed critique of the principal institution governing women in English society in *Some Reflections upon Marriage* (1700).

As experimental science advanced, philosophers struggled to assess the limits of knowledge and rationality, while religious thinkers decided, in increasing numbers, to abandon traditional–and, to them, superstitious–dogma in favor of the apparently more rational and more moderate precepts of deism. Progressive thinkers began more and more to see revealed Christianity as a species of "enthusiasm" intrinsically bound up with moral and political excess and misery. Defenders of religious orthodoxy were also keen to support the moderate, rational, and modern project of natural theology, but in contrast with many of their deist peers they set out to demonstrate its compatibility with Christianity. Funded by a bequest from Robert Boyle (1627–1691), author of *The Sceptical Chymist* (1661) and the most important natural philosopher between Bacon and Newton, the Boyle lectures were established to prove "the Christian Religion, against notorious Infidels, viz. Atheists, Theists, Pagans." The first lecturer in the series was Richard Bentley (1662–1742). Much in the way that recent opponents of evolutionary theory have done, Bentley maintains in *Matter and Motion Cannot Think* (1692) that the complexity of living organisms, the wonders of the starry heavens, and even the force of gravity testify to an intelligent and benevolent Creator.

In both power and influence, however, Bentley's lectures were eclipsed by those of Samuel Clarke. Clarke delivered two series of Boyle lectures in 1704 and 1705. The first series, published in 1705 as *A Demonstration of the Being and Attributes of God: more particularly in Answer to Mr. Hobbs, Spinoza, and their followers,* maintains that reason is able to prove that God exists and is immaterial, free, intelligent, and good. Clarke's assertion that God is both temporal and spatial stimulated a lively correspondence with Leibniz, who argued, contrary to Clarke and Newton, that space and time are in part ideal (that is, creations of the mind).

In his second series of Boyle lectures, published in 1706 as *A Discourse concerning the Unchangeable Obligations of Natural Religion,* Clarke sets out a highly rationalistic ethical theory. Like Locke, he attempts to provide a secure foundation for morality by rendering moral truth analogous to mathematical truth. Like the Cambridge Platonists, he argues that goodness is not the product of divine commands but precedes them: that is, what is good is not so because God wills it; on the contrary, God wills it because it is good. Clarke's rationalistic method drew wide support among the religious. Deists, too, found much to admire in the scope and power of Clarke's view of rationality, as well as in the fact that his method made little use of revelation. British philosophers who held more naturalistic convictions, however, reacted against Clarke's views, generating powerful new moral theories and critiques of natural religion.

Joseph Butler (1692–1752), Anglican bishop of Durham and clerk of Queen Caroline's closet, led the secular and naturalistic response to Clarke in a series of letters published in 1713 and in his *Fifteen Sermons preached at the Rolls Chapel* (1726). Butler argues that philosophers must abandon the rationalistic study of "abstract relations" in ethics in favor of focusing on "matters of fact, namely, what the particular nature of man is, its several parts, their economy or constitution; from whence it proceeds to determine what course of life it is which is correspondent to this whole nature." In his *Inquiry into the Original of Our Ideas of Beauty and Virtue* (1725) Francis Hutcheson (1694–1747), like Butler, bases ethical and aesthetic reasoning strictly on human beings' natural capacities—especially on their feelings—rather than on the logical analysis of relations among ideas carried out by Clarke. While rationalism was defended by Price, the empiricist-naturalistic project in ethics was carried on by Adam Smith (1723–1790), who in his own time was better known for the stoic and benevolent theory of sympathy presented in his *The Theory of the Moral Sentiments* (1759) than for his antimercantilist, pro–free-market economic treatise, *An Inquiry into the Nature and Causes of the Wealth of Nations* (1776).

Similarly, during his own time Smith's fellow Scot David Hume was best known not for his philosophical treatises but for his social, literary, and aesthetic criticism and especially for his *History of England* (1754–1762), which became the preeminent text on the subject until well into the nineteenth century. Today, however, Hume is widely regarded as the eighteenth century's greatest philosopher. Embracing, rather than struggling to overcome, the skeptical implications of the empiricist "Way of Ideas," Hume in *A Treatise of Human Nature: Being an Attempt to introduce the experimental Method of Reasoning into Moral Subjects* (1739–1740) and *An Enquiry Concerning Human Understanding* (1758) eliminates Locke's and Berkeley's metaphysical conclusions concerning primary qualities, God, and mental substance or spirit. Although Hume was a strong advocate of experimental science, his theory of knowledge severely limits the capacities of reason, and his critical analysis of the cause-effect relation-

ship as merely a habit or "custom" of the mind in which the constant conjunction of similar events produces an association of the ideas of those events undermines rationalistic science, just as his attack on the proof of the existence of God from the design of the universe undermines natural theology. (While he may never have read Hume's works, David Hartley [1705–1757] developed a theory of the association of ideas similar to, but simpler than, that advanced by Hume, resulting in tremendous advances in naturalistic psychology.)

In ethics, Hume rooted moral reasoning in human sentiment, remarking in *An Enquiry concerning the Principles of Morals* (1751) that "Reason is, and ought only to be, the slave of the passions." Following Hume, Jeremy Bentham (1748–1832) and, in the nineteenth century, John Stuart Mill (1806–1873) and Henry Sidgwick (1838–1900) developed one of the most important modern ethical theories: utilitarianism. Maintaining that happiness is the proper end of human action, that happiness must be considered collectively, and that conditions of greater or lesser happiness can be empirically determined, utilitarian theorists sundered moral theory from metaphysical speculation, logical analyses of ideas, and religious dogma, tying it instead to the findings of empirical social science and psychology.

The Irishman Edmund Burke (1729?–1797) joined with the naturalists in his aesthetic treatise *On the Sublime and Beautiful* (1756), but he is principally remembered for his political philosophy. Holding that the inevitable political consequence of ethical rationalism would be violence and tyranny, Burke channeled the naturalists' criticisms of rationalism into a powerful conservative critique of liberal and radical political theory. Belief in the power of human reason to grasp metaphysical truths about the good of society (for example, natural rights) tempts political thinkers to abolish existing social institutions in favor of the purportedly more-perfect visions of theory. Accordingly, Burke argues in *Reflections on the Revolution in France* (1790), political philosophers should respect the accumulated wisdom invested in the traditional institutions. Burke's text has remained one of the most influential conservative critiques of radical politics.

Burke's work did not, however, mean an end to radical political theory in Britain. Burke's contemporary Mary Wollstonecraft (1759–1797), the wife of the anarchist political theorist William Godwin (1756–1836) and mother of the author of *Frankenstein; or, The Modern Prometheus* (1818), Mary Wollstonecraft Shelley (1797–1851), put forth such theories in *Thoughts on the Education of Daughters; with Reflections on Female Conduct, in the More Important Duties of Life* (1787) and *A Vindication of the Rights of Woman: With Strictures on Political and Moral Subjects* (1792). Wollstonecraft's liberal ideals on the equality and improvement of women are woven together with insights from the Swiss-born French philosopher Jean-Jacques Rousseau (1712–1778), as well as with modern social theories and philosophies of mind.

Undaunted by Hume's criticisms, William Paley (1743–1805) continued to uphold the proof from design but emphasized biological rather than cosmological manifestations of order in the universe. Hume's thought came under assault by the Scottish Common Sense school led by Thomas Reid (1710–1796). The Common Sense theorists argued that sensory experience is not just a succession of ideas but yields knowledge of the existence of physical objects. This position aimed at securing knowledge of the material world, in opposition to the idealism of Berkeley and the radical skepticism of Hume. Its refreshing realism and down-to-earth quality made Common Sense philosophy the dominant school of thought in both Britain and the United States until its claims were unraveled by Mill in 1865. Since then, Common Sense philosophy has fallen into near oblivion; its general claims, however, have been partially resurrected by philosophers such as Alvin Plantinga (1932–) who have developed theories of epistemological realism.

The Common Sense school was not the only response to the results of early modern British philosophy. Other movements were taking shape that locked horns in the nineteenth century with the mechanistic and scientist sort of empiricism with which British thought was so deeply engaged. With some inspiration from the Germans Johann Wolfgang von Goethe (1749–1832) and Immanuel Kant (1724–1804), the Romantics rejected the passive, artificially constrained, and machinelike rendering of the mind the eighteenth century had produced, opposing to it a more dynamic view. Romantic poets such as William Blake (1757–1827), William Wordsworth (1770–1850), Samuel Taylor Coleridge (1772–1834), George Gordon, Lord Byron (1788–1824), and Percy Bysshe Shelley (1792–1822) demanded a more expansive and more creative role for the imagination. They sought to gain, through engagement with feeling, aesthetic experience, and the natural world, a comprehension of the self and the universe that was never conceived by their skeptical and rationalistic predecessors.

The Romantics, however, did not end the empiricist current in British philosophy. They merely established another current. Empiricism in new and more complex forms drove onward. The mix of these competing movements produced a fertile concoction, and the tension between enthusiastic, revolutionary, idealistic Romanticism and rationalistic, moderate liberal empiricism set down the roots of the powerful philosophical movements that flowered in Britain in the centuries ahead—movements from which the yield is still being harvested.

–*Philip B. Dematteis and Peter S. Fosl*

Acknowledgments

This book was produced by Bruccoli Clark Layman, Inc. Karen L. Rood is senior editor. Charles Brower was the in-house editor. He was assisted by Philip B. Dematteis, Jan Peter F. van Rosevelt, and Angela Shaw-Thornburg.

Production manager is Philip B. Dematteis.

Administrative support was provided by Ann M. Cheschi, Amber L. Coker, and Angi Pleasant.

Accountant is Ann-Marie Holland.

Copyediting supervisor is Sally R. Evans. The copyediting staff includes Phyllis A. Avant, Brenda Carol Blanton, Melissa D. Hinton, Charles Loughlin, Rebecca Mayo, Nancy E. Smith, and Elizabeth Jo Ann Sumner. Freelance copyeditors are Brenda Cabra and Thom Harman.

Editorial associates are Michael S. Allen, Michael S. Martin, and Pamela A. Warren.

Database manager is José A. Juarez.

Layout and graphics supervisor is Janet E. Hill. The graphics staff includes Karla Corley Brown and Zoe R. Cook.

Office manager is Kathy Lawler Merlette.

Photography supervisor is Paul Talbot. Photography editor is Scott Nemzek.

Digital photographic copy work was performed by Joseph M. Bruccoli.

The SGML staff includes Frank Graham, Linda Dalton Mullinax, Jason Paddock, and Alex Snead.

Systems manager is Marie L. Parker.

Typesetting supervisor is Kathleen M. Flanagan. The typesetting staff includes Jaime All, Patricia Marie Flanagan, Mark J. McEwan, and Pamela D. Norton. Freelance typesetter is Wanda Adams.

Walter W. Ross did library research. He was assisted by Jaime All and the following librarians at the Thomas Cooper Library of the University of South Carolina: circulation department head Tucker Taylor; reference department head Virginia W. Weathers; Brette Barclay, Marilee Birchfield, Paul Cammarata, Gary Geer, Michael Macan, Tom Marcil, Rose Marshall, and Sharon Verba; interlibrary loan department head John Brunswick; and interlibrary loan staff Robert Arndt, Hayden Battle, Barry Bull, Jo Cottingham, Marna Hostetler, Marieum McClary, Erika Peake, and Nelson Rivera.

British Philosophers, 1500–1799

Dictionary of Literary Biography

Mary Astell

(12 November 1666 – 9 May 1731)

Jacqueline Broad
Monash University

BOOKS: *A Serious Proposal to the Ladies, For the Advancement of their true and greatest Interest. By a Lover of Her Sex,* anonymous (London: Printed for Richard Wilkin, 1694);

Letters Concerning the Love of God, Between the Author of the Proposal to the Ladies and Mr. John Norris: Wherein his late Discourse, shewing That it ought to be intire and exclusive of all other Loves, is further cleared and justified, anonymous, by Astell and John Norris (London: Printed for Samuel Manship and Richard Wilkin, 1695; revised and enlarged edition, 1705);

A Serious Proposal to the Ladies, Part II: Wherein a Method Is Offer'd for the Improvement of Their Minds, anonymous (London: Printed for Richard Wilkin, 1697); republished with part 1 as *A Serious Proposal to the Ladies for the Advancement of Their True and Greatest Interest. In Two Parts. By a Lover of Her Sex* (London: Printed by J. R. for Richard Wilkin, 1697);

Some Reflections Upon Marriage, Occasion'd by the Duke & Dutchess Of Mazarine's Case; which is also consider'd, anonymous (London: Printed for John Nutt, 1700); republished as *Reflections Upon Marriage. The Third Edition. To which is Added A Preface, in Answer to some Objections* (London: Richard Wilkin, 1706);

A Fair Way With The Dissenters And Their Patrons. Not writ by Mr L--Y, or any other Furious Jacobite, whether Clergyman or Layman; but by a very Moderate Person and Dutiful Subject to the Queen, anonymous (London: Printed by E. P. for Richard Wilkin, 1704);

An Impartial Enquiry Into The Causes Of Rebellion and Civil War In This Kingdom: In an Examination of Dr. Kennett's Sermon, Jan. 31, 1703/4. And Vindication of the Royal Martyr, anonymous (London: Printed by E. P. for Richard Wilkin, 1704);

Moderation Truly Stated: or, A Review Of A Late Pamphlet, Entitul'd, Moderation a Vertue. With A Prefatory Discourse To Dr. D'Aveanant, Concerning His Late Essays on Peace and War, as Tom Single (London: Printed by J. L. for Richard Wilkin, 1704);

The Christian Religion, As Profess'd by a Daughter Of The Church of England. In a Letter to the Right Honourable, T.L. C.I., anonymous (London: Printed by S. H. for Richard Wilkin, 1705);

*Bart'lemy Fair: Or, An Enquiry after Wit; In which due Respect is had to a Letter Concerning Enthusiasm, To my LORD ***,* as Mr. Wotton (London: Printed for Richard Wilkin, 1709); republished as *An Enquiry After Wit: Wherein the Trifling Arguing and Impious Raillery of the Late Earl of Shaftsbury, In his Letter concerning Enthusiasm, and other Profane Writers, Are fully Answer'd, and justly Exposed* (London: Printed for John Bateman, 1722).

Editions and Collections: *The First English Feminist: 'Reflections Upon Marriage' and Other Writings by Mary Astell,* edited, with an introduction, by Bridget Hill (Aldershot, U.K.: Gower/Maurice Temple Smith, 1986);

Astell, Political Writings, edited by Patricia Springborg (New York & Cambridge: Cambridge University Press, 1996);

A Serious Proposal to the Ladies: Parts I and II, edited, with an introduction, by Springborg (London & Brookfield, Vt.: Pickering & Chatto, 1997).

OTHER: "Mary Astell's Preface to the Embassy Letters," in *The Complete Letters of Lady Mary Wortley Montagu,* volume 1, edited by Robert Halsband (New York & Oxford: Oxford University Press, 1965), pp. 466–468.

St. Nicholas Church, Newcastle, where Mary Astell's uncle Ralph Astell was curate. Ralph Astell is believed to have tutored his niece in philosophy and logic before his death when she was not yet thirteen (From John Baillie, Newcastle upon Tyne, *1801).*

Mary Astell is regarded as one of the earliest British feminists. In a time when women were seen as intellectually deficient by nature, she was one of the first thinkers to embrace Cartesian rationalism in support of arguments for the equal rational capacities of the sexes; she advocated dualism as a way in which women could define their selfhood in terms of their minds, rather than their bodies; and she used these insights to oppose the inferior education bestowed upon her sex. Although Astell is best known for her feminist writings, her other works are also an important reminder that a woman philosopher was once a clear and articulate critic of her famous male contemporaries in general seventeenth-century debates.

Born in Newcastle-upon-Tyne on 12 November 1666, Mary Astell was the first child of Mary Errington and Peter Astell, a gentleman and member of the Company of Hostmen. From a staunch Royalist background Astell developed early in life a conservative political and religious outlook. She and her brother Peter were educated by their unmarried uncle Ralph, the curate of

St. Nicholas Church in Newcastle, who was also a student of Emmanuel College during the heyday of the Cambridge Platonists, a group of mid-seventeenth-century philosopher-theologians. Ralph Astell is supposed to have tutored his niece in philosophy and logic, but since he died when she was not yet thirteen years old, her philosophical career likely was inspired by his example rather than his instruction. From an early age she faced an uncertain and possibly dismal future. Her father's death in 1678 had left the family in financial straits, and without a reasonable dowry Astell could not expect to marry someone of her own social standing. She apparently decided on a writing career as an alternative to marriage, however (she remained unmarried all her life), and after her mother's death in 1684 Astell moved to London in her early twenties, probably with the intention of pursuing this ambition.

By 1688, alone, orphaned, and poverty-stricken, Astell was forced to appeal to the charity of William Sancroft, Archbishop of Canterbury, who may have encouraged her plans to write. The next year she made him a gift of her religious poetry, thanking the archbishop for his kindness "when even my Kinsfolk had failed, and my familiar Friends had forgotten me." She was saved from further hardship by the financial support and friendship of a group of gentlewomen, including Lady Ann Coventry, Lady Elizabeth Hastings, and Lady Catherine Jones. From the 1690s onward Astell lived near her friends in Chelsea, where she spent her time, like a true Cartesian, teaching herself the basic principles of philosophy and religion. According to her first biographer, George Ballard, Astell was such a dedicated scholar that when she saw visitors coming, rather than have her meditations interrupted by "idle twaddle and vain amusements," she would open the window and inform the callers that she was "not at home." This self-assertive character is confirmed by the granddaughter of Lady Mary Wortley Montagu, Lady Louisa Stuart, who upon hearing Astell described as "fair and elegant" remarks that she was "a very pious, exemplary woman, and a profound scholar, but as far from fair and elegant as any old schoolmaster of her time: in outward form, indeed, rather ill-favoured and forbidding, and of a humour to have repulsed the compliment roughly, had it been paid her while she lived."

In Astell's subsequent writings, one can easily discern the impression left by her religious upbringing, her uncle's Cambridge background, and her friendships with women. As a Christian, Astell is critical of those philosophers who denigrate the spiritual or rational aspects of human beings. Like the Cambridge Platonists, such as Ralph Cudworth and Henry More, she opposes any form of "atheistic" materialism, and she blends René Descartes's rationalist arguments with the moral spirit of Platonism in order to affirm the reality of the spiritual world. Moreover, as a strong supporter of her sex, Astell believes that women should be encouraged to improve their reason so that they might fulfill their part in God's supremely rational design.

Not surprisingly, Astell's first venture into intellectual debate was a correspondence with "the last of the Cambridge Platonists," John Norris, who was in fact the Oxford-trained advocate of Nicolas Malebranche's occasionalist philosophy. Their exchange, initiated by Astell on 21 September 1693 and concluded a year later, was privately published by Norris as *Letters Concerning the Love of God, Between the Author of the Proposal to the Ladies and Mr. John Norris: Wherein his late Discourse, shewing That it ought to be intire and exclusive of all other Loves, is further cleared and justified* in 1695. These epistles give an early indication of Astell's impressive gift for philosophical analysis: although she supports the Malebranchean view that one must desire and love God above everything else, and that love for one's fellow humans ought to be purely disinterested, Astell often

William Sancroft, Archbishop of Canterbury, to whom Astell dedicated an unpublished collection of her poetry in 1689 in gratitude for his financial assistance (National Portrait Gallery, London)

presents sharp and perceptive objections to Norris's arguments.

In her first letter, after introducing her remarks as the "Impertinencies of a Womans Pen," Astell points to a difficulty she found when reading the third volume of Norris's *Practical Discourses upon Several Divine Subjects* (1693). While Astell agrees with Norris's conclusion, that God ought to be the sole object of human love, she is critical of his reasoning. Following Malebranche, Norris had argued that God is the sole cause of all human sensations, including pleasure; and since people only love that which causes pleasure, God must therefore be the sole object of human love. But, Astell points out, if God is the only true cause of all sensations, then he is also the only true cause of pain; yet, people do not love that which causes pain; and thus "if the Author of our Pleasure be upon that account the only Object of our Love, then by the same reason the Author of our Pain can't be the Object of our Love." To avoid Norris's inconsistency, she suggests that the experience of pain may in fact do a person good, and that one ought to love God because he alone does good, not merely

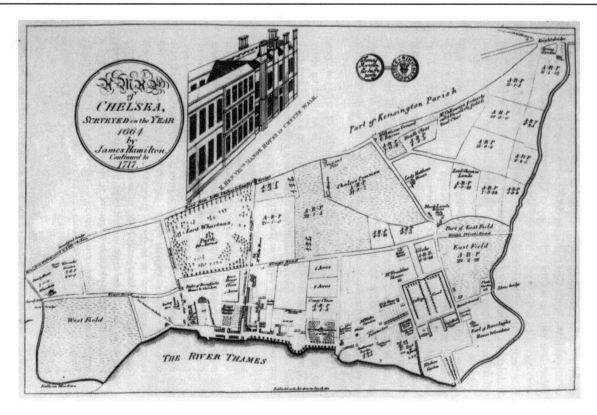

Map of the area of London where Astell settled in the 1690s (Royal Borough of Kensington and Chelsea Libraries and Arts Service)

because he is the author of pleasure. After expressing surprise "to see such a Letter from a Woman," Norris accepts Astell's argument and qualifies his view accordingly.

Astell's pertinent criticisms do not end there, however. Indeed, Astell's final letter (14 August 1694) issues a challenge to Norris's central premise that God is the only efficient cause of all human sensations. Anticipating John Locke's objection in "Remarks Upon Some of Mr. Norris's Books," published posthumously in *A Collection of Several Pieces of Mr. John Locke* (1720), Astell maintains that Norris's theory renders "a great Part of God's Workmanship vain and useless." She argues that if external objects are not able to produce sensations, then these objects cannot serve any relevant purpose; but if this premise is correct, then Norris's theory is contrary to the idea that an infinitely wise being creates nothing in vain. Instead, Astell suggests that there could be a natural efficacy in bodies to produce sensations in the soul, especially since it is more agreeable to God's majesty, she believes, "to say that he produces our Sensations *mediately* by his Servant Nature, than to affirm that he does it *immediately* by his own Almighty Power."

Overall, Astell's carefully thought-out objections did little to sway the man whom John Passmore, in his

entry on Norris in the *Encyclopedia of Philosophy* (1967), describes as "so concerned to leave nothing lovable in the world, nothing which could be a source of happiness to us, that he reduced it to a nonentity." Norris obviously admired the strength and clarity of her reasoning, however. At his entreaty Astell agreed to the letters being published, on the assurance that her name would not appear in print (she always published anonymously), and she requested that the volume be dedicated to her friend and patron, Lady Catherine Jones, the daughter of the earl of Ranelagh. After their publication the letters may have fulfilled Astell's desire "to excite a generous Emulation" in her sex: according to Ruth Perry's 1985 article "Radical Doubt and the Liberation of Women," other women writers were likely inspired to initiate intellectual correspondences with learned men, and the eighteenth-century bluestocking Sarah Chapone told Ballard that she thought *Letters Concerning the Love of God* was Astell's most "sublime" piece of writing.

Astell's best-known work is *A Serious Proposal to the Ladies, For the Advancement of their true and greatest Interest. By a Lover of Her Sex* (1694), an inspiring and witty feminist treatise written and published during the correspondence with Norris. In an earlier letter to Norris (31 October 1693) Astell says she plans to persuade women to care for "the Embellishment of their minds" rather than "the Adornation of their bodies." This idea is given philosophical strength in *A Serious Proposal to the Ladies,* a carefully reasoned argument for the establishment of an all-female academic institute, a safe retreat for single gentlewomen like Astell and her friends, where they could divorce themselves from "the hurry and noise of the World" and "the rude attempts of designing Men" in order to meditate and improve their minds and to study the grounds of religion.

A Serious Proposal to the Ladies, like Astell's final letter to Norris, draws on the idea that a supremely wise being performs nothing in vain: God would not have granted women rationality, Astell argues, if they were not meant to use and improve it. This teleological premise is united with Cartesian principles, particularly the claim that all human beings are essentially thinking things. Given their essential rationality, Astell argues, women can no longer be deemed inferior on the basis of their biology. Proclaiming herself "a Lover of her Sex," she calls on women to consider the welfare of their true selves—their minds—and rails against the "unthinking mechanical way of living" expected of them. Like Descartes, she takes a critical perspective toward custom, arguing that a woman's incapacity is the outcome of irrational prejudices perpetuated in the interests of men. But to every woman, Astell maintains, it is self-evident and indubitable that she possesses a rational faculty. Therefore, she says, "Let us . . . not entertain such a degrading thought of our own *worth,* as to imagine that our Souls were given us only for the service of our Bodies, and that the best improvement we can make of these, is to attract the Eyes of Men." The intellectual deficiency of women, she declares, is solely due to a neglected education, and their transformation could easily be effected through meditative study.

Astell's lively manifesto was received with great enthusiasm by literary London. Her prose was frequently remarked on for its eloquence: John Evelyn praised her work in *Numismata* (1697), Daniel Defoe emulated her in *An Essay upon Projects* (1697), and John Dunton advertised the tract in his publications. Her ideas also inspired other talented young women, including her friends Lady Mary Wortley Montagu, Elizabeth Elstob, and Lady Mary Chudleigh. *A Serious Proposal to the Ladies* was Astell's best-selling work, and by 1701 four editions had been published.

Nonetheless, Astell's early publications were also greeted with criticism. In 1696 there appeared a caustic reply to both *Letters Concerning the Love of God* and *A Serious Proposal to the Ladies* in an anonymous work, *A Discourse Concerning the Love of God,* written by Damaris Masham, the daughter of Ralph Cudworth. Curiously, in a 12 March 1743 letter to Ballard, Thomas Rawlins observed that "Lady Masham . . . was supposed to be Author of Mrs Astells Serious Proposal to the Ladies." In reality, although Masham was a feminist, she was also sympathetic to the empiricist views of Locke, a paying guest at her house in Essex since 1691. Overlooking Astell's criticisms of Norris, Masham attacked both writers for espousing an impractical ethical system based on abstract, rationalist principles rather than common sense. God has obviously designed his creatures for a sociable life, she wrote, and they can no more love and desire him alone, than fishes can fly in the air. Dismissing Astell's letters as "pompous rhapsodies," Masham also attacked *A Serious Proposal to the Ladies* for its utopian visions of "Monasteries and Hermitages," which she believed could only "draw in Discontented, Devout People, with an Imaginary Happiness."

The most damaging response to Astell's work was the suspicion that her idea for a women's college was a call for the restoration of Catholic nunneries. A wealthy woman (possibly Queen Anne) was apparently willing to contribute £10,000 to Astell's plan but was dissuaded by Gilbert Burnet, the Bishop of Salisbury, who warned her that it looked like preparing a way for popery. Astell's next work, *A Serious Proposal to the Ladies, Part II: Wherein a Method Is Offer'd for the Improvement of Their Minds* (1697), was dedicated to Anne and emphasized that her institute would be more academic than monastic, unlike certain "Foreign" establishments. Disappointed that no one was roused to build her college, Astell wrote this second part to provide a philosophical method for women to practice at home. Calling on women to awaken their minds for the sake of their spiritual welfare, she writes: "Can you be in Love with servitude and folly? Can you dote on a mean, ignorant and ignoble Life? An Ingenious Woman is no Prodigy to be star'd on, for you have it in your power to inform the World, that you can every one of you be so, if you please your selves."

Astell's methodology, like Descartes's, does not require any specialized training in Latin, Greek, or mathematics, only the exercising of one's "natural logic." She teaches her readers that "all may *Think,* may use their own Faculties rightly," if only they follow the proper procedures for rigorous thought. They must start, for instance, by defining the terms of the question under consideration, making sure they have cut themselves off from all irrelevant matters, and only reason about things of which they have clear and distinct ideas. A good philosopher, Astell says, always conducts her thoughts in an orderly manner, from the most simple to the most complex, judging no further than she perceives and taking nothing for truth which is not evidently known to be so. In "Cartesian Reason and

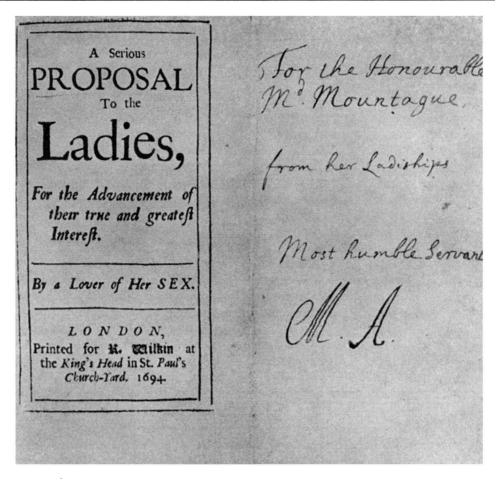

Title page, with the author's inscription to Lady Mary Wortley Montagu, for the work in which Astell exhorts women to develop their rational faculty (British Library)

Gendered Reason" (1993) Margaret Atherton focuses on this second part of *A Serious Proposal to the Ladies,* contrasting Astell's concept of reason with modern feminist critiques of Cartesianism. Whereas some writers maintain that Descartes's rationalism implicitly excludes women, Atherton writes, Astell's feminist arguments are a healthy reminder that there is another conception of Cartesian reason, one that emphasizes the general characteristics underlying all human thought processes, including those of women.

Shortly after the second part of *A Serious Proposal to the Ladies,* Astell published her second most popular feminist work, *Some Reflections Upon Marriage, Occasion'd by the Duke & Dutchess Of Mazarine's Case; which is also consider'd* (1700), written in response to the unhappy situation of her Chelsea neighbor, Hortense Mancini, the Duchess of Mazarin. Starting with her neighbor's divorce, Astell launches into a general assessment of marriage. This sacred and venerable "Institution of Heaven," she says, has been defiled by the "ill Choice" and "foolish Conduct" of men and women. There are few successful alliances, according to Astell, because the majority of men marry for irrational motives, such as power, money, vanity, and passion, rather than true friendship. Continuing the theme of *A Serious Proposal to the Ladies,* Astell argues that women should be pitied because they lack the education to make rational decisions; and if their husband is a tyrant or a fool, she says, women also lack the mental fortitude to endure lives of misery and abuse.

In the preface to the third edition of *Reflections Upon Marriage* (1706), Astell's critique of marriage goes even further, articulating one of the first feminist analogies between domestic despotism and political tyranny: "If *all Men are born free,*" she writes, "how is it that all Women are born slaves? as they must be if the being subjected to the *inconstant, uncertain, unknown, arbitrary Will* of Men, be the *perfect Condition of Slavery?*" While she does not advocate a woman's right to resist tyranny within marriage, Astell uses this analogy to highlight the hypocrisy of Whigs, such as Locke, who distinguish between a man's freedom (in the public sphere) and a woman's subjection (in private) on purely arbitrary grounds. Indeed, starting with *Some Reflections Upon Mar-*

riage, Astell became increasingly active in party political debates, and in 1704 she published three tracts along conservative Tory lines: *A Fair Way with the Dissenters, An Impartial Enquiry* and *Moderation Truly Stated.* Until recently most critics agreed with Florence Smith's opinion that these pamphlets "passed into oblivion" largely because they held no relevance beyond the conflicts of the day. Patricia Springborg, however, makes a convincing case for their significance, arguing that Astell's forgotten works, together with *Some Reflections Upon Marriage,* include some of the earliest and most astute criticisms of Locke's entire corpus.

The culmination of Astell's attack against Locke is *The Christian Religion, As Profess'd by a Daughter Of The Church of England. In a Letter to the Right Honourable, T.L. C.I.* (1705), a 418–page treatise in the form of a letter to Lady Catherine Jones. Regarded as the definitive statement of Astell's religious and philosophical views, this work was designed to acquaint women with the rational principles behind their religious convictions, claiming that most of "the Follies and Vices that Women are subject to . . . are owing to our paying too great a deference to other Peoples judgments, and too little to our own." *The Christian Religion* also aims to meet common threats to religious orthodoxy, its main targets being Locke's *An Essay Concerning Humane Understanding* (1690), his *Reasonableness of Christianity* (1695), and his letters to Edward Stillingfleet, the bishop of Worcester, as well as Masham's *A Discourse Concerning the Love of God* and the anonymous *The Ladies Religion* (1697), both of which were assumed by Astell to have been written by Locke.

In particular, Astell is disturbed by Locke's controversial suggestion in *An Essay Concerning Humane Understanding* that it might be possible that God could endow some systems of matter with the power of thought. Like many writers of her time, Astell believes that if thought can be attributed to matter, then there is no philosophical proof that the soul is distinct from the body and therefore immaterial and immortal. Her strategy of refutation is to point out inconsistencies in Locke's own writings. In some passages of *An Essay Concerning Human Understanding* and in his letters, she writes, Locke admits that although human understanding is limited, one can have knowledge of the "Repugnancy of Ideas": that it is contradictory to say that a substance is solid and not solid at the same time, for instance, or that it is impossible for God to change the essential property of a thing. Astell writes that the ideas of extension and thought are "repugnant" or incompatible in this way. As a Cartesian dualist, she believes that thought is the essence of mind and extension the essence of body; each substance and its essential attributes are necessarily inseparable; therefore, says Astell, one can know that "an Extended Being does not,

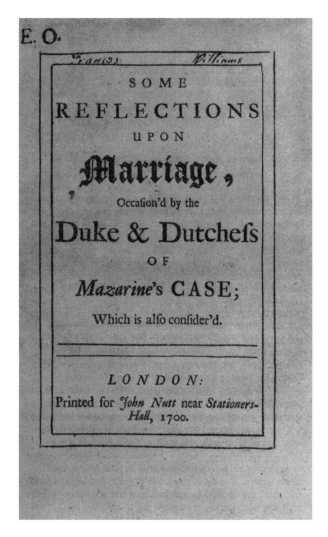

Title page for Astell's feminist critique of matrimony, written in response to the divorce of her neighbor Hortense Mancini, Duchess of Mazarin (Folger Shakespeare Library)

cannot Think, any more than a Circle can have the Properties of a Triangle." Mimicking Masham's criticisms in *A Discourse Concerning the Love of God,* Astell supposes that Locke can hardly despise her arguments as "the *Rhapsodies* and *Strong Imaginations* of a silly Woman" when they thus proceed by his own principles.

Her approach is commended by William Parry, an associate of Ballard, who in a letter dated 12 February 1743 remarks that "the Learned Authoress hath with great Dexterity and Success retorted Mr. Locke's Metaphysical Artillery against himself, confuted his whimsical Idea of *Thinking* Matter, and given him a genteel Foil." Modern commentators such as Kathleen Squadrito and Richard Acworth, however, note that although Astell's argument is perceptive, her critique of thinking matter overlooks a significant difference between Locke's views and the Cartesian conception of substance.

Following *The Christian Religion,* Astell's only other major tract is *Bart'lemy Fair: Or, An Enquiry after Wit; In which due Respect is had to a Letter Concerning Enthusiasm, To my LORD **** (1709), a defense of orthodox Christianity. The same year she was twice satirized by either Richard Steele or Jonathan Swift in issues 32 and 63 of *The Tatler* (23 June and 3 September 1709). They presented her as "Madonella," the head of a reclusive "Order of Platonics" whose retreat is infiltrated by a group of rakish men. The assembly of nuns hide behind doors "pale, trembling, and fretting," until Madonella confronts the men, only to be wooed by deceitful flattery for her book, "an excellent and seraphic discourse." Not wishing to remain prominent in public controversy, Astell stopped writing after 1709 in order to become the director of a girls' charity school in Chelsea. Leading a relatively quiet life in her later years, she was almost completely forgotten soon after she died of breast cancer, at age sixty-four, on 9 May 1731. The efforts of recent historians and feminist scholars, however, have made it possible to pay tribute to this impressively consistent woman philosopher, one of the first thinkers to employ Cartesian ideas against the subjugation of women, and a worthy opponent to some of the foremost intellectuals of her age.

Biographies:

Florence M. Smith, *Mary Astell* (New York: Columbia University Press, 1916);

George Ballard, "Mary Astell," in his *Memoirs of Several Ladies of Great Britain, who have been celebrated for their writings or skill in the learned languages, arts and sciences,* modernized edition, edited, with an introduction, by Ruth Perry (Detroit: Wayne State University Press, 1985), pp. 382–392;

Ruth Perry, *The Celebrated Mary Astell: An Early English Feminist* (Chicago & London: University of Chicago Press, 1986).

References:

Richard Acworth, "The Theory of Love" and "Essence and Substance, and the Immortality of the Soul," in his *The Philosophy of John Norris of Bemerton (1657–1712)* (Hildesheim & New York: Olms, 1979), pp. 172–180, 237–238;

Margaret Atherton, "Cartesian Reason and Gendered Reason," in *A Mind of One's Own: Feminist Essays on Reason and Objectivity,* edited by Louise M. Antony and Charlotte Witt (Boulder, Colo. & Oxford: Westview Press, 1993), pp. 19–34;

Joan K. Kinnaird, "Mary Astell and the Conservative Contribution to English Feminism," *Journal of British Studies,* 19 (Autumn 1979): 53–75;

John McCrystal, "Revolting Women: The Use of Revolutionary Discourse in Mary Astell and Mary Wollstonecraft Compared," *History of Political Thought,* 14 (Summer 1993): 189–203;

Jane Elizabeth Norton, "Some Uncollected Authors XXVII: Mary Astell, 1666–1731," *Book Collector,* 10 (Spring 1961): 58–65;

Ruth Perry, "Radical Doubt and the Liberation of Women," *Eighteenth-Century Studies,* 18 (Summer 1985): 472–493;

Hilda L. Smith, "'A New Path to Honour,' English Feminists, 1690–1710," in her *Reason's Disciples: Seventeenth-Century English Feminists* (Urbana: University of Illinois Press, 1982), pp. 115–139;

Patricia Springborg, "Astell, Masham, and Locke: religion and politics," in *Women Writers and the Early Modern British Political Tradition,* edited by Hilda L. Smith (Cambridge: Cambridge University Press, 1998), pp. 105–125;

Springborg, "Mary Astell (1666–1731), Critic of Locke," *American Political Science Review,* 89 (September 1995): 621–633;

Kathleen M. Squadrito, "Mary Astell," in *A History of Women Philosophers,* volume 3, edited by Mary Ellen Waithe (Dordrecht, Netherlands & Boston: Kluwer, 1991), pp. 87–99;

Squadrito, "Mary Astell's Critique of Locke's View of Thinking Matter," *Journal of History of Philosophy,* 25 (July 1987): 433–439.

Papers:

The 1689 manuscript of Mary Astell's *A Collection of Poems humbly presented and Dedicated To the most Reverend Father in God William By Divine Providence Lord Archbishop of Canterbury &c* (Rawlinson MSS Poet. 154:50) can be found in the Bodleian Library, Oxford. There are full transcriptions of this item and other materials in Ruth Perry's biography of Astell.

Francis Bacon

(22 January 1561 – 9 April 1626)

Rosalind Davies
University College London

See also the Bacon entries in *DLB 151: British Prose Writers of the Early Seventeenth Century* and *DLB 236: British Rhetoricians and Logicians, 1500–1660, First Series.*

BOOKS: *Essayes. Religious Meditations. Places of perswasion and disswasion. Seene and allowed* (London: Printed by John Windet for Humfrey Hooper, 1597); revised and enlarged as *The Essaies Of S͏ͬ Francis Bacon Knight, the Kings Solliciter Generall* (London: Printed by John Beale, 1612); revised and enlarged as *The Essayes Or Covnsels, Civill And Morall, Of Francis Lo. Vervlam, Viscovnt S͏ͭ Alban. Newly Enlarged* (London: Printed by John Haviland for Hanna Barret & Richard Whitaker, 1625);

A Letter written out of England to an English Gentleman remaining at Padua, containing a true Report of a strange Conspiracie, contriued betweene Edward Squire, lately executed for the same treason as Actor, and Richard Wallpoole a Iesuite, as Deuiser and Suborner against the person of the Queenes Maiestie, anonymous (London: Printed by the Deputies of Christopher Barker, 1599);

A Declaration of the Practises & Treasons attempted and committed by Robert late Earle of Essex and his Complices, against her Maiestie and her Kingdoms, and of the proceedings as well at the Arraignments & Conuictions of the said late Earle, and his adherents, as after: Together with the very Confessions and other parts of the Euidences themselues, word for word taken out of the Originals, anonymous (London: Printed by Robert Barker, 1601);

A Briefe Discovrse, Touching The Happie Vnion Of The Kingdomes Of England, And Scotland. Dedicated In Private To His Maiestie, anonymous (London: Printed by Richard Read for Faelix Norton & sold by William Aspley, 1603); republished as *The Union Of The Two Kingdoms Of Scotland And England: Or, The elaborate Papers of Sir Francis Bacon, Lord Verulam, Viscount of St. Alban, sometime High Chancellor of England; The greatest Sates-man* [sic] *of his Nation, and Schollar of his Age, concerning that Affair. Published in this form, for the publick satisfaction* (Edinburgh, 1670);

Francis Bacon; portrait from the studio of Paul van Somer (National Portrait Gallery, London)

Sir Francis Bacon His Apologie, In Certaine imputations concerning the late Earle of Essex. Written to the right Honorable his very good Lord, the Earle of Deuonshire, Lord Lieutenant of Ireland (London: Printed by Richard Field for Felix Norton, 1604);

Certaine Considerations touching the better pacification and Edification of the Church of England: Dedicated to his most Excellent Maiestie, anonymous (London: Printed by Thomas Purfoot for Henriè Tomes, 1604);

The Twoo Bookes of Francis Bacon. Of the proficience and aduancement of Learning, diuine and humane. To the King (London: Printed by Thomas Purfoot & Thomas Creede for Henrie Tomes, 1605); translated and enlarged as *Opera Francisci Baronis De Vervlamio, Vice-Comitis Sancti Albani; Tomvs Primvs: Qui continet De Dignitate & Augmentis Scientiarum Libros IX. Ad Regem Svvm* (London: Printed by John Haviland, 1623); translated by Gilbert Wats as *Of The Advancement And Proficience Of Learning or the Partitions of Sciences. IX Bookes. Written in Latin by the Most Eminent, Illustrious & Famous Lord Francis Bacon Baron of Verulam Vicont St. Alban Counsilour of Estate and Lord Chancellor of England. Interpreted by Gilbert Wats* (Oxford: Printed by Leonard Lichfield for Robert Young & Edward Forrest, 1640);

Francisci Baconi Eqvitis Avrati, Procvratoris Secvndi, Iacobi Regis Magnæ Britanniæ, De Sapientia Vetervm Liber, Ad Inclytam Academiam Cantabrigiensem (London: Printed by Robert Barker, 1609); translated by Arthur Gorges as *The Wisedome Of The Ancients, Written In Latine By the Right Honourable Sir Francis Bacon Knight, Baron of Verulam, and Lord Chancelor of England. Done into English by Sir Arthur Gorges Knight* (London: Printed by John Bill, 1619);

The Charge of Sir Francis Bacon Knight, His Maiesties Attourney generall, touching Duells, vpon an information in the Star-chamber against Priest and Wright. With The Decree of the Star-chamber in the same cause (London: Printed by George Eld for Robert Wilson & sold by Robert Wilson & George Potter, 1614);

Francisci De Verulamio Summi Angliæ Cancelsaris Instauratio Magna. Multi pertransibunt & augebitur scienta (London: Printed by Bonham Norton & John Bill, 1620)—includes *Novum Organum* and *Parasceve ad Historiam Naturalem et Experimentalem*);

The Historie Of The Raigne of King Henry the Seuenth. Written By the Right Honourable, Francis, Lord Verulam, Viscount St. Alban (London: Printed by William Stansby for Matthew Lownes & William Barret, 1622);

Francisci Baronis De Vervlamio, Vice-Comitis Sancti Albani, Historia Natvralis Et Experimentalis Ad Condendam Philosophiam: Sive, Phænomena Vniversi: Quæ est Instaurationis Magnæ Pars Tertia (London: Printed by John Haviland for Matthew Lownes & William Barret, 1622); translated by R. G. [Robert Gentili?] as *The Naturall And Experimental History of Winds, &c. Written in Latine by the Right Honorable Francis Lo: Veru-*

lam, Viscount St. Alban (London: Printed for Humphrey Moseley & Thomas Dring, 1653);

Francisci Baronis De Vervlamio, Vice-Comitis Sancti Albani, Historia Vitae & Mortis. Sive, Titvlvs Secvndvs in Historia Naturali & Experimentali ad condendam Philosophiam: Quae est Instavrationis Magnae Pars Tertia Historia Vitae et Mortis (London: Printed by John Haviland for Matthew Lownes, 1623); translated anonymously as *The Historie of Life and Death. With Observations Naturall and Experimentall for the Prolonging of Life. Written by the Right Honorable Francis Lord Verulam, Viscount S. Alban* (London: Printed by John Okes for Humphrey Mosley, 1638); translated, and edited, by William Rawley as *History Naturall And Experimentall, Of Life and Death, Or Of the Prolongation of Life. Written in Latine by the Right Honorable Francis Lo. Verulam, Vis-Count St. Alban* (London: Printed by John Haviland for William Lee and Humphrey Mosley, 1638);

Apophthegmes New And Old. Collected By The Right Honovrable, Francis Lo. Vervlam, Viscount St. Alban (London: Printed by John Haviland for Hanna Barret, & Richard Whittaker, 1625 [i.e., 1624]);

Sylva Sylvarvm Or A Naturall Historie. In Ten Centuries. Written By The Right Honourable Francis Lo. Verulam Viscount St. Alban. Published after the Authors death, By William Rawley Doctor of Diuinitie, late his Lordships Chaplaine, edited by Rawley (London: Printed by John Haviland & Augustine Mathewes for William Lee, 1626)—includes *New Atlantis, Magnalia Naturae,* and *Praecipue Quoad Usus Humanos;*

Considerations Tovching A Warre with Spaine. Written by the Right Honourable Francis Lo. Verulam, Vi. St. Alban (London, 1629);

The Elements Of The Common Lawes of England, Branched into a double Tract: The One Contayning a Collection of some principall Rules and Maximes of the Common Law, with their Latitude and Extent. Explicated for the more facile Introduction of such as are studiously addicted to that noble Profession. The Other The Vse of the Common Law, for preseruation of our Persons, Goods, and good Names. According to the Lawes and Customes of this Land. By the late Sir Francis Bacon Knight, Lo: Verulam and Viscount S. Alban (London: Printed by Robert Young for the Assignes of John More, 1630);

Three Speeches of The Right Honorable, Sir Francis Bacon Knight, then his Majesties Sollicitor Generall, after Lord Verulam, Viscount Saint Alban. Concerning the Post-Nati, Naturalization of the Scotch in England, Vnion of the Lawes of the Kingdomes of England and Scotland. Published by the Authors Copy, and Licensed by Authority (London: Printed by Richard Badger for Samuel Broun, 1641);

Cases Of Treason. Written By Sir Francis Bacon, Knight, His Maiesties Solicitor Generall (London: Printed by the Assignes of John More & sold by Matthew Walbancke & William Coke, 1641); reprinted in part as *The Office of Constables. Written by Francis Bacon Knight, His Majesties Atturney Generall in the yeare of our Lord 1610. Being an Answer to the Questions proposed by Sir Alexander Hay, touching the Office of Constables. Declaring what power they have, and how they ought to be cherished in their Office* (N.p.: Printed for Francis Coules, 1641);

A Wise and Moderate Discourse, Concerning Church-Affaires. As it was written, long since, by the famous Authour of those Considerations, which seem to have some reference to this. Now published for the common good (London, 1641); republished as *True Peace: Or A Moderate Discourse To Compose the unsettled Consciences, and Greatest Differences In Ecclesiastical Affaires. Written long since by the no less famous then Learned Sir Francis Bacon, Lord Verulam, Viscount St. Alban* (London: Printed for A. C., 1663);

A Confession Of Faith. Penned By an Orthodox man of the reformed Religion: Dedicated to some eminent Persons, now assembled in Parliament (London: Printed for William Hope, 1641);

A Speech Delivered By Sir Francis Bacon, In the lower House of Parliament quinto Iacobi, concerning the Article of Naturalization of the Scottish Nation (London, 1641);

An Essay Of A King, With An explanation what manner of persons those should be that are to execute the power or ordinance of the Kings Prerogative. Written By the Right Honorable Francis, Lord Verulam Viscount Saint Alban. Decemb. 2, attributed to Bacon (London: Printed for Richard Best, 1642); republished as *XVI Propositions Concerning The Raign and Government of a King. Propounded, by The Right Honourable, Sir Francis Bacon, late Lord Chancellour of England. Wherein is shewed, 1. The Power which God hath given to Kings. 2. How a King ought to wear His Crown. 3. To make Religion the Rule of Government. 4. The danger in alteration of Government. 5. The love which a King oweth to His Subjects* (London: Printed for R. Wood, 1647);

The Learned Reading Of Sir Francis Bacon, One of the Maiesties learned Counsell at Law, upon the Statute of Uses: Being his double Reading to the Honourable Society of Grayes Inne. Published for the Common good (London: Printed for Mathew Walbancke & Lawrence Chapman, 1642);

Ordinances made By The Right Honourable Sir Francis Bacon Knight, Lord Verulam and Viscount of Saint Albans, being then Lord Chancellor. For the better and more regular Administration of Iustice in the Chancery, to be daily observed saving the Prerogative of this Covrt (London:

Printed for Mathew Walbanke & Lawrence Chapman, 1642);

The Remaines Of The Right Honorable Francis Lord Verulam Viscount of St. Albanes, sometimes Lord Chancellor of England. Being Essayes and severall Letters to severall great Personages, and other pieces of various and high concernment not heretofore published. A Table whereof for the Readers more ease is adjoyned (London: Printed by Bernard Alsop for Lawrence Chapman, 1648); republished as *The Mirrour of State and Eloqvence. Represented In the Incomparable Letters of the Famous St. Francis Bacon, Lord Verulam, St. Albans, to Queene Elizabeth, King James, and other Personages of the highest trust and honour in the three Nations of England, Scotland, and Ireland. Concerning the better and more sure Establishment of those Nations in the affaires of Peace and Warre. With an ample and admirable accompt of his Faith, written by the express Command of King Iames: Together with the Character of a true Christian, and some other adjuncts of rare Devotion* (London: Printed for Lawrence Chapman, 1656);

The Felicity Of Queen Elizabeth: And Her Times, With other Things; By the Right Honorable Francis Ld. Bacon Viscount St Alban (London: Printed by T. Newcomb for George Latham, 1651);

A True and Historical Relation Of the Poysoning of Sir Thomas Overbury. With the Severall Arraignments and Speeches of those that were executed thereupon. Also, all the passages concerning the Divorce between Robert late Earle of Essex, and the Lady Frances Howard: with King James and other large Speeches. Collected out of the Papers of Sir Francis Bacon, the Kings Attorney-General, attributed to Bacon (London: Printed by T. M. & A. C. for John Benson & John Playford, 1651);

New Atlantis. A Work unfinished. Written by the Right Honorable Francis, Lord Verulam, Viscount St. Albans (London: Printed by Thomas Newcomb, 1659); bound with *Mr Bushell's Abridgment Of the Lord Chancellor Bacon's Philosophical Theory In Mineral Prosecutions* (London, 1659);

A Letter Of Advice Written by Sr. Francis Bacon To the Duke of Buckingham, When he became Favourite to King James, Never before Printed (London: Printed for R. H. & H. B., 1661);

A Charge Given by the most Eminent and Learned Sr. Francis Bacon Kt. Late Lord Chancellor of England, at a Sessions holden for the Verge, in the Reign of the Late King James. Declaring The Latitude of the Jurisdiction thereof, and the Offences therein inquireable, as well by the Common-Law, as by several Statutes herein particularly mentioned (London: Printed for Robert Pawley, 1662);

Letters and Remains of the Lord Chancellor Bacon, edited by Robert Stephens (London: W. Bowyer, 1734)–

includes *Valerius Terminus of the Interpretation of Nature with the Annotations of Hermes Stella;*

The Works of Francis Bacon, Baron of Verulam, Viscount St. Alban, and Lord High Chancellor of England, 7 volumes, edited by James Spedding, Robert Leslie Ellis, and Douglas Denon Heath (London: Longman/ Simpkin/Hamilton/Whittaker/J. Bain/E. Hodgson/ Washbourne/Richardson Brothers/Houlston/Bickers & Bush/Willis & Sotheran/J. Cornish/L. Booth/J. Snow/Aylott, 1858–1861; 15 volumes, Boston: Brown & Taggard, 1860–1864)—comprises volume 1 (1858); volume 2 (1859); volume 3 (1859); volume 4, *Translations of the Philosophical Works, Vol. I* (1860); volume 5, *Translations of the Philosophical Works, Vol. II* (1861); volume 6, *Literary and Professional Works, Vol. I* (1861); and volume 7, *Literary and Professional Works, Vol. II* (1861);

The Promus of Formularies and Elegancies (Being Private Notes, Circ. 1594, Hitherto Unpublished), edited by Mrs. Henry Pott (London: Longmans, Green, 1883);

Collotype Facsimile & Type Transcript of an Elizabethan Manuscript Preserved at Alnwick Castle, Northumberland, by Bacon, Thomas Radcliffe, Philip Sidney, and Robert Dudley, edited by Frank James Burgoyne (London, New York & Bombay: Longmans, Green, 1904)—includes "Of Tribute, or Giving What Is Due," "Of Magnaminitie," "Advertisement Touching Private Censure," "Advertisement Touching the Controversies of the Church," and "Letter to a French Gentleman Touching the Proceedings in England in Ecclesiastical Causes";

Francis Bacon's Natural Philosophy: A New Source: A Transcription of Manuscript Hardwick 72A, Monograph Series, no. 5, edited by Grahan Rees and Christopher Upton (Chalfont St. Giles, U.K.: British Society for the History of Science, 1984)—comprises *De viis mortis.*

Editions: *Certaine Miscellany Works Of The Right Honovrable, Francis Lo. Verulam, Viscount S. Alban. Pvblished By Willaim Rawley, Doctor of Divinity, one of his Maiesties Chaplaines* (London: Printed by John Haviland for Humphrey Robinson, 1629)—comprises *Considerations touching a vvarre with Spaine, An advertisement touching an holy vvarre,* and *An offer to our late soveraigne King Iames, of a digest to be made of the lawes of England;*

Francisci Baconi Baronis De Vervlamio, Vice-Comitis Sancti Albani, Opervm Moralivm Et Civilivm Tomus. Qui continet: Historiam Regni Henrici Septimi, Regis Angliae. Sermones Fideles, sive Interiora Rerum. Tractatum de Sapientia Veterum. Dialogum de Bello Sacro. Et Novam Atlantidem. Ab ipso Honoratissimo Auctore, praeterquam in paucis, Latinitate donatus. Cura & Fide Guilielmi Rawley, Sacrae Theologiae Doctoris, olim Dominationi *suae, nunc Serenissimae Majestati Regiae, a Sacris. In hoc volumine, iterum excusi, includuntur: Tractatus de Augmentis Scientiarum. Historia Ventorum. Historia Vitae & Mortis* (London: Printed by Edward Griffin & John Haviland & sold by Richard Whitaker & Joyce Norton, 1638);

Francisci Baconi De Verulamio Scripta In Natvrali Et Vniversali Philosophia, edited by Isaac Gruter (Amsterdam: Elzevir, 1653);

Resuscitatio, Or, Bringing into Publick Light Severall Pieces, Of The Works, Civil, Historical, Philosophical, & Theological, Hitherto Sleeping; Of the Right Honourable Francis Bacon, Baron of Verulam, Viscount Saint Alban. According to the best Corrected Coppies. Together, With his Lordships Life. By William Rawley, Doctor of Divinity, His Lordships First, and Last, Chapleine. Afterwards, Chapleine, to His late Maiesty, edited by William Rawley (London: Printed by Sarah Griffin for William Lee, 1657); republished in part as *Several Letters Written By This Honourable Author, To Queen Elizabeth, King James, Divers Lords, and Others* (London: Printed by T. R. for William Lee, 1671);

Opuscula Varia Posthuma, Philosophica, Civilia, Et Theologia, Francisci Baconi, Baronis de Verulamio Vice-Comitis Sancti Albani, Nunc primum Edita. Cura & Fide Guilielmi Rawley, Sacrae Theologiae Doctoris, primo Dominationi suae, postea Serenissimae Majestati Regiae, a Sacris. Vna cum Nobilissimi Auctoris Vita, edited by Rawley (London: Printed by Roger Daniel, 1658)—comprises "Nobilissimi auctoris vita," "Historia densi & rari," "Opuscula sex philosophica simul collecta," "Opus illustre in felicem memoriam Elizabethae Angliae Reginae," and "Confessio fidei";

Francisci Baconi . . . opera omnia, quae extant, philosophica, moralia, politica, historica . . . in quibus complures alii tractatus, quos brevitatis causa praetermittere visum est, comprehensi sunt, hactenus nunquam conjunctim edita, jam vero summo studio collecta, uno volumine comprehensa, & ab innumeris mendis repurgata: cum indice rerum ac verborum universali absolutissimo. His praefixa est auctoris vita, edited by Johann Baptist Schonwetter (Frankfort am Main: Printed by Mathias Kempffer for Johann Baptist Schonwetter, 1665);

The Second Part Of The Resuscitatio Or A Collection Of several pieces of the Works Of the Right Honourable Francis Bacon, Baron of Verulam, and Viscount of St. Albans. Some of them formerly Printed in smaller Volumes, and being almost lost, are now Collected and put into Folio, with some of his other Pieces, which never yet was published. Collected By William Rawley Doctor of Divinity, his Lordships first and last Chaplain, and lately Chaplain in Ordinary to his Majesty, edited by Rawley (London: Printed by S. G. & B. G. for William Lee,

1670); republished in part as *A Preparatory To The History Natural & Experimental. Written Originally in Latine, by the Right Honourable Francis Lord Verulam, Lord High Chancellour of England, and now faithfully rendred into English. By a Well-wisher to his Lordships Writings* (London: Printed by Sarah Griffing & Ben. Griffing, for William Lee, 1670);

Baconiana. Or Certain Genuine Remains of Sr. Francis Bacon, Baron of Verulam, and Viscount of St. Albans; In Arguments Civil and Moral, Natural, Medical, Theological, and Bibliographical; Now the First time faithfully Published. An Account of these Remains, and of all his Lordship's other Works, is given by the Publisher, in a Discourse by way of Introduction, edited by Thomas Tenison (London: Printed by J. D. for Richard Chiswell, 1679);

Francisci Baconi Baronis de Verulamio . . . Opera omnia, quatuor voluminibus comprehensa: hactenus edita, ad autographorum maxime fidem, emendantur; nonnulla etiam, ex MSS. codicibus deprompta, nunc primum prodeunt, 4 volumes, edited by John Blackbourne (London: R. Gosling, 1730);

The Philosophical Works of Francis Bacon, Baron of Verulam, Viscount St. Albans, and Lord High Chancellor of England; Methodized and Made English, from the Originals, with Occasional Notes, to Explain What Is Obscure, and Shew How Far the Several Plans of the Author, for the Advancement of All Parts of Knowledge, Have Been Executed to the Present Time, 3 volumes, edited by Peter Shaw (London: J. J. & P. Knapton/D. Midwinter & A. Ward/A. Bettesworth & C. Hitch/J. Pemberton/ Osborn & Longman/C. Rivington/F. Clay/J. Batley/R. Hett/T. Hatchett, 1733);

The Works of Francis Bacon, Baron of Verulam, Viscount St. Alban, Lord High Chancellor of England. In Four Volumes. With Several Additional Pieces, Never Before Printed in Any Edition of His Works. To Which Is Prefixed, a New Life of the Author, 4 volumes, edited by David Mallet (London: Printed for A. Millar, 1740);

The Works of Francis Bacon: Baron of Verulam, Viscount St. Alban, and Lord High Chancellor of England, 5 volumes, edited by Thomas Birch (London: Printed for A. Millar, 1765);

The Works of Francis Bacon, Lord Chancellor of England: A New Edition, 16 volumes in 17, edited by Basil Montagu (London: William Pickering, 1825–34);

The New Organon, and Related Writings, edited, with an introduction, by Fulton H. Anderson (New York: Liberal Arts Press, 1960);

"Cogitata et Visa de Interpretatione Naturae, sive de Scientia Operativa," "Tempus Partus Masculus, sive Instauratio Magna Inperii Humani in Argumentum," and "Redargutio Philosophiarum,"

translated by Benjamin Farrington in his *The Philosophy of Francis Bacon: An Essay on its Development from 1603 to 1609, with New Translation of Fundamental Texts* (Liverpool: University of Liverpool Press, 1964);

The History of the Reign of King Henry the Seventh, edited by F. J. Levy (New York: Bobbs-Merrill, 1972);

The Advancement of Learning, edited by G. W. Kitchin (London: Dent, 1973);

The Advancement of Learning, and New Atlantis, edited by Arthur Johnson (Oxford: Clarendon Press, 1974);

Gli 'Essayes' di Francis Bacon: Studio introduttivo, testo critico e commento, edited by Mario Melchionda (Florence: L. S. Olschki, 1979);

The Great Instauration; and, New Atlantis, edited by Jerry Weinberger (Arlington Heights, Ill.: AHM Publishing, 1980);

The Essayes or Counsels, Civill and Morall, edited by Michael Kiernan (Oxford: Clarendon Press, 1985; Cambridge, Mass: Harvard University Press, 1985);

Novum Organum with Other Parts of the Great Instauration, translated and edited by Peter Urbach and John Gibson (Chicago: Open Court, 1994);

Francis Bacon, edited by Brian Vickers (Oxford & New York: Oxford University Press, 1996);

The Advancement of Learning, edited, with an introduction, by Kiernan (Oxford: Clarendon Press, 2000);

The New Organon, edited by Lisa Jardine and Michael Silverthorne (Cambridge & New York: Cambridge University Press, 2000).

OTHER: Descriptions of dumb-shows, in *Certaine Devises and shewes presented to her Maiestie by the Gentlemen of Grayes-Inne at her Highnesse Court in Greenewich, the twenty eighth day of Februarie in the thirtieth yeare of her Maiesties most happy Raigne,* by Thomas Hughes and others (London: Printed by Robert Robinson, 1587);

The Translation Of Certaine Psalmes Into English Verse: By The Right Honovrable, Francis Lo. Vervlam, Viscount St. Alban, translated by Bacon (London: Printed by John Haviland for Hanna Barret, & Richard Whittaker, 1625);

"The Vse Of The Law. Provided for Preservation of Our Persons. Goods, and Good Names. According to the Practise of The Lawes and Customes of this Land," attributed to Bacon, in *The Lawyers Light: Or, A due direction for the study of the Law,* by John Doddridge (London: Benjamin Fisher, 1629);

"Speeches of the Counsellors," in *Gesta Grayorum: Or, The History Of the High and mighty Prince, Henry Prince of Purpoole, Arch-Duke of Stapulia and Bernardia, Duke of High and Nether Holborn, Marquis of St. Giles and Tottenham, Count Palatine of Bloomsbury and Clerkenwell, Great Lord of the Cantons of Islington, Kentish-Town, Paddington and Knights-bridge, Knight of the most Heroical Order of Helmet, and Sovereign of the Same; Who Reigned and Died, A. D. 1594. Together With A Masque, as it was presented (by His Highness's Command) for the Entertainment of Q. Elizabeth; who, with the Nobles of both Courts, was present thereat* (London: Printed for W. Canning, 1688).

Francis Bacon is a major figure in the intellectual tradition of Europe. Statesman, philosopher, supreme promoter of natural science based on observation and experiment, Bacon was the patron saint of the Royal Society and of Restoration science, the dedicatee of Immanuel Kant's *Kritik der reinen Vernunft* (1781; translated as *Critique of Pure Reason,* 1855), and the lawyer whose legal reforms were embodied in the Code Napoléon of France in the nineteenth century. As the subject of popular myth Bacon's reputation has been dramatically shaped by the execution of his patron, the Earl of Essex (which in the eyes of many historians of the nineteenth and twentieth centuries defined Bacon as an arch betrayer), and by his own fall from power near the end of his life (charged with bribery in his dealings in the court of Chancery). The portrait of Bacon as corrupt has been widely recycled, providing a seductive set of contradictions, expressed by Alexander Pope in an epigram in his *An Essay on Man* (1734): "If parts allure thee, think how Bacon shin'd, / The wisest, brightest, meanest of mankind."

Francis, born on 22 January 1561, and his brother, Anthony, were the two surviving sons of Sir Nicholas Bacon by his second marriage. Sir Nicholas had risen from his birth into the family of an Ipswich abbot's sheep reeve to become lord keeper of the Great Seal in the reign of Elizabeth I. In *The Arte of English Poesie* (1589) the poet George Puttenham described Sir Nicholas as "a most eloquent man, and of rare learning and wisdom, as I ever knew England to breed." With his first wife, a merchant's daughter named Jane Fernley, Sir Nicholas had seven children. Within weeks of his wife's death in 1552 he married Anne Cooke, one of the five daughters of Sir Anthony Cooke, an eminent scholar who had been the tutor to Henry VIII's son Prince Edward, later Edward VI. The Cooke daughters were known for their erudition, and Anne later published her translations of sermons of Bernardino Ochino as well as an English-language version of John Jewel's *Apologia ecclesiae anglicanae* (Apology for the Church of England, 1562). This marriage set in place another crucial relationship that later bore significantly on Bacon's career. Anne's sister Mildred became the

second wife of William Cecil, Baron Burghley, who rose to the position of principal secretary under Elizabeth, providing his nephew Francis with a tantalizingly close source of power and influence in government, but one that failed to affect his career materially.

Lady Bacon was also a woman of strong religious conviction, and the education of her sons by Sir Nicholas was shaped by both their mother's radical Protestantism and her reverence for learning. A tutor was appointed to the boys while they lived at home, and for at least three years from 1566, when Anthony was eight years old and Francis was five, John Walsall, a graduate from Christ Church, Oxford, filled this role. Their education was a traditional one, and in the seven or eight years of tutoring that the boys received before they went up to Cambridge in 1573 they would have been taken through the standard classical diet of the grammar-school curriculum. As an introduction to an analysis of "Bacon and Rhetoric" in *The Cambridge Companion to Bacon* (1996), edited by Markku Peltonen, Brian Vickers describes the conventional progress through Cato, Aesop, Ovid, Horace, and Virgil, culminating in the orations of Cicero, which provided the training in formal rhetoric essential to political life. In Bacon's career the ends of such learning were not purely contemplative but practical, and they are expressed, for example, in his legal occupations; in the illustrations, digressions, and conceits of *Essayes. Religious Meditations. Places of perswasion and disswasion. Seene and allowed* (1597; conventionally referred to as the *Essays*); and in his presentation of advice to Elizabeth, and after her, King James.

In April 1573, at the age of twelve, Bacon was sent to Trinity College, Cambridge, as companion to his brother Anthony, although he was younger than the customary age for boys to join the university. The boys were placed under the care of the master of Trinity, John Whitgift, later to become Archbishop of Canterbury. Accounts kept by Whitgift in the 1570s reveal that he bought for Anthony and Francis the major classical texts and commentaries, including (as cited by Vickers) "2 aristotells" costing 36s., two copies of Plato for 24s., "tullies workes" (probably Cicero's philosophical writings), and a separate edition of "ciceronis rheto," that is, the rhetorical works of Cicero. The list of texts bought for the use of the Bacon brothers runs on, covering the orations of Demosthenes, the *Commentarii* of Julius Caesar, works by Salust and Xenophon, and a Latin Bible. As Vickers notes, these records illustrate the "triple emphasis" on philosophy, rhetoric, and history typical of Renaissance humanism, and the components of a grounding in the skills necessary for persuasive speaking and arguing, vital for anyone entering public life.

Bacon's residence at Cambridge between 1573 and 1575 was twice interrupted by outbreaks of the plague. The university was shut between August 1574 and March 1575, and Francis and Anthony departed again for the sake of their health in August 1575. The year after he left Cambridge, Bacon joined the train of the English diplomat Sir Amias Paulet in his embassy to France. As his most recent biographers, Lisa Jardine and Alan Stewart, comment in their *Hostage to Fortune: The Troubled Life of Francis Bacon 1561–1626* (1998), contrary to the stereotype, this journey was not a youthful intermission or "finishing" experience in the style of the European Grand Tour. Bacon himself recommended in his essay "Of Travel" that young men go abroad not "hooded" but in the company of someone able to educate them in the language, places, and people of the country. In Bacon's case the practicalities of arranging a period of residence abroad were as relevant as its advantages in the minds of Sir Nicholas and Lady Bacon, who obtained for their son a license to travel and placed him in a diplomatic household, hence avoiding some of the extreme expense of continental travel.

The English embassy in Paris was the center of news-gathering operations, providing reports to the government at home on political events, religious sensitivities, and accounts of the French court and its personalities. It was strategically important in its proximity to mainland routes and access to London. Attached to the resident ambassador were a host of translators, exiles, intelligencers, secretaries, and officials, and in this environment Bacon acted as secretary, copyist, intelligencer, and, on at least one occasion, as the bearer of confidential messages across the channel to the court of Elizabeth. The working methods of Paulet's embassy became, as Jardine and Stewart suggest, an integral part of Bacon's intellectual practices in years to come. In return for a sum of money from Thomas Bodley (later the founder of the Bodleian Library at Oxford), which Bacon had requested because of the increasing difficulties of living within his allowance, he became the supplier of information to Bodley, who had been for much of his life a Protestant exile on the continent. Bacon was charged with giving an account of the state of the two faiths, Catholicism and Protestantism, in France, and "how both are supported, balanced and managed by the state." Another skill Bacon learned during this period in France is cryptography and deciphering. In his later work *De augmentis scientiarum* (The Advancement of Learning), first published in 1623 as part of *Opera Francisci Baronis De Verulamio, Vice-Comitis Sancti Albani; Tomvs Primvs: Qui continet De Dignitate & Augmentis Scientiarum Libros IX* (Works of Francis Baron of Verulam, Viscount St. Alban: Volume One: Which Contains The Proficiency & Advancement of Learning in Nine Books), he describes a code that he devised "when I

William Cecil, first Baron Burghley, Bacon's uncle and patron (National Portrait Gallery, London)

was at Paris in my early youth, and which I still think worthy of preservation."

Also part of the embassy was the miniaturist Nicholas Hilliard, who had joined Paulet at the queen's command, and this coincidence produced one of the few lasting images of the young Bacon. The art historian Roy Strong, in *Burlington Magazine* (1964), prizes the miniature as "of superlative quality. The features are delicately rendered, the eyes turned out towards the spectator, the lips thin and compressed. The sitter is altogether a superior young man, and the inscription leaves us in no doubt as to his intelligence: *1578 Si tabula daretur digna / Animum mallem Æ[tatis] S[uae] 18* (If the face as painted is deemed worthy, yet I prefer the mind, in his eighteenth year)."

The death of Sir Nicholas Bacon on 20 February 1579 prompted Bacon's return to England, and within weeks he was established, with Anthony, at Gray's Inn in London. His father's concern that his sons should receive a practical education in diplomacy, languages, and the law—which in the last months before Bacon's departure from France had led to his removal from Paulet's embassy in favor of residence with a civil lawyer—stood him in good stead in the absence of any substantial inheritance. Besides receiving daily training in French, his placement in such an environment was the ideal complement for the theoretical university background from which he had come. In 1579, unlike his elder brother and half brothers, Bacon turned with dedication to the law and to politics, although he expressed the view to Lady Bacon and Lord Burghley that men with friends or money or "at their own free election" did not choose to practice at the bar. Bacon's first experience of Parliament was in 1581 and his second in 1584, at which he took a seat at Weymouth. In later parliaments he sat for Taunton and Ipswich.

Bacon's legal career has received less attention than any other aspect of his life. Although there was a gap of seventeen years between the death of his father in 1579 and the publication of his *Essays* and *Maximes of the Law* in 1597, these years, while not productive of greatly influential work, hold much significance for the development of Bacon's mind and are indicative of his enthusiasm for argument and the principle behind the argument. William Holdsworth, author of *A History of English Law* (1903), places his early legal forays in the context of his self-confessed province of "all knowledge": "It is significant that the philosopher who taught that man is the minister and interpreter of nature, and that he can only accomplish and understand in proportion as he has actually and intelligently observed the order of nature, was a lawyer, taught to reason out his rules and principles from diverse decisions upon the concrete facts of individual cases."

The most significant of Bacon's early work does not survive. In 1625 he said about a youthful effort at natural philosophy: "it being now forty years as I remember, since I composed a juvenile work on this subject which, with great confidence and a magnificent title, I named *The Greatest Birth of Time*." What does survive from this early period are four technical legal projects, some speeches in Parliament, and certain sections of Gray's Inn masques or entertainments. As Daniel Coquillette suggests in *Francis Bacon* (1992), these early pieces establish him as a conventional Elizabethan lawyer—a description contrary to the summary of his persistent opponent in legal theory and rival for the attorney generalship, Edward Coke, that Bacon had dangerous "foreign" tendencies and "superficial" legal expertise. Bacon's earliest surviving legal work, *A Brief Discourse Upon the Commission of Bridewell,* was written in 1587 and was unpublished until the nineteenth century. The Bridewell Hospital in London, established in 1557, faced a challenge to its royal commission as being unlawful. Bacon assessed whether the charter stood with "the laws, customs, and statutes of this Realm" and tested it against judicial and statutory law. As is the case with much of Bacon's work, the conventional use of legal sources, analysis, and precedent anticipates the future directions of his thought. Notably, he made an attempt to clarify and classify the sources of the law—"The Law is the most highest inheritance that the King hath; for by the law both the King and all his subjects are ruled and directed"—and the maxims, customs, and statutes by which the king is directed.

Throughout his career Bacon acted as an adviser to Elizabeth and her successor, King James. Several of his advice tracts have been mistakenly thought to be the work of his uncle and main (though unreliable) patron, Burghley. At the end of 1584 Bacon offered to Elizabeth and her ministers advice as to the course to be taken for protection against the Catholic threat at home and abroad. In 1592 a similar theme occupied Bacon's thoughts, and he was engaged to write a formal response to a vigorous attack on Elizabeth's government by the Jesuit Robert Parsons, the *Responsio ad edictum Reginæ Anglicæ,* occasioned by Elizabeth's edict against the Jesuits. Bacon's reply, "Certaine Observations made upon a libel published this present year, 1592," has been mistaken for the work of Burghley; although he wrote from the perspective of his marginal, insecure existence, his writing was taken for the output of a figure at the center of power.

In the early 1590s Bacon composed some performance pieces for entertainments at Gray's Inn. One such device, "Of Tribute, or Giving What Is Due," offers an homage to Elizabeth. Another, *A Conference of Pleasure* (1592), offers the speeches of "Mr Bacon in praise of knowledge" and "Mr Bacon's discourse in praise of his sovereign." At Gray's Inn revels in 1594 a satire about government, *Gesta Grayorum,* was performed; Bacon wrote the part consisting of advice from fictional "councillors" to the real and powerful personages in office. Though Bacon's pen was behind the composition of some of these pieces, he did not always intend for his identity to be remembered in connection with them. In a performance prepared for the annual Accession Day festivities of 1595 Bacon created an allegorical conceit as a vehicle for the presentation and recommendation of the Earl of Essex before the queen and court. Bacon became friends with Essex, one of the heroes of the 1596 naval battle at Cadiz, Spain, and a favorite of Elizabeth's in the late 1580s. In his retrospective *Sir Francis Bacon His Apologie, In Certaine imputations concerning the late Earle of Essex. Written to the right Honorable his very good Lord, the Earle of Deuonshire, Lord Lieutenant of Ireland* (1604; conventionally known as the *Apology*), written after Essex's execution, Bacon spoke of the earl as "the fittest instrument to do good to the state," to whom he appealed for favor while offering "to the best of my understanding, propositions and memorials of anything that might concern his Lordship's honour, fortune or service."

In the early years of this relationship Bacon worked with Anthony Bacon, forming a small kind of foreign office and supplying Essex with a network of correspondence and continental intelligence. A letter from Essex to Bacon in 1593, at the time at which Essex was elevated to the Privy Council, describes the services he sought from Bacon: "Mr Phillips hath known Mr Secretary's courses in such matters," he wrote, with reference to activities in Rheims and Rome, "so as I may have counsel from you and precedents from him. I pray you, as your leisure will serve, send me your conceipt as soon as you can. . . . I will draw some notes of my own which I will reform and enlarge by yours." At this time Bacon pushed for the appointment of the position of attorney general, and when it was given to his rival Coke, Essex promoted Bacon's cause for the solicitor general's position that Coke had vacated. Eventually the queen made him a member of her learned counsel, a largely honorific title that brought no financial reward. Essex was more generous to his protégé; after Bacon's failure to secure the post of solicitor general, Essex bestowed upon him a gift of land in Twickenham Park.

In 1597 Bacon's first printed book, the *Essays,* appeared, dedicated not to his famous patron but to "his loving and beloved brother," Anthony. The dedicatory epistle reveals that the threat of a pirated edition of the essays, which had been circulating in manuscript form for a few months, motivated Bacon to produce an authorized volume. The essays communicate precepts for the conduct of persons in public affairs, based on Bacon's own political experience. The first edition comprises ten essays; an enlarged version appeared in 1612, and the text was amplified again in the edition of 1625, which comprises fifty-eight individual essays. In *De augmentis scientiarum* Bacon recognized the gap in contemporary instruction that his essays aimed to fill, declaring "there is no great concurrence between learning and practical wisdom." His essays are explicit performances of that learning–the practice of rhetoric–in the political and public domain. As Jardine describes in *Francis Bacon: Discovery and the Art of Discourse* (1974), the essays are a condensation of practical precepts on chosen topics, "backed up by the maximum compression of colouring, persuasive and illustrative *exempla,* and interspersed with apt apophthegms." The essay "Of Truth" opens with a strictly rhetorical provocation, "*What is truth?* said jesting Pilate, and would not stay for an answer," and is followed by an evaluation of the qualities of untruthfulness, which merges the condemnation of falsehood with examples that "bring lies in favour": "Doth any man doubt, that if there were taken out of men's minds vain opinions, flattering hopes, false valua-

Miniature of Bacon at eighteen by Nicholas Hilliard. The motto means "If I could only paint his mind" (Collection of the Duke of Rutland, Belvoir Castle)

tions, imaginations as one would, and the like, but it would leave the minds of a number of men poor shrunken things, full of melancholy and indisposition, and unpleasing to themselves?"

Bacon's relationship with Essex is, rightly or wrongly, central to his posthumous reputation, a view that is perhaps fueled by the romantic appeal of Essex, who has become, as proclaimed by Bacon himself in the *Apology,* an Elizabethan "Icarus." In 1598 Essex was appointed to the post of commander of the expedition to Ireland. Elizabeth was greatly angered to hear that he had undertaken secret negotiations with the rebel Earl of Tyrone, a situation that was inflamed when Essex returned to London unexpectedly without the queen's permission in September 1599. Bacon's loyalties were now compromised by the breakdown in relations between the earl and the queen, which inevitably had an effect on Elizabeth's dealings with Essex's chief advocate as well. Living "privately" at Essex House in London, his letters and suits to the queen unanswered, Essex was in fact gathering his allies and planning with them to surprise the court and seize the queen. Essex and his three hundred men failed to ignite the people of London, however. At the same time as they marched through the city he was declared a traitor, and shortly afterward he surrendered and was imprisoned.

Besides involuntarily having pleaded a rebel's cause, Bacon was teamed with Coke in the role of the prosecution in Essex's trial. As with his forays into political pamphleteering and his reply to Jesuit propaganda, his role in the trial proceedings was the result of a special commission of state. The uncompromising nature of Bacon's professional concerns and his powers of rational argument are clear: from the first he had advised Essex against accepting the Irish commission. As he wrote in the *Apology*, "I alwaies vehemently disswaded him from seeking greatnes by a military dependance, or by a popular dependance, as that would breed in the Queene jealousy, in himself presumption, and in the State perturbation." During the trial Bacon's frustrations with Coke's methods of proceeding and the shabby conduct of the trial led him to denounce the case along with the integrity of the defendant. "I have never yet seen in any case," he said to the court, "such favour shown to any prisoner: so many digressions, such delivering of evidence by fractions, and so silly a defence of such great and notorious treasons." Essex ultimately admitted his guilt and implicated others of his followers, and on 25 February 1601 he was executed.

Bacon's connection to the downfall of Essex resulted in his writing two political works: *A Declaration of the Practises & Treasons attempted and committed by Robert late Earle of Essex and his Complices, against her Maiestie and her Kingdoms, and of the proceedings as well at the Arraignments & Conuictions of the said late Earle, and his adherents, as after: Together with the very Confessions and other parts of the Euidences themselues, word for word taken out of the Originals* (1601) and the *Apology*. The fixing of Bacon's formal relationship to the execution of Essex in the printed text of *A Declaration of the Practises & Treasons attempted and committed by Robert late Earle of Essex and his Complices* is another indication of the disgust that has been leveled at Bacon for accepting the earl's patronage and then sealing his fate. The work was prepared at the order of Elizabeth, who decided that an account of the trial proceedings needed to be published and chose Bacon to be the author. It includes the confessions and testimonies of the conspirators, because, as Bacon wrote in the preface, "it is requisite that the world do understand as well the precedent practices and inducements to the treasons, as the open and actual treasons themselves." As he stated three years later in the *Apology,* Bacon was given specific instructions as to how the text was to be written, so particular "as never secretary had more particular and express directions and instructions in every point how to guide my hand in it." His draft of the piece was then submitted to the Privy Council, which

"perused, weighed, censured, altered, and made almost a new writing, according to their Lordships' better consideration." Once the council had approved the text, the queen herself made some alterations, and the tract was given to the queen's printer, Robert Barker, in April 1601. After it was set in print, however, the queen decreed that Bacon had been too deferential in his stylization of Essex as "My Lord of Essex," and she ordered that all copies of this first text be suppressed in favor of a second in which its subject was denoted simply "Essex" or "the late earl of Essex." One year after the death of Elizabeth, Bacon attempted to reconcile himself with the earl's supporters by publishing the *Apology,* in which he described his dedication to the "honor, fortune or service" of Essex, summarizing that "in two maine points we alwaies directly & contradictorily differed. . . . The one was, I ever set this downe, that the onely course to be held with the Queene, was by obsequiousness and obseruance. . . . My Lord on the other side had a setled opinion, that the Queene could be brought to nothing, but by a kind of necessitie and authority."

King James acceded to the English throne in 1603, and Bacon joined the scramble for official positions and favor at the new court. The *Apology* belongs to this period of readjustment, with the added pertinence for Bacon that his reputation, as far as it had reached the Scottish king, was as the ruthless prosecutor of the Earl of Essex. Bacon reflected on this time after the queen's death when he wrote his "Opus illustre in felicem memoriam Elizabethae Angliae Reginae" (On the Fortunate Memory of Elizabeth), published in 1608. *A Briefe Discourse, Touching The Happie Vnion Of The Kingdomes Of England, And Scotland. Dedicated In Private To His Maiestie* (1603) is Bacon's well-targeted attempt to place himself in the service of James, appealing to the king's wish to unite the two kingdoms. In it he argues that natural law could be the basis upon which to build legal union, necessitating a careful study of the core laws of each state. Bacon lent his support in the House of Commons to the principle of unification, and in the Parliament of April 1603 he added weight to the king's position and delivered a powerful speech in favor of union. On 23 July 1603 Bacon received his knighthood, along with three hundred other recipients, at a ceremony to mark the king's coronation. Also at this time he was granted the office of learned counsel, which brought with it a modest pension of £60 a year for life. Subsequently, he was chosen by Parliament to survey all the questions and issues involved in the subject of unification, the outcome of which was Bacon's second publication on union, *Certaine Articles or Considerations Touching the Union of the Kingdoms of England and Scotland* (1604). Bacon's advice to the king on ecclesiastical matters is included in his *Certaine Considerations touching the better pacification and Edification of the Church of England: Dedicated to his most Excellent Maiestie,* published the same year but probably written in August or September 1603.

Approaching the body of Bacon's philosophical writings is rather like entering a maze, in which many paths lead to each other and most of them lead to the center. Hence, alongside apparently discrete writings there is a subtext in which works are unfinished or incomplete, chapters and whole sections are reproduced in, or digested into, several places, and everything is underlined by the complicated progress of Bacon's ideas. At the center is Bacon's project for the renewal of learning, the *Instauratio magna* (Great Instauration), a project easily but misleadingly glossed as a complete entity, when in fact it was the raison d'être for Bacon's intellectual structure; it was published as a preface to the second of its "parts," the *Novum organum,* in 1620. The *Novum organum* (The New Tool, or Method) was begun in 1608 and took twelve years to complete. As Bacon commented to his friend Tobie Matthew in a letter of 1610: "My great work goeth forward; and after my manner, I alter ever when I add. So that nothing is finished till all be finished."

In the arrival of King James, a monarch with intellectual inclinations, and in the course of debate over the union of the two kingdoms, Bacon saw the possibility for joining politics and natural philosophy, the laws of men and the laws of nature. In 1603 he wrote the *Valerius Terminus of the Interpretation of Nature with the Annotations of Hermes Stella,* a work written in English, probably to gain its author financial support, though it was not published until 1734 in *Letters and Remains of the Lord Chancellor Bacon,* edited by Robert Stephens. The commentator Hermes Stella may, according to Coquillette, have been a symbol for James I. In the first chapter of the *Valerius Terminus* (Authoritative Limit, or True Goal) Bacon integrates the prophecy of Daniel in the Old Testament (a text that later fascinated Sir Isaac Newton), and it stands as the guide to the inquiries of his philosophical program. In reference to the end times Daniel is told (12:4) that "many will go here and there to increase knowledge." Later Bacon deployed these words on the frontispiece of the *Novum organum,* which carries an engraving of a ship in full sail passing between classical pillars (the pillars of Hercules), with the inscription *multi pertransibunt et augebitur scienta* (many shall go to and fro and knowledge will increase), as if the opening of the world to navigation and commerce was an analogy for the furtherance of knowledge. The *Valerius terminus* poses the dilemma facing the Protestant intellectual, which followed from the humanist ambitions encapsulated in the Latin inscription: if man originally transgressed and fell owing to his pursuit of knowledge, how can it be possible for him again to seek knowledge without falling from grace? The description of the "limits and end of knowledge," which is Bacon's subject in the first chapter, involves the reconstruction of the story of the fall of Adam:

> Man on the other side, when he was tempted before he fell, had offered unto him this suggestion, *that he should be like unto God.* But how? Not simply, but in this part, *knowing good and evil.* For being in his creation invested with sovereignty of all inferior creatures, he was not needy of power or dominion; but again, being a spirit newly inclosed in a body of earth, he was fittest to be allured with appetite of light and liberty of knowledge; therefore his approaching and intruding into God's secrets and mysteries was rewarded with a further removing and estranging from God's presence.

Bacon concluded that all knowledge was to be protected by the parameters of religion, which would lead to the increase in the glory and exaltation of God, rather than of man. If knowledge could be limited in this way, it could also be subjected to the priorities of use and action. The pleasure of curiosity and the temptations of ambition, honor, or fame were not the true ends of knowledge. The true goals of knowledge were "a discovery of all operations and possibilities of operations and possibilities of operations from immortality to the meanest mechanical practice. And therefore knowledge that tendeth but to satisfaction is but as a courtesan, which is for pleasure and not for fruit or generation."

Such critical preliminaries are formulated across the chronological and intellectual spectrum of Bacon's work. A fundamental tenet of Bacon's philosophy of science is the throwing out of the deductive system of reasoning of Aristotle and his followers. In his *The Life of the Right Honourable Francis Bacon, Baron of Verulam, Viscount St. Alban* (1670), William Rawley, Bacon's chaplain and editor of some of his works, claimed that his master was at Cambridge when he "first fell into the dislike of the philosophy of Aristotle; not for the worthlessness of the author, but for the unfruitfulness of the way; being a philosophy (as his lordship used to say) only strong for disputations and contentions, but barren of the production of works for the benefit of the life of man." The picture of an intellectually "precocious" Bacon, as biographers Jardine and Stewart put it, needs to be offset against the dominance of Aristotle and the scholastics in the university curriculum. As he made clear in *The Advancement of Learning* (1605), Bacon did not deny that the scholastics exhibited a great "thirst of truth," but he argued that they neglected "the oracle of God's works," that is, the natural world. Medieval philosophers, who

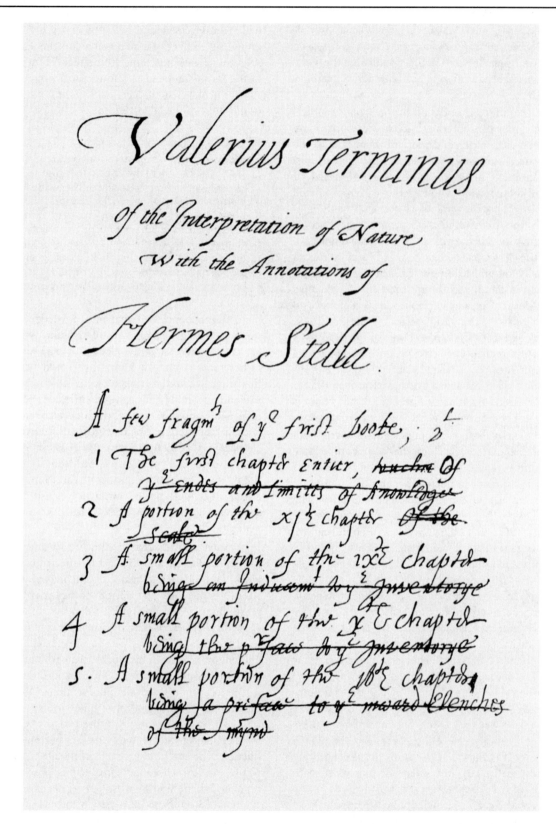

Contents list for a manuscript, written in 1603 but not published until 1734, which includes material that was later incorporated into Bacon's The Advancement of Learning *(British Library, Harleian MS 6463)*

Of the Interpretacon

6. A small portion of the iiij^th chapter
~~of the in poincts of knowledge in generall~~

7th A small portion of the vth chapter ~~of y^e~~
~~division of ~~

8 The vj^th chapter Entire

9 A portion of the v^ith chapter

10 The vij^th chapter Entire

11 Another portion of the ix^th chapter

12 The Abridgm^t of the 12. 13. 14. 15. 16. 17.
18. 19. 21. 22. 25. 26th chapters
of ye first booke

13. The first chapter of ~~the~~ a booke of
the same argum^t wrytten in Latine
and desti^med ~~for~~ to be ~~traditionary~~ separate and
not publike.

None of ye Annotations of Stella
are sett down in these fragments.

Philosophy

Sp. St. 26. — . 1603. B. 45. x^o. /
Libri dimidiū est, pag^a 34. —
Pagellarū numeri veri. /

23

revered Aristotle, saw themselves as organizers and preservers of knowledge, not as its creators. Bacon's principles were based on empiricism, or inductive methods of inquiry, in which knowledge always starts from sensory experience. His concerns are comprehensive, practical and civil as well as intellectual. Sachiko Kusakawa, writing on Bacon's classification of knowledge in *The Cambridge Companion to Bacon* (1996), describes his scientific method as one that touched questions such as how to unify all sciences under one comprehensive system; how to unify theoretical and practical parts of science; how to govern and control people; and how to map out human knowledge. This inductive method opened the field of law as well as science to Bacon; the examination of common-law precedents and the examination of scientific propositions are parallel in Baconian logic. Aristotelian programs began with "first principles" and ended with consequences; Baconian science, on the other hand, asked how the mind acquired the knowledge of these primary truths. How does one get from an empirical knowledge of things or phenomena to their fundamental nature? In Bacon's view the old logic of Aristotle and the scholastics had forgotten to interrogate the construction of the first principles themselves.

With respect to the lengthy composition process of the *Novum organum,* Rawley calculated that he had seen "at the least twelve copies revised year by year, one after another, and amended in the frame thereof." As is clear from any account of Bacon's works, one work cannot be described in isolation from the others, and each contributes to the overall texture of Bacon's thought and scholarly output. *The Advancement of Learning,* for example, corresponds to the first ten chapters of the *Valerius terminus,* especially the first and the tenth. The remainder of the former work can largely be found in the *Novum organum.* The fragmentary last chapter of *Valerius terminus,* "The inventory, or an enumeration and view of inventions already discovered and in use," corresponds not only to the second book of *The Advancement of Learning,* but also to the last eight books of *De dignitate et augmentis scientiarum.* A surviving fragmentary work, *De interpretatione naturæ proœmium,* written at the same time as *Valerius terminus* and first published in *Francisci Baconi De Verulamio Scripta In Natvrali Et Vniversali Philosophia* (Francis Bacon of Verulam's Writings on Natural and Universal Philsophy, 1653), was probably designed to stand as a general introduction to a greater work bearing that title. Most of this short piece, essentially autobiographical in nature, was digested into the first book of the *Novum organum.* In *De interpretatione naturæ proœmium* Bacon reveals that he saw his life as essentially bifurcate, as moving between the ambitions and necessities of politics and civic life (the *vita activa*) and the higher concerns of his scientific program, the

bettering of human life (the *vita contemplativa*). Bacon and his apologists returned to this theme with special urgency at the time of his forced move from public life into retirement after charges of bribery were brought against him in 1621.

In *De interpretatione naturæ proœmium* Bacon describes himself, at forty years of age, as a man no longer young (*cum ætis iam consisteret*) but not yet old (*hominem non senem*). Interestingly, even at this time of moderate success and promise under the new king, he illustrates the divergent paths of his career to date, holding open the possibilities they held for him and referring to himself as one who had been a candidate for office of state but who had resolved to abandon that pursuit in favor of his own study. A book of notes or memoranda dating from 1608, during this stage in his life, provides valuable insight into Bacon's occupations at this time; contrary to his self-protective and self-congratulatory claims in *De interpretatione naturæ proœmium,* the notes testify to the combined intellectual and political interests of Bacon's career. The general title Bacon gave to these loose notes was *transportata,* suggesting—as James Spedding, one of the editors of the seven-volume *The Works of Francis Bacon, Baron of Verulam, Viscount St. Alban, and Lord High Chancellor of England* (1858–1861), observes—that these were notes transferred from a former notebook or group of notebooks. The evidence of these papers makes clear too that Bacon was in the habit of reviewing his business from time to time, and written as they are in a sometimes unintelligible shorthand intended for his eyes only, they are a fascinating glimpse into the private organization of his affairs. In one part of the *transportata,* headed "Comentarius Solutus, sive pandecta" (A book or collection of loose notes), Bacon labeled his jottings as "all remembrances touching my private of what nature soever and hath 2 parts; Diarum and Schedulae. The one being a journall of whatsoever occureth; The other Kalenders of Titles of things of the same nature, for better help of memory and judgment." One memorandum reminds its author "To make a stock of 2000*l* allwaies in readyness for bargaines and occasions"; another instructs him "To prepare eyther collect or at lest advise towching the equalling of Lawes." In other entries Bacon recollects that he has been "Proceeding with the translation of my book of Advancement of Learnyng." Perhaps trying out his wit (or sympathetic tone), he notes elsewhere: "Death comes to young men and old men goe to death. That is all the difference. To send message of complement to my Lady Dorsett the wydowe."

In 1605 Bacon published his first important piece of writing concerned with a defense of learning, *The Tvvoo Bookes of Francis Bacon. Of the proficience and aduancement of Learning, diuine and humane. To the King,* composed

Bacon's coat of arms as Baron Verulam, Viscount St. Albans

between 1603 and 1604. The main business of the work is the development of the classification of knowledge, but it is also noteworthy for its lavish praise of King James in its opening paragraphs. In dedicating *The Tvvoo Bookes of Francis Bacon* to James, Bacon had written that the wisdom and virtues of such a ruler demanded to be expressed "in some solid work, fixed memorial, and immortal monument, bearing a character or signature both of the power of a King, and the difference and perfection of such a King": "Therefore I did conclude with myself, that I could not make unto your Majesty a better oblation than of some Treatise tending to that end, whereof the sum will consist of these two parts; the former, concerning the excellency of Learning and Knowledge, and the excellency of the merit and true glory in the augmentation and propagation thereof."

The Advancement of Learning maps out a plan for the reform of education and research, a project that Bacon believed would bring credit to the Stuart monarchy. The bid for favor with James also explains Bacon's decision to write and publish the book in English; he chose Latin for the expanded version of *The Advancement of Learning, De augmentis scientiarum.* Hence scholars have assumed that Bacon's hope of political and financial support for his philosophical scheme was the greatest concern for the author, over and above impressing a scholarly international audience.

In the first of *The Tvvoo Books of Francis Bacon,* the aim was to show what knowledge was not. Bacon said that knowledge was discredited by the argument that men were emasculated, made slothful and unfit for war or government, by learning. Bacon countered these imputations, saying that they had no grounds of gravity, citing the achievements in arms and learning of celebrated military leaders such as Alexander the Great, Julius Caesar, Epaminondas, and Xenophon. Against the view that learning made men slothful, Bacon wrote that the love of learning made men indefatigable, "that no kind of men love business for itself but those that are learned; for other persons love profit, as a hireling, that loves the work for the wages. . . . only learned men love business as an action according to nature, as agreeable to health of mind as exercise is to health of body, taking pleasure in the action itself, and not in the purchase."

Bacon then criticizes the false philosophies of his age, what he terms "vanities in studies." Anthony Quinton notes in his useful essay on Bacon in *Renaissance Thinkers* (1993) that Bacon's target was essentially humanism, which he challenges for its "ornamental vacuity, for concentration on style at the expence of substance." The first of these empty philosophies was "fantastical learning," the thoughtless acceptance of marvels, fables, and miracles—"things weakly authorised or warranted." This vice has two branches, "delight in deceiving and aptness to be deceived" and "imposture and credulity."

The second science Bacon attacks is contentious or disputatious learning. Here the pre-Renaissance scholastics, who had Aristotle for their "dictator," are likened to monks "shut up in the cells of a few authors," who "out of no great quantity of matter and infinite agitation of wit spin out unto those laborious webs of learning which are extant in their books." These methods were unprofitable by Bacon's standards, in direct opposition to the *scientia operativa*—an operative or productive science—that he promoted. Bacon called the third category "delicate" learning and claimed that greater interest in "words" over "matter" was the first failing of traditional learning. Here his subject is Reformation humanism and its reorientation away from an oral culture toward the word of God and scriptural exegesis. By consequence, he writes, the Lutherans "did draw on a necessity of a more exquisite travail in the languages of the original," which grew into an excess of interest in style, phrase, and composition.

The classification of the sciences is found in the second book of *The Advancement of Learning* and in a considerably enlarged form in books 2 through 6 of *De augmentis scientiarum*. Bacon made a threefold distinction among history, poesy, and philosophy (or science), and the divisions are pursued through theoretical and practical categories—divine and nondivine, physical and metaphysical—until at the end of the book he writes: "Thus I have made as it were a small globe of the intellectual world." The archives offer evidence of the circulation of Bacon's *The Advancement of Learning* among scientific enthusiasts and European scholars, and often Bacon's friend Tobie Matthew, living in Paris, was an intermediary, lending out his copy. In an exchange of letters with the Genevan classical scholar Isaac Casaubon, who became popular with King James, Bacon wrote in Latin regarding Casaubon's reading of some of his works: "You are right in supposing that my great desire is to draw the sciences out of their hiding-places into the light. For indeed to write at leisure that which is to be read at leisure matters very little; but to bring about the better ordering of man's life and business, with all its troubles and difficulties, by the help of sound and true contemplations,—this is the thing I am at."

On 10 May 1606 Bacon married Alice Barnham, a girl not quite fourteen years old—"an alderman's daughter, an handsome maiden, to my liking." The occasion of his marriage probably explains Bacon's lower-than-usual profile in the parliamentary session of early 1606, but when Parliament met again in November he is recorded as again speaking in favor of the Union. He referred to his parliamentary career when he pressed the king and two of his most powerful ministers, Thomas Egerton, Lord Chancellor Ellesmere, and Robert Cecil, Lord Salisbury, for the vacant post of solicitor general in 1607. To the king he summarized his services "in the commission of Union . . . and this last parliament, in the bill of the Subsidy (both body and preamble); in the bill of Attainders . . . in the matter of Purveyance; in the Ecclesiastical Petitions; in the Grievances, and the like." After sixteen years of waiting for a crown office, and after several tortuous near misses, Bacon was appointed to the post of solicitor general on 25 June 1607, with an income of £1000 per annum. The following year he was also sworn in as clerk of the Star Chamber, adding the post's salary of £2000 to his income, an emolument that caused the review of business in the notebooks of the *transportata*.

Around this time, as indicated by the evidence of letters and the memoranda in the "Comentarius Solutus, sive pandecta," Bacon wrote *Cogitata et visa* (Thoughts and Conclusions; first published in *Francisci Baconi De Verulamio Scripta In Natvrali Et Vniversali Philosophia*). As one of Bacon's minor works it can be regarded as preliminary to the *Novum organum,* and indeed it covers most of the ground taken up by the first book of the later work. *Cogitata et visa* was clearly intended to be followed by an example of a true inductive investigation, with an apparatus and tables, and had such a work been written it would have corresponded to the second book of the *Novum organum.* Thomas Bodley, who had employed Bacon in Paris, commented on his argument in this text, displaying skepticism at his rejection of assumptions in scientific knowledge "that are left by tradition from our elders unto us, which (as it is to be intended) have passed all probations of the sharpest wits that ever were." As a letter in *Reliquiæ Bodleianæ: Or Some Genuine Remains of Sir Thomas Bodley* (1703) reads: "Because it may seem, that being willing to communicate your treatise with your friends, you are likewise willing to listen to whatsoever I, or others can except against it, I must deliver unto you for my private opinion, that I am one of the crew that say there is, and we possess a far greater holdfast of certainty in your sciences, than you by your discourse will seem to acknowledge." If the sciences were to be rebuilt from first principles upward, as Bacon argued, Bodley asserted that humanity would arrive back with the precepts passed down from the ancients. Biographers Jardine and Stewart annotate this letter with the conclusion that Bodley entirely failed "to comprehend the sweeping nature of Bacon's altered vision of the sciences."

The *Cogitata et visa* is one of the earliest of Bacon's writings (preceded only by the brief *Temporis partus masculus* of 1603), known to posterity through a copy text printed after Bacon's death and one of thirteen works by Bacon printed in 1653 by the Dutch scholar Isaac Gruter. Gruter was a book collector who had built up a substantial private library, and a group of Bacon manuscripts came into his hands on the death of William Boswell, one of Bacon's executors. As quoted in the introduction to *Philosophical Studies, c. 1611–c. 1619* (1996), Gruter explained to a friend:

> For the last few weeks I have had in my possession manuscript *opuscula* of Bacon of Verulam—some of them moral and political, others natural-philosophical—corrected by the author himself. A few of the former have been published in English, but I shall offer them in Latin, together with other unpublished ones which I have translated long since. Of the latter, written in Latin by Lord Verulam himself, nothing save a few grains scattered in the *Novum organum* and the books of the *De augmentis scientiarum* has been processed for public consumption.

He adds elsewhere that all the pieces are genuine, many of them bearing the marks of revision by Bacon himself. Some of Gruter's valuable bundle of manuscripts consists of prefaces, drafts, and fragments that scholars have concluded to belong to, or to have been designed for, the *Instauratio magna*. Neither Gruter's transcription nor the original manuscripts are now extant, and his editorship and others' in the seventeenth century remains a significant intervention in the transmission of Bacon's canon.

Like *The Advancement of Learning, Francisci Baconi Equitis Avrati, Procvratoris Secvndi, Iacobi Regis Magnæ Britanniæ, De Sapientia Vetervm Liber, Ad Inclytam Academiam Cantabrigiensem* (The Wisdom of the Ancients), published in 1609, was a popular success. It was republished in 1617, translated into English by Arthur Gorges and published as *The Wisedome Of The Ancients, Written In Latine By the Right Honourable Sir Francis Bacon Knight, Baron of Verulam, and Lord Chancelor of England* in 1619, and translated into French in the same year. Its popularity with the next generation of Bacon's admirers led to its translation into Italian and German as well as to several Latin editions on the continent. The text was based on a collection of ancient myths with Bacon's interpretations. It appears

Title page for Bacon's Novum organum, *the first part of his projected "Great Instauration of Learning" (from J. G. Crowther,* Francis Bacon: The First Statesman of Science, *1960)*

to have grown out of an idea in *The Advancement of Learning,* in which Bacon considered poesy as a branch of knowledge. He questioned what the relationship was, if any, between the poet Homer and "a more original tradition" of fable telling and concluded that it was a difficult matter to decide. In *De sapientia veterum* Bacon interrogates several parables, making a comparison across all extant traditions, and pares each fable down in order to recover the original. This combination of scholarship, speculation, and interpretation was based on what Spedding describes as Bacon's belief that "before the days of Homer and Hesiod a generation of wise men had flourished on the earth who taught the mysteries of nature in parables."

A sequence of six texts written between 1607 and 1611 sharpens the picture of the promised *Instauratio magna* with its subsidiary and superseded texts: *Phænomena universi, sive historia naturalis et experimentalis ad condendam philosophia* (circa 1611), *De vijs mortis* (circa 1611–1612), *De fluxu et refluxu maris* (circa 1612), *Descriptio globi intellectualis* (1612), *Thema coeli* (circa 1612), and *De principiis atque originibus secundam fabulas cupidinis et coeli* (circa 1612). This group is the subject of *Philosophical Studies, c. 1611–c. 1619,* the first volume of a new edition of Bacon's works and correspondence under the editorship of Graham Rees. In the introduction to the volume Rees writes that it is proper to see these six writings as superseded contributions to the works that are known as the *Instauratio magna.* Usefully, he goes on to draw further conclusions from this sequence, arguing that there is no evidence to show that Bacon ever abandoned or altered the fundamentals of the six-book scheme for the *Instauratio magna,* and hence it makes most sense to assume that any work of natural philosophy produced by Bacon after about 1607 was produced for that larger work. One of the texts from this group, *De vijs mortis* (An Inquiry Concerning the Ways of Death), was published for the first time in 1984 in an edition by Rees. It was unknown to Bacon scholars until it was discovered by Peter Beal among manuscripts at Chatsworth House in 1980. *De vijs mortis* is a work on a topic of enduring interest to Bacon—the prolongation of life. As Rees writes in the introduction to *Philosophical Studies,* Bacon marked out longevity as the first objective of the new philosophy: "Confident that he lived in an age ordained by providence for great advances in knowledge, he believed that philosophy could improve material conditions and so in part restore prelapsarian felicity."

The partial fulfillment of plans for parts of the *Instauratio magna* can be seen in the *Phænomena universi, sive naturalis & experimentalis ad condendam philosophia* (Natural and Experimental History for the Foundation of Philosophy: or the Phenomena of the Universe), an unfinished preface to Bacon's natural-historical program. The duplication between the full title of this text and the title of the third part of the *Instauratio magna* suggests that it was almost certainly designed as the opening to the third part of the later work. *De fluxu et refluxu maris* (On the Ebb and Flow of the Sea) is a short tract on tidal motion, probably written with part 1 of the *Instauratio magna* in mind. *Thema coeli* (Theory of the Heavens) is a brief essay on cosmology and astrology and is connected to the astronomical part of the *Instauratio magna. De principiis atque originibus* (On Principles and Origins) was designed as a revision of the *De sapientia veterum* and is an interpretation of myths about Cupid. As it outgrew its prototype, it became Bacon's most thorough mythological work, presenting myths as doctrines of the principles of things.

Descriptio globis intellectualis (A Description of the Intellectual Globe) was the beginning of a massive piece of writing proposed as part 1 of the *Instauratio magna,* which, according to the plan in the *Distributio operis* of the *Instauratio magna,* was titled *Partitiones scientiarum* (Division of the Sciences). A glance at the birth and generation of the *Descriptio globis* reveals a characteristic web of cross-fertilization. To locate the *Descriptio globis* properly, one must start with the *Valerius terminus,* of which the ninth chapter was the predecessor of *The Advancement of Learning,* later expanded into *De augmentis scientiarum.* The *Descriptio globis* runs parallel to this development of ideas in that it was conceived as a revision and Latinization of book 2 of *The Advancement of Learning,* and its materials were expanded into *De augmentis scientiarum.*

In October 1612 a revised volume of Bacon's essays was ready for print, and Bacon, still pushing at the door of high office, had spread his clientage beyond the king to the young Prince of Wales. This time the dedicatory letter prefacing the *Essays* was addressed to Prince Henry. A month later, however, the prince died of a fever, and Bacon's hopes as well as those of others, such as Sir Walter Ralegh, who had begun to find favor with Prince Henry to counter the disfavor of James, were disappointed. Bacon wrote another dedication, this time to his brother-in-law Sir John Constable. Another death in November, that of Sir George Carew, the master of the wards, changed Bacon's prospects, and he renewed his campaign for the mastership. He was unsuccessful—the job went to Sir Walter Cope—but the event marked the start of several reshuffles and Bacon's ever-ready, often overconfident plea to secure another income. On 7 August 1613 Sir Thomas Fleming, chief justice for the King's Bench, died, and key legal appointments were on the table once more. Bacon's proposals went further than himself, as he presented to James a reorganization in which his old rival Coke would become chief justice; Sir Henry Hobart, the current attorney general, would take Coke's place as chief justice of the common pleas; and Hobart's vacant position would then be filled by Bacon. In presenting this scenario to the king, he inferred the limitations of Coke and Hobart in their present positions. He showed that he was the man who could safeguard the king's prerogative, whereas Coke, who in dealing with civil suits generally had to adjudicate between king and subject, had come into conflict with royal prerogative. Unlike Coke and Hobart, Bacon wrote in a document headed "Reasons for the remove of Coke" now at Lambeth Palace Library, he was "of a quicker and more earnest temper, and more effectual in that he dealeth in, is like to recover that strength to the King's prerogative which it hath in times past, and which is due to unto it. And for that purpose there must be brought in to be solicitor some man of courage and speech and a grounded lawyer; which done, his Majesty will speedily find a marvellous change in his business." Bacon's schemes were, this time, taken up: Coke departed the office of common pleas for the King's Bench, and Bacon gratefully took up the attorneyship.

Another aspect of Bacon's work on legal theory, besides the issues he engages on paper, was his advocacy at the bar—that is, his judicial decisions. In the case of *De rege inconsulto,* brought to the King's Bench between 1615 and 1616, Bacon spoke in defense of the king, claiming that the case directly weighed on the king's prerogative. It concerned one of James's favorites, John Murray, groom of the bedchamber, who got the king to appoint a friend to a newly created office "for the role of making writs of *supersedeas* . . . in the Common Pleas," a move that deprived other court officers of their profits. Bacon argued that the king's title "shall never be discussed in a plea between common persons" and entered into what Coquillette terms "genuine legal discourse" on the royal prerogative. As legal advocate and later as judge, Bacon brought a tremendous breadth and scope to his legal activities. He argued on behalf of private clients in the published arguments *Chudleigh's Case* (1594) and *Slade's Case* (1602) as well as on important doctrinal issues and policy. In addition, he was involved in special commissions of state such as *The Case of the Post-Nati* (1608), concerning the nationality and rights of those born after the accession of James to the English throne. Coquillette concludes: "In all of these cases Bacon demonstrated three traits. The first, often overlooked by his critics, was his dedication to the advocacy process, his love of the give-and-take of rational discourse and legal argument. This love of 'testing' propositions and theories was directly linked to his second great trait, his systematic and scientific approach to legal advocacy. . . . Finally, Bacon's later arguments revealed his growing interest in a legal science that was directly instructed by natural philosophy and the study of linguistics."

In the years from 1616 to 1618 Bacon equaled his father's achievement, first by becoming a member of James' Privy Council and then, in March 1617, lord keeper of the Privy Seal. In January of the following year the lord keeper became the lord chancellor, a move that was accompanied by the rumor that Bacon would shortly be made a baron. The court gossips were proved right when, on 12 July 1618, Bacon was created Baron Verulam of Verulam. There are limited resources relating to Bacon's years as lord chancellor, the formal head of the national legal system. The best record is a set of rules allegedly adopted by Bacon to govern practice in Chancery, *Ordinances made By The Right Honourable Sir Francis Bacon Knight, Lord Verulam and Viscount of Saint Albans, being then Lord Chancellor. For the better and more regular Administration of Iustice in the Chancery, to be daily observed saving the Prerogative of this Covrt* (1642). The rules

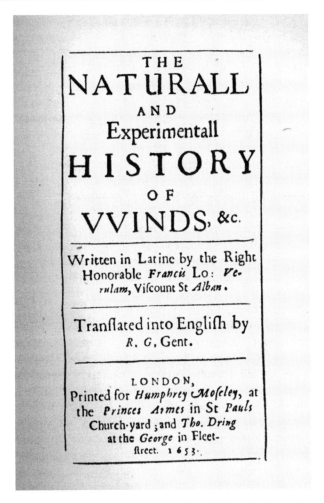

Title page for the English translation of Bacon's Historia Natvralis Et Experimentalis Ad Condendam Philosophiam *(1622), intended as the third part of his "Great Instauration" (from George Walter Steeves,* Francis Bacon: A Sketch of His Life, Works, and Literary Friends, Chiefly from a Bibliographical Point of View, *1910)*

incorporated in the work were designed to increase the accuracy of record keeping, with an emphasis on speed of decision making and fairness. In rule 18, for example, Bacon prohibited abuses such as repeated filing of the same bill, filing pleadings of "immoderate length," and bringing lawsuits in more than one court: "18. Double vexation is not to be admitted; but if the party sue for the same cause at the common law and in chancery, he is to have a day given to make his election where he will proceed, and in default of making such election to be dismissed."

Bacon tackled obsolete laws that impaired the authority of new laws in *An offer to our late soveraigne King Iames, of a digest to be made of the lawes of England,* better known as the *Digest of the Laws of England,* written in 1621 and published after Bacon's death by Rawley as part of *Certaine Miscellany Works Of The Right Honovrable,*

Francis Lo. Verulam, Viscount S. Alban (1629). The *Digest of the Laws of England* omitted all obsolete rules, resolved contradictions in favor of the best interpretations, weeded out and erased the least perfect of repeating laws, and compressed and abridged "laws found to be wordy and too prolix."

Only six months before he faced charges of accepting bribes, on 12 October 1620, Bacon published the *Novum organum*. The title of the work made clear Bacon's ambition to replace Aristotle's *organon* (meaning "instrument of thought or knowledge"), the traditional title of his treatises on logic. *Novum organum* is doubly important for its preface, the twenty-page *Instauratio magna*, little more than a fragment of things promised but enormously important in terms of its *Distributio operis*–its presentation of the organization of Bacon's various writings subsumed within the guiding principle of his scientific project. The greater part of the plan traced in the *Distributio operis* remained unfulfilled, and it is estimated that there exists, across all earlier texts and separately published works, perhaps one-twentieth of the material Bacon outlined of the *Instauratio magna.*

In the *Proœmium* or the preliminary comment, Bacon explained his haste in setting forth sections of the *Instauratio magna* in 1620. Referring to himself, he wrote: "because he knew not how long it might be before these things would occur to any one else, judging especially from this, that he has found no man hitherto who has applied his mind to the like, he resolved to publish at once so much as he has been able to complete. The cause of which haste was not ambition for himself, but solicitude for the work; that in case of his death there might remain some outline and project of that which he had conceived, and some evidence likewise of his honest mind and inclination towards the benefit of the human race."

The first part outlined in the *Distributio operis* is the *Partitiones scientiarum;* Bacon noted elsewhere that this section was missing, though it could be supplied, in part, from the second book of *The Advancement of Learning.* Its purpose was to "exhibit a summary or general description of the knowledge which the human race at present possesses." Greater fulfillment of this section was provided in *De augmentis scientiarum.* The third part, *Phænomena universi, sive historia naturalis & experimentalis ad condendam philosophiam,* was never completed. Its purpose was to present a storehouse of "materials on which the new method is to be employed." Bacon set out six heads for this work: *Historia ventorum, Historia gravis et levis, Historia sympathiae et . . . , Historia sulphuris,* and *Historia vitae et mortis.* Published in 1622, the *Historia naturalis et experimentalis ad condendam philosophiam* was Bacon's effort to begin work on the third part of the *Instauratio magna,* in which only the section on winds, *Historia ven-*

torum, was completed, the other five titles amounting to no more than fragmentary prefaces. The next section, finished a year later, is the *Historia vitae et mortis,* published in 1623. The fourth part of the *Instauratio magna* was *Scala intellectus* (The Ladder of Understanding), which was to have included examples of the operation of Bacon's new method and results. This section was never completed. The fifth part, for which only a brief preface was completed, is *Prodromi, sive anticipationes philosophiae secundae* (Forerunners or Anticipations of the Second Philosophy). Lastly, *Philosophia secunda, sive scientia activa* (The Second Philosophy or Active Science) was never started. Bacon indicated that he was looking to others to take on the burden of this work.

The *Instauratio magna* was dedicated to King James, and in respect of its patron, the dedication alluded to Bacon's other royal appointments and commissions, admitting that he had "stolen" time from James's affairs in order to produce this work. He commended the work to the king, who, he said, resembled King Solomon "in the gravity of your judgements, the peacefulness of your reign, in the largeness of your heart, in the noble variety of the books which you have composed." For his part James is reported as finding the second part of the *Instauratio magna,* printed as the *Novum organum,* rather taxing. A letter passed between the court gossips John Chamberlain and Dudley Carleton, now in the State Papers, records that James had declared that Bacon's book "like the peace of God passeth all understanding." In an earlier letter Chamberlain hinted at the popular verdict on the *Novum organum,* that "A fool could not have written such a book and a wise man would not." In the front of his presentation copy, a gift from the author, Coke wrote with unsurprising scorn: "It deserveth not to be read in schooles, But to be freighted in the ship of Fooles."

In the *Proœmium* Bacon described the *Instauratio magna* as a "total reconstruction of sciences, arts, and all human knowledge, raised upon proper foundations." The foundation on which to rebuild was inductive reasoning, "that form of demonstration which upholds the sense, and closes with nature." Aristotelian logic was explicitly rejected for its disputation, propositions, and syllogisms, which consisted, in Bacon's view, of words, tokens, and signs and which were "barren of works, remote from practice, and altogether unavailable for the active department of the sciences." Expanding on the allusions in the frontispiece and its inscription, the *Instauratio magna* uses metaphors of discovery and navigation to show Baconian science coasting past "ancient arts" and voyaging into the new world with the second phase of the project, equipping the intellect "for passing beyond"–the *plus ultra* of the inscription. "Now what the sciences stand in need of," wrote Bacon, "is a form of induction which shall analyse experience and take it to pieces, and by a due process of exclusion and rejection lead to an inevitable conclusion."

The *Novum organum* is developed through aphorisms. Book 1 is incomplete, consisting of 130 aphorisms designed to set out the intellectual inadequacies of existing scientific methods. Book 2 was intended to demonstrate the new method by the analysis of a single phenomenon, heat. Bacon's writing is most criticized when it moves from the spirit to the letter of the new science, as is the case with the concrete scientific examples he attempts to give in the second book. In the middle of an analysis of "aids to induction" he brings his investigation suddenly to a close, and he never completed it. In the first book the attack on existing systems of knowledge is presented in the form of the doctrine of "idols." As Quinton explains, "The idols of the mind are various tendencies of the human intellect which explain its frequent lapses into error." Bacon divides these tendencies into idols of the tribe, the cave, the market, and the theater. The idols of the tribe are mental weaknesses typical of the human race. By contrast those of the cave are idiosyncrasies and limitations peculiar to one style of thought or another. To explain his meaning, Bacon borrows Plato's famous simile of the cave wherein prisoners are trapped, with a fire behind them, and only able to see shadows, which eventually they come to perceive as reality. Aphorism 42 reads: "The Idols of the Cave are the idols of the individual man. For every one (besides the errors common to human nature in general) has a cave or den of his own, which refracts and discolours the light of nature." In the third category, "idols of the market-place," are words and the confusions of communication and linguistics. Bacon deems these idols the most dangerous of all, as words, he writes, have a power independent of men's reason, so that although men think they can govern words and names, words can resist change and impede order and definition. The idols of the theater had been first described fifteen years earlier in *The Advancement of Learning;* Bacon refers to the vain systems of thought "which have immigrated into men's minds from the various dogmas of philosophies, and also from wrong laws of demonstration."

Spedding has argued that Bacon's greatness was not due to "the technical part of his method," and, as a book about experimental science, the *Novum organum* is flawed. As Coquillette suggests, Bacon's most important failing was his inability to comprehend the limitations of the inductive method. Yet, Bacon's theories of the limits and traditions of human understanding "directly anticipated modern social science," and Coquillette goes on to identify Bacon's categories of idols with modern anthropology, ethnology, psychology, and linguistics. Built into

Title page for the translation of Bacon's De Dignitate & Augmentis Scientiarum, *which was published in 1623*
(Cambridge University Library)

the cornerstones of his critique are the tools for analytical jurisprudence. The fullest and most fruitful connection between scientific and legal methods, however, is in *De augmentis scientiarum.*

Jardine and Stewart, in *Hostage to Fortune,* utilize both familiar and underused documents in their superb account of Bacon's fall in 1621. His public image was progressively undermined on two fronts. First, there was an increase in the gibes that had always attended him, largely based on his weakness for court finery and ostentation. Jardine and Stewart cite a verse that circulated in manuscript, "On the Lord Chancellor Bacons stinking breath": "the Muses nine upon a time / as gaping he lay winking / Shit on his tongue, when he was young, / and made his breath so stinking." Secondly, and more seriously, Bacon faced a series of challenges, the origin of which lay in disputes of judgments made by him in Chancery, which generated a variety of public denouncements of the chancellor. In one conflict of May 1619 a canon of St Paul's, Isaac Singleton, exorcized his wrath at a legal decision by Bacon in a sermon, and his attack slides from the professional, legal character of Bacon into speculation about the private arrangements of his household. Singleton bemoaned Bacon's "court" and then "glanced" toward what he called Bacon's "catamites," so formulating the two interrelated charges of professional and private misconduct that surfaced again later. In early modern England the charge of sodomy implied in the relation between Bacon and his so-called catamites is best understood as a pejorative term rather than as a practice or identity. The common factor between the charge of sodomy and the procedures of Chancery was Bacon's servants, who acted for him in the courts and at home. Taken together they created a chain of association that went from prodigality to ambition to bribery. The giving of gifts in Chancery was normal practice, and lower officials, who in Bacon's case were also his servants, accepted gifts on his behalf. The slur on his morals comes with the fact that he was too indulgent of his servants and allowed them to keep gifts that were intended for him. Indeed, Bacon argued before the king in a matter-of-fact manner that these bribes were *vitia temporis* (abuses of the times) rather than evidence of his personal culpability.

Bacon reached his greatest public height in January 1621, at the time of his sixtieth birthday, when he was created Viscount St. Alban's with the king in attendance. A comment by the diarist Simonds D'Ewes, punning on the new honor, exemplifies the detractions leveled at Bacon and the joining of personal and professional slander:

> . . . all men wondering at the exceeding vanity of his pride and ambition: for his estate in land not above four or five hundred pounds per annum at the uttermost, and his debts were generally thought to be near £30,000. Besides he was fain to support his household expenses, being very lavish, by taking great bribes in all causes of moment that came before him. So as men raised very bitter sarcasms or jests of him; as that he was *very lame,* alluding to his barony of *Verulam,* but now having fallen into a consumption of purse, without all question he was become *All-bones,* alluding to his new honour of St. *Alban;* nay, they said, *Nabal* being folly or foolishness, and the true anagram of *Alban,* might well set forth his fond and impotent ambition.

On 14 March two charges of accepting bribes were brought against Bacon on twenty-eight counts, and the lord chancellor was impeached, held "incapable of any office, place, or employment in the state or commonwealth . . . never to sit in Parliament, nor to come within the verge of the court." Jardine and Stewart iden-

tify three defenses that Bacon used to exempt himself from the charge of corruption. He said that some gifts had been received during the season for gift-giving, at New Year, when it was natural for gifts to be exchanged. On these occasions, Bacon said, "I neglected to enquire whether the cause was ended or depending." On other counts he argued that it was a question of timing, saying that he had received the gift after sentence had been passed, hence it was "to be for favours past, and not in respect to favours to come." Lastly he implicated his servants, saying that he had "given way to great exactions by his servants" and was guilty of neglecting the actions of those in his employ. Bacon's amanuensis, Thomas Bushell, confirmed this last point in his account of the events of 1621, printed as *Mr Bushell's Abridgment of the Lord Chancellor Bacon's Philosophical Theory in Mineral Prosecutions* (1659). Bushell noted the irony with which a great man "should be thus brought upon the public stage for the foolish miscarriages of his own servants whereof (with grief of heart) I confess my self to be one."

In assessing Bacon's career, the author of the collection of biographical portraits published as *Brief Lives* (1898), John Aubrey, wrote: "He was a *paiderastos*. His Ganimeds and Favourites tooke bribes; but his Lordship always gave Judgement secundum aequum et bonum [according as was just and good]. His Decrees in Chancery stood firme, i.e. there are fewer of his Decrees reverst then of any other Chancellor." Aubrey's judgment is noticeably different from that of D'Ewes; he implies that Bacon's career as chancellor should be untainted by the alleged facts of his sodomitical practices.

The alternatives that Bacon self-consciously nurtured, between a life on "the stage of civil action" and the retired life of intellectual contemplation and letters, came to fruition after his impeachment in 1621. In a letter to King James, Bacon carefully orchestrated his forced "retirement" to the family home of Gorhambury. He presented himself as the last in a line of classical scholars and state heroes who had emerged from banishment restored to honor or replete with masterpieces for posterity. This picture was reinforced by Rawley, who, in his biography of Bacon, described the last five years of Bacon's life as years when he was "withdrawn from civil affairs and from an active life," absorbed entirely in contemplation and study. On 8 October 1621 Bacon sent James the manuscript of his new work, *The History of the Reign of Henry the Seventh* (unpublished until 1972). At this time he petitioned the king for release from the £40,000 fine imposed upon him in the course of his removal from office. He cited his years of royal service, and James agreed to a reallocation of the debt, so that, in effect, the fine was shifted onto creditors named by Bacon who became a layer of insulation between Bacon and the debt itself: effectively, the crown no longer levied the fine.

The *De augmentis scientiarum,* probably written by June 1622, was to be the completion of the first part of the *Instauratio magna,* the *Partitiones scientiarum. The Advancement of Learning* was translated into Latin to form the first part of the mature work, together with "several enrichments and enlargements," as Rawley put it. In December 1624 Bacon published his *Apophthegmes New and Old* and *The Translation Of Certaine Psalmes Into English Verse.* These pieces, described as lackluster by Jardine and Stewart, may have met immediate needs rather than the call of posterity and helped to relieve Bacon of some of his debts. Also at this time Bacon was compiling data for the *Sylva sylvarum,* published after his death by Rawley in 1627. Its title literally means "wood of woods," a pastoral trope suggesting a forest of useful materials or collection of collections.

The *Sylva sylvarum* is the continuation of Bacon's focus on intellectual work and the product of an attempt to finish part 3 of the *Instauratio magna.* Like the *Novum organum,* the *Sylva sylvarum* is another unfinished but separately published part of the *Instauratio magna.* The *Historia naturalis* (the only previously completed and published section of part 3) had called for a demonstration of inductive methods through concrete scientific experiments, and Bacon intended to fulfill this aim in the *Sylva sylvarum.* The collection was presented to the new king, Charles I, by William Rawley, who wrote in his dedication "To the Reader" that Bacon had often complained that he who was the architect of the building "should be forced to be a workman and a labourer, and to dig the clay and burn the brick; and more than that . . . to gather the straw and stubble all over the fields to burn the bricks withal." Filling the gap in Baconian science—of experimental observation—was the weakest, often absent part of Bacon's published work. Again, the intention was clear and even took clarity as its subject. Bacon's aim was "to make wonders plain, not plain things wonders." A work of natural history, Rawley admitted, was to approach "the world as God made it, and not as men have made it." Yet Bacon's death in 1626 intervened and the *Sylva sylvarum* is, in Coquillette's words, "a hodgepodge of half-baked facts and errors." It was commonplace desire among the virtuosi of Restoration science fifty years later to continue Bacon's natural history, acknowledging its inadequacies. John Beale, horticulturist and fellow of the Royal Society, advised the chemist Robert Boyle to publish his "Promiscuous Experiments" in order "to relieve Lord Bacons Sylva, & his Novum Organum which oft times wants your ayde."

*Title page for Bacon's work of natural history that was left unfinished at his death (from George Walter Steeves, *Francis Bacon: A Sketch of His Life, Works, and Literary Friends, Chiefly from a Bibliographical Point of View, *1910)*

The volume of the *Sylva sylvarum* published by Rawley also includes Bacon's fantastical vision, *New Atlantis,* written in 1624 at the same time as the compilation of natural-history materials for the *Sylva sylvarum* was under way. Rawley indicates that Bacon specifically instructed the pairing of these two texts. Spedding provides one explanation: that *New Atlantis* represented Bacon's idea of what should be the end of the work that was begun in the *Sylva sylvarum,* and that *New Atlantis* was "nothing more than a vision of the practical results which he anticipated from the study of natural history diligently and systematically carried on through successive generations." The work is described in the preface to the reader as a "fable" of a college "for the interpreting of nature and the producing of great and marvellous works for the benefit of men," which takes the form of a voyage from Peru to China and Japan. Tantalizingly, Rawley added that "His Lordship thought also in this present fable to have composed frame of Laws, or of

Title page for the collection of thirteen of Bacon's works edited by the Dutch scholar Isaac Gruter (from George Walter Steeves, Francis Bacon: A Sketch of His Life, Works, and Literary Friends, Chiefly from a Bibliographical Point of View, *1910)*

the best state or mould of a commonwealth; but foreseeing it would be a long work, his desire of collecting the Natural History diverted him, which he preferred many degrees before it." Jurists have found Bacon's decision especially frustrating, but it is evidence of the cosmopolitan terms that Bacon's legal theories were made to operate in.

Francis Bacon died on Easter Sunday, 9 April 1626, an event magnified through its own entourage of anecdotes and ironies. Aubrey claimed that Bacon's death had been partly self-inflicted in the service of trying out an experiment of refrigeration.

As he was taking the air in a coach . . . towards Highgate, snow lay on the ground, and it came into my lord's thought, why flesh might not be preserved in snow, as in salt. [He] alighted out of the coach, and went into a poor woman's house at the bottom of Highgate Hill, and bought a hen, and made the woman gut it, and then stuffed the body full of snow, and my lord did help to do it himself. The snow so chilled him, that he immediately fell so extremely ill, that he could not return to his lodgings.

Modern biographers have dispensed with this story as the fashioning of an appropriate death for an experimental scientist, springing from Bacon's interest in the prolongation of life and the "preservation of flesh." Given the fact that he was already unwell in 1625 and had depended on opiates all his life, and based on his own references to his physical condition in his last months, Bacon is generally believed to have died from an overdose of nitre or opium.

In the century after Bacon's death, science, particularly in the years 1660 to 1680, was self-consciously Baconian. Its protagonists in England, in the circle of scientists brought together in the foundation of Gresham College and the Royal Society, were committed to ousting the dominant sterile scholastic science and furthering the program of inductive inquiry. The Royal Society, founded in 1660, specifically incorporated Bacon's natural philosophy in what Michael Hunter, in *Science and the Shape of Orthodoxy: Intellectual Change in Late Seventeenth-Century Britain* (1995), has termed a "unifying slogan" for their scientific activities. The first historian of the Royal Society, Thomas Sprat, praised Bacon in *The History of the Royal-Society of London* (1667) as "a Man of strong, clear, and powerful Imaginations," and marveled that the man who bore "the greatest Burden of Civil business" had found time for "retir'd Studies." Bacon is depicted on the elaborate frontispiece to the volume, with the first president of the society, William Viscount Brouncker, sitting alongside a bust of Charles II and surrounded by books, globes, and instruments of navigation and experiment. Like Joseph Glanvill, author of *Scepsis scientifica* (1665), many believed that "Salomon's House in the New Atlantis was a Prophetick Scheam of the Royal Society." Hunter confirms that the threat of inadequacy in Bacon's methodology, its lack of specificity, resulted in the failure of Baconian science to provide a precise focus for research—one reason, in Hunter's opinion, that the relationship between Bacon and the Royal Society loosened in the seventeenth century. Scientists such as Robert Boyle and Robert Hooke realized the need for a balance between theory and observation.

In the nineteenth century Bacon fared far worse. The popular view of Bacon borne out in dictionaries and encyclopedias was primarily generated by Thomas Babington Macaulay's "Lord Bacon," which appeared in the July 1837 issue of the *Edinburgh Review;* writing in

India without access to contemporary records, Macaulay assumed that Bacon had been driven by the search for wealth and titles and had transferred his allegiance as served him best. As Nieves Matthews concludes in *Francis Bacon: The History of a Character Assassination* (1996), Macaulay's invective was the byproduct of his main concern, a biography of Basil Montagu, who in the 1820s and 1830s edited Bacon's works, and at such a remove from Bacon himself Macaulay relied mainly on shallow moralization. Early-twentieth-century textbooks dwelled on the charges of fraud and corruption and, like Sidney Lee in *Great Englishmen of the Sixteenth Century* (1904), found Bacon's moral judgment "blurred past recovery." *Blackwood's Magazine* in 1930 declared that "Lord Bacon was a horrible old rascal, but he wrote very charming essays." Michael J. Hawkins, in his introduction to the 1972 Dent edition of the *Essays*, wrote that Bacon "showed an ungrateful and indecent eagerness in pressing the case against his former friend and benefactor," the Earl of Essex. Such naive historiography began to be toned down in the 1950s as the result of revived interest in Bacon studies, particularly through the work of scholars of the history of science such as Benjamin Farrington, Brian Vickers, and, in Italy, Paolo Rossi.

The great ideal bequeathed by Francis Bacon to Western culture has been the notion of "good" science. Bacon can be compared with King Solomon, paragon of wisdom in the Bible, who frequently appears in his writings. In *The Advancement of Learning* he wrote that Solomon made no claim to the excellencies of his rule, of treasure, shipping, architecture, or navigation, but delighted himself only in "the glory of inquisition of truth: for he saith expressly, *The glory of God is to conceal a thing, but the glory of the king is to find it out.*" Paradoxically, though, Bacon promoted his good science as good insofar as it was useful or technologically exploitable. His achievement lay chiefly in the cultivation of the relationship between classificatory systems and theories and worldly, humane interests. As another Bacon editor, Jerry Weinberger, wrote: "Bacon did not consider the new science to be an autonomous enterprise with no links to other human concerns. He knew that the scientific conquest of nature would have extraordinary moral and political consequences." Resisting the opposing appeals of "active" or "meditative" science, Bacon's scientific and philosophical ideas sought to make these connections.

Letters:

Letters of Sir Francis Bacon, Baron of Verulam, Viscount St Alban, and Lord High Chancellor of England. Written during the Reign of King James the First. Now Collected, and Augmented with Several Letters and Memoires, *Address'd by Him to the King and Duke of Buckingham, Which Were Never Before Published,* edited by Robert Stephens (London: Benjamin Tooke, 1702);

Letters and remains of the Lord Chancellor Bacon. Collected by Robert Stephens, Esq., edited by John Lockyer (London: Printed by W. Bowyer, 1734);

The Letters and the Life of Francis Bacon Including All His Occasional Works: Namely Letters, Speeches, Tracts, State Papers, Memorials, Devices and All Authentic Writings Not Already Printed among His Philosophical, Literary, or Professional Works, 7 volumes, edited by James Spedding (volumes 1–2, London: Longman, Green, Longman & Roberts, 1862; volumes 3–7, London: Longmans, Green, Reader & Roberts, 1868–1874)—comprises volume 1 (1862), volume 2 (1862); volume 3 (1868), volume 4 (1868); volume 5 (1869), volume 6 (1872), and volume 7 (1874);

Illustrations of Jack Cade's Rebellion: From Researches in the Guildhall Records; Together with Some Newly-found Letters of Lord Bacon, edited by B. Brogdon Orridge (London: John Camden Hotten, 1869);

E. R. Wood, "Francis Bacon's 'Cousin Sharpe,'" *Notes and Queries,* 196 (1951): 248–249;

Robert Johnson, "Francis Bacon and Lionel Cranfield," *Huntington Library Quarterly,* 23 (1960): 301–320;

Daniel R. Woolf, "John Seldon [sic], John Borough and Francis Bacon's *History of Henry VII* 1621," *Huntington Library Quarterly,* 47 (1984): 47–53.

Bibliographies:

R. W. Gibson, *Francis Bacon: A Bibliography of His Works and of Baconiana to the Year 1750* (Oxford: Scrivener Press, 1950);

Paolo Rossi, "Per una Bibliografia degli scritti su Francesco Bacone," *Rivista critica della storia della filosofia,* 12 (1957): 75–89;

Gibson, *Francis Bacon: A Bibliography of His Works and of Baconiana to the Year 1750: Supplement* (Oxford: Privately printed, 1959);

J. Kemp Honk, "Francis Bacon: 1926–1966," *Elizabethan Bibliographies, Supplement,* 15 (London: 1968);

Brian Vickers, *Francis Bacon* (Harlow, U.K.: Published for the British Council by Longman, 1978), pp. 38–46;

William A. Sessions, "Recent Studies in Francis Bacon," *Recent Studies in the English Renaissance,* edited by E. H. Hageman, 17 (1985): 351–371;

Biographies:

William Rawley, *The Life of the Right Honourable Francis Bacon, Baron of Verulam, Viscount St. Alban* (London: Printed by S. G. & E. G. for William Lee, 1670);

Edwin A. Abbot, *Francis Bacon: An Account of His Life and Works* (London: Seely, Jackson & Halliday, 1885);

George Walter Steeves, *Francis Bacon: A Sketch of His Life, Works, and Literary Friends, Chiefly from a Bibliographical Point of View* (London: Methuen, 1910);

Mary Sturt, *Francis Bacon: A Biography* (New York, 1932);

J. G. Crowther, *Francis Bacon: The First Statesman of Science* (London: Cresset Press, 1960);

John Aubrey, *Aubrey's Brief Lives,* edited by Oliver Lawson Dick (London: Secker & Warburg, 1949; Ann Arbor: University of Michigan Press, 1962), pp. 8–16;

Joel Epstein, *Francis Bacon: A Political Biography* (Athens: Ohio University Press, 1977);

Lisa Jardine and Alan Stewart, *Hostage to Fortune: The Troubled Life of Francis Bacon, 1561–1626* (London: Gollancz, 1998; New York: Hill & Wang, 1999).

References:

J. H. Baker, *An Introduction to English Legal History,* third edition (London: Butterworths, 1990);

Daniel R. Coquillette, *Francis Bacon* (Edinburgh: Edinburgh University Press, 1992; Stanford, Cal.: Stanford University Press, 1992);

Benjamin Farrington, *The Philosophy of Francis Bacon: An Essay on Its Development from 1603 to 1609, with New Translations of Fundamental Texts* (Liverpool: Liverpool University Press, 1964);

Samuel R. Gardiner, *History of England from the Accession of James I to the Outbreak of the Civil War, 1603–1642,* 10 volumes (London: Longmans, Green, 1895–1899);

Paul E. J. Hammer, "The Uses of Scholarship: The Secretariat of Robert Devereux, Second Earl of Essex, *c.* 1585–1601," *English Historical Review,* 109 (1994);

Nieves Matthews, *Francis Bacon: The History of a Character Assassination* (New Haven, Conn.: Yale University Press, 1996);

J. E. Neale, *Elizabeth I and Her Parliaments,* 2 volumes (London: Jonathan Cape, 1953, 1957);

Markku Peltonen, ed., *The Cambridge Companion to Bacon* (Cambridge & New York: Cambridge University Press, 1996);

Anthony Quinton, "Francis Bacon," in *Renaissance Thinkers,* edited by James Kelsey McConica (Oxford: Oxford University Press, 1993);

Paolo Rossi, *Francis Bacon: From Magic to Science,* translated by Sacha Rabinovitch (London: Routledge & Kegan Paul, 1968; Chicago: University of Chicago Press, 1968);

Brian Vickers, *Francis Bacon* (Harlow, U.K.: Longman, 1978);

Charles Webster, *The Great Instauration: Science, Medicine and Reform, 1626–1660* (London: Duckworth, 1975).

Papers:

Francis Bacon's manuscripts are found mainly in the United Kingdom at the following institutions: in London, at the British Library, Lambeth Palace Library, the Public Record Office, and Gray's Inn Library; in Cambridge at Cambridge University Library and the Fitzwilliam Museum; in Oxford at the Bodleian Library; and in the Edinburgh University Library. In the United States, Bacon's papers are held at the Henry E. Huntington Library, San Marino, and at the Folger Shakespeare Library in Washington, D.C.

Jeremy Bentham

(15 February 1748 – 6 June 1832)

Anthony J. Draper
University College London

See also the Bentham entries in *DLB 107: British Prose Writers, 1789–1832, First Series,* and *DLB 158: British Reform Writers, 1789–1832.*

BOOKS: *A Fragment on Government; Being an Examination of What is Delivered, on the Subject of Government in General in the Introduction of Sir William Blackstone's Commentaries: with a Preface, in Which is Given a Critique on the Work at Large,* anonymous (London: Printed for T. Payne, P. Elmsly & E. Brooke, 1776);

A View of the Hard-Labour Bill; Being an Abstract of a Pamphlet, Intituled, "Draught of a Bill, to Punish by Imprisonment and Hard-Labour, Certain Offenders; and to Establish Proper Places for Their Reception." Interspersed with Observations Relative to the Subject of the Above Draught in Particular, and to Penal Jurisprudence in General (London: Printed for T. Payne, T. Cadell, P. Elmsly & E. Brooke, 1778);

Defence of Usury; Shewing the Impolicy of the Present Legal Restraints on the Terms of Pecuniary Bargains. In a Series of Letters to a Friend. To which is added a Letter to Adam Smith, Esq.; LL.D. on the Discouragements Opposed by the Above Restraints to the Progress of Inventive Industry (London: Printed for T. Payne, 1787; Philadelphia: Printed for Mathew Carey by Lang & Ustick, 1796);

An Introduction to the Principles of Morals and Legislation (London: Printed for T. Payne, 1789); revised edition (London: Pickering, 1823; New York: H. Frowde, 1907);

Draught of a New Plan for the Organisation of the Judicial Establishment in France: Proposed as a Succedaneum to the Draught Presented, for the Same Purpose, by the Committee of Constitution, to the National Assembly, December 21st, 1789 (London?, 1790);

Essay on Political Tactics (London: T. Payne, 1791);

*"Panopticon": or, the Inspection-House: Containing the Idea of a New Principle of Construction applicable to any Sort of establishment, in which persons of any Description are to be

*Jeremy Bentham; portrait by an unknown artist, 1789
(University College London)*

kept under Inspection; and in Particular to Penitentiary-houses, Prisons, Houses of industry, Workhouses, Poor Houses, Manufactories, Madhouses, Lazarettos, Hospitals, and Schools; with a plan of management adopted to the principle: in a series of letters, written in the year 1787, from Crecheff in White Russia, to a friend in England* (1 volume, Dublin: Thomas Byrne, 1791; 2 volumes, London: Sold by T. Payne, 1791);

Panopticon: Postscript; Part I: Containing further particulars and alterations relative to the plan of construction originally proposed; principally adapted to the purpose of a panopticon penitentiary-house (London: Printed for T. Payne, 1791);

Panopticon: Postscript; Part II: Containing a plan of management for a panopticon penitentiary-house (London: Printed for T. Payne, 1791);

Panoptique. Mémoire sur un nouveau principe pour construire des maisons d'inspection, et nommément des maisons de force (Paris: De L'Imprimerie Nationale, 1791);

Jeremy Bentham to the National Convention of France (London: R. Heward, 1793); republished as *Emancipate Your Colonies! Addressed to the National Convention of France, A° 1793* (London: R. Heward, 1830);

A Protest against Law Taxes (Dublin, 1793); republished with *Supply without Burthen; or Escheat Vice Taxation* (London: Printed for J. Debrett, 1795);

Letter to Lord Pelham, Giving a Comparative View of the System of Penal Colonization in New South Wales, and the Home Penitentiary System, Prescribed by Two Acts of Parliament of the Years 1794 and 1799 (London: Wilkes & Taylor, 1802);

Traités de legislation civile et pénale, 3 volumes, translated by Etienne Dumont (Paris: Boussange, Masson & Besson, 1802); translated by John Neal as *Principles of Legislation: From the ms. of Jeremy Bentham . . . By M. Dumont* (Boston: Wells & Lilly; New York: G. & G. H. Carvill, 1830); translated by Richard Hildreth as *Theory of Legislation* (Boston: Weeks, Jordan, 1840; London: Trübner, 1864);

A Plea for the Constitution: Shewing the Enormities Committed to the Oppression of British Subjects, Innocent as well as Guilty, in Breach of Magna Charta, the Petition of Right, the Habeas Corpus Act, and the Bill of Rights; as Likewise of the Several Transportation Acts: in and by the Design, Foundation and Government of the Penal Colony of New South Wales (London: Printed for Mawman, Poultry & Hatchard by Wilkes & Taylor, 1803);

Scotch Reform; Considered, with Reference to the Plan, Proposed in the Late Parliament, for the Regulation of the Courts, and the Administration of Justice in Scotland . . . . In a Series of Letters, Addressed to the Right Hon. Lord Grenville (London: Printed by R. Taylor for J. Ridgway, 1808);

Théorie des peines et des récompenses, 2 volumes, translated by Dumont (London: Printed by Vogel & Schulze, sold by B. Dulau, 1811); translated and edited by Richard Smith as *The Rationale of Reward* (London: J. & H. L. Hunt, 1825) and *The Rationale of Punishment* (London: R. Heward, 1830);

Panopticon versus New South Wales; or, The Panopticon Penitentiary System and the Penal Colonization System Compared. Containing 1. Two Letters to Lord Pelham. 2. Plea for the Constitution, anno 1803, printed now first published (London: Sold by R. Baldwin & J. Ridgway, 1812);

Pauper Management Improved: Particularly by Means of an Application of the Panopticon Principle of Construction.

Anno 1797, first published in Young's Annals of Agriculture; now first published separately (London: Sold by R. Baldwin & J. Ridgway, 1812);

Tactique des Assemblées legislatives, suivie d'un Traité des Sophismes politiques, 2 volumes, translated by Dumont (Geneva & Paris: J. J. Paschoud, 1816);

Chrestomathia, Being a Collection of Papers, Explanatory of the Design of an Institution, Proposed to be Set on Foot, Under the Name of the Chrestomathic Day School, or Chrestomathic School, for the Extension of the New System of Instruction to the Higher Branches of Learning, for the Use of the Middling and Higher Ranks of Life, 2 parts (London: Printed for Payne & Foss & J. Ridgway by J. M'Creery, 1815 [i.e., 1817]);

A Table of the Springs of Action, Shewing the Several Species of Pleasures and Pains, of which Man's Nature is Susceptible (London: Printed by R. & A. Taylor, 1815 [i.e., 1817]);

"Swear Not at All": Containing an Exposure of the Needlessness and Mischievousness, as well as Anti-Christianity, of the Ceremony of an Oath (London: Sold by R. Hunter, 1817);

Papers Relative to Codification and Public Instruction; Including Correspondence with the Russian Emperor, and Divers Constituted Authorities in the American United States (London: Printed by J. M'Creery, sold by Payne & Foss, Pall-Mall; and R. Hunter (Successor to Mr. Johnson), St. Paul's Church-Yard, 1817);

Supplement to Papers on Codification (London: Printed by J. M'Creery, 1817);

Jeremy Bentham, an Englishman, to the Citizens of the Several American United States (London: Printed by J. M'Creery, 1817);

Plan of Parliamentary Reform, in the Form of Catechism, with Reasons for Each Article, with an Introduction, Shewing the Necessity of Radical, and the Inadequacy of Moderate, Reform (London: Printed for R. Hunter, 1817);

Church of Englandism and its Catechism Examined (London: E. Wilson, 1818);

Bentham's Radical Reform Bill (London: E. Wilson, 1819);

The King against Edmonds and Others: Set Down for the Trial, at Warwick, on the 29th of March, 1820. Brief Remarks Tending to Show the Untenability of This Indictment (London: Printed by J. M'Creery, 1820);

The King against Sir Charles Wolseley, Baronet, and Joseph Harrison, Schoolmaster: Set Down for Trial at Chester on the 4th of April, 1820. Brief Remarks Tending to Show the Untenability of This Indictment (London: Printed by J. M'Creery, 1820);

Observations on the Restrictive and Prohibitory Commercial System; Especially with a Reference to the Decree of the Spanish Cortes of July 1820, edited by John Bowring (London: E. Wilson, 1821);

The Elements of the Art of Packing, as Applied to Special Juries, Particularly in Cases of Libel Law (London: E. Wilson, 1821);

On the Liberty of the Press and Public Discussion (London: Printed for W. Hone, 1821);

Three Tracts Relative to Spanish and Portugueze Affairs; With a Continual Eye to English Ones (London: Printed for W. Hone, 1821);

An Analysis of the Influence of Natural Religion on the Temporal Happiness of Mankind, as Philip Beauchamp, edited by George Grote (London: R. Carlile, 1822);

Letters to Count Toreno on the Proposed Penal Code (London: E. Wilson, 1822);

Codification Proposal, Addressed by Jeremy Bentham to All Nations Professing Liberal Opinions (London: Printed by J. M'Creery, 1822);

Truth Versus Ashhurst; or Law As It Is, Contrasted With What It Is Said to Be (London: T. Moses, 1823);

Leading Principles of a Constitutional Code for Any State (London: A. Valpy, 1823);

Traité des preuves judiciares, ouvrage extrait des manuscrits de Jérémie Bentham, 2 volumes, translated by Dumont (Paris: Bossages fréres, 1823); translated as *A Treatise on Judicial Evidence, Extracted from the Manuscripts of Jeremy Bentham, Esq., by M. Dumont,* 1 volume (London: Baldwin, Cradock & Joy, 1825; Philadelphia: T. & J. W. Johnson, 1858);

Not Paul, but Jesus, as Gamaliel Smith (London: Printed for John Hunt, 1823);

The Book of Fallacies: From the Unfinished Papers of Jeremy Bentham, edited by Peregrine Bingham (London: J. & H. L. Hunt, 1824); republished as *Bentham's Handbook of Political Fallacies,* edited by Harold A. Larrabee (Baltimore: Johns Hopkins University Press, 1952);

Indications Respecting Lord Eldon, Including History of the Pending Judges'-Salary-Raising Measure (London: J. & H. L. Hunt, 1825);

Observations on Mr. Secretary Peel's House of Commons Speech, 21st March, 1825, Introducing His Police Magistrates' Salary Raising Bill. Date of Order for Printing, 24th March, 1825. Also on the Announced Judges' Salary Raising Bill, and the Pending County Courts Bill (London: J. & H. L. Hunt, 1825);

Extract from the Proposed Constitutional Code, Entitled Official Aptitude Maximized, Expense Minimized (London, 1816 [i.e., 1826]);

The Rationale of Judicial Evidence, Specially Applied to English Practice, 5 volumes, edited by John Stuart Mill (London: Hunt & Clarke, 1827);

De l'Organisation judiciaire, et de la Codification: Extraits de divers ouvrages de Jérémie Bentham, edited by Dumont (Paris: H. Bossange, 1828);

Justice and Codification Petitions (London: R. Heward, 1829);

Constitutional Code: For the Use of All Nations and All Governments Professing Liberal Opinions, Vol. I (London: R. Heward, 1830);

Official Aptitude Maximized, Expense Minimized; As Shewn in the Several Papers in This Volume (London: R. Heward, 1830);

Law Reform Association Proposal (London: Printed by C. & W. Reynell, 1830);

Equity Dispatch Court Proposal: Containing a plan for the Speedy and Unexpensive Termination of the Suits Now Pending in Equity Courts (London: R. Heward, 1830);

Jeremy Bentham to his Fellow-Citizens of France on House of Peers and Senates (London: R. Heward, 1830);

Jeremy Bentham to his Fellow Citizens of France, on Death Punishment (London: R. Heward, 1831);

Parliamentary Candidate's Proposed Declaration of Principles: or Say, A Test Proposed for Parliamentary Candidates (London: R. Heward, 1831);

Lord Brougham Displayed: Including I. Boa Constrictor, alias Helluo Curiarum; II. Observations on the Bankruptcy Court Bill, Now Ripened into an Act. III. Extracts from Proposed Constitutional Code (London: R. Heward, 1832);

Deontology: or, the Science of Morality, 2 volumes, edited by Bowring (London: Longman, Rees, Orme, Brown, Green & Longman, 1834);

Observations: On the Poor Bill, Introduced by the Right Honourable William Pitt. Written February, 1797. Not for Publication (London: W. Clowes, 1838);

Anti-Senatica. An Attack on the U.S. Senate, Sent by Jeremy Bentham to Andrew Jackson, President of the United States, Now First Published by Permission of the University College Committee from the MSS. Owned by the University of London, and Contained in the Library of University College, London, edited, with an introduction, by Charles Warren Everett (Northampton, Mass.: Department of History of Smith College, 1926).

Editions and Collections: *The Works of Jeremy Bentham, Published under the Supervision of His Executor, John Bowring,* 11 volumes (Edinburgh: W. Tait, 1838–1843; New York: Russell & Russell, 1962);

A Comment on the Commentaries: A Criticism of William Blackstone's Commentaries on the Laws of England, edited by Charles Warren Everett (Oxford: Clarendon Press, 1928);

Jeremy Bentham's Economic Writings, 3 volumes, edited by W. Stark (London: Published for the Royal Economic Society for Allen & Unwin, 1952);

The Collected Works of Jeremy Bentham, general editors J.H. Burns and others (3 volumes, London: Athlone Press, 1968–1981; 10 volumes, Oxford, 1983–   )

—comprises *An Introduction to the Principles of Morals and Legislation,* edited by Burns and H.L.A. Hart (London: Athlone Press, 1970); *Of Laws in General,* edited by Hart (London: Athlone Press, 1970); *A Comment on the Commentaries and A Fragment on Government,* edited by J.H. Burns and Hart (London: Athlone Press, 1977); *Deontology together with A Table of the Springs of Action and Article on Utilitarianism,* edited by Amnon Goldworth (Oxford: Clarendon Press, 1983); *Chrestomathia,* edited by M.J. Smith and W.H. Burston (Oxford: Clarendon Press, 1983); *Constitutional Code,* Vol. I, edited by F. Rosen and Burns (Oxford: Clarendon Press, 1983); *First Principles preparatory to Constitutional Code,* edited by Philip Schofield (Oxford: Clarendon Press, 1989); *Securities against Misrule and other Constitutional Writings for Tripoli and Greece,* edited by Schofield (Oxford: Clarendon Press, 1990); *Official Aptitude Maximized; Expense Minimized,* edited by Schofield (Oxford: Clarendon Press, 1993); *Colonies, Commerce, and Constitutional Law: Rid Yourselves of Ultramaria and other writings on Spain and Spanish America,* edited by Schofield (Oxford: Clarendon Press, 1995); *"Legislator of the World": Writings on Codification, Law, and Education,* edited by Scholfield and Jonathan Harris (Oxford: Clarendon Press, 1998); *Political Tacticsm,* edited by Michael James, Cyprian Blamires, and Catherine Pease-Watkin (Oxford: Clarendon Press, 1999) *Writings on the Poor Laws,* volume 1, edited by Michael Quinn (Oxford: Clarendon Press, 2001);

De l'ontologie et autres textes sur les fictions, text established by P. Schofield, translation and commentary by Jean-Pierre Cléro and Christian Laval (Paris: Editions du Seyil, 1997).

OTHER: François-Marie Arouet Voltaire, *The White Bull, an Oriental History,* 2 volumes, translated, with an introduction, by Bentham (London: J. Bew, 1774);

Jean-François Marmontel, *Novels,* volume 1 (London: Elmsley, 1777)—includes Bentham's translation of *Les Incas;*

Sir Torbern Bergman, *An Essay on the Usefulness of Chemistry . . . ,* translated by Bentham (London: Printed for J. Murray, 1783).

SELECTED PERIODICAL PUBLICATIONS—UNCOLLECTED: Three letters, as Irenius, *Gazetteer,* 3 December 1770, 1 March 1771, 18 March 1771;

"Defence of Economy Against the Late Mr. Burke," *Pamphleteer,* 9, no. 22 (1817);

"Defence of Economy against the Right Hon. George Rose," *Pamphleteer,* 10, no. 20 (1817);

"Observations on Mr. Secretary Peel's House of Commons Speech, 21st March, 1825," *Pamphleteer,* 25, no. 50 (1825);

"Observations on the actual State of the English Law of Real Property," *Westminster Review,* 6 (October 1826): 446–507;

"Jeremy Bentham to Henry Brougham, old and familiar friend, the administration of justice in England needs improvement," *New York Globe,* 25 May 1830.

Jeremy Bentham is widely accepted as the founder of modern utilitarianism, and his ideas continue to influence moral and political philosophy. While he was not the first to draw on the notion of utility (usefulness) and the principle of the greatest happiness, the manner in which he developed such philosophical ideas into a standard for moral action has ensured his continued prominence. Bentham's unambiguous identification of happiness as the fundamental element, the driving force, behind understandings of social, political, and economic questions has established him as the quintessential classical utilitarian thinker.

Long before the end of his remarkably productive life Bentham's many contributions, in terms both of analytic theory and of practical application, had made their presence felt across many areas of study, including philosophy, law, politics, political economy, social welfare, and public policy. Bentham's combination of critical rationality and clear empiricism, both of which he employed with a relentless consistency throughout his varied writings, has established him as one of the best-known legal, political, and social theorists. Yet, Bentham was primarily a philosopher of the law, and he unremittingly maintained that his prime goal was to correct the failures and inadequacies he saw in the legal process and especially within the British legal process. This element of practicality makes Bentham's philosophy quite distinctive.

Jeremy Bentham was born in Houndsditch, London, on 15 February 1748, the son of Jeremiah Bentham, a prosperous London attorney who significantly enlarged his wealth through dealings in real estate. In regard to his eldest son, Jeremiah was more ambitious than affectionate; and, clearly proud of his son's early signs of intellectual ability, he suggested that with "pushing," Jeremy might one day become lord chancellor. Bentham's mother, Alicia, was kindly but overshadowed by his father, and she died when Jeremy was ten years old, leaving Jeremy and Samuel, his junior by nine years, the only survivors of seven siblings. Jeremy's relationship with Samuel, who later became a distinguished naval architect and administrator, was perhaps the most important of his adult life, and Bentham developed a deep and affectionate concern for his younger brother's welfare. Bentham was a precociously talented child, who is said to have been able to read Latin at the age of three and who showed an interest in the world of literature and learning from a young age. He remembered his childhood as rather monotonous, however, as he was kept largely without the company of children his own age, and without frivolous amusements in general; he relished the frequent visits to his grandmothers' houses at Reading and Barking and found pleasure in flowers, music, and books.

At seven Bentham was sent to Westminster School to be educated alongside the sons of the wealthy and the aristocratic, and there his talents for classical languages emerged; by age ten he was composing verse in Greek and Latin, and he became thoroughly familiar with the Bible. Yet, Bentham was a sensitive boy with a frail constitution, and besides his recognition for academic ability he gained a reputation only for being the smallest boy in the school. He did not remember school life as a pleasant experience. From Westminster, Bentham moved on to Queen's College, Oxford in 1761, and there he found even less comfort, writing of his fear of ghosts in the graveyard outside the window of his room and seeing even less value in the pedestrian teaching offered. In *Church of Englandism and its Catechism Examined* (1818) he describes Oxford life as characterized by "mendacity and insincerity . . . the only sure effects of an English university education." The most lasting impression provided by the university experience was his being constrained to subscribe to the Thirty-nine Articles. Bentham resented this requirement for the rest of his life, and it underlay much of his thinking regarding toleration and the questionable validity of oaths when taken as the proof of any fact or belief. In 1764 he graduated from Oxford, was admitted to Lincoln's Inn, and started his professional training as a lawyer. His later education confirmed his belief that there was little that could be looked upon with confidence in the practice of English law.

Until the end of the 1760s all appeared to be progressing as Bentham's father would have wished. In 1768, however, inspired by his reading of Claude-Adrien Helvétius's *De l'esprit* (Of the Spirit, 1758), Bentham declared that he had found the direction in which his particular genius could best be used, which was not in the practice of the law but in its criticism and correction. While Bentham was, therefore, called to the bar in 1769, his career as a barrister progressed no further; and although he provided a few legal opinions he never pleaded a case in court. From

Bentham as a student of Queen's College, Oxford, circa 1761; portrait by Thomas Frye (National Portrait Gallery, London)

this point Bentham's relations with his father became more strained as he enthusiastically began his analysis of the English legal system in a manner and style that changed little over the course of the next sixty years.

Much of the work produced by Bentham was never published and remains in manuscript form, of which some seventy thousand sheets still in existence. He developed the habit of working on several subjects concurrently, sometimes publishing completed works immediately but more usually leaving them in an unfinished state to be returned to at a later date; the result is a complex publication history. A further problem exists in regard to Bentham volumes published by various editors: the editing process usually involved considerable changes to both content and arrangement, raising questions regarding the authenticity of such works. The first attempt to produce a comprehensive collection of Bentham's writings, *The Works of Jeremy Bentham, Published under the Supervision of His Executor, John Bowring* (1838–1843), includes many flaws and excludes several important works. The publication of a new edition of *The Collected Works of*

Jeremy Bentham (1968–) seeks to remedy these defects by carefully reconstructing Bentham's own work and providing full annotation and thorough introductions to each volume.

From the early 1770s until the middle of the following decade Bentham made substantial progress in the exploration of the major themes and principles that provided the foundations for his philosophy throughout his life. His formidable publishing career began in 1771 with three modest letters in the *Gazetteer* defending the eminent English judge William Murray, first Earl of Mansfield; he was also forced to turn his hand to translation, producing *The White Bull, an Oriental History,* a version of François-Marie Arouet Voltaire's *Le Taureau blanc* (1774), and Jean-François Marmontel's *Les Incas* (1777). These works not only illustrate the practical results of going against his father's wishes and having to supplement his meager allowance but also display quite clearly the source of Bentham's inspiration for his literary efforts. The thought of the Enlightenment–the philosophical ideas of Helvétius, Jean Le Rond d'Alembert, Cesare Beccaria, and Charles Louis Secondat, Baron de Montesquieu–drove Bentham to develop his philosophy through an examination of the motives that produced the actions of individuals and governments and of the means by which systems of law could be designed to benefit all in the societies they controlled.

Bentham soon began a valuable collaboration with a family friend, John Lind, a clergyman who acted as the unofficial London agent for the king of Poland. Bentham fell in love with Mary Dunkley, a friend of Lind's sister, but this relationship brought further conflict between Bentham and his father. Mary–or Polly, as she was frequently called–was the orphaned daughter of a surgeon and without fortune. In the eyes of Jeremiah she was quite unsuitable for his eldest son. For a while Bentham considered abandoning all financial reliance on his father; but eventually the relationship ended, and he continued as before. Throughout these early years Bentham's grand ideas regarding the reorganization of the law continued to grow, and the first public offerings of his enthusiastic critique of the existing system of jurisprudence were seen in *A Fragment on Government; Being an Examination of What is Delivered, on the Subject of Government in General in the Introduction of Sir William Blackstone's Commentaries: with a Preface, in Which is Given a Critique on the Work at Large* (1776), which was published anonymously. *A Fragment on Government* proved to be important not only for the recognition it brought Bentham once his identity became known but also as a fundamental statement of his critical approach. It certainly developed into a far more fundamental assault than Bentham had initially envisaged. The observations in the small volume attack a remarkable range of theories then prevalent in jurisprudence and political philosophy. So sophisticated was the criticism that many reckoned it to be the work of some legal or philosophical master such as Lord Mansfield, Lord Camden, or the solicitor general John Dunning, the legal star of the government opposition; few could believe that it was the young Bentham's work when his authorship finally became known.

In the preface to *A Fragment on Government* Bentham declares it to be a fundamental axiom that "it is the greatest happiness of the greatest number that is the measure of right and wrong." This premise was the core not only of his science of legislation but also of his entire conception of the nature and value of social and political society. With this idea he proceeded to analyze what went under the name of English law as presented by Sir William Blackstone, the preeminent English legal theorist and the first Vinerian Professor of English Law at Oxford, in the four-volume *Commentaries on the Laws of England* (1765–1769). *A Fragment on Government* purported to look only at the introduction to Blackstone's work; yet, in examining the fundamental concepts of natural law and social contract that underpinned all of what Blackstone was saying, Bentham's critique extended far beyond the limits he ostensibly set.

In his presentation of utility as the proper foundation on which legitimate government must rest Bentham took direct issue with the well-established doctrine that political society was legitimated by a hypothetical social contract. Such Lockean thinking was prominent within eighteenth-century English political theory, and in following such concepts Blackstone was only restating what many accepted to be a central pillar for the understanding of society and the role of government. The contractarian view had not, however, been immune from attack, and the philosophy of David Hume had already substantially criticized the doctrine. Hume argued in his *Treatise of Human Nature* (1738) that the basis of the citizen's obligation to obey sovereign power was not tacit consent to some contract but the interests and necessities of human society. Without obedience no society could be maintained.

On reading Hume's attack, Bentham says in *A Fragment on Government,* he "felt as if scales had fallen from my eyes, I then, for the first time learnt to call the cause of the people the cause of Virtue." Bentham saw great value in the concept of obedience as presented by Hume and, accordingly, attempted a definition of political society as one in which the "subjects" had become accustomed to the habit of obeying a certain person or set of persons, called the "governors." In *A Fragment on Government* Bentham suggests that this habit of obedience was secure only so long as the subjects conceived of it as being in their interests to continue to obey. His most powerful suggestion was that once individuals reached the stage where they were said to be disposed to revolt—in other words, once they believed their interests would be better served by destroying the sovereign body—then no hypothetical contract or "metaphysico-legal" argument would prevent them from doing just that. This point was defined by Bentham as the "juncture for resistance" and provided one of the primary messages of *A Fragment on Government*: that freedom of criticism is essential for the continual improvement of society and provides the only way to avoid an accumulation of discontent that could lead to the destruction of political society. One of his key concerns with Blackstone's analysis and with its overwhelming reliance on contract theory was that such latitude for "censorial" analysis was removed, and all that was presented was an "expository" view of English law and society that did little but seek submission from the reader. The need for subjects to feel able to censure freely, to criticize the system of politics and law under which they lived, was basic to Bentham's vision of stable and justified government.

Heavily enmeshed in Blackstone's use of contract theory was John Locke's notion of natural law as provider of social and political rights. To claim that natural law could furnish such rights was incomprehensible to Bentham, who stated in *A Fragment on Government* that "the natural tendency of such doctrine is to impel a man, by the force of conscience, to rise up in arms against any law whatsoever that he happens not to like." Nothing in such notions of natural law bound people to any form of behavior in relation to the political society in which they lived unless the reason for their obedience was mischief or inexpediency; but then these concepts of natural law would be grounded not on natural right but on pain and pleasure and, hence, on the principle of utility. For Bentham, Blackstone's reliance on natural law and the social contract failed to explain the antagonism between liberty and government, and only the principle of utility could balance their conflicting demands. A concern with the fallacious nature of contractarian and natural-law arguments stayed with Bentham throughout his life, and he returned to the theme with great effect in his analysis of French politics in the period following the Revolution of 1789.

The value of *A Fragment on Government* owes much to the vigor and vitality that filled this introduc-

Bentham's brother, Samuel, in the service of Prince Potemkin in St. Petersburg, Russia, in 1784

tory tract. Yet, the piece was but a small part of a more extended analysis of Blackstone's *Commentaries on the Laws of England;* Bentham completed his critique in the 1770s, but it remained unpublished until it appeared as *A Comment on the Commentaries: A Criticism of William Blackstone's Commentaries on the Laws of England* (1928). Here he continues his critique of Blackstone's method and principles, and his criticism of Blackstone is severe. But Blackstone's influence on Bentham was not wholly negative: Blackstone's influential expression of the foundations of common-law theory provided the essential exposition of English practice against which he could react.

Systematic arrangement and classification were a prime concern for Bentham, and this interest arose partly from his deep dissatisfaction with the perceived inaccuracies and imprecision in the accepted common-law foundation provided for English jurisprudence. Statute law was generally regarded as inferior to common or unwritten law, but the common-law reliance on legal precedent and the opportunity for judicial discretion encouraged Bentham to regard much of the law of England as simply fictitious. All the common law amounted to for him was an "assemblage of fictitious regulations feigned after the images of these real ones which compose the Statute Law." From the earliest period, therefore, Bentham's analysis directed him toward the rationalization of the law as a principal task, and by 1782 he had come to regard codification of the entire legal system as the only answer to the problems produced by the existing confusion. From the late 1770s he drafted many sheets of manuscript on the codification of the penal and civil law, as well as essays on the foundations of jurisprudence, to which he gave titles such as "Preparatory Principles" and "Elements of Critical Jurisprudence." Until the mid 1780s codification was constantly at the forefront of his endeavors to establish a new "science of legislation," as he refers to it in *An Introduction to the Principles of Morals and Legislation* (1789), in the form of a complete code, or *pannomion,* of laws. *A Fragment on Government,* rather than his writings on codification, first brought him to the attention of others, however.

In July 1781 Bentham was visited at his Lincoln's Inn chambers by William Petty, second Earl of Shelburne, a Whig aristocrat who became prime minister for a short period during 1782–1783. Shelburne was seeking a copy of *A Fragment on Government,* and this contact and recognition began a particularly fulfilling episode in Bentham's life. Shelburne (created marquess of Lansdowne in 1784) was interested in ideas, and at his country mansion at Bowood, Wiltshire, a coterie of intellectuals were gathered. Shelburne invited Bentham to visit Bowood, and after a somewhat tentative acceptance Bentham developed a close and valuable relationship with the earl. Bentham became a frequent visitor to Lansdowne House, the London residence of Shelburne, and visited Bowood in 1781 and in 1789, for several weeks on each occasion. These stays left him with some happy memories. Not only was Bentham free to converse with fellow intellectuals such as the dissenting philosopher Joseph Priestley, but he also met the second young woman for whom he felt romantic affection. Caroline Fox, the niece of Lady Shelburne, was at Bowood on both occasions Bentham visited, and during his stays he wrote playful and romantic letters to her, but no closer relationship appears to have developed. In 1805 the two met again, and Bentham made her an offer of marriage that was politely refused. This tentative encounter appears to have put an end to Bentham's attempts at romance, and he remained a bachelor.

At Bowood, too, Bentham met his future editor, a Genevan named Etienne Dumont, where popular-

ization of his writings propelled Bentham to international recognition. While many of the manuscripts used by Dumont were produced by Bentham in the 1770s and 1780s, however, Dumont's editions did not appear until *Traités de legislation civile et pénale* (1802), in three volumes, and the two volumes of *Théorie des peines et des récompenses* (1811) were published. This selection and presentation of Bentham's difficult texts was vitally important for his career; by the end of the first decade of the nineteenth century his writings were being read in French throughout France, Russia, Switzerland, and Spain. Following their translation into Spanish in 1821–1822, the Dumont recensions also became widely read in Spanish America. This foreign interest led William Hazlitt to remark in *The Spirit of the Age* (1825) that Bentham's reputation grew in size according to the distance traveled from his home in Westminster.

Bentham's attention had always been directed beyond the British Isles, and Continental connections were important from the beginning; his interest in penal codification, in particular, was constantly assisted by reformist influences from abroad. In 1778, for example, the Oeconomical Society of Bern advertised a competition for the best "Plan of Legislation on Criminal Matters," which may have provided the stimulus for Bentham to begin codification of his penal theory. Bentham had already written a considerable quantity of preparatory material on the subject, and penal law and the theory of punishment were of substantial importance in the development of his work at this period; they brought him into contact with the most famous prison reformers and theorists of the day, including John Howard, Thomas Hanway, and William Eden. Yet, the material was under constant reworking and revision and was clearly unsuitable for wide dissemination in its original form; editing was essential for its true value to be revealed to a wider audience. Dumont provided that service for Bentham: he presented the most complex of analyses in a convenient and accessible form for general public consumption; and while the authenticity of Dumont's texts has been questioned, their powerfully effective communication and accord with the ideas of Bentham's reformist thinking is not in doubt. But English readers had to wait to read Bentham; the punishment material in Dumont's edition of 1802, for example, was not translated back into English until 1830, when Richard Smith published *The Rationale of Punishment.* Thus, what Bentham had written in English in 1775 was not published in English until 1830. It is hardly surprising that his reputation at home took so long to grow.

Despite Bentham's reluctance to concentrate on preparing material for the press, his early ideas on the theory and reform of punishment did find their way into print in the form of *A View of the Hard-Labour Bill; Being an Abstract of a Pamphlet, Intituled, "Draught of a Bill, to Punish by Imprisonment and Hard-Labour, Certain Offenders; and to Establish Proper Places for Their Reception." Interspersed with Observations Relative to the Subject of the Above Draught in Particular, and to Penal Jurisprudence in General* (1778). *A View of the Hard-Labour Bill* was an important work in support of the extension of punishment by imprisonment in opposition to the excessive use of the death penalty in England, and it may well have played a role in the preparation and passing of the landmark Penitentiary Act of 1779. Bentham's ideas thus took a practical turn even at this early stage. More practical applications were found for his ideas in the 1790s, but during the preceding decade Bentham continued to explore his utilitarian principles.

At Bowood, Bentham drafted the material that became one of his best-known works, *An Introduction to the Principles of Morals and Legislation.* This work has proved to be of profound influence in philosophy; yet, its full value is still only beginning to be recognized. The piece was intended as an introduction to a penal code rather than as a preliminary view of more general moral and legal questions, and the relationship between Bentham's discussion of utility and the detailed analysis of human motivation and penal theory is, accordingly, difficult to appreciate on a first reading.

The work opens with a proposition copied, as Elie Halévy noted in *The Growth of Philosophic Radicalism* (1928), virtually word for word from Helvétius: "Nature has placed mankind under the governance of two sovereign masters, *pain* and *pleasure*. It is for them alone to point out what we ought to do, as well as to determine what we shall do. On the one hand the standard of right and wrong, on the other the chain of causes and effects, are fastened to their throne." Bentham claims that only the principle of utility, or, as he later called it, "the greatest happiness principle," can recognize this subjection. Bentham was not the first to use such terminology, and he makes regular mention of earlier thinkers whose ideas he develops. He claims to have discovered the phrase "the greatest happiness of the greatest number" in the work of the philosopher Priestley. None of Priestley's works include these exact words, however, and after tracing the history of the phrase, Robert Shackleton has concluded that "there can be no reasonable doubt" that Bentham first set eyes on it in Beccaria's *Dei delitti e delle pene* (1764; translated as *An Essay on Crimes and Punishments,* 1767). Other eighteenth-century consequentialist formulations of pain and pleasure can be found in the work of Francis Hutcheson or in that of the scientist and mathematician Pierre Louis Moreau de Maupertuis, but Beccaria was particularly influential for Bentham. On his general indebtedness to Beccaria, Bentham states in *A Fragment on Government* that "he was received by the intelligent as an Angel from heaven would be by the faithful. He may be styled the father of 'Censorial Jurisprudence.'" While Bentham was the first, therefore, to describe himself as a "utilitarian," a wide range of eighteenth-century thinkers pursued similar consequentialist discussions, viewing social happiness as a justifiable goal for moral and political philosophy. In England, William Paley published a rival utilitarian analysis in *Principles of Moral and Political Philosophy* (1785), and the appearance of this work has been seen as a spur to the final publication of Bentham's *An Introduction to the Principles of Morals and Legislation* some nine years after its composition in 1780.

From *An Introduction to the Principles of Morals and Legislation* it is apparent that the principle of utility relies on a particular view of individual motivation: that human beings consistently act to maximize their own pleasure or minimize their own pain. Human motivation is, therefore, dependent upon experience, on the knowledge of enjoyment and suffering and on the experienced sensations of pleasure and pain. Only by reference to such experience, in which all share, can any source of a standard of right and wrong be established. Any action that could be seen to increase aggregate happiness would be pronounced by Bentham as right, while any action deemed to reduce the sum of happiness would be wrong. Bentham thought that the "value" of pain might be measured in terms of "intensity, duration, certainty, propinquity, fecundity, purity and extent," and he enumerated the various categories into which pleasure and pain could be divided. This "felicific calculus" theory has been criticized as an unrealistic approach to morality and human motivation and a naive understanding of human psychology. But such critiques fail to acknowledge that for Bentham pain and pleasure were not simple tools but complicated sensations, and he develops a sophisticated assessment of them.

In *An Introduction to the Principles of Morals and Legislation* the complex motivating forces operating in individuals are divided into three general categories: social, dissocial, and self-regarding. The social motive is subdivided into semisocial motives, such as love of reputation, desire for friendship and religion, and a purely social one that consists only of goodwill toward others. An agent feeling sympathetic gains

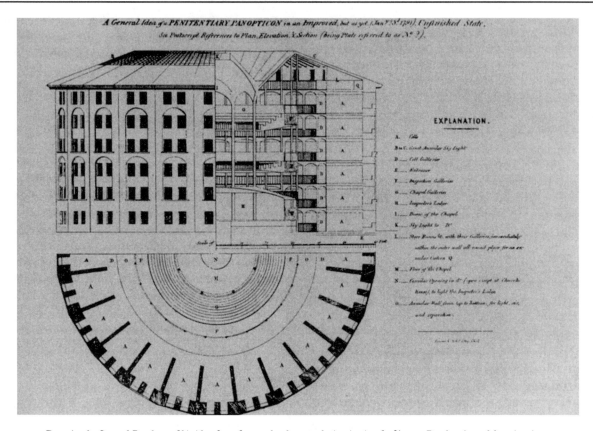

Drawing by Samuel Bentham of his idea for a factory that became the inspiration for Jeremy Bentham's model penitentiary, the "panopticon" (from Jeremy Bentham's "Panopticon": or, the Inspection-House, 1791; Houghton Library, Harvard University)

pleasure from contemplating the happiness of others. In *An Introduction to the Principles of Morals and Legislation* Bentham moves toward the development of an egoistic psychology that does not rule out the possibility of benevolent conduct.

The way in which Bentham's use of the concept of utility relates to earlier thinking has been the subject of careful analysis, and the role played by Hume's philosophy, in particular, has been consistently prominent. The opinion has been expressed by writers such as H. L. A. Hart and Ross Harrison that Bentham adopted the term "utility" from Hume but produced a markedly differing use of it by emphasizing the maximization of happiness as a critical standard to assess individual acts, common and statute law, and social and political institutions.

Others, however, have seen the distinction between Hume and Bentham as less dramatic. Frederick Rosen has argued that while Bentham did link utility more directly with pleasure, and that this connection eventually led to the abandonment of the phrase "principle of utility" in favor of "the greatest happiness principle," both thinkers established utility as a critical factor in the sentiment of "approbation"– that is, they both use it to explain why individuals

feel drawn to approve of actions or rules that are socially useful. Also, for both Hume and Bentham, utility is taken to mean public utility, while any individual utility is a part of the public utility in which the individual shares. The most important element in Bentham's understanding of motivation, as Rosen sees it, is that even self-regarding motives that appear opposed to the public interest can actually advance it. In this interpretation Bentham does not have to be separated so distinctly from Hume in connecting happiness, individual or communal, with the public interest.

Despite the valuable discussion of motivation in *An Introduction to the Principles of Morals and Legislation* the book remains essentially a treatise on the theory of punishment. Asserting that "all punishment in itself is evil" because it is painful, he concludes that "Upon the principle of utility, if it ought at all to be admitted, it ought only to be admitted in as far as it promises to exclude some greater evil." Of preeminent value for the development of penal theory in *An Introduction to the Principles of Morals and Legislation* is Bentham's demonstration of how a deterrent theory of punishment might accommodate a concept of proportionality in the assignment of punishments to offenses of greater or lesser severity. It has been of deep and lasting influence throughout every penal system in the Western world.

Bentham concludes this work with a chapter on the division of offenses, in keeping with his demand for coherence and completeness in the penal law. Without clarity in the law, citizens could not be secure in their pursuit of happiness. In a "Concluding Note," added in 1789 to the original 1780 manuscript, he asks, "What is a law?" and explains that penal law requires a coercive element. This notion led in a later manuscript, "Of Laws in General," to his definition of law as the command of a sovereign. The highly original material in "Of Laws in General" was never published in Bentham's lifetime; it appeared in 1945 as *The Limits of Jurisprudence Defined* and was republished under its original title in 1970 with substantial changes by Hart. Hart suggests in *Essays on Bentham: Studies in Jurisprudence and Political Theory* (1982) that had this material on the nature of a law been published earlier, Bentham would have dominated English jurisprudence throughout the nineteenth century rather than Bentham's follower, John Austin, author of *the Province of Jurisprudence Determined* (1832), who beginning in 1827 held the first Chair in Jurisprudence and the Law of Nations at the newly established University of London.

An Introduction to the Principles of Morals and Legislation has been recognized as a milestone in the development of Bentham's thought. Yet, much on which he was working during this period appears nowhere in it. Of particular interest is the emphasis he placed on the subordinate ends of government, those of security, subsistence, abundance, and equality. He outlined these ends in his civil-law writings of the 1780s, which were published as part of *Traités de legislation civile et pénale*, and further developed his ideas about them in the 1820s. Of the four elements, security is of paramount importance. One of the prime factors that set human beings apart from animals is, for Bentham, their ability to look to the future and to build expectations. Positive expectations are the source of much social happiness, and, as a consequence, a proper end of government is the provision of security for the members of society in which the opportunity of fulfilling their individual expectations is offered. Another word for security in this sense is *liberty;* Bentham occasionally used the term for the sake of its familiarity, but he believed that *liberty* originated from an incorrect understanding that implied security against those in authority. Bentham, himself, on occasion, equated liberty with the absence of government, but his political philosophy required restrictions on individual freedoms for the sake of order and security in which

individual expectations could be fulfilled. Of the other subordinate ends, subsistence and abundance are closely connected with security. Economic equality is subordinate not only to utility but also to security, since in Bentham's opinion no rapid movement toward equality should be allowed that might threaten the security of property.

By the end of the 1780s Bentham had spent about fifteen years concentrating on the theory of law and legislation. At this point he began to examine more practical matters, the shift perhaps being encouraged by his change of location. In 1785 he had left England for Russia, and in February 1786 he arrived at Krichev in the Crimea to join his brother, who had entered the service of Prince Potemkin. In Russia, Bentham traveled little; he visited neither Moscow nor St. Petersburg but devoted his time to study. He produced a work on political economy, *Defence of Usury; Shewing the Impolicy of the Present Legal Restraints on the Terms of Pecuniary Bargains. In a Series of Letters to a Friend. To which is added a Letter to Adam Smith, Esq.; LL.D. on the Discouragements Opposed by the Above Restraints to the Progress of Inventive Industry* (1787), which proved an important addition to arguments in favor of the free circulation of capital. *Defence of Usury* was a further application of his utilitarian philosophy to questions of political organization, penology, public administration, social policy, and economics.

The most substantial of Bentham's practical applications of his ideas during this period was the panopticon prison project, the inspiration for which came from his brother. Samuel had developed the idea of an inspection house for the supervision of unskilled laborers by skilled workers; on the basis of this idea Bentham developed the concept of a building that could be used for the control and handling of prisoners, indigent poor, and those requiring education. The panopticon was a circular building with a single row of cells around the circumference arranged on several floors, with an inspection tower placed at the center from which the activities in each of the cells could be constantly observed. The letters forming the text of the work were sent back to England during 1786 and were published in three parts in 1791 as *"Panopticon": or, the Inspection-House: Containing the Idea of a New Principle of Construction applicable to any Sort of establishment, in which persons of any Description are to be kept under Inspection; and in Particular to Penitentiary-houses, Prisons, Houses of industry, Workhouses, Poor Houses, Manufactories, Madhouses, Lazarettos, Hospitals, and Schools; with a plan of management adopted to the principle: in a series of letters, written in the year 1787, from Crecheff in White Russia, to a friend in England; Panopticon: Postscript; Part I: Containing further particulars and alterations relative to the plan of construction originally proposed; principally adapted to the purpose of a panopticon penitentiary-house;* and *Panopticon: Postscript; Part II: Containing a plan of management for a panopticon penitentiary-house.* Bentham placed his proposal for the panopticon penitentiary before Prime Minister William Pitt in 1791 with the suggestion that he himself should be appointed governor. The government reacted favorably but slowly, and legislation was passed in 1794 for the purchase of land. Aristocratic opposition, however, first from the Spencer and then the Grosvenor families, mired the scheme and brought its implementation to an end in 1803. Bentham's father had died in 1792, leaving Bentham his house in Queen's Square Place, along with a fairly substantial inheritance. Bentham poured a good part of his new fortune into the panopticon scheme and endeavored for nearly twenty years to persuade, cajole, and convince the administration of the validity of the project. When his efforts failed, he was left with an acute sense of the lack of accountability in public administration and the dangers presented to good government by private influence. He recouped his financial losses when Parliament voted him compensation of £23,000 in 1813. Nevertheless, many commentators see Bentham's experience of government incompetence and intransigence as contributing to the development of his political radicalism.

The years surrounding the 1789 revolution in France were busy ones for Bentham. Along with many others in England he was swept up in a wave of enthusiasm for events that seemed at first to provide the opportunity for a rational reconstruction of a government in the most prominent state in Europe. While Bentham found much in the regime of 1789 to support, he had misgivings regarding its philosophical foundation on the principles of natural law and natural rights.

Bentham provided an influential analysis of parliamentary procedure in his *Essay on Political Tactics* (1791), but of more philosophical importance was his rigorous attack on natural-rights theory that Dumont published, in combination with the earlier material on tactics, as *Tactique des Assemblées legislatives, suivie d'un Traité des Sophismes politiques* (Tactic of Legislative Assemblies, with a Treatise on Political Fallacies, 1816). The second volume includes the essays "Traité des sophismes politiques," translated as *The Book of Fallacies: From the Unfinished Papers of Jeremy Bentham* (1824), and "Sophismes anarchiques," which was first published in English as "Anarchical Fallacies" in *The Works of Jeremy Bentham.* In his discussion of the Declaration of the Rights of Man and the Citizen embodied in the French Constitution, Bentham argued that the claim that no law that infringed such rights should be

regarded as valid was irreconcilable with any effective system of law and government. He went further, arguing that such rights were not even in accord with themselves, for if people had a naturally unrestricted right to liberty, then they could never be justifiably restrained and would be free to take whatever property they chose; no government would be able to impose taxation, since that would be an infringement of the individual's natural right to freedom. Further, reading in the same declarations how such rights were to be restricted or limited, Bentham felt compelled in "Anarchical Fallacies" to describe the notion of natural rights as "simple nonsense" and that of natural and imprescriptible rights as "nonsense upon stilts." This analysis was described by Sir William Holdsworth, the historian of English law, as "the most complete exposure of the logical absurdity of the doctrine of natural rights that has ever been written." Nevertheless, Bentham's opposition to the claims made for natural law and natural rights did not mean that he was opposed to those rights that were created by the existence and enforcement of the law, for these were not the fictions of the French declaration but were real rights guaranteed by government sanction.

Despite these serious reservations with the philosophical foundations on which the French Revolution rested, Bentham showed himself to be a capable defender of the revolution's ideals of reform and improvement. When Sir William Ashhurst, Puisne Justice of King's Bench, pronounced on the superiority of the English law and attacked the supporters of the French Revolution in England, Bentham quickly responded with *Truth Versus Ashhurst; or Law As It Is, Contrasted With What It Is Said to Be,* written in 1792 but not published until 1823. *Truth Versus Ashhurst* is a direct attack on the complacency of English law and the fallacious glorification of the judicial institutions of England. Clearly, Bentham's objections to French natural-law theory did not dull his criticism of English law nor reduce his excitement at the opportunities for reform presenting themselves across the English Channel. Indeed, his enthusiasm was considerable, and in the spirit of assistance and encouragement for the democratic cause he composed and sent to Paris *Draught of a New Plan for the Organisation of the Judicial Establishment in France: Proposed as a Succedaneum to the Draught Presented, for the Same Purpose, by the Committee of Constitution, to the National Assembly, December 21st, 1789,* which was published in the *Courier de Province* throughout May 1790, and *Essay on Political Tactics.* His writings on penal reform were edited and translated by Dumont and put before the National Assembly, with the help of Jacques Pierre Brissot de Warville, as *Panoptique. Mémoire sur un nouveau principe Our construire des maisons d'inspection, et nommément des maisons de force* (Panopticon. Notes on a New Principle for Construction of Houses of Inspection, also Known as Houses of Correction, 1791). Bentham's efforts were rewarded when he was made an honorary citizen of France in 1792, and he responded by contributing a further tract, *Jeremy Bentham to the National Convention of France* (1793), in which he encourages the deputies to free the colonies of France from domination.

The tumultuous events in France did not distract Bentham from other practical aspects to which his developing philosophy of law and motivation could be applied. By the end of the 1780s he had embarked on his analysis of economics with his attack on statutory restrictions on interest rates in *Defence of Usury,* which had provided an influential critique of Adam Smith's lack of support for a free trade in money in his *Inquiry into the Nature and Causes of the Wealth of Nations* (1776). In the 1790s economic aspects appeared in many of Bentham's writings, including *A Protest against Law Taxes* (1793), republished with *Supply without Burthen; or Escheat Vice Taxation* (1795). In this work he demands the abolition of taxes on the law, which made justice expensive and provided judges and lawyers with self-interested reasons for prolonging lawsuits, and suggested that the revenue lost to the exchequer be replaced by a new tax extending the law of escheat. The latter proposal sought to return inheritances to the state when an heir stood beyond the degree of relationship to the decedent within which marriage is forbidden. Bentham also began a general treatise on the "art" of political economy, which remained unfinished. Many of his economic writings between 1790 and 1800 consisted of proposals or critiques on specialized practical issues and met with little immediate success.

One problem to which Bentham paid much attention was poor relief, which was seen as a growing threat to the propertied classes. In *Pauper Management Improved: Particularly by Means of an Application of the Panopticon Principle of Construction. Anno 1797, first published in Young's Annals of Agriculture; now first published separately* (1797) he suggests the formation of a national joint-stock company for the management of the indigent. The company would construct 250 workhouses on the panopticon model, the occupants of which would work to cover the cost of their maintenance. Bentham expected that this enterprise would not only relieve the state of the burden of the poor but would also provide a profit for company shareholders. The scheme was never adopted, and in 1800 private enterprise was ruled out by Parliament as an acceptable basis on which to found a state system of poor relief.

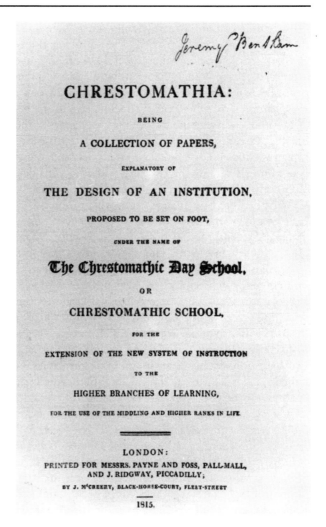

Title page for Bentham's work on educational reform. Although the year of publication is given as 1815, the book actually appeared in 1817 (courtesy of Special Collections, Thomas Cooper Library, University of South Carolina).

Bentham continued his assault on conventional ideas on punishment, presenting in *Letter to Lord Pelham, Giving a Comparative View of the System of Penal Colonization in New South Wales, and the Home Penitentiary System, Prescribed by Two Acts of Parliament of the Years 1794 and 1799* (1802) and *A Plea for the Constitution: Shewing the Enormities Committed to the Oppression of British Subjects, in and by the Design of the Penal Colony of New South Wales; Including an Inquiry into the Right of the Crown to Legislate without Parliament in Trinidad, and Other British Colonies* (1803) powerful arguments against the transportation of convicts to Australia. The works were republished together as *Panopticon versus New South Wales; or, The Panopticon Penitentiary System and the Penal Colonization System Compared. Containing 1. Two Letters to Lord Pelham. 2. Plea for the Constitution, anno 1803, printed now first published* (1812).

Bentham's move away from pure theory in these years provided him with a new understanding of the operation of bureaucracy and the importance of administrative detail when putting ideas into practice. Nevertheless, these projects absorbed an enormous amount of time and distracted him from his vocation of codifying the law. In the early years of the nineteenth century, however, Bentham returned to jurisprudential theory, with an emphasis on judicial procedure. Beginning in 1803 he drafted a considerable body of work analyzing the effective, efficient, and justified use of evidence, from which John Stuart Mill compiled the five volumes of *The Rationale of Judicial Evidence, Specially Applied to English Practice* (1827). Bentham's work laid the foundations for a whole new area of the law; as Mill wrote in "Remarks on Bentham's Philosophy" (1833), "the theory of Procedure" had been in an "utterly barbarous state," but "there is scarcely a question of practical importance in this most important department, which he has not settled. He has left next to nothing for his successors." Bentham applied his analysis of basic principles of judicial evidence to a topical question when he entered the debate over the reform of the Scottish legal system. His *Scotch Reform; Considered, with Reference to the Plan, Proposed in the Late Parliament, for the Regulation of the Courts, and the Administration of Justice in Scotland . . . . In a Series of Letters, Addressed to the Right Hon. Lord Grenville* (1808) argued that the existing "technical" system of legal procedure in Scotland and England ought to be replaced by a "natural" one. In Bentham's view, only lawyers benefited from the technical process; he positioned himself as an enemy of the entire lawyer class, whose interests were directly opposed to those of nonlawyers who suffered nothing but "delay, vexation and expense" at lawyers' hands.

Bentham's attack on the processes of English law increased in ferocity in *The Elements of the Art of Packing, as Applied to Special Juries, Particularly in Cases of Libel Law,* written in 1810, in which he uses language so strident that his friend Samuel Romilly warned him against publication for fear that Bentham would be prosecuted under the very libel law he condemned; on this occasion Bentham listened to the advice and did not publish the work for eleven years. Many of the writings on evidence produced at this time were later published by Dumont in French versions, the most important being *Traité des preuves judiciaires, ouvrage extrait des manuscrits de Jérémie Bentham* (1823; translated as *A Treatise on Judicial Evidence, Extracted from the Manuscripts of Jeremy Bentham, Esq., by M. Dumont,* 1825) and *De l'Organisation judiciaire, et de la Codification: Extraits de divers ouvrages de Jérémie Bentham*

(1828). Once again nearly twenty years passed before important parts of Bentham's applied philosophy were available to an English audience.

The compensation awarded in 1813 as reimbursement for the sums Bentham had invested in the panopticon project allowed him to rent a magnificent house in the West Country, Ford Abbey, where he spent summers and autumns. It is clear from the names of those who stayed with him that, despite the many stories of his reclusive nature, he was in regular contact with men deeply involved in the politics of the day. He could count not only notable members of Parliament, including Romilly, Joseph Hume, and Francis Horner, among his visitors but also prominent intellectuals such as the economists David Ricardo and Jean-Baptiste Say and famous radicals such as Francis Place.

In 1814 Bentham began work on *Chrestomathia, Being a Collection of Papers, Explanatory of the Design of an Institution, Proposed to be Set on Foot, Under the Name of the Chrestomathic Day School, or Chrestomathic School, for the Extension of the New System of Instruction to the Higher Branches of Learning, for the Use of the Middling and Higher Ranks of Life* (1817), an attempt to show how the failings of the contemporary education system, as he saw them, could be dealt with. The typically Benthamic name for the institution means "useful education," and the proposed syllabus reflects Bentham's desire to see the introduction of new subjects, including physical science, mathematics, modern languages, law, economics, and music. The school was to be designed around the monitorial system of education devised by the Quaker educationalist Joseph Lancaster. Under this method teachers would only be required to educate the older pupils, who would teach the younger ones. *Chrestomathia* was one of the first attempts to apply the monitorial method to children from the "middling and higher ranks of life."

Also during this period, Bentham worked on his writings on logic and language, which were connected in many ways to his interest in education. These philosophical works are some of his most original. As was the case with other Enlightenment thinkers, an assessment of the manner in which the mind perceived and interacted with the external world was central to his philosophy, and he was led to pay great attention to language and logic. While the greater part of Bentham's material on this subject was produced between 1813 and 1815, much has remained in manuscript form. Some were included in Bowring's edition of Bentham's collected works; some were included by his nephew, George Bentham, in George's *Outline of a New System of Logic* (1827); and a further collection of these writings was edited by

C. K. Ogden as *Bentham's Theory of Fictions* (1932). Yet, this area of Bentham's research still requires further attention.

Bentham believed, as had Locke and Hume before him, that all knowledge was constructed on foundations presented by sense perceptions; but for Bentham any impression received from the outside world was inescapably compounded with feelings of pain and pleasure. This natural process was required to be respected in any rational and sustainable philosophy. The result of this distinctive epistemological perspective was an emphasis on the "clearness of discourse"—that is, on the exposition of meaning, the correct definition of terms, and the distinction between real and fictitious entities.

Bentham's important ontological writings between 1813 and 1821 remained unpublished until Bowring included parts of them in *The Works of Jeremy Bentham;* they were first published in their entirety in French more than 150 years later as *De l'ontologie et autres textes sur les ficions* (On Ontology and Other Texts on Fictions, 1997). Bentham distinguishes between real and fictitious entities by defining real entities as those that can be perceived. He does not reject fictitious entities, since most general terms, and especially the main terms of law and government, belong to this category; but they are only meaningful insofar as they are related in a precise way to real entities. This relationship can only be achieved by "paraphrasis," which Bentham had described some forty years earlier in *A Fragment on Government* as a method whereby a sentence including the word to be defined is "translated into another sentence; the words of which latter are expressive of such ideas as are simple, or are more immediately resolvable into simple ones than those of the former." But resolving complex ideas into simple ones does not imply that the terms being defined refer to real things. Bentham had to go a step further in his ontological writings, saying in his "Essay on Logic" (1843) that "by the word paraphrasis may be designated that sort of exposition which may be afforded by transmuting into a proposition, having for its subject some real entity, a proposition which has not for its subject any other than a fictitious entity." Paraphrasis is the method Bentham developed for finding meaning for terms such as *power, right, duty,* and *obligation.* As Bentham showed in his criticism of the Declaration of the Rights of Man, unless abstract notions, such as political rights, are both defined and supported by enforced law, the fictitious entities they represent lack meaning. This careful attention to the correlation between the accurate definition of words and the process of political reform is an element in many of his most influential works.

By 1815 Bentham had turned to a further development of the motives first analyzed in *An Introduction to the Principles of Morals and Legislation;* he printed a new work, later completed and published as *A Table of the Springs of Action, Shewing the Several Species of Pleasures and Pains, of which Man's Nature is Susceptible* (1817). Bentham distinguishes among desires, aversions, needs, hopes, and fears. *A Table of the Springs of Action* is therefore a substantial contribution to Bentham's analysis of the individual will. Closely connected with this continuing investigation of motivation is Bentham's analysis of what he calls "private ethics," on which he worked periodically from 1814 onward and which appeared posthumously as *Deontology: or, the Science of Morality* (1834). Private ethics is an educational method for showing individuals how to promote the happiness of others while maximizing their own happiness in the process. Such instruction always has to start from the individual rather than the social perspective, for the direct object of ethics cannot be the maximization of general happiness: private ethics and public legislation are distinct arts. But this method of private instruction could provide substantial assistance to the legislator whose objective was the maximization of the happiness of the community as a whole. Practical deontology is divided into two branches: "self-regarding prudence," which refers to the procurement of individual happiness independent of any other member of the community; and "extra-regarding prudence," referring to the sphere of action in which individual happiness is affected by one's behavior in relation to others in the community. Maximizing individual long-term happiness would increase aggregate happiness; the teaching of "extra-regarding prudence" would enable individuals to recognize how their own long-term happiness would be best increased by showing an "intermediate regard" for the happiness of the wider community.

The years around 1809–1810 have been seen as a transition point for Bentham, a time when a more dramatic form of political radicalism appears in his thinking. Whereas Bentham had previously taken the view that enlightened monarchs would eagerly adopt proposals that would benefit their subjects once they were made aware of them, he now became convinced of the need for substantial political reform. By the 1820s he supported democracy as the only form of government capable of enacting good utilitarian legislation. Bentham's move toward a more radical position coincides with his meeting in 1808 with James Mill, an historian and philosopher with a radical reformist agenda. Mill's precise influence is difficult to assess, however, since Bentham was acquainted with many other leading social and political reformers of the period, including the opponent of slavery William Wilberforce, the fierce advocate of universal suffrage Major John Cartwright, and the founder of modern British socialism, Robert Owen. The extent of Bentham's new radicalism is displayed in *Plan of Parliamentary Reform, in the Form of Catechism, with Reasons for Each Article, with an Introduction, Shewing the Necessity of Radical, and the Inadequacy of Moderate, Reform* (1817), which stresses that moderate reform is inadequate and that universal male suffrage, annual parliaments, equal electoral districts, payment of members of Parliament, and the secret ballot are vital for the security of the greatest happiness. This tract was followed by *Bentham's Radical Reform Bill* (1819), which sought to provide the foundations for the institution of representative democracy in Britain. It calls for massive constitutional renovation, including the abolition of the House of Lords, of all titles, and, most dramatically, of the monarchy. Without these measures Bentham saw no way for the government to be open and accountable to those it was in existence to serve. Needless to say, his proposals attracted little interest among those in power, for it was precisely their interests that Bentham's proposals threatened–although they were eagerly welcomed by radicals of many persuasions. Of crucial importance in the development of his political radicalism was the identification of what he terms in *Constitutional Code: For the Use of All Nations and All Governments Professing Liberal Opinions, Vol. 1* (1830) the "sinister interests" of the governing classes. This concept explains why those controlling society are not interested in promoting the greatest happiness of the greatest number but in protecting and increasing their own happiness. There can be little doubt that Bentham's dealings with the Pitt administration over the panopticon scheme deeply affected his view of the motivation of power holders, and within this category he included not just officials in office but also the aristocratic interest that exerted such an overwhelming influence. The undermining of his plans for the establishment of a national penitentiary under his governorship left a permanent impression of the corrupt forces at the head of the political establishment in England.

Although he had become disenchanted with the aristocracy and the power holders in the government, he endeavored to show that utilitarian political reform would not threaten their own happiness. Between November 1819 and April 1820 he drafted a manuscript, "Radicalism not Dangerous," which was first published in Bowring's *The Works of Jeremy Bentham.* He wrote in support of those taking an active role in protests against the establishment in *The King against Edmonds and Others: Set Down for the Trial, at Warwick, on the 29th of March, 1820. Brief Remarks Tending to Show the Untenability of This Indictment* (1820), and *The King against Sir Charles Wolseley, Baronet, and Joseph Harrison, Schoolmaster: Set Down for Trial at Chester on the 4th of April, 1820. Brief Remarks Tending to Show the Untenability of This Indictment* (1820). Bentham became progressively more outspoken and by 1820 he was ignoring the advice of friends not to publish and seeking out radical publishers who were not intimidated by the threat of imprisonment for sedition.

Bentham was clearly a leading figure in the radical movement by the early 1820s. Although he often encouraged the vision of his life as reclusive–for example, describing his house at Queen's Square Place as a "hermitage"–he actually received a steady stream of visitors. While his guests were generally admitted because they brought some information or influence by which he sought to further his causes, the common image of Bentham as cloistered, naive, and emotionally detached is far from accurate. He was recognized throughout the world. The *Westminster Review,* which he helped establish in 1823 to combat the dominant Whig and Tory periodicals, added to his fame at home and was beginning to disseminate his brand of utilitarianism. Recognition was flowing in from abroad, as well, with the American codifier Edward Livingstone praising his "science of legislation" and José del Valle of Guatemala creating for him the title "Legislador del mundo" (Legislator of the World).

The works produced by Bentham in the early decades of the nineteenth century reflect an increasingly clear vision of how the "ruling few" managed their domination over the "subject many" by controlling civil and political institutions. From 1815 onward many of Bentham's writings attempt to expose the influence of these institutions. His attacks on the Anglican Church, for instance–material that Bowring, a committed Unitarian, suppressed from his edition of Bentham's collected works–show the power exerted by this traditional authority over English society. While Bentham had a philosophical opposition to the ascetic principles promoted by most strands of Christianity, since these went against his fundamental principle that anything productive of pleasure or happiness could not be immoral, he had a greater antipathy for Anglicanism for the political role it played. In *"Swear Not at All": Containing an Exposure of the Needlessness and Mischievousness, as well as Anti-Christianity, of the Ceremony of an Oath* (1817), *Church of Englandism and its Catechism Examined* (1818), the pseudonymously published *An Analysis of the Influence of Natural Religion on the Temporal Happiness of Mankind* (1822), and *Not Paul, but Jesus* (1823), Bentham attacks the established church as an ally of the political elite that aimed to instill intellectual submission among the English population.

The government fared no better in the face of Bentham's attacks on opposition to reform. In two articles for *The Pamphleteer*, "Defence of Economy Against the Late Mr. Burke" and "Defence of Economy against the Right Hon. George Rose," both written in 1810 but not published until 1817, he unleashed a furious attack on "waste and corruption," as he termed it in the former essay. Bentham was in no doubt that both Whig and Tory administrations were corruptly pursuing the protection of their own interests.

Bentham reserved his most ferocious attacks for lawyers, whom he saw as encouraging delay, vexation, and expense in the legal process. Some of his gravest accusations against the lawyer class are included in *Indications Respecting Lord Eldon, Including History of the Pending Judges'-Salary-Raising Measure* (1825), an attack on the lord chancellor that led Bentham's friends to fear that he was in real danger of prosecution. Bentham continued his critique of complacency that reigned in the upper echelons of English law in "Observations on Mr. Secretary Peel's House of Commons Speech, 21st March, 1825," which appeared in *The Pamphleteer* in 1825.

As Bentham developed his radical political philosophy the need for codification of the law became a central practical and theoretical concern once more, and during the last twenty years of his life he produced many publications on the subject. Indeed, the energy he displayed in his later years stands as a testament to his health and vitality and contrasts sharply with his frail constitution in his youth. In old age Bentham suffered few major illnesses and engaged in a surprising amount of physical activity. John Neal, a young American visiting him in 1826, reported that at the age of seventy-eight he "trotted" the entire distance from Fleet Street to Queen's Square Place, south of St. James's Park. His young secretaries were kept busy as he worked vigorously toward the fulfillment of his plans for codification.

Bentham had begun to lay out his practical codification proposals in *Papers Relative to Codification and Public Instruction; Including Correspondence with the Russian Emperor, and Divers Constituted Authorities in the American United States* (1817). In this work and his other writings on codification the emphasis is on completeness of the code and the "rationalized" definitions with which each provision was to be accompanied. The civil code, with its definition of rights and duties, is of prime importance, and work on it is to be followed by the drafting of penal, procedural, and constitutional

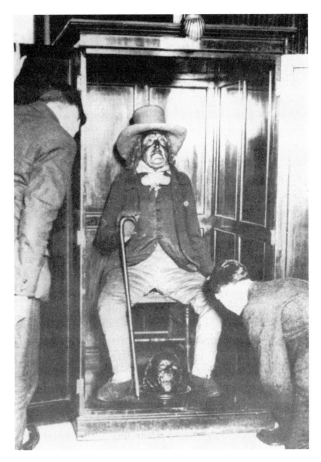

Bentham's "Auto-icon": his skeleton padded and dressed in his own clothes, with a wax effigy of his head, placed in a glass case in the lobby of University College London in accordance with the provisions of his will. His skull has since been removed from between his feet.

codes. Bentham offered his codification services to any regime he thought might benefit, sending out *Three Tracts Relative to Spanish and Portugueze Affairs; With a Continual Eye to English ones* (1821), *Letters to Count Toreno on the Proposed Penal Code* (1822), and *Codification Proposal, Addressed by Jeremy Bentham to All Nations Professing Liberal Opinions* (1822). Nevertheless, he was outspokenly critical of the governments he contacted if he believed they were in error. In *On the Liberty of the Press and Public Discussion* (1821), for example, he provided a sharp response to the 1820 restrictions on the freedom of speech levied by the Spanish legislature, the Cortes, and he wrote *Observations on the Restrictive and Prohibitory Commercial System; Especially with a Reference to the Decree of the Spanish Cortes of July 1820* (1821) in support of free trade, when the Cortes imposed higher customs charges.

At the end of 1821 the Portuguese Cortes accepted Bentham's codification offer, and on receiving the news in April 1822 he set to work on a constitutional code for the country. The Portuguese regime fell shortly after the acceptance was made; but Bentham continued to develop his constitutional code, with his attention directed first to the political regime in Tripoli and then to Greece. The code he had begun for Portugal was published in 1830 as *Constitutional Code: For the Use of All Nations and All Governments Professing Liberal Opinions, Vol. I.* Throughout the last decade of his life Bentham kept a constant eye on international developments, often drawing up pieces relevant to local circumstances, such as *Three Tracts Relative to Spanish and Portugueze Affairs* in response to the rapidly changing situation in Spain and *Anti-Senatica,* written between 1822 and 1824 but not published until 1926, which attempted to draw the attention of President Andrew Jackson to the mischievousness of having a second legislative chamber. Bentham continued to develop his ideas on codification and economy in government in *Justice and Codification Petitions* (1829) and *Official Aptitude Maximized, Expense Minimized; As Shewn in the Several Papers in This Volume* (1830). A full set of codes was never completed, however, and only the one volume of the three he projected on the constitutional code was published before his death. During the 1820s he drafted much on the penal and procedure codes, and while he made less progress on the civil code, he produced a good deal between 1828 and 1830. Bentham saw codification of the law as the means of implementing his utilitarian philosophy.

In his later years Bentham developed some idiosyncrasies, the most obvious being his ascription of bizarre terms and expressions to everyday activities—for example, *circumgyration* for walking and *antepostjentacular* for the time just after breakfast. Bentham's egocentrism increased with age, as he surrounded himself with young, uncritical admirers, the most favored of whom was Bowring. He also quarrelled with former colleagues, including both Mill and Dumont, two of his staunchest and most reliable supporters.

Yet, despite these frailties of age, Bentham never faltered in the pursuit of improvement. Encouraged by a growing interest in law reform as seen in the efforts of such prominent individuals as Sir Robert Peel and Henry Brougham, Bentham produced a series of works pressing for improvement across many fronts. "Observations on the actual State of the English Law of Real Property," published in the *Westminster Review* in October 1826, attempted to influence the Real Property Commission of 1828; *Law Reform Association Proposal* (1830) was aimed at drawing moderate figures into the reform process; and *Equity Dispatch Court Proposal* (1830) showed how benefits could be provided by reform of judicial organization and

procedure. Toward the end of his life, however, frustration at the constant lack of progress led him to attack fellow reformers. Brougham, for example, said in the *Edinburgh Review* in 1830 that Bentham's exposure of the defects in English law was "the greatest service ever rendered to the country . . . by any of her political philosophers"; yet, on 25 May of the same year Bentham published an article in the *New York Globe,* "Jeremy Bentham to Henry Brougham, old and familiar friend, the administration of justice in England needs improvement," which included a sharp critique of Brougham. The attack was continued in *Lord Brougham Displayed: Including I. Boa Constrictor, alias Helluo Curiarum; II. Observations on the Bankruptcy Court Bill, Now Ripened into an Act. III. Extracts from Proposed Constitutional Code* (1832), in which he argues that Brougham's suggestions for reform are far too moderate and advocates more drastic and systematic measures.

Bentham was clearly demanding of his supporters when their recommendations failed to reach the standard set by his own rigorous philosophy. He was, however, as hard on himself, and his tireless and rather impatient approach to improvement was applied to his own philosophy. He constantly returned to reexamine issues and themes to which he had already devoted considerable effort. For example, by 1778 he had adopted the position that imprisonment was far superior to the mass of capital penalties then enacted; but his most powerful critique of the death penalty, *Jeremy Bentham to his Fellow Citizens of France, on Death Punishment,* appeared in 1831.

To the end of his career Bentham was prepared to confront difficulties presented by even his most fundamental conceptions. Concerned by a growing awareness that a simple aggregate of social happiness implied that the majority of a society could justifiably oppress the minority, so long as such oppression resulted in an ultimate increase in the quantity of pleasure in the society as a whole, Bentham sought to promote a more distributive notion of happiness by extension of the idea of equality. In *Parliamentary Candidate's Proposed Declaration of Principles: or Say, A Test Proposed for Parliamentary Candidates* (1831) he defines the greatest happiness principle as a theory that optimally seeks an "equal quantity of happiness" for each member of society. Bentham was always prepared to examine his arguments anew and was ready, if utility required, to change.

When Bentham died on 6 June 1832 his plans for continued change were put into effect. According to his will his body was to be dissected for the furtherance of anatomical knowledge, and his skeleton and head were to be preserved, dressed in his own clothes, and displayed. It had been his desire to leave his body to science since the age of twenty-one–at that time medical dissection was carried out only as a further humiliation and desecration to the bodies of hanged murderers. Bentham wanted to break the many taboos surrounding dissection. Thomas Southwood Smith duly carried out his wishes on the afternoon of 9 June, when he delivered an oration over Bentham's body at the Webb Street School of Anatomy on dissection and the value the dead could provide for the living. In *Auto-Icon; or, Farther Uses of the Dead to the Living* (1842?), a piece he had worked on until days before his death, Bentham described how his corpse might be of use to others, perhaps as an inspiration to future generations and certainly in the attempt to undermine any mystical and superstitious beliefs concerning the life to come. While vanity must have played some role in the creation of the "Auto-Icon" (some believe Bentham was serious in suggesting that his remains were to be ceremoniously present when his ideas were discussed), the image of the "Auto-Icon," which is on display to this day in a glass box in the lobby of University College London, which he helped to found, provides tangible evidence of the strength of Bentham's conviction that empirical science is the way to improvement.

The most important legacy of Jeremy Bentham's life is the considerable body of work that stands as the repository of his utilitarian philosophy. The central emphasis on pain and pleasure as a practical standard of moral value has remained alive despite the best efforts of religious revivalism, late-nineteenth-century philosophical idealism, twentieth-century psychology with its concentration on the unconscious and the irrational as forces of human motivation, and, more recently, philosophies that further rework contract theory and principles of natural right. While influential attempts have been made to restate the value of utilitarianism by James Mill's son John Stuart Mill, Henry Sidgwick, and R. M. Hare, Bentham's thought remains distinctive for its internal consistency and thorough.

Letters:

The Correspondence of Jeremy Bentham, edited by Timothy L. S. Sprigge, Ian R. Christie, Alexander Taylor Milne, J. R. Dinwiddy, Stephen Conway, and Catherine Fuller, in *The Collected Works of Jeremy Bentham,* 11 volumes to date, edited by Dinwiddy, J. H. Burns, F. Rosen, and P. Schofield (volumes 1–5, London: Athlone Press, 1968–1981; volumes 6–11, Oxford: Clarendon Press, 1984–1994).

Bibliographies:

A. Siegwart, *Bentham's Werke und ihre Publikation* (Bern, 1910);

C. W. Everett, "Bibliography," in *The Growth of Philosophic Radicalism,* by Elie Halévy, translated by Mary Morris (London: Faber & Gwyer, 1928; New York: Kelly & Millman, 1928), pp. 522–546;

Sadao Ikeda, Michihiro Otonashi, and Tamihiro Shigemori, *A Biographical Catalogue of the Works of Jeremy Bentham* (Tokyo: Chuo University, 1989).

Biography:
Charles M. Atkinson, *Jeremy Bentham: His Life and Work* (London: Methuen, 1905).

References:
David Baumgardt, *Bentham and the Ethics of Today: With Bentham Manuscripts Hitherto Unpublished* (Princeton, N.J.: Princeton University Press, 1952);

Hugo Bedau, "Bentham's Utilitarian Critique of the Death Penalty," *Journal of Criminal Law and Criminology,* 74 (1983): 1033–1065;

Lea Campos Boralevi, *Bentham and the Oppressed* (Berlin & New York: De Gruyter, 1980);

James Burns, "Bentham and Blackstone: A Lifetime's Dialectic," *Utilitas,* 1 (May 1989): 22–40;

Burns, "Jeremy Bentham: From Radical Enlightenment to Philosophic Radicalism," *Bentham Newsletter,* 8 (June 1984): 4–14;

Stephen Conway, "Bentham and the Nineteenth-Century Revolution in Government," in *Victorian Liberalism: Nineteenth-Century Political Thought and Practice,* edited by Richard Bellamy (London: Routledge, 1990), pp. 71–90;

John Dinwiddy, *Bentham* (Oxford: Oxford University Press, 1989);

Anthony Draper, "'To Exclude Some Greater Evil': Distributions of Pain in Bentham's Theory of Punishment," in *Contemporary Political Studies* (Nottingham: Political Studies Association of the United Kimgdom, 1998), pp. 269–278;

Elie Halévy, *The Growth of Philosophic Radicalism,* translated by Mary Morris (London: Faber & Gwyer, 1928; New York, 1928);

Ross Harrison, *Bentham* (London: Routledge & Kegan Paul, 1983);

H. L. A. Hart, *Essays on Bentham: Studies in Jurisprudence and Political Theory* (Oxford: Clarendon Press, 1982);

L. J. Hume, *Bentham and Bureaucracy* (Cambridge: Cambridge University Press, 1981);

P. J. Kelly, *Utilitarianism and Distributive Justice: Jeremy Bentham and the Civil Law* (Oxford: Clarendon Press, 1990);

David Lieberman, *The Province of Legislation Determined: Legal Theory in Eighteenth-Century Britain* (Cambridge: Cambridge University Press, 1989), pp. 217–290;

Douglas Long, *Bentham on Liberty: Jeremy Bentham's Idea of Liberty in Relation to His Utilitarianism* (Toronto & Buffalo: University of Toronto Press, 1977);

David Lyons, *In the Interest of the Governed: A Study in Bentham's Philosophy of Utility and the Law* (Oxford: Clarendon Press, 1973);

Bhikhu Parekh, ed., *Jeremy Bentham: Ten Critical Essays* (London: Cass, 1974);

Parekh, ed. *Jeremy Bentham: Critical Assessments,* 4 volumes (London: Routledge, 1993);

Gerald Postema, *Bentham and the Common Law Tradition* (Oxford: Clarendon Press, 1986);

Postema, ed., *Jeremy Bentham: Moral, Political, and Legal Philosophy,* 2 volumes (Aldershot & Burlington, Vt.: Ashgate, 2001);

Michael Quinn, "Jeremy Bentham on the Relief of Indigence: An Exercise in Applied Philosophy," *Utilitas,* 6 (May 1994): 81–96;

Frederick Rosen, "Individual Sacrifice and the Greatest Happiness: Bentham on Utility and Rights," *Utilitas,* 10 (July 1998): 129–143;

Rosen, *Jeremy Bentham and Representative Democracy: A Study of the Constitutional Code* (Oxford: Clarendon Press, 1983);

Rosen, "Utilitarianism and the Punishment of the Innocent: The Origins of a False Doctrine," *Utilitas,* 9 (March 1997): 23–37;

Philip Schofield, "Jeremy Bentham: Legislator of the World," *Current Legal Problems 1998, Volume 51: Legal Theory at the End of the Millennium* (Oxford: Oxford University Press, 1998), pp. 115–147;

Schofield, "Jeremy Bentham and Nineteenth-Century English Jurisprudence," *Journal of Legal History,* 12 (May 1991): 57–88;

Schofield, "Professing Liberal Opinions: The Common Law, Adjudication and Security in Recent Bentham Scholarship," *Journal of Legal History,* 16 (December 1995): 350–367;

Janet Semple, *Bentham's Prison: A Study of the Panopticon Penitentiary* (Oxford: Clarendon Press, 1993);

Semple, "Foucault and Bentham: A Defence of Panopticism," *Utilitas,* 4 (May 1992): 105–120;

Robert Shackleton, "The Greatest Happiness of the Greatest Number: The History of Bentham's Phrase," *Studies on Voltaire and the Eighteenth Century,* 90 (1972): 1461–1482;

William Twining, *Theories of Evidence: Bentham and Wigmore* (Oxford: Clarendon Press, 1985; Stanford, Cal.: Stanford University Press, 1985);

Colin Tyler, "The Metaethics of Pleasure: Jeremy Bentham and His British Idealist Critics," *Contemporary Political Studies* (Nottingham: Political Studies Association, 1998), pp. 261–268.

Papers:

The main body of Jeremy Bentham's papers is the Bentham Papers at University College London and consists of approximately fifty thousand folios of manuscript. Further large collections of Bentham manuscripts can be found in the Additional Manuscripts of the British Library, where many relate to his correspondence, and the Etienne Dumont papers held by the Bibliothèque Publique et Universitaire at Geneva. The Keynes Collection at King's College, Cambridge University, also houses some of Bentham's correspondence.

Richard Bentley
(27 January 1662 – 14 July 1742)

Susan Spencer
University of Central Oklahoma

BOOKS: *The Folly of Atheism, and (what is now called) Deism, Even with Respect to the Present Life: A Sermon Preached in the Church of St. Martin in the Fields, March the VII, 1691/2: Being the First of the Lecture Founded by the Honourable Robert Boyle, Esquire* (London: Printed for Thomas Parkhurst & Henry Mortlock, 1692);

Matter and Motion cannot Think; or, A Confutation of Atheism from the Faculties of the Soul: A Sermon Preached at St. Mary-le-Bow, April 4, 1692. Being the Second of the Lecture Founded by the Honourable Robert Boyle, Esquire (London: Printed for Thomas Parkhurst & Henry Mortlock, 1692);

A Confutation of Atheism from the Structure and Origin of Humane Bodies. Part I: A Sermon Preached at Saint Martin's in the Fields, May 2, 1692: Being the Third of the Lecture Founded by the Honourable Robert Boyle, Esquire (London: Printed for Thomas Parkhurst & Henry Mortlock, 1692);

A Confutation of Atheism from the Structure and Origin of Humane Bodies. Part II: A Sermon Preached at St. Mary-le-Bow, June 6, 1692. Being the Fourth of the Lecture Founded by the Honourable Robert Boyle, Esquire (London: Printed for Thomas Parkhurst & Henry Mortlock, 1692);

A Confutation of Atheism from the Structure and Origin of Humane Bodies. The Third and Last Part: A Sermon Preached at Saint Martin's in the Fields, September the 5th, 1692: Being the Fifth of the Lecture Founded by the Honourable Robert Boyle, Esquire (London: Printed for Henry Mortlock, 1692);

A Confutation of Atheism from the Origin and Frame of the World. Part I: A Sermon Preached at St. Mary-le-Bow, October the 3d. 1692. Being the Sixth of the Lecture Founded by the Honourable Robert Boyle, Esquire (London: Printed for Henry Mortlock, 1692);

A Confutation of Atheism from the Origin and Frame of the World. Part II: A Sermon Preached at St. Martin's in the Fields, November the 7th 1692. Being the Seventh of the Lecture Founded by the Honourable Robert Boyle, Esquire (London: Printed for Henry Mortlock, 1692);

Richard Bentley; portrait by John Thornhill, 1710 (Master's Lodge, Trinity College, University of Cambridge)

A Confutation of Atheism from the Origin and Frame of the World. The Third and Last Part. A Sermon Preached at St. Mary-le-Bow, December the 5th. 1692. Being the Eighth of the Lecture Founded by the Honourable Robert Boyle, Esquire (London: Printed for Henry Mortlock, 1693);

Of Revelation and the Messias. A Sermon preached at the Publick Commencement at Cambridge. July 5th 1696 (London: Printed by J.H. for Henry Mortlock, 1696);

A Dissertation upon the Epistles of Phalaris: With an Answer to the Objections of the Honourable Charles Boyle, Esquire (London: Printed by J.H. for Henry Mortlock & John Hartley, 1699);

The Present State of Trinity College in Cambridg, in a Letter from Dr. Bentley, Master of the Said College, to the Right Reverend John Lord Bishop of Ely, as a gentleman of the Temple (London: Printed for Anne Baldwin, 1710; revised, 1710);

Emendationes in Menandri et Philemonis Reliquias, ex nupera Editione Joannis Clerici ubi multa Grotii & aliorum plurima vero Clerici errata castigantur, as Phileleutherus Lipsiensis (Utrecht: Sold by Willem van de Water, 1710; Cambridge: Printed for Cornelius Crownfield, 1713);

Remarks Upon a Late Discourse of Free-Thinking: In a Letter to F.H.D.D., as Phileleutherus Lipsiensis (London: Printed for John Morphew, 1713; enlarged seventh edition, London: Printed for William Thurlbourn, 1737);

A Sermon upon Popery: Preach'd before the University of Cambridge, November v^th. MDCCXV (Cambridge: University-Press, 1715);

A Sermon preach'd before His Majesty, King George, at his Royal Chapel of St. James's, on Sunday, February 3. 1716/17 (London: W. Innys, 1717);

Η Καινη Διαθηκη Græce. Novum Testamentum versionis vulgatæ, per S^tum Hieronym ad vetusta exemplaria Græca castigatæ & exactæ. Utrumque ex antiquissimis Codd. MSS. cum Græcis tum Latinis, edidit Richardus Bentlius (Cambridge, 1720); enlarged as *Dr. Bentley's Proposals for Printing a New Edition of the Greek Testament, and St. Hierom's Latin Version. With a full Answer to all the Remarks of a late Pamphleteer, by a Member of Trinity College in Cambridge,* as J.E. (London: Printed for J. Knapton, 1721);

Bentleii Critica Sacra: Notes on the Greek and Latin Text of the New Testament, Extracted from the Bentley MSS. in Trinity College Library: With the Abbé Rulotta's Collation of the Vatican Codex B, a Specimen of Bentley's Intended Edition, and an Account of His Collations, edited by Arthur Ayres Ellis (Cambridge: Deighton, Bell / London: Bell & Daldy, 1862);

Bentley's Plautine Emendations from His Copy of Grovinius, edited by E. A. Sonnenschein, Anecdota Oxoniensia: Classical Series, volume 1, part 3 (Oxford: Clarendon Press, 1883).

Editions and Collections: *The Folly and Unreasonableness of Atheism demonstrated from the Advantage and Pleasure of a Religious Life, the Faculties of Human Souls, the Structure of Animate Bodies, & the Origin and Frame of the World: In Eight Sermons, Preached at the Lecture Founded by the Honourable Robert Boyle, in the First Year MDCXCII* (London: Printed by J.H. for Henry Mortlock, 1693; revised, 1699); enlarged as *Eight Sermons Preach'd at the Honourable Robert Boyle's Lecture, in the first year, MDCXVII. To Which is Now added a Sermon Preach'd at the Publick-*

Commencement at Cambridge July V. MDCXCVI (Cambridge: Printed by Cornelius Crownfield & sold by James Knapton & Robert Knaplock, London, 1724); enlarged again as *Eight Sermons preach'd at the Honourable Robert Boyle's Lecture, in the first year, MDCXVII. To Which are Added, Three Sermons: One at the Public Commencement, July 5, 1696. When he proceeded Doctor in Divinity; another before the University, Nov. 5, 1715, and one before his late majesty King George I. Feb 3, 1716/17* (Cambridge: Printed by M. Fenner for William Thurlbourn, 1735);

The Works of Richard Bentley, D.D., 3 volumes, edited by Alexander Dyce (London: Francis Macpherson, 1836–1838; New York: AMS Press, 1966);

Dr. Richard Bentley's Dissertations upon the Epistles of Phalaris, Themistocles, Socrates, Euripides and upon the Fables of Æsop, edited, with an introduction and notes, by Wilhelm Wagner (Berlin: S. Calvary, 1874; London: Bell, 1882);

Epistola ad Joannem Millium: Reprinted from the Edition of Alexander Dyce, introduction by G. P. Goold (Toronto: University of Toronto Press, 1962).

OTHER: *Epistola ad Joannem Millium S. T. P.,* in Ioannes Malalus's *Joannis Antiocheni, cognomento Malalæ, Historia chronica: E mso cod. Bibliothecæ Bodleianæ nunc prima edita. Cum interpret. & notis Edm. Chilmeadi & triplice indice rerum, autorem, & vocum barbararum. Præmittitur dissertatio de autore, per Humfredum Hodium,* edited by John Mill (Oxford: Sheldonian Theatre 1691);

Callimachus, *Callimachi hymni, epigrammata, et fragmenta ex recensione Theodori J.G. f. Grævii; cum ejusdem animadversionibus; accedunt N. Frischlini, H. Stephani, B. Vulcanii, P. Voetii, A. T. f. Daceriæ, R. Bentleji, commentarius, et annotationes viri illustrissimi, Ezechielis Spanhemii. Nec non præter fragmenta, quae ante Vulcanius & Daceria publicarant, nova, quæ Spanhemius & Bentleius collegerunt, & digesserunt; hujus cura & studio quædam quoque inedita epigrammata Callimachi nunc primum in lucem prodeunt,* edited by Joannes Georgius Grævius, 2 volumes (Utrecht: Sold by Halmam & Willem van de Water, 1697)—includes contribution by Bentley;

William Wotton, *Reflections upon Ancient and Modern Learning, Second Edition, with Large Additions, with a Dissertation upon the Epistles of Phalaris, Themistocles, Sophocles, Euripides, &c. and Aesop's Fables. By Dr. Bentley* (London: Printed by John Leake for Peter Buck, 1697);

Horace, *Q. Horatius Flaccus, ex Recensione & cum Notis atque Emendationibus,* edited, with notes, by Bentley (Cambridge, 1711); republished as *Dr. Bentley's Dedication of Horace, translated, To which is added, a*

Poem in Latin and English, inscribed to the Right Honourable the Lord Hallifax, written by the Reverend Dr. Bentley (London: Printed for John Morphew, 1712);

Terence, *Publii Terentii Afri Commoediæ, Phædri Fabulæ Æsopiæ, Publii Syri et aliorum Veterum Sententiæ, ex recensione et cum notis,* edited, with notes, by Bentley (Cambridge: Printed for & sold by Cornelius Crownfield / London: Sold by James Knapton, Robert Knapbek & Paul Vaillant, 1726);

John Milton, *Milton's Paradise Lost: A New Edition,* edited by Bentley (London: Printed for Jacob Tonson, John Poulson & for John Darby, Arthur Bettesworth & Francis Clay, in trust for Richard, James & Bethel Wellington, 1732;

Marcus Manilius, *M. Manilii Astronomicon ex recensione et cum notis Richardi Bentleii,* edited, with notes, by Bentley (London: Printed by Henry Woodfall for Paul & Isaac Vaillant, 1739).

Classical scholar and theologian Richard Bentley, master of Trinity College, was one of the most controversial personalities at Cambridge University in the early eighteenth century. Students of British literature are familiar with Bentley as the pompous and ill-mannered pedant ridiculed by Jonathan Swift, Alexander Pope, and their "Scriblerian Club." Classicists know him as perhaps the greatest philologist of all time and the founder of modern textual criticism. He is remembered among Greek Testament scholars as the first to devise a plan for reconstructing the entire text directly from the oldest documents available. Although most of his works are in Latin, he was one of the outstanding exponents of the plain English prose style in the transitional period between the seventeenth and eighteenth centuries. With regard to philosophy, his main role was to lay groundwork that made possible several different modes of philosophical speculation, resulting from this distinctive combination of attributes.

Bentley was born on 27 January 1662 in the village of Oulton, near Wakefield in the West Riding of Yorkshire, into a family of wealthy yeomen whose fortune had suffered somewhat as a result of Royalist loyalties during the English Civil War. He was taught Latin grammar by his mother, Sarah Willie Bentley, attended Wakefield Grammar School as a child, and was sent to St. John's College at Cambridge at the age of fourteen, shortly after the death of his father, Thomas Bentley.

Although little is known of the young Bentley's undergraduate career, he took high honors in all fields of study then offered at Cambridge: logic, ethics, natural philosophy, and mathematics. At the age of twenty he was appointed to the mastership of Spalding School

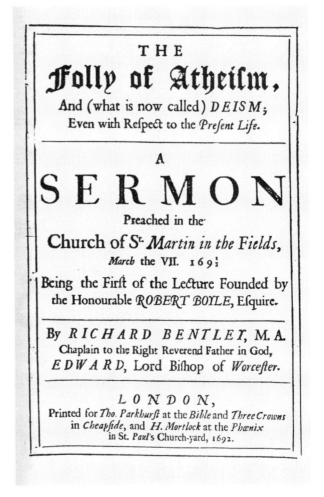

THE
Folly of Atheism,
And (what is now called) *DEISM;*
Even with Respect to the *Present Life.*

A
SERMON
Preached in the
Church of St *Martin in the Fields,*
March the VII. 169½

Being the First of the Lecture Founded by the Honourable *ROBERT BOYLE,* Esquire.

By *RICHARD BENTLEY,* M. A.
Chaplain to the Right Reverend Father in God,
EDWARD, Lord Bishop of *Worcester.*

LONDON,
Printed for *Tho. Parkhurst* at the *Bible* and *Three Crowns* in *Cheapside,* and *H. Mortlock* at the *Phœnix* in St. *Paul's* Church-yard, 1692.

Title page for Bentley's first book (Beinecke Library, Yale University)

in Lincolnshire. After a year he took a post as tutor to James Stillingfleet, the second son of Edward Stillingfleet, the dean of St. Paul's, London, which he retained for six years. Stillingfleet was foremost among the scholarly divines who opposed the idea of deism, or materialism, a subject that Bentley also later tackled.

Bentley's relationship with Stillingfleet's family, as well as his access through them to one of the finest private libraries in England and the company of the cream of London literary society, did much to shape his classical learning, his religious views, and the development of his straightforward writing style. He was not a particularly amiable individual, and throughout his long lifetime he retained a high opinion of his own brilliance; biographers such as Richard Claverhouse Jebb report that Stillingfleet once said of him that "had he but the gift of humility, he would be the most extraordinary man in Europe." As Jebb notes, Bentley, according to an accusation of misconduct and misappropriation of college funds submitted against him in July of 1710 by the Fellows of Trinity College to John Moore, the bishop of Ely, frequently referred to himself as "the Genius of the Age."

When Bentley took religious orders in 1690 at the age of twenty-eight, he had already followed his pupil to Oxford and taken an *ad eundem* (literally, "to same") degree of M.A. that recognized his work at Cambridge and allowed him to be placed on the books at Wadham College. At Oxford he enjoyed access to the Bodleian Library, where, Jebb reports in his *Bentley* (1882), he conceived the idea of editing "the fragments of all the Greek poets." This idea, especially given the methods and materials available at the time, was overly ambitious, but within two years he had managed to edit the fragments of the works of Callimachus.

At this point in his career Bentley was engaged by John Mill in the unpromising pursuit of writing a commentary for the only known copy of a chronicle written in Greek by John of Antioch, sometimes called "Malelus," or "rhetor," and thus also known as Ioannes Malalus, a tedious Christian compiler from sometime between the sixth and tenth centuries who attempted to give a chronological sketch of universal history down to his own time. Embedded within the narrative, however, were the names of lost works and excerpts from ancient texts, and there was some interest in publishing it. When Mill's edition appeared in 1691, with Bentley's ninety-eight page *Epistola ad Joannem Millium, S. T. P.* (Letter to John Mill, Professor of Theology) attached as an appendix, it caused an immediate sensation. Ranging across almost the entire field of ancient literature and suggesting corrections or explanations for more than sixty Greek and Latin authors, Bentley's incisive observations showed an enormous range of learning and an unprecedented sensitivity for meter. In this work he announced his discovery of the metrical continuity, or *synapheia,* of the anapestic system, a key that enabled scholars easily to detect false metrical quantities in Greek texts. Such errors, Bentley pointed out, indicated either forgery (since no true classical Greek author would have ignored the rule) or a corruption of the original through scribal carelessness. In the manner that became his trademark, and the source of most of the praise and criticism that was heaped on him throughout his lifetime, he suggested hundreds of possible emendations. The most celebrated of these emendations was in a passage where the Malalus manuscript referred to the founders of tragedy as "Themis, Minos, and Auleus"; Bentley corrected these names to the familiar Thespis, Ion of Chios, and Aeschylus.

Perhaps most importantly, Bentley's *Epistola ad Joannem Millium* showed the relevance of historical and linguistic context to establish a work's authenticity and antiquity—concerns that changed classical scholarship forever. Before Bentley, intellectuals and scholars both in England and on the Continent generally viewed Greek and Latin classics as a single block of "ancient wisdom" to be mined almost indiscriminately for bits and pieces that might be useful for the purpose of imitation or to give the weight of authority to a scientific treatise. One author was as good as another, and there was little distinction made even between Greeks and Romans; in fact, for most seventeenth- and early-eighteenth-century writers almost all knowledge of Greek writers came secondhand through Latin sources. Despite the classical education of the time, only a few scholars, most of them French, had a solid knowledge of the Greek language. Yet, it was largely Bentley's philological achievements that, within his lifetime, began the revolution in Greek studies so evident in the late eighteenth and early nineteenth centuries. Since education at the time was so focused on classical learning, the methods he introduced in the *Epistola ad Joannem Millium* came to represent in many minds the rigorous empirical approach that had entered English sciences, including historiography, philosophy, astronomy, and geology.

As a result of the *Epistola ad Joannem Millium,* when Robert Boyle died in December of 1691, leaving a bequest for an annual series of eight lectures, ostensibly "for proving the Christian Religion against notorious Infidels, viz. Atheists, Deists, Pagans, Jews, and Mohometans," but actually meant to reconcile the sciences with Christianity, Bentley was considered an obvious choice to deliver the first set: "The Folly of Atheism, and (what is now called) Deism" (1692), "Matter and Motion cannot Think" (1692), "A Confutation of Atheism from the Structure and Origin of Humane Bodies" (three parts, 1692), and "A Confutation of Atheism from the Origin and Frame of the World" (three parts, 1692–1693). These lectures were so popular that they were quickly published separately; the lectures were bound together and issued with a collective title page in 1693 under the general title *The Folly and Unreasonableness of Atheism demonstrated from the Advantage and Pleasure of a Religious Life, the Faculties of Human Souls, the Structure of Animate Bodies, & the Origin and Frame of the World.*

Although primarily devoted to condemning as atheistic Thomas Hobbes's view, stated in the *Leviathan* (1651), that all ideas could be resolved into sensations, Bentley's Boyle lectures did much to popularize Isaac Newton's theory of gravitation. Since Newton had shown that planets are held in their orbits by the force of gravity, drawing them toward the sun, combined with a transverse impulse that projects them at tangents, Bentley suggested that one could thus prove the existence of an "Intelligent Providence." In his eighth and final lecture, he remarked that since the transverse impulse is not uniform but has been adjusted so that each planet has its own velocity proportioned to its distance from the sun and to "the quantity of its [solar] matter," such complexity must imply an intelligent and omnipotent creator. Newton himself was delighted with this application of his theory and agreed with Bentley's findings wholeheartedly. The two entered into correspondence and a lasting friendship; when Newton was knighted in 1705, the ceremony took place at Bentley's house, Trinity Lodge.

At the end of 1693 the post of royal librarian became vacant in London, and Bentley was appointed to that position in 1694; in that year he also became a member of the Royal Society. In a letter to John Evelyn dated 21 October 1697 he mentions a small group of friends who had arranged to meet in the evenings, once or twice a week, at his lodgings in St. James's: Evelyn, Sir Christopher Wren, John Locke, and Newton. In that same year his collation of Callimachus first appeared in an edition published in Utrecht, edited by Joannes Georgius Grævius; it was widely hailed as the first systematic attempt to reconstruct an ancient author's body of work along scientific principles. Again Bentley had been a pioneer of critical method.

The first, and perhaps most serious, crisis of Bentley's career also came in 1697. At that time the "Ancients vs. Moderns" controversy was raging in the Royal Society, touched off by Sir William Temple's 1690 *Essay on Ancient and Modern Learning,* which refuted assertions by patriotic French authors Charles Perrault and Bernard Le Bovier de Fontenelle. In his essay Temple claims that ancient authors had surpassed the moderns in every field, including science, even though the records of that science have vanished. Using Thales and Pythagoras as his models, Temple complains that while the ancient Greeks had traveled the world pursuing original research, "the Moderns gather all their learning out of Books in the Universities." Regarding literature, he cites Aesop's *Fables* and *The Epistles of Phalaris,* supposedly the letters of the sixth-century B.C. tyrant of Agrigentum in Sicily, as "the best" examples of ancient "profane" authors.

In reply, Bentley's friend William Wotton published *Reflections on Ancient and Modern Learning* (1694), an attempt to take the middle ground by claiming superiority for the ancients in literature, but for the moderns in science. When he published the second edition in 1697, he appended Bentley's *Dissertation upon The Epistles of Phalaris, Themistocles, Socrates, Euripides; &c. and Æsop's Fables,* which proved, by exposing hundreds of anachronisms, that the fables had been corrupted through transmission and *The Epistles of Phalaris* were rank forgery, probably written by a sophist some

seven centuries later. While none could deny the accuracy of Bentley's proofs, his dissertation was seen as a direct attack on Temple, uncalled for and unfair. Temple and his followers, the "Ancients," felt that the aim of classical learning was not to accumulate knowledge but to develop a moral philosophy—and Bentley's behavior was not quite moral. The question came down to one of who was more qualified to judge texts: a statesman and gentleman-scholar who had experienced events of the sort described in epic and tragedy, or a "Modern" pedant who had known nothing but the academic cloister.

Matters might have ended there had Temple not had a powerful protégé: the satirist Jonathan Swift. Swift's scathing attacks on Bentley and Wotton in two works written between 1696 and 1699 and published in 1704, *The Battle of the Books* and *A Tale of a Tub* led to a spirited pamphlet exchange in which, for once, Bentley did not prevail. In 1699 he published *A Dissertation upon the Epistles of Phalaris: With an Answer to the Objections of the Honourable Charles Boyle, Esquire,* a revised and much expanded version of the work that had appeared in Wotton's book, which spread his reputation throughout Europe but at home invited renewed attacks from the "Ancients." Jebb describes the Phalaris episode as "the first controversy in English letters that had made anything like a public stir" and *A Dissertation upon the Epistles of Phalaris* as "the beginning of a new epoch of criticism." It is certainly true that this exchange is the source of Bentley's dual reputation: classicists view *A Dissertation upon the Epistles of Phalaris* as a work of genius, while students of British literature, influenced by Swift, tend to view it as evidence of small-mindedness.

In 1701 Bentley was appointed to the position of master of Trinity College, Cambridge—the post he occupied for the rest of his life, though he also retained the title and privileges of king's librarian. That same year he married Joanna Bernard. The marriage was happy and produced three surviving children: Elizabeth, Joanna, and Richard. Joanna Bentley's charm and even temper often rescued her husband from the effects of his public irascibility and despotic management style, but in 1717, shortly after Bentley had been appointed Regius Professor of Divinity, even she could not shield him from scandal. Honorary doctor of divinity degrees were customarily conferred upon members of the university on the occasion of royal visits; when George I arrived on such a visit, Bentley as Regius Professor was asked to officiate at the conferring of the honorary degrees. He flatly refused unless each of the thirty-two recipients paid him four guineas in advance. The "created" doctors reluctantly complied, but later one of them, Conyers Middleton, sued Bentley for return of the sum he had paid. When Bentley failed to appear in

Bentley's wife, Joanna Bernard Bentley (Master's Lodge, Trinity College, University of Cambridge)

contends that objections against matter having the ability to think—the subject of Bentley's second Boyle lecture—apply equally against immaterial substance, and he refutes Samuel Clarke's argument that immaterial memory (an analogy for the soul) remains even though the cells of the brain are continually in flux, by reminding readers that memory is only maintained by periodic recollections that refresh it. Collins was socially ostracized as an atheist, but nevertheless, Bentley felt compelled to compose a reply, published in 1713 as *Remarks Upon a Late Discourse of Free-Thinking: In a Letter to F.H.D.D.* ("F.H." is Francis Hare, a doctor of divinity and the bishop of Chichester). This time he and Swift fought on the same side—Swift with satire and Bentley with logic. Swift's 1713 tract, titled *Mr. C——n's Discourse of Free-Thinking, Put into Plain English,* is similar in tone to pamphlets he later published ridiculing Bentley's suggestions for revised editions of the New Testament and John Milton's *Paradise Lost* (1674).

As an aside in his reply to Collins's pamphlet, Bentley anticipates by seventy-two years the German scholar F. A. Wolf's assertion that Homer's epics were a series of detached pieces rather than a single effort. The public outrage that greeted Wolf's *Prolegomena ad Homerum, sive de operum Homericorum prisca et genuina forma vareisque mutationibus* (1795) and its revisionist approach to a revered text might well have been Bentley's lot had he completed either his own edition of Homer or, even more, his edition of the Greek Testament, a proposal for which was published in Greek and Latin in 1720 and in English in 1721. He spent years preparing for the latter, studying manuscripts from English libraries and arranging for collations from several libraries abroad, declaring in the 1721 proposal for the work that he could "set out an edition . . . without using any book under 900 years old." The work was almost ready for press by 1726 but left unpublished until 1862, when a partial edition was printed. Christian Europe was probably not ready for critical scrutiny of sacred texts in the style of *A Dissertation upon the Epistles of Phalaris;* even Bentley's proposals for the project drew fire, particularly from his old nemesis, Middleton.

Bentley's proposed edition of Homer's *Iliad* and *Odyssey* and the Homeric hymns was only slightly less controversial. In 1713 Bentley had rediscovered the *digamma* or "w" sound that had dropped out of the Greek language before the Homeric epics were committed to writing. By applying this letter to certain metrical peculiarities in Homer he was able to verify that, contrary to general opinion, Homeric verse followed strict metrical rules and could be scanned. Bentley worked from 1732 to 1734 on restoring the text with the aid of all manuscripts and scholia available, replacing *digammas* and including all quotations he had found in ancient

court, the university stripped him of all his degrees, though he retained his position as master of Trinity College. He in turn sued both Middleton and the university. Middleton was fined for libel, but Bentley did not regain his degrees until 1724.

After becoming master of Trinity, Bentley had slowed his scholarly publication, having other responsibilities. He fitted up a chemical laboratory for the first professor of chemistry at Cambridge, Francis Vigani, appointed the eminent Oriental and Hebrew scholar Henry Sike, and conferred a professorship of astronomy on Newton's young disciple Roger Cotes. He also introduced written examinations for fellowships and annual elections to scholarships, which permanently improved the quality of both student body and faculty and made Trinity a formidable research center.

In 1713 the deist Anthony Collins published his pamphlet *A Discourse of Free-Thinking, occasion'd by the Rise and Growth of a Sect call'd Free-Thinkers,* in which he calls for the right of free inquiry into religious affairs. Collins challenged Bentley's Newtonian arguments by remarking that it is as logical to maintain that matter gravitates as the result of powers originally placed in it by God as to assume that an immaterial being puts an object into motion and continues to keep it moving. Collins also

authors. Although unpublished, the manuscript was used extensively by scholars long after Bentley's death.

Bentley made many other contributions to the field of classics, among them new editions of the works of Horace (1711) and Terence (1726). His last work was a recension of the work of the astronomical poet Marcus Manilius (1739). On 14 July 1742, at the age of eighty, Richard Bentley died of pleuritic fever. He was buried in the chapel of Trinity College.

Bentley had less luck with editing the works of Latin authors than he had with Greek writers, and he was often criticized for excessive daring in his conjectures. However, the only serious mistake of his career as a critic was his attempt in 1732 to revise John Milton's *Paradise Lost* (1674) using the metrical and contextual methods he had developed for emendation of classical texts. Arguing that the blind Milton's poem had been subject to clerical errors by a careless amanuensis, Bentley made "corrections" to passages he thought unsuitable. The result was widely condemned, especially by Swift, who wrote a pamphlet, *Milton Restor'd, and Bentley Depos'd* (1732), ridiculing the replacement of such powerful images as "darkness visible," which Bentley thought physically impossible, with "a transpicuous gloom," and Satan's famous statement "To be weak is miserable" with "Here to dwell is miserable," which, Bentley pointed out, had superior theological precedent. Mercifully, Bentley's "emendation" of *Paradise Lost* never went into a second edition. Nevertheless, Bentley was never allowed to forget it, as evidenced in the portrait of him that appeared shortly before his death in book 4 of *The New Dunciad* (1742), Alexander Pope's revised and enlarged version of his 1728 poem, *The Dunciad:* "mighty Scholiast, whose unweary'd pains / Made Horace dull, and humbled Milton's strains."

Letters:

Richardii Bentleii et doctorum virorum Epistolæ, partim mutuæ: Accedit Richardi Dawesii ad Joannem Taylorum epistola singularis, edited by Charles Burney (London: Printed by William Bulmer, 1807);

Christopher Wordsworth, ed., *The Correspondence of Richard Bentley, Master of Trinity College, Cambridge* (2 volumes, London: J. Murray, 1842; 1 volume, New York & Hildesheim: G. Olms Verlag, 1977);

Elfriede Hulshoff Pol, ed., *Some Letters of Richard Bentley Published from the University Library, Leyden, on the Occasion of the Third International Congress of Classical Studies, London* (Leiden: E. J. Brill, 1959).

Bibliography:

Augustus Theodore Bartholomew and John Willis Clark, *Richard Bentley, D.D.: A Bibliography of His Works and of All the Literature Called Forth by His Acts or His Writings* (Cambridge: Bowes & Bowes, 1908).

Biographies:

James Henry Monk, *The Life of Richard Bentley, D.D.: With an Account of His Writings, and Anecdotes of Many Distinguished Characters During the Period in Which He Flourished* (1 volume, London: C. J. G. & F. Rivington, 1830; revised and corrected, 2 volumes, 1833; Osnabrück: Biblio Verlag, 1969);

Jacob Maehly, *Richard Bentley: Eine Biographie* (Leipzig: Teubner, 1868);

Richard Claverhouse Jebb, *Bentley* (New York: Harper, 1882; London: Macmillan, 1882);

Reginald James White, *Dr. Bentley: A Study in Academic Scarlet* (London: Eyre & Spottiswoode, 1965; East Lansing: Michigan State University Press, 1968).

References:

John Arbuthnot, John Gay, Robert Harley, Thomas Parnell, Alexander Pope, and Jonathan Swift, *Memoirs of the Extraordinary Life, Works, and Discoveries of Martinus Scriblerus* (Dublin: George Faulkner, 1741); republished, edited by Charles Kerby-Miller (New Haven: Yale University Press, 1950; New York: Oxford University Press, 1988);

Francis Atterbury, and others, *A Short Account of Dr Bentley's Humanity and Justice, to Those Authors Who Have Written Before Him: With an Honest Vindication of Tho. Stanley, Esquire, and His Notes on Callimachus. To Which Are Added, Some Other Observations on That Poet. In a Letter to the Honourable Charles Boyle, Esq.; With a Postscript, in Relation to Dr. Bentley's late Book against Him. To Which is Added an Appendix, by the Bookseller; wherein the Doctor's Mis-Representations of all the Matters of Fact wherein he is concern'd, in his late Book about Phalaris's Epistles, are modestly consider'd; with a Letter from the Honourable Charles Boyle, Esq; on that subject* (London: Printed for Thomas Bennet, 1699);

Charles Boyle, *Dr. Bentley's Dissertations on the Epistles of Phalaris and the Fables of Aesop Examin'd* (London: Printed for Thomas Bennet, 1698);

C. O. Brink, *English Classical Scholarship: Historical Reflections on Bentley, Porson, and Housman* (Cambridge: Clarke / New York: Oxford University Press, 1985);

Eustace Budgell, *Memoirs of the Life and Character of the Late Earl of Orrery, and of the Family of the Boyles: Containing Several Curious Facts, and Pieces of History, from the Reign of Queen Elisabeth to the Present Times: Extracted from Original Manuscripts and Papers Never*

Yet Printed. With a Short Account of the Controversy between the late Earl of Orrery and the Reverend Doctor Bentley; and Some Select Letters of Phalaris, the Famous Sicilian Tyrant (London: Printed for W. Mears, 1732);

Anthony Collins, *A Discourse of Free-Thinking, occasion'd by the Rise and Growth of a Sect call'd Free-Thinkers* (London, 1713);

Richard Cumberland, *Memoirs of Richard Cumberland; Written by Himself: Containing an Account of His Life and Writings, Interspersed with Anecdotes and Characters of Several of the Most Distinguished Persons of His Time, with Whom He Has Had Intercourse and Connexion* (1 volume, London: Lackington, Allen, 1806; revised and enlarged, 2 volumes, 1807);

J. A. Davison, ed., "The Bentley Commemorative Lectures," *Proceedings of the Leeds Philosophical and Literary Society: Literary and Historical Section,* 10, no. 3 (1963): 89–128;

Adam Fox, *John Mill and Richard Bentley: A Study of the Textual Criticism of the New Testament 1675–1729,* Aularian Series, no. 3 (Oxford: Blackwell, 1954);

Harold Richard Joliffe, "The Critical Methods and Influence of Bentley's Horace," dissertation, University of Chicago, 1939;

William King, *Dialogues of the Dead: Relating to the present Controversy concerning the Epistles of Phalaris* (London: A. Baldwin, 1699);

Conyers Middleton, *Remarks, Paragraph by Paragraph, upon the Proposals Lately Publish'd by Richard Bentley, for a New Edition of the Greek Testament and Latin Version* (London: J. Roberts, 1721);

Middleton, *Some Farther Remarks, paragraph by paragraph, upon Proposals lately publish'd for a new edition of a Greek and Latin Testament, by Richard Bentley: Containing a full answer to the Editor's late defence of his said Proposals, as well as to all his objections there made against my former remarks* (London: Printed by T. Bickerton, 1721);

L. D. Reynolds and N. G. Wilson, *Scribes and Scholars: A Guide to the Transmission of Greek and Latin Literature,* third edition (Oxford: Clarendon Press / New York: Oxford University Press, 1991);

John Edwin Sandys, "Richard Bentley," in *From the Revival of Learning to the End of the Eighteenth Century* (in Italy, France, England, and the Netherlands), volume 2 of his *A History of Classical Scholarship* (Cambridge: Cambridge University Press, 1908), pp. 401–410;

Jonathan Swift, *Milton Restor'd, and Bentley Depos'd* (London: E. Curll, 1732);

Swift, *A Tale of a Tub. Written for the Universal Improvement of Mankind. Diu multumque desideratum. To which is added, An Account of a Battel between the Antient and Modern Books in St. James's Library* (London: Printed for John Nutt, 1704); republished, edited by Angus Ross and David Woolley (Oxford & New York: Oxford University Press, 1986);

Sir William Temple, *Miscellanea. The Second Part. In Four Essays. I. Upon Ancient and Modern Learning. II. Upon the Gardens of Epicurus. III. Upon Heroick Virtue. IV. Upon Poetry* (London: R. Simpson, 1690);

Vita et Colloquia Richardi Bentleii, ut plurimum ab Ipso Conscripta/The Life and Conversation of Richard Bentley, delivered in his own Words, for the most part from his own Writings (London: Printed for John Morphew, 1712);

Ulrich von Wilamowitz-Moellendorff, *History of Classical Scholarship,* translated by Alan Harris (London: Duckworth, 1982; Baltimore: Johns Hopkins University Press, 1982), pp. ix, xxi, 54, 73, 78–82, 84–87, 108–109, 114, 117, 129, 131, and 134.

Papers:

Most of Richard Bentley's papers are in the Trinity College and University libraries, Cambridge, and the British Library, London.

George Berkeley
(12 March 1685 – 14 January 1753)

James Whitlark
Texas Tech University

See also the Berkeley entries in *DLB 31: American Colonial Writers, 1735–1781,* and *DLB 101: British Prose Writers, 1660–1800, First Series.*

BOOKS: *Arithmetica Absque Algebra aut Euclide Demonstrata. Cui Accesserunt, Cogitata Nonnulla de Radicibus Surdis, de Æstu Æris, de Ludo Algebraico, &c.,* as Art. Bac. Trin. Col. Dub. (London: Printed by J. Matthews for A. & J. Churchill, 1707);

An Essay Towards a New Theory of Vision (Dublin: Printed by Aaron Rhames for Jeremy Pepyat, 1709; revised, 1709);

A Treatise Concerning the Principles of Human Knowledge. Part I. Wherein the Chief Causes of Error and Difficulty in the Sciences, with the Grounds of Scepticism, Atheism, and Irreligion, are Inquir'd Into (Dublin: Printed by Aaron Rhames for Jeremy Pepyat, 1710); revised and republished with *Three Dialogues Between Hylas and Philonous* (London: Printed for J. Dodsley and J. Wilkie, 1734);

Passive Obedience, or the Christian Doctrine of not Resisting the Supreme Power, Proved and Vindicated upon the Principles of the Law of Nature. In a Discourse Deliver'd at the College-Chappel (Dublin: Printed by Francis Dickson for Jeremy Pepyat, 1712; corrected and enlarged edition, London: Printed for H. Clements, 1713);

Three Dialogues Between Hylas and Philonous. The Design of Which Is Plainly to Demonstrate the Reality and Perfection of Humane Knowledge, the Incorporeal Nature of the Soul, and the Immediate Providence of a Deity: In Opposition to Sceptics and Atheists. Also, to Open a Method for Rendering the Sciences More Easy, Useful, and Compendious (London: Printed by G. James for Henry Clements, 1713);

Advice to the Tories who have Taken the Oaths, anonymous (London: Printed by R. Baldwin and sold by R. Burleigh, 1715);

An Essay Towards Preventing the Ruine of Great Britain (London: J. Roberts, 1721);

George Berkeley; portrait by John Vanderbank (Regent House, Trinity College, Dublin)

De Motu; Sive, de Motus Principio & Natura, et de Causa Communicationis Motuum, Auctore G. B. (London: J. Tonson, 1721);

A Proposal For the Better Supplying of Churches in our Foreign Plantations, and for converting the savage Americans to Christianity, By a College to be Erected in the Summer Islands, Otherwise Called the Isles of Bermuda, anonymous (London: Printed by H. Woodfall, 1724);

Alciphron: or, the Minute Philosopher. In Seven Dialogues. Containing an Apology for the Christian Religion, Against those who are Called Free-thinkers, anonymous, 2 volumes (London: Printed for J. Tonson, 1732; revised, 1732); revised again (London: Printed for

J. R. Tonson and S. Draper, 1752); republished, with a foreword by T. Dwight (New Haven, Conn.: Printed by Sidney's Press for Increase Cooke, 1803);

A Sermon Preached Before the Incorporated Society for the Propagation of the Gospel in Foreign Parts; At their Anniversary meeting in the Parish-Church of St. Mary-le-Bow, on Friday, February 18, 1731 (London: Printed by J. Downing, 1732);

The Theory of Vision, or Visual Language, Shewing the Immediate Presence and Providence of a Deity, Vindicated and Explained (London: Printed for J. Tonson, 1733);

The Analyst; or, a Discourse Addressed to an Infidel Mathematician. Wherein it is Examined Whether the Object, Principles, and Inferences of the Modern Analysis are More Distinctly Conceived, or More Evidently Deduced, than Religious Mysteries and Points of Faith (London: Printed for J. Tonson, 1734);

A Defence of Free-thinking in Mathematics. In Answer to a Pamphlet of Philalethes Cantabrigiensis, Intituled, Geometry no Friend to Infidelity, or a Defence of Sir Isaac Newton, and the British Mathematicians. Also an Appendix Concerning Mr. Walton's Vindication of the Principle of Fluxions Against the Objections Contained in the Analyst. Wherein it is Attempted to Put this Controversy in such a Light as that Every Reader may be Able to Judge Thereof (Dublin: Printed by M. Rhames for R. Gunne, 1735);

Reasons for not Replying to Mr. Walton's Full Answer in a Letter to P.T.P. (Dublin: Printed by M. Rhames for R. Gunne, 1735);

The Querist, Containing Several Queries, Proposed to the Consideration of the Public, anonymous, 3 volumes (Dublin: Printed by R. Reilly for G. Risk, G. Ewing, and W. Smith, 1735–1737); revised edition (Dublin: George Faulkner, 1750);

Queries Relating to a National Bank, Extracted from the Querist. Also the Letter Containing A Plan of Sketch of such Bank. Republished with Notes (Dublin: George Faulkner, 1737);

A Discourse Addressed to Magistrates and Men in Authority. Occasioned by the Enormous Licence, and Irreligion of the Times, anonymous (Dublin: George Faulkner, 1738; revised, 1738);

Siris: A Chain of Philosophical Reflexions and Inquiries Concerning the Virtues of Tar-Water, and Divers Other Subjects Connected Together and Arising One from Another (Dublin: Printed by M. Rhames for R. Gunne, 1744; revised edition, London: Printed for W. Innys, C. Hitch & C. Davis, 1747);

A Letter to T– P–, Esq; from the Author of Siris, Containing Some Farther Remarks on the Virtues of Tar-Water, and The Methods for Preparing and Using it (Dublin: George Faulkner, 1744);

A Letter from the Author of Siris to Thomas Prior, Esq; Concerning the Usefulness of Tar-Water in the Plague. Wherein also it is Considered, Whether Tar-Water Prepared with the Distilled Acid of Tar should be Preferred, to that made in the Common Way, by Mixing Tar with Water, and Stirring them Together (Dublin: George Faulkner, 1747);

Two Letters from the Right Reverend Dr. George Berkeley . . . the One to Thomas Prior, Esq; Concerning the Usefulness of Tar-Water in the Plague . . . the Other to the Rev. Dr. Hales, on the Benefit of Tar-Water in Fevers, for Cattle as well as the Human Species. Published at his Lordship's Desire, on Occasion of the present Distemper among the Cattle, and for the General Good of Mankind (Dublin: Printed for W. Innys, C. Hitch, M. Cooper & C. Davis, 1747);

A Word to the Wise: or, an Exhortation to the Roman Catholic Clergy of Ireland. By a Member of the Established Church, anonymous (Dublin: George Faulkner, 1749; Boston: Printed and sold by S. Kneeland, 1749);

Maxims Concerning Patriotism. By a Lady, anonymous (Dublin, 1750);

A Miscellany, Containing Several Tracts on Various Subjects (Dublin: George Faulkner, 1752);

The Danger of Popery to the Present Government, Examined. To which are Annexed, Queries, Relative to the Same Subject, by Dr. Berkley, [sic] *Bishop of Cloyne* (Dublin: George Faulkner, 1761);

Berkeley's Philosophical Commentaries Generally Called the Commonplace Book, An Editio Diplomatica, edited by A. A. Luce (London: Thomas Nelson, 1944).

Editions: *The Medicinal Virtues of Tar Water, Fully Explained . . . to Which Is Added, the Receipt for Making It . . . ; Designed for the Benefit of All Who Drink It . . .* (London: Printed for the Proprietors of the Tar Water Warehouse, 1744);

Siris: or, an Abstract of the Treatise on the Virtues of Tar-Water, anonymously abridged and annotated (Dublin: Printed by and for Augustus Long, 1744);

An Abstract from Dr. Berkley's [sic] *Treatise on Tar-Water with some Reflexions Thereon. Adapted to Diseases Frequent in America,* anonymous abridgement of *Siris* by Cadwallader Colden (New York: Printed and sold by J. Parker, 1745);

A Treatise Concerning the Principles of Human Knowledge. With Remarks on Each Section, In which his Doctrines are Candidly Examined, and Shewn to be Repugnant to Facts, his Principles Incompatible with the Constitution of Human Nature, and the Reason and Fitness of things. To Which are Added, his Dialogues between Hylas and Philonous. And a Philosophical Discourse on the Nature of Human Being, Containing a Defence of Mr. Locke's Principles, and Some Remarks on Dr. Beattie's Essay on Truth, anonymously edited (London: Printed for J. Dodsley and J. Wilkie, 1776);

The Measure of Submission to Civil Government (Edinburgh: Printed for G. Robinson and C. Elliot, 1784);

The Works of George Berkeley, D.D, late Bishop of Cloyne in Ireland: To Which Is Added, an Account of His Life and Several of His Letters to Thomas Prior, esq. Dean Gervais, and Mr. Pope, 2 volumes, edited by Joseph Stock (Dublin: Printed by John Exshaw, 1784);

The Works of George Berkeley: Including His Letters to Thomas Prior, Dean Gervais, Mr. Pope, etc.: To Which Is Prefixed an Account of His Life, 2 volumes, edited by G. N. Wright (London: Printed for T. Tegg, 1843);

A Treatise Concerning the Principles of Human Knowledge, edited by J. R. B[allantyne] in *Metaphysics and Mental Philosophy,* volume 1, Reprints for the Pandits, no. 4 (Allahabad, India: Orphan School Press, 1852);

The Theory of Vision, or Visual Language, Shewing the Immediate Presence and Providence of a Deity, Vindicated and Explained, edited, with annotations, by H. V. H. Cowell (London, 1860);

The Works of George Berkeley, D.D., formerly Bishop of Cloyne, 3 volumes, edited by Alexander Campbell Fraser (Oxford: Clarendon Press, 1871; revised, 4 volumes, 1901);

Selections from Berkeley: With an Introduction and Notes, for the Use of Students in the Universities, edited by Fraser (Oxford: Clarendon Press, 1874);

A Treatise Concerning the Principles of Human Knowledge . . . with Proleomena and Annotations, Select, Translated, and Original, edited by Charles P. Krauth, Philosophical Classics (Philadelphia: Lippincott, 1874);

The Works of George Berkeley, D.D., formerly Bishop of Cloyne, 3 volumes, edited by George Sampson (London: G. Bell, 1897–1898);

Three Dialogues between Hulas and Philonous, edited by T. J. McCormack (Chicago: Open Court, 1901);

A Treatise Concerning the Principles of Human Knowledge, edited by McCormack (Chicago: Open Court / London: Kegan Paul, Trench & Trübner, 1907);

The Querist: Containing Several Queries, Proposed to the Consideration of the Public, Johns Hopkins University Reprints of Economic Tracts (Baltimore: Johns Hopkins University Press, 1910);

A New Theory of Vision and Other Select Philosophical Writings, introduction by A. D. Lindsay (London: Dent / New York: Dutton, 1910);

Berkeley: Essay, Principles, Dialogues, with Selections from Other Writings, edited by Mary Whiton Calkins (London & New York: Scribners, 1929);

The Querist: Containing Several Queries, Proposed to the Consideration of the Public, edited by Joseph Maunsell Hone (Dublin: Talbot, 1935);

The Works of George Berkeley, Bishop of Cloyne, 9 volumes, edited by Luce and T. E. Jessop (London: Thomas Nelson, 1948–1957);

Hermathena, no. 82 (1953) [contains previously unpublished sermons by Berkeley as well as essays on him];

Principles, Dialogues, and Philosophical Correspondence, edited, with an introduction, by Colin Murray Turbayne (Indianapolis: Bobbs-Merrill, 1954);

A Treatise Concerning the Principles of Human Knowledge, edited, with an introduction, by Turbayne (New York: Liberal Arts Press, 1957);

The Principles of Human Knowledge and Three Dialogues between Hylas and Philonous, edited by Geoffrey James Warnock (Cleveland: World, 1963);

Berkeley's Philosophical Writings, edited by David M. Armstrong, Collier Classics in the History of Thought (New York: Collier, 1965);

Berkeley's Philosophical Works, edited by M. R. Ayers (London, 1975);

George Berkeley's Manuscript Introduction: An Editio Diplomatica, edited, with an introduction, by Bertil Belfrage (Oxford: Doxa, 1987);

Alciphron, or, The Minute Philosopher: In Focus, edited by David Berman, Routledge Philosophers in Focus (London & New York: Routledge, 1993);

Principles of Human Knowledge and Three Dialogues Between Hylas and Philonous, edited, with an introduction, by Howard Robinson (Oxford & New York: Oxford University Press, 1996);

Philosophical Texts, edited by Jonathan Dancy (Oxford: Oxford University Press, 1997);

A Treatise Concerning the Principles of Human Knowledge, edited by Dancy (Oxford: Oxford University Press, 1998).

OTHER: Two letters by Berkeley, in Thomas Prior, *Authentic Narrative of the Success of Tar-Water, In Curing a Great Number and Variety of Distempers, With Remarks, And Occasional Papers Relative to the Subject, To which are Subjoined Two Letters from the Author of Siris* (Dublin: Printed by Marg.t Rhames for R. Gunne, 1746).

SELECTED PERIODICAL PUBLICATION– UNCOLLECTED: "Extract of a Letter by Mr. Edw. [*sic*] Berkeley from Naples, Giving Several Curious Observations and Remarks on the Eruptions of Fire and Smoak from Mount Vesuvio," *Philosophical Transactions of the Royal Society,* 30 (October 1717): 708–713.

According to John Stuart Mill, George Berkeley made "three first-rate philosophical discoveries, each

Berkeley as a young man (Collection of George Fitz-Hardinge Berkeley)

sufficient to have constituted a revolution in psychology, and which by their combination have determined the whole course of subsequent philosophical speculation." Mill was praising Berkeley's theory of vision, critique of abstractions, and recognition that sensations provide humanity's only knowledge of reality. The last of these influenced David Hume and, through him, Immanuel Kant. These three discoveries guarantee Berkeley's place in the history of philosophy. Beyond it, however, his name appears widely, from William Butler Yeats's poetry to discussions of quantum mechanics and of Asian religion (such as the Mahayana Buddhist doctrine that all is mind). This greater renown comes for the controversial core of his philosophy: an attack on materialism so thorough that he denied even the existence of matter. Consequently, he has been considered a precursor by many who, for whatever reason, challenge traditions that spring from eighteenth-century Occidental science and materialism.

Berkeley's family had been royalists, loyal to Charles I. As a reward for his loyalty Berkeley's grandfather became collector of Belfast after the Restoration. His father, William, served as a military officer and as collector for a port. His mother, Elisabeth, was the daughter of a Dublin brewer. Born on 12 March 1685 in Kilcrene, Ireland, about a mile from the city of Kilkenny, George

Berkeley lived at Dysart Castle or in a house erected on its remains. At eleven he enrolled at the Duke of Ormond's College at Kilkenny (the "Irish Eton"), joining the second from highest class. In 1700 he entered Trinity College, Dublin, where he received his bachelor of arts degree in 1704, his master of arts in 1707, and both a bachelor of divinity and doctorate of divinity in 1721.

Berkeley wrote in *Siris: A Chain of Philosophical Reflexions and Inquiries Concerning the Virtues of Tar-Water, and Divers Other Subjects Connected Together and Arising One from Another* (1744) that "man is a compound of contrarieties," and he was himself a union of opposites. On the one hand, he continued his family's conservatism; on the other hand, he questioned intellectual authority radically. In an entry in his notebooks, published in 1944 as *Berkeley's Philosophical Commentaries Generally Called the Commonplace Book, An Editio Diplomatica* he remarked that his discoveries derived from his being "distrustful" since he was eight years old. Repeatedly, he ridicules those who accept theories because they come from a venerable figure such as Aristotle. A biography of Berkeley in the *Weekly Magazine* in 1759–1760 recounts a story that illustrates his hunger to understand and judge directly. On seeing an execution, he asked his friend Thomas Contarine to hang him for a few seconds, so he could know the experience. Some later scholars doubted this anecdote, but David Berman has argued for its authenticity now that it has been established that the author of the biography was Oliver Goldsmith, who could have heard it from his uncle, Contarine. Offended by the idea that Berkeley might have committed so rash an act, the Reverend A. A. Luce wrote that "no wise, or indeed Christian, student would perform it, or allow it to be performed." Such recklessness, however, merely brings into another sphere of life the daring that Berkeley showed in championing his startling philosophy. In his introduction to Joseph Hone and M. M. Rossi's *Bishop Berkeley* (1931), Yeats limits Berkeley's boldness entirely to his youth, before his mellowing into a bishop. But Berkeley spent his last years championing tar water, despite opposition from virtually the entire medical profession. Conversely, his willingness to bow to social authority appears during his years in school, where submissiveness, not intelligence alone, was necessary for success. A synthesis of willing acquiescence to power and intellectual independence pervades his thought. According to his philosophy, all phenomena consist of sensations sent by God into human minds. Ceaselessly under the direction of God, each person could know reality directly without resort to any human intellectual authority. Despite being markedly innovative, his theory was politically conservative, emphasizing perpetual, divine generation of the whole physical world, including the government. Thus, he devotes the sermons in his *Passive Obedience, or the Christian Doctrine of not Resisting the Supreme Power, Proved and Vindicated upon the Prin-*

ciples of the Law of Nature. In a Discourse Deliver'd at the College-Chappel (1712) to the doctrine: he who resists the authorities resists what God has appointed (Rom. 13:2).

Berkeley's philosophical career dates from 1707, the year he published his *Arithmetica* and *Miscellanea Mathematica* together as *Arithmetica Absque Algebra aut Euclide Demonstrata. Cui Accesserunt, Cogitata Nonnulla de Radicibus Surdis, de Æstu Æris, de Ludo Algebraico, &c.* The first of these pieces demonstrates the rules of arithmetic without recourse to algebra or Euclidean geometry. The second advocates using Greek letters instead of radical signs, criticizes Richard Mead's theory of the atmospheric tide, belittles one of Andree Tacquet's discoveries, and provides a "game of algebra" to amuse students. With a reticence more common in the eighteenth century than thereafter, his title page simply identifies the author as a B.A. from Trinity College, Dublin. His letters show that he sometimes presented his works to an acquaintance as having been written by a friend; if it was well received, he would acknowledge it as his own. Being published (even in this cautious manner) may have helped him gain the fellowship he received that year, but the book is otherwise insignificant. What most makes 1707 notable is that it is the year he began keeping the notebooks in which he sketched his major theories.

These jottings commence with random speculations about duration as a "succession of ideas." Since time is experienced as a string of sensations, it is "only in ye mind." After about a page he mentions the "immaterial hypothesis," so he has already decided that phenomena consist entirely of the sensations by which they are known; there is no matter to give them any existence separate from the perceiving mind. At about this point he writes: "fall of Adam, rise of Epicurism & Hobbism dispute about divisibility matter &c expounded by material substances." Luce explains that "the mention of the Fall suggests Berkeley thought of the substitution of matter for God as the original sin of intellect." Berkeley is making great mental leaps from Adam to the undatable beginnings of idolatry, to Epicurus's belief in atoms, to the scientific materialism of Thomas Hobbes, and, finally, to Berkeley's own day, when philosophers generally assumed that matter was a substance that could be divided infinitely–a presumption he attacks in an unpublished paper, "Of Infinities" (circa 1707). In his *Philosophical Commentaries,* behind various instances of what he considers evil and heretical, he sees the belief in matter. Near the beginning of his second notebook he reiterates that such belief is "the chief source of all that scepticism & folly all those contradictions & inextricable puzling absurdities, that have in all ages been a reproach to Human Reason, as well as of that Idolatry whether of Images or of Gold etc that blinds the Greatest part of the World, as well as of that shamefull immorality that turns us into Beasts." He also castigates

human language for trying to describe spiritual concerns with physical metaphors. In calling attention to how speech is "metaphorical more than we imagine," he anticipates Friedrich Nietzsche, but to opposite conclusions. For Nietzsche, the self-proclaimed anti-Christian, humanity is trapped in a prison of its own languages. For Berkeley there is also another communication system: what appears to be an external world but is actually God's signs. The signs' purpose limits them to what can be perceived; thus, they are not infinite or infinitely divisible. Their presence and benign orderliness teach that their Author is both benevolent and intelligent.

Berkeley wished to refute the heretical tendencies in scientific materialism. For instance, he warns of "The great danger of making extension exist without the mind." The danger is that if God is given extension, one of the attributes of a material world, he may be thought to be material. If, however, God is outside of space, then space, as an eternal being, would virtually constitute another God. Berkeley's denial of infinite space perhaps makes him a precursor of relativistic physics. His motive, however, was to strengthen traditional theology so that it might resist what he considered the irreligious implications of Newtonian mechanics.

Strengthening, however, involves changing. Michelangelo Fardella and Nicolas de Malebranche had argued that the existence of the external world could not be demonstrated by reason but was proved through Scripture. In contrast, Berkeley's immaterialism runs against a common-sense interpretation of every word in the Bible. As a Christian, Berkeley faced the frightening question of whether Scripture could be reconciled with his philosophy. For instance, according to Psalm 90:4, a thousand years are like a day to the Lord. In *Philosophical Commentaries* entry 92, Berkeley asks himself "whether if succession of ideas in the Eternal mind, a day does not seem to God a 1000 years rather than a 1000 years a day?" To be aware of everything, God's mind must experience eons of sensations while a human being experiences a single one. Berkeley's worry eventually receded. In entry 281 he contends that nothing in the Bible absolutely contradicts him and says that there are "perhaps, many things for me." He notes that the philosophical revolution of René Descartes did not offend Christians, so his own need not do so, either (especially since he is so decidedly on the side of religion). Nonetheless, he warns himself "not to give the least Handle of offence to the Church or Church-men."

In 1708 Berkeley completed the notebooks and was ready to share his hypothesis. As his friends were to tell him and virtually every commentator since Hume has remarked, it was both irrefutable and unconvincing. The London wit Dr. Samuel Johnson reputedly thought that he refuted the hypothesis by kicking a rock. Such an act, however, is still within the realm of perception, and the

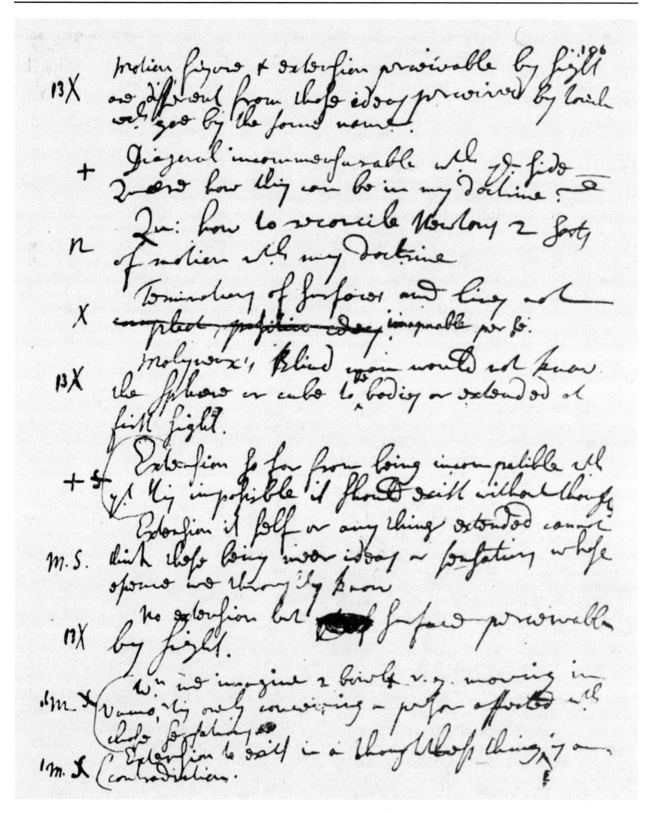

Page from one of Berkeley's notebooks, published in 1944 as Berkeley's Philosophical Commentaries
Generally Called the Commonplace Book *(British Library)*

touch, sight, and sound of the moving rock could be provided by the Almighty, who furnishes all neutral, pleasurable, and painful sensations.

To Berkeley's contemporaries the cosmos was external and physical. If God gave humanity every reason to believe the universe material but actually made it immaterial, he could be accused of deception. Berkeley had to defend God against this charge. Furthermore, he had to explain what advantage there was in disproving matter. The rise of science from Galileo Galilei to Sir Isaac Newton had shown how rigorously and mathematically the material model could be applied. Berkeley needed to demonstrate that his hypothesis was both more convincing and more useful by illustrating how sensations follow psychological rather than physical laws. For instance, that time sometimes seems to flow more quickly is easier to explain from a psychological than a mechanical vantage point. If the laws of nature were psychological, then God was not being deceptive. His communication system (the world) might be what the structure of thought required. He could not be blamed that in some ways, coincidentally, it resembled an external, material universe.

In investigating the psychology of sensations Berkeley became fascinated with sight. Newton and others had made major advances in optics, so Berkeley was here challenging material science at one of its firmest points. The result was *An Essay Towards a New Theory of Vision* (1709)—the considerable achievement of which was not in any singular innovation but in its unprecedented thoroughness. In his first sentence he announces his three-part organization: he will explain how "distance, magnitude, and the situation of objects" are perceived not through unconscious mathematics but through association of ideas. From the Renaissance onward, painters had understood that as objects recede, they appear to grow smaller, proportional to the distance. With the invention of microscopes, telescopes, and spectacles, opticians discovered that an image is only clear if the rays from it converge on the retina. Consequently, a common presumption, first promulgated by Descartes, was that vision judges distance by the angle of the rays. Berkeley objected that he was not aware of using his eyes like a protractor. Moreover, a small object that is close and a large one at a distance might have the same angle. Only experience teaches which is large, which small. Additionally, other determinants, such as faintness or closeness to the horizon, figure in assessing distance. All of these factors must be learned and are far from infallible. Intervening haze or the state of the viewer's eyes affect the outcome. What is blurred by being too far or too close may seem equally distant. Refraction through lenses changes the angle of the rays, yet the mind can compensate for the displacement. By showing how perceptual skills are acquired, he resolves a problem with the optical properties of bent mirrors that the previous standard text

in the field, Isaac Barrows's *Optical Lectures* (1669), found inexplicable. In summary of all the difficulties of assessing distance, Berkeley maintains that a person born blind, then suddenly restored to sight, would have to learn to judge distance.

In explaining perception of magnitude, Berkeley distinguishes between sight and touch. For vision, distance from an object affects its perceived size. Touch, however, always gives the same report, whether applied at arm's length or closer. With sight, other factors also enter, such as context. Seen in the sky, where there are no earthly features by which to compare it, an object appears smaller. Thus, the moon looks larger at the horizon than at the zenith. Like distance, judgment of magnitude would elude someone suddenly restored to sight.

Situation of objects must also be learned, since images on the retina are inverted. How does the mind restore them to their correct orientation? According to William Molyneux, the process is like a blind person's touching an object with a stick and distinguishing above from below by the angle. Again, Berkeley denies that his sight discerns by computing angles or that it functions like touch. Perception of magnitude, situation, and form requires experience. A person born blind who knew a globe and a cube by touching would not, at first seeing, be able to recognize them. Similarly, Molyneux and John Locke had both predicted that a blind person whose sight was restored would still be visually challenged. Berkeley suggests that this admission was, for them, quite inconsistent: elsewhere they presume that the senses give closely comparable information to one another and that sight involves a geometry of angles. For Berkeley, however, geometry has more to do with touch than sight, as, for example, knowing what is meant by a solid. He ends by stressing a major theme of the book: vision is like language; both have to be learned.

Within months of publication, the book received a second edition. It significantly influenced R. Smith's monumental *A Compleat System of Opticks* (1738), which, nonetheless, includes a few criticisms of it. In France it impressed Voltaire, Etienne Bonnot de Condilac, Jean Le Rond d'Alembert, Denis Diderot, and Georges Louis Leclerc, Comte de Buffon. In Scotland it not only became the established view but was, according to Adam Smith, a model of what philosophy should be. Berkeley himself later recommended it as a prelude to his immaterialism and republished it in the same volume with his *Alciphron: or, the Minute Philosopher. In Seven Dialogues. Containing an Apology for the Christian Religion, Against those who are Called Free-thinkers* (1732).

And the work did lay the foundations for that immaterialism, for both good and ill. Berkeley continued to hold that the senses differ so much that they only seem to corroborate one another. Such corroboration

Berkeley (standing, far right), and others associated with his plan to found a college in Bermuda for colonists and Native Americans: (standing) John Smibert, John Moffatt, and John James; (seated) Richard Dalton, Miss Handcock, and Berkeley's wife and infant son, Henry (painting by Smibert, 1731; Yale University Art Gallery)

was commonly employed to demonstrate that some object is external to the mind, and he wished to deprive materialists of this support. His insistence on the radical difference of the senses, however, was not always helpful to his purpose. In *Essay Towards a New Theory of Vision* he makes it sound as if sight constitutes an independent language, while touch discloses an external world. As he later explained in *The Theory of Vision, or Visual Language, Shewing the Immediate Presence and Providence of a Deity, Vindicated and Explained* (1733), in *Essay Towards a New Theory of Vision* he only pretended to accept the existence of matter so as to introduce the British public to his hypothesis gradually. *A Treatise Concerning the Principles of Human Knowledge. Part I. Wherein the Chief Causes of Error and Difficulty in the Sciences, with the Grounds of Scepticism, Atheism, and Irreligion, are Inquir'd Into* (1710) reveals that all sensory impressions come from God. Nonetheless, he continues to consider vision the only sense complex enough to be deemed a "language." If the senses could corroborate one another, then together they might form a single divine tongue. Instead, sight alone attains to that dignity, while the others are, for some unclear reason, lesser signs. Comparably, in *Alciphron* he argues that vision is

the only sense capable of conveying beauty. His letters remark beauties in written poetry, but this is also a visible language. Much of *Siris* is spent on the close relationship of God to light. Together, these instances suggest a hierarchy of senses with sight at the summit, like God above the Great Chain of Being. Perhaps his philosophy is here colored by habits of thought drawn from his theology and politics.

Even for vision, Berkeley's theory does not prove the completely mental nature of that sense. Why, for instance, are there eyes? He provides no immaterial answer. His later tendency is to treat such particulars of God's language—the human body and the world around it—as arbitrary, just as the sounds of human languages have only an arbitrary relationship to their meaning. Understandably, he shies away from trying to reconstruct all of God's grammar, the complete rules by which appearances function. Nonetheless, *Essay Towards a New Theory of Vision* was an appreciable accomplishment. Having shown that (within certain limits) he could outdo the scientists in their own territory, he felt confident to make a less disguised presentation of his hypothesis.

The next year he did so with *A Treatise Concerning the Principles of Human Knowledge*. Its subtitle indicates that his target is error not only in science but also in religion. His brief preface claims that as a counter against skepticism, the work offers a proof of God and of the immortality of the soul. He dedicates it to Thomas, Earl of Pembroke, an acquaintance—but more significantly, the one to whom Locke dedicated *An Essay Concerning Humane Understanding* (1690). Considering the similarity of the titles and the revolution Locke's essay had brought, Berkeley seems to have had exalted hopes for his own work.

Its introduction reveals what Mill prized as the second of Berkeley's major discoveries: his critique of abstractions. Berkeley begins by remarking that the wise ought to be more serene than the ignorant; yet, academics are constantly at risk of skepticism by contemplating paradoxes about infinity and abstraction. Surprisingly, he promises to lead mankind out of paradox, when the impression he has always made is quite the reverse. He is not unaware of his challenging style, however. The preface of *A Treatise Concerning the Principles of Human Knowledge* warns that his individual sentences may be misunderstood if construed apart from the whole of his argument. Whatever its difficulties, that argument offers to make clear the previously undisclosed nature of the universe. If abstract and infinite, the cosmos would transcend human comprehension; nonetheless, humanity longs to understand it. Therefore, it must be without abstraction and infinity; a benevolent God would not have created mankind with desire for universal knowledge if it could not be fulfilled. Since Berkeley has not yet proved that there is a God, arguing from his benevolence might seem premature; but he proceeds in a characteristically double manner. He proves each point with theology, to appeal to Christians, and with natural philosophy for skeptics. Christians already believe in a benevolent God. For the skeptics he contends that the contradictions into which all previous natural philosophy has fallen show that its principles are false. His double logic is one more expression of his conservative/radical temperament. The conservative side is deductive, beginning with an omnipotent God and proceeding to particulars. The radical side is inductive, basing all argument firmly on sense perception. The style is challenging, since Berkeley's audience encounters two fundamentally different methodologies almost simultaneously.

From his radical vantage point (but with pretended modesty), he states that he has made his discovery because he is intellectually "short-sighted," forced to look more closely than better minds. Thus limited, he has found that abstract ideas of the sort postulated by Locke are a contradiction in terms. If they are totally abstract, they are not definite enough to be ideas; thus, they cannot even be imagined. The method Berkeley employs to prove this contention is surprising. In *Essay*

Towards a New Theory of Vision he had insisted that the senses, usually presumed to corroborate one another, must be treated as separate. In *A Treatise Concerning the Principles of Human Knowledge* he contends that supposedly distinct qualities—form, extension, color, and movement—are always perceived together and are thus inseparable from one another. He is, however, not being inconsistent: these qualities are all visual. Whether stressing the division of senses or the blending of qualities in one sense, he is in his radically inductive mode, detailing sensations exactly as he perceives them. (This technique is called "phenomenology," and modern phenomenologists consider him an ancestor.)

The Lockean theory is that, for example, in thinking the idea "triangle," one imagines a colorless figure without a definite size or a definite degree to its angles. Sarcastically, Berkeley counters that although some people may possess the ability to imagine such a triangle, all he can manage is to look at a variety of them, noting the details they have in common. From their similarities he may arrive at a definition of *triangle*. This definition, however, never becomes an abstract idea that can be imagined apart form actual examples. Rather, the definition operates as a series of directions for identifying triangles. His sarcasm becoming more blatant, he shows how illusory and pretentiously elitist are abstract ideas, which Locke admits are unknown to the "unexercised mind." Berkeley appoints himself as a champion for the attitude of children and the uneducated. In their pedantry, his opponents teach that each word has only one definite thing meant by it. According to this false notion, to give a meaning to the word *triangle* there must somewhere be a colorless, sizeless figure with three angles that have no definite measure. Actually, Berkeley asserts, words are vague, connotative, and ambiguous. Consequently, the definition "plane surface comprehended by three right lines" describes all real triangles not by denoting an abstract idea but simply by leaving out the specifics that distinguish one triangle from another. The words of this definition function as letters do in algebra: they allow for a series of operations (in this case, identifying a triangle).

The purpose of his introduction is to prove the "impossibility" of abstract ideas, so that he can then demonstrate that matter is simply one of these meaningless terms used by confused Scholastics. In *Philosophical Commentaries* he marks arguments against abstract ideas for the "Introduction," so he had long planned to begin *A Treatise Concerning the Principles of Human Knowledge* this way. As a churchman, however, he must have been aware of the peril that by limiting human knowledge to what can be imaged distinctly, he may seem to rule out the existence of such spiritual entities as God. Many critiques have subsequently charged that he unintentionally did so (for example, D. M. Datta's "Berkeley's Objective Ideal-

Whitehall, the house in Newport, Rhode Island, where Berkeley lived from 1729 to 1732 while pursuing his Bermuda project

ism: An Indian View" in Warren E. Steinkraus's *New Studies in Berkeley's Philosophy,* 1966). This charge usually involves labeling his philosophy nominalism: the belief that words are only meaningful to the extent that they name sensed particulars. Berkeley, however, is not precisely a nominalist, since he notes functions of language other than naming. Furthermore, his philosophy is sufficiently unusual that, as he has already warned, snap judgments are unwarranted. The sole way of assessing his success is to follow his details.

He commences by defining all objects of knowledge as "ideas." This term stands for sensations, as well as the thoughts and emotions that ultimately derive their imagery from the senses. Of these ideas he employs the aphorism "*esse* is *percipi*"–to be is to be perceived. As he explains in section 81, *existence* is an abstract idea; therefore, strictly speaking, in and of itself, *esse* (to be) is empty verbiage. It has no meaning except when employed as a term for the perception of something.

Human perceptions are of at least two radically different kinds. First, there are sensations, over which the mind has little control. Ordering a real mountain to float in the air will not cause it to do so. Second, there is imagination. If one commands an imagined mountain to levitate, it is more likely to comply. These two kinds of perceptions can be distinguished, he explains, in that the former are

more vivid and coherent than the latter. Therefore, a sensed world may be deemed real, an imagined one illusory. Since ideas, particularly sensory ones, are not always obedient, ideas are different from the will.

A common but unfair objection to his hypothesis is that it offers no way to distinguish real from imaginary. He admits, for example, that dreams sometimes provide sensations of pain and pleasure as vivid as daily life. If materialists had any infallible test for the difference between imaginary and real, they might object to Berkeley, but he has merely articulated the common-sense process by which people contrast vivid, coherent "reality" with the usually dim ramblings of the imagination.

Berkeley postulates that imaginings are controlled by the human mind. What, then, is the source of the real? Answering this question leads him into his long proof of divine activity. The first step is to show that ideas (thoughts and sensations) are by nature mental. In Berkeley's day, scientists realized that color does not exist in the physical world; they termed color a "secondary" quality to differentiate it from "primary" ones, such as size and shape, that were thought to exist in the objects themselves. Berkeley, however, points out that size and shape are only known by sensations of them–in other words, ideas. Ideas could represent an external, material world only if they resembled non-ideas. Berkeley cannot imagine how such a likeness could exist or be proved since, by definition, they differ absolutely in kind.

Ideas are only known as components of minds. Consequently, Berkeley does not believe himself justified in postulating that they could have any other origin. Weakly coherent ideas come from the human imagination; the closely related ones of reality must, thus, issue from some vastly greater intellect–that of God. This formulation is only in a casual sense a proof of the existence of God and other minds, since *existence* is to Berkeley a nonsense word. He tries usually to confine himself to describing his perceptions. Sensing reality occasions the inference that it is created by a mind analogous to the human but greater. There is no point asking about the independent existence of anything, such as an unseen tree in the forest. Seeing the tree each time one visits it makes likely that it persists as an idea in God's mind. Aside from an entity's relation to perception, however, discussion of it is baseless. Because he experiences will and thought, he applies the terms *will* and *understanding* to an otherwise unknown something–for lack of a better term called a "self," "soul," or "spirit." He admits that he has no idea but only a "notion" of it. If, as he sometimes contends, there are only spirits and ideas, what is a "notion"? In eighteenth-century usage, it meant a vague, possibly erroneous idea. In section 308 of *Siris* Berkeley defines it as an act or operation of a spirit, though previously it tends to signify the "intuition" of such an act–in other words, his perceiving of the effects of these spirits.

God and other selves are known only through their acting on ideas as by "willing, imagining, remembering." How they do these things is also a mystery, particularly since Berkeley rejects speculation about unconscious processes. (In *Essay Towards a New Theory of Vision* he ridiculed the Cartesian assumption that vision unconsciously measures angles to perceive distance.) Rejection of the unconscious raises a problem in regard to memory, since the process of forgetting and recalling requires ideas to leave consciousness and return. Although Berkeley does not discuss this problem, to be consistent he would have to place the storage of memories in the divine mind. One problem with this contention is that it gives the largest share of the process of thinking to God. Cognition consists of perceiving and manipulating either ideas that God provides to the senses or copies of them that memory stores in, and subsequently withdraws from, the divine bank. Thinking follows patterns of reasoning largely learned through divine assistance and then furnished by God to memory. Does thinking have enough autonomy to be morally responsible for actions? Based on his intuition of his own will, Berkeley says that it does.

Berkeley can only give a largely negative description of spirits: they are "simple, undivided, active." "Simple" and "undivided" sound as if they mean "unified," but in section 13 he condemns the term *unity* as another abstract idea. It is not a property of objects, which are aggregates of ideas and thus open to dissolution; nor can any idea be predicated of a spirit. Since spirits are not aggregates of ideas, they are not "mortal," if that term means the death of a body when its ideas disassociate themselves from one another. A spirit, however, is only conscious (knowing and knowable) when it has ideas to perceive. These depend on God, so only belief in divine benevolence offers hope that each human mind will function forever.

In the nineteenth century Charles Baudelaire composed the poem "Correspondances" (Correspondences), in which symbols (or ideas) are described as alive and capable of perceiving humanity. Without discussion, Berkeley rejects the possibility that ideas might perceive. Introspection, he contends, should teach any sane person that ideas are inanimate and, therefore, perceivers must be other than ideas; perceivers must be "spirits." In other words, Berkeley's phenomenalist method consists of using his own mind as the test of mental normality. The prose poet Chuang Tzu wondered if he were a man who had dreamed that he was a butterfly or a butterfly now dreaming that he was a man. Typical in this respect of his epoch, Berkeley assumes that there is no monumental difficulty in distinguishing between dream and reality. For his British contemporaries the problem with his philosophy was not that it ignores rare states described by poets but that it was itself exotic.

Berkeley, however, thought his theory the most plausible available. He contended that there are only four options: a material world produced by chance; a material world long ago created by God; a material world constantly generated by God; or a nonmaterial world constantly generated by God. In his age the first of these possibilities was easily rejected in that there was no well-developed theory of evolution, chaos, or complexity to explain how order could arise spontaneously from disorder. The second option requires matter to be created from nothing–a notion that Berkeley notes, has often been deemed impossible. The third, a theory of some medieval Scholastics, is at least as incredible. Berkeley invokes the principle of Occam's razor, according to which, when several theories describe a situation, a philosopher must choose the simplest–in this case, Berkeley's, since it has one less component: matter.

Berkeley feared that his age was moving God further into the background. Reference to the Lord was still presumed useful to frighten the populace into morality and to account for the origin of the world. Aside from these residual pieties, many of the educated turned science. Somewhat plaintively, Berkeley insists that he is not depriving anyone of the useful discoveries of science: the mathematical relations between ideas hold whether there is matter or not. In either case, one must still ponder why

God created things as they are. His readers, though, were aware that science discovered its physical laws by assuming an external world. For instance, in conventional optics light travels through space and is focused through the eyes, its data eventually reaching the brain. Why, if there is no external world, would Berkeley's God arrange sensations as if they arose from such a spatial sequence? Berkeley might have argued that, for moral education, God needed to teach humanity through ideas arranged as an intricate, vulnerable body, susceptible to disease and other corporeal punishments. Perhaps he considered this argument too obvious to state. Instead, he criticized science: for instance, Newton's so-called universal gravitation did not seem to affect the fixed stars. More accurate observations have since supported Newton in this regard, but some evidence corroborates other of Berkeley's views. His assumption that space was finite, for example, was affirmed by Albert Einstein. Furthermore, in quantum mechanics some particles lack determinate form except when they are perceived.

Berkeley's book was generally ignored. His friend Sir John Percival brought it to the attention of acquaintances, but even Percival's wife doubted that it could be reconciled with the biblical account of creation. Berkeley wrote to reassure her on 6 September 1710. Perhaps he was already planning *Three Dialogues Between Hylas and Philonous. The Design of Which Is Plainly to Demonstrate the Reality and Perfection of Humane Knowledge, the Incorporeal Nature of the Soul, and the Immediate Providence of a Deity: In Opposition to Sceptics and Atheists. Also, to Open a Method for Rendering the Sciences More Easy, Useful, and Compendious* (1713), which includes a section on this question, but three busy years elapsed before its publication. After 1710 he had duties as a newly made priest and various junior appointments at the university.

Of the many sermons he preached, three became the book *Passive Obedience*. He had to publish to contradict rumors about them that were damaging his prospects. The political philosophy of the book follows more or less logically from *A Treatise Concerning the Principles of Human Knowledge,* in which God, to keep from throwing the world into disorder, almost never breaks the rules of physics, which are the associations of ideas in the divine mind. The sermons echo this theme of divine constancy. They explain that although a prince who fell from a cliff might be saved by God's suspending gravitation, for the greater good of consistency he would allow the prince to perish. If God seldom makes exceptions, mankind should never stray from the moral rules. Among these rules is that since God ordains the civil authorities, they should not be resisted, lest anarchy ensue. One might think that this tract on submission would please the government; and it might have, if the current sovereign, Queen Anne, already in ill health, had been succeeded by the Stuarts. Instead, power

remained with the Whigs, the slightly more liberal party. Their ascendancy had come with the so-called Glorious Revolution against a Stuart monarch; thus, by denouncing all revolution, Berkeley had branded them sinners. One of their champions, Archbishop William King, had contended that God worked eighteen virtual miracles to support the revolution–precisely the kind of massive divine rule-breaking that *Passive Obedience* argues against. In 1716 Berkeley failed to attain appointment to St. Paul's in Dublin, probably because of reports that he was a Jacobite (a defender of the Stuarts), even though in 1715 he had published *Advice to the Tories who have Taken the Oaths*. Both it and *Passive Obedience* denounce rebellion but show Tory sympathies and are otherwise subtly ambiguous. For instance, in addition to condemning and supporting the present government simultaneously, *Passive Obedience* is based on a major theological paradox: to teach his moral laws, which should not be transgressed because they are like natural ones, God broke those natural laws, performing miracles connected with his promulgation of the Ten Commandments. Berkeley skirts this problem. These sermons and two other early ones that have survived are notable for their infrequent biblical citations. Indeed, he begins *Passive Obedience* by admitting that people interpret Scripture according to their prejudices, so that trying to convince his opponents through quotation would be less useful than recourse to philosophy.

In 1713 Berkeley made another attempt to promulgate a detailed version of his philosophy by publishing *Three Dialogues Between Hylas and Philonous* in London; *A Treatise Concerning the Principles of Human Knowledge* had been published in Dublin, perhaps too far from the British capital to attract fashionable society. Also, to arouse public attention he recast his doctrine in dialogue form. The result is a literary classic with a style sometimes ahead of its time–for instance, in its opening praise of the morning: "The purple sky, these wild but sweet notes of birds, the fragrant bloom upon the trees and flowers, the gentle influence of the rising sun, these and a thousand nameless beauties of nature inspire the soul with secret transports. . . ." In denying the generally accepted idea that language is a representation of the external world, Berkeley approached composition in a manner that anticipated Romanticism. That movement was also obsessed with the "nameless" and "secret," connected with the private perceptions of a self that can never be fully described. Moreover, with his belief in nature as God's communication, Berkeley's sense of how its "beauties . . . inspire the soul" anticipates Romantic meditations on the subject.

The dialogues are between Hylas (Greek for "materialist") and Philonous ("mind-lover"). As Luce notes, Berkeley was at the time junior lecturer in Greek and thus probably had Plato's dialogues in mind. Berkeley's differ, however, in that most of Plato's dialogues close before forcing issues to ultimate conclusions (which, perhaps, were given orally as part of Plato's courses in his Academy). Berkeley's dialogues present the doctrine of *A Treatise Concerning the Principles of Human Knowledge,* but with more explanation, particularly about certain scientific terms such as "secondary qualities." As his name testifies, Hylas champions the existence of matter, which he redefines each time his previous conception of it is disproved. As a churchman, however, he accepts unquestioningly Philonous's theology. For example, God knows all phenomena without sensory perception and without pain or pleasure. Philosophically, this premise requires more explanation, but it is fairly standard Christianity—except that it ignores Jesus, his Incarnation, and his suffering. Being derived from revelation, these issues are, perhaps, not to be expected in a work of natural philosophy. Nonetheless, Philonous does devote his conclusion to Genesis. To Philonous, creation of the world means that God caused the ideas, which eternally abide in the divine mind, to be perceivable by other beings. He thus interprets Scripture as an imprecise or, as Berkeley terms it in *A Treatise Concerning the Principles of Human Knowledge,* "vulgar" version of what philosophy reveals more clearly. Philonous insists, however, that he is not making a religious change but only a philosophical one: "That innovations in government and religion, are dangerous, and ought to be discountenanced I freely own. But is there like reason why they should be discouraged in philosophy?" Here he is a totally transparent version of Berkeley, trying to reconcile political and theological conservatism with philosophical revolution. Largely oblivious to the strangeness of this goal, Philonous claims his hypothesis to be an articulation of common sense: "Ask the gardener, why he thinks yonder cherry-tree exists in the garden, and he shall tell you, because he sees and feels it; in a word, because he perceives it by his senses."

Three Dialogues between Hylas and Philonous brought few converts but was received as the stylish work of a metaphysical wit able to create elegant paradoxes. That reputation, his personal charm, and the influence of his friend Jonathan Swift brought Berkeley within the dazzling circle of such London writers as Joseph Addison, Alexander Pope, and John Arbuthnot. In 1713, at the instigation of another of these writers, Richard Steele, Berkeley contributed a series of essays to *The Guardian.* Although they are anonymous and thus difficult to identify, Berman argues well for attributing to Berkeley perhaps 3, part of 9, 27, 35, part of 39, 49, 55, 62, 69, 70, 77, at least part of 81, 83, 88, 89, 126, and possibly 130. Whoever wrote them, these works evidence skill in satire, as in a continued article in numbers 35 and 39 in which "philosophical snuff" allows a character to separate his soul from his body and enter the pineal gland of a freethinker who is composing a confused, vanity-generated book. Most of the articles

attributed to Berkeley are attacks on atheism, using arguments he later employed in *Alciphron.*

While nominally retaining his post at Trinity College, Berkeley spent eight years away except for a brief return in 1715. Even by the relaxed standards of the time, this sabbatical was a rather long one. He attracted some criticism, but he was adding polish to his education. From October 1713 to August 1714 he traveled to Italy as chaplain to the earl of Peterborough. From 1716 to 1720 he toured the Continent again, this time as a tutor to the bishop of Clogher's son. Berkeley's travel journals testify to his particular interest in the seemingly psychological cure of tarantula bites, precisely the kind of data that, if conclusive, might have supported his hypothesis. In October 1717 he published in *Philosophical Transactions* "Extract of a Letter by Mr. Edw. [*sic*] Berkeley from Naples, Giving Several Curious Observations and Remarks on the Eruptions of Fire and Smoak from Mount Vesuvio," based on personal experience. Despite being away, he became senior fellow at Trinity that year. During his return to London in 1720, he wrote *De Motu; Sive, de Motus Principio & Natura, et de Causa Communicationis Motuum* (1721), which alleges that scientists have forgotten that the ultimate cause of motion cannot be any inanimate object; only God can be that cause. Berkeley also reminds the reader that mathematics "depends on the notion of the definer." He was ahead of his time in recognizing that scientific theories are only rigorously applied metaphors, not permanent truths. But the book presents this important insight in an undeveloped way, then hurries into rather conventional theology.

When Berkeley arrived in London, the city was in turmoil because of the South Sea Bubble—the first stock market crash in history, which was followed by an unsettling investigation of government corruption. Berkeley wrote *An Essay Towards Preventing the Ruine of Great Britain* (1721), the title of which captures his almost apocalyptic mood. So bleak is he that he even admits that monarchies easily lose the thrift and simplicity of manners typical of a republic, but he immediately adds that by setting the right example a court can help the nation recover these more speedily than a republic can if it slips from virtue. His basic argument is that the South Sea Bubble is a symptom of the turn within the country from Christianity to greed and materialism.

Berkeley had his own financial concerns, and he directed his attention to acquiring a remunerative church post. After receiving the degrees of bachelor of divinity and doctor of divinity, he gained a Crown appointment to the deanery of Dromore. Its bishop appointed another candidate, however, who took possession of the position before Berkeley could. In 1724 he became dean of Derry but had other ambitions. He wanted to found a college in Bermuda, which was rumored to have an Edenic climate. Furthermore, since the South Sea Bubble he had many

GEORGE BERKELEY D.D.
Fellow 1707, *Bishop of Cloyne* 1733

Portrait of Berkeley by James Latham, circa 1738
(Trinity College, Dublin)

misgivings about the Old World, as he voices in "Verses . . . on the Prospect of Planting Arts and Learning in America." It begins with the muse "disgusted at Age and Clime" and ends:

> Westward the Course of Empire takes its Way;
> The four first Acts already past,
> A fifth shall close the Drama with the Day;
> Time's noblest Offspring is the last.

In *A Proposal For the Better Supplying of Churches in our Foreign Plantations, and for converting the savage Americans to Christianity, By a College to be Erected in the Summer Islands, Otherwise Called the Isles of Bermuda* (1724) Berkeley expresses his hope to transform young colonists and Native Americans into missionaries. Christianity, he explains, can spread more quickly throughout the New World, where it is impeded only by ignorance, than in the Old World, where it combats "Error." If the king grants the proposal "it will cast no small Lustre on his Majesty's Reign, and derive a Blessing from Heaven on his Administration and those who live under the Influence thereof." Parliament voted an appropriation, but, then opposition became more audible, focusing particularly on the site for the school. One of his reasons for choosing the location was so that Native Americans from continental America would not

"find Opportunities of running away to their Countrymen." In other words, they were to be kept by force. Even by the standards of the time, this means of conversion seemed oppressive. Louder objections were voiced because Bermuda was too far from centers of population and commerce. Berkeley had contended that this distance would make the scheme cheaper and better ensure the innocence of the students, but it was ultimately impractical. In fact, Berkeley never went to Bermuda. Instead, he visited Virginia, then spent almost three years in Newport, Rhode Island.

When Berkeley first proposed the college, a girl delivered to him in Dublin a satirical broadside that began:

> Dear Doctor, here comes a Young Virgin untainted
> To your Shrine at Bermudas to be Married and Sainted;
> I am Young, I am Soft, I am Blooming and Tender,
> Of all that I have I make you a Surrender. . . .

Whether or not he recalled these words about taking a bride with him, in August 1728, immediately before leaving for the Americas that September, he did marry. His wife was Anne, the eldest daughter of Sir John Forster, former speaker of the Irish House of Commons and chief justice. Her uncle was a bishop who had assisted at Berkeley's consecration.

Waiting in America for the money from Parliament, Berkeley preached relatively unphilosophical sermons that abound with biblical references. For philosophical stimulation he ran a study circle and corresponded with the colonial Anglican minister Samuel Johnson, who later became first president of King's College in New York. Berkeley also confronted a practical problem in political philosophy and theology. He feared that slaves might be freed automatically on converting to Christianity and that masters would, therefore, refrain from giving them a Christian education. He appealed to the king's attorney and solicitor general for a ruling on the issue; to Berkeley's delight, the decision was that Christians might remain slaves. He had the ruling printed and widely distributed. Thereafter, he bought and baptized three slaves. Some colonists justified the owning of slaves by saying that Native Americans and Africans were racially inferior to themselves. In *A Sermon Preached Before the Incorporated Society for the Propagation of the Gospel in Foreign Parts* (1732) Berkeley condemned this prejudice but said that just as the government is ordained by God, so one's status as free or slave must be accepted without revolt. Masters ought to be kind; but if they were not, redress would come in the afterlife.

In 1731 Berkeley learned informally that Parliament would never supply the funding it had voted for the college. Partly with his own money he established at Yale University the first graduate fellowship offered in the Americas and then left for England. This endowment and some massive subsequent gifts of books were all he could accomplish for education in the New World. His stay in Rhode Island had been a financial setback for him, but he had managed to write his clever dialogue *Alciphron* there, combating what he perceived as a conspiracy of atheists. Blaming them for the failure of the college scheme, he intended his book as revenge. It also probably helped him become bishop of Cloyne in 1734, since the queen was impressed by it. Its subtitle, *The Minute Philosopher,* is his phrase for an atheist (taken from Cicero), since he judged the term *freethinker* too complimentary. His targets are such philosophers as Anthony Collins, Bernard de Mandeville, and Anthony Ashley Cooper, Lord Shaftesbury, all of whom Berkeley suspected of secret atheism or of doctrines inclining in that direction. The villains of the dialogue are Alciphron (a satire of Shaftesbury and Collins) and Lysicles (a travesty of Mandeville). The heroes are Crito, who has only a small part, and Euphranor, the spokesman for Christianity and Berkeley's philosophy. The only real innovation in the work is a more developed presentation of Berkeley's emotive theory of language than he offered in *A Treatise Concerning the Principles of Human Knowledge.* Alciphron admits that such theological terms as *Grace* and *Trinity* are not definite ideas but contends that belief in them may arouse emotions and thereby "serve to regulate and influence our wills, passions or conduct." Therefore, they are meaningful because they have a significant function. Whereas the eighteenth century thought that meaning comes from representation of an external world, Berkeley assigns it instead to the way a word is used. This revolution in thought is equal to the three mentioned by Mill. Edmund Burke adopted it in his *Philosophical Enquiry into the Sublime and Beautiful* (1757). Nonetheless, Anthony Flew's "Was Berkeley a Precursor of Wittgenstein?" in Berman's edition of *Alciphron* shows that Berkeley's insight largely disappeared from philosophy until it resurfaced in the twentieth century, when it was presumed to be the discovery of Ludwig Wittgenstein.

Following the publication of *Alciphron* Berkeley continued his assault on materialism with four minor works. In answer to a critic, the first of these books, *The Theory of Vision, or Visual Language, Shewing the Immediate Presence and Providence of a Deity, Vindicated and Explained* (1733), indicates that Berkeley's previous work on vision tried to move its readers gently beyond belief in an external world and thus partly concealed its immaterialist orientation. Berkeley also notes that an actual case of a person born blind and restored to sight had corroborated his contention that vision must be learned gradually. In 1734, suspecting a certain mathematician (probably Edmund Halley) to be an atheist, Berkeley addressed to him *The Analyst; or, a Discourse Addressed to an Infidel Mathematician. Wherein it is Examined Whether the Object, Principles, and Inferences of the Modern Analysis are More Distinctly Conceived, or More Evidently*

Deduced, than Religious Mysteries and Points of Faith. It asserts that Newton's "fluxions," or calculus, reaches accurate results but only by compensating for errors that come from the metaphysical inconsistencies on which it is based. After 1713, when he rejected the existence of "infinitesimals" (infinitely small quantities intermediate between something and nothing), Newton tacitly continued to use them. Berkeley's target is the postulate that matter can be divided infinitely. Additionally, he wishes to undermine the authority of science, which was becoming a competitor to religion as an explanation of the world.

In an attack on *The Analyst* James Jurin, a fellow of Trinity College, Cambridge, suggested that bishops leave mathematics to mathematicians. Berkeley replied with *A Defence of Free-thinking in Mathematics. In Answer to a Pamphlet of Philalethes Cantabrigiensis, Intituled, Geometry no Friend to Infidelity, or a Defence of Sir Isaac Newton, and the British Mathematicians. Also an Appendix Concerning Mr. Walton's Vindication of the Principle of Fluxions Against the Objections Contained in the Analyst. Wherein it is Attempted to Put this Controversy in such a Light as that Every Reader may be Able to Judge Thereof* (1735). Because, Berkeley supposes, scientists incline toward free thought in religion, he claims a right to introduce liberty into mathematics, which, he asserts, idolatrously follows even the errors of its heroes. As usual, he champions the reverse: freethinking in philosophy (including mathematics) and conservatism regarding religion. In defending *The Analyst* he argues that the metaphysical foundations of the fluxions are abstract ideas. To another critic, the Dublin schoolteacher J. Walton, Berkeley addressed the satiric pamphlet *Reasons for not Replying to Mr. Walton's Full Answer in a Letter to P.T.P.* (1734). These reasons, Berkeley demonstrates, are Walton's own inconsistencies, which already refute him.

Somewhat more interesting is Berkeley's three-volume *The Querist, Containing Several Queries, Proposed to the Consideration of the Public* (1735–1737), which the economist John Maynard Keynes praised as one of the shrewdest essays of its times. Nonetheless, its intentions are sometimes obscured by its consisting entirely of questions. These range from the sarcastic to ones to which the answers so clearly implied that they function more like statements. Generally, however, the form keeps him from completely committing himself. It resembles his sometimes publishing anonymously in order to feel his way cautiously. Archly, he inquires in query 316, "Whether he who only asks asserts? And whether any man can fairly confute the querist?"

The primary subject of his interrogation is potentially explosive: the economic plight of Ireland, oppressed by laws designed to give England the financial advantage even at the cost of ruining such Irish businesses as the wool industry. Politically conservative, he does not expect England to be equitable, nor does he broach the possibility

*Recumbent sculpture of Berkeley by Bruce Joy in the cathedral in Cloyne, Ireland, where Berkeley
was bishop from 1734 until his death in 1753*

of Ireland rebelling. Rather, he applies his linguistic insights to economics. Locke had claimed that paper money owes its value entirely to being backed by precious metals. For Berkeley, however, money is a system of signs, with no such inherent need (just as God's language, the visible world, requires no matter to support it). Since a lack of currency restricted trade, Berkeley advocated an Irish national bank to issue notes that could substitute for coins. Furthermore, he understood that the health of an economy depended on the people's desires, which made them labor and buy. Desire is a languagelike system in that it is learned and bestows meaning on actions. The eighteenth-century tendency was to assume that, as language refers to an external world, so desire comes from people's material needs, which are largely fixed. Berkeley stresses that through fashion, legislation, and other means desire can be manipulated and, with it, the economy. Given a taste of those luxuries that the English considered necessities, the Irish would become more industrious, and the wealth of the nation would increase. Despite going through ten editions, *The Querist* persuaded no authority with the power to turn its hints into government policies. Consequently, Berkeley confined his assault on poverty to his own diocese, where he established a spinning school, a workhouse for

the homeless, and other relief projects. Although he had previously often been an absentee cleric, drawing income without performing services, he was a model bishop, making only rare departures from Cloyne.

One of those departures was in 1737, when, as part of his episcopal duties, he took his seat in the House of Lords in Dublin. His only speech was against an alleged society of "Blasters." Accused of mock Satanism and atheism, these practitioners of religious free speech may have been one of the so-called Hellfire Clubs. Reference to the latter occurs sporadically throughout the century (albeit more at the level of legend than of history). Whatever their reality, stories of them crystallized the epochal fear that Christianity was being taken less seriously. In his pamphlet *A Discourse Addressed to Magistrates and Men in Authority. Occasioned by the Enormous Licence, and Irreligion of the Times* (1738), quoting Plato and Confucius among others, Berkeley says that impiety, since it undermines morality, threatens society; therefore, blasphemers must be punished as criminals.

This advocacy of censorship, along with his founding of a workhouse and his Tory sympathies, made Berkeley an example of eighteenth-century attitudes that nineteenth-century liberals such as Charles Dickens found repugnant. In Dickens's *Great Expectations* (1861) a pint of tar water is poured down the protagonist's throat because "some medicinal beast" had revived its use. The original vogue for this medicine derived from Berkeley's *Siris*, but his advocacy of the concoction was well intentioned. Having heard of its being used in the Carolinas, he experimented with it on his many ailments. Luce speculates that the famine of 1739 also inclined him to seek a remedy for the disease and death surrounding him. At any rate, he found that it alleviated respiratory and digestive problems and concluded that it was an inexpensive preventative and cure for every disease. *Siris* begins with empirical evidence and recipes, then turns to philosophical and theological reasons why tar water might be a panacea. Although the title refers to the Nile River, it denotes primarily a cord or chain, which is related both to the association of ideas that loosely structures the essay and to the Great Chain of Being. According to Berkeley's poem "On Tar," affixed to some copies of *Siris*:

> Causes connected with effects supply
> A golden chain, whose radiant links on high
> Fix'd to the sovereign throne from thence depend
> And reach e'en down to the tar the nether end.

As in alchemy, that is, the bottom reflects the pinnacle. The curative property in the tar is an acid that, Berkeley implies, is liquid flame. According to a host of ancient sources, fire (equated by Berkeley to ether) is the part of creation that is most like God. Although all foods and medicines allegedly provide this element, Berkeley cites Plato to show that tar is the best natural source, since wine, a more famous fiery liquid, is fermented and thus unnatural. He makes the drinking of tar water sound like a Eucharistic partaking of the divine. His ruminations come at last to what some Christian apologists contended were pagan philosophers' discovery of the Holy Trinity. Berkeley adapts his terminology to his new genre, a mixture of practical advice and religious consolation. Formerly, for instance, he emphasized the value of the senses as sources of knowledge. The meditative mood of *Siris*, however, occasions his dwelling instead on true knowledge as a product of thought (previously thought was treated largely in terms of the perceptions it involves). Nonetheless, his basic philosophy remains the same, and it reached its largest audience through this popular work. Probably because of a placebo effect, many cures were attributed to tar water. Public confidence in it grew to the point that physicians had to campaign against Berkeley to protect their incomes. He counterattacked by publishing letters on the subject, including two in his friend Thomas Prior's *Authentic Narrative of the Success of Tar-Water, In Curing a Great Number and Variety of Distempers, With Remarks, And Occasional Papers Relative to the Subject* (1746).

In his last years, aside from defenses of his panacea, Berkeley published other minor works. In 1745 a Jacobite rebellion occasioned a letter to his clergy and another to the Roman Catholics of the diocese, urging that neither support the Stuart cause. The latter epistle was friendlier than Anglican clerics usually were to Catholics. In *The Querist* he had questioned various discriminatory practices against Roman Catholics, notably their being barred from Trinity College Dublin, and suggested that the political charges against them might be largely a misunderstanding. They responded cordially, and he pursued the same line in his pamphlet *A Word to the Wise: or, an Exhortation to the Roman Catholic Clergy of Ireland. By a Member of the Established Church* (1749), which urges Catholic priests to stimulate the industriousness of their parishioners. This advice was considered both well intentioned and inherently insulting. Aside from an abridged version of *Siris*, it was the only one of Berkeley's volumes to have an American edition. Perhaps its advocacy of hard labor appealed to American sentiments, or its stereotyped portrayal of Irish sloth to American prejudices. In 1750 he published anonymously *Maxims Concerning Patriotism*, ascribing it simply to "a Lady." It consists of aphorisms teaching that no one can be a true patriot without all the Christian virtues. He republished it in his last book, *A Miscellany, Containing Several Tracts on Various Subjects* (1752).

To publish a revised edition of *Alciphron*, Berkeley sailed to London, then traveled to Oxford for a long visit with his son George, who was attending the university there. On Sunday evening, 14 January 1753, while listening to his wife read him a sermon, he died suddenly. He was survived by his children: Henry, George, and Julia; four others, Lucia, John, Sarah, and William, predeceased him.

George Berkeley's influence ultimately assumed forms he might barely have recognized. A reader of *Siris*, Thomas De Quincey changes significantly its imagery of low mirroring high and of the world as language:

> The pulses of the heart, the motions of the will, the phantoms of the brain, must repeat themselves in secret hieroglyphics uttered by the flying footsteps. Even the articulate or brutal sounds of the globe must be all so many languages and ciphers that somewhere have their corresponding keys–have their own grammar and syntax; and thus the least things in the universe must be secret mirrors to the greatest.

Berkeley's divine language had become De Quincey's palimpsest of messages, with no explicit reference to God. According to Mary Shelley's preface to her husband's collected works, Percy Bysshe Shelley was a "disciple of the Immaterial Philosophy of Berkeley. This theory gave unity and grandeur to his ideas, while it opened a wide field for his imagination" but without converting him to

Christianity. Samuel Taylor Coleridge named his second son after Berkeley. Nonetheless, in marginalia in a 1744 edition of *Siris,* Coleridge observes that Berkeley should have broken more fully from science. In the margins of another copy of the 1744 *Siris,* William Blake disagrees with it but in ways that show him actually close to Berkeley's basic philosophy. Blake insists that "Knowledge is not by deduction but Immediate by Perception or Sense," which was Berkeley's definition of knowledge. Furthermore, in adding that phenomena stem from the divine imagination, that the common person's perceptions are to be preferred to academicians' cogitations and Christianity to classic philosophy, Blake is (unconsciously or not) seconding Berkeley. By examining how everything known of reality is constructed by the mind, Berkeley's philosophy contributed unintentionally to disparate traditions, including an almost religious Romantic devotion to the imagination. He feared that if the colonies did not adopt the Anglican faith they would eventually rebel, and that if science continued in its established direction, it would undercut religion. His fears were prophetic on both counts, but his singlehanded efforts could not change the course of history. The synthesis of Christianity with the science of the age that he seems to have been attempting was no longer possible—if it had ever been. He deserves credit, however, for joining philosophical originality with a piety so extreme that, according to Pope in the epilogue to his *Satires* (1734–1738), he possessed "ev'ry virtue under Heav'n."

Bibliographies:

Herman Ralph Mead, *A Bibliography of George Berkeley, Bishop of Cloyne,* Library Bulletin, no. 17 (Berkeley: California University Press, 1910);

T. E. Jessop, *A Bibliography of George Berkeley,* with an inventory of Berkeley's manuscript remains by A. A. Luce (New York: Burt Franklin, 1934);

Raymond Clare Archibald, *Bibliography of George Berkeley* (New York: Scripta Mathematica, 1935);

Colin Murray Turbayne, *A Bibliography of George Berkeley, 1933–1962* (Rochester, N.Y.: University of Rochester Press, 1963);

G. Keynes, *A Bibliography of George Berkeley, Bishop of Cloyne: His Works and Critics in the Eighteenth Century* (Oxford: Clarendon Press, 1976).

Biographies:

Joseph Stock, *An Account of the Life of George Berkeley: D.D. late Bishop of Cloyne in Ireland. With notes, Containing Strictures upon His Works* (London: Printed for J. Murray, 1776); revised as *Memoirs of George Berkeley* (London: Printed for J. Murray and R. Faulder, 1784);

Alexander Campbell Fraser, *Life and Letters of George Berkeley, D.D., former Bishop of Cloyne: and an Account of His Philosophy; with Many Writings of Bishop Berkeley Hitherto Unpublished: Metaphysical, Descriptive, Theological* (Oxford: Clarendon Press, 1871);

Benjamin Rand, *Berkeley's American Sojourn* (Cambridge, Mass.: Harvard University Press, 1932);

John Wild, *George Berkeley: A Study of His Life and Philosophy* (Cambridge, Mass.: Harvard University Press, 1936);

Alice Brayton, *George Berkeley in Apulia* (Boston: Merrymount, 1946);

A. A. Luce, *The Life of George Berkeley: Bishop of Cloyne* (London: Thomas Nelson, 1949);

Brayton, *George Berkeley in Newport* (Portland, Me.: Authoessen, 1954);

Edwin S. Gaustad, *George Berkeley in America* (New Haven: Yale University Press, 1979);

David Berman, *George Berkeley: Idealism and the Man* (Oxford & New York: Oxford University Press, 1994).

References:

Gavin W. R. Ardley, *Berkeley's Renovation of Philosophy* (The Hague: Martinus Nijhoff, 1968);

David Malet Armstrong, *Berkeley's Theory of Vision: A Critical Examination of Bishop Berkeley's Essay towards a New Theory of Vision* (New York: Garland, 1988);

Armstrong and Charles Burton Martin, eds., *Locke and Berkeley: A Collection of Critical Essays* (New York: Garland, 1988);

Samuel Bailey, *A Review of Berkeley's Theory of Vision: Designed to Show the Unsoundness of That Celebrated Speculation* (London: J. Ridgway, 1842);

Bertil Belfrage, "A Summary of Berkeley's Metaphysics in a Hitherto Unpublished Berkeleian Manuscript," *Berkeley Newsletter,* 3 (1979): 1–4;

J. Bennett, "Berkeley and God," *Philosophy,* 40 (1965): 207–221;

Berkeley and Modern Problems: The Symposia Read at the Joint Session of the Aristotelian Society and the Mind Association at Dublin, July 10–12th, 1953, Aristotelian Society, Supplementary, no. 27 (London: Harrison, 1953);

David Berman, ed., *George Berkeley: Eighteenth-Century Responses,* 2 volumes (New York: Garland, 1989);

Sigmund Bonk, *"We See God": George Berkeley's Philosophical Theology* (Frankfurt am Main & New York: Peter Lang, 1997);

Harry McFarland Bracken, *The Early Reception of Berkeley's Immaterialism, 1710–1733* (The Hague: Martinus Nijhoff, 1959);

Richard J. Brook, *Berkeley's Philosophy of Science* (The Hague: Martinus Nijhoff, 1973);

Joseph W. Browne, *Berkeley* (New York: St. Martin's Press, 1974);

Browne, *Berkeley's Intellectualism* (Jamaica, N.Y.: St. John's University Press, 1975);

Edmund Burke, *Philosophical Enquiry into the Origin of Our Ideas of the Sublime and Beautiful* (London: Printed for R. and J. Dodsley, 1757);

Stephen R. L. Clark, ed., *Money, Obedience, and Affection: Essays on Berkeley's Moral and Political Thought* (New York & London: Garland, 1989);

Walter E. Creery, ed., *George Berkeley: Critical Assessments,* 3 volumes (London: Routledge, 1991);

Jonathan Dancy, *Berkeley: An Introduction* (Oxford & New York: Basil Blackwell, 1987);

Nagendra Kumar Dey, *Berkeley's Philosophy: A Critical Study* (Calcutta: Sanskrit Pustak Bhandar, 1989);

Willis Doney, ed., *Berkeley on Abstraction and Abstract Ideas,* The Philosophy of George Berkeley, no. 3 (New York: Garland, 1989);

Gale W. Engle and Gabriele Taylor, eds., *Berkeley's Principles of Human Knowledge: Critical Studies* (Belmont, Cal.: Wadsworth, 1968);

John Foster and Howard Robinson, eds., *Essays on Berkeley: A Tercentennial Celebration* (Oxford: Clarendon Press, 1985);

Alexander Campbell Fraser, *Berkeley and Spiritual Realism* (London: Constable, 1908);

E. J. Furlong, "An Ambiguity in Berkeley's *Principles,*" *Philosophical Quarterly,* 14 (1964): 334–344;

Furlong, "Berkeley and the Tree in the Quad," *Philosophy,* 41 (1969): 169–173;

D. Grey, "Berkeley on Other Selves: A Study in Fugue," *Philosophical Quarterly,* 4 (1954): 28–44;

Ingemar Hedenius, *Sensationalism and Theology in Berkeley's Philosophy,* translated by Gerda Wingqvist (Uppsala: Almqvist & Wiksells, 1936);

G. Dawes Hicks, *Berkeley* (New York: Russell & Russell, 1932);

Joseph Maunsell Hone and M. M. Rossi, *Bishop Berkeley: His Life, Writings, and Philosophy,* introduction by William Butler Yeats (London: Faber & Faber, 1931);

Raymond W. Houghton, Berman, and Maureen T. Lapan, *Images of Berkeley* (Dublin: National Gallery of Ireland / Wolfhound, 1986);

Thomas Henry Huxley, *Hume with Helps to the Study of Berkeley: Essays* (New York: Appleton-Century-Crofts, 1986);

Douglas Michael Jesseph, *Berkeley's Philosophy of Mathematics* (Chicago: University of Chicago Press, 1993);

T. E. Jessop, "Berkeley and Contemporary Physics," *Revue Internationale de Philosophie,* 7 (1953): 101–133;

George Alexander Johnston, *The Development of Berkeley's Philosophy* (London: Macmillan, 1923);

J. Kupfer, "Universalization in Berkeley's Rule Utilitarianism," *Revue Internationale de Philosophie,* 28 (1974): 511–531;

A. A. Luce, *Berkeley and Malebranche: A Study in the Origins of Berkeley's Thought* (New York: Garland, 1988);

Luce, *Berkeley's Immaterialism: A Commentary on His* A Treatise Concerning the Principles of Human Knowledge (New York: Russell & Russell, 1968);

Luce, *The Dialectic of Immaterialism: An Account of the Making of the Principles* (London: Hodder & Stoughton, 1963);

Luce, "More Unpublished Berkeley Letters and New Berkeleiana," *Hermathena,* 23 (1933): 25–53;

John Stuart Mill, "Berkeley's Life and Writings" in *Collected Works,* volume 11, edited by J. M. Robson (Toronto: University of Toronto Press, 1978);

Gabriel Moked, *Particles and Ideas: Bishop Berkeley's Corpuscularian Philosophy* (Oxford: Clarendon Press / New York: Oxford University Press, 1988);

Robert G. Muehlmann, *Berkeley's Ontology* (Indianapolis: Hackett, 1990);

Muehlmann, ed., *Berkeley's Metaphysics: Structural, Interpretive, and Critical Essays* (University Park: Pennsylvania State University Press, 1995);

Paul J. Olscamp, *Moral Philosophy of George Berkeley* (The Hague: Martinus Nijhoff, 1970);

George Pitcher, *Berkeley,* Arguments of the Philosophers (London & Boston: Routledge & Kegan Paul, 1977);

J. P. Pittion, Berman, and Luce, "A New Letter by Berkeley to Browne on Divine Analogy," *Mind,* 78 (1969): 375–392;

Karl Popper, "A Note on Berkeley as Precursor of Mach and Einstein," *British Journal for the Philosophy of Science,* 4 (1953): 37–45;

K. Raine, "Berkeley, Blake and the New Age," *Thought,* 51 (1976): 356–376;

Benjamin Rand, *Berkeley and Percival: The Correspondence of George Berkeley, afterwards Bishop of Cloyne, and Sir John Percival, afterwards Earl of Egmont* (Cambridge, Mass.: Harvard University Press, 1914);

Arthur David Ritchie, *George Berkeley: A Reappraisal,* edited by G. E. Davie (Manchester: Manchester University Press / New York: Barnes & Noble, 1967);

Thomasine Rose, *Verbi-voco-visual: The Presence of Bishop Berkeley in* Finnegans Wake (Netherlands: Bellefonte, 1981);

Roberts Schwartz, *Vision: Variations on Some Berkeleian Themes* (Oxford & Cambridge, Mass.: Blackwell, 1994);

Edward Augustus Sillem, *George Berkeley and the Proofs for the Existence of God* (London & New York: Longmans, Green, 1957);

Ernest Sosa, ed., *Essays on the Philosophy of George Berkeley* (Dordrecht & Boston: Reidel, 1987);

George J. Stack, *Berkeley's Analysis of Perception,* Studies in Philosophy, no. 21 (The Hague: Mouton, 1970);

Warren E. Steinkraus, ed., *New Studies in Berkeley's Philosophy* (New York: Holt, Rinehart & Winston, 1966);

Charles Richard Teape, *Berkeleian Philosophy* (Edinburgh: Colston, [1860]);

Ian C. Tipton, *Berkeley: The Philosophy of Immaterialism* (Bristol: Thoemmes, 1974);

Colin Murray Turbayne, "Berkeley's Two Concepts of Mind," *Philosophy and Phenomenological Research,* 20 (1959): 85–92; 22 (1962): 577–580;

Turbayne, ed., *Berkeley: Critical and Interpretive Essays* (Minneapolis: University of Minnesota Press, 1982);

J. O. Urmson, *Berkeley* (Oxford: Oxford University Press, 1982);

David Vernon, *An Essay Towards a New Theory of Vision: Berkeley in the Modern Context* (Dublin: Trinity College Press, 1992);

Godfrey Vesey, *Berkeley: Reason and Experience* (Milton Keynes, U.K.: Open University Press, 1982);

Geoffrey James Warnock, *Berkeley* (Harmondsworth, U.K.: Penguin, 1953);

John Daniel Wild, *George Berkeley: A Study of his Life and Philosophy* (Cambridge, Mass.: Harvard University Press, 1936);

Kenneth P. Winker, *Berkeley: An Interpretation* (Oxford: Oxford University Press, 1989);

J. O. Wisdom, *The Unconscious Origin of Berkeley's Philosophy,* International Psychoanalytical Library, no. 47 (London: Hogarth, 1953);

Theodore A. Young, *Completing Berkeley's Project: Classical vs. Modern Philosophy* (Lanham, Md.: University Press of America, 1985).

Papers:
A large collection of George Berkeley's manuscripts is at the British Museum, and another is at Trinity College, Dublin. Others are at Yale University, the Egmont Papers in the Public Record Office (London), the Diocesan Office in Dublin, the Johnston Collection at Columbia University Library, the Fulham Papers of the Lambeth Palace Library, the British Library, the National Library of Ireland, the O'Conor Papers in the Royal Irish Academy Library, and the Historical Society of Pennsylvania.

Edmund Burke
(12 January 1729 – 9 July 1797)

Keith E. Welsh
Webster University

See also the Burke entry in *DLB 104: British Prose Writers, 1660–1800, Second Series.*

BOOKS: *A Vindication of Natural Society; or, a View of the Miseries and Evils arising to Mankind from every Species of Artificial Society. In a Letter to Lord ****. By a late Noble Writer* (London: Printed for M. Cooper, 1756; revised edition, with a new preface, London: Printed for Robert & James Dodsley & sold by M. Cooper, 1757);

An Account of the European Settlements in America: In Six Parts. I. A Short History of the Discovery of That Part of the World. II. The Manners and Customs of the Original Inhabitants. III. Of the Spanish Settlements. IV. Of the Portuguese. V. Of the French, Dutch, and Danish. VI. Of the English, 2 volumes, attributed to Burke and William Burke (London: Printed for Robert & James Dodsley, 1757);

A Philosophical Enquiry into the Origin of our Ideas of the Sublime and Beautiful (London: Printed for Robert & James Dodsley, 1757); revised and enlarged as *A Philosophical Enquiry into the Origin of our Ideas of the Sublime and Beautiful: With an introductory Discourse Concerning Taste, and several other Additions* (London: Printed for Robert & James Dodsley, 1759; Philadelphia: Printed for S. F. Bradford by J. Watts, 1806);

Observations on a Late State of the Nation (London: Printed for James Dodsley, 1769);

Thoughts on the Cause of the Present Discontents (London: Printed for James Dodsley, 1770);

Mr. Edmund Burke's Speeches at His Arrival at Bristol: And at the Conclusion of the Poll (London: Printed for John Wilkie, 1774);

Speech of Edmund Burke, Esq. On American Taxation, April 19 1774 (London: Printed for James Dodsley, 1775; New York: Printed by James Rivington, 1775);

The Speech of Edmund Burke, Esq. On Moving His Resolutions for Conciliation with the Colonies, March 22, 1775 (London: Printed for James Dodsley, 1775; New York: Printed by James Rivington, 1775);

Edmund Burke; portrait by James Barry, 1771
(Trinity College, Dublin)

The Political Tracts and Speeches of Edmund Burke, Esq. Member of Parliament for the City of Bristol (Dublin: Printed for William Whitestone, 1777);

A Letter from Edmund Burke, Esq; One of the Representatives in Parliament for the City of Bristol, to John Farr, and John Harris, Esqrs. Sheriffs of that City, on the Affairs of America (Bristol: Printed by William Pine, 1777);

Two Letters from Mr. Burke to Gentlemen in the City of Bristol, on the Bills Depending in Parliament Relative to the Trade of Ireland (London: Printed for James Dodsley, 1778);

The Speech of Edmund Burke, Esq.; in the House of Commons, on Friday, the 11th of February, 1780, on His Motion for a Plan of Public Oeconomy; The Outlines of that Plan, and An Addenda, of other curious Particulars [unauthorized edition] (London: Printed for John Hay, 1780); revised as *Speech of Edmund Burke, Esq. Member of Parliament for the City of Bristol, On presenting to the House of Commons (On the 11th of February, 1780) A Plan for the Better Security of the Independence of Parliament, and the Oeconomical Reformation of the Civil and Other Establishments* [authorized edition] (London: Printed by William Bowyer for James Dodsley, 1780);

A Letter from a Gentleman in the English House of Commons, in Vindication of His Conduct, with Regard to the Affairs of Ireland, Addressed to a Member of the Irish Parliament (London: Printed for John Bew, 1780); republished as *A Letter from Edmund Burke, Esq.; in Vindication of His Conduct with Regard to the Affairs of Ireland. Addressed to Thomas Burgh, Esq. Member of Parliament for Athy* (Dublin: Printed by Patrick Byrne, 1780); republished as *A Letter from Edmund Burke, Esq. in Vindication of His Conduct with Regard to the Affairs of Ireland, Addressed to Thomas Burgh, Esq. Member of the Irish Parliament* (London: Printed for John Bew, 1780);

A Speech of Edmund Burke, Esq. at the Guildhall, in Bristol, Previous to the late Election in that City, upon Certain Points Relative to His Parliamentary Conduct (London: Printed for James Dodsley, 1780);

Ninth Report from the Select Committee, Appointed to Take into Consideration the State of the Administration of Justice in the Provinces of Bengal, Bahar, and Orissa (London: Printed by William Strahan for the House of Commons, 1783);

Eleventh Report from the Select Committee, Appointed to Take into Consideration the State of the Administration of Justice in the Provinces of Bengal, Bahar, and Orissa (London: Printed by William Strahan for the House of Commons, 1783);

A Letter from a Distinguished English Commoner, to a Peer of Ireland on the Penal Laws Against Irish Catholics; Previous to the Late Repeal of a Part Thereof, in the Session of the Irish Parliament, Held A.D. 1782 (Dublin: Printed for Matthew Doyle, 1783);

Mr. Burke's Speech, on the 1st December 1783, Upon the Question for the Speaker's Leaving the Chair, in Order for the House to Resolve Itself into a Committee on Mr. Fox's East India Bill (London: Printed for James Dodsley, 1784);

A Representation to His Majesty, Moved in the House of Commons, by the Right Honourable Edmund Burke, and Seconded by the Right Honourable William Windham, on Monday, June 14, 1784, and negatived. With a Preface and Notes (London: Printed for John Debrett, 1784);

Mr. Burke's Speech on the Motion Made for Papers Relative to the Directions for Charging the Nabob of Arcot's Private Debts to Europeans, on the Revenues of the Carnatic, February 28th, 1785. With an Appendix, containing several Documents (London: Printed for James Dodsley, 1785);

Articles of Charge of High Crimes and Misdemeanors, Against Warren Hastings, Esquire, Late Governor General of Bengal, 5 parts, by Burke and others (London: Printed for the House of Commons, 1786);

The Committee, to whom it was referred to prepare Articles of Impeachment against Warren Hastings, Esquire, late Governor General of Bengal, have, pursuant to the Order of the House, prepared several Articles accordingly: Which Articles are as followeth; viz. Articles of Impeachment of High Crimes and Misdemeanors against Warren Hastings, Esquire, late Governor General of Bengal, three parts, by Burke and others (London: Printed for the House of Commons, 1787);

A Letter to Phillip Francis, Esq. From the Right Hon. Edmund Burke, Chairman, . . . Members of the Committee for managing the Impeachment of Mr. Hastings. With Remarks (London: Printed for John Murray & John Stockdale, 1788);

Substance of the Speech of the Right Honourable Edmund Burke, in the Debate on the Army Estimates in the House of Commons, on Tuesday, the 9th Day of February, 1790, Comprehending a Discussion of the Present Situation of Affairs in France (London: Printed for John Debrett, 1790);

Reflections on the Revolution in France, and on the Proceedings in Certain Societies in London Relative to that Event. In a Letter Intended to Have Been Sent to a Gentleman in Paris (London: Printed by Henry Hughes for James Dodsley, 1790; revised, 1790; New York: Printed by Hugh Gaine, 1791);

Lettre de M. Burke à un membre de l'Assemblée nationale de France (Paris: L'Assemblée nationale, Chez Artaud, 1791); English version published as *A Letter from Mr. Burke to a Member of the National Assembly; in Answer to Some Objections to his Book on French Affairs* (London: Printed for James Dodsley, 1791; New York: Printed by Hugh Gaine, 1791);

Two Letters from the Right Honourable Mr. Burke, on the French Revolution: One to the Translator of His Reflections on the Revolution in France: the Other to Captain W——, On the same Subject (London: Printed for H. D. Symonds, 1791);

An Appeal from the New to the Old Whigs, in Consequence of Some Late Discussions in Parliament, Relative to the Reflections on the French Revolution (London: Printed for James Dodsley, 1791; revised, 1791; revised and enlarged, 1791; New York: Printed by Childs & Swaine & sold by Berry & Rogers, New York;

the principal booksellers in Philadelphia; Thomas & Andrews, Boston; and W. P. Young, Charleston, S.C., 1791);

Lettre de M. Burke à M. l'Archevêque d'Aix; Et Réponse de M. l'Archevêque d'Aix, à M. Burke (N.p., 1791);

Lettre de M. Burke, sur les affaires de France et des Pays-Bas; adressée à M. le vicomte de Rivarol. Traduite de l'Anglais (Paris: Chez Denné, 1791);

A Letter from the Right Hon. Edmund Burke, M.P. in the Kingdom of Great Britain, to Sir Hercules Langrishe, Bart. M.P. on the Subject of Roman Catholics of Ireland, and the Propriety of Admitting Them to the Elective Franchise, Consistently with the Principles of the Constitution as Established at the Revolution (Dublin: Printed by Patrick Byrne, 1792; revised edition, London: Printed for John Debrett, 1792);

Mr. Burke's Speech, in Westminster-Hall, on the 18th and 19th of February, 1788, With Explanatory Notes. This Speech Contains What Mr. Burke, in His Letter to the Chairman of the East India Company, Calls "Those Strong Facts Which the Managers For the Commons Have Opened as Offences, And Which Go Seriously to Affect Mr. Shore's Administration, As Acting Chief of the Revenue Board." With a Preface, Containing Mr. Burke's Letter to the Chairman on Sir John Shore's Appointment to the Government of Bengal, and Remarks Upon That Letter (London: Printed for John Debrett, 1792);

Report from the Committee of the House of Commons, appointed to inspect the Lords Journals, in relation to their Proceeding on the Trial of Warren Hastings, Esquire (London: Printed for the House of Commons, 1794);

Substance of the Speech of the Right Honourable Edmund Burke, in the House of Commons, On Friday the 23rd Day of May, 1794, in Answer to Certain Observations on the Report of the Committee of Managers, Representing that Report to have been a Libel on the Judges (London: Printed for John Debrett, 1794);

A Letter from the Right Honourable Edmund Burke to a Noble Lord, on the Attacks Made Upon Him and His Pension, in the House of Lords, by the Duke of Bedford and the Earl of Lauderdale, Early in the present Sessions of Parliament (London: Printed for John Owen & Francis & Charles Rivington, 1796; revised, 1796; revised again, 1796; New York: Printed for T. Allen & A. Drummand, 1796);

Thoughts on the Prospect of a Regicide Peace, in a Series of Letters [unauthorized edition] (London: Printed for John Owen, 1796); revised as *Two Letters Addressed to a Member of the Present Parliament, on the Proposals for Peace with the Regicide Directory of France* [authorized edition] (London: Printed for F. & C. Rivington, 1796; revised, 1796; Philadelphia: Printed for William Cobbett by Bioren & Madan, 1797);

A Letter from the Rt. Honourable Edmund Burke to His Grace The Duke of Portland on the Conduct of the Minority in Parliament. Containing Fifty-Four Articles of Impeachment Against The Rt. Hon. C.J. Fox. From the Original Copy in the Possession of The Noble Duke [unauthorized edition] (London: Printed for the editor & sold by John Owen, 1797; Philadelphia: Printed for James Humphreys, 1797); revised and enlarged as *Two Letters on the Conduct of Our Domestick Parties, With Regard to French Politicks; Including, "Observations on the Conduct of the Minority, in the Session of M.DCC.XCIII." By the Late Right Hon. Edmund Burke* [authorized edition] (London: Printed for Francis & Charles Rivington & sold also by John Hatchard, 1797);

Three Memorials on French Affairs Written in the Years 1791, 1792, and 1793 by the Late Right Hon. Edmund Burke, edited by Walker King and French Laurence (London: Printed for Francis & Charles Rivington and sold also by John Hatchard, 1797);

A Third Letter to a Member of the Present Parliament, on the Proposals for Peace with the Regicide Directory of France. By the Late Right Hon. Edmund Burke, edited by King and Laurence (London: Printed for Francis & Charles Rivington & sold also by John Hatchard, 1797);

Thoughts and Details on Scarcity, Originally Presented to the Right Hon. William Pitt, in the Month of November, 1795. By the Late Right Hon. Edmund Burke, edited, with a preface, by King and Laurence (London: Printed for Francis & Charles Rivington & John Hatchard, 1800);

The Works of the Right Honourable Edmund Burke, 16 volumes, edited by King and Laurence (volume 1, London: Printed by T. Gillet for Francis, Charles & John Rivington & sold also by John Hatchard, 1803; volume 2, London: Printed by Bye & Law for Francis, Charles & John Rivington & sold also by John Hatchard, 1803; volumes 3–8, London: Printed by T. Gillet for Francis, Charles & John Rivington & sold also by John Hatchard, 1803; volumes 9–10, London: Printed by Luke Hansard & Sons for Francis, Charles & John Rivington and sold also by John Hatchard, 1812; volumes 11–12, London: Printed by Luke Hansard & Sons for Francis, Charles & John Rivington & sold also by John Hatchard, 1813; volumes 13–14, London: Printed by Luke Hansard & Sons for Francis, Charles & John Rivington, 1822; volumes 15–16, London: Charles & John Rivington, 1827);

The Catholic Claims, Discussed; in a Letter from the Late Right Hon. Edmund Burke, to the Hon. William Smith, L.L.D. F.R.S. & M.R.I.A. Then a Member of the Irish Parliament; Now Third Baron of the Court of Exchequer in Ireland (Dublin: Printed by Graisberry & Campbell for John Archer, 1807; London: Printed by T. Curson Hansard & sold by Francis, Charles & John Rivington & John Hatchard, 1807);

The Works of Edmund Burke, 12 volumes, revised edition (Boston: Little, Brown, 1865–1867);

A Note-Book of Edmund Burke: Poems, Characters, Essays and Other Sketches in the Hands of Edmund and William Burke, Now Printed for the First Time in Their Entirety, edited by H. V. F. Somerset (Cambridge: Cambridge University Press, 1957);

The Writings and Speeches of Edmund Burke, edited by Paul Langford and others (Oxford: Clarendon Press / New York: Oxford University Press, 1981–)—includes volume 1, *The Early Writings* (1997), edited by T. O. McLoughlin and James T. Boulton; volume 2, *Party, Parliament, and the American Crisis, 1766–1774* (1981), edited by Langford; volume 3, *Party, Parliament, and the American War, 1774–1780* (1996), edited by W. M. Elofson and John A. Woods; volume 5, *India, Madras and Bengal, 1774–1785* (1981), edited by P. J. Marshall; volume 6, *India, the Launching of the Hastings Impeachment, 1786–1788* (1991), edited by Marshall; volume 7, *India, the Hastings Trial, 1789–1794* (2000), edited by Marshall; volume 8, *The French Revolution, 1790–1794* (1990), edited by L. G. Mitchell; and volume 9, part 1, *The Revolutionary War, 1794–1797,* and part 2, *Ireland* (1991); edited by R. B. McDowell.

Editions and Collections: *The Writings and Speeches of Edmund Burke,* Beaconsfield Edition, 12 volumes (Boston: Little, Brown, 1901);

Burke's Speeches: On American Taxation; On Conciliation with America & Letter to the Sheriffs of Bristol, edited, with an introduction and notes, by F. G. Selby (London: Macmillan, 1908; London: Macmillan / New York: St. Martin's Press, 1954);

Edmund Burke: Selected Prose, edited, with an introduction, by Philip Magnus (London: Falcon, 1948);

Burke's Politics: Selected Writings and Speeches of Edmund Burke on Reform, Revolution and War, edited by Ross J. S. Hoffman and Paul Levack (New York: Knopf, 1949);

A Philosophical Enquiry into the Origin of Our Ideas of the Sublime and Beautiful, edited, with an introduction and notes, by James T. Boulton (London: Routledge & Kegan Paul, 1958; Notre Dame, Ind.: University of Notre Dame Press, 1968; revised edition, Oxford: Blackwell, 1987);

Reflections on the Revolution in France and on the Proceedings of Certain Societies in London Relative to That Event, edited by William B. Todd (New York: Rinehart, 1959);

The Philosophy of Edmund Burke: A Selection from His Speeches and Writings, edited, with an introduction, by Louis I. Bredvold and Ralph G. Ross (Ann Arbor: University of Michigan Press, 1960);

Selected Writings of Edmund Burke, edited by W. J. Bate (New York: Modern Library, 1960);

An Appeal from the New to the Old Whigs, edited, with an introduction, by John M. Robson (Indianapolis: Bobbs-Merrill, 1962);

Selected Writings and Speeches: Edmund Burke, edited by Peter J. Stanlis (Garden City, N.Y.: Anchor, 1963);

On the American Revolution: Selected Speeches and Letters, edited by Elliott Robert Barkan (New York: Harper & Row, 1966; republished, with new preface, Gloucester, Mass.: Smith, 1972);

Reflections on the Revolution in France: And on the Proceedings in Certain Societies in London Relative to That Event, edited, with an introduction, by Conor Cruise O'Brien (London & New York: Penguin, 1968);

A Vindication of Natural Society, Or, a View of the Miseries and Evils Arising to Mankind from Every Species of Artificial Society: In a Letter to Lord **** by a Late Noble Writer, edited, with an introduction, by Frank N. Pagano (Indianapolis: Liberty Classics, 1982);

The Political Philosophy of Edmund Burke, compiled by Iain Hampsher-Monk (London: Longman, 1987);

Reflections on the Revolution in France, edited, with an introduction and notes, by J. G. A. Pocock (Indianapolis: Hackett, 1987);

A Philosophical Enquiry into the Origin of Our Ideas of the Sublime and Beautiful, edited, with an introduction, by Adam Phillips (Oxford & New York: Oxford University Press, 1990);

Reflections on the Revolution in France, edited, with an introduction, by L. G. Mitchell (Oxford & New York: Oxford University Press, 1993);

A Philosophical Enquiry into the Origin of Our Ideas of the Sublime and Beautiful, and Other Pre-Revolutionary Writings, edited by David Womersley (London & New York: Penguin, 1998);

The Portable Edmund Burke, edited by Isaac Kramnick (London: Penguin, 1999; New York: Penguin, 1999);

Reflections on the Revolution in France, edited by J. C. D. Clark (Stanford, Cal.: Stanford University Press, 2001).

Eighteenth-century man of letters, politician, and member of Parliament (MP), Edmund Burke is usually regarded as the father of modern political conservatism and an advocate for what has become party politics. His philosophy is revealed not in a series of systematic treatments of philosophical issues but rather in an array of speeches, letters, books, and pamphlets dealing with specific political and social issues of his day, including taxation of the American colonies, the treatment of Ireland, the responsibility of the British Parliament toward India, and the French Revolution. He is variously heralded as a champion of liberty, party politics, limited government, tradition, prescription, and natural law.

Burke was born on 12 January 1729 in Dublin, Ireland Son of a convert to Protestantism, Richard Burke, an attorney of the Irish Court of Exchequer, and Catholic Mary Burke (nee Nagle) of County Cork, Edmund Burke was raised Protestant while his mother remained Catholic, a division that profoundly shaped Burke's ideas on toleration and political suffrage. From 1744 to 1749 he attended Trinity College, Dublin, ostensibly to study law and follow in his father's profession, but at the same time he cultivated an interest in literature, manifested in his editorship of a short-lived periodical, *The Reformer*. In 1750 he journeyed to London to continue his legal education at the Middle Temple.

Eighteenth-century London was a major center of intellectual and literary exchange, and Burke's literary pursuits brought him into the society of such men as Samuel Johnson, Joshua Reynolds, and fellow Irishman Oliver Goldsmith. During the course of the early 1750s Burke abandoned legal study in favor of a literary career. His desire for literary fame led to the production of his early essays on ideas of natural society and aesthetics: works both literary and philosophical.

A Vindication of Natural Society; or, a View of the Miseries and Evils arising to Mankind from every Species of Artificial Society. In a Letter to Lord ****. *By a late Noble Writer* (1756) offers a satiric response—a reductio ad absurdum—to the rationalist philosophy of Henry St. John, first Viscount Bolingbroke, and provides a vision of political society replicating the Hobbesian world of life in nature: nasty, brutish, and short. Burke's satiric method in this work—a direct imitation of Bolingbroke's rationalist style—reveals more about Burke's intellectual style than about his philosophical tenets. Throughout his career Burke eschewed purely theoretical and speculative approaches for practical and applied reasoning, and he brought to bear all the powers of rhetoric and language in defense of his cause. Specifically, Burke responded to Bolingbroke's attack on the irrationality of religion as dangerous and irrational. Using Bolingbroke's own method, Burke demonstrates that every form of political society—despotism, aristocracy, democracy, or mixed—is tyrannical and threatens the very lives of those it is supposed to protect. Consequently, in *A Vindication of Natural Society* Burke satirically suggests humans would be better off with no government at all, an unstated proposition that implicitly explodes the whole project. At

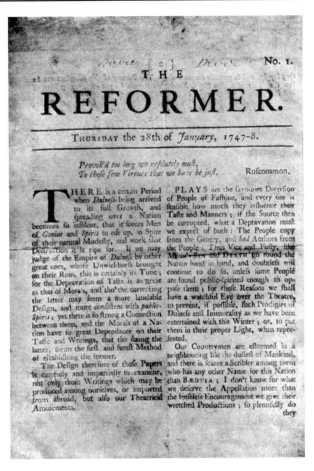

First page of the first issue of the literary periodical that Burke edited while a student at Trinity College, Dublin (from Arthur P. I. Samuels, The Early Life, Correspondence and Writings of The Rt. Hon. Edmund Burke, *1923)*

root, *A Vindication of Natural Society* implies that life in society is the human state of nature—a position Burke developed over the course of his career—and that reasoning from a conjectured prior "state of nature" (as Hobbes, John Locke, Jean-Jacques Rousseau, and Bolingbroke do) is to create a useless fiction that has nothing to do with the immediate political and social condition of humankind. As a literary work, *A Vindication of Natural Society* displays Burke's ability to manipulate voice and image for rhetorical effect—the tools of a statesman and orator as well as an author.

A Vindication of Natural Society was quickly followed by *A Philosophical Enquiry into the Origin of our Ideas of the Sublime and Beautiful* (1757), a work that has its origins in Burke's college days. With this book Burke addressed a major aesthetic topic of the day and established himself in the literary society he sought. While not as sophisticated or significant as Immanuel Kant's *Beobachtungen über das Gefühl des Schönen und Erhabenen* (Observations on the Feeling of the Beautiful and Sublime, 1764), Burke's work nevertheless offers insight into the issues

SPEECH

OF

EDMUND BURKE, Esq.

MEMBER OF PARLIAMENT FOR THE
CITY OF BRISTOL,

On presenting to the House of Commons

(On the 11th of February, 1780)

A PLAN FOR THE BETTER SECURITY OF
THE INDEPENDENCE OF PARLIAMENT,

AND THE

OECONOMICAL REFORMATION OF THE
CIVIL AND OTHER ESTABLISHMENTS.

LONDON.
Printed for J. DODSLEY, in PALL-MALL.
M.DCC.LXXX.

Title page for the printed version of the address in which Burke outlined a program to modernize British government finances and to curb the ability of the king to influence Parliament through the dispensation of sinecures (Beinecke Library, Yale University)

of literary and visual aesthetics in the mid eighteenth century and into his method as thinker and writer. His approach appears systematic and rational: he neatly divides his larger themes into smaller and seemingly exhaustive subcategories, a regular Enlightenment taxonomy of aesthetic categories. But Burke's approach is experiential, not theoretical; his analysis proceeds not from some idealized notion of human feeling but from what he characterizes as actual experience. He seeks to delineate and catalogue emotive responses to events, things, and persons (and posits a fictional universal male in the process). The sublime emerges from anything that overwhelms the senses or suggests potential destruction (with the concomitant desire for self-preservation). The sublime leads humans to contemplate the delight in terror, vastness, obscurity—the uncontainable. The beautiful, by contrast, arises from the knowable and emphasizes human sociability as represented in that which is pleasing, visible, regular, and containable. In this typology the sublime is necessarily masculine and is associated with dominance (and hence government and religion) while the beauti-

ful is feminine and is associated with submission (and hence the domestic and sexual). The topic gives Burke ample range to display his knowledge of classical and British literature, as well as the visual arts, and in this sense *A Philosophical Enquiry into the Origin of our Ideas of the Sublime and Beautiful* can be read as a kind of literary audition, a portfolio piece, which, taken with *A Vindication of Natural Society,* asserts Burke's right to be classed as a literary man.

On 12 March 1757 Burke married Jane Mary Nugent, the daughter of an Irish Catholic doctor, and in the following year they had two children, Richard (born on 9 February), who died in 1794, and Christopher (born on 14 December), who died in infancy. As a man of letters, Burke's finances were at best unstable. Few men could support themselves solely on literary production and conversation, and while Burke was popular with the literary clubs, that was hardly a guarantee of income. In 1757 he had contracted with the booksellers Robert and James Dodsley to write "An Essay Towards an Abridgement of the English History," which he never finished. In his 1964 bibliography of Burke's writings, William B. Todd notes that though a fragment of the first part, extending chronologically up to A.D. 388, was printed circa 1760, the work was not published until it was included in the fifth volume (1803) of *The Works of the Right Honourable Edmund Burke* (1803–1827), with the history extending up to A.D. 1216. In 1758 Burke undertook the editorship of *The Annual Register,* a yearbook of politics and literature published by Robert Dodsley, which Burke edited until 1765. Both projects served to prepare Burke for his ensuing political career, in which he displayed an impressive command of history and a meticulous mastery of economic and social detail. These qualities gave him the authority to support his varying (and sometimes seemingly self-contradictory) positions in parliamentary debate over the next thirty years.

Burke's political career formally began in 1759 when William Gerard Hamilton, chief secretary for Ireland, employed him as his personal secretary, a position Burke held until 1764, and which took him back to Ireland twice. While in Ireland, Burke began his "Tracts relative to the Laws against Popery in Ireland" (not published until 1813 when it was included in volume 12 of his collected works), a work that deals with the relationship of the people to the legislature, and with higher principles of natural law handed down from God. In this work Burke contends that any law that persecutes a majority of the people cannot be a law, for the law is the expression of the people through its legislature. Far from being a democrat, Burke sees the government as holding a trust for the people with an eye on their greater good that they may not themselves perceive.

Pages from the 1780 Dublin edition of A Letter from Edmund Burke, Esq.; in Vindication of His Conduct with Regard to the Affairs of Ireland, *with Burke's holograph corrections (Boston Athenaeum)*

That being a given, the law must proceed on the bases of utility and equity, and in Burke's analysis the Popery laws (laws prohibiting Catholics from voting, holding political office, and otherwise curtailing basic rights) are neither useful nor equitable. Such arguments were highly unpopular in anti-Catholic Whig England (which explains why Burke did not publish his tracts), but they reveal Burke's strong-minded willingness to argue for what he believed to be just. He returned to this cause more publicly in the last years of his life.

After Burke separated from Hamilton in 1764, he remained in London, editing the *Annual Register* and mixing in political and intellectual circles. On 17 July 1765 he accepted the post of private secretary to Charles Watson-Wentworth, the second Marquis of Rockingham, at that time First Lord of the Treasury. Through the patronage of the marquis, a Whig leader, Burke was elected to Parliament for Wendover on 23 December. Burke remained in Parliament until 1794, representing various constituencies (chiefly "pocket boroughs," election districts that were controlled by, or "in the pocket" of, major landowners). His political philosophy, as such, emerges from his experience as a politician, not from abstract speculation upon the human condition, an approach Burke deeply distrusted. His

interests focused on real people in actual circumstances and his guiding light was the British Constitution.

The constraints that run through Burke's political writings include a veneration of tradition and the inherited wisdom of the past as articulated in the British Constitution; a general commitment to maintain the economic status quo with an emphasis on the protection of landed property as this has acquired authority through long usage (prescription); a strong faith in God and religion as guarantors of a general humanitarian compassion and civility; an abhorrence to sudden, radical change, but also a willingness to reform gently, but thoroughly, when reform would improve government for the people. His thought shows the influence of Hobbes and Locke, though he distrusts their abstractions, particularly the abstract state of nature, and shares Adam Smith's faith in the economic marketplace as the arena for the gradual improvement of the human condition, though Burke was quick to guard the prerogatives of property in that marketplace.

Burke's major writings emerge from his responses to the central issues that he considered during his career: the treatment of the American colonies and Ireland, British responsibility to India (and his subsequent impeachment of and prosecution of Warren Hastings, who had been governor general of India for the East India Company), and the nature and ramifications of the French Revolution, which he spent the last years of his life denouncing. Behind these specifics is a general concern to protect the tradition of the British Constitution as a bulwark of liberty.

Burke's earliest significant political work is *Thoughts on the Cause of the Present Discontents* (1770), which touches on a range of affairs troubling Parliament, including the unrest in the American colonies, the conflict over the election and seating of John Wilkes, and a general Whig resentment of the growing power of George III. In *Thoughts on the Cause of the Present Discontents* Burke articulates a model of the political party, "a body of men united for promoting by their joint endeavors the national interest upon some particular principle in which they are all agreed." Underpinning this model is Burke's concept of the duties of political representation. The MP must be responsive to his constituents, but his job is not to represent their narrow interests alone, but rather to weigh competing interests in the quest for a greater national good. In Parliament, party affiliation allows for a give and take of interests and aims to keep the individual representative focused on the larger goals of government, always with the eye to the national good. While Burke remained a loyal party member and servant during his entire career, he did not seek to create or to promote a two-party system of government. In fact, his adherence to his views on the French Revolution led to a split in the Whig Party. For Burke, party was an expedient method to counterbalance the powers of the Crown, a means of controlling power rather than creating it.

Burke is justly famous for his support of the American colonies prior to the American Revolution. However, this support needs to be seen as a response to specific circumstances rather than a commitment to abstract rights. Burke did not seek direct representation from the colonies in Parliament. Rather, he sought to maintain the economic advantages of the colonies for Britain while also recognizing that at the distance of an ocean, the colonies naturally desired internal autonomy and ought not be taxed or harassed directly when there were in existence other means to extract their submission to the British Parliament. The larger issue that underpins both the *Speech of Edmund Burke, Esq. On American Taxation, April 19 1774* (published January 1775) and *The Speech of Edmund Burke, Esq. On Moving His Resolutions for Conciliation with the Colonies, March 22, 1775* (published May 1775) is the question of liberty and the British Constitution. If the court of George III could contravene the liberty of citizens in a distant colony through arbitrary taxation supported by military force, what guarantee did the home country have? Burke urged

Parliament to abandon the newly imposed taxes that the Americans resented, and to return to the former model of relationship, including the Navigation Acts and payments from the colonial legislatures to the Crown. He thus argues from history and tradition rather than considering the abstract question of whether or not Parliament has the right to tax the colonies. Indeed, he does not deny that the right may be presumed, but suggests that it should be judged by its practicality rather than its theoretical soundness. If citizens refuse to pay the taxes, the theoretical right is useless.

In 1774 Burke stood for open election for one of the seats from Bristol, a major port and manufacturing center. Although he was elected MP for Bristol on 11 October of that year, his relationship with the Bristol constituency was a rocky one, since he refused to act within what he saw as their narrow interests. He was criticized for his stand on the American question and on free trade with Ireland, as both were seen as contrary to the good of Bristol. This state of affairs produced some of his most impassioned writing and speaking on the duty of a representative and the function of Parliament, the most significant being *A Letter from Edmund Burke, Esq; One of the Representatives in Parliament for the City of Bristol, to John Farr, and John Harris, Esqrs. Sheriffs of that City, on the Affairs of America* (1777), *Two Letters from Mr. Burke to Gentlemen in the City of Bristol, on the Bills Depending in Parliament Relative to the Trade of Ireland* (1778) and his 6 September 1780 speech at the Bristol Guildhall. Burke considered Parliament as the deliberative body for the entire British empire, responsible for the happiness of all its people; members therefore had to consider the good of the entire empire, not just that of their commercial interests, and did not reelect Burke in 1780. To keep Burke in Parliament, Rockingham found for him the pocket borough of Malton, where he was elected 7 December 1780. Hereafter, Burke represented only pocket boroughs, though this circumstance did not diminish his influence in Parliament.

In 1780 Burke began his quest to reform the patronage system of the Crown with his *Speech of Edmund Burke, Esq. Member of Parliament for the City of Bristol, On presenting to the House of Commons (On the 11th of February, 1780) A Plan for the Better Security of the Independence of Parliament, and the Oeconomical Reformation of the Civil and Other Establishments.* Burke's approach in this work, which is supremely calm and reasonable, is variously interpreted as either a high-minded, rational plan to streamline and make more efficient the financial apparatus of the Crown and Parliament or as a move in the name of reason to contain the ability of the Crown to dispense influence through its disposition of sinecures. It served to accomplish both goals when a scaled-down

Broadside by James Gillray (20 May 1788) showing Burke driving the Whigs into "the Slough of Despond" through his determination to impeach Warren Hastings for Hastings's actions as governor general of India. The man with the blunderbuss on top of the carriage is the politician Charles James Fox.

version was passed into law in 1782 during a brief Rockingham ministry, and is part and parcel of the general Whig interest in limiting the power of the Crown.

During the 1780s the governance of India dominated Burke's attentions, revealing a shift from the more narrow concern of party politics that dominated his thought and action in the 1770s to a broader arena of human justice and responsibility that transcended the merely political. Scholars who view Burke as a natural-law thinker focus on this project as the major manifestation of Burke's faith in and defense of natural law.

Eighteenth-century India was governed by a private corporation, the East India Company, and its government was run as a capitalist enterprise; the company extracted wealth from the country, often through violent means, and exported it to Britain. The new wealth had the power to buy influence and titles in Britain, potentially changing the course of domestic politics and posing a threat to the traditional power base of the landed order, and consequently to the British Constitution, at least in Burke's assessment. The principle of government represented by the East India Company was further anathema, since it was government in the best interests of the governors rather than the people. Both of these factors deeply worried Burke, and, begin-

ning in 1781, he formally undertook the issue in Parliament, serving on the Select Committee of the Commons appointed to consider colonial abuses in India (writing two of its published reports) and subsequently bringing about the impeachment of Governor General Hastings by the House of Commons and managing his prosecution before the House of Lords (from 1786 to 1794). At the opening of the prosecution before the House of Lords in 1788, he delivered a four-day speech for the prosecution, and he fervently pursued the issue as his health and strength allowed until the trial ended.

For Burke, Hastings became the representative of everything bad and dangerous in the British government of India. Since Hastings had broken no law established by Parliament, Burke had to appeal in his prosecution to higher ideals of justice, governmental responsibility, and common humanity. His Indian writings reveal a passionate humanity that transcends mere political pragmatism. He used the impeachment and trial as theater for dramatizing the true ideals of colonial government and the responsibilities of the governors. The conqueror, Burke argued, has a moral responsibility to the conquered and must govern in their best interests, which the East India Company had not done.

Furthermore, the new government has a responsibility to recognize and accept the existing governmental institutions since they reflect the traditional constitution of the nation. Imposing an arbitrary system is wrong because it neglects the needs and desires of the governed and because no one has the right to such arbitrary power.

Burke hoped to be remembered for his work and writings on the India question. However, he is most famous for his writings on the French Revolution, particularly *Reflections on the Revolution in France, and on the Proceedings in Certain Societies in London Relative to that Event. In a Letter Intended to Have Been Sent to a Gentleman in Paris* (1790). This work, as the full title indicates, is cast in the form of a letter to a young French gentleman, recounting in impassioned detail why the French Revolution is essentially different from the British Glorious Revolution of 1688 and why Burke cannot support the French Revolution, even though he had been a friend to the American revolutionaries. It represents Burke at his most traditional, conservative, and antitheoretical. Burke's antirevolutionary stance, which came as a surprise to many of his friends and colleagues, divided the Whig Party, essentially isolating Burke in the rump of the party, and spawned a plethora of responses—a veritable pamphlet war—the most notable being Mary Wollstonecraft's *A Vindication of the Rights of Men, in a Letter to the Right Honourable Edmund Burke Occasioned by His Reflections on the Revolution in France* (1790), Thomas Paine's *The Rights of Man* (1791), and James MacIntosh's *Vindiciae Gallicae* (1791).

In Burke's view the French Revolution was not just a change in government but a change in fundamental "sentiments, manners, and moral opinions"—the very fabric that connected people and allowed for social intercourse. Burke reiterates his condemnation of abstracted states of Nature and abstract conceptions of rights, particularly the Rousseauian natural man which was at the heart of Revolutionary doctrine. He concedes that all people should have equal rights, but not to equal things, and that a governmental order is necessary to preserve these rights: rights, in fact, flow from an orderly, governed society, not from a state of nature. Burke argues that people are by nature social beings, that they have their life and death in a social order, and that they must therefore respect the inheritance of that order as the inheritance of wisdom. Indeed, an individual's reason is so faulty that he or she must frequently be checked by external constraints (social and legal) for the good of both society and the individual. Moreover, Burke contends that humans have a "just prejudice" that leads them to venerate their leaders, families, homes, and religion, and such prejudice should be cherished as part of their humanity.

Burke is more concerned with tradition and the preservation of property as a social concept than he is with individual rights and the social contract. In Burke's view the unequal distribution of property—that is, land and agricultural wealth—is the source of much social good. Those who own the land have the leisure to study, think, and lead the nation, and have the duty to watch out for the best interests of their tenants, retainers, and dependents. Since property is obviously a limited resource, not everyone can own it, and since it is vulnerable to insurrection, the State must zealously guard it, and guard against sources of newer, but less stable, wealth. However, property owners must guard the civil rights of those below them: the model is, in short, paternalistic and communal.

In Burke's model of paternalism the Church and the State together are responsible for preserving and perpetuating the common good. The Church provides education and a model of behavior for all, and the State works to protect the inherited order from the behavior of rash individuals so as to perpetuate the gradual improvement of the human condition. Burke articulates this concept most succinctly when he offers his vision of the social contract:

> Society is . . . a contract. . . . It is a partnership in all science; a partnership in all art; a partnership in every virtue and in all perfection. As the ends of such a partnership cannot be obtained in many generations, it becomes a partnership not only between those who are living, but between those who are living, those who are dead, and those who are to be born. Each contract of each particular state is but a clause in the great primeval contract of eternal society, linking the lower with the higher natures, connecting the visible and invisible world, according to a fixed compact sanctioned by the inviolable oath which holds all physical and all moral natures, each in their appointed place.

Burke's major concern was to prevent the ideals of the French Revolution from being exported to Great Britain, and his commitment to this cause forced him to break with the leader of the Whig opposition, Charles James Fox (a vocal supporter of the Revolution), and throw his support to the Tory government of William Pitt the Younger, splitting the Whig Party, some of whom left Fox in the opposition and joined the Pitt coalition. This division was certainly painful to Burke, particularly as he was charged with inconsistency and bad faith, having supported the American Revolution some fifteen years earlier.

Burke addresses these charges of inconsistency in *An Appeal from the New to the Old Whigs, in Consequence of*

Some Late Discussions in Parliament, Relative to the Reflections on the French Revolution (1791). He reviews his career as MP and casts his actions in relation to the mixed Constitution of Great Britain, supporting the rights of each part against encroachments of another. He insists that his actions must be judged within the context of specific circumstances rather than against some abstract ideal of behavior. His consistency emerges in his commitment to the Constitution in diverse situations and not in a commitment to an ideal of rights abstracted from practical circumstance.

In the last years of his life Burke's activities and writings followed three intertwined strands: the conclusion of his prosecutions of Hastings for violations of the rights of Indians, renewed attempts to influence the British and Irish Parliaments to expand the rights of Irish Catholics, and increasingly strident attacks on the French Revolution. The Hastings prosecution concluded in 1794 and coincided with the end of Burke's parliamentary career; to Burke's dismay Hastings was acquitted by the House of Lords in 1795. For a time Burke had great hopes for improving the conditions for Catholics in Ireland, writing a letter to Sir Hercules Langrishe, an Irish MP (published in 1792), arguing that an increase in rights for Catholics would benefit all of Ireland as well as working fervently behind the scenes to influence the Pitt administration. These hopes were dashed with the recall of Burke's friend and Whig leader, William Wentworth, second Earl Fitzwilliam, from the post of lord lieutenant of Ireland in 1795. Burke's campaign against the French Revolution continued with *Two Letters Addressed to a Member of the Present Parliament, on the Proposals for Peace with the Regicide Directory of France* (1796) as well as several other letters and documents. Burke's beloved son, Richard, died in 1794, dashing Burke's hopes for a legacy and leaving him desolate. In that year he accepted a royal pension of £1,200 and retired to Beaconsfield, his estate. The pension provoked attacks from the Whig lords Francis Russell, fifth Duke of Bedford, and James Maitland, eighth Earl of Lauderdale, which Burke ably and brilliantly refuted in *A Letter from the Right Honourable Edmund Burke to a Noble Lord, on the Attacks Made Upon Him and His Pension, in the House of Lords, by the Duke of Bedford and the Earl of Lauderdale, Early in the present Sessions of Parliament* (1796). In this letter Burke turns his assailants' attack on royal patronage against the attackers, themselves major recipients of the beneficence of the Crown. It is of a piece with the rhetorical force of the early *A Vindication of Natural Society,* and it reflects Burke's lifelong commitment to the art and power of political rhetoric.

In his last years Burke suffered declining health but maintained his lively correspondence. He died, probably of tuberculosis of the stomach, on 9 July 1797.

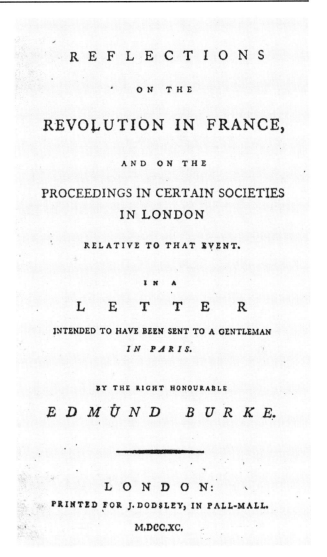

Title page for Burke's best-known work, in which he explains his reasons for opposing the French Revolution and the spread of revolutionary ideals to England (New York Public Library)

Tradition suggests he may have been converted to the Roman Catholic Church before his death; however, he received an Anglican burial.

Taken as a whole, Edmund Burke's writings and career reveal a mind deeply engaged with the political and social issues of his age at a practical, detailed level. In every case, as much as possible, Burke attempted to examine the circumstances before making a judgment or taking action, and his close observation of human nature contributed to his prescience in forecasting the atrocities of the French Revolution (though some scholars attribute this accurate prediction to luck). Burke was committed to concepts of tradition, prejudice, and government as guarantors of freedom and rights. He respected but distrusted power and constantly advocated that power be held in check within traditional institutions. In these terms he should be seen as a conservative, but in his commitment to expanding individual rights within the context of established social order, he is a liberal communitarian.

Letters:

The Correspondence of Edmund Burke, 10 volumes, edited by Thomas Copeland and others (Cambridge: Cambridge University Press / Chicago: University of Chicago Press, 1958–1978);

Selected Letters of Edmund Burke, edited, with an introduction, by Harvey C. Mansfield Jr. (Chicago: University of Chicago Press, 1984).

Bibliographies:

William B. Todd, *A Bibliography of Edmund Burke,* The Soho Bibliographies, no. 17 (London: Hart-Davis, 1964);

Clara I. Gandy and Peter J. Stanlis, *Edmund Burke: A Bibliography of Secondary Studies to 1982* (New York: Garland, 1983);

Leonard W. Cowie, *Edmund Burke, 1729–1797: A Bibliography,* Bibliographies of British Statesmen, no. 19 (Westport, Conn. & London: Greenwood Press, 1994).

Biographies:

Robert Bisset, *The Life of Edmund Burke, Comprehending an Impartial Account of His Literary and Political Efforts and a Sketch of the Conduct and Character of His Most Eminent Associates, Coadjutors, and Opponents* (London: Printed by George Cawthorn and sold by W. J. & J. Richardson, 1798);

James Prior, *Memoir of the Life and Character of the Right Hon. Edmund Burke: With Specimens of His Poetry and Letters and an Estimate of His Genius and Talents Compared with Those of His Great Contemporaries* (London: Printed for Baldwin, Cradock & Joy, 1824; Philadelphia: A. Small, 1825);

John Morley, *Edmund Burke: A Historical Study* (London: Macmillan, 1867; New York: Harper, 1879);

Robert H. Murray, *Edmund Burke: A Biography* (London & New York: Oxford University Press, 1931);

Philip Magnus, *Edmund Burke: A Life* (London: Murray, 1939; New York: Russell & Russell, 1973);

Carl B. Cone, *Burke and the Nature of Politics,* 2 volumes (Lexington: University of Kentucky Press, 1957, 1964);

Alice P. Miller, *Edmund Burke: A Biography* (New York: Allwyn, 1976);

Isaac Kramnick, *The Rage of Edmund Burke: Portrait of an Ambivalent Conservative* (New York: Basic Books, 1977);

Stanley Ayling, *Edmund Burke: His Life and Opinions* (London: Murray, 1988; New York: St. Martin's Press, 1988);

Russell Kirk, *Edmund Burke: A Genius Reconsidered* (Peru, Ill.: Sherwood Sugden, 1988; revised edition, Wilmington, Del.: Intercollegiate Studies Institute, 1997);

Conor Cruise O'Brien, *The Great Melody: A Thematic Biography and Commented Anthology of Edmund Burke* (Chicago: University of Chicago Press, 1992; London: Sinclair-Stevenson, 1992);

Nicholas K. Robinson, *Edmund Burke: A Life in Caricature* (New Haven: Yale University Press, 1996);

F. P. Lock, *Edmund Burke* (Oxford: Clarendon Press / Oxford & New York: Oxford University Press, 1998–)—includes volume 1, *1730–1784.*

References:

Steven Blakemore, *Burke and the Fall of Language: The French Revolution as a Linguistic Event* (Hanover, N.H.: Published for Brown University Press by University Press of New England, 1988);

Blakemore, *Intertextual War: Edmund Burke and the French Revolution in the Writings of Mary Wollstonecraft, Thomas Paine, and James Mackintosh* (Madison, N.J.: Fairleigh Dickinson University Press / London: Associated University Presses, 1997);

Stephen H. Browne, *Edmund Burke and the Discourse of Virtue* (Tuscaloosa: University of Alabama Press, 1993);

Francis P. Canavan, *Edmund Burke: Prescription and Providence* (Durham, N.C.: Carolina Academic Press/ Claremont Institute for the Study of Statesmanship and Political Philosophy, 1987);

Canavan, *The Political Economy of Edmund Burke: The Role of Property in His Thought* (New York: Fordham University Press, 1995);

Canavan, *The Political Reason of Edmund Burke* (Durham, N.C.: Duke University Press, 1960);

Gerald W. Chapman, *Edmund Burke: The Practical Imagination* (Cambridge, Mass.: Harvard University Press, 1967);

Alfred Cobban, *Edmund Burke and the Revolt against the Eighteenth Century,* second edition (London: Allen & Unwin, 1960; New York: Barnes & Noble, 1960);

Ian Crowe, ed., *Edmund Burke: His Life and Legacy* (Dublin: Four Courts Press, 1997);

Michel Fuchs, *Edmund Burke, Ireland, and the Fashioning of Self* (Oxford: Voltaire Foundation, 1996);

Tom Furniss, *Edmund Burke's Aesthetic Ideology: Language, Gender, and Political Economy in Revolution* (Cambridge & New York: Cambridge University Press, 1993);

Paul Hindson and Tim Gray, *Burke's Dramatic Theory of Politics* (Aldershot, U.K.: Avebury, 1988);

C. B. Macpherson, *Burke* (Oxford: Oxford University Press, 1980; New York: Hill & Wang, 1980);

Harvey C. Mansfield, *Statesmanship and Party Government: A Study of Burke and Bolingbroke* (Chicago: University of Chicago Press, 1965);

Frank O'Gorman, *Edmund Burke: His Political Philosophy* (Bloomington: Indiana University Press, 1973; London: Allen & Unwin, 1973);

Charles Parkin, *The Moral Basis of Burke's Political Thought: An Essay* (Cambridge: Cambridge University Press, 1956; New York: Russell & Russell, 1968);

J. G. A. Pocock, *Virtue, Commerce, and History: Essays on Political Thought and History, Chiefly in the Eighteenth Century* (Cambridge: Cambridge University Press, 1985);

Christopher Reid, *Edmund Burke and the Practice of Political Writing* (Dublin: Gill & Macmillan / New York: St. Martin's Press, 1985);

Peter J. Stanlis, *Edmund Burke: The Enlightenment and Revolution,* foreword by Russell Kirk (New Brunswick, N.J.: Transaction, 1991);

Stanlis, *Edmund Burke and the Natural Law* (Ann Arbor: University of Michigan Press, 1958);

Stanlis, ed., *The Relevance of Edmund Burke* (New York: Kenedy, 1964).

Papers:
Edmund Burke's papers are located principally in the Fitzwilliam Mss. Collection (formerly known as Wentworth Woodhouse Mss.) in Sheffield Central City Library; in the Fitzwilliam Mss. Collection (formerly known as the Milton Mss.) in the Northhamptonshire Record Office, Lamport Hall; and the British Library, London.

Joseph Butler

(18 May 1692 – 16 June 1752)

Terry G. Harris
Louisiana State University at Shreveport

BOOKS: *Fifteen Sermons preached at the Rolls Chapel* (London: Printed by W. Botham for James & John Knapton, 1726; revised, with a preface, 1729); enlarged as *Fifteen Sermons preached at the Rolls Chapel: To Which Is Added Six Sermons Preached on Publick Occasions* (London: Printed for John & Paul Knapton, 1749);

The Analogy of Religion, Natural and Revealed, to the Constitution and Course of Nature. To Which Are Added Two Brief Dissertations: I. Of Personal Identity II. Of the Nature of Virtue (London: Printed for James, John & Paul Knapton, 1736);

A Sermon Preached Before the Incorporated Society for the Propagation of the Gospel in Foreign Parts at their anniversary meeting in the Parish-Church of St. Mary-le-Bow, on Friday, February 16, 1738–9 (London: Printed for John & Paul Knapton, 1739);

A Sermon Preached before the Right Honourable the Lord-Mayor, the Court of Aldermen, the Sheriffs, and the Governors of the several Hospitals of the City of London, at the Parish Church of St. Bridget, on Monday in Easter-week, 1740 (London: Printed for John & Paul Knapton, 1740);

A Sermon Preached Before the House of Lords, in the Abbey-Church of Westminster, on Friday, Jan. 30, 1740–41. Being the Day appointed to be observed as the Day of the Martyrdom of King Charles I (London: Printed for John & Paul Knapton, 1741);

A Sermon Preached in the Parish-Church of Christ-Church, London; On Thursday May the 9th 1745. Being the Time of the Yearly Meeting of the Children Educated in the Charity-Schools, in and about the Cities of London and Westminster. To which is annexed, an Account of the Society for promoting Christian Knowledge (London: Printed by John Oliver & sold by Benjamin Dod, 1745);

A Sermon preached before the House of Lords in the Abbey Church of Westminster, on Thursday, June 11, 1747, being the anniversary of His Majesty's happy accession to the throne (London: Printed for John & Paul Knapton, 1747);

Joseph Butler (National Portrait Gallery, London)

A Sermon Preached before His Grace Charles Duke of Richmond, Lenox, and Aubigny, president; and the Governors of the London Infirmary, for the relief of sick and diseased persons, especially manufacturers, and seamen in merchant-service, &c. At the Parish-church of St. Lawrence-Jewry, on Thursday, March 31, 1748 (London: Printed by Henry Woodfall, 1748);

A Charge deliver'd to the clergy, at the primary visitation of the diocese of Durham, in the year, MDCCLI (Durham: Printed by Isaac Lane & sold by J. Richardson, 1751);

Some Remains (Hitherto Unpublished) of Joseph Butler, L.L.D. Sometime Lord Bishop of Durham, edited, with a preface, by Edward Steere (London: Gilbert & Rivingtons, 1853).

Editions and Collections: *Six Sermons Preached on Publick Occasions* (London: Printed for John & Paul Knapton, 1749);

Six Sermons on Moral Subjects: A Sequel to the Three Sermons on Human Nature, edited, with a preface, by W. Whewall (Cambridge: Deighton, 1848);

The Sermons and Remains of the Right Reverend Father in God, Joseph Butler, D.C.L., Late Lord Bishop of Durham, edited, with a memoir and indices, by Edward Steere (London: Bell & Daldy, 1862);

The Works of Joseph Butler, D.C.L. Sometime Lord Bishop of Durham: Divided into Sections; with Some Occasional Notes, Also Prefatory Matter, 2 volumes, edited by W. E. Gladstone (Oxford: Clarendon Press, 1896; republished, with a new introduction by R. G. Frey, Bristol: Thoemmes Press, 1995);

The Works of Bishop Butler, 2 volumes, edited by J. H. Bernard (London & New York: Macmillan, 1900).

The youngest of eight children, Joseph Butler was born 18 May 1692 at Wantage, Berkshire. His father, Thomas Butler, had been a successful and respected linen draper but was retired at the time of Joseph's birth. A Presbyterian, Thomas Butler decided early to educate his youngest son for the Presbyterian ministry. He first attended the free grammar school at Wantage, where he received a basic classical education under the direction of the Reverend Philip Barton, an Anglican clergyman. He then was sent to a Dissenting academy operated by Samuel Jones, first at Gloucester and then at Tewkesbury. The academy enjoyed a high reputation, and among Butler's contemporaries were several individuals who later distinguished themselves in public and religious life, both Anglican and Dissenting. The close friendship Butler established with Thomas Secker, who later became archbishop of Canterbury, is especially notable.

Butler's progress at the academy was remarkable, and he demonstrated a natural affinity for philosophy and metaphysics, as evidenced by his earliest writings. In 1713, while at Tewkesbury, he began corresponding with Dr. Samuel Clarke, author of *A Demonstration of the Being and Attributes of God* (1705), the third edition of which had been published two years earlier. For reasons that are not totally clear, Butler carried on his correspondence anonymously, identifying himself only as "a gentleman from Gloucester" and prevailing upon his friend Secker to deliver the letters to the post office in Gloucester and bring back Clarke's replies. Over the next several years Butler and Clarke corresponded with

each other, Butler admitting his desire to seek out truth but acknowledging his dissatisfaction with the explanations Clarke had provided as demonstrative proof of the existence of God. Butler was never completely pleased with Clarke's responses to the objections, but Clarke was so impressed with the candor and sincerity of the inquiries that he included the correspondence in the fourth (1716) and subsequent editions of his work. The Butler-Clarke correspondence is included in J. H. Bernard's edition of Butler's works (1900).

Near the end of his time at Tewkesbury, Butler decided to leave the Presbyterians and join the Church of England. Few specifics are known, but some reports indicate that his father enlisted the aid of several Presbyterian ministers in an effort to dissuade him. However, when it became clear that Butler's resolve was firm, his father consented and allowed him to enter Oriel College, Oxford, as a commoner on 17 March 1714. He was not particularly impressed or stimulated by the intellectual life of Oxford, and he expressed his dissatisfaction in letters to Dr. Clarke, who was becoming his confidant and friend. Having come from a progressive Dissenting academy with a distinguished academic reputation, it is no wonder Butler found little to excite him at Oxford, where the main intellectual activity seemed to be a defense of the thought of Aristotle against the criticisms of John Locke. At one point in 1717 Butler even considered transferring to Cambridge, but he stayed at Oxford after learning he would lose academic credit for the terms he had already completed.

On 16 October 1718 Butler took his B.A. degree. Edward Talbot, a close friend and Oriel Fellow, had helped persuade Butler to embark on an ecclesiastical career in the Anglican church, and ten days after graduating from Oxford he was ordained a deacon by Bishop William Talbot of Salisbury, his friend's father, who also ordained him a priest on 21 December 1718. Bishop Talbot appointed Butler preacher at the Rolls Chapel in London in 1719, a position he held until 1726.

Edward Talbot died of smallpox in December 1720, but he had recommended Butler to his father. Through the patronage of Bishop Talbot and with the support of Dr. Clarke, Butler became prebendary of Salisbury in 1721, and in 1722 he was appointed rector of Haughton le Skerne in Durham, after Talbot became bishop of Durham in October 1721. Secker, Butler's close friend from their days at Tewkesbury, had followed Butler in taking Anglican orders, being ordained by Bishop Talbot in 1723. Secker married Catherine Becker, sister of the bishop of Gloucester, in 1725, and after his marriage Edward Talbot's widow, Mary, and daughter, Catherine, came to live with the couple. That same year Secker prevailed upon the bishop to transfer

A deed of gift by Butler in the parish books at Stanhope, where he served as minister from 1725 to 1736
(from William Morley Egglestone, Stanhope Memorials of Bishop Butler, 1878)

Butler to the wealthy benefice of Stanhope in Durham. In accepting this appointment Butler retired from London life to country living, resigning his appointment at the Rolls Chapel the following year.

Upon resigning, Butler published a collection of sermons selected from the many he had delivered during his eight years at the chapel. His *Fifteen Sermons preached at the Rolls Chapel* (1726) has come to be regarded as his most important contribution to ethics. In the preface he wrote for the second edition of the collection in 1729, Butler suggests that the sermons were chosen randomly as typical representatives of his work. While that may be technically accurate, the selection and arrangement also indicate a more focused effort:

"Upon Human Nature" (Sermons I, II, and III)
"Upon the Government of the Tongue" (Sermon IV)
"Upon Compassion" (Sermons V and VI)
"Upon the Character of Balaam" (Sermon VII)
"Upon Resentment" (Sermon VIII)
"Upon Forgiveness of Injuries" (Sermon IX)
"Upon Self-Deceit" (Sermon X)
"Upon the Love of our Neighbour" (Sermons XI and XII)
"Upon the Love of God" (Sermons XIII and XIV)
"Upon the Ignorance of Man" (Sermon XV)

As these titles indicate, the first three sermons lay the foundation of Butler's theory of human nature, and the remaining sermons illustrate and apply his principles. That Butler recognized such a relationship among the sermons is borne out by his comments near the beginning of the preface, where he acknowledges two approaches to the study of morals: "One begins from inquiring into the abstract relations of things: the other from a matter of fact, namely, what the particular nature of man is, its several parts, their economy or constitution; from whence it proceeds to determine what course of life it is, which is correspondent to this whole nature." Some have assumed that Butler thought of Clarke as representing the first approach and Anthony Ashley Cooper, Earl of Shaftesbury as representing the second. In any case, he recognizes that both approaches lead to the same conclusion, that man is to practice virtue. Nevertheless, he notes that the second is "adapted to satisfy a fair mind" and "is more easily applicable to the several particular relations and circumstances in life." With those comments the reader finds the basic justification for Butler's ethical philosophy and discovers that Butler stands in conflict with the self-preservation philosophy of Thomas Hobbes. Butler's interest was in applying the principles of human nature to an individual's own life and to the relationships that exist between individuals.

Butler then notes that his discourses follow the latter method. His examination of human nature begins with the recognition that, as he states in the preface, "virtue consists in following, and vice in deviating from" the nature of man. Shaftesbury had expressed the same idea in his *An Inquiry Concerning Virtue: In Two Discourses, Viz., I. of Virtue and the Belief of a Deity, II. Of the*

Obligations to Virtue (1699). With that foundation, then, the first three sermons explore human nature. In the first sermon Butler acknowledges the existence of various "appetites, passions, and particular affections" that are distinct from the two other principles of self-love and benevolence. A third component of human nature is "the principle of reflection or conscience." The second and third sermons argue for the supremacy of conscience. In his preface to the sermons Butler asserts that failing to consider a claim for the supremacy of conscience is a deficiency in Shaftesbury's work. According to Butler, the mere existence of these components does not identify man's moral nature. The whole of natural, moral life cannot be glimpsed or determined unless all the passions are related and subordinated, and the conscience is the faculty by which the relationship can be illustrated and by which man learns virtue. Conscience has its own authority because it is "the guide assigned us by the Author of our nature." The importance of this last claim lies in the fact that it clearly reveals Butler's ethics to be firmly grounded in theism, and, of course, those who cannot accept a theistic position will have difficulty accepting Butler's complete scheme.

As he attempts to illustrate his theory of ethics in the remaining twelve sermons, he re-emphasizes the position of self-love and benevolence as separate principles that regulate the particular passions in human nature. Furthermore, because to Butler man's purpose is virtue, following nature cannot mean acting as one pleases or following one's strongest passions. To follow nature means to follow conscience, and to follow conscience is virtue, which is more than an inner faculty. If an individual has virtue he will act accordingly. As Butler says in his fifteenth sermon, "Upon the Ignorance of Man," virtue "consists in good actions, proceeding from a good principle, temper, or heart." In addition, these actions can be observed in the two spheres of self-love and benevolence, which are not opposed to but merely distinguished from one another in the focus of their attention. Self-love does not mean selfishness or self-centeredness, but it concerns the effort to control and manage passions so that the individual can live happily—in virtue rather than in vice. Benevolence, on the other hand, focuses on the individual's relationship to society. A person who is benevolent will assist others to live happily. Whether they are private actions arising from self-love or public actions arising from benevolence, virtuous actions are the result of man's constitution.

At times it seems as though Butler refers to benevolence in the sermons not as the general principle he identified in the first sermon but as a particular appetite or passion. The confusion over this seeming contradiction can be resolved easily, however, by recognizing that benevolence occupies a dual position in Butler's hierarchy. The challenge is to recognize when he refers to it as a general principle and when he refers to it as a particular passion. The potential for argument and discussion of this matter as well as discussion of the relationship between conscience, self-love, benevolence, and the various appetites and passions is great. Nevertheless, when all the evidence is considered, it seems that Butler establishes a hierarchy that subordinates the particular appetites and passions to the principles of self-love and benevolence, which in turn become subordinated to conscience. Indeed, the supremacy of conscience is central to Butler's ethical philosophy.

Butler's life at Stanhope can be characterized as solitary but by no means unproductive. He had ample time for his own studies, and he conscientiously performed the duties of a parish priest. There he planned and wrote his most famous work, *The Analogy of Religion, Natural and Revealed, to the Constitution and Course of Nature. To Which Are Added Two Brief Dissertations: I. Of Personal Identity II. Of the Nature of Virtue* (1736). Nevertheless, while he kept busy, it is almost certain that he missed the association with friends and the more active life he had led before retiring to Stanhope. In any case, through the influence of his old friend Secker, Butler was appointed chaplain to Lord Chancellor Charles Talbot, first Baron Talbot of Hensol, when Talbot became lord chancellor in 1733. On 8 December of that same year Butler took his Doctor of Law degree at Oxford. The elder brother of Butler's friend Edward Talbot, Charles Talbot appointed Butler to a prebendary of Rochester Cathedral in July 1736. Despite his new appointments, Butler divided his time and, by agreement with Talbot, resided in Stanhope for one half of the year.

In July 1732 Secker had become chaplain to King George II. While in conversation with Queen Caroline he mentioned his friend Butler, and she remarked that she thought he was dead. When she repeated her comment to Lancelot Blackburne, the archbishop of York, he is supposed to have remarked that "he is not *dead*, but he is *buried*." Taking an interest in Butler, the queen appointed him her clerk of the closet in 1736. The queen was a deeply intellectual woman who took great pleasure discussing philosophy and theology, and by her command Butler attended her every evening from seven to nine. *The Analogy of Religion* was published the same year as his appointment, and it became a prominent part of the queen's studies.

The Analogy of Religion was written to counteract the claims of the Deists and other rationalists who argued that the deity who created the world was separated from man and therefore had no interest in human affairs. Revelation occupied no place in the Deist

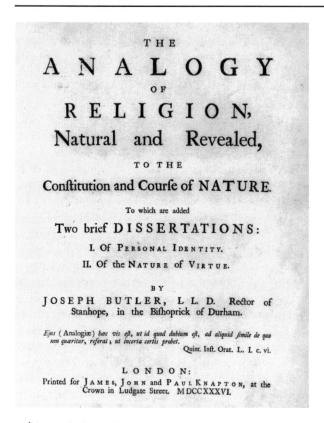

THE

ANALOGY

OF

RELIGION,

Natural and Revealed,

TO THE

Conſtitution and Courſe of NATURE.

To which are added

Two brief DISSERTATIONS:

I. Of PERSONAL IDENTITY.

II. Of the NATURE of VIRTUE.

BY

JOSEPH BUTLER, L. L. D. Rector of
Stanhope, in the Biſhoprick of Durham.

Ejus (Analogiæ) *hæc vis eſt, ut id quod dubium eſt, ad aliquid ſimile de quo
non quæritur, referat; ut incerta certis probet.*
Quint. Inſt. Orat. L. I. c. vi.

LONDON:

Printed for JAMES, JOHN and PAUL KNAPTON, at the
Crown in Ludgate Street. MDCCXXXVI.

*Title page for Butler's best-known work, written to combat deism and
defend revealed Christianity (courtesy of The Lilly Library,
Indiana University)*

scheme, and a concern with morals and spirituality was strictly a matter of rational interpretation derived from what one could make out by observing the natural world. Butler objected to such thinking, but the defensive posture he adopts in the "Advertisement" and the "Introduction" to *The Analogy of Religion* goes beyond merely pleading the case of traditional Christianity. As the full title indicates, his approach is to meet the Deists on their own ground and demonstrate that his revealed religion and their natural religion both conform to nature. Such conformity means that "the system of religion, both natural and revealed, considered only as a system, . . . is not a subject of ridicule, unless that of nature be so too." Thus, Butler approaches the matter rationally, attempting to defuse the Deist attack on traditional Christianity by turning the basis of the attack on itself. In other words, for many of the problems Deists find in their criticism of traditional theology, an analogy can be found in their natural religion.

Obviously, such an argument from analogy depends upon a shared belief in a natural governor of the universe. The next step is to evaluate the viability of the analogy. To do so, Butler invokes the concept of probablity, which, though imperfect, is the only means

available to human beings. Nevertheless, it is sufficient to guide their actions as they live the virtuous life outlined in the sermons. For Butler the important point is that the mere presence of any degree of probability is sufficient to establish any principle of practical or revealed religion. As he notes in the introduction to *The Analogy of Religion,* even though there may be "the lowest presumption on one side" of an issue "and none on the other," individuals are still in matters of practice bound by prudence "to act upon that presumption or low probability."

As the title indicates, the work is divided into two halves, the first focusing on the analogy of natural religion to human knowledge and understanding of nature, and the second focusing on the analogy of revealed religion to nature. Part 1 begins with a chapter arguing the probability of a future life, followed by a chapter on rewards and punishments and a chapter on the moral government of God. The next two chapters focus on the probationary state as a time of trials and challenges to promote moral discipline and improvement. A chapter arguing that the doctrine of necessity does not hinder belief, a chapter explaining the imperfect human understanding of God's scheme of government, and a final chapter summarizing the entire argument complete part 1.

In part 2 Butler turns to revealed religion, and, following his procedure in part 1, he begins with an assumption and proceeds to explain its credibility. In this instance the assumption is that revelation has been given. Chapter 1, therefore, examines the importance of revelation in its Christian context. In Butler's work revealed religion means Christianity. Chapter 2 examines the argument against revelation because it is miraculous. The next two chapters focus on the ability of people to judge the morality of revelation, asserting that apparent inconsistencies are the result of limited human abilities to comprehend the entire scheme of revealed religion. Chapter 5 explains the concept of redemption by means of a mediator and acknowledges Jesus Christ as the Redeemer. Chapter 6 invokes the principle of probability as a guide because of the supposed lack of demonstrable proof for revelation, and chapter 7 cites particular evidence for Christianity from miracles and prophecy. The next chapter offers a final apology for the argument from analogy, and a brief concluding chapter brings part 2 to an end.

As indicated by the full title, Butler appended two dissertations to *The Analogy of Religion:* "Of Personal Identity" and "Of the Nature of Virtue." As its title hints, the first of these is in part a criticism of Locke. The second is a development of the ethical scheme outlined in Butler's sermons and should be read in conjunction with them. *The Analogy of Religion* is often cited as the source for Butler's natural theology, and the sermons are cited as the source for his ethical theory and moral philosophy. While such an appropriation is true, the presence of the dissertations at the end of *The Analogy of Religion* suggests the two categories need not be as distinct as might be supposed. Indeed, both parts of *The Analogy of Religion* emphasize the morality of both natural and revealed religion; correlating moral philosophy and traditional Christianity is ultimately a large part of Butler's rational defense of Christianity.

Two examples from *The Analogy of Religion* illustrate the nature of the correlation. In part 1 Butler argues for a future life: as the physical states of this life change from one's existence in the womb to infancy and on to maturity, so may one presume a continuance of life after death. The probability of life after death rests in the individual's observation and experience of this life. In part 2 he argues that all living creatures are brought into the world and are nurtured, protected, and preserved by the instrumentality and mediation of others. Thus, there should be no objection to the notion of a mediator between God and man: Christ as Redeemer. In both instances, accepting the existence of a future life and the existence of a mediator is an incentive to live virtuously, to regulate passions and desires to principles of self-love and benevolence with conscience reigning supreme. Of course, such arguments are not likely to help those who do not believe; they will only strengthen the convictions of believers and perhaps assist those who are uncertain or wavering in their faith. Thus, it is fair to say that even though Butler meets the Deists head-on, in reality one of his main purposes in *The Analogy of Religion* was to strengthen the converted. True, in both examples probability is limited to a temporal world, not an eternal one, but the fact that Butler makes the leap from a temporal to a transcendental realm reveals him to be one who can balance religious faith and reason. In so doing he anticipates the Romantic theological tradition of Samuel Taylor Coleridge and John Henry Newman, both of whom knew and admired Butler's works.

Butler served only a short time under Queen Caroline, for she died in 1737, one year after Butler's appointment as clerk of the closet. As she lay dying, however, the queen requested that Butler be taken care of, and in 1738 George II appointed Butler bishop of Bristol. As the poorest bishopric in England, the appointment to Bristol was a disappointment to Butler, who openly expressed his dissatisfaction. Thus, he was allowed to keep the rectory at Stanhope. Two years later he was appointed dean of St. Paul's in London by the king. At that time he resigned his living at Stanhope, but he retained his position at Bristol. It would be easy to assume that Butler was worldly because of his concern over the income attached to the appointment at Bristol and his occupation of two positions simultaneously. However, that seems not to be the case. Butler lived at a time when plural appointments were the norm rather than the exception, and evidence suggests that he gave away most of his wealth. In fact, while at Stanhope he was noted for never being able to turn away beggars, and it is said that at times he had to stay at home to avoid them. In his 1839 memoir of Butler, Thomas Bartlett records a tradition that on one occasion Butler had to ride away on a black pony to flee from a group of beggars following him. In 1746 Butler added to his preferments when George II made him his clerk of the closet. When John Potter, the archbishop of Canterbury, died in 1747, the position was offered to Butler after it had been offered to Thomas Sherlock, Bishop of London, who refused. Butler also refused the appointment, but not because it had not been offered to him first. Bartlett reports a tradition that Butler's explanation for his refusal was "it was too late for him to try to support a falling Church." If accurate, that comment is interesting in light of his efforts in *The Analogy of Religion* to defend revealed religion, and thus the Church, against the Deists.

While he was bishop of Bristol, he preached several public sermons; six that he preached in London were published separately between 1739 and 1748 and then collected as *Six Sermons Preached on Publick Occasions* (1749). Four of these sermons reveal his interest in missionary work, poor relief, charity schools, and hospitals. The other two were preached before the House of Lords, one on the anniversary of the martyrdom of Charles I and the other on the anniversary of the accession of George II. Clearly the public mission of the church was on Butler's mind.

On 16 October 1750 Butler was translated to the See of Durham (his friend Secker replacing him as dean of St. Paul's), and there he delivered and published in 1751 his famous charge to the clergy of Durham, in which he emphasized the use and importance of external religion. He began by lamenting the decline of religion in England and reminding the clergy of their duty to revive the religious spirit. That task, he says, can be accomplished best by emphasizing the form of religious worship, which includes focusing not only on what is done in the service but also on how the service is conducted in terms of adherence to established patterns and ritual. Butler also encouraged an emphasis on frequent worship services throughout the week and the practice of other forms of worship such as teaching the catechism to children at home and conducting family prayer.

This charge to the clergy led to the revival of a strange claim that had been made against him a few years earlier at Bristol. After becoming bishop of Bristol, Butler

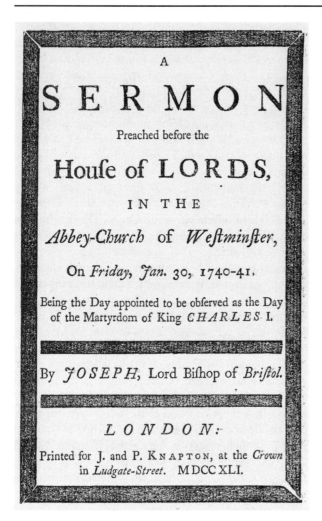

A

SERMON

Preached before the

Houfe of LORDS,

IN THE

Abbey-Church of *Weftminfter*,

On *Friday, Jan.* 30, 1740-41.

Being the Day appointed to be obferved as the Day
of the Martyrdom of King *CHARLES* I.

By *JOSEPH*, Lord Bifhop of *Briftol*.

LONDON:

Printed for J. and P. KNAPTON, at the *Crown*
in *Ludgate-Street*. MDCCXLI.

Title page for one of Butler's sermons that was collected in 1749 as Six
Sermons Preached on Publick Occasions *(Pitts Theology Library,
Emory University)*

restored the episcopal palace and chapel there, erecting in
the chapel an altarpiece of black marble with an inlaid
cross of white marble. The introduction of that cross was
taken by some to be a sign of Butler's inclination toward
Catholicism. Thus, when he delivered the charge at
Durham and emphasized the use and importance of external religion, his remarks became connected to the erection
of the cross and resulted in a renewed claim of "popish"
tendencies against him, most notably in an anonymous
pamphlet, attributed to Francis Blackburne, *A Serious
Enquiry into the Use and Importance of External Religion: Occasioned by some passages in the Right Reverend the Lord Bishop of
Durham's Charge to the clergy of that diocese in the year MDCCLI*
(1752). While it is true that Butler urged dignity and careful attention in conducting church services, his emphasis
was on awakening personal spirituality by encouraging
appropriate worship both in the church and in individual
homes, and that emphasis was far removed from any
claims of Roman Catholic tendencies.

Butler's health began to decline soon after becoming bishop of Durham. He suffered from stomach and
intestinal disorders and was first taken to Bristol to
recover. The change did not produce the desired remedy, so he was then taken to Bath, where he died on 16
June 1752. He was interred in the cathedral at Bristol.
Butler never married, but he divided his estate among
relatives and left a modest sum each to the Newcastle
Infirmary and to the Society for the Propagation of the
Gospel in Foreign Parts. One of his last requests was
that all his letters, sermons, and papers locked in a
wooden box in a room within his library at Hampstead
be burned at his death without being read. Apparently
his survivors honored his request, for the only known
manuscripts in his writing today are two account books,
some letters, and a few other fragments.

By the end of his life Butler's emphasis had
changed. He began with abstract reasoning concerning
a priori arguments for the existence of God in his letters
to Clarke and ended with public sermons and a charge
to the clergy of Durham emphasizing ecclesiastical privilege and responsibility. In the middle are the two works
upon which his reputation rests, his sermons preached
at the Rolls Chapel and *The Analogy of Religion*. That his
renown continued into the twentieth century speaks
well of the impact of a decidedly small body of work.

His modern reputation is most certainly not as
strong as it was in his own lifetime and in the century
following his death. For example, in his own lifetime
four editions each of his *Fifteen Sermons preached at the
Rolls Chapel* and *The Analogy of Religion* appeared in
England. Later in the eighteenth century and into the
nineteenth century the depth of his influence can be
gauged by the fact that his two main works were used
as texts in courses of study at universities. Scores of editions of his works appeared in England, Scotland, Ireland, Wales, and the United States, with at least eighty
editions of *The Analogy of Religion* published during the
nineteenth century in the United States alone. In the
nineteenth century prominent figures such as Coleridge, John Keble, Cardinal Newman, Hurrell Froude,
and Edward Pusey provided more measured but deeply
praiseworthy responses. Interestingly, most of these
individuals were connected to or participated directly in
the Oxford Movement, and one must only remember
the focus of Butler's charge to the Durham clergy and
its analogous goal with the objectives of the Oxford
Movement to understand why he would appeal to its
members. While detractors existed in his own time, the
intellectual climate of the nineteenth century provided a
ready-made situation for detractors as the rise of science
brought new challenges to religion. Among those of an
actual or supposed scientific bent who found fault with
either Butler's theology or his ethical system are James

Martineau, John Stuart Mill, Walter Bagehot, Thomas Henry Huxley, Leslie Stephen, and Matthew Arnold. The overwhelming and dominant strategy of these individuals was to point out that Butler's views were unsatisfactory, but a few are not totally negative. For example, in his essay "Bishop Butler and the Zeit-Geist," first collected in *Last Essays on Church and Religion* (1877), Arnold praises Butler for his profound religious sense, but Arnold cannot accept the basic assumptions upon which Butler's arguments rest. Butler was willing to use reason in matters of faith, but he still accepted a spiritual, otherworldly realm for religion. Arnold simply could not accept such a balance of reason and religious faith.

At the end of the nineteenth century and the beginning of the twentieth century Butler's position was declining but still relatively strong. At this time two editions of his works by the statesman W. E. Gladstone and by J. H. Bernard were published in 1896 and 1900, respectively. Since then there have been no major modern editions of Butler's works published, so Bernard's and Gladstone's editions are still considered the best and the most authoritative (Gladstone's was republished, with a new introduction, in 1995). Butler's works are no longer included in courses of study at universities, but given his connection to several prominent figures such as Coleridge, Newman, and Arnold, Butler certainly will not be entirely forgotten. Furthermore, his ethical theory is still attractive to philosophers who continue to wrestle with the meanings of and the relationships among conscience, self-love, benevolence, and individual passions. Book-length studies are few, but articles assessing his ideas continue to appear regularly. To paraphrase the response given by the archbishop of York when Queen Caroline remarked that she thought Butler was dead, as a subject of investigation today he is not dead, nor is he buried, though admittedly his reputation and fame are modest in comparison to what they were during his life and in the century and a half immediately following his death.

Biographies:

Thomas Bartlett, *Memoirs of the Life, Character, and Writings of Joseph Butler, D.C.L., late Lord Bishop of Durham* (London: John W. Parker, 1839);

William Morley Egglestone, *Stanhope Memorials of Bishop Butler* (London: Simpkin, Marshall, 1878);

W. A. Spooner, *Bishop Butler* (Boston & New York: Houghton, Mifflin, 1901; London: Methuen, 1901).

References:

Matthew Arnold, "Bishop Butler and the Zeit-Geist," in *The Complete Prose Works of Matthew Arnold,* edited by R. H. Super, volume 8 (Ann Arbor: University of Michigan Press, 1972), pp. 11–62;

Albert Edward Baker, *Bishop Butler* (London: Society for Promoting Christian Knowledge / New York & Toronto: Macmillan, 1923);

Alan Brinton, "'Following Nature' in Butler's Sermons," *Philosophical Quarterly,* 41 (1991): 325–332;

C. D. Broad, "Butler as a Theologian," *Hibbert Journal,* 21 (1923): 637–656;

Broad, *Five Types of Ethical Theory* (London: Kegan Paul, Trench, Trübner / New York: Harcourt, Brace, 1930);

P. Allan Carlsson, *Butler's Ethics,* Studies in Philosophy, no. 3 (The Hague & London: Mouton, 1964);

Webster Cook, *Ethics of Bishop Butler and Immanuel Kant,* University of Michigan Philosophical Papers, second series, no. 4 (Ann Arbor: Andrews, 1888);

Christopher Cunliffe, ed., *Joseph Butler's Moral and Religious Thought: Tercentary Essays* (Oxford: Clarendon Press / New York: Oxford University Press, 1992);

Austin Duncan-Jones, *Butler's Moral Philosophy: The Foundations of Ethics as Treated by a Great Eighteenth-Century Bishop: A Critical Exposition Introducing the Subjects to Modern Readers* (Harmondsworth, U.K.: Penguin, 1952);

Peter Fuss, "Sense and Reason in Butler's Ethics," *Dialogue: Canadian Philosophical Review,* 7 (1968): 180–193;

W. E. Gladstone, *Studies Subsidiary to the Works of Bishop Butler* (Oxford: Clarendon Press, 1896; New York: Macmillan, 1896);

S. A. Grave, "Able and Fair Reasoning of Butler's *Analogy,*" *Church History,* 47 (1978): 298–307;

Grave, "The Foundation of Butler's Ethics," *Australasian Journal of Philosophy,* 30 (1952): 73–89;

Kenneth E. Harris, "Important Shifts in Argumentation: The Empirical Apologetic of Joseph Butler's *The Analogy of Religion,*" Ph.D. thesis, Indiana University, 1998;

Terry G. Harris, "Matthew Arnold, Bishop Joseph Butler, and the Foundation of Religious Faith," *Victorian Studies,* 31 (1988): 189–208;

Henry Hughes, *A Critical Examination of Butler's "Analogy,"* (London: Kegan Paul, Trench, Trübner, 1898);

Reginald Jackson, "Bishop Butler's Refutation of Psychological Hedonism," *Philosophy,* 18 (1943): 114–132;

Edward W. James, "Butler, Fanaticism and Conscience," *Philosophy,* 56 (1981): 517–532;

Anders Jeffner, *Butler and Hume on Religion: A Comparative Analysis* (Stockholm: Diakonistyrelsens Bokförlag, 1966);

Clifford Johnson, "Joseph Butler, Laodicean Rationalist?" *Modern Language Studies,* 4 (1974): 78–85;

John Kleinig, "Butler in a Cool Hour," *Journal of the History of Philosophy,* 7 (1969): 399–411;

John Betts Koehne, *Bishop Butler's Challenge to Modernism: Retribution from "The Analogy," an Interpretation* (Fort Wayne, Ind.: Glad Tidings Publishing, 1929);

Alan R. Lacey, "Comment on P. A. Moritz's Essay on Joseph Butler," *Ultimate Reality and Meaning,* 4 (1981): 248–253;

Edmund Leites, "A Problem in Joseph Butler's Ethics," *Southwestern Journal of Philosophy,* 6 (1975): 43–57;

Michael W. Martin, "A Defense of the Rights of Conscience in Butler's Ethics," *Philosophy Research Archives,* 3, no. 1203 (1977), pp. 88–98;

Thomas H. McPherson, "The Development of Bishop Butler's Ethics," parts 1 and 2, *Philosophy,* 23 (1948): 317–331; 24 (1949): 3–22;

Alan Millar, "Following Nature," *Philosophical Quarterly,* 38 (1988): 165–185;

Philip A. Moritz, "Joseph Butler and His Ideas on Ultimate Reality and Meaning," *Ultimate Reality and Meaning,* 4 (1981): 213–224;

Ernest Campbell Mossner, *Bishop Butler and the Age of Reason* (New York: Macmillan, 1936; Bristol: Thoemmes, 1990);

William Joseph Norton Jr., *Bishop Butler: Moralist and Divine,* Rutgers University Studies in Philosophy, no. 1 (New Brunswick, N.J.: Rutgers University Press, 1940);

Wendell O'Brien, "Butler and the Authority of Conscience," *History of Philosophy Quarterly,* 8 (1991): 43–57;

Terence Penelhum, *Butler* (London & Boston: Routledge & Kegan Paul, 1985);

Thomas W. Platt, "Self-Love and Benevolence: In Defense of Butler's Ethics," *Southwestern Journal of Philosophy,* 3 (1972): 71–79;

Michael S. Pritchard, "Conscience and Reason in Butler's Ethics," *Southwestern Journal of Philosophy,* 9 (1978): 39–49;

Thomas Ruggles Pynchon, *Bishop Butler, a Religious Philosopher for All Time: A Sketch of His Life with an Examination of The Analogy* (New York: Appleton, 1889);

D. Daiches Raphael, "Bishop Butler's View of Conscience," *Philosophy,* 24 (1949): 219–238;

Charles H. Reynolds with Riggins R. Earl, "Alexander Crummell's Transformation of Bishop Butler's Ethics," *Journal of Religious Ethics,* 6 (1978): 221–239;

Glenn K. Riddle, "The Place of Benevolence in Butler's Ethics," *Philosophical Quarterly,* 9 (1959): 356–362;

J. Robinson, "Newman's Use of Butler's Arguments," *Downside Review,* 76, no. 24 (1958): 161–181;

Amélie Oksenberg Rorty, "Butler on Benevolence and Conscience," *Philosophy,* 53 (1978): 171–184;

James Rurak, "Butler's *Analogy:* A Still Interesting Synthesis of Reason and Revelation," *Anglican Theological Review,* 62 (1980): 365–381;

M. J. Scott-Taggart, "Butler on Disinterested Actions," *Philosophical Quarterly,* 18 (1968): 16–28;

Nicholas J. Sturgeon, "Nature and Conscience in Butler's Ethics," *Philosophical Review,* 85 (1976): 316–356;

Béla Szabados, "Butler on Corrupt Conscience," *Journal of the History of Philosophy,* 14 (1976): 462–469;

Joseph M. Walsh, "Benevolence and Self-Love in Butler's Moral Philosophy," part 1, *Culture,* 19 (1958): 419–425; part 2, 20 (1959): 63–72;

George Watson, "Joseph Butler," in *The English Mind: Studies in the English Moralists Presented to Basil Willey,* edited by Hugh Sykes Davies and George Watson (London: Cambridge University Press, 1964), pp. 107–122;

John H. Watson, "Bishop Butler as Philosopher-Theologian," *Evangelical Quarterly,* 24 (1952): 168–174;

A. R. White, "Conscience and Self-Love in Butler's Sermons," *Philosophy,* 27 (1952): 329–344;

Alexander Whyte, *Bishop Butler, An Appreciation: With the Best Passages of His Writings* (London: Oliphant, Anderson & Ferrier, 1903);

A. C. Windsor, "Bishop Butler and Contemporary Ethics," *Church Quarterly Review,* 168 (1967): 181–190.

Papers:

Because Joseph Butler directed that the papers he kept be burned at his death, few items have survived: the British Library, London, has a collection of several letters, including two addressed to Samuel Clarke, along with miscellaneous extracts and papers, and his will and codicil; two of Butler's account books are at Oriel College, Cambridge University; and the Bodleian Library, Oxford University, has a manuscript index of subjects in *The Analogy of Religion,* made by Edward Bentham, with three pages of corrections and additions by Butler.

Margaret Cavendish, Duchess of Newcastle

(1623 – 15 December 1673)

Erin Lang Bonin
University of North Carolina at Chapel Hill

BOOKS: *Poems and Fancies* (London: Printed by Thomas Roycroft for John Martin & James Allestrye, 1653); revised as *Poems and Phancies* (London: Printed by William Wilson, 1664); revised as *Poems; or, Several Fancies in Verse: With the Animal Parliament, in Prose* (London: Printed by A. Maxwell, 1668);

Philosophicall Fancies (London: Printed by Thomas Roycroft for John Martin & James Allestrye, 1653);

The Worlds Olio (London: Printed for John Martin & James Allestrye, 1655);

The Philosophical and Physical Opinions (London: Printed by Thomas Roycroft for John Martin & James Allestrye, 1655); enlarged as *Philosophical and Physical Opinions* (London: Printed by William Wilson, 1663); revised as *Grounds of Natural Philosophy: Divided into Thirteen Parts: With an Appendix Containing Five Parts* (London: Printed by A. Maxwell, 1668);

Natures Pictures Drawn by Fancies Pencil to the Life. Written by the thrice Noble, Illustrious and Excellent Princess, the Lady Marchioness of Newcastle. In this Volume there are several feigned Stories of Natural Descriptions, as Comical, Tragical, and Tragi-Comical, Poetical, Romancical, Philosophical, and Historical, both in Prose and Verse, some all Verse, some all Prose, some mixt, partly Prose, and partly Verse. Also, there are some Morals, and some Dialogues; but they are as the Advantage Loaves of Bread to a Bakers dozen; and a true Story at the end wherein there is no Feignings (London: Printed for John Martin & James Allestrye, 1656); revised as *Natures Picture Drawn by Fancies Pencil to the Life. Being Several Feigned Stories, Comical, Tragical, Tragi-Comical, Poetical, and Moral. Some in Verse, Some in Prose; Some Mixt, and Some by Dialogue* (London: Printed by A. Maxwell, 1671);

Plays Written by the Thrice Noble, Illustrious and Most Excellent Princess, the Lady Marchioness of Newcastle (London: Printed by Alice Warren for John Martyn, James Allestry & Thomas Dicas, 1662);

Margaret Cavendish, Duchess of Newcastle; portrait attributed to Abraham van Diepenbeke (Collection of the Duke of Portland)

Orations of Divers Sorts, Accommodated to Divers Places (London: Printed by A. Maxwell, 1662);

CCXI Sociable Letters (London: Printed by William Wilson, 1664);

Philosophical Letters; or, Modest Reflections Upon some Opinions in Natural Philosophy maintained by several Famous and

Learned Authors of this Age, Expressed by way of Letters (London, 1664);

Observations upon Experimental Philosophy. To which is added, The Description of a New Blazing World (London: Printed by A. Maxwell, 1666);

The Life of the Thrice Noble, High and Puissant Prince William Cavendishe, Duke, Marquess, and Earl of Newcastle; Earl of Ogle; Viscount Mansfield; and Baron of Bolsover, of Ogle, Bothal, and Hepple: Gentleman of His Majesties Bed-Chamber; one of His Majesties most Honourable Privy-Councel; Knight of the most Noble Order of the Garter; his Majesties Lieutenant of the County and Town of Nottingham; and Justice in Ayre Trent-North: Who had the honour to be Governour to our most Glorious King, and Gracious Sovereign, in his Youth, when He was Prince of Wales; and soon after was made Captain-General of All the Provinces beyond the River of Trent, and other Parts of the Kingdom of England, with Power, by a special Commission, to make Knights (Printed by A. Maxwell, 1667); translated as *De vita et rebus gestis nobilissimi illustrissimque principis, Guilielmi Ducis Novo-Castrensis, commentarii. Ab excellentissima principe, Margareta ipsius uxore sanctissima conscripti. Et ex anglico in Latinum conversi* (London: Printed by T. M., 1668);

The Description of a New World, called the Blazing-World (London: Printed by A. Maxwell, 1668);

Plays, Never before Printed (London: Printed by A. Maxwell, 1668).

Editions and Collections: *The Lives of William Cavendishe, Duke of Newcastle, and of His Wife, Margaret, Duchess of Newcastle: Written by the Thrice Noble and Illustrious Princess, Margaret, Duchess of Newcastle,* edited, with a preface and notes, by Mark Antony Lower (London: J. R. Smith, 1872);

The Life of William Cavendish Duke of Newcastle to Which Is Added The True Relation of My Birth, Breeding and Life, edited by C. H. Firth (London: J. C. Nimmo, 1886);

Sociable Letters, 1664 (Menston: Scolar, 1969);

Poems and Fancies, 1653 (Menston: Scolar, 1972);

The Description of a New World Called the Blazing World and Other Writings, edited by Kate Lilley (London: Pickering & Chatto, 1992); republished as *The Blazing World and Other Writings* (London & New York: Penguin, 1994);

The Convent of Pleasure: A Comedy Written by the Duchess of Newcastle, edited by Jennifer Rowsell (Oxford: Seventeenth Century Press, 1995);

Grounds of Natural Philosophy, introduction by Colette V. Michael, Women in the Sciences, volume 2 (West Cornwall, Conn.: Locust Hill, 1996);

The Sociable Companions: Or, The Female Wits: A Comedy, Written by the Thrice Noble, Illuftrious, and Excellent Princesse, the Duchefs of Newcaftle, edited, with an introduction, by Amanda Holton (Oxford: Seventeenth Century Press, 1996);

Sociable Letters, edited by James Fitzmaurice, Garland Reference Library of the Humanities, volume 2009 (New York: Garland, 1997);

The Convent of Pleasure and Other Plays, edited by Anne Shaver (Baltimore, Md. & London: Johns Hopkins University Press, 1999);

Paper Bodies: A Margaret Cavendish Reader, edited by Sylvia Lorraine Bowerbank and Sara Heller Mendelson (Peterborough, Ont. & Orchard Park, N.Y.: Broadview Press, 2000);

Observations upon Experimental Philosophy, edited by Eileen O'Neill (Cambridge: Cambridge University Press, 2001).

One of the most prolific women writers in seventeenth-century England, Margaret Cavendish, Duchess of Newcastle, published poems, plays, prose romances, science fiction, philosophical treatises, and a biography. She even wrote an autobiography, *A True Relation of my Birth, Breeding, and Life,* which appeared as book 11 of the first edition of *Natures Pictures Drawn by Fancies Pencil to the Life* (1656). A bewildering assortment of contradictions animated Margaret Cavendish's life and thought. Although painfully shy, she fashioned herself into one of the most talked-about spectacles of Restoration England. Enchanted by philosophy and the new science, she nevertheless doubted her capacity to participate in these pursuits, often questioning their validity. She was at once a visionary radical and a political conservative, both a pre-Enlightenment feminist and a dogged misogynist. The voluminous writings Cavendish left behind attest to a paradoxical, always interesting mind.

Born in Essex near the town of Colchester in 1623, Margaret Lucas was the eighth and last child of Thomas and Elizabeth Lucas. When she was still an infant, her father died, leaving his widow to manage the aristocratic family's household and lands capably; Cavendish writes in her autobiography that "I observe she took a pleasure, and some little pride in the governing thereof: she was very skilfull in Leases, and setting of Lands, and Court-keeping, ordering of Stewards, and the like affaires." As a girl, Lucas received a spotty education, even by seventeenth-century standards. Under the tutelage of an elderly, somewhat lackadaisical governess, she dabbled in music, dancing, reading, writing, and needlework. As a self-taught adult, she regretted her childhood course of study, analyzing the problem in gendered terms. "But as for Learning, that I am not versed in it," she wrote in her preface to the reader in *Observations upon Experimental Philosophy. To which is added, The Description of a New Blazing World* (1666), "no body, I

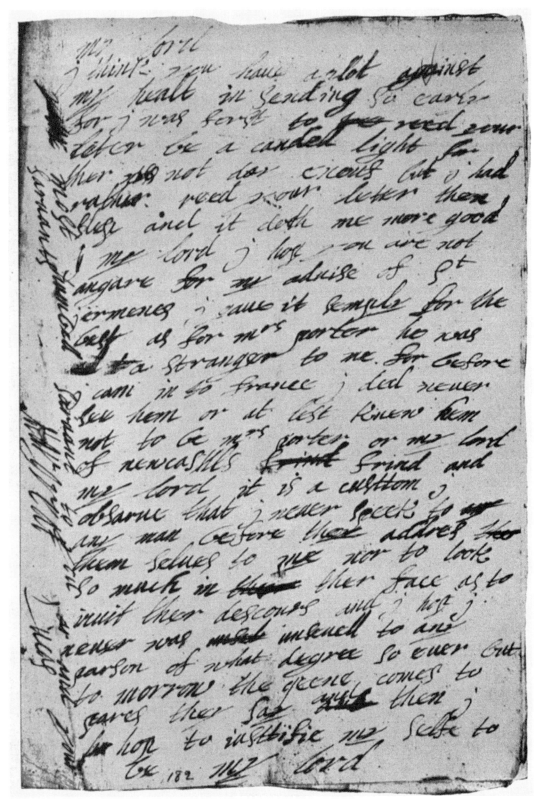

Letter written in 1645 by Margaret Lucas to her future husband, William Cavendish (from Douglas Grant, Margaret the First: A Biography of
Margaret Cavendish, Duchess of Newcastle, 1623–1673, *1957)*

hope, will blame me for it, since it is sufficiently known, that our Sex is not bred up to it, as being not suffer'd to be instructed in Schools and Universities."

Lucas was in her late teens when the Civil War began. In August 1642 an anti-Royalist mob stormed the Lucas estate, destroying the grounds, the house, and even the family vault. The event marked her life and politics. A staunch Royalist, she had little use for Parliamentarians or middling sorts. A few months after the riot, she traveled to Oxford, where the embattled Stuart court had taken up residence. She became a lady-in-waiting to Queen Henrietta Maria, later accompanying the French-born queen when she fled to Paris in July 1644. The codes of behavior and political intrigues of the court baffled Lucas. She missed her family and was miserable.

Then she met William Cavendish, first Marquess of Newcastle, a widower nearly thirty years her senior. Newcastle had fought valiantly, if ineptly, for his king, raising a large army in the north of England in support of Charles I. He had some successes against the Parliamentarian forces, but a Royalist army led by Newcastle and Prince Rupert, Count Palatine of the Rhine, was resoundingly defeated by the Roundheads under Oliver Cromwell on 2 July 1644 at the battle of Marston Moor in Yorkshire, a defeat for which Newcastle was widely, though perhaps unjustly, blamed. After the Royalist defeat at Marston Moor—in which Margaret Lucas's youngest brother, Sir Charles Lucas, also fought—Newcastle escaped to the Continent, disgraced and impoverished. But he soon secured sufficient credit to restore his dashing cavalier image and to launch a passionate courtship with Margaret Lucas. When she refused to become his mistress, Newcastle asked her to be his bride. She recalls in *A True Relation of my Birth, Breeding, and Life* that "though I did dread Marriage, and shunn'd Mens companies, as much as I could, yet I could not, nor had not the power to refuse him, by reason my Affections were fix'd on him, and he was the onely Person I ever was in love with." The Newcastles married in December 1645 and then spent fifteen years on the Continent, residing first in Paris and later in Antwerp. Despite their financial difficulties and their childlessness, they were happy. William Cavendish, who was created first duke of Newcastle in 1650, loved his wife's intellect, and with his encouragement, she renewed her childhood passion for writing.

Margaret Cavendish wrote with unbounded vigor, frequently composing aloud and pacing about the room as she spoke. Often, her thoughts flowed too swiftly for her to record them on paper: "many fancies are lost, by reason they ofttimes out-run the pen," she writes in *A True Relation of my Birth, Breeding, and Life,* so "to keep speed in the Race," she hastily scribbled and

seldom revised. Her writing process spawned a chaotic style that has influenced perceptions of her philosophy among contemporaries and later critics. Replete with contradictions, her texts seem like roller-coaster rides because readers encounter and grapple with paradoxes alongside her. She intended at least part of this disorder; she wanted her language to capture the irregularities of dialogic thought. She explicitly describes her approach in *Grounds of Natural Philosophy: Divided into Thirteen Parts: With an Appendix Containing Five Parts* (1668), in which she structures discussions around the "minor" and "major" parts of her mind. Although my thoughts "often dispute and argue for recreation and delight-sake," she declares, "yet they were never so irregular, as to divide into parties like facetious fellows." Clearly, Cavendish relished the creative force of contradictions.

When she was composing her earliest works, Cavendish was surrounded by some of the most innovative thinkers of her day. While in exile, the Newcastles entertained a coterie of learned men, including English writer Kenelm Henry Digby, French mathematicians Marin Mersenne and Gilles Personne de Roberval, French mathematicians and philosophers Pierre Gassendi and René Descartes, and the English philosopher Thomas Hobbes. Like most early moderns, the "Newcastle Circle" did not draw rigid distinctions between "philosophy" and "science." Instead, they engaged in what they called "natural philosophy," a pursuit that valued both speculation and experimentation. Their ideas influenced Margaret Cavendish's writing for the next two decades. During this time, for instance, she learned about the "new astronomy." She and her husband acquired seven telescopes and began to gaze at the heavens. The possibility of many inhabitable worlds energized her philosophy and eventually inspired her science-fiction fantasy, *The Description of a New Blazing World,* first published together with her *Observations upon Experimental Philosophy* (1666).

Despite her proximity to learned men and scientific novelties, Cavendish's access to philosophy was limited. Language barriers sometimes precluded serious intellectual engagement. Interregnum politics, however, granted her an extended period of contact with the Cavendish family's real virtuoso, William Cavendish's brother Charles Cavendish. An amateur scientist and mathematician, Charles Cavendish possessed knowledge and skill as well as enthusiasm. In November 1651, Margaret Cavendish traveled with her brother-in-law to England to petition Parliament for some compensation for the Cavendish properties, which had been sequestered, or seized, because of the brothers' Royalist sympathies and were about to be sold. For the year and a half that she and Charles Cavendish waited in London for the wheels of bureaucracy to turn, she learned about his intellectual interests and began to experiment with some of them in her writing. In her *The Mental World of Stuart Women: Three Studies* (1987) Sara Heller Mendelson argues that the discursive environment in interregnum London motivated Cavendish to offer up her ideas for public scrutiny. Encouraged by relaxed censorship rules and religious fervor, many women were publishing pamphlets and preaching in the streets. In 1653 Cavendish published her first book, *Poems and Fancies,* which she dedicated to Charles Cavendish.

Many poems in the volume explored the idea of atoms. As were many seventeenth-century thinkers, Cavendish was captivated by the ancient philosophies of Democritus, Epicurus, and Lucretius, who posited an unbounded universe filled with atoms and voids. For them and their early modern adherents, atoms harbored infinitesimal worlds that human sense could not perceive. "And if thus *small,* then Ladies well may weare / A *World* of *Worlds,* as *Pendents* in each *Eare,*" Cavendish conjectures in "*Of many* Worlds *in this* World" in *Poems and Fancies.* Despite her initial enchantment, Cavendish later rejected atomism because it emphasized chance and contingency, principles she could not fully accept. She was, after all, a Royalist who craved a unified world with a single organizing principle. As her encounter with atomism illustrates, Cavendish's philosophical interests often clashed with her political convictions.

After her stay in England, Cavendish returned to Antwerp and gathered together some of her old manuscripts, publishing them in *The Worlds Olio* (1655). The collection includes a preface to the reader in which Cavendish attempts to explain the differences between men and women. This piece encapsulates Cavendish's paradoxical thoughts on gender. On one hand, the preface asserts men's biological supremacy. Just as the moon is the lesser light of the sun, so woman is the inferior of man. Such unalterable distinctions justifiably dictate social inequities. Cavendish advocates separate spheres for the two genders, announcing that "Man is made to Govern Common Wealths, and Women their privat Families." Men's superiority is self-evident; they are responsible for every major achievement on earth. On the other hand, despite this antifeminist stance, Cavendish includes in her preface lengthy passages voicing the "great complaints" of "our Sex." Through this rhetorical strategy she hints that social inequalities are what make women inferior, not natural weaknesses.

The ideological tensions evident in the preface to *The Worlds Olio* continued to plague (and inspire) Cavendish's "feminism." When she writes about women as a social group in the real world, she generally takes a conservative position, expressing essentialist arguments

William Cavendish, first Duke of Newcastle; engraving circa 1657 by Peter Clouwet from a painting by Abraham van Diepenbeke (from Douglas Grant, Margaret the First: A Biography of Margaret Cavendish, Duchess of Newcastle, 1623–1673, *1957)*

on the nature of women. When she writes about her fictional heroines or even herself, she often assumes a constructivist and more recognizably feminist perspective. Hilda Smith argues that "no work of a seventeenth-century feminist poses so many interpretive problems" as the writings of Margaret Cavendish. "She appears to have understood better than any of her sisters the multi-faceted nature of women's oppression," Smith adds.

In 1656 Cavendish published *Natures Pictures Drawn by Fancies Pencil to the Life. Written by the thrice Noble, Illustrious and Excellent Princess, the Lady Marchioness of Newcastle. In this Volume there are several feigned Stories of Natural Descriptions, as Comical, Tragical, and Tragi-Comical, Poetical, Romancical, Philosophical, and Historical, both in Prose and Verse, some all Verse, some all Prose, some mixt, partly Prose, and partly Verse. Also, there are some Morals, and some Dialogues; but they are as the Advantage Loaves of Bread to a Bakers dozen; and a true Story at the end wherein there is no Feignings,* a charming collection of stories and essays. Although she had a flair for fiction and poetry, she considered philosophy to be a more serious, and thus a more admirable, pursuit. She wrote some plays in the 1660s, but she increasingly invested her energies in philosophy. While her early philosophical texts professed

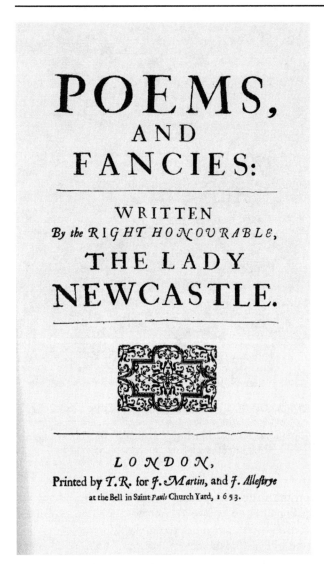

*Title page for Cavendish's first book. It includes "*Of many *Worlds* in this *World*," one of her poems about the atomic theory of matter (from Cavendish,* Poems and Fancies, *1653, 1972)*

gression. "When any of our Sex doth Write," Cavendish comments in *CCXI Sociable Letters* (1664), "they Write some Devotions, or Romances, or Receits of Medicines, for Cookery or confectioners, or Complemental Letters, or a Copy or two of Verses." In her view such frivolous texts were consistent with women's flighty, domestic natures. As Cavendish puts it, she and her female counterparts expressed "our Brief Wit in our Short Works." By writing philosophy, though, Cavendish set herself apart from her sex and its frailties. Throughout her career she attempted to represent herself as a singular personality who was different from other women.

Contemporary reactions to Cavendish's eccentric persona varied. Dorothy Osborne's letters hint that people looked upon the notorious authoress with a mixture of fascination and disgust. When Osborne first heard about *Poems and Fancies,* she was anxious to peruse it. "For God's sake if you meet with it send it to me," she begged her lover, William Temple. Nevertheless, Osborne later condemned Cavendish. In a subsequent letter to Temple, written 7 May 1653, she declared that she had read *Poems and Fancies* and there were "many soberer people in Bedlam," adding that Cavendish's friends were "much to blame to let her go abroad." An accomplished writer herself, Osborne may well have been intrigued by a woman who dared to make her writing public. But Osborne was also a proper lady, and this identity spurred her to castigate Cavendish's textual antics.

In 1660 Charles II was restored to the English throne, and after years on the Continent, the Newcastles were able to come home. Once back in England, Margaret Cavendish continued to cut an outlandish figure. Onlookers were struck by her peculiar sense of style. In *A True Relation of my Birth, Breeding, and Life,* she wrote that even as a girl she "took great delight in attiring, fine dressing and fashions, especially such fashions as I did invent my self, not taking that pleasure in such fashions as was invented by others." Contemporary accounts describe extravagant, androgynous costumes. For instance, she may have worn breeches with long, ornate trains, thus combining masculinity with an exaggerated femininity. In his diary entry for 11 April 1667 Samuel Pepys described the duchess's "antique dress" and "footmen in velvet coats," adding that the court was as breathlessly anticipating the arrival of the duchess "as if it were the Queen of Sheba." Such acts of self-representation earned Cavendish the nickname "Mad Madge." The sobriquet stuck. For years critics focused on her idiosyncrasies, often at the expense of serious discussions of her writing. More recently, however, feminist critics have urged the study of Cavendish's texts as well as her colorful personality.

an originality grounded in ignorance, later works directly challenged the ideas of major early modern thinkers including Hobbes, Descartes, the poet and philosopher Henry More, the Belgian naturalist and philosopher Franciscus Mercurius van Helmont, the physicist and chemist Robert Boyle, and the physicist and architect Robert Hooke. Londa Schiebinger notes that though Cavendish was a materialist, she believed nature possessed a unifying, organizing principle. She occasionally leaned toward atheism but finally resolved theological tensions by placing religion in a category separate from science. Her *Grounds of Natural Philosophy,* for example, describes an "immaterial," "uncreated" God who presides over nature.

Mendelson convincingly argues that Cavendish believed her commitment to philosophy was a trans-

Despite her efforts to cultivate a singular, androgynous persona, Cavendish experienced the sting of sexism. Although she corresponded informally with male philosophers and scientists, her sex barred her from intellectual institutions. She did not receive a university education, and as a result, she craved formal recognition from the academic community, frequently sending presentation copies of her books to Oxford and Cambridge. She was also excluded from the emergent scientific profession–as a woman, she was not invited to join the newly formed Royal Society. On 30 May 1667, after much debate within the group, Cavendish was permitted to attend a Royal Society meeting. Her gender, however, strongly influenced men's perceptions of her scientific acumen. For instance, Boyle conducted an experiment he deemed especially appealing to the ladies. Writing about the occasion in his diary entry for 30 May 1667, Pepys focused on her body and her attire, saying that the "Duchesse hath been a good comely woman; but her dress so antic and her deportment so unordinary, that I do not like her at all," adding that he did not "hear her say anything that was worth hearing, but that she was full of admiration, all admiration." Also writing about the Royal Society visit in his diary for 30 May 1667, John Evelyn wrote in a similar vein, calling Cavendish "a mighty pretender to Learning, Poetrie & Philosophie."

Cavendish's marginal intellectual status instilled within her a persistent utopianism. Throughout the 1660s she imagined academic, political, and aesthetic communities controlled by women. For instance, *The Female Academy*, which appears in *Playes Written by the Thrice Noble, Illustrious and Most Excellent Princess, the Lady Marchioness of Newcastle* (1662), features a fantasy college where "Academical Ladies" engage in intellectual pursuits usually limited to men. The same volume includes *Bell in Campo*, in which a pack of disgruntled wives form an army of "she Souldiers." *The Convent of Pleasure* appears in a 1668 volume, *Plays, Never before Printed*. In this play Cavendish tells the story of a wealthy young heiress who, having resolved to remain unmarried, transforms her late father's estate into an enclosed women's community. Cavendish's utopian texts contain her most adamant feminist expressions. In constructing these fantasy spaces, she temporarily sets aside obstacles to feminist thought that loom in her own culture. Her utopias interrogate natural law, common sense, and gendered hierarchies. Her imagined communities often lack traditional family structures, and they thus release their female characters from subordinate positions as daughters, wives, and mothers to envision new arenas for female thought, voice, and action. Cavendish's utopian texts typically end with the collaspse of imagined society. This narrative strategy both emphasizes the inevitability of patriarchal constraints and implies that seventeenth-century society is fundamentally dystopian for women.

Cavendish's best-known utopia is her 1666 science-fiction fantasy, *The Description of a New Blazing World*, which appears in the same volume as her *Observations upon Experimental Philosophy* and was separately published two years later as *The Description of a New World, called the Blazing-World*. On the surface the two texts seem extremely different. *Observations upon Experimental Philosophy* is a serious treatise on seventeenth-century science while *The Description of a New Blazing World* is, as Cavendish puts it, "romancical" and "fantastical." But together these two books, which are joined "as two worlds at the ends of their poles," provide a comprehensive portrait of Cavendish's philosophical interests.

Observations upon Experimental Philosophy mainly consists of a series of essays on astronomy, natural history, the physics of color, atoms, telescopes, microscopes, and other early modern scientific discoveries. Essay titles are as whimsical as "Of a Butter-Flye" and as rigorous as "Des Cartes Opinion of Motion Examined." Cavendish evaluates contemporary scientific advances with a mixture of interest and skepticism. She comments on the epistemological shift that her century has witnessed, that is, that scholars increasingly value observation and experimentation over speculation. She herself endorses older, more speculative modes of inquiry, challenging the positivist, empirical stance of the new science. She condemns the reliance of the fledgling discipline on human sense, questioning its capacity to reveal the truth. Throughout *Observations upon Experimental Philosophy*, she insists upon the existence of things beyond human perception.

In *The Description of a New Blazing World*, Cavendish imagines alternatives to aspects of scientific culture that trouble her most. As if to reinforce her point about the limits of knowledge, she positions her celestial utopia in an imaginary universe that differs markedly from those described by classical and early modern authors. For instance, she does not scatter her worlds in space but rather strings them together at their poles like a strand of pearls. And, instead of traversing over vast distances and noting familiar astronomical locales along the way, her celestial travelers move from world to world within strange subterranean passages. Finally, *The Description of a New Blazing World* includes casual asides that defy the tenets of early modern astronomy, such as the insistence that the moon generates a light of its own.

In Cavendish's story a lady is kidnapped by the lustful merchant who loads her into his packet boat and sails away. The merchant and his sailors lose themselves in Arctic seas and freeze to death, but God's grace protects the lady, and she drifts across the

Frontispiece, supposedly depicting Cavendish and her family, for her
Natures Pictures Drawn by Fancies Pencil to the Life,
Cavendish's 1656 collection of poems and tales; engraving by
Peter Clowet from a painting by Abraham van Diepenbeke
(from Douglas Grant, Margaret the First: A
Biography of Margaret Cavendish,
Duchess of Newcastle,
1623–1673, *1957)*

The Description of a New Blazing World features a female character who not only wields religious and political power but also participates in intellectual communities. Cavendish's utopian heroine converses with bear-men experimental philosophers, bird-men astronomers, ape-men chemists, lice-men mathematicians, and other scholarly groups that bear more than a coincidental resemblance to the Royal Society. The text celebrates the empress's ability to orchestrate research collaborations, set scientific agendas, and most importantly, hold her own in intellectual disputes. She expresses views similar to those Cavendish outlines in *Observations upon Experimental Philosophy,* with one crucial difference: she enjoys an unqualified respect. In this way *The Description of a New Blazing World* presents alternatives to the prejudices Cavendish and other early modern women thinkers endured.

Despite its radicalism, *The Description of a New Blazing World* is in some ways a deeply conservative text. Because the utopia is a peaceful, monolinguistic monarchy with no religious differences, some critics have dismissed it as a singular, elitist wish for the world English aristocrats enjoyed before the Civil War. Perhaps most disturbingly for a modern reader, the feminist ideas in the text apply only to upper-class women. *The Description of a New Blazing World* reminds readers to consider Cavendish's feminism through the lens of history, attending to its limitations as well as its triumphs.

Cavendish published her last book in 1668 but continued to express her ideas in letters and in manuscripts for unpublished works. On 15 December 1673 she died suddenly at Welbeck, her country house. Biographers do not know the cause of her death. They do know, however, that she had experienced stomach problems since the mid 1660s and had perhaps worsened her condition by dieting, purging, and eschewing exercise. She was buried in Westminster Abbey. An eighty-year-old William Cavendish composed an epitaph for her tomb, calling his remarkable wife a "wise, witty, and learned Lady" who "was with her Lord all the time of his banishment and miseries, and when he came home never parted from him in his Solitary Retirements."

Writing in 1666, in her preface to the reader for *Observations upon Experimental Philosophy,* Margaret Cavendish remarks of her philosophy (referring to it with the feminine pronoun) that "if she be slighted now and buried in silence, she may perhaps rise more gloriously hereafter . . . She may meet with an age where she will be more regarded, then she is in this." The age Cavendish envisioned has arrived. Since the 1980s critical interest in Cavendish's writing has surged. Feminist literary critics were initially attracted to Cavendish as a rare example of a pre-Enlightenment feminist. Begin-

North Pole into the Blazing World, a kingdom of animal-human hybrids ruled by an emperor. The lady so enchants the emperor that he marries her, grants her full sovereignty over his realm, and benevolently disappears from notice. As empress, Cavendish's utopian heroine explores the knowledge, religion, and politics of "the Blazing World"; communicates with spirits; and befriends a female soul from another world, a character based on Cavendish herself. Together, the two women travel from world to world in spirit and in body, eventually rescuing the empress's home country from military disaster.

ning in the 1990s critics increasingly have interpreted her not as a lone visionary who thought beyond her time but rather as a participant in a wide range of early modern conversations.

Letters:

Letters Written by Charles Lamb's "princely woman, the thrice noble Margaret Newcastle" to Her Husband: By His "fine old Whig" William Plumer to the Third Duke of Portland and Lord William Bentinck; Also by His "old bencher" Samuel Salt. From the Originals at Welbeck Abbey. Together with a Reprint of a Rare Pamphlet, Entitled "Considérations sur l'état actuel de la France au mois de juin 1815; par un Anglais," edited by Richard William Goulding (London: Murray, 1909);

The Phanseys of William Cavendish Marquis of Newcastle Addressed to Margaret Lucas and her Letters in Reply, edited by Douglas Grant (London: Nonesuch, 1956).

Biographies:

Douglas Grant, *Margaret the First: A Biography of Margaret Cavendish, Duchess of Newcastle, 1623–1673* (London: Hart-Davis, 1957);

Kathleen Jones, *A Glorious Fame: The Life of Margaret Cavendish, Duchess of Newcastle, 1623–1673* (London: Bloomsbury, 1988).

References:

Anna Battigelli, "Between the Glass and the Hand: The Eye in Margaret Cavendish's *Blazing World*," *1650–1850: Ideas, Aesthetics, and Inquiries in the Early Modern Era,* 2 (1996): 25–38;

Battigelli, *Margaret Cavendish and the Exiles of the Mind* (Lexington: University Press of Kentucky, 1998);

Erin Lang Bonin, "Margaret Cavendish's Dramatic Utopias and the Politics of Gender," *Studies in English Literature 1500–1900,* 40, no. 2 (2000): 339–354;

Sylvia Bowerbank, "The Spider's Delight: Margaret Cavendish and the 'Female' Imagination," *English Literary Renaissance,* 14 (Autumn 1984): 392–408;

Sylvia Brown, "Margaret Cavendish: Strategies Rhetorical and Philosophical against the Charge of Wantonness: Or Her Excuses for Writing so Much," *Critical Matrix: The Princeton Journal of Women, Gender, and Culture,* 6, no. 1 (1991): 20–45;

Catherine Gallagher, "Embracing the Absolute: The Politics of the Female Subject in Seventeenth-Century England," *Genders,* 1 (March 1988): 24–39;

Elaine Hobby, *Virtue of Necessity: English Women's Writing 1649–88* (Ann Arbor: University of Michigan Press, 1989);

Randall Ingram, "First Words and Second Thoughts: Margaret Cavendish, Humphrey Moseley, and 'the Book,'" *Journal of Medieval and Early Modern Studies,* 30, no. 1 (2000): 101–124;

Lee Cullen Khanna, "The Subject of Utopia: Margaret Cavendish and Her *Blazing World*," in *Utopian and Science Fiction by Women: Worlds of Difference,* edited by Jane L. Donawerth and Carol A. Kolmerten (Syracuse, N.Y.: Syracuse University Press, 1994), pp. 15–34;

Kate Lilley, "Blazing Worlds: Seventeenth-Century Women's Utopian Writing," in *Women, Texts, and Histories: 1575–1760,* edited by Clare Brant and Diane Purkiss (London & New York: Routledge, 1992);

B. G. MacCarthy, *The Female Pen: Women Writers and Novelists 1621–1818,* second edition (New York: New York University Press, 1994);

Sara Heller Mendelson, *The Mental World of Stuart Women: Three Studies* (Amherst: University of Massachusetts Press, 1987);

Rebecca Merrens, "A Nature of 'Infinite Sense and Reason': Margaret Cavendish's Natural Philosophy and the 'Noise' of a Feminized Nature," *Women's Studies,* 25, no. 5 (1996): 421–456;

Gerald Dennis Meyer, *The Scientific Lady in England 1650–1760: An Account of Her Rise, with Emphasis on the Major Roles of the Telescope and Microscope* (Berkeley & Los Angeles: University of California Press, 1955);

Samuel I. Mintz, "The Duchess of Newcastle's Visit to the Royal Society," *Journal of English and Germanic Philology,* 51 (April 1952): 168–176;

Lisa T. Sarasohn, "A Science Turned Upside Down: Feminism and the Natural Philosophy of Margaret Cavendish," *Huntington Library Quarterly,* 47 (Autumn 1984): 289–307;

Londa Schiebinger, *The Mind Has No Sex?: Women in the Origins of Modern Science* (Cambridge, Mass.: Harvard University Press, 1989);

Sandra Sherman, "Trembling Texts: Margaret Cavendish and the Dialectic of Authorship," *English Literary Renaissance,* 24 (Winter 1994): 184–210;

Hilda Smith, *Reason's Disciples: Seventeenth-Century English Feminists* (Urbana: University of Illinois Press, 1982);

Jay Stevenson, "The Mechanist-Vitalist Soul of Margaret Cavendish," *Studies in English Literature 1500–1900,* 36, no. 3 (1996): 527–543;

Sophie Tomlinson, "'My Brain the Stage': Margaret Cavendish and the Fantasy of Female Performance," in *Women, Texts, and Histories: 1575–1760,* edited by Brant and Purkiss (London & New York: Routledge, 1992), pp. 134–163;

Women's Writing, special Cavendish issue, 4, no. 3 (1997).

Samuel Clarke

(11 October 1675 – 17 May 1729)

J. Dybikowski
University of British Columbia

BOOKS: *Three Practical Essays, viz. On Baptism, Confirmation, Repentance. Containing Full Instructions for a Holy Life: With Earnest Exhortations, especially to young Persons, drawn from the Consideration of the Severity of the Discipline of the Primitive Church* (London: Printed for James Knapton, 1699); republished as *The Whole Duty of a Christian, Plainly Represented in Three Practical Essays, on Baptism, Confirmation, and Repentance. Containing Full Instructions for a Holy Life with Earnest Exhortations, especially to young Persons, drawn from the Consideration of the Severity of the Discipline of the Primitive Church* (London: Printed for James Knapton, 1704); republished as *Three Practical Essays, on Baptism, Confirmation, and Repentance. Containing Full Instructions for a Holy Life with Earnest Exhortations, especially to young Persons, drawn from the Consideration of the Severity of the Discipline of the Primitive Church* (London: Printed by William Botham for James Knapton, 1721);

Some Reflections on that Part of a Book called Amyntor, or The Defence of Milton's Life, which relates to the Writings of the Primitive Fathers and the Canon of the New Testament. In a Letter to a Friend, anonymous (London: Printed for James Knapton, 1699);

A Paraphrase on the Gospel of St. Matthew (London: Printed for James Knapton, 1701);

A Paraphrase on the Gospels of St. Mark and St. Luke (London: Printed for James Knapton, 1702);

A Paraphrase on the Gospel of St. John (London: Printed for James Knapton, 1703);

A Demonstration of the Being and Attributes of God: More Particularly in Answer to Mr. Hobbs, Spinoza, And their Followers. Wherein the Notion of Liberty is Stated, and the Possibility and Certainty of it Proved, in Opposition to Necessity and Fate, Being the Substance of Eight Sermons Preach'd at the Cathedral-Church of St. Paul, in the Year 1704, at the Lecture founded by the Honourable Robert Boyle Esq. (London: Printed by William Botham for James Knapton, 1705);

The Great Duty of Universal Love and Charity. A Sermon Preached before the Queen, at St. James's Chapel. On

Samuel Clarke (National Portrait Gallery, London)

Sunday December the 30th (London: Printed by Henry Hills, 1706);

A Discourse concerning the Unchangeable Obligations of Natural Religion and the Truth and Certainty of the Christian Revelation. Being eight sermons preach'd at the Cathedral-Church of St Paul, in the year 1705, at the Lecture founded by the Honourable Robert Boyle Esq (London: Printed by William Botham for James Knapton, 1706); revised and enlarged as *A Discourse concerning the*

Being and Attributes of God, the Obligations of Natural Religion, and the Truth and Certainty of the Christian Revelation. In answer to Mr. Hobbs, Spinoza, the Author of The Oracles of Reason, and other deniers of natural and revealed religion: Being Sixteen sermons preach'd at the Cathedral-Church of St Paul, in the years 1705 and 1706, at the Lecture founded by the Honourable Robert Boyle, Esq. (London: Printed by William Botham for James Knapton, 1711); revised and enlarged fourth edition (London: Printed by William Botham for James Knapton, 1716)—includes *Several Letters to Dr. Clarke from a Gentleman in Glocestershire Relating to the first volume of Sermons preached at Mr Boyle's Lecture,* by Joseph Butler; revised and enlarged sixth edition (London: Printed by William Botham for James Knapton, 1725)—includes *A Discourse concerning the Connexion of the Prophesies in the Old Testament, and the Application of them to Christ* and *An Answer to a seventh letter, concerning the Argument à priori;*

A Letter to Mr Dodwell; wherein All the Arguments in his Epistolary Discourse against the Immortality of the Soul are particularly answered, and the Judgment of the Fathers concerning that Matter truly represented (London: Printed by William Botham for James Knapton, 1706); enlarged as *A Letter to Mr. Dodwell; wherein all the Arguments in his Epistolary Discourse against the Immortality of the Soul are particularly answered, and the Judgment of the Fathers concerning that Matter truly represented. Together with A Defense of an Argument made use of in a Letter to Mr. Dodwell to prove the immateriality and natural immortality of the soul. The Third Edition. To which is added, Some Reflections on that Part of a Book called Amyntor, or The Defense of Milton's Life, which relates to the Writings of the Primitive Fathers and the Canon of the New Testament,* by Clarke and Anthony Collins (London: Printed by William Botham for James Knapton, 1718);

A Defense of an Argument made use of in a Letter to Mr. Dodwel, to prove the Immateriality and Natural Immortality of the Soul (London: Printed by William Botham for James Knapton, 1707);

A Second Defense of an Argument made use of in a Letter to Mr Dodwel, to prove the Immateriality and Natural Immortality of the Soul. In a Letter to the Author of A Reply to Mr Clarke's Defense, etc. (London: Printed by William Botham for James Knapton, 1707);

A Third Defense of an Argument made use of in a Letter to Mr. Dodwel, to prove the Immateriality and Natural Immortality of the Soul. In a Letter to the Author of the Reflexions on Mr Clarke's Second Defense, &c. (London: Printed by William Botham for James Knapton, 1708);

A Fourth Defense of an Argument made use of in a Letter to Mr. Dodwel, to prove the Immateriality and Natural Immortality of the Soul. In a Letter to the Author of the Answer to Mr. Clark's Third Defense, &c. With a Postscript, relating to the Book, entitled, A Vindication of Mr Dodwel's Epistolary Discourse, &c. (London: Printed for James Knapton, 1708);

A Sermon Preach'd at the Parish-Church of St. Mary White-Chapel, on Tuesday, October 11. 1709. At the Funeral of Dame Mary Cooke, Late Wife of Sir John Cooke, of Doctor's-Commons, London, Knight, Doctor of Laws, &c. (London: Printed by J.B. for James Knapton, 1709);

A Sermon Preach'd before the Honourable House of Commons, At the Church of St. Margaret Westminster. On Tuesday, Nov. 22. 1709. Being the Day of Thanksgiving For the Signal and Glorious Victory obtained near Mons, and for the other Great Successes of Her Majesties Arms, this last Year, Under the Command of the Duke of Marlborovgh (London: Printed by William Botham for James Knapton, 1709);

A Sermon preach'd at the Parish-Church of St James's Westminster, on Tuesday November. 7. 1710: Being the Day of Thanksgiving for the Successes Of the fore-going Campaign (London: Printed by William Botham for James Knapton, 1710);

A Sermon preach'd before the Queen at St James's Chapel, on Wednesday the 8th of March, 1709/10. Being the anniversary of Her Majesties happy accession to the throne (London: Printed by William Botham for James Knapton, 1710);

The Government of Passion. A Sermon Preach'd before the Queen at St. James's Chapel, on Sunday the 7th of January, 1710/11 (London: Printed by William Botham for James Knapton, 1711);

The Scripture-Doctrine of the Trinity. In Three Parts. Wherein all the Texts in the New Testament relating to that Doctrine, and the Principal Passages in the Liturgy of the Church of England are collected, compared and explained (London: Printed for James Knapton, 1712); revised as *The Scripture-Doctrine of the Trinity. Wherein Every Text in the New Testament relating to that Doctrine, is distinctly considered; and the Divinity of our Blessed Saviour according to the Scriptures, proved and explained* (London: Printed by W. Wilkins for James Knapton, 1719);

A Letter to the Reverend Dr Wells, Rector of Cotesbach in Leicestershire. In Answer to his Remarks, &c. (London: Printed for James Knapton, 1714);

A Reply to the Objections of Robert Nelson, Esq; and of an Anonymous Author, against Dr Clarke's Scripture-Doctrine of the Trinity. Being a Commentary upon Forty Select Texts of Scripture. To which is added, An Answer to the Remarks of the Author of Some Considerations concerning the Trin-

ity, and the Ways of managing that Controversy (London: Printed for James Knapton, 1714);

Three Letters to Dr Clarke, from a Clergyman of the Church of England; concerning his Scripture-Doctrine of the Trinity. With the Doctor's Replies. Published by the Author of the said Three Letters, by Clarke and John Jackson (London: Printed for John Baker, 1714);

A Collection of Papers, which passed between the late Learned Mr. Leibnitz, and Dr. Clarke, in the Years 1715 and 1716. Relating to the Principles of Natural Philosophy and Religion. With an Appendix. To which are added, Letters to Dr. Clarke concerning Liberty and Necessity; From a Gentleman of the University of Cambridge: With the Doctor's Answers to them. Also Remarks upon a Book, Entituled, A Philosophical Enquiry concerning Human Liberty (London: Printed for James Knapton, 1717);

The Modest Plea, &c. continued. Or, A Brief and Distinct Answer to Dr Waterland's Queries, relating to the Doctrine of the Trinity (London: Printed for James Knapton, 1720);

Observations on Dr Waterland's Second Defense of his Queries, By the Author of the Reply to his First Defense (London: Printed for James Knapton, 1724);

XVII Sermons on Several Occasions: (Eleven of Which, Never Before Printed). Particularly of the Great Duty of Universal Love and Charity. Of the Government of Passion. Discourses upon Occasion of the Plague. Of St Peter being the Rock on Which Christ built his Church. Of the Faith of Abraham. Of Christ being the Bread of Life. Of the Original of Sin and Misery. Of Election and Reprobation, being a Paraphrase on Rom. IX. The Present Life a State of Probation in order to a Future Life. That Christ's Admonitions to his Apostles, belong Universally to all Christians (London: Printed by William Botham for James Knapton, 1724); enlarged as XVIII Sermons on Several Occasions (London: Printed for James, John & Paul Knapton, 1734;

A Paraphrase upon Our Saviour's Sermon on the Mount (London: Printed for James Knapton, 1724);

A Discourse concerning the Connexion of the Prophecies in the Old Testament, and the Application of them to Christ. Being an extract from the Sixth Edition of A Demonstration of the Being and Attributes of God, &c. To which is added, A Letter concerning the Argument a priori (London: Printed for James & John Knapton, 1725);

A Sermon Preach'd at the Parish-Church of St James's Westminster, on Sunday April 18, 1725. Upon Occasion of the Erecting a Charity-School, as a House of Education for Women-Servants (London: Printed for James & John Knapton, 1725);

An Exposition of the Church-catechism: Published from the Author's Manuscript, edited by John Clarke (London: Printed by William Botham for James & John Knapton, 1729);

Sermons on the Following Subjects, viz. Of Faith in God, Of the Unity of God, Of the Eternity of God, Of the Spirituality of God, Of the Immutability of God, Of the Omnipresence of God, Of the Omnipotence of God, Of the Ominiscience of God, Of the Wisdom of God, Of the Goodness of God, Of the Patience of God, Of the Justice of God. By Samuel Clarke, D.D. Published from the Author's Manuscript, edited by John Clarke, preface by Benjamin Hoadley, 10 volumes (London: Printed by William Botham for James & John Knapton, 1730–1731).

Editions and Collections: A Paraphrase on the Four Evangelists. Wherein, for the Clearer Understanding of the Sacred History, the Whole Text and Paraphrase Are Printed in Separate Columns Against Each Other. Together with Critical Notes on the More Difficult Passages, two volumes (London: Printed for James Knapton, 1703);

Six Sermons on Several Occasions (London: Printed by William Botham for James Knapton, 1714);

The Works of Samuel Clarke, D.D. Late Rector of St. James's, Westminster, 4 volumes (London: Printed for John & Paul Knapton, 1738); reprinted as The Works of Samuel Clarke (New York & London: Garland, 1978);

The Leibniz-Clarke Correspondence: Together with Extracts from Newton's Principia and Opticks, edited, with an introduction and notes, by H. G. Alexander (Manchester: Manchester University Press, 1956; Manchester: Manchester University Press / New York: Barnes & Noble, 1970);

Samuel Clarke: A Demonstration of the Being and Attributes of God. 1705: A Discourse Concerning the Unchangeable Obligations of Natural Religion. 1706. Faksimile-Neudruck der Londoner Ausgaben (Stuttgart-Bad Canstatt: Friedrich Frommann Verlag, 1964);

A Demonstration of the Being and Attributes of God And Other Writings, edited by Ezio Vailati (Cambridge: Cambridge University Press, 1998);

G. W. Leibniz & Samuel Clarke: Correspondence, edited, with an introduction, by Roger Ariew (Indianapolis & Cambridge: Hackett, 2000).

OTHER: Jacques Rohault, Jacobi Rohaulti Physica. Latinè reddidit, & annotatiunculis quibusdam illustravit S. Clarke. Accessit index rerum & Phænomenorum præcipuorum, translated, with notes, by Clarke (London: Printed for James Knapton, 1697); revised and enlarged as Jacobi Rohaulti Physica. Latinè vertit, recensuit, & uberioribus jam Adnotationibus, ex illustrissimi Isaaci Newtoni Philosophiâ maximam partem haustis, amplisicavit & ornavit Samvel Clarke (London:

Printed for James Knapton, 1702; revised, 1710; revised, 1718); translated by John Clarke as *Rohault's System of Natural Philosophy, Illustrated with Dr. Samuel Clarke's Notes Taken mostly out of Sir Isaac Newton's Philosophy, with Additions: Done into English*, 2 volumes (London: Printed for James Knapton, 1723);

Isaac Newton, *Optice, sive de Reflexionibus, Refractionibus, Inflexionibus, et Coloribus Lucis libri tres. Latine reddidit Samuel Clarke. Accedunt tractatus duo ejusdem Authoris de Speciebus & Magnitudine Figurarum Curvilinearum, Latine scripti*, translated by Clarke (London: Printed for Samuel Smith & Benjamin Walford, 1706; enlarged edition, London: Printed for William & John Innys, Printers for the Royal Society, 1719);

Julius Caesar, *C. Julii Cæsaris quæ extant. Accuratissimè cum libris editis & MSS optimis collata, recognita & correcta. Accesserunt annotationes Samuelis Clarke. S.T.P. Item indices locorum, rerumque & verborum utilissimæ; Tabulis ænis ornata*, edited by Clarke (London: Printed for Jacob Tonson, 1712);

John Moore, *Sermons on Several Subjects By the Right Reverend Father in God, John, Late Lord Bishop of Ely*, 2 volumes, edited by Clarke, (volume 1, London: Printed for William Taylor, Thomas Caldecott & John Hooke, 1716; volume 2, London: Printed for Thomas Caldecott, 1716);

Homer, *Homeri Ilias Græce et Latine annotationes in usum Serenissimi Principis Gulielmi Augusti, Ducis de Cumberland, & c. regio jussu scripsit atque edidit Samuel Clarke*, 2 volumes, edited and translated by Clarke and Samuel Clarke Jr. (London: Printed for James & John Knapton, 1729, 1732);

Homer, *Homeri Odyssea Græce et Latine, item Batrachomyomachia, Hymni, et Epigrammata, Homero vulgò ascripta. Edidit, Annotationesque, ex Notis nonnullis MStis a Samuele Clarke S.T.P. defuncto relictis partim collectas, adjecit Samuel Clarke, S.R.S.*, 2 volumes, edited and translated by Clarke and Samuel Clarke Jr. (London: Printed for John & Paul Knapton, 1740);

Theophilus Lindsey, ed., *The Book of Common Prayer Reformed According to the Plan of the Late Dr. Samuel Clarke Together with The Psalter or Psalms of David and A collection of Hymns for Public Worship* (London: Printed for J. Johnson, 1774).

Edition: Jacques Rohault, *A System of Natural Philosophy*, translated by John Clarke, introduction by L. L. Laudan, Sources of Science Series, no. 50 (New York & Londo: Johnson Reprint Corporation, 1965);

Rohault, *Rohault's System of Natural Philosophy: Illustrated with Dr. Samuel Clarke's Notes, Taken Mostly out of Sir*

Isaac Newton's Philosophy, 2 volumes, translated by John Clarke (New York: Garland, 1987).

SELECTED PERIODICAL PUBLICATION— UNCOLLECTED: "A Letter from the Rev. Dr. Samuel Clarke to Mr. Benjamin Hoadly, F. R. S. occasion'd by the present Controversy among Mathematicians, concerning the Proportion of Velocity and Force in Bodies in Motion," *Philosophical Transactions of the Royal Society of London*, 35 (1729): 381–388.

In a passage in his *Lettres philosophiques* (Philosophical Letters, 1734), translated by Leonard Tancock in *Letters from England* (1980), Voltaire describes Samuel Clarke as "a man of unswerving virtue and a gentle disposition, more interested in his opinions than excited about making converts, solely concerned with calculations and demonstrations—a real reasoning machine." Clarke was versatile: he was a scrupulous and dedicated clergyman of high moral character in the Church of England, an accomplished classical scholar, an expert in Isaac Newton's natural philosophy, a courtier admired by Princess Caroline, and a gifted theologian, controversialist, and philosopher. His philosophy focuses on a set of metaphysical issues where theology and philosophy converge and where his approach is marked by the discoveries of Newtonian natural philosophy. Central to his thought is his claim that reason can demonstrate God's existence and attributes by a proof so compelling even a dispassionate atheist must accept its premises and reasoning; that it can establish the immateriality and immortality of the soul as well as the freedom of the will; and that it illuminates the nature of virtue and its foundation in eternal relations, binding on God as much as on human beings. On these foundations of natural religion he attempts to justify by powerful, but not demonstrative, arguments the truth of Christianity. While he contrasted himself with René Descartes, repudiated Benedict de Spinoza, and crossed swords with Gottfried Wilhelm Leibniz in a celebrated epistolary debate published in 1717, he, like them, was a rationalist who was himself strongly influenced by the Cambridge Platonists Henry More and Ralph Cudworth. His thought developed and matured on some issues, but there is a remarkable consistency of outlook that takes shape early in his writings.

Clarke was born in Norwich, England on 11 October 1675 to Hannah Clarke and Edward Clarke, a worsted-cloth manufacturer who was a prominent alderman as well as a member of Parliament for a brief term to which he was elected as a Whig in 1701. His Whig outlook was shared by his son, who was educated at the Free Grammar School in Norwich and sent to Cambridge, where he matriculated at Gonville

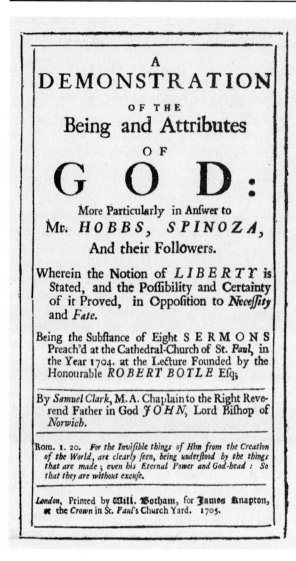

A

DEMONSTRATION

OF THE

Being and Attributes

OF

GOD:

More Particularly in Anſwer to
Mr. *HOBBS, SPINOZA,*
And their Followers.

Wherein the Notion of *LIBERTY* is
Stated, and the Poſſibility and Certainty
of it Proved, in Oppoſition to *Neceſſity*
and *Fate.*

Being the Subſtance of Eight S E R M O N S
Preach'd at the Cathedral-Church of St. *Paul,* in
the Year 1704. at the Lecture Founded by the
Honourable *ROBERT BOTLE* Eſq;

By *Samuel Clark,* M.A. Chaplain to the Right Reverend Father in God *JOHN,* Lord Biſhop of
Norwich.

Rom. I. 20. *For the Inviſible things of Him from the Creation
of the World, are clearly ſeen, being underſtood by the things
that are made ; even his Eternal Power and God-head : So
that they are without excuſe.*

London, Printed by **Will. Botham,** for **James Knapton,**
at the *Crown* in St. *Paul's* Church Yard. 1705.

*Title page for the series of sermons in which Clarke seeks to prove the
existence and nature of God and the reality of free will
(Beinecke Library, Yale University)*

and Caius College in 1691 and took his first degree in 1695. As a student Clarke was precocious, reputedly the first Cambridge undergraduate to defend a thesis drawn from Newton in the public exercises that were then a staple of Cambridge education. His talents were wide-ranging: he was accomplished in mathematics, natural philosophy, the ancient languages, ecclesiastical history, philosophy, and theology. He draws on all of these disciplines in his writings.

In 1696 Clarke was appointed a fellow of his college and about this time was asked by his former tutor, John Ellis, to retranslate Jacques Rohault's *Traité de physique* (Treatise on Physics, 1671), then a standard text at Cambridge, but in a faulty Latin translation. Clarke had doubts about the undertaking, since Rohault's natural philosophy was not only dated, but based on Cartesian

principles that Newton believed he had comprehensively undermined. Clarke sought advice from William Whiston, himself a convinced Newtonian, who, impressed by Clarke's knowledge of Newton's system, advised him to proceed in the absence of any existing text making Newton's thought more accessible than his forbidding masterwork, *Philosophiæ Naturalis Principia Mathematica* (Mathematical Principles of Natural Philosophy, 1687).

Clarke added notes that refer to Newton's ideas, but largely restricted himself to updating Rohault's natural philosophy and adding references to observations from ancient authors in the first edition, published in 1697. In later, revised editions (1702, 1710, and 1718), however, his notes became increasingly subversive, explaining Newton's theory of universal gravitation as well as his challenge to Cartesian views of space, matter, and the vacuum. No longer content to note the incompatibility between Rohault and Newton, Clarke says that Rohault is wrong. Whereas Rohault defines matter as extension, Clarke takes it to be impenetrable solidity. Whereas Rohault cannot separate space from matter, Clarke does, claiming the existence of a vacuum and holding space to be absolute. Whereas Rohault subscribes to the vortex theory to avoid positing occult causes, Clarke asserts the existence of the force of gravitational attraction. Rejecting the possibility of matter acting at a distance, Clarke argues for an immaterial cause, God, who is extended, infinite, and omnipresent, but also indivisible and able, unlike material objects, to penetrate the solidity of matter. Whereas Rohault claims God's existence on the basis of Descartes's ontological argument, Clarke asserts that God's existence should be proved on other grounds. He draws the philosophical battle lines between Newtonians and Cartesians sharply.

Whiston drew Clarke to the attention of John Moore, Bishop of Norwich, who had been rewarded for his support of William of Orange and the Glorious Revolution of 1688 with a bishopric. The liberal Moore, a patron of bright young men entering the ministry, appointed Clarke as his chaplain in 1698 and used his influence to promote him. His favor led to Clarke's appointment as rector of Drayton, Norfolk in 1699, and Clarke soon married the daughter of a Norfolk clergyman, Catherine Lockwood, with whom he had seven children, although only five survived him when his life was cut short after a brief illness at the age of fifty-three. As Moore's chaplain, Clarke catalogued his magnificent library of some 29,000 books and 1,500 manuscripts and pursued his scholarly interests in ideal circumstances. He acknowledged his debt by dedicating some of his writings to Moore, including his translation of Rohault. After Moore's death in 1714 he collected two volumes of his sermons, which he saw through the press. In them there are striking resemblances between Clarke's and Moore's views on such issues as proofs of God's existence and the natural basis for an expectation of a future state of rewards and punishments.

Three Practical Essays, viz. On Baptism, Confirmation, Repentance. Containing Full Instructions for a Holy Life: With Earnest Exhortations, especially to young Persons, drawn from the Consideration of the Severity of the Discipline of the Primitive Church (1699), Clarke's first book, sketches a defense of the certainty of Christianity that he takes as proof against all but thorough skeptics and determined libertines. He later filled in this sketch in his Boyle Lectures in 1704–1705. He anchors his argument in reason and natural religion, arguing for God's existence and attributes, including his justice and goodness, as determined not by his will or power but by the unalterable nature of things discoverable by reason. From this basis he infers God's providence and the necessity of religion. Since rewards and punishments in this life are not proportioned to virtue and vice, a providential God must provide for a future state of rewards and punishments for the immaterial souls of human beings. Since human reason is weak and vulnerable to the passions, it needs help from divine revelation to remedy its shortcomings. This revelation is unique to Christianity, the teaching of which conforms with human reason and is proven by the evidence of miracles and fulfilled biblical prophecies. To establish God's existence, Clarke relies on the easily grasped argument from design, which he later supplemented and effectively displaced in his Boyle Lectures with a less easily understood but more powerful argument that restricts itself to premises that even an atheist, so Clarke claims, must accept. Otherwise his scheme of argument in the two works is the same.

In 1699 Clarke anonymously published *Some Reflections on that Part of a Book called Amyntor, or The Defence of Milton's Life, which relates to the Writings of the Primitive Fathers and the Canon of the New Testament. In a Letter to a Friend,* which responds to John Toland's *Amyntor: or, A Defence of Milton's Life* (1699). Clarke believed that Toland's work constituted an attack on the essential canon of the New Testament, raising doubts about its scope and the authenticity of its texts in order to undermine religion. Clarke defends the existing canon, crucial to his conception of Protestantism as recognizing Scripture as the sole and sufficient rule of faith. The significance of the work is as the first in a series of encounters between himself and the "free-thinkers," Toland and Anthony Collins especially.

In 1701 Clarke began to publish paraphrases of the evangelists, which were collected in two volumes in 1703. In the preface to his *A Paraphrase on the Gospel of St. Matthew* (1701) he observes: "I have sincerely endeavoured to represent the Doctrine of our Saviour in its Original Simplicity, without respect to any Controversies in Religion." For him, controversies over speculative and minor issues of faith pose as great a

threat to religion as the attacks of atheists and deists, needlessly disturbing church peace and unity. Doctrinal imposition should give way, at least for the learned, to full liberty of examination. The doctrines most significant and essential to Christianity are those which, on a full and balanced reading of Scripture, are most secure and certain. What matters most for salvation is virtuous action in imitation of God whose moral attributes are within the reach of human understanding, albeit more perfect than their human counterparts. Were they beyond the reach of human understanding, the moral and consolational purposes of Christianity would be defeated.

Clarke's most ambitious and seminal contribution to philosophy and theology are his Boyle Lectures. In them by a single chain of reasoning, he seeks to demonstrate God's existence and attributes as well as the moral certainty of the truth of Christianity. His later writings are anchored in these lectures, as his earlier works anticipate them. The lecture series had been endowed by the scientist Robert Boyle in 1691 as a showcase for the defense of Christianity against "notorious Infidels, viz. Atheists, Deists, Pagans, Jews, and Mahometans," but without reference to the divisions among Christians. The platform was to Clarke's liking and the response to the first set of lectures he delivered in 1704 was so favorable that he was invited to deliver a second in 1705.

The full title of the first set of lectures, as published in 1705, reveals Clarke's intentions: *A Demonstration of the Being and Attributes of God: More Particularly in Answer to Mr. Hobbs, Spinoza, And their Followers. Wherein the Notion of Liberty is Stated, and the Possibility and Certainty of it Proved, in Opposition to Necessity and Fate, Being the Substance of Eight Sermons Preach'd at the Cathedral-Church of St. Paul, in the Year 1704, at the Lecture founded by the Honourable Robert Boyle Esq.* His main object is to demonstrate God's existence by a method approximating mathematical proof. His polemical aim is to refute Thomas Hobbes, Spinoza, and their followers—Toland included—whom he regards as atheists, their denials notwithstanding. Key to his demonstration is his defense of liberty. He represents it as a beginning of motion, uncaused by the motives or reasons of agents that influence how they act but do not cause or necessitate their actions. Liberty is incompatible with the necessity that governs only the behavior of passive material objects. For Clarke, God's existence is not established until God is shown to be intelligent, an impossibility unless God is also free. But neither God nor human agents can be intelligent or free unless they are immaterial. Dualism, accordingly, is at the heart of his project, but not the Cartesian variety, since Clarke follows the Platonist More in attributing extension to immaterial substances while denying their divisibility, whereas Descartes makes extension the defining property of matter. Being incomposite and not depending on matter, the soul, whether human or divine, is naturally indestructible and thus immortal.

Clarke begins by noting that, whether or not God exists, everyone must agree it would be preferable if he does. It follows that to mock religious belief or to make light of it, as atheists and freethinkers characteristically do, is indefensible. Even the bare possibility of God's existence ought to determine fair-minded thinkers to live piously, soberly, and virtuously.

The starting point of Clarke's proof is the cosmological argument whose ancestry extends back to Thomas Aquinas. From the bare premise that something now is, he infers that something always must have been. Arguing dialectically, as he characteristically does, he claims that it would be a contradiction to assert the contrary, for then something could exist without a cause. At once, then, Clarke relies on a rationalist principle, since his claim, appearing where it does in his argument, can claim no sanction from experience.

Clarke then argues that this something that always existed must be one, unchangeable and independent. Otherwise there could be an infinite succession of beings, one depending on nothing more than its predecessor. But if there were, there would be no cause of the series external to it and hence no reason for the existence of the chain, an effect once more without a cause. In dialogue 11 of his *Dialogues concerning Natural Religion* (1779) David Hume questions the principle of sufficient reason that Clarke invokes: "Did I show you the particular causes of each individual in a collection of twenty particles of matter I should think it very unreasonable should you afterwards ask me what was the cause of the whole twenty. This is sufficiently explained in explaining the cause of the parts."

Clarke then infers that this being exists necessarily. Unlike Descartes, who argues from the idea of God as containing all perfections that God necessarily exists, Clarke starts by proving a necessary existent and then argues it must have the perfections traditionally attributed to God. From this point, his argument is, with one notable exception, a priori, or argued from the nature of causes rather than from effects to causes, as in the contrasting argument from design. In defending his strategy, he claims that attributes such as infinity, omnipresence, eternity and oneness, cannot be demonstrated simply from a knowledge of effects. A cause with such attributes is not necessary to produce the universe as humans know it.

For Clarke, if God exists necessarily, he cannot be identified with the material world because of the existence of a vacuum, among other reasons. If matter existed necessarily, the same necessity would exist everywhere. Since matter is not everywhere, while God must be, absolute space must be one of God's attributes, but God cannot be

material. Clarke's argument illustrates his use of Newtonian natural philosophy in support of his position.

For Clarke, all this argument would be for naught, however, unless this necessary being is shown to be intelligent. For him, this attributing of intelligence to God is the real divide separating the theist from the atheist, but he acknowledges that intelligence must be established by experience of observable effects. He argues intelligence is a distinct property not derivable, as materialists claim, from material properties such as figure and motion. Since intelligent beings are known to exist by experience, and given the rationalist principle of causal adequacy that there must be as much reality in a cause as in its effect, the necessary being must be intelligent. Once more, Hume lays down the basic challenge to Clarke's argument when he argues in his *Treatise of Human Nature* (1739–1740) that, for all that human beings know independent of experience, anything can produce anything. In any case, Clarke must exercise ingenuity to avoid the inference that since the world has material characteristics, God as its cause must have them as well.

Intelligence is not possible, however, for necessitated beings. Intelligent beings must be free, but being free is incompatible with being necessitated. To act freely is to exercise the power to act or not to act; it is to be a cause, while not being caused and only inclined by reasons and motives. It is morally impossible for God, being good, to act contrary to his perfections. Still, even if God is "morally necessitated," this necessity is neither real nor natural but only a manner of speaking that rests on nothing stronger than the prediction that God will not—not that he cannot—act otherwise.

If Clarke's first series of Boyle Lectures targets the atheist, the second sets its sights on showing the untenability of deism. These lectures were published as *A Discourse concerning the Unchangeable Obligations of Natural Religion and the Truth and Certainty of the Christian Revelation. Being eight sermons preach'd at the Cathedral-Church of St Paul, in the year 1705, at the Lecture founded by the Honourable Robert Boyle Esq* (1706). In these lectures Clarke does not claim the same demonstrative certainty for much of his argument—although he does for his moral theory—as for his proof of God's existence, but he claims it is enough to convince any reasonable person. But Clarke is Janus-faced about the powers of human reason, since it is not so strong that it can do without help from divine revelation, as deists claim. If it were, the achievements of ancient thinkers should have been more systematic and imposing than they are. For Clarke, not only is revelation a source of truths consistent with, but not discoverable by unaided human reason, it also spurs reason's exercise, directing it to great discoveries in moral theory and natural philosophy alike. For him, it is no accident that Newton's natural philosophy is the product of a Christian mind.

For Clarke, deism takes many forms: one, akin to ancient Epicureanism, rejects God's active and continual governance of the world; another effectively rejects the existence of good and evil by making them artifacts of human conventions; another rejects the human soul's immortality, supposing death to be the end of its existence; while a last rejects the truth or need of divine revelation. For Clarke, most of these forms directly collapse into atheism, while the last gives way to Christianity unless its real purpose is to disguise atheism. He believes that he can refute the first three on the strength of reason alone.

Clarke opposes the first position from Newton's natural philosophy. Not only are mechanical laws inadequate to explain living beings, but gravity, being nonmechanical, is inexplicable unless through the continual and providential action of an immaterial being who alone can penetrate the core of matter. The tools available to the materialist cannot explain the power of gravity, since it is a function of mass rather than of impacts on the surfaces of material objects.

Clarke's moral theory, as rationalist as his proof of God's existence, is the real center of his second set of Boyle Lectures and his reply to the second type of deist. He rejects Hobbes's contractual approach to morals, since, applied to God, it undermines his moral attributes and implies atheism. Unless there is a justice and goodness independent of God's will, there can be no God. For Clarke, there are eternal relations and proportions, akin to geometrical relations, from which follow the fitness or unfitness of indefeasible principles of actions binding on God and human agents alike. To deny them would be equivalent to denying that a square is not double a triangle of equal base and height. These principles include the duty to promote the universal good, to preserve the lives of the innocent, and to act justly. To apprehend them is to assent to them, even if appetite or perverseness result in a failure to act on them. While Clarke rejects Plato's celebrated doctrine of recollection (the theory that memory is the true source of human knowledge about the fundamental features of reality, resting on the belief that the soul is not only eternal but also preexistent), he is impressed by the questioning of an uneducated boy described in Plato's *Meno* (circa 387 B.C.), where Socrates demonstrates that the boy already knows the solution to a mathematical problem, suggesting that a knowledge of virtue is likewise innate to human beings.

In 1706, when he was only thirty, Clarke already enjoyed a formidable reputation as a metaphysician and defender of Christianity. That year he was appointed chaplain to Queen Anne; received his first London parish, St. Benet's, Paul Wharf; and published a refutation of a provocative book by the nonjuror Henry Dodwell, who had been stripped of his Oxford professorship for refus-

William Whiston, the mathematician and minister who encouraged Clarke and brought him to the attention of his patron, John Moore, bishop of Norwich; portrait by Sarah Hoadly (National Portrait Gallery, London)

ing to take the oaths of allegiance and supremacy to William of Orange when James II was deposed in 1688. In his *An Epistolary Discourse: Proving, from the Scriptures and the First Fathers, That the Soul is a Principle Naturally Mortal; but Immortalized Actually by the Pleasure of God, to Punishment; or to Reward, by its Union with the Divine Baptismal Spirit* (1706) Dodwell argues that the human soul is naturally mortal, but immortalized by God through acquaintance with the gospel. He defends his claim more on the strength of Scripture and the early Church Fathers than philosophical argument. In his response, *A Letter to Mr Dodwell; wherein All the Arguments in his Epistolary Discourse against the Immortality of the Soul are particularly answered, and the Judgment of the Fathers concerning that Matter truly represented* (1706), Clarke charges Dodwell with advocating a view that is not only dangerous by encouraging infidels to question the existence of a future state of rewards and punishments, but also indefensible as philosophy. For the soul as the bearer of personal identity can be demonstrated to be immaterial, independent of anything material and, accordingly, immortal. Clarke's argument became the focus of a protracted debate with Collins, who challenged Clarke's demonstration and illustrated, in Clarke's eyes, the danger of Dodwell's book.

Clarke defines his philosophical position against John Locke, who argues it is beyond the power of human reason to show God cannot make a material substance think. For Clarke, since consciousness is incomposite and individual, it cannot inhere in a divisible, material subject. All properties inhering in material subjects, such as size, necessarily belong to their parts. If consciousness were such a property, there would be an infinite number of individual consciousnesses, not one. Hence consciousness can only belong to an indivisible, albeit extended immaterial subject.

In the exchanges between Clarke and Collins published from 1706 to 1708, the issue of divine and human free will is always close at hand, but their clash on this issue came to a head with Collins's publication of *A Philosophical Inquiry concerning Human Liberty* (1717), which Clarke answered with *Remarks upon a Book, Entituled, A Philosophical Enquiry concerning Human Liberty,* included in the 1717 collection of his correspondence with Leibniz. For Clarke, the idea of a necessary agent is a contradiction in terms, since to be caused or necessitated is by its nature to be passive, not active. Collins questions the argument for free will based on the experience of acting freely. For Clarke, such experience cannot strictly demonstrate the freedom of the will. However, it could only fail to be convincing if God formed human minds so that individuals could be systematically deceived. Since human beings know God cannot intend this condition, freedom of the will can be claimed with certainty. Nor is it undermined by God's foreknowledge. If God knows how human beings will choose to act in advance of their choices, his predictions must be true. But it does not follow that what God predicts is a necessary truth. Without the freedom of the will, there could be no personal merit or demerit, no personal justice or injustice, no just reward or punishment and, indeed, no religion.

Nearly a decade later Clarke again challenged Collins in *A Discourse concerning the Connexion of the Prophecies in the Old Testament, and the Application of them to Christ. Being an Extract from the Sixth Edition of A Demonstration of the Being and Attributes of God, &c. To which is added, A Letter concerning the Argument a priori* (1725) for his attempted subversion of the argument from prophecy. In his Boyle Lectures, Clarke defended both miracles and prophecies as proving the truth of Christianity. Ever the metaphysician, he is more concerned with the nature of miracles than with epistemological questions of the sort that preoccupy Locke, such as proving they have occurred. For him, miracles ought not to be viewed as violations of the laws of nature, since such so-called laws are nothing other than expressions of God's

will and governance, just as miracles are, except these miracles are unusual actions as opposed to regular or chance events. Indeed, a miracle need not be performed by God, only by an intelligent agent superior to man, whether good or evil. Their attributability to God or his agents rests on the moral character of the doctrines or the authority, notably Jesus Christ's, which they attest. But they can only attest doctrines or claims that are probable or possible, since those that are certain require no support from miracles, and an impossible one can receive none.

Clarke's claim that fulfilled prophecy proves the truth of Christianity is challenged by Collins, who argues in his *Discourse of the Grounds and Reasons of the Christian Religion* (1723) and subsequent works that since Christianity depends on Christ's identity as the Messiah prophesied in the Old Testament, it fails because those prophecies apply to Christ, if at all, only typically and not uniquely. In *A Discourse concerning the Connexion of the Prophecies in the Old Testament, and the Application of them to Christ,* Clarke challenges Collins's argument, but he concedes a great deal to it. Now he allows that the prophecies do not prove Christ's status but are only needed to confirm it. Christ effectively proves his divine mission by his works. This proof only needs confirmation from the applicability of the prophecies to Christ. They do fit Christ, however, since Clarke argues that they prophecy a spiritual Messiah, unlike Collins, who claims that they prophecy a temporal one.

If Clarke's challenges to nonjurors and freethinkers strengthened his standing in the Church of England (in 1709 he was appointed to St. James, Westminster, an important and demanding parish where he remained the rest of his life), the application of his views on natural religion to the doctrine of the Trinity, a flash point in eighteenth-century Christianity, did the reverse. The doctrine of the Trinity tests his account of the relation of reason to revealed religion as well as his ability to accommodate it to orthodoxy. In his Boyle Lectures, Clarke defends God's essential undivided unity and oneness as the necessary self-existent cause of the universe. If the God of Christian revelation were the Trinity rather than God the Father, however, revelation would conflict with Clarke's natural religion and his exclusion of matter's candidacy as a second necessary being would collapse.

For Clarke, the only unimpeachable source of Christian revelation is Scripture. The early Church Fathers and Church Councils can be helpful in its interpretation, but Scripture alone is the authoritative source of Christian doctrine. For him, the orthodox view of the Trinity, which claims that its persons are of the same individual substance, power, and eternity in a single Godhead, is neither founded in Scripture nor consistent with reason. It depends on accretions to Christianity that have corrupted the purity, simplicity, and intelligibility of primitive Christianity.

Clarke entertained such ideas well before he published his *The Scripture-Doctrine of the Trinity. In Three Parts. Wherein all the Texts in the New Testament relating to that Doctrine, and the Principal Passages in the Liturgy of the Church of England are collected, compared and explained* (1712). In this book he exhaustively lists 1,251 scriptural passages and formulates the doctrine he claims that they support. They provide a "demonstration"–his word–that the scriptural God is God the Father, to whom the other persons in the Trinity owe their being and power, and to whom they are subordinate. They have the same kind of spiritual substance as the Father, but they could not be the same individual being that he is. Prayers and honor are properly addressed to God the Father. Clarke was charged with Arianism, but he rejected the imputation, since he claims that the Son and Holy Spirit are eternal, not created, and acknowledges their divinity. He concludes by showing that his view is reconcilable with the liturgy of the Church of England and the Thirty-nine Articles on which the church doctrinally rests. To Clarke's critics, he was attempting to reconcile the irreconcilable. In later editions of *The Scripture-Doctrine of the Trinity* he abandoned this attempt and replaced it with an appeal to those in authority to review the liturgy and the Thirty-nine Articles with a view to change. His appeal fell on deaf ears.

The Scripture-Doctrine of the Trinity scandalized Church opinion. It led to an attempt within the Convocation, the highest constitutionally recognized body of the Church of England clergy, to take action against Clarke and his book in 1714. Clarke weathered the storm by promising not to preach further on the Trinity and to act in a manner that would not occasion further complaint. As a compromise it satisfied neither conservatives, who wanted Clarke censured, nor those such as Whiston, who found Clarke's response wavering and cowardly. The bishops insured that he would never be elevated as one of them. For his part Clarke decided not to accept any further preferment that would depend on subscribing to the Thirty-nine Articles or require him to administer their subscription. Bishops were not required to subscribe, but as a bishop he would have administered the Articles in ordaining priests. For the rest of the eighteenth century Clarke was a symbol of troubled conscience.

Clarke later made manuscript annotations to a copy of the 1724 edition of *The Book of Common Prayer* in conformity with his views for reform. Among his many revisions, he addresses all its prayers to God the Father and deletes the Nicene and Athanasian Creeds. In 1768 his son donated this copy to the British Museum. It influenced Theophilus Lindsey, a founder of Unitarianism, who used Clarke's alterations, as well as ones of his own, in the first public Unitarian service in London on 17 April 1774,

which was attended by Benjamin Franklin. That same year Lindsey published his version of *The Book of Common Prayer,* based in part on Clarke's unpublished notes.

When Princess Caroline of Brandensburg-Ansbach, wife of George Augustus, Prince of Wales (the future George II), arrived in England in August of 1714, she was already a woman with formidable intellectual credentials and a friend to Leibniz, whom she had first met in 1704. She met and took to Clarke early, receiving personal instruction in Newton's system from him and suggesting that he might translate Leibniz's *Essais de Théodicée sur la Bonte de Dieu, la Liberté de l'Homme et l'Origine du Mal* (Theodicy: Essays on the Goodness of God, the Freedom of Man, and the Origin of Evil, 1710) which he declined. The clarity of Clarke's mind impressed her. Their relation proved to be long-standing, and by it Clarke enjoyed influence at court. She would have liked to be his patron, whether by supporting his appointment as a bishop or Newton's successor at the Royal Mint, but Clarke declined such marks of favor. Caroline, who became queen after her husband ascended to the throne in 1727, even adorned the Hermitage, a grotto she had built in Richmond in 1732, with a bust of Clarke as well as ones of Newton, Locke, and the rationalist philosopher William Wollaston.

It is not known when Clarke first came to know Newton personally, but by the time of his first set of Boyle Lectures in 1704 they were already on close personal terms. Newton invited him to translate his *Opticks; Or, A Treatise of the Reflexions, Refractions, Inflexions and Colours of Light: Also, Two Treatises of the Species and Magnitude of Curvilinear Figures* (1704) into Latin and rewarded him handsomely for his performance, published in 1706 and in an enlarged version in 1719, with £500, or £100 for each of his children. Of his friends Newton held Clarke in the highest regard, seeing him frequently and referring to him affectionately as his chaplain. Their views, however, were not identical. Clarke was metaphysically more daring, at least in public, and, as a defender of the natural immortality of the soul, he did not share Newton's mortalism. But on a wide range of issues–natural philosophy and the rejection of the Athanasian view of the Trinity–they agreed. Newton was notoriously secretive; Clarke, more open on public issues and more affable, maintained a reserve about private matters that his friend Arthur Ashley Sykes characterized as "impenetrable."

In Clarke's translation of the *Opticks,* Newton made significant additions to the "Queries" with which the book concludes. One of special significance concerns God and his relation of the world, infinite space serving as his sensorium, although Newton revised his language in some copies by the qualification that space serves "as it were" as God's sensorium. As luck would have it, Leibniz possessed an uncorrected copy of Clarke's translation that he cited in a letter to Princess Caroline to illustrate the pov-

THE

WORKS

OF

SAMUEL CLARKE, D.D.

Late Rector of St JAMES's Weftminfter.

In Four VOLUMES.

VOLUME the FIRST.

CONTAINING

SERMONS on Several Subjects:

WITH A

PREFACE, giving fome Account of the LIFE,
WRITINGS, and CHARACTER of the AUTHOR:
By BENJAMIN, now Lord Bifhop of WINCHESTER.

LONDON:
Printed for JOHN and PAUL KNAPTON in Ludgate-Street.
MDCCXXXVIII.

*Frontispiece and title page for the first edition of Clarke's collected works, which includes a biographical preface by Benjamin Hoadly
(Beinecke Library, Yale University)*

erty of the treatment of natural religion in English philosophy. Leibniz's letter is the starting point of a celebrated exchange with Clarke on the relation between natural religion and natural philosophy, Newtonianism in particular. Clarke repeatedly attempts to disarm Leibniz's misinterpretation of Newton's claim. It does not imply, as Leibniz supposed, a perceptual model of omniscience. Newton's intention is only to explain God's omniscience by way of his omnipresence. The princess relished the role of mediator, and the exchange was ended only by Leibniz's death late in 1716. When Clarke published the correspondence the following year, he dedicated it to Princess Caroline.

The edition of 1717 was published in a parallel French-English text, with Clarke's English answers translated into French by Michel de La Roche and an appendix that included Clarke's correspondence with John Bulkeley of the University of Cambridge, as well as his

reply to Collin's *Philosophical Inquiry concerning Human Liberty*. The Clarke-Leibniz correspondence is Clarke's best known contribution to philosophy, even if much of it is strongly rooted in his Boyle Lectures and his exchanges with Collins. Clarke and Leibniz cross swords on a wide range of questions, including the relation between soul and body, God and his relation to the creation, space and time, matter and the existence of a vacuum, gravity, the liberty of the will, and the nature of miracles.

The theme that pervades the correspondence, however, is their difference over the principle of sufficient reason, which both accept but interpret differently. For Leibniz, the principle requires that nothing can happen without a reason why it should be so and not otherwise and, since God always acts for the best, there can be no sufficient reason for action unless one action is preferable to the alternatives. For Leibniz, it follows that absolutist conceptions of space and time must be mistaken, as are claims for the existence of a vacuum or atomist conceptions of undifferentiated matter. In such a view, God could create the universe at one time rather than another and in one location rather than another, but since there can be no sufficient reason for preferring one to the other, Leibniz argues such a view is absurd. Similarly, no drop of water can be exactly like any other, since God would then have no sufficient reason to create it. For Clarke, on the other hand, Leibniz's account effectively deprives God of free will. A material balance cannot move unless there is a greater weight on one side rather than the other, but God, as an agent who is altogether unlike passive matter, can have a sufficient reason for acting even if it is indifferent which alternative he chooses.

When Clarke died 17 May 1729, among his literary remains were manuscripts of 173 sermons not previously published. Most of them had been delivered in his church at St. James, Westminster. Clarke published only a few sermons individually or in collections during his lifetime. His brother John Clarke prepared a ten-volume edition of his father's sermons, published in 1730–1731, while his son, Samuel Clarke Jr., completed the second volume of his father's edition of Homer's *Iliad* (1729, 1732) and completed his father's edition of the *Odyssey* (1740). In a preface to the posthumously collected sermons (also included in the first volume of Clarke's *Works,* 1738) Benjamin Hoadly, then bishop of Salisbury and after 1734 bishop of Winchester, observes that Clarke's intent as a preacher was "not to move the Passions," but to illuminate Scripture by reason. As such, the sermons are expressive of his philosophical outlook. Contemporaries admired their lucidity, none more so than Samuel Johnson, who judged them the best in English "bating a little heresy." One theme that pervades them is a pastoral conception of the priest's role, whether in their subordination of the sacramental to moral virtue, their constraint of religious doctrine by reason, or their insistence that eternal salvation is secured by sincere individual inquiry into what is plain and clear in Scripture, whatever the inquirer's intellectual ability. The priest exercises authority by moral example rather than any supposed appointment from Christ or any monopoly over the indispensable means to salvation. Clarke's impeccable conduct made him a paradigm for the role his sermons define.

Samuel Clarke was widely regarded in the first half of the eighteenth century as the greatest English philosopher after Locke. His rationalism, in which he joins theology, ethics, and the best science of the day into a seamless web of Anglican Christian apologetics, was the foundation of his appeal as well as of the attacks of those such as Hume, who viewed it as the root cause of his failure. To the critics, the confidence he invests in the power of human reason is misplaced and, indeed, causes him to

stray beyond the limits of what it can establish. For a long time afterward Clarke was ignored, partly because his rationalism seemed at odds with the empiricist mainstream of English philosophical thought. As this picture of English philosophy has become recognized as a caricature–rationalist elements of even Locke, for example, have been acknowledged–and as the history of Newtonianism and its religious background has become prominent, Clarke's contributions to British philosophical thought have come to be better appreciated.

Bibliography:
J. Dybikowski, "Samuel Clarke Bibliography," *Enlightenment and Dissent,* 16 (1997): 198–207.

Biographies:
William Whiston, *Historical Memoirs of the Life of Dr. Samuel Clarke: Being a Supplement to Dr. Sykes's and Bishop Hoadley's Accounts: Including certain memoirs of several of Dr. Clarke's Friends* (London: Sold by Fletcher Gyles and by J. Roberts, 1730); enlarged as *Historical Memoirs of the Life and Writings of Dr. Samuel Clarke: Including Certain Memoirs of Several of His Friends* (London: Printed for John Whiston, 1748)–includes *Dr. Sykes's Elogium of Dr. Clarke,* by Arthur Ashley Sykes and *Mr. Emlyn's Memoirs of the Life and Sentiments of Dr. Clarke,* by Thomas Emlyn;

J. P. Ferguson, *An Eighteenth Century Heretic: Dr. Samuel Clarke* (Kineton, U.K.: Roundwood, 1976).

References:
Enlightenment and Dissent, special Clarke issue, 16 (1997);

J. P. Ferguson, *The Philosophy of Dr. Samuel Clarke and its Critics* (New York: Vantage, 1974);

Edward Grant, *Much Ado About Nothing: Theories of Space and Vacuum from the Middle Ages to the Scientific Revolution* (Cambridge & New York: Cambridge University Press, 1981);

Margaret C. Jacob, *The Newtonians and the English Revolution 1689–720* (Hassocks, U.K.: Harvester, 1976; Ithaca, N.Y.: Cornell University Press, 1976);

William L. Rowe, *The Cosmological Argument* (Princeton: Princeton University Press, 1975);

Ezio Vailati, *Leibniz & Clarke: A Study of their Correspondence* (New York: Oxford University Press, 1997);

Maurice Wiles, *Archetypal Heresy: Arianism through the Centuries* (Oxford: Clarendon Press / New York: Oxford University Press, 1996).

Papers:
Small collections of Samuel Clarke's papers are held by the Cambridge University Library and the British Library, London, which also holds his annotated copy of the *Book of Common Prayer.*

Anthony Collins

(21 June 1676 – 13 December 1729)

J. Dybikowski
University of British Columbia

BOOKS: *A Letter to the Learned Mr. Henry Dodwell; containing Some Remarks on a (pretended) Demonstration of the Immateriality and Natural Immortality of the Soul, in Mr. Clark's Answer to his late Epistolary Discourse,* anonymous (London: Printed for Anne Baldwin, 1707 [i.e., 1706]);

A Reply to Mr. Clark's Defence of his Letter to Mr. Dodwell. With a postscript relating to Mr. Milles's Answer to Mr. Dodwell's Epistolary Discourse, anonymous (London, 1707);

An Essay concerning the Use of Reason in Propositions, the evidence whereof depends on Human Testimony, anonymous (London, 1707);

Reflections on Mr. Clark's Second Defence of his Letter to Mr. Dodwell, anonymous (London: Printed by John Darby, 1707);

An Answer to Mr. Clarke's Third Defence of his Letter to Mr. Dodwell, anonymous (London: Printed for Anne Baldwin, 1708);

Priestcraft in Perfection, or, A Detection of the Fraud of Inserting and Continuing this Clause (The Church hath Power to Decree Rites and Ceremonys, and Authority in Controversys of Faith) in the Twentieth Article of the Articles of the Church of England, anonymous (London: Printed for Benjamin Bragg, 1710);

A Vindication of the Divine Attributes. In some Remarks On His Grace the Archbishop of Dublin's sermon, intituled, Divine Predestination and Foreknowledg consistent with the Freedom of Man's will, anonymous (London: Printed for Anne Baldwin, 1710);

Reflections on a late Pamphlet, intitled, Priestcraft in Perfection, anonymous (London: Printed for John Baker, 1710);

A Discourse of Free-Thinking, occasion'd by the Rise and Growth of a Sect call'd Free-Thinkers, anonymous (London, 1713 [i.e., 1712]);

A Philosophical Inquiry concerning Human Liberty, anonymous (London: Printed for Ranew Robinson, 1717);

A Discourse of the Grounds and Reasons of the Christian Religion. In two Parts: The first containing some Consider-

Anthony Collins (Pascotts Farm, Haywards Heath, Sussex)

ations on the Quotations made from the Old in the New Testament, and particularly on the Prophecies cited from the former and said to be fulfill'd in the latter. The second containing an Examination of the Scheme advanc'd by Mr. Whiston in his Essay towards restoring the true Text of the Old Testament, and for vindicating the Citations thence made in the New Testament. To which is prefix'd an Apology for free debate and liberty of writing, anonymous (London, 1724 [i.e., 1723]);

An Historical and Critical Essay, on the Thirty nine Articles of the Church of England. Wherein it is demonstrated, that this Clause The Church has power to decree Rites and Ceremonies, and Autority in Controversies of Faith, inserted in the 20th Article, is not a Part of the Articles, as they were established by Act of Parliament in the 13th of Eliz. or agreed on by the Convocations of 1562 and 1571, anonymous (London: Printed for Richard Francklin, 1724);

The Scheme of Literal Prophecy considered; in a View of the Controversy, Occasion'd by a late Book, intitled, A Discourse of the Grounds and Reasons of the Christian Religion, anonymous (London [i.e., The Hague]: Printed by Thomas Johnson for the Booksellers of London & Westminster, 1726);

A Letter to the Author of the Discourse of the Grounds and Reasons of the Christian Religion, In Answer to Mr. Green's Letters, &c. With a Postscript Occasion'd by Dr. Lobb's Brief Defence, &c., anonymous (London: Printed for A. Moore [fictitious], 1726);

A Letter to the Reverend Dr. Rogers, on Occasion of his Eight Sermons, concerning The Necessity of Divine Revelation, and the Preface prefix'd to them. To which is added, A Letter printed in the London Journal, April 1. 1727. with an Answer to the same, anonymous (London, 1727);

A Discourse concerning Ridicule and Irony in Writing, in a letter to the Reverend Dr. Nathanael Marshall, anonymous (London: Printed for John Brotherton & sold by Thomas Warner & Anne Dodd, 1729).

Editions and Collections: *A Philosophical Inquiry Concerning Human Liberty Republished with a Preface by Joseph Priestley, L.L.D.F.R.S.,* preface by Joseph Priestley (Birmingham, U.K.: Printed by Thomas Pearson & sold by Joseph Johnson, London, 1790);

A Discourse of Free-Thinking: Faksimile-Neudruck der Erstausgabe London 1713 mit deutschem Paralleltext, edited and translated, with notes, by Günter Gawlick and preface by Julius Ebbinghaus (Stuttgart-Bad Canstatt: F. Fromann Verlag, 1965);

A Discourse Concerning Ridicule and Irony in Writing (1729), introduction by Edward A. Bloom and Lillian D. Bloom, Augustan Reprint Society Publication, no. 142 (Los Angeles: Willam Andrews Clark Memorial Library, 1970);

Determinism and Freewill: Anthony Collins' A Philosophical Inquiry Concerning Human Liberty: With a Discussion of the Opinions of Hobbes, Locke, Pierre Bayle, William King and Leibniz, edited and annotated by James O'Higgins, Archives internationales d'histoire des idées: Series minor, no. 18 (The Hague: Nijhoff, 1976);

Discourse of the Grounds and Reasons of the Christian Religion (New York: Garland, 1976);

An Essay Concerning the Use of Reason in Propositions; A Discourse of Free-Thinking, The Philosophy of John Locke, no. 2 (New York: Garland, 1984);

A Philosophical Inquiry Concerning Human Liberty: Republished with a Preface by Joseph Priestley, introduction by John Stephens (Bristol: Thoemmes Press, 1990);

An Answer to Mr. Clarke's Third Defence of his Letter to Mr. Dodwell; A Discourse of Free-Thinking, Atheism in Britain, volume 1, edited by David Berman (Bristol: Thoemmes Press, 1996).

OTHER: *The Independent Whig; Or, A Defence of Primitive Christianity, and of Our Ecclesiastical Establishment, Against the Exorbitant Claims and Encroachments of Fanatical and Disaffected Clergymen,* fifth edition, 2 volumes, edited by John Trenchard and Thomas Gordon (London: Printed by John Peele & sold by John Osborne, 1732)–includes contributions by Collins, as C.

Marcus Tullius Cicero, *M. Tullius Cicero Of the Nature of the Gods; in Three Books. With critical, philosophical, and explanatory notes. To which is added, An Enquiry into the Astronomy and Anatomy of the Ancients* (London: Printed for Richard Francklin, 1741).

Anthony Collins, the most philosophically acute of the early eighteenth-century freethinkers, is best known for his defense of freedom of thought or "free-thinking." His approach to philosophical questions is strongly influenced by John Locke as well as other freethinkers such as John Toland. At the heart of his inquiries is a set of philosophical issues that center on religion, natural and revealed: the freedom of the will, the immateriality of the soul, God's existence and attributes, the relation of reason to religion, and the nature and interpretation of evidence that purports to establish the truth of revelation. Collins was early identified by critics as a dangerous enemy of Christianity and a none-too-secret atheist, even if clever enough to cover his tracks against the threat of prosecution. In his writings he rejects the charge that he is motivated by hostility to Christianity or religion generally, or, for that matter, that he has a system of thought to defend. Instead, he strongly commits himself to following reason, wherever it leads.

Collins was born in Isleworth, a village near London, on 21 June 1676, the eldest child of Henry and Martha Collins. His father was a lawyer, who added to the substantial property near London and in rural Essex that Collins's grandfather (also a lawyer) had accumulated. He was educated at Eton and King's College, Cambridge, where he was admitted in 1693, but without any intention of taking a degree. Following family tradition, he was admitted to the Middle Temple in 1694, but a legal career did not interest him, and he spent most of his time through 1696 at Cambridge.

294391

AN
ESSAY
Concerning the
Uſe of Reaſon
IN
PROPOSITIONS,

The Evidence whereof depends
upon Human Teſtimony.

LONDON,
Printed in the Year 1707.

*Title page for the early work in which Collins argues that the claims
of religion must meet the test of reason (Beinecke Library,
Yale University)*

In 1697 Collins married Martha Child, daughter of an influential banker, Sir Francis Child, who was lord mayor of London and a member of Parliament. The marriage agreement stipulated that the Collins family properties were to be held in a trust by Anthony and Martha Collins and their descendants. The couple had four children (Henry, Elizabeth, Anthony, and Martha), the first dying in infancy while the last occasioned her mother's death in childbirth in April 1703.

Collins spent part of each year in Essex looking after the family properties and permanently moved there around 1715, participating actively in county government. His life as a country gentleman was exemplary, so much so that he was compared to Sir Roger de Coverley, the fictional character created by Joseph Addison, who represents the ideal of the benevolent landed country gentleman. He remarried in 1724, but only after the death of Anthony less than a year before. His second wife was Elizabeth Wrottesley, daughter of Sir Walter Wrottesley. Collins had no children by his second marriage.

Early on, Collins showed a passion for books. By the early eighteenth century he boasted in a letter to Henry Dodwell (19 October 1706) that his collection of works by the Church of England divines rivaled anyone's. He later put his extensive library to use in his writings to illustrate existing and historical differences "about every Point in the whole Christian Religion, as well as about the Meaning of almost every Text in the Bible." His books, his knowledge of where to find them, no matter how rare, and the encouragement he gave to friends and acquaintances for their publishing projects were at the heart of his life.

Also central were the friendships he formed early with several controversial freethinkers, notably Toland and Matthew Tindal. These relationships were significant and influential, but by far the most important was with Locke. It began with an invitation to visit Locke early in 1703. Locke was impressed by Collins and encouraged him to visit as often as possible. They also corresponded, often several times a week. The newly widowed Collins was treated by Locke as though he were the older man's son. The experience was a giddy one for Collins, who found himself engaged without reserve by the greatest English philosopher of his time on issues that mattered to him. They discussed innate ideas, the powers of animals, the possibility of thinking matter, toleration, and Locke's *An Essay concerning Humane Understanding* (1690), over which Locke praised Collins's mastery. They also discussed such Continental figures as the French philosophers Nicolas Malebranche and Pierre Bayle, the many books and pamphlets then being published that were hostile to Locke's thought, and the efforts of senior academics at Oxford to discourage or suppress the reading by undergraduates of Locke's *An Essay concerning Humane Understanding*.

The theme that dominates their correspondence and friendship is the love of truth pursued with indifference as to whom it pleases or displeases. Locke and Collins regarded it, together with friendship, as the key human virtues. When Locke confided to Collins that he possessed this quality to as great a degree as anyone he knew, Collins accepted his praise as the highest compliment he could wish. He told Locke that it was in religion above all that he wished to do justice to this love.

Locke's philosophy and his epistemology in particular established a framework for Collins's thought, but while Collins held Locke in the highest regard–once, in a 27 May 1704 letter to Locke, dubbing him as "the Great Lay Priest among us"–he was not prepared as a lover of truth to defer to Locke's opinions simply because they were his. He presses Lockean modes of analysis in directions Locke did not, particularly in his examination of Christian revelation. To Locke's critics, Collins's philosophy demonstrates the underlying subversive tendency of Locke's ideas; to some of Locke's admirers, it is a testimonial to Collins's betrayal of his mentor. Collins's personal tribute to Locke came with his publication in 1720 of some of Locke's unpublished manuscripts, scarce publications, and private correspondence (including several letters to Collins), in a collection edited by his longstanding friend, the Huguenot biographer and editor Pierre Des Maizeaux, who befriended Collins around 1704 and played a significant role in making Collins's works known in Europe.

The defense of free inquiry or the liberty of thought and examination informs all Collins's writing from the opening sentences of *A Letter to the Learned Mr. Henry Dodwell; containing Some Remarks on a (pretended) Demonstration of the Immateriality and Natural Immortality of the Soul, in Mr. Clark's Answer to his late Epistolary Discourse* (1707), to *A Discourse concerning Ridicule and Irony in Writing, in a letter to the Reverend Dr. Nathanael Marshall* (1729). Sometimes the occasion is the defense of others with unconventional views, ranging from the ultraconservative non-juror Dodwell to the heretical William Whiston. More often, the occasion is supplied by attacks on Collins and his writings, which were portrayed as potent threats to religion and the social order.

Collins's *A Letter to the Learned Mr. Henry Dodwell,* his first published work, appeared anonymously, a practice to which he consistently adhered. Contemporaries usually had little trouble identifying his writings, but it was a principle with him not to acknowledge them publicly as his. The uproar they generally provoked makes his continued adherence to this policy unsurprising. Collins's work was written as a rebuttal to the Newtonian clergyman and philosopher Samuel Clarke's *A Letter to Mr Dodwell; wherein All the Arguments in his Epistolary Discourse against the Immortality of the Soul are particularly answered, and the Judgment of the Fathers concerning that Matter truly represented* (1706), in which Clarke had criticized as doctrinally and philosophically unsound Dodwell's *An Epistolary Discourse, Proving, from the Scriptures and the First Fathers, That the Soul Is a Principle Naturally Mortal:* *but Immortalized Actually: By the Pleasure of God to Punishment; Or, to Reward by its Union with the Divine Baptismal Spirit* (1706).

As well as defending free inquiry, in *A Letter to the Learned Mr. Henry Dodwell* Collins challenges Clarke's influential proof of the human soul's immateriality, from which Clarke infers its immortality. Clarke argues that since consciousness is incomposite and individual, it cannot inhere in a divisible, material subject. All properties in material subjects, such as size, are only the sums of the same properties of their parts. If consciousness were such a property, as materialist philosophers such as Thomas Hobbes argued, each human being would have an infinite number of individual consciousnesses, not one: an absurd conclusion. Hence, consciousness can only belong to indivisible, immaterial subjects. But if the subject of consciousness is simple and indivisible, it must be naturally indestructible and immortal. As the bearer of personal identity, it is a proper object of rewards and punishments in a future state for a life of virtue and vice respectively.

Collins accuses Clarke of failing to prove what he claims to establish. His object is not to demonstrate the materiality of the soul, although he believes such a view to be reasonable in light of the close and evident relation between consciousness and the body, in light of perception's role as the initial source of the mind's ideas or the connection between thought and action. For him, as for Locke, human reason cannot demonstrate the immateriality of the human soul and, accordingly, it cannot show that a material subject is incapable of thinking. Such a claim can only be established with any certainty by divine revelation.

Collins's most important objection to Clarke is that properties may belong to a complex or system that do not belong to its parts, such as the power of a rose to produce agreeable sensations or the roundness of a circle. Accordingly, thought and consciousness might well be modes of motion, for example, of suitably organized material systems, though human ignorance of the nature of thought makes it impossible to prove or to disprove this theory.

Even if this objection could be overcome, Clarke's argument would only show at best that the soul is immortal, not that it is conscious and thinks when separated from the body. If so, his argument does not prove personal survival, which is constituted by consciousness and continued by memory. The motivational effectiveness and justice of a future state of rewards and punishments for actions in this life depends not on the continued existence of some bare subject with which human beings cannot identify, but on the connectedness of conscious states in a

A

DISCOURSE

OF THE

GROUNDS and REASONS

OF THE

CHRISTIAN RELIGION.

In two Parts:

The firſt containing ſome CONSIDERATIONS on the Quotations made from the Old in the New Teſtament, and particularly on the Propheſies cited from the former and ſaid to be fulfill'd in the latter.

The ſecond containing an EXAMINATION of the SCHEME advanc'd by Mr. WHISTON in his *Eſſay towards reſtoring the true Text of the Old Teſtament, and for vindicating the Citations thence made in the New Teſtament.*

To which is prefix'd an Apology for free debate and liberty of writing.

Who hath alſo made us able Miniſters of the New Teſtament, not of the Letter, but of the Spirit ; for the Letter killeth, but the Spirit giveth Life. 2 Cor. iii. 6.

Omnia a *MOSE* ordinata enumerans, oſtendere poſſem figuras & notas & *denunciationes* eſſe eorum quæ CHRISTO eventura erant, eorumq; qui in ipſum ut crederent præcogniti fuerant, atq; item eorum quæ CHRISTUS ipſe erat faĉturus. JUSTINI MARTYRIS *Opera.* p. 261.

Sin dixerint poſt adventum Domini ſalvatoris & prædicationem Apoſtolorum libros Hebræos fuiſſe falſatos, cachinnum tenere non potero: Ut Salvator, & Evangeliſtæ, & Apoſtoli ita teſtimonia protulerint, ut Judæi poſtea falſaturi erant! HIERON. *Oper.* tom. 3. p. 64. c. 6. in ISAIAM.

LONDON. MDCCXXIV.

Title page for the book in which Collins critiques some of the common arguments in favor of the truth of Christianity (Beinecke Library, Yale University)

future state with those in this life. Unless an individual can remember performing certain actions deserving of punishment in his or her past life, how, on that account, can he or she be motivated in this life to avoid them? The supposed indivisibility of an immaterial soul, for that matter, makes it unsuitable to be the bearer of personal identity, since it would make it impossible to explain human thinking and consciousness, which is successive and has parts. Properties such as these demand a complex and divisible subject. But even if Clarke's argument proved personal survival, it would prove too much. For if animals are conscious and think, which Collins takes to be obvious from common experience, would not Clarke's proof apply to them equally as well? To Clarke, such views are not only mistaken but are also destructive of religion.

In his exchanges with Clarke, Collins also challenged Clarke's demonstration of God's existence and the role he assigns to God. As he wryly comments, those such as Clarke, who purport to demonstrate God's existence, make it a question for many to whom it otherwise would not have been: an observation that rang true to such readers as Benjamin Franklin. Collins questions, for example, whether, in view of Clarke's claim that human beings are entirely ignorant of the nature of substance, he can prove, as he must to show God's distinctness from the created universe, that there is more than one substance. But even if Clarke can, his proof would still fall short of what Christianity requires because it does not show God to have created the universe from nothing.

In his *A Vindication of the Divine Attributes. In some Remarks On His Grace the Archbishop of Dublin's Sermon, intituled, Divine Predestination and Foreknowledg consistent with the freedom of Man's Will* (1710), Collins returns to the difficulties that bar the way to a coherent and compelling argument for God's existence and attributes, while discussing Archbishop William King's sermon advocating negative theology preached and published in Dublin the year before. This time the difficulty is the problem of evil. How is it that an all-powerful and beneficent God could create a morally imperfect world in which sin and pain exist? The French Protestant philosopher Bayle found the problem intractable. The facts as human beings know them, he argues, would be better explained on the supposition of Manicheanism, which posits two eternal beings who control the world: the one good, the other evil, but that has nothing else to be said for it. He concludes that there is no alternative to subordinating reason to the obedience of faith against the evidence. Bayle's solution holds no attraction for Collins, since faith on his view of freethinking must also be constrained by reason. But if Bayle's solution is unacceptable, his critics, like King, fare no better.

King's solution claims that the moral and intellectual attributes traditionally ascribed to God do not apply to God in the same sense they apply to humans. According to King, Bayle's difficulty arises only if God's beneficence, for example, is like human beneficence. Similarly, the apparent contradiction between divine foreknowledge and human liberty disappears when "foreknowledge" does not have the same meaning when applied to God. Collins argues that the solution comes at a great cost. If these attributes apply to God in a different sense of which human beings can have little idea, humans can have correspondingly little idea of God, save perhaps that God is an incomprehensible being who causes effects: nothing an atheist need deny. Bayle has a clear conception of God, which is irreconcilable with his creation; in King's opposing viewpoint the problem disappears, but at the cost of removing God.

The method of argument that *Vindication of the Divine Attributes* illustrates is derived from the ancient skeptics and is characteristic of Collins's writings. He asserts few claims in his own right but sets alternative views against each other. The strengths of each expose fatal weaknesses of its rival. Collins's declared aim, however, is not to justify any general skepticism but to show the need for freethinking, if a true intellectual system comparable in power to the discoveries of natural philosophy is to be found.

Collins's first systematic defense of free inquiry is his *A Discourse of Free-Thinking, occasion'd by the Rise and Growth of a Sect call'd Free-Thinkers* (1713), copies of which were seized and burned by the public hangman, while the work itself was attacked with ferocity by, among others, the philosopher George Berkeley, bishop of Cloyne, the prodigious classical scholar Richard Bentley, and the satirical writer Jonathan Swift. They all did their best to savage the book and, they hoped, bury it.

A notable feature of *A Discourse of Free-Thinking* is that it is the first time Collins defends the liberty of thought and examination under the rubric of "free-thinking." "Free-thinking" and "free-thinker" were then modish expressions used contemptuously to refer to those such as Collins and Toland whose inquiries were viewed not as the fair-minded examination of received opinions but as pretexts for attacking clerical authority and Holy Scripture in order to advance an anti-Christian and atheistic agenda through a sect of libertines who would displace Christianity. The title of Collins's book—*A Discourse of Free-Thinking, occasion'd by the Rise and Growth of a Sect call'd Free-Thinkers*—is his ironic response to these charges. He deliberately adopts the abusive language of his critics in order to restore "free-thinking" to its proper meaning.

For Collins, freethinking is the impartial use of understanding or reason to determine the meaning of propositions; assess the evidence for and against them; and judge their truth or falsity, as well as their probability or improbability by the strength or weakness of the available evidence. Freethinking, he argues, is a universal right grounded in the human interest in knowledge that can only be secured by rational examination. Without it, opinions would be adopted on nothing stronger than tradition, interest, reputation, or deference to authority, grounds equally supportive of falsehood. Even if they happen to be true, they will be better understood and defended if they are exposed to challenge. For Collins, the reluctance to subject, or to permit the subjec-

tion of commonly received views to examination, and the willingness to treat certain views as sacred and beyond the reach of rational examination is the main reason for the persistence of confused and contradictory ideas on subjects of importance, such as God, liberty, and the soul. He was impressed early by the weakness of the common arguments used to support the foundations of religion. They needed to be challenged so that the positions that relied on them either would be supported by stronger arguments or abandoned.

Not only does the right of freethinking apply universally to everyone, so also does its scope extend to all subjects. The effects of restraint on freethinking cannot be limited to the subject matter where it is applied. Restraint in any subject such as religion inevitably has an impact beyond it, since knowledge cannot be compartmentalized and any branch has a bearing on others. The meaning and truth of Scripture, for example, cannot be assessed without a knowledge of ethics or chronology. Restrictions on the right and its exercise are only warranted where it can be shown to cause harm to the peace of society or to individuals. To restrict it any further is to embrace principles destructive of all reasoning.

The right of freethinking, moreover, entails rights of public expression, including the right to publish or otherwise express one's views and the right to endeavor to convince, debate with, and teach others. Without these rights the right to think freely would atrophy and be subverted.

Collins's special concern is freethinking in religion, where he defends a duty to think freely as well as a duty to tolerate not just divergent beliefs and their expression but also divergent religious worship and practice. According to Collins, religious diversity, far from threatening civil order, contributes to its maintenance, to respect for law, and the flourishing condition of the state. He admires Locke's defense of toleration, but he extends its scope to Roman Catholics and atheists, unlike Locke, who excludes the former because they acknowledge a foreign prince in the Pope and the latter because they undermine oaths. For Collins, religious belief is "merely personal," not a proper subject of penal sanction or a condition for holding offices of public trust. This view, shocking to most of his contemporaries, is a significant step toward a secular conception of the state and its role.

Soon after Collins published *Vindication of the Divine Attributes* in 1710, he traveled to Holland, where he met leading Huguenot and Dutch intellectuals, established personal contacts in the publishing world, and, as always, purchased books and journals

A

DISCOURSE

CONCERNING

Ridicule and Irony

I N

WRITING,

I N   A

LETTER

To the Reverend

Dr. NATHANAEL MARSHALL.

———— *Ridiculum acri*
Fortius & melius magnas plerumq; fecat res.

———— *Ridentem dicere verum*
Quid vetat ?

LONDON:

Printed for J. BROTHERTON in *Cornhill*, and fold
by T. WARNER in *Pater-nofter-Row*, and
A. DODD without *Temple-Bar.* 1729.

*Title page for Collins's final book, published the year of his death (Lewis
Walpole Library, Yale University)*

for his own library and his friends. He visited Holland once more after he published *A Discourse of Free-thinking* in 1713. It was widely rumored that he did so to avoid possible prosecution for his book. Although these were the only times he traveled abroad, he, as were Locke and Anthony Ashley Cooper, third Earl of Shaftesbury, before him, was highly knowledgeable about what was being thought and written on the Continent and made good use of his knowledge in his writings.

Collins's classic statement of his view of human liberty is to be found in *A Philosophical Inquiry concerning Human Liberty* (1717), though it pervades his earlier writings as well. Joseph Priestley, who had *A Philosophical Inquiry concerning Human Liberty* republished toward the end of the eighteenth century when copies were difficult to find, admired it not only as a clear and succinct statement of Collins's position but also as the first systematic defense of *compatibilism,* the view that human liberty is compatible with determin-

ism, or necessity. Hobbes, Priestley notes in his preface to the 1790 edition of Collins's work, had advanced the same view, but Collins offered a systematic defense of it.

For Collins, liberty is properly defined as the power of acting or refraining from acting as one wills or pleases. For him, this definition is the only account of liberty that reason and experience sanction. The obscurity of other accounts arises, he argues, from their attempt to make claims about liberty beyond the limits of clear and distinct ideas and from imposing religious requirements on such an account that cannot be so justified.

Collins disentangles his account of liberty from standard materialism. He argues that perception and desire cause human actions, whether or not they have a material basis. For him, as for opponents such as Clarke, it is common ground that to be caused is to be necessitated. But whereas Clarke claims that reasons for acting only incline without necessitating, Collins defends the contrary view. If reasons only inclined without serving as causes of action, they would not explain them. The same action might just as well be done for no reason at all or an entirely opposite reason.

Collins is aware that incompatibilists—who hold that humans cannot be free and responsible if determinism is true—defend their view by appealing to the experience of acting freely. But, he argues, when experience is closely examined, it supports his view. Close attention to experience shows action to be caused by human will, which is determined by the judgment of what is best, which in turn is determined by how things are perceived. Collins approvingly cites Socrates' classic argument in Plato's *Protagoras* (before 387 B.C.) to show that individuals always act in accordance with their judgment of what is best. Collins adds that it is not only human action that is necessitated, but also, by common consent, animal action and, indeed, God's actions, since God, being necessarily good, can only act for the best.

For Collins, the same conclusion is justified by considering rewards and punishments. Far from presupposing incompatibilism, he argues, the threat of punishment depends on its serviceability as a cause of appropriate action. Far from threatening morality or virtue, compatibilism is needed to make sense of them. Without the network of connections that causally link perception to action, he argues, humans "would have no notion of morality, or motive to practise it; the distinction between morality and immorality, virtue and vice would be lost; and man would not be a moral agent."

Collins consistently argues that revealed religion necessarily rests on a foundation of natural religion. It is against natural religion that revealed religion must be understood and tested. Most of his early writings center on issues of natural religion, but *An Essay concerning the Use of Reason in Propositions, the evidence whereof depend upon Human Testimony* (1707) focuses on the role of reason in revealed religion. Collins's central aim in this work is to examine the celebrated distinction between claims contrary to reason and those said to be above it.

Collins's approach to the role of reason in revealed religion is shaped by Locke, who argues that faith cannot detract from reason without undermining both. His approach to the distinction between what is contrary to reason and what is above it, however, is shaped by Toland. In *Christianity not Mysterious* (1696), Toland claims that the genuine doctrines of Christianity are neither contrary to reason nor above it. For him, they are not above reason, since their real point is to remove the veil from what would otherwise be obscure. That Christianity no longer appears in this light is explained by the impositions of priests and their allies who corrupt and mystify its doctrines to justify their authority. "Priestcraft," the expression Toland regularly uses to describe this practice, is regularly used by Collins to the same effect.

While Locke, for his part, allows there may be truths above reason, his claim is only that some truths are known by divine revelation rather than unaided reason. Since claims of divine revelation characteristically rely on human testimony, reason is still charged with determining what they mean and deciding the probability that the testimony is true and its source is God. God cannot be wrong, but human testimony that mediates divine revelation certainly can be.

For Toland, on the other hand, those who say that there are truths above reason intend to make a different and narrower claim in defense of the mysteries of religion, such as the Trinity. On this view, truths above reason are not those that unaided reason fails to discover, but ones that human reason cannot comprehend, although it is required to assent to them as a condition of religious faith.

Collins's approach is similar to Toland's, but his analysis is more comprehensive and acute. He sets out to show that the distinction of what is above and what is contrary to reason is the product of murky thinking. Its proponents divide propositions as the objects of possible assent or dissent into three categories: those agreeable to reason, those contrary to it, and those above it. Collins, by contrast, argues that propositions divide only into the first two.

Locke's account would not meet the objectives of the advocates of the mysteries because the contrast it draws is between what is according to reason, being discoverable by it, and what is above it, relying on testimony. A proposition may be agreeable to reason, even if not according to it. For Collins, the terms of propositions as objects of human understanding, even when they testify to a revelation from God, must stand for ideas that individuals can only know from experience or reflection, and then only to the extent that they are known. Thus, when one hears people speaking a foreign language that one does not understand or when one, being blind, hears people talk of colors, one may justifiably believe that they speak sensibly, but one cannot assent to what they say since one has no idea what they are saying.

For Collins, accounts of what is above reason fail to satisfy the demands made of them either because they only distinguish ways in which something comes to be known (by testimony, for example, as distinct from direct experience), or because, by identifying what is above reason with an unknown cause or the inadequacy of an idea, these accounts fail to identify an object in the mind to which assent or dissent can be given, as in hearing an unknown language. It is one thing to agree that some matters are not understood; it is quite another to assent to an account of the Trinity intended to stagger human understanding.

The key arguments used to vindicate revealed religion and Christianity in particular were miracles and fulfilled biblical prophecies. In *A Discourse of the Grounds and Reasons of the Christian Religion. In two Parts: The first containing some Considerations on the Quotations made from the Old in the New Testament, and particularly on the Prophecies cited from the former and said to be fulfill'd in the latter. The second containing an Examination of the scheme advanc'd by Mr. Whiston in his Essay towards restoring the true Text of the Old Testament, and for vindicating the Citations thence made in the New Testament. To which is prefix'd an Apology for free debate and liberty of writing* (1723) as well as the works that follow, Collins subjects the argument from prophecy in particular to sustained and corrosive analysis. He claims that this argument is fundamental to Christianity since it does not purport to be an entirely new religion, but is rooted in the Old Testament. Its claims rely on the identification of Jesus Christ as the Messiah prophesied in the Old Testament. If the argument from prophecy succeeds, Collins allows that it would demonstrate the truth of Christianity; if it fails, however, Christianity would lack a just foundation.

For Collins, miracles apart from prophecy cannot show Christ to be the Messiah or "render a foundation valid, which is in itself invalid." He discusses them only glancingly, though skeptically. A note in his translation of Marcus Tullius Cicero's *De natura deorum* (On the Nature of the Gods, 45 B.C.), published in 1741, has more than once been credited with anticipating David Hume's critique of miracles. In this note Collins argues that even credible testimony must be balanced against the incredibility of the alleged miracle, although he adds that testimony often does not meet this standard and supports contradictory religious views, while claims of miracles are more frequent when and where free inquiry and the use of reason are restricted. Beyond that, such extraordinary works need not be the work of God. When they are claimed as God's because of the beneficent and defensible character of the doctrines these alleged miracles are said to attest, then not only does this attestation apply to a limited set of doctrines–excluding, for example, God's instruction to Abraham to sacrifice Isaac or the doctrine of the Trinity–but the doctrines that satisfy this condition would serve to prove the miracle rather than the miracle serve to prove the doctrine.

Scriptural prophecies, viewed as proofs, are problematic for different reasons. For, as Collins argues in his *Discourse of the Grounds and Reasons of the Christian Religion,* if the text of Scripture is taken as a given, the prophecies of the Old Testament frequently refer to events closer at hand to the utterance of the prophecy and so apply only secondarily to Christ. Still worse, they do not apply to Christ in any obvious way but only in a "mystical, or allegorical, or enigmatical sense." The prophesied Messiah, for example, was understood to be a temporal deliverer, unlike Christ. If the Messiah of Prophecy is a temporal deliverer, however, Collins argues that the applicability of Old Testament prophecies to Christ is weak and not sufficiently robust to prove the truth of Christianity.

This argument is valid, however, only if Scripture is reliable and not radically corrupted. If it has been corrupted, as Whiston claims in his *An Essay Towards Restoring the True Text of the Old Testament; and for Vindicating the Citations Made Thence in the New Testament* (1722), arguing that the text was tampered with by opponents of Christianity, it might support the unique and literal fulfillment of the Old Testament prophecies in Christ. But how can the scriptural text be judged to have been corrupted in the way required without some textual warrant or, for that matter, without casting doubt on the inspired character of Scripture? Without textual warrant, there would be nothing to constrain the amendment of the

text other than a critic's wish to make it say whatever he thinks it should.

Collins draws his arguments from distinguished apologists for and interpreters of Christianity, as he reminds his readers. From some he draws the weakness of arguments not based on the unique, clear, and literal fulfillment of prophecy as proofs for what is claimed on their behalf. From others he shows the futility of attempts to make the text read this way, while he still accepts their arguments showing the insecurity of the scriptural text. He characteristically concludes with a defense of freedom of inquiry. Little wonder that he provoked dozens of replies, thirty-five of which he painstakingly lists in the preface and its postscript of *The Scheme of Literal Prophecy considered; in a View of the Controversy, Occasion'd by a late Book, intitled, A Discourse of the Grounds and Reasons of the Christian Religion* (1726), and many of which appealed to the magistrate to put an end to his mischief making.

At the end of the eighteenth century, Priestley noted that Collins's examination of the argument from prophecy had yet to be convincingly refuted. He concedes that it cannot be refuted unless the claim of Christ and his apostles' infallibility is abandoned. This solution would exact a great price, since it undermines the status of the New Testament as divine revelation and, as such, its immunity from error. To the late eighteenth-century philosopher William Godwin, the obscurity into which Collins's writings fell is a prime example of how the worse argument can triumph over the better.

In the last years of his life Collins was afflicted by kidney and urinary stones that ultimately caused his death on 13 December 1729. In his will he left his manuscripts to his friend Des Maizeaux, who was prevailed upon by Collins's widow, Elizabeth, to sell them to her. In his writings and correspondence Collins indicates that he had prepared a response to Clarke's attack on his views on liberty and necessity, a treatise on biblical miracles, an ecclesiastical history of the Church of England since the Reformation, and a dissertation on the Sybilline Oracles. There may well have been others, but Collins's widow took care that none ever saw the light of day. Des Maizeaux regretted his precipitate sale of the manuscripts as a betrayal of his closest friend, but his efforts to recover them were unavailing.

In philosophy Anthony Collins belongs to a skeptical tradition with respect to natural and revealed religion that extends from Hobbes through Hume. Collins is critical of Hobbes's dogmatism and illiberal authoritarianism, defending free thought, toleration, and a liberal conception of the role of the state. On all these last points Locke was his mentor.

After his death Collins's influence waned in England, proving to be greater and more enduring on the Continent, where it was propagated through the writings of Voltaire, Paul-Henri Dietrich, Baron d'Holbach, and Jacques-André Naigeon; however, he has always been admired by British historians of free thought, who have come to think of him, in the memorable epithet from *T. H. Huxley's Hume: with Helps to the Study of Berkeley* (1901), as "the Goliath of Freethinking." His style of argument was well adapted to the cause that mattered most to him: the advancement of free thought.

Letters:

A Collection of Several Pieces of Mr. John Locke, Never before printed, or not extant in his Works. Publish'd by the author of the Life of the ever-memorable Mr. John Hales, &c., edited by Pierre Des Maizeaux (London: Printed by James Bettenham for Richard Francklin, 1720);

Correspondence of John Locke, 8 volumes, edited by E. S. De Beer (Oxford: Clarendon Press, 1976–1989)— volumes 7 (1982) and 8 (1989) include what survives of Collins's correspondence with Locke.

Biography:

James O'Higgins, S. J., *Anthony Collins: The Man and His Works* (The Hague: Martinus Nijhoff, 1970).

References:

David Berman, "Anthony Collins: Aspects of his Thought and Writings," *Hermathena,* 119 (1975): 49–70;

Berman, "Anthony Collins' Essays in the *Independent Whig*," *Journal of the History of Philosophy,* 13 (1975): 463–469;

Berman, *A History of Atheism in Britain: From Hobbes to Russell* (London & New York: Croom Helm, 1988);

Berman, "Hume and Collins on Miracles," *Hume Studies,* 6 (1980): 150–154;

John M. Robertson, *The Dynamics of Religion: An Essay in English Culture History,* second edition, revised with additions (London: Watts, 1926);

Paul Russell, "Hume's Treatise and the Clarke-Collins Controversy," *Hume Studies,* 21 (1995): 95–115;

Pascal Taranto, *Du déisme à l'athéisme: La libre-pensée d'Anthony Collins* (Paris: Honoré Champion, 2000);

Norman L. Torrey, *Voltaire and the English Deists* (New Haven: Yale University Press, 1930).

Papers:

Collections of Anthony Collins's letters are at the British Library, London; the Bodleian Library, Oxford University; and the Universiteitsbibliotheek, Leiden University. A single letter to Sir William Simpson is at the Department of Special Collections, Kenneth Spencer Research Library, University of Kansas, Lawrence. John Locke's letters to Collins are dispersed in several collections, the largest group being at the Harry Ransom Humanities Research Center, University of Texas at Austin. The manuscript catalogue Collins maintained of his library is at King's College, Cambridge. Documents relating to his civic role are in the Essex Record Office, Chelmsford. The marriage settlement that governed his marriage and property is in the Greater London Record Office.

Anne Conway

(14 December 1631 – 23 February 1679)

Patricia Sheridan
University of Western Ontario

BOOK: *Opuscula Philosophica Quibus Continentur Principia Philosophiae antiquissimae et recentissimae Ac Philosophiae Vulgaris Refutatio* (Amsterdam: M. Brown, 1690); translated by J.C. as *The Principles of the Most Ancient and Modern Philosophy, concerning God, Christ, and the Creatures, viz. of Spirit and Matter in General; Whereby may be Resolved all Those Problems or Difficulties, which Neither by the School nor Common Modern Philosophy, nor by the Cartesian, Hobbesian, or Spinosian could be Discussed. Being a Little Treatise Published since the Authors Death, Translated out of the English into Latin, with Annotations Taken from the Ancient Philosophy of the Hebrews* (London, 1692).

Editions: *The Principles of the Most Ancient and Modern Philosophy*, edited, with an introduction, by Peter Loptson (The Hague & Boston: Martinus Nijhoff, 1982);

The Principles of the Most Ancient and Modern Philosophy, translated and edited by Allison P. Coudert and Taylor Corse (Cambridge: Cambridge University Press, 1996).

Anne Conway is one of the interesting yet overlooked figures in the history of Western philosophy. She demonstrates that women were active participants in philosophical debates as early as the seventeenth century and offers an original philosophical theory that stands in direct opposition to some of the most influential theories in her own period. Conway's work offers a distinctive approach to the philosophical debates of the seventeenth century by attempting to fuse the rigorous methodology of the mechanistic sciences with the spiritualistic metaphysics of vitalism. Conway stands as an important figure both as a woman philosopher and as an innovator with new solutions to the problems inherent in the philosophical debates of her time.

Anne Finch was the second daughter of Elizabeth Bennet Finch and Heneage Finch, recorder of London, speaker of the House of Commons, and friend and defender of Francis Bacon. Both of her parents settled at their residence, Kensington House, with children from previous marriages. Their first child was a daughter, Francis. Heneage Finch died one week prior to the birth of their second daughter, Anne, on 14 December 1631. There is little existing record of Anne's childhood. One incident of note, however, was her illness from fever at the age of twelve. A lasting effect of this illness was that she suffered from debilitating headaches for the rest of her life, for which neither a successful diagnosis nor cure were ever discovered. Her correspondence clearly indicates that these headaches had a profound effect on her life and often left her utterly incapacitated for days and even months at a time.

While growing up, Finch was surrounded by a large family of children, among whom, according to Marjorie Hope Nicolson, editor of *Conway Letters: The Correspondence of Anne, Viscountess Conway, Henry More, and Their Friends, 1642–1684, Collected from Manuscript Sources* (1930), she was "the link which bound the family together." She was the one family member with whom all the others maintained correspondence, and their letters to one another make clear that she was beloved by all of them for her intelligence and warmth of personality. She was, however, a solitary person, and of all her large family, Finch's most intimate friendship was with her brother John, who was five years her senior.

As was typical of the period, girls were not sent to school but were expected to learn the arts of housekeeping and deportment with a view of their marrying. While her brothers were being educated at the most prestigious institutions in the country, Finch educated herself at home. She taught herself French and Latin and later studied Greek and Hebrew. From her youth, and throughout her life, Finch's favorite reading was philosophy, which she approached with great zeal. According to Nicolson, she engaged in her studies so voraciously that her family considered them the cause of her headaches. She carried on, however, with the help of her brother John, who took the time to provide Finch with a more organized and systematic program of study. He wrote her letters from school engaging her in philosophical debate and sent her books that he thought essential to philosophical education. Most importantly, though, John was instrumental in forging an alliance for Finch that was to transform her previously chaotic and voracious studies into mature and sophisticated philosophical thought. He brought about the intellectual friendship between his sister and the renowned Cambridge Platonist Henry More.

Prior to this introduction to her later mentor and friend, Finch married Edward Conway on 11 February 1651. They later settled at Ragley Hall, a Conway family estate in Warwickshire. Anne Conway was fortunate in finding a husband who would turn out to be sympathetic to and encouraging of her intellectual pursuits. Edward Conway, who later became third viscount of Conway and Killutagh and first earl of Conway, was born in 1623. In the course of his political career he became governor of Counties Armagh, Tyrone, Monaghan, and part of Down, as well as joint commissioner of customs, lieutenant governor of horse, and secretary of state for the north. In addition to being a successful statesman, he was also an avid reader of philosophy. In the midst of his political duties he became one of the early members of the Royal Society, read René Descartes at a time when Cartesianism was little known in England, and found time to study Euclid. He could not have been unimpressive as a scholar, as is seen from More's dedication to him of his work *The Immortality of the Soul* (1659). While Edward Conway always preferred the life of a politician to the retired life of Ragley Hall, he came to take an active interest in furthering the careers not only of More but also of Jeremy Taylor and Ralph Cudworth, both of whom were also intellectual companions of his learned wife.

For a woman of the seventeenth century, Conway was in an unusually hospitable environment for intellectual work. Her brother actively encouraged her philosophical development, while her husband was sympathetic to her interests. While Edward Conway's career often took him away from home, Anne Conway opened Ragley Hall to some of the great intellectuals of the period. She found herself in a position many women of her period were denied. Not only was she intellectually gifted, but she was also in a position to express and develop her intellect. She did so despite the impediments posed by her physical condition. In the early years of her marriage she was kept under the eye of her physician, the famous William Harvey, the first in a long line of physicians she consulted throughout her life.

John Finch studied at Cambridge under his tutor, More, leader of the group that later came to be known as the Cambridge Platonists. They were a group of philosophers who appreciated immensely the methods of new science and valued empirical observation as a basis

Anne, Viscountess Conway; portrait by Samuel van Hoogstraten (Royal Gallery, The Hague)

for objective knowledge, but who saw purely empirical enquiry as lacking any regard for what they felt was the ultimately spiritual fabric of nature. Finch believed his sister would benefit greatly from such a tutor as More and effected an introduction between them. More and Conway began to correspond in 1650, and over time the two came to be intellectual companions, sharing their interests in Platonic and Cartesian philosophies. Conway agreed with More that the new scientific theories relied on too limited a concept of nature. She shared More's concern that spiritual enrichment was necessary in order for science to fully unlock the casual relations between all aspects of creation. More clearly held Conway in high regard, referring to her as his "heroine Pupil." In his dedication to her of his work *An Antidote against Atheisme* (1653), More wrote of Conway as "one whose Genius I know to be so speculative, and Wit so penetrant, that in the knowledge of all things as well Natural as Devine, you have not only outgone all of your own Sex, but even of that other also, whose ages have not given them over-much on you." More had an enormous impact on Conway's intellectual development, introducing her to the ideas of the modern scientific age and providing her with the back-

Letter from Conway to her husband, Edward (British Museum)

ground for her critical writings on Thomas Hobbes, Benedict de Spinoza, and Descartes.

Late in her life Conway was still beset with debilitating headaches, and another in a long line of reputable physicians was sent to her aid. Francis Mercury van Helmont sought to meet with More in order to discuss their mutual interest in the Cabala. On his arrival in 1670 Van Helmont was asked to see Conway concerning her condition. Van Helmont was a scholar, as well as a physician, and though he was unable to cure Conway's headaches, he did introduce her to the mysteries of the Cabala. The Cabala comprises many of the mystical teachings of Judaism, teachings thought to derive from unwritten revelations given to Moses on Mount Sinai. Conway was greatly fascinated by the Cabala and found in its doctrines much that mirrored her own philosophy of nature. One aspect of the Cabalistic teaching similar to that of Conway's thought is the belief that matter and spirit are not distinct but exist together on a continuum. Conway attacks Descartes's dualistic metaphysics and the purely materialistic ontology of Hobbes largely from this point of view. According to some versions of the Cabalistic teachings, all material objects have some spiritual aspect. They gradually gain greater and greater levels of spiritual content through successive reincarnations. This theme appears in Conway's antimaterialistic philosophy, where she argues for a protoevolutionary view of the development of the species along the matter-spirit continuum. According to Conway, because all matter is created by God, it is imbued with a spiritual dimension that provides the impetus for greater spiritual perfection. Scholars are not certain whether she got these ideas from the Cabala, but at any rate it is clear why she would have found it highly insightful and why she would choose to refer to it at several points in her work.

Van Helmont became another influential thinker in Conway's life, opening the way for her eventual conversion to Quakerism. More disagreed with Quakerism, and Conway's adoption of Quaker beliefs caused a tension in their relationship. The strain was not enough to bring an end to their friendship, but for the rest of Conway's life More remained concerned about her adherence to the views of such a suspicious and radical religion. At Ragley Hall she regularly entertained such Quaker eminences as founder George Fox, Robert Barclay, and William Penn. One aspect of Quakerism that attracted her was the view that the individual's understanding of God, rather than doctrinal teachings, could lead people to their own salvation. The Quaker view of salvation harmonized with Conway's broader view of universal progress along the spiritual continuum. According to her, created beings have the capacity within themselves to reach higher levels of spiritual

growth. Allison P. Coudert, in the introduction to her and Taylor Corse's 1996 edition of Conway's work, suggests that she also found personal comfort in the company of Quakers, because of their philosophy of serenity and forbearance in times of physical suffering.

In the later years of her life Conway made notes that were later compiled as her only philosophical tract, the posthumously published *The Principles of the Most Ancient and Modern Philosophy, concerning God, Christ, and the Creatures, viz. of Spirit and Matter in General; Whereby may be Resolved all Those Problems or Difficulties, which Neither by the School nor Common Modern Philosophy, nor by the Cartesian, Hobbesian, or Spinosian could be Discussed. Being a Little Treatise Published since the Authors Death, Translated out of the English into Latin, with Annotations Taken from the Ancient Philosophy of the Hebrews* (1692). In her notes she sought to show that the new science need not rely on the view that matter is dead and entirely divorced from the spiritual realm. She argued for the organic unity of mind and matter. While More had argued for a stronger presence of the spiritual in the material world, he did not go as far as Conway, who sought to collapse the mind-matter distinction altogether. More still believed that spirit and matter were distinct substances, something Conway rejected in favor of a monistic conception of spiritualized matter. Her view yielded a theory of motion based on vital principles internal to matter itself. Conway opposed this theory to the mechanistic view of matter as essentially inert and as requiring an external cause of motion, which marks another important difference between Conway and More. More's critique of mechanism was primarily animated by theological concerns about the role of God in nature. Conway focused more on the weakness of mechanistic theories in explaining motion in nature. She believed that the notion of vital spirits was necessary to any physics that claimed to understand laws of motion. Though Conway clearly was influenced greatly by More, her view is nevertheless her own. Her work is certainly strongly theological, but there is also an earnest desire to address and correct weaknesses in mechanistic theories of nature.

Conway sought to prove that it is not necessary to divorce matter from spirit in order to maintain an empirical science. Her ultimate purpose was to enrich the various scientific theories of the period by proving that they could be rigorous without leading to atheistic and materialistic conclusions. Conway's work is an interesting contribution to the history of antimechanistic philosophy. She did not reject the new scientific project but sought to save it from the limited perspective she thought it had adopted. While Conway was influenced by many different sources, her work itself is an original synthesis, not reducible to any or all of her

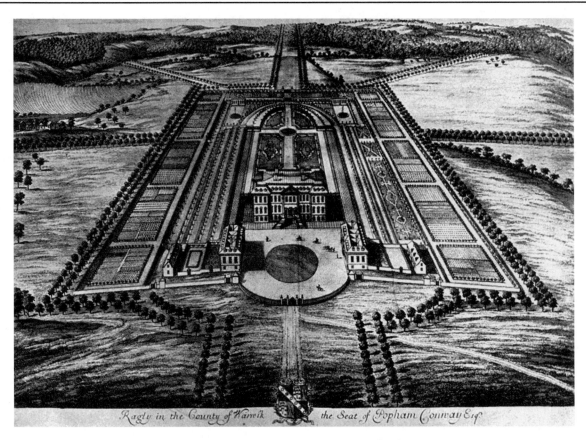

Eighteenth-century engraving of Ragley Hall and the surrounding grounds, the Conways' home

influences. She benefited from her tutors, but her work is the product of a keen and original intellect.

Near the end of her life Conway's headaches worsened, and she was often in severe pain for months at a time. She died on 23 February 1679. Her husband was away at the time, and Van Helmont laid out her body and preserved it in wine until his return. She was placed in a casket encased in lead at a small church in Arrow. Edward Conway, Van Helmont, and More all oversaw the funeral, which was, as she had requested, a simple one. Her only epitaph consists of the words "Quaker Lady" scratched on the lead casing.

After her death her philosophical notes were found by More, who described them as being written "abruptly and scatteredly." More and Van Helmont set out to prepare them for publication. Although the text was prepared from Conway's notes, of which only a portion appears, it reads as a continuous and complete document, which would indicate that the editors added to the notes themselves, although it is difficult to determine the precise extent of their contributions. Since the original notes have been lost, there is no longer any basis for a conclusive judgment on the matter. In the introduction to his 1982 edition of *The Principles of the*

Most Ancient and Modern Philosophy, Peter Loptson points out that while Conway's early editors lay claim only to their own annotations, there are sections in the body of the work that refer to these annotations and to chapter numbers that would certainly not have been present in the notes. Such evidence clearly indicates that while the work is based on Conway's notes, their contents were unalloyed. The editors likely did not tamper greatly with the ideas expressed by Conway, however, given the great intellectual esteem in which she was held by both men. Since the learned texts of the time were generally published in Latin, the resulting text was translated as *Opuscula Philosophica Quibus Continentur Principia Philosophiae antiquissimae et recentissimae Ac Philosophiae Vulgaris Refutatio* and published in Amsterdam. It was published in English in 1692, and it is conjectured that the original English edition is lost. The editor of the 1692 edition, identified in that work only as "J. C.," translated his edition from the Latin text. The *Dictionary of National Biography* identifies J. C. as Jacobus Crull, but Nicolson proposes that Van Helmont's translator, John Clark, is a more likely candidate.

Scant information is available regarding the critical reception of Conway's work. Van Helmont traveled extensively in the years that followed, however, and spread word of Conway's philosophical achievements. One of the most famous names to come into contact with her ideas was Gottfried von Leibniz, who was a pupil of Van Helmont's. He was greatly interested in Conway's philosophical system and wrote of her frequently in his correspondence. In his *Nouveaux Essais* (New Essays, 1765) he refers to her in several places as one whose ideas are close to his own. Caroline Merchant, in her "The Vitalism of Anne Conway: Its Impact on Leibniz's Concept of the Monad" (1979), argues that Leibniz's philosophy was strongly influenced by Conway's work.

One of the most interesting sources on Conway's life is Nicolson's *Conway Letters*. Not only has Nicolson thoroughly researched Conway and all those who came into contact with her, but also she has brought together a collection of letters that offer a fascinating glimpse of Conway's world. These letters most fully describe the effects of her illness, as well as the many consultations made and remedies attempted, sometimes at the hands of questionable physicians. Throughout the correspondence Conway is clearly determined to continue in her philosophical pursuits no matter how difficult it became for her to do so.

Letters:

Conway Letters: The Correspondence of Anne, Viscountess Conway, Henry More, and Their Friends, 1642–1684, Collected from Manuscript Sources, edited by Marjorie Hope Nicolson (New Haven: Yale University Press, 1930; revised, with an introduction and new material, by Sarah Hutton, Oxford: Clarendon Press, 1992).

References:
Allison P. Coudert, "A Cambridge Platonist's Kabbalist Nightmare," *Journal of the History of Ideas,* 36 (1975): 633–652;

Coudert, "A Quaker-Kabbalist Controversy," *Journal of the Warburg and Courtauld Institutes,* 39 (1976): 171–189;

Jane Duran, "Anne Viscountess Conway: A Seventeenth-century Rationalist," *Hypatia,* 4 (1989): 64–79;

Lois Frankel, "Anne Finch, Viscountess Conway," in *A History of Women Philosophers,* volume 3, edited by Mary Ellen Waithe (Dordrecht: Kluwer, 1991), pp. 41–58;

Alan Gabbey, "Anne Conway et Henri More, Lettres sur Descartes," *Archives de Philosophie,* 40 (1977): 379–404;

Caroline Merchant, "The Vitalism of Anne Conway: Its Impact on Leibniz's Concept of the Monad," *Journal of the History of Philosophy,* 17 (1979): 255–269;

Gilbert R. Owen, "The Famous Case of Lady Anne Conway," *Annals of Medical History,* 9 (1937): 567–571;

Richard H. Popkin, "The Spiritualistic Cosmologies of Henry More and Anne Conway," in *Henry More (1614-1687),* edited by Sarah Hutton (Dordrecht: Kluwer, 1990), pp. 97–112.

Ralph Cudworth
(1617 – 26 June 1688)

Sarah Hutton
Middlesex University

BOOKS: *The Union of Christ and the Church; in a Shadow* (London: Richard Bishop, 1642);

A Discourse Concerning the True Notion of the Lord's Supper (London: Printed for Richard Cotes, 1642); republished as *A Discourse Concerning Our Evidence of Knowing Christ* (New York: Printed & sold by H. Gaine, 1770);

A Sermon, Preached Before the Honourable the House of Commons, at Westminster, March 31. 1647 (Cambridge: Printed by Roger Daniel, 1647);

Dantur rationes boni et mali aeternae et indispensabiles (London, 1651);

A Sermon Preached to the Honourable Society of Lincolne's Inne (London: Printed by J. Flesher for Richard Royston, 1664);

The True Intellectual System of the Universe: The First Part; Wherein, All the Reason and Philosophy of Atheism Is Confuted; and Its Impossibility Demonstrated (London: Printed for Richard Royston, 1678);

A Treatise Concerning Eternal and Immutable Morality (London: Printed for James & John Knapton, 1731);

A Treatise of Freewill, edited by John Allen (London: Parker, 1838).

Editions: *Systema intellectuale huius universi seu De veris naturae rerum originibus commentarii . . . Accedunt reliqua eius opuscula*, 2 volumes, translated into Latin by Johann Lorenz Mosheim (Jena, 1733);

The True Intellectual System of the Universe: The First Part; Wherein, All the Reason and Philosophy of Atheism Is Confuted, and Its Impossibility Demonstrated. With A Discourse Concerning the True Notion of the Lord's Supper; and Two Sermons, on I John II. 3, 4, and I Cor. XV. 57. 2d ed., in Which Are Now First Added References to the Several Quotations in the Intellectual System; and an Account of the Life and Writings of the Author, 2 volumes, edited by Thomas Birch (London: J. Walthoe, D. Midwinter, J. & J. Bonwick, 1743);

The True Intellectual System of the Universe; with A Treatise Concerning Eternal and Immutable Morality, 3 volumes, edited by John Harrison (London: Tegg, 1845);

Ralph Cudworth (from his Systema Intellectuale Huius Universi, *1733; Thomas Cooper Library, University of South Carolina)*

A Treatise Concerning Eternal and Immutable Morality and A Treatise of Freewill, edited by Sarah Hutton (Cambridge: Cambridge University Press, 1996).

Ralph Cudworth was the leading philosopher of the group of philosophical divines known as the Cambridge Platonists. Cudworth's philosophical reputation rests on his two major works, *The True Intellectual System of the Universe: The First Part; Wherein, All the Reason and Philosophy of Atheism Is Confuted; and Its Impossibility Demonstrated* (1678) and *A Treatise Concerning Eternal and Immutable Morality* (1731). In philosophy he was an opponent of Thomas Hobbes and a forebear of John Locke. He is best remembered for his moral philosophy. In his own day he sought an accommodation between the new natural philosophy of his time and religion. In theology he was a moderate who contributed significantly to the mainstream of tolerationist thought. He was also one of the first philosophers to write consistently in English.

Cudworth was the third son of Ralph Cudworth and his wife, Mary Machell. He was born in Aller, Somerset, in 1617, where his father was rector from 1616 until his death in 1624. After Cudworth's father died his mother married Richard Stoughton, who took responsibility for Cudworth's education. In 1630 he was admitted pensioner at Emmanuel College, Cambridge, where his father had once been a fellow. He matriculated in 1632 and was elected to a fellowship in 1635. Emmanuel College was a relatively new college, having been founded in 1588 by Sir Walter Mildmay. The college had enormous shaping influence on interregnum Cambridge, since it was from Emmanuel that a high proportion of the vacancies for heads and fellows of other colleges were filled following the ejection of Cambridge dons by Edward Montagu, second Earl of Manchester, in 1644. Cudworth was a beneficiary of the new round of appointments. Although Emmanuel was noted for the rigorous Calvinism of some of its masters (notably Laurence Chaderton and Antony Tuckney), it also nurtured puritanism of a different stamp. The leading exponent of theological liberalism was Benjamin Whichcote. The temper of Whichcote's theology, with its message of toleration, its optimism about the power of human reason, and its emphasis on the moral content of Christianity, was to be the hallmark of Cambridge Platonists. That such a liberal temper could flourish alongside more doctrinaire Calvinism may be due to Richard Holdsworth, who was appointed master in 1637 but deprived of the post in 1645 and whose theological moderation was underpinned by deep humanist learning. Cudworth's contemporaries at Emmanuel included so many of the Cambridge Platonists that they were at one time known as the "Emmanuel Platonists": besides Whichcote, these included John Smith, Peter Sterry, and Nathaniel Culverwel. Other theological moderates at Emmanuel included Cudworth's friends Samuel Cradock, John Wallis, John Worthington, and the future archbishop of Canterbury, William Sancroft.

Little is known of Cudworth's activities as a young don. In the 1640s he was in correspondence with Samuel Hartlib and also with John Selden. There is evidence, however, that he had already arrived at the fundamentals of his philosophy at this time and that he had a reputation for erudition. In 1645 his career received a boost when he was appointed Regius Professor of Hebrew. In 1646 he gave a series of lectures on the Temple of Jerusalem, and on 31 March 1647 Cudworth preached a sermon to the House of Commons. The irenic message of this sermon, which urged his listeners to put into practice the Christian message of love of one another, must have struck a chord with war-weary Englishmen. Holdsworth, the ousted master of Emmanuel, noted to Sancroft that Cudworth "hath gained well by his sermon," observing that it was selling at "ye great prices wch have bene given for poetry." Also in 1647 Cudworth was appointed master of Clare Hall to fill a vacancy resulting from the earl of Manchester's purge of Cambridge dons. In 1650 he succeeded Whichcote in the living of North Cadbury, Somerset. The next year he published his dissertation. In 1651 he defended the thesis that "Dantur rationes Boni et Mali aeternae, et Indispensabiles" (There are eternal and indispensable rules of good and evil) and also that "Dantur substantiae incorporeae natura sua immortales" (There are incorporeal substances immortal by nature). In 1654 he was appointed master of Christ's College, where Henry More was a fellow. In the same year he married Damaris Andrewes (née Cradock), a widow with two children. Cudworth became the father of four children, Ralph, John, Charles (who died in India), and Damaris (who became a close friend of Locke and a philosopher in her own right).

During the interregnum Cudworth was a respected figure who was consulted by the government over various matters relating to religion and learning. Oliver Cromwell's secretary of state, John Thurloe, sought his advice on suitable candidates for positions in the administration. In 1655–1656 he served on the commission appointed to advise Cromwell on the question of the readmission of Jews to England. In 1656–1657 he was nominated to advise Parliament on a new translation of the Bible. He also advised on the statutes for Cromwell's proposed college at Durham. After Cromwell's death he contributed to the collection *Luctus et gratio* on the death of Cromwell and succession of Richard Cromwell. His position thereafter was not secure, however. John Beale told Hartlib in 1658 that Cudworth "hath been affronted by many discouragements" from "vulgar spirits . . . too narrowe to understand him." Along with More, he came in for attack after the Restoration as a latitude man–in other words, a "Vicar of Bray," whose theological tolerance was con-

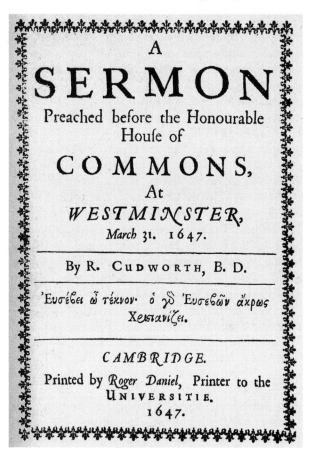

Title page for the published version of Cudworth's sermon on the virtue of Christian love (Library of the Union Theological Seminary)

strued as political timeserving. Cudworth found it prudent to contribute a verse to the collection presented to the restored Charles II by the University of Cambridge. In the event he was one of only two heads of college appointed during the interregnum to retain his post at the Restoration. He was no doubt assisted by influential figures like Viscount Edward Conway and his brother-in-law, Heneage Finch, future lord chancellor. He continued as master of Christ's College and as professor of Hebrew until his death in 1688.

Another indication of his acceptance by the new ecclesiastical order was the fact that in 1662 he was presented to a living in Hertfordshire by Archbishop Gilbert Sheldon. The grounds of Cudworth's accommodation with the newly restored Anglican Church are evident in the sermon he preached at Lincoln's Inn in 1664, in which he argued that religious differences should be put aside in the interest of ecclesiastical peace. Nevertheless, his liberal theological temper was one that was out of kilter with that of the Restoration ecclesiastical regimen. His de-emphasis of the institutional aspect of religion and his latitudinarianism, together with imputations of

questionable orthodoxy (notably in respect of the heterodox early Christian father, Origen) and his millenarianism did not sit well with Anglican orthodoxy. One respect in which he was in tune with the establishment view was his stance against the perceived atheist Hobbes: in 1669 Cudworth was one of the signatories of the order expelling the self-confessed Hobbesian, Daniel Scargill, from Cambridge. He did not receive any further preferment. He claimed lack of ambition. A letter of 1678 gives some indication that his financial circumstances were somewhat straitened, however. In this letter he sought preferment from Archbishop Sancroft on account of the fact that he had to provide for a family and that his expenditures exceeded his income from his various appointments. He told Sancroft that he "could not have subsisted in this place, had I not had something of my own, a great part of wch I have onely during my wives Life." At the same time, Cudworth stressed that he was content with his current position and that he was not "ambitious of High titles or Dignities." The notes that Thomas Birch gathered in preparation for his 1743 edition of Cudworth's works include a story that when he was dying, he insisted on being carried thirty miles to Cambridge, that he might die at Christ's College. The same notes show that imputations of heterodoxy clung to Cudworth's name after his death: he is said on his deathbed to have refused spiritual consolation and denied that he was a Deist, thus dying "a very infidel."

The static character of Cudworth's post-Restoration career is paralleled in his published output. For most of his life his only publications were a handful of sermons. His magnum opus, *The True Intellectual System of the Universe,* was published ten years before his death in an incomplete version. In 1664 he was working on a major treatise of ethics, but he still had not completed this work in 1667 when More published his *Enchiridion ethicum.* The fact that More had embarked on a similar project to his was, he told his friend John Worthington, the reason why he abandoned his own. Although More's unintended upstaging of Cudworth's work on ethics put their friendship under strain, this episode did not lead to a lasting rupture. Cudworth's delay in producing *The True Intellectual System of the Universe* is probably owing to a variety of factors—the pressures of college business (which More reports), native caution, and, possibly, external opposition. According to Birch there was opposition emanating from court circles to his publishing *The True Intellectual System of the Universe.* The imprimatur is dated seven years before the book appeared, and it was not completed as planned.

The True Intellectual System of the Universe is the only major work Cudworth published in his lifetime. It was originally conceived as the first of three books on liberty and necessity. His posthumously published *A Treatise Concerning Eternal and Immutable Morality* and his writings on free will were originally intended as part of the same project. The latter consist of three manuscripts, with overlapping subject matter, only one of which has ever been printed–*A Treatise of Freewill* (1838). Cudworth also prepared a commentary on the biblical book of Daniel, which has never been published.

In philosophy Cudworth was an antideterminist who set out to defend theism in rational terms and to establish the certainty of knowledge and the existence of unchangeable moral principles. In natural philosophy he was a vitalist who opposed the materialist tendencies of contemporary natural philosophy, especially that of Hobbes, by arguing for the existence of immaterial substance or spirit. His philosophy is Platonist in fundamentals, especially in his conviction that mental reality transcends and precedes the physical world ("mind precedes the world," as he put it) and that goodness is a sovereign principle inscribed in the order of things.

He was, nonetheless, receptive to other currents of thought, both ancient and modern. Among the ancient philosophers on whom he drew, besides Plato and Plotinus, are Aristotle, the Stoics, and Sextus Empiricus. He had a high regard for René Descartes but was also a critic of aspects of Cartesianism and the philosophies of Hobbes and Benedict de Spinoza. Cudworth's idea of philosophy is shaped by the Renaissance concept of *philosophia perennis* (perennial philosophy), supposed to have been the same since the beginning of time. This view stresses continuities between philosophies and treats contemporary philosophy not as a new departure, as its exponents claim, but as a recent manifestation of doctrines and arguments for which there are precedents in antiquity. In Cudworth's conception, true and original philosophy is a combination of atomistic, mechanistic natural philosophy and a metaphysics concerned with the immortality of the soul and the existence of God. This true philosophy is, moreover, in origins a *philosophia sacra* (sacred philosophy) that can be traced back to Moses and possibly also Adam. Cudworth's invocation of the accumulated wisdom of antiquity in his writings is an elaborate version of the argument from universal consent (*consensus gentium*), which underpins Cudworth's philosophy in three important areas: his demonstration of the existence of God, his vindication of corpuscularian natural philosophy, and his arguments against ethical relativism.

Although incomplete as Cudworth originally intended, *The True Intellectual System of the Universe* is a self-contained work of philosophy. The book is an antideterminist treatise that seeks an accommodation of theology and philosophy. It is in large part devoted to a philosophical refutation of atheism and a demonstration of the true idea of God as essentially good and wise. The constant reference to the perennial model accounts in large measure for the erudite character of the work. It is a magisterial compendium of humanist erudition. Paradoxically, the solidity of its scholarly foundations has become an obstacle to reading it in the twenty-first century.

The central purpose of the book is to give a rational demonstration of the existence and nature of God. A major component of Cudworth's apologetic is to show that belief in a deity is natural to man by demonstrating that all men at all times have had some kind of belief in God as a fully perfect being, infinitely powerful, wise, just, and good. Cudworth is concerned, therefore, to demonstrate not just the existence of God but also the true character of the deity. He argues not just as a theist against atheists and a monotheist against polytheists, but he also argues as the exponent of one type of Christian theology against another. Cudworth's conception of the deity, which emphasizes divine goodness, wisdom, and justice rather than the divine will, marks him as an anti-voluntarist in theology. It also has profound implications for his philosophy. Cudworth's critique of theological voluntarism is the counterpart of his critique of philosophical determinism. Firstly, he argues that voluntarism leads to skepticism: if truth depends on God's arbitrary will, there can be no certainty. Conversely, the wisdom and goodness of God guarantees certainty. Secondly, voluntarism undermines morality: if the will of God were to determine all human actions, then human beings would not be responsible for their actions and could not act morally. Furthermore, if right and wrong were determined by the arbitrary will of God, there could be no principles of morality. The philosophical system that Cudworth expounds is derived directly from his conception of God. From God's wisdom and justice derives the order and intelligibility of nature. God's wisdom and justice guarantee certainty of knowledge and sustain the fundamental goodness of the created world. It follows from such an idea of God that divine justice and moral principles are not arbitrary but are founded in the goodness and rationality of God. The laws of morality and God's providential design being thus evidently rational, it also follows that human beings must bear responsibility for their actions. Cudworth is also at pains to emphasize divine providence, the visible hand of God in his creation being clear demonstration of the wisdom and goodness of God. In this fundamental sense Cudworth's philosophy is integrally connected to his theology.

Just as Cudworth's survey of classical philosophy was intended to support his theism, so also his survey

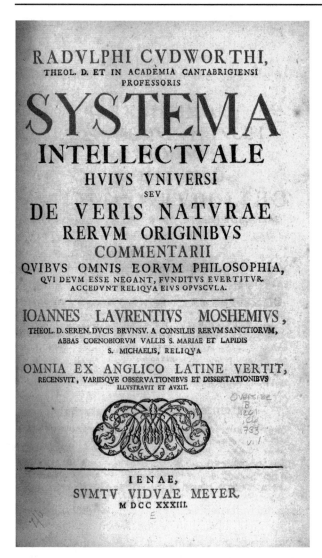

RADVLPHI CVDWORTHI,
THEOL. D. ET IN ACADEMIA CANTABRIGIENSI
PROFESSORIS

SYSTEMA
INTELLECTVALE
HVIVS VNIVERSI
SEV
DE VERIS NATVRAE
RERVM ORIGINIBVS
COMMENTARII
QVIBVS OMNIS EORVM PHILOSOPHIA,
QVI DEVM ESSE NEGANT, FVNDITVS EVERTITVR.
ACCEDVNT RELIQVA EIVS OPVSCVLA.

IOANNES LAVRENTIVS MOSHEMIVS,
THEOL. D. SEREN. DVCIS BRVNSV. A CONSILIIS RERVM SANCTIORVM,
ABBAS COENOBIORVM VALLIS S. MARIAE ET LAPIDIS
S. MICHAELIS, RELIQVA

OMNIA EX ANGLICO LATINE VERTIT,
RECENSVIT, VARIISQVE OBSERVATIONIBVS ET DISSERTATIONIBVS
ILLVSTRAVIT ET AVXIT.

IENAE,
SVMTV VIDVAE MEYER,
M DCC XXXIII.

Title page for Johann Lorenz Mosheim's 1733 Latin translation of
Cudworth's collected works, which was responsible for most of the
interest in Cudworth among eighteenth-century Europeans
(Thomas Cooper Library, University of South Carolina)

of classical writings was intended to support his atomistic natural philosophy. By citing examples of good and bad among earlier proponents of atomism he sought to prove that atomism and atheism do not necessarily go together. As he explained, one of his reasons for writing *The True Intellectual System of the Universe* was his desire to clear atomistic philosophy of the imputation of atheism: "But so many seem to be so strongly possessed with the prejudice, as if Atheism were a Natural and Necessary Appendix to Atomism and therefore will conclude that the same persons could not possibly be Atomists, and Incorporealists or Theists, we shall further make it Evident that there is not only no Inconsistency betwixt the Atomical Physiology and Theology, but also that there is on the contrary, a most natural cognation between

them." Cudworth's subscription to atomism was not mere antiquarianism. Rather, he was a modern in his support of it, regarding it as a rationally grounded theory able to account for the phenomena of nature. He accepted the view of contemporary philosophers, such as Descartes, that material substance is merely "Extended bulk" and that "the onely Principles of Body are Magnitude, Figure, Site, Motion, and Rest." He takes up this point again in *The True Intellectual System of the Universe* when he observes that "atomical, corpuscular or mechanical philosophy . . . solves all the phenomena of the corporeal world by those intelligible principles of magnitude, site, and motion, and thereby makes sensible things intelligible." In *The True Intellectual System of the Universe* he develops this position into an argument for the existence of immaterial beings by arguing that it is impossible to explain movement, life, or thought in terms of these properties: "neither can Life and Cogitation, Sense, and Consciousness, Reason and Understanding, Appetite and Will, ever result from Magnitudes, Figures, Sites and Motions, and therefore they are not Corporeally generated and Corrupted." Therefore there must be some other cause, necessarily immaterial, namely a spirit or soul. Modern corpuscularian theory therefore had apologetic value for Cudworth, who was persuaded that it was the best argument for belief in incorporeal substance and hence in the existence of God. Ancient atomists were thus necessarily theists, for "the same Principle of Reason which made the Ancient Physiologers to become Atomists, must needs induce them also to be Incorporealists." Furthermore, since true atomism leads to the recognition of an intellectual faculty able to judge the appearances of things, it is an antidote to skepticism.

Cudworth's most distinctive contribution to discussions of causality was his hypothesis of "Plastic nature," by which he sought to account for the interaction of God with creation and the orderly operation of the physical universe. He conceives plastic nature as an intermediary between God and nature, the indirect means by which God puts his purposes into effect, governs the physical universe, and maintains the orderly day-to-day operations of nature. Cudworth describes plastic nature as "an Inferior and Subordinate Instrument [which] doeth Drudgingly Execute that Part of his Providence, which consists in the Regular and Orderly Motion of Matter." It is in many ways the epitome of the laws of nature. In Cudworth's conception it is a spirit or immaterial substance, however—not unlike Plato's *anima mundi*. Although a spiritual agent, it operates unconsciously, performing the directives of God without question or foresight. Cudworth put forward his theory of plastic nature as a third alternative to, on the one hand, theories that explain all physical phenomena as the result of chance and, on the other, the occasionalism that entails the direct intervention of God in all occurrences to intervene in even the minutest details of day-to-day natural occurrences. The doctrine of plastic nature is thus designed to ensure a role for divine Providence. It is the means whereby God imprints his presence on his creation, displaying his wisdom and goodness and rendering nature intelligible.

Cudworth's epistemology and moral philosophy are most fully set out in several writings that were not published in his lifetime: the work published with the title *A Treatise Concerning Eternal and Immutable Morality* and the manuscripts on the topic "Of Liberty and Necessity." Cudworth was a moral realist: that is, he held that ethical principles exist independently in nature. He was, therefore, strongly opposed to ethical conventionalism. His target here was Hobbes, in opposition to whose ethical relativism he argued that good and evil, justice and injustice, are "eternal and self-subsistent." Moral principles belong in the same category, ontologically, as wisdom, knowledge, and understanding. Most of *A Treatise Concerning Eternal and Immutable Morality* is devoted to expounding the epistemological basis of his position. In epistemology, as in ethics, Cudworth set out his position in opposition to Hobbes. Cudworth denies that the principles of morality can be deduced from sense knowledge, for he did not regard sense data as true knowledge. Rather, the mind contains within it the ideas of things, and the process of cognition entails a process of recollection from within: as he put it, "to know a thing is nothing else but to comprehend it by some inward ideas that are domestic to the mind, and actively exerted from it." As this quotation makes plain, the knowing mind is not a passive recipient of knowledge from outside itself but an active participant in the process of producing knowledge.

Since the mind contains the principles of knowledge within itself, recollection is a key element in the process of cognition. Recollection is, Cudworth writes, the mind's "power of raising intelligible ideas and conceptions of things from within itself." This idea does not mean that the mind derives nothing from the external world; but sense perception has a secondary role in cognition. Without the addition of a comprehending mind knowledge cannot be derived from sense impressions. Knowing entails mental activity, "the active power of the mind exerting its own intelligible ideas upon that which is passively perceived." True knowledge being the product of the soul's reflection on itself and its own ideas, the mind brings to bear preexisting "conceptions or intelligible ideas" on sensory input. Cognition therefore entails not just recollection but anticipation. Cudworth denominates the preexisting

ideas of things *prolepses,* a term from Stoicism, where they are the common notions with which the mind is furnished. Knowledge is therefore to be acquired by the soul turning inward to contemplate its own inward notions or ideas. The mind is a mental microcosm of knowable reality. Certain knowledge is possible by the fact that it participates in the wisdom of God: "all the knowledge and wisdom that is in cretures, which angels or men, is nothing else but a participation of that one eternal immortal, and increated wisdom of God, or several signatures of that one archetypal soul, or like so many multiplied reflections of one and the same face, made in several glasses, whereog some are clearer, some obscurere, some standing nearer, some further off." Certain knowledge of the external world is possible because the cosmos bears the stamp of its creator. The order and harmony of the world is the "stamp of intellectuality" that renders the natural world intelligible to the observing mind. The mind grasps not external properties but the essences of things. This idea does not mean that sense perception has no role to play. On the contrary, it is vital for making human subjects aware of the external world and for ensuring that the mind is aware of the needs of the body. The mind operates with the "intelligible principles," such as the properties of matter, "magnitude, figure, site and motion," which may be deduced by analyzing sense data.

The practical aspect of Cudworth's ethics is most fully treated in his unpublished writings, the three surviving manuscripts on "Liberty and Necessity." They were probably intended as a continuation of topics dealt with in *A Treatise Concerning Eternal and Immutable Morality* and overlap with one another in subject matter. In these papers Cudworth argues that freedom of the will is an essential attribute of rational beings and freedom of action is the prerequisite for moral responsibility. People are not constrained to act morally by outside incentives or disincentives (such as rewards and punishments in the afterlife). Rather, the individual soul contains within it the principles of virtue and vice, "all moral habits," and conscience. The soul also has the capacity of directing itself toward the good. Without the power to direct itself, the soul would not be free to act but would be a passive respondent to external causes, like a mechanism operated from without. Free choice is not a matter of indifference, but involves end-directed action. Fundamental to Cudworth's understanding of moral action is his concept of "self-power," or *autexousion,* as he calls it.

The central concept of Cudworth's account of free will is *hegemonikon,* or his concept of will as a "ruling principle" of the soul. This quality directs the actions of the individual being (or "self-powerful things"). *Hegemonikon* is the foundation of moral responsibility (that which earns one "praise or blame") and gives human

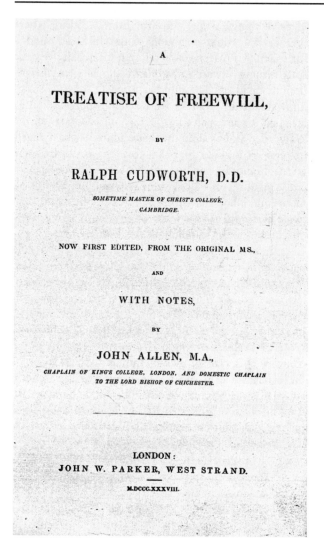

A

TREATISE OF FREEWILL,

BY

RALPH CUDWORTH, D.D.

SOMETIME MASTER OF CHRIST'S COLLEGE,
CAMBRIDGE.

NOW FIRST EDITED, FROM THE ORIGINAL MS.,

AND

WITH NOTES,

BY

JOHN ALLEN, M.A.,

CHAPLAIN OF KING'S COLLEGE, LONDON, AND DOMESTIC CHAPLAIN
TO THE LORD BISHOP OF CHICHESTER.

LONDON:
JOHN W. PARKER, WEST STRAND.

M.DCCC.XXXVIII.

Title page for a work that was first published 150 years after Cudworth's death

beings control over themselves and frees them from being determined by outside forces. Strictly, Cudworth's theory of free choice is not a theory of free will but a theory of autodeterminism. The *hegemonikon* is, in fact, the means of self-determination. The moral psychology that underlies Cudworth's ethics is based on a unitary concept of the soul and its powers. The will is not, as in scholastic philosophy, a separate faculty of the soul. Rather, the will is the ruling principle that coordinates the functions of the soul and directs the actions of the individual being. The soul, according to Cudworth, is a single, uncompartmentalized unity, compounded of powers or principles, two higher and one lower. The *hegemonikon* acts as a unifying principle uniting the lower and higher functions of the soul. Since the *hegemonikon* also ensures close interaction between mind and body, Cudworth avoids the problems associated with Cartesian dualism of mind and body. The empha-

sis here is on the whole person, the unity of body and mind. Cudworth's theory has further features of a theory of personhood: the *hegemonikon* individuates not only by coordinating the functions of the soul but differentiating one soul from others. By virtue of the *hegemonikon,* "men have something in their own power, add something of their own, so that they can change themselves and determine themselves." As a principle of self-determination the *hegemonikon* is therefore a principle of individuation. The freedom to act for oneself also defines the self.

As he puts it in one of the "On Liberty and Necessity" manuscripts, the unifying soul constitutes the self, "denominates the whole man as such," and "determines all ye passive capability of every mans nature, and makes every an such as he is." In the course of his discussion Cudworth employs a range of reflexive terms, many of them new coinages that emphasize the concept of soul as self, such as "self-reflexive," "self-comprehensive," "self-forming," and "self-framing." Furthermore, since the *hegemonikon* is that whereby the soul may strive for the better, it is, by definition, the mark of those beings capable of improvement. Consequently it is not an attribute of perfect beings and does not pertain to God. Rather, it defines people as essentially human. Cudworth's ethics, therefore, is the basis of a theory of the human subject, autonomous to the extent that it is capable of self-determination. Indeed, many of the defining terms of modern psychology and the philosophy of the self are to be found for the first time in Cudworth's philosophy, including "consciousness," "self-determination," and "self-reflection."

Ralph Cudworth died on 26 June 1688. Given the fact that key aspects of his philosophy were published posthumously or not at all, it is difficult to assess his influence. There are certainly important echoes of Cudworth in Locke, their differences with regard to epistemology notwithstanding. Locke was acquainted with Cudworth and was a particularly close friend of his daughter, Damaris, in whose house he spent his last years. It is thus not beyond the bounds of possibility that Locke had access to Cudworth's manuscripts. Samuel Clarke's debt to Cudworth is more certain. Cudworth's posthumous fame was boosted by the republication of his works in the eighteenth century–Birch's 1743 edition and Johann Lorenz Mosheim's Latin translation, which appeared in 1733. These editions account for the interest in Cudworth's philosophy in both Britain and Europe throughout the eighteenth century. His British readers included John Ray; Nehemiah Grew; Anthony Ashley Cooper, third earl of Shaftesbury; and Le Chevalier Ramsay. Mosheim's Latin translation had a relatively wide diffusion in Europe. Cudworth's doctrine of plastic nature was debated in Europe and defended by Paul Janet in France as late as the nineteenth century. Continuing interest in Cudworth in nineteenth-century Britain can be gauged from the publication of one of his manuscripts, edited by John Allen as *A Treatise of Freewill* in 1838, and of *The True Intellectual System of the Universe; with A Treatise Concerning Eternal and Immutable Morality,* an edition of his two most important works, edited by John Harrison in 1845. Modern interest in Cudworth's philosophy focuses on his ethics, where he is regarded as one of the founders of the English ethical tradition extending through Clarke, William Wollaston, Thomas Balguy, Richard Price, and Thomas Reid. His latterday reputation therefore derives largely from his posthumously published writings.

Bibliography:

G. A. J. Rogers, "Die Cambridge Platoniker" and "Ralph Cudworth," in *Ueberwegs Grundriss der Geschichte der Philosophie: Die Philosophie des 17. Jahrhunderts,* edited by Friedrich Ueberweg, volume 3, book 1 (Basel: Schwabe, 1988).

References:

G. Aspelin, "Ralph Cudworth's Interpretation of Greek Philosophy: A Study in the History of English Philosophical Ideas," *Göteborgs Högskolas Arsskrift* (1943): 49;

E. M. Austin, *The Ethics of the Cambridge Platonists,* thesis, University of Pennsylvania, 1935;

Stephen L. Darwall, *British Moralists* (Cambridge: Cambridge University Press, 1992);

G. Giglioni, "Automata Compared: Boyle, Leibniz and the Debate on the Notion of Life and Mind," *British Journal for the History of Philosophy,* 3 (1995), pp. 249–278;

T. Gregory, "Studi sull'atomismo del seicento: III Cudworth e l'atomismo," *Giornale critico della filosofia italiana,* 46 (1967): 528–541;

W. B. Hunter, "The Seventeenth-century Doctrine of Plastic Nature," *Harvard Theological Review,* 4 (1950): 197–213;

G. Musca, "'Omne genus animalium': Antichità e Medioevo in una biblioteca privata inglese del Seicento," *Quaderni Medievali,* 25 (1988): 25–76;

John A. Passmore, *Ralph Cudworth: An Interpretation* (Cambridge: Cambridge University Press, 1951);

Richard H. Popkin, "Cudworth," in his *The Third Force in Seventeenth-Century Thought* (Leiden: Brill, 1992), pp. 333–350;

D. B. Sailor, "Cudworth and Descartes," *Journal of the History of Ideas,* 23 (1962): 133–140;

Dominic Scott, "Platonic Recollection and Cambridge Platonism," *Hermathena,* 149 (1990): 73–97;

Luisa Simonutti, "Bayle and Le Clerc as Readers of Cudworth: Elements of the Debate on *Plastic Nature* in the Dutch Learned Journals," *Geschiedenis van de Wijsbegeerte in Nederland,* 4 (1993): 147–165;

Udo Thiel, "Cudworth and Seventeenth-Century Theories of Consciousness," in *The Uses of Antiquity: The Scientific Revolution and the Classical Tradition,* edited by Stephen Gaukroger (Dordrecht & Boston: Kluwer, 1991);

Yves-Charles Zarka, "Critique de Hobbes et Fondement de la Morale chez Cudworth," in *The Cambridge Platonists in Philosophical Context: Politics, Metaphysics, and Religion,* edited by G. A. J. Rogers, J. M. Vienne, and Zarka (Dordrecht & London: Kluwer, 1997), pp. 39–52.

Papers:

Ralph Cudworth's three manuscript treatises "On Liberty and Necessity" (Additional MSS 4978–4982) and his commentary on the book of Daniel (Additional MSS 4987) are held at the British Library, London. A few of his letters are also held at the British Library (Additional MSS) and the Bodleian Library, Oxford (Selden and Tanner MSS).

Nathaniel Culverwel

(1619? – 1651?)

Jay G. Williams
Hamilton College

BOOKS: *Spiritual Optiks, or, A Glasse Discovering the Weakness and Imperfection of a Christian Knowledge of This Life,* edited by William Dillingham (Cambridge: Printed by Thomas Buck & sold by A. Nicholson, 1652);

An Elegant and Learned Discourse of the Light of Nature, With Several Other Treatises (London: Printed by T. R. & E. M. for John Rothwell, 1652); republished as *Of the Light of Nature: A Discourse,* edited by John Brown with a critical essay by John Cairns (Edinburgh: T. Constable, 1857); excerpted in *The Cambridge Platonists: Being Selections from the Writings of Benjamin Whichcote, John Smith and Nathaniel Culverwel,* edited by Ernest Trafford Campagnac (Oxford: Clarendon Press, 1901); republished as *An Elegant and Learned Discourse on the Light of Nature,* edited by Robert A. Greene and Hugh MacCallum (Toronto: University of Toronto Press, 1971);

The White Stone: or, A Learned and Choice Treatise of Assurance Very Usefull For All, But Especially For Weak Believers (London: J. Rothwell, 1654).

Nathaniel Culverwel is usually portrayed as a minor member of the school of Cambridge Platonists, which flourished during the Interregnum, the period in English history between the execution of Charles I in 1649 and the ascension of Charles II in 1660, at Emmanuel College of Cambridge University. He was an articulate spokesman for the more Puritan side of the school represented by Benjamin Whichcote and John Worthington. Unlike the mystical and theosophical Henry More, Culverwel had much more in common with the Calvinistic Puritan and Aristotelian Scholastic traditions in which he was educated. Nevertheless, his emphasis on reasoning in theology clearly foreshadows the opinions of Enlightenment thinkers such as John Tillotson and John Locke.

Little is known of Culverwel's life. His father, Richard, was serving as rector of St. Margaret Moses Church, Friday Street, London, when Nathaniel was

christened on 13 January 1619. He had four brothers and sisters and seems to have been related to a variety of well-established Elizabethans with Puritan sympathies. Nathaniel attended the same school as his father, St. Paul's, and in 1633 was admitted to Emmanuel College, the Cambridge institution most closely associated with Puritanism. He received a B.A. in 1636 and an M.A. in 1640. There is no evidence that he received a theological degree, though he may have been ordained. When Culverwel entered Emmanuel, Benjamin Whichcote, the founder of Cambridge Platonism, was already a fellow at the college; John Smith, Ralph Cudworth, and John Worthington were contemporary students, while Henry More was an undergraduate at Christ's College.

No biographical information exists about Culverwel's undergraduate years. He contributed a Latin poem to a volume to celebrate the birth of Princess Anne, the daughter of Charles I, in 1637. Another Latin poem appeared in *Irenodia Cantabrigiensis* in 1641, and there exists "On the Death of Mr. Holden," an elegy, written in English, for a contemporary student. On 27 July 1641 Culverwel delivered a sermon that was later published by William Dillingham under the title *Spiritual Optiks, or, A Glasse Discovering the Weakness and Imperfection of a Christian Knowledge of This Life* (1652).

According to Worthington's diary, Culverwel was chosen as a fellow of Emmanuel College on 19 November 1642 and held that position until his death in 1651 or 1652. *An Elegant and Learned Discourse of the Light of Nature, With Several Other Treatises,* published in 1652, includes several of Culverwel's treatises that were probably originally delivered as sermons and "An Elegant Discourse of the Light of Nature." The projected second half of Culverwel's most famous work, which was to deal more specifically with "positive religion" and revelation, was apparently never completed. Culverwel dedicated the work to Anthony Tuckney—the master of Emmanuel and a sometime Westminister divine—and to the fellows of Emmanuel, indicating that Culverwel, the only Cambridge Platonist to remain at Emmanuel after Tuckney was appointed master, was far closer to the Puritan movement than many interpreters have suggested.

Although *An Elegant and Learned Discourse of the Light of Nature* concentrates primarily upon the role of reason in religion, Culverwel had intended this work to be prefatory to a second volume that was to treat the grace and revelation given to man through Jesus Christ. His death prevented him from completing his projected works, although his sermons and scattered comments in *An Elegant and Learned Discourse of the Light of Nature* give some indication of the approach Culverwel intended to take in the second volume.

In *An Elegant and Learned Discourse of the Light of Nature* Culverwel expands and clarifies some of the ideas treated in a less systematic way by Whichcote. Essentially, Culverwel attempts to establish the importance of reason in the life of the believer and to show that the use of this god-given faculty is not only consistent with, but necessary for, an orthodox theology. The basis for this sustained argument is laid out in the introduction to the work.

In this introduction Culverwel defends the position that there is no gap between faith and reason, and that acknowledgment of imperfection of reason does not necessarily entail the position that reason should not be used at all. On the contrary, without reason there is no basis for sound judgment and thus for theology. A theologian who denies the use of "the candle of the Lord," as Culverwel characterizes reason, denies one of the essential tools of his trade. Culverwel argues that to abandon reason because groups such as the Socinians and Arminians have misused reason and consequently drawn false conclusions concerning theology is a serious error. Rather, a Christian theologian must understand the proper role of reason within the theological enterprise so that erroneous arguments of this sort can be refuted. In chapter 2 Culverwel attempts to explain and justify his interpretation of Prov. 20:27—that the spirit of humans is the "candle of the Lord"—by a careful analysis of the various Hebrew words for "spirit" and "soul." His conclusion is that *n'shmath* is the rational human soul, which is breathed into him by God, and that *n'shmath* should be distinguished from both *nephesh,* the sensitive soul, and *ruah,* the seat of feeling and passion.

Although he emphasizes reason in theology, Culverwel spends little time attempting to prove the existence of God. God, for him, is the source of all reason, not a being whose existence is a conclusion to be arrived at by a rational process that begins without theological presuppositions. He therefore turns to the external world not to prove God's existence but to dis-

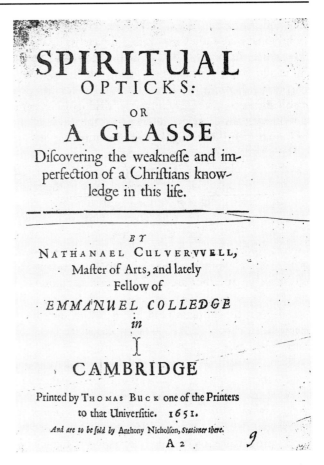

SPIRITUAL
OPTICKS:
OR
A GLASSE
Difcovering the weakneffe and imperfection of a Chriftians knowledge in this life.

BY
NATHANAEL CULVERVVELL,
Mafter of Arts, and lately
Fellow of
EMMANUEL COLLEDGE
in
Ï
CAMBRIDGE

Printed by THOMAS BUCK one of the Printers to that Univerfitie. 1651.
And are to be fold by Anthony Nicholfon, Stationer there.
A 2   9

Title page for Nathanael Culverwel's first published work, a sermon he had given ten years previously (Bodleian Library, Oxford)

cover God's law. Before considering the laws of nature, however, Culverwel attempts to define the natural itself.

In this attempt Culverwel reveals his affinity with both the Calvinists and the Platonists. First he repudiates any attempt to distinguish between the natural and the spiritual, including in nature the physical and the spiritual, the measurable and the immeasurable, and the human and the angelic. Nature, according to Culverwel, is simply equivalent to what has been created, the *natura naturata.* Culverwel also responds to attempts, be they Aristotelian or Cartesian, to regard this nature as having independent existence. God, he argues, is being itself, the *natura naturans.* All motion, all change, and all action takes place according to God's will. Thus nature, for Culverwel, means two things: the *natura naturans,* the "origin of existence," and the *natura naturata,* "the action of existence."

Culverwel does not emphasize any human need to examine the "reason in things" in order to know God's laws for humanity. Rather, he contends that this law is "written upon the heart." The eternal law that has been from the beginning is a fountain that bubbles and flows forth to the "sons of men." Thus, humans are theonomous rather than autonomous. Humans do not rightly make laws; they only reflect the eternal law over which they have no control. The theonomous state of humanity does not mean that all obey this law naturally and necessarily, for the very nature of law implies that disobedience is possible. Culverwel distinguishes carefully between natural law, intended for the government of humans, and those regularities of nature that are the result of God's providence and that are commonly studied by the physical scientists. "A law," he says, "is founded in intellectuals, in the reason, not in the sensitive principle. It supposes a noble and free born creature, for where there is no liberty there is no law." Therefore, to speak of God governing the world of physical objects in the way that a governor rules a state is illegitimate. Physical objects have no independent will of their own and thus are totally dependent upon God for their being and their motion. Although human souls are also dependent upon God for existence, they have freedom of choice. Hence, God promulgates laws for human beings; God does not pull strings.

Culverwel does not explain how this position regarding the freedom of humans and the possibility of disobedience is consistent with his position in regard to the unity of nature. On the one hand, he seems to imply that humans are controlled at every moment by God's providence; on the other, he allows humans freedom and a kind of semi-independent will.

According to Culverwel, God's law is known by humans through "the candle which burns within" and on the heart is written plainly a transcript of the original and eternal law of God necessary for the welfare of humanity. Culverwel, rather than accepting as axiomatic a belief in innate ideas, explicitly attacks Plato's doctrine of recollection and the belief that humans are born with innate ideas, thus committing himself to what appear to be two contrary propositions, that is, that the natural law is written upon the heart and that the mind is a tabula rasa. Culverwel reconciles these two notions by slightly modifying them. In the first place, the natural law that is written on the heart is not conceived of as explicit information or rules that are somehow inscribed in a common tongue on the minds of all. Rather, Culverwel argues that humans have within them "natural instincts," which are enlivened when confronted by sense-experience. These instincts are the "candle" that experience lights. When the natural world affects the human mind, the mind produces ideas that are implicit in the natural instincts.

Although Culverwel emphasizes the importance of reason, he also cautions that there are important doctrines that reason can never apprehend by itself. Revelation complements and fulfills reason; it does not destroy rationality. Unlike Whichcote, however, Culverwel does not accept reason as the norm for interpretation of Scripture; although not opposed to reason, some doctrines and events—the Trinity, the Incarnation, and the Resurrection, for example—can never be understood by it. These doctrines and events, according to Culverwel, are not against reason but above it. Confronted by the paradoxes of faith, Reason should not put out her eye, but should, perhaps, close it.

Given these paradoxes, certain questions immediately arise for Culverwel: How can one "know" the doctrines by revelation? If there is no correlation between the doctrine of the Trinity, for instance, and the "natural instincts" of reason, in what sense can a person claim to "know" this doctrine to be true? In answering this question Culverwel returns to the thought of the Calvinists. The best interpreter of Scripture, he argues, is not reason, but the Holy Spirit, who wrote it. The Holy Spirit confirms the testimony of Scripture and makes revelation possible. The Holy Spirit provides the correspondence between what humans can know and divine reality.

Culverwel also distinguishes between what is revealed in the Bible and what was known to the people of Israel through natural reason. Throughout his work he resists strongly the idea that the Jews in essence had in their moral law anything that the Gentiles did not know through reason. According to Culverwel, the Jews incorrectly supposed that the light of nature shone only upon them. Greek and Jew, circumcision and uncircumcision, barbarian and Scythian are all one in respect to nature, nature's law, and nature's light, according to Culverwel. For this reason there is no purpose in arguing, as Cudworth later did, that the Gentiles lighted their lamps at the Jew's sun. The Gentiles were created by God and thus had their own light that revealed to them the moral law.

In order to substantiate this idea Culverwel appeals to the consent of the nations in regard to matters of virtue. There are, he says, in every nation some corrupted people who will disagree; yet, those who have culture and morality basically affirm that murder, the dishonoring of parents, and lies are wrong. Culverwel argues that this consent shows the Jews were incorrect in claiming any particular revelation in the Ten Commandments. These laws are not peculiarly Jewish but are universal.

The obvious circularity of Culverwel's appeal to the consent of the nations to prove the universality of agreement concerning moral law precludes the use of empirical evidence contrary to his position as a means of critique. Culverwel accepts the moral standards of the Decalogue and then affirms that anyone who does not agree is corrupt. Since all people are sinners through the fall of Adam, the logical conclusion of this

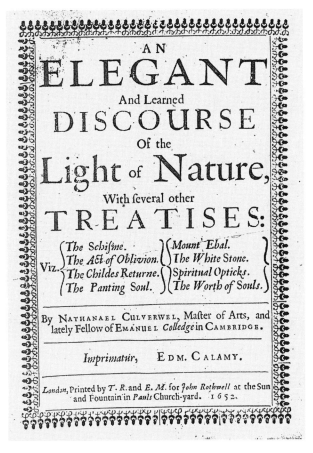

Title page for Culverwel's best-known work, a collection of his sermons on the role of reason in religion
(Henry E. Huntington Library, San Marino, California)

position is that there could be a universal moral law that everyone in theory would know but with which everyone in fact disagrees. Culverwel does not, for obvious reasons, carry his argument to this conclusion because he wishes to maintain that most people can apprehend the basic moral principles that God has ordained for human welfare. Nevertheless, his acknowledgment of the corrupting effect of sin upon this apprehension places him closer to the Calvinistic tradition than might at first be suspected.

In the final two chapters of his treatise Culverwel identifies the "candle of the Lord" as both a pleasant and an ascendant light. Epicurus, he says, may have been right in thinking that pleasure is the end of humanity, but he utterly failed to understand the true meaning of, or source for, pleasure. Had Epicurus truly known the meaning of pleasure, argues Culverwel, he would have realized that the pleasures of reason and the intellect far surpass the pleasure of sense-experience. In this realization, he claims, Plato and Aristotle far surpass the Epicureans; yet, even they fall short of an understanding of the true end of humanity. Culverwel

ends by arguing that the pleasures of natural reason fall far short of "Gospel delights." The true end of humanity is to glorify God and to enjoy him forever. This end can only be fulfilled when the love of God revealed in Jesus Christ is known and accepted.

Culverwel sees the end of humanity as the beatific vision of God; yet, he qualifies his description of this vision so that he avoids the possible heresies inherent in extreme mysticism. First, he makes clear that humans are humans and God is God. Culverwel accepts that the more humans exercise reason the more they are similar to God, but he maintains that there remains, even when the end is reached, a great chasm between humanity and divinity. Humans remain subservient beings who do not really partake of the divine essence.

Culverwel also emphasizes that humans cannot save themselves through the light of their own "candle": God stoops to become incarnate and thereby gives humanity its salvation. Culverwel's emphasis on reason, then, in no way precludes a belief in free grace and election. Humans may use their faculties to discover how they should live in this world and can apprehend God as the illuminator of reason, but God alone blots out iniquity and acts to complete human nature, bringing it to its ultimate end and happiness.

One of the central impulses that pervades and shapes Culverwel's theology is his concern for the charitable unity of the church. In "The Schism," another sermon in *An Elegant and Learned Discourse of the Light of Nature, With Several Other Treatises,* Culverwel directs his attention to this problem, using 1 Cor. 3:4 as his text. The church, Culverwel laments, has become militant against itself and thus "the enemy" becomes triumphant. He sees that an overemphasis on precision and absolute agreement in all doctrine can only lead to disaster for the church. Culverwel is not attempting to dispense with the central doctrines of the church but is expressing concern that if there is no latitude within the church that will allow for variations in faith and practice, the church can only fragment and decay. Culverwel's theology can be understood as an attempt to heal the division of the church that troubled seventeenth-century England. He appeals to reason, charity, and the clear revelation of God's mercy for sinners as a basis for unity.

Although he is often described as a minor member of the Cambridge movement, Culverwel's work constitutes a real contribution to one major strand of Cambridge Platonism. In his *Platonic Renaissance in England* (1953) Ernst Cassirer barely mentions him at all. Even Tulloch treats him only briefly in *Rational Theology and Christian Philosophy in England in the Seventeenth Century* (1872). His association with a particular theological strand of the Cambridge school perhaps explains why he has been overlooked. Critics and readers who take the imaginative and speculative thought of More to be characteristic of the movement as a whole have difficulty fitting Culverwel into their preconceptions of Cambridge Platonism. He is not an anti-Puritan. He is not an Arminian. He is not an enthusiastic follower of either Plato or Plotinus. Rather, he continued and developed Benjamin Whichcote's theology.

The major difference between Whichcote and Culverwel is that Culverwel stands somewhat closer to the Puritan tradition than Whichcote, particularly in his greater emphasis on the doctrines of election, free grace, and the testimony of the Holy Spirit. Such a difference, however, is a matter of degree and not of kind. These two men, along with Worthington, show how closely Puritanism and Cambridge Platonism were related. Together they represent an important but unheralded school of thought within the Cambridge movement, which is distinct from that of Henry More.

Nathaniel Culverwel's treatise "A Discourse of the Light of Nature" is one of the clearest and best theological statements to be written by any of the members of the Cambridge school. He puts in systematic order many of the ideas promulgated by Whichcote and clarifies the way these men arrived at and justified their positions. His writings reveal not only a great appreciation for the philosophers of antiquity but also a deep understanding of the Scholastics as well. The pages of his magnum opus are dotted with references to Thomas Aquinas, Francis Suaréz, and the philosophers of the Renaissance. Nevertheless, he accepts no theologian or philosopher as authoritative but works out his own theological position in his own way.

References:

Robert A. Greene and Hugh MacCallum, eds., introduction to *An Elegant and Learned Discourse on the Light of Nature,* by Nathaniel Culverwel (Toronto: University of Toronto Press, 1971), pp. ix–lv;

Frederick J. Powicke, *The Cambridge Platonists: A Study* (Cambridge, Mass.: Harvard University Press, 1926), pp. 130–149;

John Herman Randall Jr., *The Career of Philosophy,* 2 volumes (New York: Columbia University Press, 1962), I: 481–482;

John Tulloch, *Rational Theology and Christian Philosophy in England in the Seventeenth Century* (Edinburgh: W. Blackwood, 1872), II: 410–425.

Joseph Glanvill
(1636 – 4 November 1680)

William E. Burns
Howard University

BOOKS: *The Vanity of Dogmatizing: or, Confidence in Opinions Manifested in the Discourse of the Shortness and Uncertainty of Our Knowledge, and Its Causes; with Some Reflexions on Peripatecism; and An Apology for Philosophy* (London: Printed by E. Cotes for Henry Eversden, 1661); revised as *Scepsis Scientifica: or, Confest Ignorance, the Way to Science, in an Essay on the Vanity of Dogmatizing, and Confident Opinion. With a Reply to the Exception of the Learned T. Albius (A Letter to a Friend Concerning Aristotle)*, 2 volumes (London: E. Cotes for Henry Eversden, 1665)–includes "Sciri tuum nihil est: or, The Author's Defense of the Vanity of Dogmatizing";

Lux Orientalis; or An Enquiry into the Opinion of the Eastern Sages Concerning the Praeexistence of Souls: Being a Key to Unlock the Grand Mysteries of Providence, in Relation to Man's Misery and Sin (London, 1662);

A Philosophical Endeavour Towards the Defence of the Being of Witches and Apparitions. In a Letter to the Much Honoured, Robert Hunt, as a member of the Royal Society (London: Printed by J. Macock for James Collins, 1666); republished as *Some Philosophical Considerations Touching the Being of Witches and Witchcraft, Written in a Letter to the Much Honour'd Robert Hunt, esq.* (London: Printed by E.C. for James Collins, 1667); revised and enlarged as *A Blow at Modern Sadducism in Some Philosophical Considerations about Witchcraft. To Which is Added, the Relation of the Fam'd Disturbance by the Drummer, in the House of Mr. John Mompesson: With Some Reflections on Drollery, and Atheisme*, as J.G., a member of the Royal Society (London: Printed by E.C. for James Collins, 1668); revised and enlarged as *Saducismus Triumphatus: or, Full and Plain Evidence Concerning Witches and Apparitions. In Two Parts. The First Treating of Their Possibility, The Second of Their Real Existence*, edited by Henry More (London: Printed for J. Collins & S. Lownds, 1681);

A Loyal Tear Dropt on the Vault of Our Late Martyred Sovereign: In an Anniversary Sermon on the Day of His Mur-

Joseph Glanvill (engraving by W. Faithorne)

ther (London: Printed by E. Cotes & sold by James Collins, 1667);

Plus Ultra: or, The Progress and Advancement of Knowledge Since the Days of Aristotle. In an Account of Some of the Most Remarkable Late Improvements of Practical, Useful Learning: To Encourage Philosophical Endeavours. Occasioned by a Conference With One of the Notional Way (London: Printed for James Collins, 1668);

Catholick Charity Recommended in a Sermon Before the Right Honorable Lord Mayor, and Aldermen of London, in Order to the Abating the Animosities among Christians, That Have Been Occasion'd by Differences in Religion

(London: Printed by H. Eversden for James Collins, 1669);

ΛΟΓΟΥ ΘΡΗΣΚΕΙΑ [Logou Threskeia]; or, A Seasonable Recommendation, and Defence of Reason; in the Affairs of Religion; Against Infidelity, Scepticism, and Fanaticisms of All Sorts (London: Printed by E.C. & A.C. for James Collins, 1670);

The Way of Happiness: Represented in Its Difficulties and Incouragements; and Cleared From Many Popular and Dangerous Mistakes (London: Printed by E.C. & A.C. for James Collins, 1670); republished as *The Way to Happiness: Represented in Its Difficulties and Incouragements; and Cleared From Many Popular Mistakes* (London: Printed for G. Schaw of Edinburgh, 1671);

A Praefatory Answer to Mr. Henry Stubbe, the Doctor of Warwick. Wherein the Malignity Hypocrisie Falshood of His Temper, Pretences, Reports, and the Impertinency of His Arguings and Quotations in His Animadversions on Plus Ultra Are Discovered (London: Printed by A. Clark for J. Collins, 1671);

A Further Discovery of M. Stubbe, in a Brief Reply to His Last Pamphlet Against Jos. Glanville (London: Printed for H. Eversden, 1671);

Philosophia Pia; or, A Discourse of the Religious Temper, and Tendencies of the Experimental Philosophy which is Profest by the Royal Society; To Which is Annext a Recommendation, and Defence of Reason in the Affairs of Religion, 2 volumes (London: Printed by J. Macock for James Collins, 1671);

An Earnest Invitation to the Sacrament of the Lord's Supper (London: Printed for John Baker, 1673; revised and enlarged, 1677, 1681, and 1684); republished as *An Earnest Invitation to the Sacrament of the Lord's Supper. Wherein All the Excuses That Men Ordinarily Make For Their Not Coming to the Holy Communion Are Answered* (London: Printed for J. Phillips & M. Wotten, 1700);

An Apology and Advice for Some of the Clergy, Who Suffer Under False, and Scandalous Reports. Written on the Occasion of the Second Part of the Rehearsal Transprosed: In A Letter To a Friend: And By Him Publish'd, anonymous (London: Printed for A. E., 1674);

An Account of Mr. Ferguson His Common-Place Book, in Two Letters, Glanvill with William Sherlock (London: Printed by Andrew Clark for Walter Kettilby, 1675);

Essays on Several Important Subjects in Philosophy and Religion (London: Printed by J. D. for John Baker & Henry Mortlock, 1676);

Seasonable Reflections and Discourses, in Order to the Conviction and Cure of the Scoffing and Infidelity of a Degenerate Age (London: Printed by R.W. for H. Mortlock, 1676);

An Essay Concerning Preaching: Written for the Direction of a Young Divine; and Useful Also For the People, In Order To Profitable Hearing (London: Printed by A.C. for H. Brome, 1678);

A Seasonable Defence of Preaching: And the Plain Way of It (London: M. Clark, for H. Brome, 1678);

Some Discourses, Sermons, and Remains of the Reverend Mr. Jos. Glanvil (London: Printed for Henry Mortlock & James Collins, 1681);

The Zealous, and Impartial Protestant, Shewing Some Great, But Less Heeded Dangers of Popery. In Order to Thorough and Effectual Security Against It. In a Letter to a Member of Parliament (London: Printed by M.C. for Henry Brome, 1681);

Mr. J. Glanvil's Full Vindication of the Late, Reverend, Pious, and Learned Mr. Richard Baxter (London: Printed for John Salusbury, 1691).

SELECTED PERIODICAL PUBLICATIONS–
UNCOLLECTED: "Answers to some of the Inquiries formerly publish'd concerning Mines," *Philosophical Transactions of the Royal Society of London (1665–1678),* 3 (21 October 1667): 525–527;

"Additional Answers to the Queries of Mines," *Philosophical Transactions of the Royal Society of London (1665–1678),* 3 (21 September 1668): 767–771;

"Observations Concerning the Bath-Springs," *Philosophical Transactions of the Royal Society of London (1665–1678),* 4 (19 July 1669): 977–983;

"'The Cupri-Cosmits': Glanvill on Latitudinarian Anti-Enthusiasm," edited by Jackson I. Cope, *Huntington Library Quarterly,* 17 (May 1954): 269–286.

Joseph Glanvill is significant both as a popularizer of the ideas of the Cambridge Platonists and the Restoration natural philosophers, and as a philosophical thinker who prefigured David Hume's doctrine of causation. He was also an important and prolific apologist for the Restoration-era Church of England, and a leader in the development of plain prose. In the disputatious intellectual world of the Restoration, Glanvill was a particularly tireless controversialist: most of his written work either provoked or responded to dispute.

Glanvill was born in 1636 in Plymouth, England, the third son of the Puritan merchant Nicholas Glanville (Joseph Glanvill later dropped the terminal *e* from his name) and his wife Joan. He matriculated at Exeter College, Oxford, in 1652 and left Exeter with a B.A. in 1655, going up to Lincoln College in 1655. Both of these Oxford colleges were dominated by Puritans during the Interregnum–the period in English history between the execution of Charles I and the ascension of Charles II–and the young Glanvill found Puritanism and the Scholastic Aristotelianism that still dominated the Oxford curriculum to be increasingly uncongenial. He later expressed the wish that he had gone to Cambridge, home of the intellectually innovative Platonist movement led by Benjamin Whichcote. During the Interregnum, Oxford boasted an active intellectual life outside the institutional structure of the university, including the Oxford Philosophical Society—an informal group interested in the then-new natural philosophy—of John Wilkins and Robert Boyle. Although there is no evidence of Glanvill having attended the meetings of the Oxford Philosophical Society, he was probably aware of its work. After taking his M.A. from Lincoln in 1658, Glanvill became the chaplain of Francis Rous, a Cromwellian and provost of Eton College. Following Rous's death shortly thereafter, Glanvill returned to Oxford, where he remained until the Restoration.

He took Anglican orders in 1660 after the Restoration. His brother Benjamin, a London tin merchant, purchased the rectory of Wimbish, Essex, for him. While at Wimbish, Glanvill published his first philosophical work, *The Vanity of Dogmatizing: or, Confidence in Opinions Manifested in the Discourse of the Shortness and Uncertainty of Our Knowledge, and Its Causes; with Some Reflexions on Peripatecism; and An Apology for Philosophy* (1661), an attack on Scholastic Aristotelianism. With the publication of this work, Glanvill became publicly associated with the Latitudinarian movement to defend the Church of England from Roman Catholic superstition, the enthusiasm of Protestant Dissenters, and the materialistic atheism associated with Thomas Hobbes. Like other Latitudinarians, he believed in a comprehensive Church of England emphasizing the fundamental tenets of the Christian faith and allowing a wide range of opinions and liturgical practices on other issues. The Latitudinarians were not believers in the toleration of Dissenters outside the Church of England, although Glanvill had friendly relations with the eminent Presbyterian minister Richard Baxter.

In *The Vanity of Dogmatizing* Glanvill demonstrates the fallacy of dogmatic belief by asserting the unknowability of the inner workings of the universe. He opposes all forms of certainty, arguing that certain knowledge of the external world was possible only for the unfallen Adam—given perfect sensory organs: "Adam needed no spectacles" to perceive any phenomenon of nature. The Fall, by limiting human sensory awareness, made it impossible for humans to truly understand the cosmos. Influenced by the Cambridge Platonist Henry More (at that time a Cartesian), Glanvill includes in *The Vanity of Dogmatizing* a great deal of praise of "the Grand Secretary of Nature, the illustrious Des-cartes," seen as a great opponent of outmoded dogma, the inventor of the method of doubt, and the

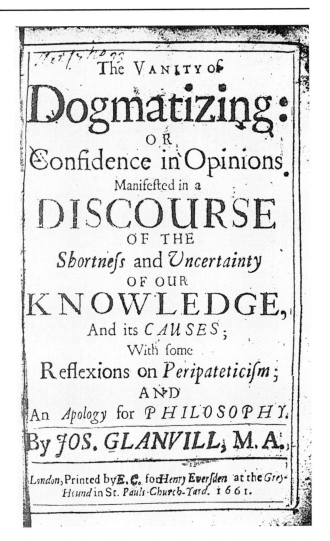

Title page for Glanvill's first work, a defense of the Church of England against Roman Catholicism, Protestant Dissent, and atheism (Henry E. Huntington Library, San Marino, California)

creator of the best system of natural philosophy extant. Glanvill does, however, criticize some aspects of Cartesian physics and psychology, such as Descartes's explanation of memory as caused by intellectual spirits traveling the paths in the brain formed by the original sense impressions being remembered. Glanvill argued that the spirits would be extremely unlikely to find the proper path among so many and that the paths would not be permanently etched into the soft material of the brain.

Glanvill, who studied ancient Greek thought mainly in translation, was neither a system builder nor a profound student of philosophical texts. He used skeptical arguments, but was not a skeptic. Granvill was an advocate of an eclectic Platonism that opposed Aristotelian dogmatizing, Cartesian dualism, and Hobbesian materialism. In *The Vanity of Dogmatizing* Granville endorsed skepticism as a method of attack on Aristotelian philosophy. Ultimately, though, Glanvill saw skepticism as a solvent of dogmatism rather than as an adequate philosophy itself.

As part of this skeptical project of denying the dogmatic foundation of knowledge, Glanvill attacked the idea of a necessary connection between a cause and its effect. A passage on causality in *The Vanity of Dogmatizing* has been claimed by some critics as a precursor of Hume's argument about the nonintrinsic nature of the causal relationship, although no one has ever demonstrated a direct influence on Glanvill from Hume, and Hume does not seem to have been very familiar with Glanvill's works. The connection between Glanvill and Hume on causality was first made by historians of philosophy—including Dugald Stewart—in the late eighteenth century and was responsible for a nineteenth-century revival of interest in Glanvill as a philosopher.

Glanvill's second philosophical work, *Lux Orientalis; or An Enquiry into the Opinion of the Eastern Sages Concerning the Praeexistence of Souls: Being a Key to Unlock the Grand Mysteries of Providence, in Relation to Man's Misery and Sin* (1662), an elaborate attempt to demonstrate the preexistence of the human soul before conception, draws on the ideas of Plato, the Alexandrian theologian Origen, and Glanvill's friend More. The work was quite popular. The same year it was published, Glanvill moved from Wimbish to a vicarage in Somersetshire. During this time Glanvill probably married his first wife, Mary Stocker, with whom he had three sons—Joseph, who died in infancy, Maurice, who followed his father into the church, and Henry—and two daughters, Sophia and Mary. After the death of his first wife, Glanvill married Margaret Selwyn, with whom he had another son, Charles.

The Vanity of Dogmatizing led to a controversy with the eminent Catholic priest and Aristotelian philosopher Thomas White, one of the most able defenders of the rational foundations of certain knowledge. White responded to Glanvill in a Latin work, *Scirri, sive sceptices et scepticorum à jure disputationis exclusio* (1663)—translated into English as *An Exclusion of Scepticks from All Title to Dispute: Being an Answer to the Vanity of Dogmatizing* (1665)—which asserted that many positions denied by the skeptics could indeed be logically demonstrated. Glanvill's rebuttal to White, *Scepsis Scientifica: or, Confest Ignorance, the Way to Science, in an Essay on the Vanity of Dogmatizing, and Confident Opinion. With a Reply to the Exception of the Learned T. Albius (A Letter to a Friend Concerning Aristotle)* (1665), is a reworking of *The Vanity of Dogmatizing* with two appended sections, one addressing White's criticisms and titled "Sciri tuum nihil est: or, The Author's Defense of the Vanity of Dogmatizing," the other "A Letter to a Friend concerning Aristotle." *Scepsis Scientifica* was shorn of much of the praise of Descartes,

as Glanvill was becoming disenchanted with Cartesianism because of its mechanistic aspects. The work also included some new prefatory material including a dedication to the Royal Society of London for the Promotion of Natural Knowledge. The dedication led to Glanvill's election to the Royal Society the same year.

In 1666 Glanvill received a living at the Abbey church of the resort town of Bath. He lived in Bath and retained the living for the rest of his life, although he continued to accumulate other desirable church posts, including a chaplaincy in ordinary to King Charles II in 1672. A conscientious if not always popular parish clergyman, Glanvill published for the benefit of his parishioners a very successful manual for communicants, *An Earnest Invitation to the Sacrament of the Lord's Supper* (1673), which went through several editions in the seventeenth and early eighteenth centuries.

Glanvill also served as secretary to a Somerset natural philosophical society that corresponded with the Royal Society, and in the 1660s he made some contributions to the Society's journal, *Philosophical Transactions of the Royal Society of London (1665–1678),* including the results of inquiries he had made concerning local mines and baths. However, his major writings related to his membership in the Society were *Plus Ultra: or, The Progress and Advancement of Knowledge Since the Days of Aristotle. In an Account of Some of the Most Remarkable Late Improvements of Practical, Useful Learning: To Encourage Philosophical Endeavours. Occasioned by a Conference With One of the Notional Way* (1668) and *Philosophia Pia; or, A Discourse of the Religious Temper, and Tendencies of the Experimental Philosophy which is Profest by the Royal Society; To Which is Annext a Recommendation, and Defence of Reason in the Affairs of Religion* (1671).

Plus Ultra was written in response to a conflict between Glanvill and Robert Crosse, a local Puritan minister and Aristotelian. This conflict was much less civil than the one between Glanvill and White, and Crosse even composed anti-Glanvill ballads to be sung in alehouses. Conceived as a supplement to Thomas Sprat's *History of the Royal Society* (1667), *Plus Ultra* praised the new philosophy of the Royal Society by placing it in the context of the advancement of natural knowledge since the days of Aristotle, demonstrating that the Society's methods were the most productive yet found. The work particularly emphasized the achievements of Robert Boyle. *Plus Ultra* was one of the earliest attempts at a history of science. Conceived in one conflict, it led to another, an elaborate pamphlet war that paired Glanvill and Sprat in defense of the Royal Society against the attacks of physician Henry Stubbe, an Aristotelian associate of Crosse and author of *Legends No Histories: or, A Specimen of Some Animadversions upon the History of the Royal Society wherein Sundry Mistakes about the*

Making of Salt Petre and Gun-powder Are Detected and Rectified; Whereunto Are Added Two Discourses, One of P. Sardi, and Another of N. Tartaglia, Relating to That Subject; Translated Out of Italian. Together with the Plus Ultra of Mr. J. Glanvill Reduced to a Non-Plus (1670), which accused the society of being intellectually elitist and a stalking-horse for the reimposition of Catholicism. Glanvill responded in *A Praefatory Answer to Mr. Henry Stubbe, the Doctor of Warwick. Wherein the Malignity Hypocrisie Falshood of His Temper, Pretences, Reports, and the Impertinency of His Arguings and Quotations in His Animadversions on Plus Ultra Are Discovered* (1671).

Philosophia Pia developed from the controversy with Stubbe and was explicitly positioned as a defense of the religious functions of "the Experimental Philosophy, which is profest by the Royal Society." Glanvill argued that natural philosophy, as rightly understood, glorified God in his works and did not lead to atheism or unbelief. Instead, the study of nature confuted atheism, materialism, and superstition. Ironically, given Glanvill's intellectual pugnaciousness, he also recommended philosophy as an aid against "the Humour of Disputing."

Like his friends More and Baxter, Glanvill was an important contributor to the movement to apply empirical techniques to the spiritual world in order to prove its reality and confute atheists. He took an active role, journeying to areas of alleged spiritual activity and investigating them for himself, as in the famous case of the phantom drummer at the house of a Mr. Mompesson in Tedworth, Wiltshire, which Glanvill visited in 1663. At Bath he also produced *A Philosophical Endeavour Towards the Defence of the Being of Witches and Apparitions. In a Letter to the Much Honoured, Robert Hunt* (1666), one of the foremost defenses of the belief in witches in the late seventeenth century. Glanvill used this book to make the acquaintance of the aristocratic natural philosopher Margaret Lucas Cavendish, first Duchess of Newcastle, to whom he sent a copy with a flattering letter. They entered into a correspondence, and several of Glanvill's letters to her discussing philosophical problems, including the nature of the soul and the reasons for belief in witchcraft, were printed in a tribute volume appearing after Newcastle's death, *Letters and Poems in Honour of the Incomparable Princess, Margaret, Dutchess of Newcastle* (1676).

The first edition of *A Philosophical Endeavour Towards the Defence of the Being of Witches and Apparitions* was mostly destroyed in the Great Fire of London in 1666, but two subsequent editions appeared in 1667, the second under the title *Some Philosophical Considerations Touching the Being of Witches and Witchcraft, Written in a Letter to the Much Honour'd Robert Hunt, esq.* (1667), and the third as *A Blow at Modern Sadducism in Some Philosophical*

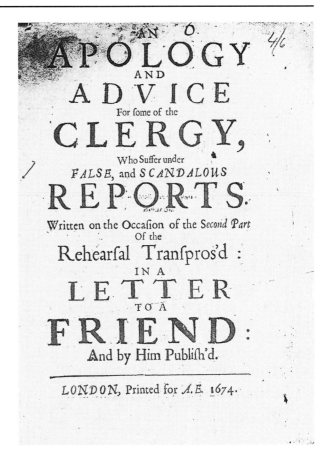

Title page for Glanvill's defense of the Anglican clergy against attacks in print by the poet Andrew Marvell (Union Theological Seminary Library)

Considerations about Witchcraft. To Which is Added, the Relation of the Fam'd Disturbance by the Drummer, in the House of Mr. John Mompesson: With Some Reflections on Drollery, and Atheisme (1668). The third edition included the drummer of Tedworth story. The work was finally posthumously published with material added by More, as *Saducismus Triumphatus: or, Full and Plain Evidence Concerning Witches and Apparitions. In Two Parts. The First Treating of Their Possibility, The Second of Their Real Existence* (1681) and went through several editions through the first quarter of the eighteenth century. Throughout his intellectual engagement with witchcraft, Glanvill was less concerned with witchcraft than he was with the question of the reality of the spiritual world and its interaction with the material world. He believed that those who attacked belief in witchcraft were denying the reality of demons and the possibility of their affecting the material world and were therefore contributing to the menace of atheistic materialism.

Many, beginning with the late-eighteenth-century historians of philosophy who revived Glanvill's reputation, have found Glanvill's philosophical skepti-

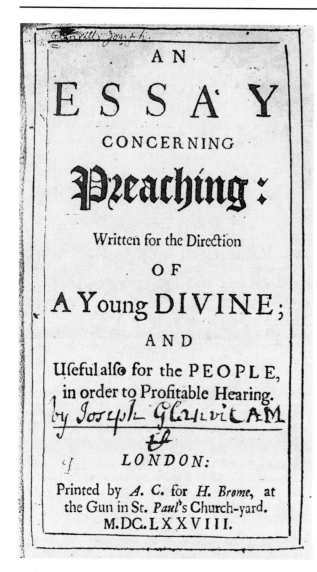

Title page for Glanvill's essay advocating a plain preaching style for clergymen (University of Michigan Libraries)

Glanvill became particularly identified as England's foremost defender of the reality of witchcraft through his debate with the physician John Webster. Webster, a believer in the hermetic philosophy of Robert Fludd, published *The Displaying of Supposed Witchcraft: Wherein Is Affirmed That There Are Many Sorts of Deceivers and Impostors, and Divers Persons under a Passive Delusion of Melancholy and Fancy, but That There Is a Corporeal League Made betwixt the Devil and the Witch, Is Utterly Denied. Wherein also Is Handled, the Existence of Angels and Spirits, Etc.* in 1677, asserting that although evil spirits existed, God prevented them from entering into compacts with witches. Webster's work was an attempt to vindicate the occult sciences from the charge of satanic witchcraft. Recognizing Glanvill as his principal opponent, Webster made him a particular target of his attacks. Glanvill responded in *Saducismus Triumphatus*. He asserted that by arguing against the belief in possession by claiming that demonic spirits were "subtle bodies" unable to occupy the same space as other bodies, Webster, despite his proclaimed piety, was playing into the hands of Hobbesian materialism, which denied the spiritual world. Glanvill was considered by most judges to have vanquished Webster. After his death he continued to be seen in England, New England, and continental Europe as one of the greatest champions of the belief in witches.

As an Anglican controversialist, Glanvill published an attack on Andrew Marvell's *The Rehearsal Transpros'd: or, Animadversions upon a Late Book, Intituled, A Preface Shewing What Grounds There Are of Fears and Jealousies of Popery* (1672). *An Apology and Advice for Some of the Clergy, Who Suffer Under False, and Scandalous Reports. Written on the Occasion of the Second Part of the Rehearsal Transprosed: In A Letter To a Friend: And By Him Publish'd* (1674) appeared anonymously but was included in a subsequent list of Glanvill's works appended to his *Essays on Several Important Subjects in Philosophy and Religion* (1676). In the battle to defend the good name of the Anglican clergy from Marvell's scurrilous assaults, Glanvill found himself on the same side as his old enemy Stubbe.

Glanvill's frequent attacks on the Dissenters as dogmatists and enemies of reason drew a response from Robert Ferguson, the notorious radical Dissenter and plotter. Ferguson's *The Interest of Reason in Religion, with the Import and Use of Scripture Metaphors; and the Nature of the Union betwixt Christ and Believers. (With Reflections on Several Late Writings, Especially Mr. Sherlock's Discourse Concerning the Knowledge of Jesus Christ)* (1675) argued that Dissenters were not enemies of reason but accepted it in its proper place in religious affairs. Glanvill and William Sherlock—another Anglican divine attacked by Ferguson—replied in *An Account of Mr. Ferguson His Common-Place Book, in Two Letters* (1675), ignoring Fergu-

cism and role as a defender of the natural philosophy of the Royal Society incompatible with his defense of the reality of witchcraft. However, there was in reality no incompatibility between the two positions during his time. The witchcraft stories, like much of the rest of Glanvill's work, were devoted to the struggle against atheism, which, like other Christian apologists of the time, Glanvill associated with the materialistic doctrines of Hobbes. Glanvill attempted to rebut atheist assaults on the reality of the spiritual world empirically, through the compilation of supernatural anecdotes, including witch stories. Glanvill was careful to credit witnesses and recount his own investigations of the phenomena. Indeed, his compilations of witchcraft and other supernatural stories can be seen as models of Baconian empiricism.

son's arguments but charging him with extensive plagiarism of Glanvill and other authors.

Glanvill's most significant philosophical work was collected in *Essays on Several Important Subjects in Philosophy and Religion,* published in 1676. Of the seven essays included in this book, only the last is entirely original. The others were reworkings of *Scepsis Scientifica,*; "Sciri Tuum"; *Plus Ultra*; *Philosophia Pia*; *ΛΟΓΟΥ ΘΡΗΣΚΣΙΑ [Logou Threskeia]; or, A Seasonable Recommendation, and Defence of Reason; in the Affairs of Religion; Against Infidelity, Scepticism, and Fanaticisms of All Sorts* (1670), and *Some Philosophical Considerations Touching the Being of Witches and Witchcraft.* The seventh essay, "Anti-Fanatical Religion and Free Philosophy," is an intellectual history and encomium of the Cambridge Platonists and Latitudinarians, in the form of a continuation of Francis Bacon's "New Atlantis: A Worke unfinished" (1626).

Glanvill's writings have often been seen as symptomatic of the rise of plain prose in English, following the ornate metaphysical style of the early seventeenth century. The changes from *The Vanity of Dogmatizing* to *Scepsis Scientifica* to the final version of the work in *Essays on Several Important Subjects in Philosophy and Religion* have particularly been seen as exemplars of this cultural shift. Beginning with an ornate and highly metaphorical prose reminiscent of Sir Thomas Browne in *The Vanity of Dogmatizing,* each successive version grew simpler and less metaphorical, ending with a plain prose resembling that of such admired authors of the Restoration period as Sprat and John Tillotson.

Essays on Several Important Subjects in Philosophy and Religion marked the end of Glanvill's philosophical writing. For the remaining years of his life Glanvill's intellectual energies were mainly spent in collecting witchcraft anecdotes and producing homiletic and religious tracts. His homiletic works are two treatises produced in 1678, *An Essay Concerning Preaching: Written for the Direction of a Young Divine; and Useful Also For the People, In Order To Profitable Hearing,* bound with *A Seasonable Defence of Preaching: And the Plain Way of It.* Both argued for a plain and practical preaching style, attacking the Dissenting "enthusiasts" for their rhetorical and canting preaching.

During the intense political crisis of the popish plot–fabricated in 1678 by Protestant Titus Oates, who claimed that Jesuits intended to assassinate Charles II and place the Catholic Duke of York (later James II) on the throne–Glanvill wrote his most partisan Anglican work, published posthumously as *The Zealous, and Impartial Protestant, Shewing Some Great, But Less Heeded Dangers of Popery. In Order to Thorough and Effectual Security Against It. In a Letter to a Member of Parliament* (1681). The use of the word *zealous* as a term of praise perhaps indicates that Glanvill thought his earlier critique of enthusiasm had perhaps gone too far. In this work he argued against the toleration of Dissenting religious practices, while agreeing with supporters of toleration that mere beliefs should not be the target of persecution. Still a Latitudinarian, Glanvill asserted that a Church of England that was more flexible on those liturgical and ceremonial practices that Dissenters disliked could bring moderate Dissenters into the church, thereby uniting the Protestant interest, and that this more comprehensive church would more effectively combat Catholicism. His defense of the persecution of Dissenting practices, including calls for more rigorous enforcement of the anti-Dissenter laws, caused some pain to his old friend Baxter, who reprinted a flattering letter Glanvill had written him in 1661 in Baxter's *A Second True Defence of the Meer Nonconformists. Against the Untrue Accusations, Reasonings and History of Dr. Edward Stillingfleet. With Some Notes on Mr. Joseph Glanviles Zealous and Impartial Protestant, and Dr. L. Moulins Character* (1681). The letter was published separately as a broadsheet on Baxter's death in 1691 as *Mr. J. Glanvil's Full Vindication of the Late, Reverend, Pious, and Learned Mr. Richard Baxter.* Joseph Glanvill died of a fever on 4 November 1680, and was buried in the Abbey Church of Bath.

Biographies:

Ferris Greenslet, *Joseph Glanvill* (New York: Columbia University Press, 1900);

Jackson I. Cope, *Joseph Glanvill: Anglican Apologist* (St. Louis: Committee on Publications, Washington University Press, 1956).

References:

Troy Boone, "Narrating the Apparition: Glanvill, Defoe, and the Rise of Gothic Fiction," *The Eighteenth Century: Theory and Interpretation,* 35 (Summer 1994): 173–189;

Henry G. Van Leeuwen, *The Problem of Certainty in English Thought, 1630–1690* (The Hague: Martinus Nijhoff, 1970), pp. 71–89;

Richard H. Popkin, "The Development of the Philosophical Reputation of Joseph Glanvill," *Journal of the History of Ideas,* 15 (April 1954): 305–311;

Popkin, "Joseph Glanvill: A Precursor of David Hume," *Journal of the History of Ideas,* 14 (April 1953): 292–303;

Sascha Talmor, *Glanvill: The Uses and Abuses of Scepticism* (Oxford: Pergamon, 1981);

Basil Willey, *The Seventeenth-Century Background: Studies in the Thought of the Age in Relation to Poetry and Religion* (London: Chatto & Windus, 1934), pp. 174–205.

David Hartley

(June 1705 – 28 August 1757)

James A. Harris
Balliol College, University of Oxford

BOOKS: *Some Reasons why the Practice of Inoculation ought to be Introduced into the Town of Bury at Present* (Bury St. Edmunds, 1733);

Ten Cases of Persons who have taken Mrs. Stephens's Medicines for the Stone. With an Abstract of Some of the Experiments, Tending to Illustrate These Cases (London: Printed for Samuel Harding & James Roberts, 1738);

A View of the Present Evidence for and against Mrs. Stephens's Medicines, as a Solvent for the Stone. Containing a Hundred and Fifty-five Cases. With some Experiments and Observations (London: Printed for Samuel Harding, John Robinson & James Roberts, 1739);

De Lithontriptico a Joanna Stephens nuper invento dissertatio epistolaris (Leyden: Johan & Herman Verbeek, 1741); enlarged as *De Lithontriptico a Joanna Stephens nuper invento Dissertatio Epistolaris. Cui Adjicitur Methodus exhibendi Lithontripticum sub formâ commodiore. Accedunt etiam Conjecturæ quædam de Sensu, Motu, et Idearum Generatione* (Bath, 1746);

Observations on Man, his Frame, his Duty, and his Expectations: In Two Parts, 2 volumes (London: Printed by Samuel Richardson for James Leake & William Frederick, Bookseller in Bath & sold by Charles Hitch & Stephen Austen, Booksellers in London, 1749).

Editions: *Hartley's Theory of the Human Mind, on the Principle of the Association of Ideas, with Essays Relating to the Subject of it,* edited, with introductory essays, by Joseph Priestley (London: Printed for Joseph Johnson, 1775);

Observations on Man, His Frame, His Duty, and His Expectations, biographical preface by David Hartley the Younger and notes by Herman Andrew Pistorius, 3 volumes (London: Printed for Joseph Johnson, 1791);

Metaphysical Tracts by English Philosophers of the Eighteenth Century, edited by Samuel Parr (London: Edward Lumley, 1837)—includes *Conjecturæ quædam de sensu, motu, et idearum generatione;*

Various Conjectures on the Perception, Motion, and Generation of Ideas (1746), translated by Robert E. A. Palmer,

David Hartley (from Dagobert D. Runes, A Pictorial History of Philosophy *[New York: Philosophical Library, 1959])*

introduction and notes by Martin Kallich, The Augustan Reprint Society, nos. 77–78 (Los Angeles: William Andrews Clark Memorial Library, 1959);

Observations on Man: His Frame, His Duty, And His Expectations (1749), introduction by Theodore L. Huguelet (Gainesville, Fla.: Scholars' Facsimiles & Reprints, 1966);

Hartley's Theory of the Human Mind, introduction by Thom Verhave (New York: AMS Press, 1973);

Observations on Man, 2 volumes, introduction by Jonathan Wordsworth (Poole, U.K. & Washington, D.C.: Woodstock, 1998).

David Hartley's importance for philosophy lies in his *Observations on Man, his Frame, his Duty, and his Expectations* (1749), which includes the first fully worked-out presentation of an associationist theory of mind. It makes a suggestion as to the physical basis of thought, and it defends a determinist conception of action. In addition, it presents a strikingly optimistic vision of the future of mankind and argues that the entire human race will ultimately recover the happiness lost at the Fall. While it is no longer widely read, *Observations on Man, his Frame, his Duty, and his Expectations* had a significant influence upon the poet and philosopher Samuel Taylor Coleridge, as well as upon the political radicalism of the early nineteenth century and the development of the discipline of experimental psychology. Hartley was one of the first writers in English to use the word "psychology" in its modern sense, and his work stands at the beginning of the ongoing project of formulating a scientific account of the human mind.

Hartley's father, David, who was a clergyman of the Church of England, married Hartley's mother, Everald Wadsworth, on 12 May 1702. Most references give Hartley's birth date as either 8 or 30 August 1705; however, Richard C. Allen reports that Hartley was baptized at Halifax Saint John on 21 June 1705. Evereld Hartley died 14 September 1705, some three months after her son's birth, and his father died fifteen years later, while vicar of the church of Armley, near Leeds, in Yorkshire. Hartley was sent to Bradford Grammar School and went up to Jesus College, Cambridge, in 1722. He graduated with a B.A. four years later, became a fellow in 1727, and took his M.A. in 1729. Although he trained to follow his father into the church, Hartley chose medicine as his profession because of a reluctance to subscribe to the Thirty-nine Articles. His scruples, which probably had to do with the eternal damnation of the unrepentant, did not prevent Hartley from remaining a member of the Church of England. Although he never qualified as a doctor, he was a practicing physician all his life, first in Bury St. Edmunds, then in London, and later in Bath. He married Alice Rowley in May 1730, and by his first wife he had a son, also named David, the scientist and inventor who wrote "A Sketch of the Life and Character of Dr. Hartley," a memoir of his father that was first published in the 1791 edition of *Observations on Man, his Frame, his Duty, and his Expectations.* His first wife having died in July 1731 giving birth to his son, Hartley married again in August 1735, this time to Elizabeth Packer, a woman whose for-

tune of £6,500 enabled the family to move to London. He had a daughter, Mary, by his second wife.

Hartley suffered from kidney stones, and he was a firm believer in a medicine devised by Joanna Stephens to treat the disease. He wrote several pamphlets on her behalf and even went so far as to help secure her a £5,000 grant from Parliament in 1739. He was similarly energetic in his promotion of an algebra textbook written by Nicolas Saunderson, who had taught him mathematics at Cambridge. Hartley's other friends in the scientific community included the physician Hans Sloane and the physiologist Stephen Hales. The unorthodoxy of his Anglicanism did not prevent him from being on good terms with preeminent philosophical divines of the time, such as Edmund Law, who was created bishop of Carlisle in 1768; Joseph Butler, bishop of Bristol from 1738 until 1751 when he was made bishop of Durham; and William Warburton, who became bishop of Gloucester in 1759. For Hartley, as for every philosopher of the first half of the eighteenth century, John Locke's *An Essay concerning Humane Understanding* (1689) was of enormous importance, but the principal influence on his work is Isaac Newton. In his sketch of his father's life Hartley's son writes that he was a disciple of Newton "in every branch of literature and philosophy, natural and experimental, mathematical, historical and religious."

In a letter to his friend the Reverend John Lister dated 15 November 1735 Hartley writes:

> I have for some time applied myself chiefly to moral and religious enquiries, and have got the better of every Material Doubt I ever yet had concerning either natural or revealed Religion. I could not avoid giving my thoughts in writing upon so important a Subject, and indeed have received from thence a greater Degree of Conviction in relation to both Reason and Scripture. I have no design of appearing in public on these subjects till I have fully satisfied myself and my friends, but if that ever happens it is not improbable but I may.

Not for Hartley were the youthful provocations and flourishes that appear in such works as David Hume's *A Treatise of Human Nature: Being An Attempt to introduce the experimental Method of Reasoning into Moral Subjects* (three volumes, 1739–1740). More than ten years elapsed before his first published philosophical work appeared, and even then it was written in Latin, published in Bath, and appended to the second edition of one of his essays on the virtues of Stephens's remedy for kidney stones. *Conjecturæ quædam de Sensu, Motu, & Idearum Generatione* (translated by Robert E. A. Palmer as *Various Conjectures on the Perception, Motion, and Generation of Ideas,* 1959) was published in 1746. By this time Hartley must have had almost all of his system worked out, but the

Conjecturæ quædam de Sensu, Motu, & Idearum Generatione is a highly condensed work, designed to do no more than hint at how its author's lines of thought might be extended into the domain of morals and religion. The work is described rather aptly by Martin Kallich, the editor of its English translation, as a "trial balloon."

Self-effacing though its manner of appearance was, *Conjecturæ quædam de Sensu, Motu, & Idearum Generatione* is a clear, not to say bold, statement of the elements of Hartley's theory of the human mind, presented *in ordine geometrico* (according to the geometrical method) as was Newton's *Philosophiæ Naturalis Principia Mathematica* (1687; translated as *The Mathematical Principles of Natural Philosophy*, 1809). With twenty-two propositions and demonstrations and a few corollaries, Hartley aims to explain both the manner in which the mind operates and the physical cause of that manner of operation. Newton's influence is strong in Hartley's execution of both the tasks he has set himself. In his account of the mind Hartley seeks a fundamental explanatory principle that will be as fertile in the science of the mind as Newton's theory of gravitation has been in the science of nature. In his account of the physical basis of thought and sensation, his model is rather the Newton of the speculations and hypotheses found in the "Queries" added to the *Opticks; Or, A Treatise of the Reflexions, Refractions, Inflexions and Colours of Light: Also, Two Treatises of the Species and Magnitude of Curvilinear Figures* (1704).

As was Locke before him, Hartley is an empiricist. By means of the various sensory media, objects give rise to "sensations" in the mind; and by repetition sensations imprint on the mind "*Vestigia, Typos, aut Imagines*" ("vestiges, types, or images of themselves"), as Hartley writes in *Conjecturæ quædam de Sensu, Motu, & Idearum Generatione*. These elements are called "*Ideæ sensationis simplices*" ("simple ideas of sensation"). However, Locke's influence on Hartley manifests itself otherwise than in a common rejection of innate ideas. To the fourth edition (1700) of *An Essay concerning Humane Understanding* Locke had added a chapter titled "Of the Association of Ideas," in which he explains what "is in it self really Extravagant in the Opinions, Reasonings, and Actions of other Men" in terms of a "Connexion of *Ideas* wholly owing to Chance and Custom," that is, "*Ideas* that in themselves are not at all of kin, come to be so united in some Mens [sic] Minds, that 'tis very hard to separate them, they always keep in company, and the one no sooner at any time comes into the Understanding but its Associate appears with it; and if they are more than two which are thus united, the whole gang always inseparable shew themselves together." Thus, Locke contrasts "natural" relations of ideas, where the ideas are joined together by reason according to the objective order of things, with the unnatural relations

produced by mere "Education and Prejudice," which is to say, by associations that have nothing to do with the order of nature. It is to association that Locke looks to explain that bugbear of the Enlightenment, religious "enthusiasm," as well as belief in goblins and sprites, and a wide range of mental dysfunctions.

While Locke certainly does not underestimate the power of association, and might perhaps accept that, as a matter of fact, it governs the operation of most people's minds, he believes that it is something the influence of which can and ought to be overcome. Hartley, on the other hand, is unwilling to believe that the way most, if not all, people think is fundamentally defective. Following the lead of John Gay's *Concerning the Fundamental Principle of Virtue or Morality*—which was published as a preliminary dissertation to *An Essay on the Origin of Evil* (1731), Law's translation of William King's *De Origine mali* (1704)—Hartley turns Locke's theory of the mind on its head, and makes association the central principle of his account of thought. In fact, it is not an exaggeration to say that association is all there is to that account. First, in the tenth proposition of *Conjecturæ quædam de Sensu, Motu, & Idearum Generatione*, he describes the manner in which association works: "Sensationes quævis *A*, *B*, *C*, & c. sibi mutuo associate vicibus satis repetitis, ejusmodi imperium obtinent in Ideas respondentes *a*, *b*, *c*, &c. ut Sensationum unaquæque *A*, seorsum impressa, reliquarum Ideas, *b*, *c*, &c. in Anima excitare valeat" ("Any sensations *A*, *B*, *C*, etc., by being associated with one another a sufficient number of times get such a power over the corresponding ideas *a*, *b*, *c*, etc., that any one of the sensations *A*, when impressed alone, shall be able to excite in the mind *b*, *c*, etc., the ideas of the rest"). Then, in Proposition 12 he says that "Ideæ simplices coibunt in complexas per Associationem" ("Simple ideas will run into complex ones by means of association"), and thereby establishes the nature of his science of the mind. The work of the Hartleian psychologist is to analyze complex ideas into their simple component parts and to show how those simple ideas were associated together to produce complex ones.

Hartley does not seem to regard the extremely large role he gives association as needing much defense. Proposition 10 is, he says, proved "ex observationibus frequentissimis, & maxime pervulgatis" ("from innumerable common observations"). In *Conjecturæ quædam de Sensu, Motu, & Idearum Generatione* he seems much more interested in establishing the physiological aspect of his theory of mind: the associationist picture of the operations of the mind is taken as a given, and what is sought is an account of the functioning of the brain that accords well with that picture. Three hypotheses go to make up this account: the first is that it is by means of the spongy white substance common to the nerves, the marrow of the spine, and the brain, that objects impinge upon consciousness; the second is that objects do so by making this medullary substance vibrate, in such a way that for each distinct kind of initial impact of an object there corresponds a distinct "vibratiuncle," or miniature vibration, in the brain; the third is that vibrations are communicated to the brain with the help, not only of the uniformity, continuity, softness, and active powers of the medullary substance but also of the "aether"(or ether), the invisible elastic fluid that Newton had postulated in order to explain the possibility of gravitational action at a distance.

In suggesting a vibrational account of sensation, Hartley is rejecting the Cartesian physiology of animal spirits. One reason for his doing so is a range of perceptual phenomena that he thinks naturally suggest a vibrational picture: following Newton, Hartley is particularly interested in the manner in which various sensations remain in the mind after the objects that caused them are removed. Cases include the way in which a bright light leaves an image of itself even after the eyes are closed, and the fact that a burning coal attached to a string and whirled around in a circle gives the impression of a circle of light. Perhaps more importantly, vibrations and vibratiuncles seem susceptible to association through repeated conjunction in just the way sensations and ideas are. Indeed, Hartley follows proposition 10 with a proposition identical to it, save for the substitution of "vibrationes" for "sensationes" and "vibratiunculas" for "ideas." Given how one knows the mind works, Hartley is saying, this method is how one would expect the brain to work. Of course, the doctrine of vibrations is no more than a conjecture, albeit one backed up with some controversial, and controverted, early neurophysiology; but it is a conjecture that provides an elegantly simple explanation of the appearances. In his *Essays on the Intellectual Powers of Man* (1785) Thomas Reid criticizes Hartley for violating the rules of Newtonian science with this particular inference to the best explanation, but in making this charge Reid ignores Newton's own propensity for adventurous hypotheses, such as that of the existence of "aether."

Hartley devotes much of *Conjecturæ quædam de Sensu, Motu, & Idearum Generatione* to showing how the phenomena of pleasure and pain, sleep, and, especially, muscular motion, both automatic and voluntary, are susceptible of explanation in terms of the doctrine of vibrations. Taken as a whole, *Conjecturæ quædam de Sensu, Motu, & Idearum Generatione* presents a case for what is now called psychophysical parallelism. For each and every state of mind there is a corresponding state of the brain: the mind does not operate independently of the brain, nor, indeed, of the rest of the body, and its health is, as a result, to a significant degree dependent on the

health of the body and brain. Despite the differences in physiological theory, the work constitutes a return to the theme of René Descartes's posthumously published *Traité de l'homme* (Treatise on Man, 1664). Hartley is, however, far less sure of the ontology of mind than was his seventeenth-century predecessor, and he admits that he can see no contradiction in the Lockean suggestion that matter might be endowed with the power of sensation. In fact, he accepts that his vibrational theory undermines the traditional claim that the properties of matter are obviously quite different to those of thinking substance. To those who discern atheism in the very idea of materialism, he replies, as Joseph Priestley later did, that the question of the immortality of the soul is quite distinct from that of the immateriality of the soul.

The "General Scholium" attached to *Conjecturæ quædam de Sensu, Motu, & Idearum Generatione* is an advertisement for his later work. Hartley makes it clear that he has as his goal something more ambitious than even a description of the functioning of the mind and of its physical causes. He believes that a proper understanding of the associative propensities of the mind will be conducive to both the development of science and the improvement of morals. While in the fourth edition of his *An Essay concerning Humane Understanding* Locke blames habitual association for "the greatest, I had almost said, of all the Errors in the World," on account of the fact that "so far as it obtains, it hinders Men from seeing and examining," Hartley says that, by enabling human beings to clarify the proper meanings of words, the doctrine of association will provide a more secure foundation for science. A proper understanding of association, moreover, will reveal how best to educate children into virtue and piety. To gauge the full extent of Hartley's rejection of Locke's mistrust of association, however, one needs to turn from the *Conjecturæ quædam de Sensu, Motu, & Idearum Generatione* to the *Observations on Man, his Frame, his Duty, and his Expectations*.

Whereas the *Conjecturæ quædam de Sensu, Motu, & Idearum Generatione* is short to the point of terseness, the two parts of the *Observations on Man, his Frame, his Duty, and his Expectations* together comprise almost a thousand pages. The first part comprises "Observations on the Frame of the Human Body and Mind, and on their mutual Connexions and Influences"; the second consists of "Observations on the Duty and Expectations of Mankind." In his equally monumental *History of Psychology* (three volumes, 1912–1921), George Sidney Brett claims that the three components of Hartley's work, the doctrine of vibrations, the account of the operations of the mind, and the affirmation of Christian doctrine, are "really unconnected." This argument consists of wishful thinking on the part of one who wants to claim Hartley as the originator of physiological psychology

DE

LITHONTRIPTICO

A

Joanna Stephens

NUPER INVENTO

DISSERTATIO EPISTOLARIS

AUCTORE

DAVIDE HARTLEY, A.M. & R.S.S.

EDITIO SECUNDA.

Cui Adjicitur

Methodus exhibendi Lithontripticum sub formâ
commodiore.

Accedunt etiam

Conjecturæ quædam de Sensu, Motu, & Idearum
Generatione.

BATHONIÆ: Typis T. BODDELY.

Proftant venales apud J. LEAKE & G. FREDERICK,
Bibliopolas, *Bathonienfes*: C. HITCH & S. AUSTEN,
Londinenfes. M.DCC.XLVI.

*Title page for the medical pamphlet that includes Hartley's first
published philosophical work, translated in 1959 as* Various
Conjectures on the Perception, Motion, and
Generation of Ideas *(William Andrews Clark
Memorial Library, University of California,
Los Angeles)*

and to keep the science separate from the theology. In his *Observations on Man, his Frame, his Duty, and his Expectations* Hartley himself says that all branches of knowledge "ought to be considered as mere Preparatories and Preliminaries to the Knowlege [sic] of Religion," and, more significantly still, that "Religion, as it were, comprehends all other Knowlege [sic], advances, and is advanced by all." There is no way of keeping the parts of Hartley's system separate. Indeed, it is not just that the findings of science are used to support religion; rather, for Hartley the practice of science is already a religious activity.

In the first chapter of the book Hartley elaborates upon the twin doctrines of association and vibrations already presented in *Conjecturæ quædam de Sensu, Motu, & Idearum Generatione*. Two points are important in this context. First, the reader should note that Hartley distinguishes between two sorts of association, the successive and the synchronous. As he says, "Sensations may be said to be associated together, when their Impressions are either made precisely at the same Instant of Time, or in the contiguous successive Instants." In successive association, the ideas are always "raised" in the order in which they have been impressed upon the mind, and this kind of association is what enables a single word to bring to mind an entire sentence, or string of sentences. In synchronous association, on the other hand, there will tend to be a certain blurring, or "coalescence," of the associated ideas into a complex whole. What Hartley calls "intellectual Ideas, such as those that belong to the Heads of Beauty, Honour, moral Qualities, &c." are produced in this way. What is significant about the process of coalescence is that the result "shall not appear to bear any Relation to these its compounding Parts, nor to the external Senses upon which the original Sensations, which gave Birth to the compounding Ideas, were impressed." The outcome of this coalescence of ideas is similar to a medicine or a cake, in that it appears to bear no relation to its ingredients. As Stephen H. Ford argues in his essay "*Coalescence:* David Hartley's '*Great Apparatus*'" (1987), Hartley's notion of coalescence is important in two respects. As an explanation of how it is that complex ideas appear to bear no relation to their constituent parts, it is central to Hartley's claim that all complex ideas arise ultimately from sensation, and that there is no need for what Locke had termed ideas of reflection, ideas the mind has of its own modes of operation. Coalescence also plays a significant role in explaining the possibility of the dialectical generation of higher out of lower pleasures that underlies Hartley's picture of the future of the human race.

The notion of a coalescence of ideas differentiates Hartley's conception of association from that of Hume, whose picture of the mind is distinctly atomistic in character. Where Hume gives his ideas all the independence from one other traditionally accorded to substances, the vibrational aspect of Hartley's theory of the brain prompts the reader to think of simple ideas as somewhat like waves of light, always blending with one other, hard to keep separate and distinct. Contrasting Hartley's understanding of association with Hume's brings up the second point that should be considered about Hartley's fully worked-out picture of what he calls in part 1 "the general Laws, according to which the Sensations and Motions are performed, and our Ideas generated." Whereas Hume depicts association as taking place on the basis of three relations—contiguity in space or time, resemblance, and causation–Hartley allows a role only to contiguity. In this formulation Hartley manifests a drive toward simplicity characteristic of an age in which it was imagined that all the sciences would ultimately reduce to a mathematized physics, and in which chemistry and biology had yet to establish themselves as autonomous and distinct bodies of knowledge.

Against this remarkable confidence, however, can be balanced a certain reticence on Hartley's part with respect to the status of the doctrine of vibrations. In *Observations on Man, his Frame, his Duty, and his Expectations* it remains a hypothesis only. When he turns to his account of the intellectual pleasures and pains in the fourth chapter of part 1, Hartley writes that the general law of vibrations seems of little importance in this Part of the Work, whether it be adopted or not. If any other Law can be made the Foundation of Association, or consistent with it, it may also be consistent with the Analysis of the intellectual Pleasures and Pains, which I shall here give." In general, as he writes earlier in the book, "the Doctrine of Association may be laid down as a certain Foundation, and a clue to direct our future Inquiries, whatever becomes of that of Vibrations." While vibrations are not irrelevant to Hartley's theory of the mind–they are, for example, important to his account of memories as reconstructed rather than reproduced–it is certainly not the case that the theory stands or falls with them.

The second chapter of the first part of *Observations on Man, his Frame, his Duty, and his Expectations* is devoted mainly to vindicating the doctrine of vibrations with respect to each of the five senses, to sexual attraction, and to the workings of the heart, of the "muscles of respiration," and of "convulsive" and "voluntary" motions. In the third chapter Hartley turns his attention to "the Phænomena of Ideas, or of Understanding, Affection, Memory, and Imagination." A large portion of the chapter is given over to an account of "the manner in which Ideas are associated with words, beginning with childhood," and, subsequently, to an enlargement upon the suggestions made in *Conjecturæ quædam de Sensu, Motu, & Idearum Generatione* concerning the possibility of developing a "philosophical language" perfectly suited to be unambiguous denotation of the conceptions of its speakers. The reader is given an idea of what Hartley has in mind here when he remarks that a system of shorthand developed by the poet John Byrom (whom he had met in London) "affords an accurate and elegant instance of the Possibility of proceeding in such Matters upon simple and philosophical Principles; his Short-hand being a real and adequate Representation of the Sounds of the *English* Tongue, as far as is necessary for determining the Sense, and that in the shortest manner possi-

ble." Hartley was so enthusiastic about this system of shorthand that since 1741 he had been corresponding in it with his friend Lister.

Hartley's description of association differs from Hume's. When Hartley gives his explanation of "the Nature of Assent and Dissent," however, the reader can see that the similarities between his picture of the mind and Hume's are far more significant than are the differences. Not only do both give association the principal part in their accounts of the workings of the mind, but they also agree that the thoroughgoing naturalization of the mind that this association makes possible entails the rejection of the standard philosophical picture of the understanding. For Locke as for Descartes the understanding is essentially a faculty of judgment, and judgment is an operation performed upon ideas by a subject apparently distinct from what is passing before his mind. It is an exercise of freedom. Hartley, on the other hand, says that "Assent and Dissent, whatever their precise and particular Nature might be, must come under the Notion of Ideas, being only those very complex internal Feelings, which adhere by Association to such Clusters of Words as are called Propositions in general, or Affirmations and Negations in particular." The choice of the word "feelings" here cannot help but bring to mind Hume's claim in his *A Treatise of Human Nature* that "belief is more properly an act of the sensitive, than of the cogitative part of our natures," even if, as seems possible, Hartley never actually read Hume. For both Hume and Hartley, coming to believe in the truth of a proposition is a matter of having a certain kind of affective response to it. There is no choice involved: the understanding is quite passive in its operations. After this passage it comes as no surprise to the reader to find Hartley echoing Hume again with the statement that the intellectual faculties of animals differ from those of men not in kind but in degree only. In fact, he says, "the Brute Creatures prove their near Relation to us, not only by the general Resemblance of the Body, but by that of the Mind also; inasmuch as many of them have most of the eminent Passions in some imperfect Degree, and as there is, perhaps, no Passion belonging to human Nature, which may not be found in some Brute Creature in a considerable degree."

In the fourth and final chapter of the first part of *Observations on Man, his Frame, his Duty, and his Expectations,* Hartley moves on to "the Six Classes of intellectual Pleasures and Pains," by which he means those of imagination, ambition, self-interest, sympathy, *theopathy* (contemplation of God), and moral sense. An important aspect of this chapter is an attempt to prove that "all the intellectual Pleasures and Pains are deducible ultimately from the sensible ones," and thus that there is no need to appeal to irreducible instincts when it comes to explaining how it is that human beings are interested in the various objects of these pleasures and pains. The background here is the debate sparked by Thomas Hobbes's derivation of virtuous conduct from pure self-interest, which took the form of an argument between those who, as did Anthony Ashley Cooper, third Earl of Shaftesbury, and Francis Hutcheson, postulated a distinct faculty called the moral sense and those who, as did Samuel Clarke, described moral judgments as, in Hartley's words, "grounded on the eternal Reasons and Relations of Things." Hartley disagrees with both parties. He explains the pleasure that human beings take in virtue, and the pain that vice causes humans, in terms of a combination of factors: education, the consideration of the immediate and more distant consequences of each of the virtues, "The great Suitableness of all the Virtues to each other, and to the Beauty, Order, and Perfection of the World, animate and inanimate," "The Hopes and Fears which arise from the Consideration of a future State," and, finally, "Meditations upon God." All of these factors together cause individuals to associate virtue with the highest kind of pleasure and vice with the worst kind of pain.

There is more to Hartley's analysis of the intellectual pleasures, however, than a rejection of brute instinct from the philosophy of mind. The sketch of sources of the pleasures and pains of the moral sense should give a sense of how the six types of intellectual pleasures and pains are related to each other. The pleasures and pains of the moral sense are not just higher than the other five; rather, the moral sense "is the sum total of all the rest, and the ultimate Result from them." One only comes to take pleasure in virtue, and to hate vice, once one has learned to take pleasure in the other five, beginning with the pleasures and pains of imagination, and ascending by stages to those of theopathy. And, fortunately for human beings, they are propelled upward toward the realm of the moral sense without having any choice in the matter. One is naturally subject to the pleasures and pains of sensation, but these wane once one leaves childhood behind, and so one seeks more refined pleasures in the objects of imagination—in the beauty of the natural world, works of art, the liberal arts, the sciences, and so on—and one is inevitably pushed on, as it were, to taking pleasure in the good opinions of others and feeling pain at a bad reputation (such are the pleasures and pains of ambition). Knowing the value of the objects of imagination one comes to seek to have oneself associated with them. Then one comes to pursue the means whereby the pleasures of sensation, imagination, and ambition are obtained: that is, one comes to recognize the pleasures of self-interest. What Hartley calls "gross self-interest," essentially love of money, then turns into "rational self-interest" when it becomes clear that money can neither buy lasting satisfaction nor help with keeping death and disease at bay, and then there arises a merely "abstract" desire of happiness and aversion to misery. At this point one's thoughts turn to death and one's future state, and the stage is set for cultivation of sympathy, theopathy, and, finally, the moral sense. It is important to see that self-interest drives the whole of this course of development. Human hopes and fears regarding the next world are, Hartley says, "the chief Foundation of the pure disinterested Love of God and of our Neighbour, and the principal Means of transferring our Associations, so that we may love and hate, pursue and fly, in the manner best suited to our Attainment of our greatest possible Happiness." In Hartley's scheme of things, virtue is a matter not of transcending human nature but of purifying it; and, in fact, human nature, with its permanent restlessness and tendency to become numb to the pleasures it knows, will in the end purify itself.

Association, Hartley believes, will take human beings beyond concern for self and beyond "pure disinterested Benevolence" toward a "pure disinterested love of God" in which the self is eradicated. Paradoxically, then, it is in loss of self that self-fulfillment is found. There is a strong strain of mysticism in Hartley's depiction of the future of the human race. In the first chapter of *Observations on Man, his Frame, his Duty, and his Expectations* the reader finds the following: "Since God is the Source of all Good, and consequently must at last appear to be so, *i.e.* be associated with all our Pleasures, it seems to follow . . . that the Idea of God, and of the Ways by which his Goodness and Happiness are made manifest, must, at last, take place of, and absorb all other Ideas, and He himself become, according to the Language of the Scriptures, *All in All*." In the end, all the intellectual pleasures and pains coalesce into a love of God that expresses itself in perfect moral conduct, but, as the final chapter of the second part of *Observations on Man, his Frame, his Duty, and his Expectations* ("Of the Expectations of Mankind") makes clear, Hartley does not see the final stages of human development as likely to come to pass before the advent of the thousand years of the rule of Christ announced in the Book of Revelation.

Hartley's optimism about the future of the human race is probably what reconciled him to the "Doctrine of Necessity" that he had come to believe followed from the "Doctrine of Association." In early modern Britain, determinism tended to be associated with deism, at best, and with atheism, at worst. It was abhorred largely because it was feared it would undermine morality. One worry was that the vicious and criminal would be able to excuse their actions on the grounds that it was not in their power to act otherwise; a second was that, if all were necessary and determined by God, then the eternal punishment promised the unrepentant sinner would seem malicious rather than just. As regards the first worry, Hartley is clear that, as did such determinists before him as Hobbes, Anthony Collins, and Hume, he takes necessity to be fully compatible with the possibility of voluntary action. While it is true that it follows from his theory of the mind that "every Action, or bodily Motion, arises from previous Circumstances, or bodily Motions, already existing in the Brain, *i.e.* from Vibrations, which are the immediate Effect of Impressions then made, or the remote compound of Effect of former Impressions, or both," this statement does not mean that a person is robbed of the power of "deliberating, suspending, choosing, &c. or of resisting the Motives of Sensuality, Ambition, Resentment, &c." In his account of "muscular motion" Hartley describes how the capacity for action on the basis of desire develops out of simple reactions to sensory stimuli. Like everything else in the mind, the will is not an inbuilt faculty but is rather the product of the gradual accretion of associations. The doctrine of association does not make automata of human beings but, in fact, explains how it is that humans are able to act voluntarily.

To this account one might respond that the kind of voluntariness that is compatible with necessity is incompatible with people being the object of moral judgment and of punishment or reward. After all, some animals seem capable of "deliberating, suspending, choosing, &c." but are not praised or blamed for what they do. On the necessitarian scheme, what humans do voluntarily is not really up to them, the objector might continue: one may act on the basis of one's choices, but these choices are not things one chooses. This objection brings up the second worry about the doctrine of necessity, the fear that while there is a distinction between the voluntary and the automatic, and while therefore the vicious person is probably lying if he says that he has no choice but to act as he acts, still, properly speaking, there is no morally significant difference between human actions and those of animals. As outlined in the first chapter of part 2 of *Observations on Man, his Frame, his Duty, and his Expectations,* Hartley's answer to this worry involves a distinction between "two different Methods of Speaking, and, as it were, two different Languages, used upon these Subjects; the one popular, and, when applied to God, anthropomorphical; the other philosophical." When one speaks the "popular" language, the worry does not arise:

human beings are properly agents, able to do otherwise than they do, and God is not the author of sin. When one speaks the "philosophical" language, however, moral good and evil reduce to natural good and evil; justice is merely a matter of what conduces to "a Balance of Happiness," and God is indeed "the one universal Cause" to whom all is ascribable. Hartley insists both that these two ways of speaking of human action can, and should, be kept quite separate, and also that there is no tension between them. But it is obvious that Hartley can only maintain this position because he believes that, ultimately, the entirety of mankind will be restored to the happiness Adam and Eve enjoyed before the Fall. What is objectionable about determinism is that it seems to mean that people will be punished for things that, viewed "philosophically," they did not really do. This formulation becomes especially difficult to countenance when the punishment in question is eternal. When forced to choose between determinism and orthodox Christian conceptions of the punishment of the wicked, however, Hartley rejects orthodox Christianity and the very idea of eternal punishment. In time, all will move upward through the dialectic of intellectual pleasures and pains and into union with God. This formulation dispenses with the very idea of God as judge. There are just good consequences of actions and bad consequences, and it is built into the natural order of things that bad consequences will turn individuals toward self-correction, and, eventually, to virtue for its own sake.

It seems likely that from the beginning Hartley's philosophical work was intended to vindicate the doubts about eternal punishment that prevented him from signing the Thirty-nine Articles and taking a position in the Church of England. In his 15 November 1735 letter to Lister he asked his friend what he thought of eternal punishment, for "The chief result of both Reason and Scripture as appears to me is Universal Happiness in the most absolute sense ultimately." In this letter Hartley says he has written "two small treatises" that he calls "'The Progress to Happiness deduced from Reason—and from Scripture,'" and, while *Observations on Man, his Frame, his Duty, and his Expectations* is most definitely not a small book, it could be given the same title. Hartley devotes more than a hundred pages in its second part to a demonstration of the literal truth of the entirety of the Bible, and shows that his devotion to Newton goes as far as support for the latter's chronology of the events of the Old Testament. Hartley's combination of biblical literalism and science was in fact far from unique. There was a strong fundamentalist tradition in British seventeenth-century

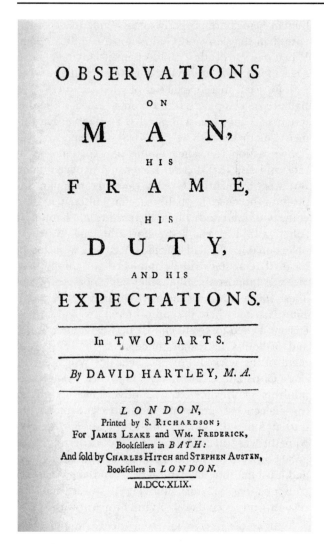

OBSERVATIONS

ON

MAN,

HIS

FRAME,

HIS

DUTY,

AND HIS

EXPECTATIONS.

In TWO PARTS.

By DAVID HARTLEY, *M.A.*

LONDON,
Printed by S. RICHARDSON;
For JAMES LEAKE and WM. FREDERICK,
Bookfellers in *BATH*:
And fold by CHARLES HITCH and STEPHEN AUSTEN,
Bookfellers in *LONDON*.

M.DCC.XLIX.

*Title page for Hartley's most important philosophical work,
in which he presents the first fully elaborated associationist
theory of the mind (British Museum)*

thought, and Newton spent a huge amount of time trying to establish the precise date of the Second Coming. But, unique or not, Hartley's optimistic necessitarianism raises a serious question as to how his book might address the duty of man. If it merely describes a process of, as he puts it in part 2 of *Observations on Man, his Frame, his Duty, and his Expectations,* "universal Restoration," could there be any sense to the idea that men ought to act otherwise than they do? If, from God's point of view, "all Individuals are actually and always infinitely happy," what in human conduct needs to be other than it is?

The best answer to these questions is perhaps that Hartley had no real desire to instruct people in their duties. His book is more a theodicy than anything else, a vindication of God's design rather than a justification of moral imperatives. When he comes

to "the Rule of Life" and finds it in adherence to the word of God as given in the Bible, this discovery is not injunction but rather a description of how it is that the happiest life might be lived, a celebration of the coincidence of virtue and the highest happiness. The entire book is marked by a curiously serene confidence. Hartley shows no appetite for philosophical discussion: thus, there is, for example, no admission of how radically he has altered Locke's philosophy of mind by giving so much importance to association. Furthermore, his son observes in his biographical sketch that once *Observations on Man, his Frame, his Duty, and his Expectations* was published, Hartley found no reason to correct or rewrite any passage of his enormous book. It is as if the very writing and publication of the book was in essence an act of devotion. "His thoughts were not immersed in worldly pursuits or contentions," the younger David Hartley writes, "and therefore his life was not eventful or turbulent, but placid and undisturbed by passion or violent ambition." Hartley finally died of his perennial kidney complaint on 28 August 1757.

Although the *Observations on Man, his Frame, his Duty and his Expectations* was not without admirers, the reviewer of Priestley's edition of the work in *The London Review* in July 1775 describes the original work as "little known even among the learned." Priestley's annotated redaction of Hartley's book, *Hartley's Theory of the Human Mind, on the Principle of the Association of Ideas, with Essays Relating to the Subject of it,* seems to have changed all that, however, going through two editions in fifteen years and prompting the publication of second and third editions of *Observations on Man, his Frame, his Duty, and his Expectations* itself in 1791, with a fourth following in 1801 and a fifth in 1810. Priestley stripped Hartley's theory of both the doctrine of vibrations and what he calls in his preface the "whole system of moral and religious knowledge; which, however excellent, is, in a great measure, foreign to it." While this redaction undoubtedly helped the cause of associational and mechanistic psychology, it should not be taken to indicate that Priestley himself was hostile to either neurophysiological speculation or Hartley's brand of millenarian theology. Robert E. Schofield, in his 1997 biography of Priestley, claims that it was in fact the second part of *Observations on Man, his Frame, his Duty, and his Expectations* that had the greatest and most immediate influence on Priestley. Priestley thought *Observations on Man, his Frame, his Duty and his Expectations* second only to the Bible, and Hartley to be a greater philosopher than either Hume or Locke.

Another with a remarkably high opinion of Hartley was of course Coleridge, who, famously, named his first son after him. In his "Religious Musings: A Desultory Poem, Written on the Christmas Eve of 1794," published in *Poems on Various Subjects* (1796), Coleridge places Hartley among those "Coadjutors of God," John Milton and Newton, and even describes him as "he of mortal kind / Wisest." While it is traditional to see Coleridge's later rejection of Hartley for Immanuel Kant, Johann Gottlieb Fichte, and Friedrich Wilhem Joseph von Schelling as a replacement of mechanist materialism for a rationalized form of Neoplatonist idealism, it seems more likely that it was precisely the mysticism in Hartley's thought that had attracted Coleridge. Hartley's writing had provided a scientific basis for believing in the veridicality of quasi-religious experiences of an annihilation of self and union with God, and it had suggested to Coleridge how he could be a mystic without being a mere "enthusiast." Coleridge's later turn to Kantian idealism should thus be seen as the exchange of one kind of explanation of mystical experience for what seemed a better kind. Insofar as Hartley's associationist theory of the mind influenced William Wordsworth, it was almost certainly more by means of Coleridge's conversation than by means of close study on the part of Wordsworth himself. Another Romantic writer affected by Coleridge's opinions of Hartley was William Hazlitt, who appended "Some Remarks on the Systems of Hartley and Helvetius" to his *Essay on the Principles of Human Action* (1805). Whereas Wordsworth had been exposed to Coleridge's first flush of enthusiasm, however, Hazlitt was present when Coleridge's enthusiasm had abated, and Hazlitt's text is an amplification of criticisms Coleridge later published in his *Biographia Literaria* (1817).

To his edition of Hartley, Priestley silently adds a two-page conclusion from his own pen titled "On the practical application of the doctrine of necessity," which seems to promise the possibility in this world of a return to "the paradisial state, in which our first parents, though naked, were not ashamed." This acceleration of Hartley's utopian scheme informs the optimism of Jeremy Bentham's *Introduction to the Principles of Morals and Legislation* (1789) and of William Godwin's *Enquiry concerning Political Justice* (1793), both of which in turn did much to shape the agenda of nineteenth-century liberalism, especially with regard to its notion of "indefinite progress." However, even though Hartley influenced the development of utilitarian philosophical radicalism, and even though he gave a central role to psychological hedonism, he was himself no utilitarian—his "Rule of Life" is to be found in the Bible, and not in the hedonistic calculus. In her essay "Mysticism Misunderstood: David Hartley and the Idea of Progress"(1972) Margaret Leslie argues that

Hartley is much closer in spirit to John Bunyan than to either Bentham or Godwin. The spiritual progress association makes possible has in Hartley's mind nothing to do with changing the world and reforming institutions. Although Hartley tells the reader in his chapter "Of the Expectations of Mankind" that "It is probable, that all the present Civil Governments will be overturned," still it is among the duties of individuals "to preserve the Government, under whose Protection we live, from Dissolution, seeking the Peace of it, and submitting to every Ordinance of Man for the Lord's sake."

David Hartley's influence has been most enduring in the realm of experimental psychology. He is routinely described in histories of psychology as one of the founders of the associational model of psychology that stands opposed to the "faculty psychology" espoused in the eighteenth century by such thinkers as Reid and Kant. As is exhaustively demonstrated by George Spencer Bower in his *Hartley and James Mill* (1881), Hartley had a profound influence on the "analytic" psychology of James Mill, and Mill used Priestley's edition of Hartley as part of the educational program to which he subjected his son John Stuart Mill. William James says of Hartley in volume 1 of his *Principles of Psychology* (2 volumes, 1890) that he was "in many essential respects, on the right track," and Hartley's ideas can be traced in several areas of twentieth-century psychology, including Pavlovian learning theory and the study of aphasia. In his book *Philosophy and Memory Traces: Descartes to Connectionism* (1998) John Sutton claims Hartley as one of the ancestors of "connectionism," the theory that cognitive processes are implemented within networks of nerve cells. Broadly stated, this theory holds that cognitive responses are the result of networked neurons creating patterns that the brain learns to recognize. Sutton enlists Hartley's support in the dispute with the modified faculty psychology of Jerry A. Fodor's "modular" theory of the mind, which holds that the mind consists of "low-level" perceptual modules that send information to "higher-level" nonmodular cognitive processes. In his biographical memoir, Hartley's son writes that his father, though he did not think *Observations on Man, his Frame, his Duty, and his Expectations* would be much read or understood, "did entertain an expectation that, at some distant period, it would become the adopted system of future philosophers." While this expectation has never quite come to pass, it is surely true to say that Hartley, largely unread though he is now, has played a significant role in the development of philosophy and psychology since the eighteenth century.

Letters:

"The Correspondence of Dr. David Hartley and Rev. John Lister," edited by Walter B. Trigg, *Transactions of the Halifax Antiquarian Society* (1938): 230–278.

References:

Richard C. Allen, *David Hartley on Human Nature* (Albany: State University of New York Press, 1999);

Arthur Beatty, *William Wordsworth: His Doctrine and Art in their Historical Relations,* University of Wisconsin Studies in Language and Literature, no. 17 (Madison: University of Wisconsin, 1927);

George Spencer Bower, *Hartley and James Mill* (London: Sampson Low, Marston, Searle & Rivington, 1881);

George Sidney Brett, *History of Psychology,* 3 volumes (volume 1, London: George Allen, 1912; volumes 2 & 3, London: Allen & Unwin / New York: Macmillan, 1921);

Hugh W. Buckingham and Stanley Finger, "David Hartley's Psychobiological Associationism and the Legacy of Aristotle," *Journal of the History of the Neurosciences,* 6, no. 1 (1997): 21–37;

Stephen H. Ford, "*Coalescence:* David Hartley's '*Great Apparatus,*'" in *Psychology and Literature in the Eighteenth Century,* edited by Christopher H. Fox (New York: AMS Press, 1987), pp. 199–224;

Élie Halévy, *The Growth of Philosophic Radicalism,* translated by Mary Morris (London: Faber & Gwyer, 1928; New York: Macmillan, 1928);

Ronald B. Hatch, "Joseph Priestley: An Addition to Hartley's Observations," *Journal of the History of Ideas,* 36 (1975): 548–550;

Gary Hatfield, "Remaking the Science of Mind: Psychology as Natural Science," in *Inventing Human Science: Eighteenth-Century Domains,* edited by Fox, Roy Porter, and Robert Wokler (Berkeley: University of California Press, 1995);

Richard Haven, "Coleridge, Hartley, and the Mystics," *Journal of the History of Ideas,* 20 (1959): 477–494;

Margaret Leslie, "Mysticism Misunderstood: David Hartley and the Idea of Progress," *Journal of the History of Ideas,* 33 (1972): 625–632;

Robert Marsh, "The Second Part of Hartley's System," *Journal of the History of Ideas,* 20 (1959): 264–273;

Barbara Bowen Oberg, "David Hartley and the Association of Ideas," *Journal of the History of Ideas,* 37 (1976): 441–454;

Richard H. Popkin, "Newton and Fundamentalism, II," in *Essays on the Context, Nature, and Influence of Isaac Newton's Theology,* edited by Popkin and James E. Force, Archives internationales d'histoire des idées, no. 129 (Dordrecht, The Netherlands, & Boston: Kluwer, 1990);

Robert E. Schofield, *The Enlightenment of Joseph Priestley: A Study of His Life and Work from 1733 to 1773* (University Park: Pennsylvania State University Press, 1997);

C. U. M. Smith, "David Hartley's Newtonian Neuropsychology," *Journal of the History of the Behavioural Sciences,* 23 (1987): 123–136;

John Sutton, *Philosophy and Memory Traces: Descartes to Connectionism* (Cambridge & New York: Cambridge University Press, 1998);

John Yolton, *Thinking Matter: Materialism in Eighteenth-Century Britain* (Minneapolis: University of Minnesota Press, 1983; Oxford: Blackwell, 1984).

Edward, Lord Herbert of Cherbury

(3 March 1582 – 20 August 1648)

R. D. Bedford

University of New England, New South Wales

See also the Herbert of Cherbury entries in *DLB 121: Seventeenth-Century British Nondramatic Poets* and *DLB 151: British Prose Writers of the Early Seventeenth Century.*

BOOKS: *De veritate, prout distinguitur a revelatione, a verisimili, a possibili, et a falso* (Paris: Privately printed, 1624; London: Per Augustinum Mathaeum, 1633); revised and enlarged with *De Causis Errorum* and *De religione laici* (London, 1645);

De Causis Errorum: Una Cum tractatu de Religione Laici (London, 1645);

The Life and Raigne of King Henry the Eighth (London: Printed by E.G. for Thomas Whitaker, 1649);

Expeditio in Ream insulam, anno 1630, translated into Latin by Timothy Baldwin (London: Printed by Humphrey Moseley, 1656); original English version published as *The Expedition to the Isle of Rhé,* edited by Edward James Herbert, Earl of Powis (London: Printed for the Philobiblon Society by Whittingham & Wilkins, 1860);

De religione gentilium errorumque apud eos causis (Amsterdam: Printed by John & Peter Blaeu, 1663); translated by William Lewis as *The Antient Religion of the Gentiles* (London: Printed for John Nutt, 1705);

Occasional Verses of Edward, Lord Herbert, Baron of Cherbury and Castle-Island. Deceased in August 1648 (London: Printed by T.R. for Thomas Dring, 1665);

The Life of Edward Lord Herbert of Cherbury, Written by Himself, dedication and advertisement by Horace Walpole (Strawberry Hill, 1764);

A Dialogue between a Tutor and His Pupil (London: Printed for W. Bathoe, 1768).

Editions: *Autobiography of Edward Lord Herbert of Cherbury* [and] *The History of England under Henry VIII* (London: Alexander Murray, 1870);

The Autobiography of Lord Herbert of Cherbury, edited, with a continuation of the life, by Sidney Lee (London: Nimmo, 1886; New York: Scribner & Welford, 1886; revised edition, London: Routledge / New York: Dutton, 1906);

Edward, Lord Herbert of Cherbury; oil painting attributed to W. Larkin (National Portrait Gallery, London)

The Poems, English and Latin, of Edward Lord Herbert of Cherbury, edited by G. C. Moore Smith (Oxford: Clarendon Press, 1923);

De veritate, translated by Meyrick H. Carré (Bristol: University of Bristol, 1937);

Lord Herbert of Cherbury's De religione laici, edited and translated by Harold R. Hutcheson, Yale Studies in English, volume 98 (New Haven: Yale University Press / London: Oxford University Press, 1944);

De veritate, facsimile of the 1645 edition, edited by Günter Gawlick (Stuttgart-Bad Cannstatt: Fromann, 1966);

De religione gentilium, facsimile, edited by Gawlick (Stuttgart-Bad Cannstatt: Fromann, 1967);

A Dialogue between a Tutor and His Pupil, facsimile, edited by Gawlick (Stuttgart-Bad Cannstatt: Fromann, 1971);

The Life of Edward, First Lord Herbert of Cherbury, Written by Himself, edited by J. M. Shuttleworth (London: Oxford University Press, 1976);

Pagan Religion: A Translocation of De religione gentilium, edited by John Anthony Butler (Ottawa: Dovehouse Editions / Binghamton, New York: Medieval and Renaissance Studies, 1996).

Edward, Lord Herbert of Cherbury, is often regarded as a curious and eccentric figure occupying an uncertain position in the first half of the seventeenth century. He asserted the chivalric, military, and philosophical ideals of an earlier age, while at the same time laying the groundwork for an apparently untimely body of thought on epistemology, metaphysics, and the philosophy of religion that had its fullest expression after his time. In his public career he was an intimate of important writers and scholars such as John Donne, Ben Jonson, Hugo Grotius, Daniel Tilenus, Marin Mersenne, and Pierre Gassendi. He corresponded with René Descartes. In his philosophical writings Herbert frequently anticipated the concerns of the Cambridge Platonists later in the seventeenth century, and his work has been seen to foreshadow that of Baruch Spinoza, John Locke, Gottfried Wilhelm Leibniz, Immanuel Kant, Thomas Reid and his followers in the Scottish Common Sense school, and the philosophy of idealism. Soldier, poet, biographer, musician, historian, metaphysician, and ecclesiastical reformer, Herbert left a body of work that includes a few dense volumes of metaphysics and religious philosophy in murky Latin, the chief of which is *De veritate, prout distinguitur a revelatione, a verisimili, a possibili, et a falso* (Concerning Truth, 1624); *The Life and Raigne of King Henry the Eighth* (1649), which was for many generations the standard account; the posthumously published *Occasional Verses of Edward, Lord Herbert, Baron of Cherbury and Castle-Island. Deceased in August 1648* (1665), a small collection of poems Platonic in tone and "metaphysical" in character; and an unpublished anthology of lute music that includes his original compositions. Herbert is perhaps best known to modern readers as the author of a racy, disconcertingly seriocomic and deeply nostalgic autobiography first published from the manuscript by Horace Walpole in 1764, and for the enduring, if inaccurate, title "father of English deism."

Edward Herbert was born in Eyton on Severn, Shropshire, on 3 March 1582, to a well-known family that had held the Welsh Marches for more than two hundred years. He was the eldest son of Richard Herbert of Montgomery Castle and Magdalen, daughter of Sir Richard Newport. His six younger brothers included George Herbert, who became a poet and Anglican priest, and Sir Henry Herbert, who became Master of the Revels at the court of James I. Edward Herbert matriculated at University College, Oxford, in May 1596 and remained there until 1600. During this time his father died, and his mother obtained wardship of her eldest son. On 28 February 1599, by her arrangement, he married a cousin who was some years older than he: Mary, the daughter of Sir William Herbert of St. Julians. After their marriage, Herbert's mother lived with them in a house they had taken in Oxford, while Herbert pursued his studies. Herbert and Mary had four children: Richard, Edward, Beatrice, and Florence, who died in infancy.

In 1600 the growing household moved to London, where Herbert continued his academic studies, learning Italian, French, and Spanish and becoming an expert lute player. He was one of the sixty or so new knights invested "upon carpet consideration" when James I ascended to the throne in 1603, and two years later he was appointed sheriff of Montgomeryshire. Herbert took his knightly vows in the chivalrous order of Knight of the Bath with great seriousness, particularly in defending distressed ladies, in retrieving stolen ribbons on a sword's point, and in barking out challenges to knaves and brigands—"not unlike," he wrote in his autobiography, "the romances of knight errantry." In 1608 he obtained a license to travel abroad and, leaving his wife and children in the country, set out for France with courtier and poet Aurelian Townshend as his companion. While in France, Herbert introduced himself to and became the intimate of the powerful Montmorency family, visiting Henri I, Duc de Montmorency-Damville, Governor of Languedoc, Constable of France, and leader of the moderate Roman Catholic party the Politiques, Herbert's thinking on religious disputes and the necessity for toleration of religious differences. After some eight months at Merlou and Chantilly, Herbert returned to Paris and lodged in the house of the irenic humanist and "incomparable scholar" Isaac Casaubon. Returning to England early in 1609, he presented himself to James at court and continued his studies while living with his family.

In 1610 Herbert saw military service in the Low Countries, assisting Philip William, Prince of Orange, at the siege of Juliers (Jülich), and serving with him again against the Spanish in 1614. He then left the army and traveled south to Cologne, visiting the Protestant German prince Frederick V, Elector Palatine (later King Frederick I of Bohemia), and his wife, Princess Elizabeth, daughter of James I of England, in Heidelberg. He continued to Ulm, Augsburg, Venice, Florence, and Rome, where—he reports in his autobiography—he called on the master of the English College, evidently with the intention of testing the ground in this center of the Catholic faith. He was assured that "men who gave no affronts to the Roman Catholic religion, received none," and Herbert replied that "I thought fit to tell him that I conceived the points agreed upon on both sides are greater bonds of amity betwixt us, than that the points disagreed on could break them; that for my part I loved everybody that was of a pious and virtuous life, and thought errors on what side soever, more worthy pity than hate."

In 1619 James I nominated Herbert as his ambassador to France. Herbert took the opportunity to revisit Merlou, "that sweet place and country." Since relations between the two countries were friendly, he had time to work on his philosophical treatise *De veritate*. His work was interrupted when James recalled him to England in July 1621 because Herbert, possessed of—in his words—a "hasty and choleric" disposition, had been involved in a duel. He was back in Paris again in 1622. A few months later he had almost completed *De veritate* and had been warmly urged to print it by the legal scholar Grotius and the theologian Tilenus. Any further doubts about publication were removed by a sign, "a loud though gentle noise . . . from the heavens" in answer to a prayer for encouragement, and the book, finished in June 1623, was printed in Paris in 1624 at Herbert's expense.

As the first proposition of his treatise, Herbert baldly states that "Truth exists." He explains: "The sole purpose of this proposition is to assert the existence of truth against imbeciles and sceptics." "Imbeciles" are Herbert's customary description of medieval Scholastics and Aristotelians, in keeping with the fashionable anti-Scholasticism of the late sixteenth century. Despite his bold opening, Herbert's approach is not merely one of assertion. In an age when voices on all sides were loudly informing each other of the "truth" according to various and competing criteria, prejudices, allegiances, or vested interests, Herbert offers to carry the discussion into the far less frequented field of basic epistemological (theory of knowledge) inquiry. His overall ambition in the work is summarized by the translation of its full title: "Concerning truth, and its distinction from revelation, probability, possibility, and falsehood." The work is, therefore, an investigation of modes of knowing and their conditions. The discussion begins formally with seven propositions regarding truth: truth exists; it is as eternal or as ancient as things themselves; it is everywhere; it reveals itself; there are as many truths as there are differences among things; the differences among things are recog-

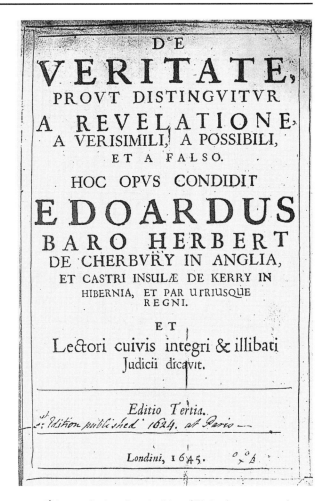

Title page for the enlarged edition of Herbert's essay on truth
(Sterling Memorial Library, Yale University)

nized by innate human powers or faculties; and there is a truth of all truths. The four main "faculties," or capacities of the mind, are Natural Instinct, the proper object of concern of which is eternal blessedness; the Internal Senses, the chief among which is "conscience"; the External Senses, the generally recognized five senses; and the *discursus*, or faculty of logical reasoning. For every object there is a faculty. When a faculty is in conformity with its object, a *sensus* occurs, and one has apprehended truth; that is, when a proper object of knowledge is perceived under the proper conditions so that a true appearance can be obtained, one is able to obtain a true concept of the thing.

There still remains, however, the problem of the criterion of truth. Herbert's elaborate system may be a method for establishing accurate appearances of true concepts, but the skeptic would ask how one knows that they are, in fact, true and that one is not deceived? There must be something outside either the faculties of perception, including the logical faculty, or *discursus*, or the things themselves that will provide the test of truth.

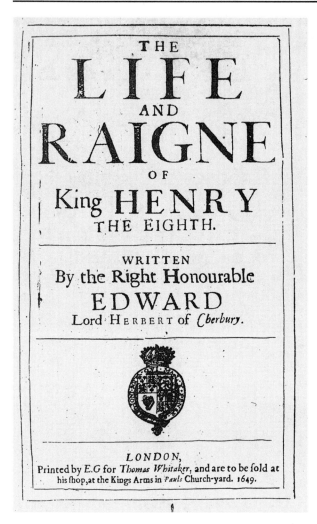

THE

LIFE

AND

RAIGNE

OF

King HENRY

THE EIGHTH.

WRITTEN

By the Right Honourable

EDWARD

Lord HERBERT of Cherbury.

LONDON,
Printed by E.G for Thomas Whitaker, and are to be fold at
his fhop, at the Kings Arms in Pauls Church-yard. 1649.

Title page for Herbert's eulogistic biography, which was the standard account of the king's life for many years (Henry E. Huntington Library, San Marino, California)

Herbert offers as the criterion the theory of Common Notions, derived from Cicero and the Stoics and from the commonplaces of Renaissance humanism: human beings have an innate capacity for comprehending truth. The Common Notions may be distinguished by their possession of several characteristics: they are assumed prior to reflection and experience; they cannot be derived from further principles; whatever imbeciles and skeptics may say to the contrary, they are universally acknowledged; they are certain; they are necessary to human preservation and salvation; and they are in immediate conformity with their objects—that is, they are intuitively grasped. Common Notions are conformities between Natural Instinct and its spiritual objects. Herbert illustrates the application of Common Notions to a particular problem in an outline of the five common religious propositions: that there is a God, that he is to be worshiped, that virtue and piety are the chief parts of worship, that people should repent of their sins,

and that there is reward or punishment after this life. These propositions are true, he asserts, because such beliefs have been maintained among peoples at all times and in all places, regardless of race or creed, however much the beliefs may have been obscured by later distortions and accretions. Despite a prefatory disclaimer that he is interested only in "truths of understanding, not truths of Faith" and that "any points bearing on the mysteries of Faith which the reader may find scattered through the book must be accepted as arising naturally out of the argument," Herbert's design can fairly be said to include the identification of religious truth with the principles of universal reason. From this strategy his pragmatic and political motives in writing *De veritate* may be discerned: he wanted to contribute to the unification and pacification of European religious diversity and its attendant wars and persecutions.

As a response to the crisis of skeptical doubt initiated, in particular, by Michel Eyquem de Montaigne, Herbert's treatise joined a large number of philosophical answers that began appearing in the 1630s, including those of Gassendi, Mersenne, and Descartes. Gassendi wrote to Herbert, praising him as "England's treasure," risen to succeed Francis Bacon, but arguing that he had failed to refute skepticism; that is, Herbert had shown more about the conditions under which truth appears to people, but not more about truth itself. In a letter to Mersenne, Descartes said that though he found much with which to sympathize in Herbert's project, the problem of the criterion of truth still remained. A 1639 French translation of *De veritate* was probably by Mersenne, and Descartes admitted that he found it much easier to read than Herbert's Latin. By the time he had read it, Descartes had published his *Discours de la méthode* (Discourse on Method, 1637) and was working on his *Méditations de Prima Philosophia* (Meditations on First Philosophy, 1641). It is noteworthy that Descartes's *Méditations de Prima Philosophia* has an apologetic aim not unlike Herbert's, and that the epistemology of the *Discours de la méthode*–though more elegant than Herbert's–is, like Herbert's, based on innate ideas of divine origin. Descartes gave Herbert a copy of the first edition of *Méditations de Prima Philosophia,* and Herbert began an English translation of the *Discours de la méthode.* Mersenne was deeply involved in many of the religious and philosophical affairs of mid-seventeenth-century Europe, at first as a publicist for the new learning and later as an indefatigable lobbyist and broker on behalf of religious peace and religious reunion, in which cause he saw the value of Herbert's discussion. He made considerable use of Herbert's writings.

After five years of costly but shrewd diplomatic service Herbert was recalled to England in April 1624, a victim of James I's political and matrimonial stratagems in France. He returned to Montgomery Castle and received no salary or expenses from the king, though he was given an Irish peerage as Lord Herbert of Castle Island, County Kerry. When Charles I succeeded his father to the throne, Herbert was raised to the English peerage in 1629 as Lord Herbert of Cherbury (a village in Shropshire). His wife died in 1634. Herbert gained no further public employment, despite his eulogistic *Life and Raigne of King Henry the Eighth* and his defense of George Villiers, first Duke of Buckingham's disastrous 1627 military expedition to aid the embattled French Huguenots, posthumously published in a Latin translation as *Expeditio in Ream insulam, anno 1630* (1656) and in the original English as *The Expedition to the Isle of Rhé* (1860). For his historical writing he had rooms in Whitehall, and from this vantage point he sought to attract the king's attention with practical schemes for naval equipment, gun carriages, and Thameside bathing establishments, but he received no further recognition or recompense. He traveled north in 1639 to join the king's forces at Alnwick in the first Bishop's War, advised the king to drive the Scots back but was ignored and withdrew again to Montgomery. In 1642 Parliament committed him briefly to the Tower of London to reflect on his ambiguous loyalties in the first Civil War. Thereafter he retired to Montgomery in what he hoped would be neutral isolation, declining Royalist invitations, though both of his sons fought for the king. Herbert wrote to his brother Henry in 1643: "I find myself grown older in this one year than in fifty-nine years before." His strategically placed castle fell bloodlessly to the Parliamentarians. (Herbert was especially anxious to preserve his library.) Left dependent on the goodwill of Parliament, he was granted a pension, and he pursued his philosophical and literary work in his London house in Queen Street, near St. Giles's.

Herbert's later philosophical writings engage more fully with "mysteries of Faith." Apart from the brief *De Causis Errorum: Una Cum tractatu de Religione Laici* (On the Causes of Errors, 1645), they leave epistemological inquiry for comparative religion, anticlericalism, irenic propaganda, and the advocacy of religious toleration. His *De religione laici* (On a Layman's Religion, 1645) attacks in a lively polemic the fragmentation of the Christian churches and the consequent bewilderment of "the Wayfarer" seeking truth, targeting especially the Calvinist articles of the Synod of Dort (1618–1619), called by the Dutch Reformed Church to respond to the Arminians' rejection of the doctrine of predestination, and all species of ecclesiastical absolutism and coercion. Many of the sentiments Herbert expressed in *De religione laici* were anticipated by others, including his friend John

Donne, and were echoed with various emphases by writers such as John Milton, Sir Thomas Browne, John Smith, Henry More, and John Locke. Herbert's posthumously published exercise in comparative religion, *De religione gentilium arrorumque apud eos causis* (1663), translated into English as *The Antient Religion of the Gentiles* (1705) is an essay on the nature of primitive belief and its development into institutional religions. It draws heavily on the work of Gerard Vossius (whose son saw the book through the press) and John Selden, but unlike most such religious anthropology it does not endorse an evolutionary progress toward Christianity. Instead, it asserts the ubiquity of the five common religious notions and concludes that all institutional religions are not only relatively true but also relatively false. (Despite these emphases, Herbert was that odd sort of religious iconoclast who, according to John Aubrey, "had prayers said twice daily in his house.") The anonymous and posthumously published *A Dialogue between a Tutor and His Pupil* (1768), which scholars generally agree is Herbert's work, furthers discussion of the relationship between "particular Christianity" and universality of the important religious truths.

In his last years Herbert continued to write and revise, corresponded with foreign scholars, and in September 1647 he made a last trip to Paris to visit Gassendi. On 1 August 1648 he made his will, providing generously for his sons and grandson, and arranged for his manuscripts and English books to be conveyed from London to Montgomery; his Latin and Greek books were bequeathed to Jesus College, Oxford, where many of them remain. Herbert died on 20 August 1648 and was buried in the Church of St.-Giles-in-the-Field. The inscription on his tombstone, which he probably wrote himself, records alone of his achievements that he was *auctoris libri, cui titulus est de Veritate* (author of the book whose title is *Concerning Truth*).

Although in his lifetime Herbert was not regarded as a dangerous or especially subversive figure–the customary epithet is simply "the learned Lord Herbert"– he was attacked or adopted by later controversialists who found in him the origins of their contemporary heresies, apostasies, and radicalism, particularly deism and the republicanism that its advocates frequently preached as well. References to Herbert's writings following his death are not extensive, though he attracted some notice on the Continent, where he was pilloried in two works as an atheist of the most dangerous kind and elevated, in the distinguished company of Spinoza and Thomas Hobbes, as one of the three great "impostors" of the age. Herbert is also not prominently mentioned in modern philosophical and religious histories of the

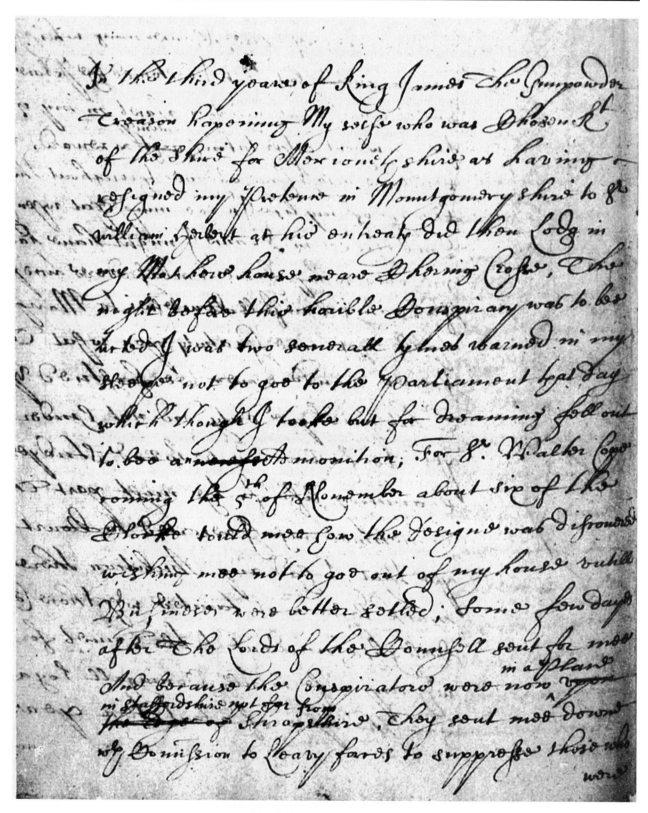

Page from the manuscript for The Life of Edward Lord Herbert of Cherbury, Written by Himself,
first published by Horace Walpole in 1764 (National Library of Wales)

seventeenth century. The facsimile reprints of his writings published in the 1960s and early 1970s supplement Meyrick H. Carré's indispensable English translation of *De veritate* (1937) and Harold R. Hutcheson's annotated translation of *Religio laici* (1944). The most comprehensive account of Herbert's life and writings is Mario M. Rossi's three-volume study (1947). For Rossi, Herbert is a crucially symptomatic, even symbolic, figure in what he calls "the passage from religious to political motives" in European culture, and Rossi admires Herbert's independence and integrity and at the same time abhors what he regards as Herbert's lack of any truly religious sensibility.

Letters:

Herbert Correspondence. The Sixteenth and Seventeenth Century Letters of the Herberts of Chirbury, Powis Castle and Dolguog, Formerly at Powis Castle in Montgomeryshire, edited by W. J. Smith (Cardiff: University of Wales Press / Dublin: Irish Manuscripts Commission, 1963).

Bibliographies:

G. H. Palmer, *A Herbert Bibliography* (Cambridge, Mass.: Harvard University Press, 1911), pp. 12–14;

Harold R. Hutcheson, "A Bibliography of Writings by and about Herbert," in *Lord Herbert of Cherbury's De Religione Laici,* edited and translated by Hutcheson (New Haven: Yale University Press / London: Oxford University Press, 1944), pp. 137–176.

Biographies:

Mario M. Rossi, *La Vita, le Opere, i Tempi di Edoardo Herbert di Chirbury,* 3 volumes (Florence: G. Sansoni, 1947);

John Butler, *Lord Herbert of Chirbury (1582–1648): An Intellectual Biography* (Lewiston, N.Y.: Edwin Mellen Press, 1990).

References:

R. D. Bedford, *The Defence of Truth: Herbert of Cherbury and the Seventeenth Century* (Manchester: Manchester University Press, 1979);

A. Carlini, "Herbert di Cherbury e la scuola di Cambridge," *Rendiconti della Reale Accademia dei Lincei,* series 5, 26 (1917): 279–357;

C. J. Fordyce and T. M. Knox, "The Library of Jesus College, Oxford: With an Appendix on the

Books Bequeathed thereto by Lord Herbert of Cherbury," *Proceedings and Papers of the Oxford Bibliographical Society,* 5, part 2 (1937): 53–115;

Carl Güttler, *Eduard Lord Herbert von Cherbury, Ein Kritische Beitrag zur Geschichte des Psychologismus und der Religionsphilosophie* (Munich, 1897);

Eugene D. Hill, *Edward, Lord Herbert of Cherbury* (Boston: Twayne, 1987);

Harold Hutcheson, "Lord Herbert and His Religious Philosophy," in *Lord Herbert of Cherbury's De Religione Laici,* edited and translated by Hutcheson (New Haven: Yale University Press / London: Oxford University Press, 1944), pp. 3–81;

Charles Lyttle, "Lord Herbert of Cherbury: Apostle of Ethical Theism," *Church History,* 5 (1935): 247–267;

W. Moelwyn Merchant, "Lord Herbert of Cherbury and Seventeenth-Century Historical Writing," *Transactions of the Honourable Society of Cymmrodorion* (1956): 47–63;

Richard H. Popkin, *The History of Scepticism from Erasmus to Descartes,* revised edition (New York: Humanities Press, 1964), pp. 155–165;

Charles de Rémusat, *Lord Herbert de Cherbury, sa vie et ses oeuvres, ou les origines de la philosophie de sens commun et de la théologie naturelle en Angleterre* (Paris, 1874);

Mario M. Rossi, "The Nature of Truth and Lord Herbert of Cherbury's Inquiry," *Personalist,* 21 (1940): 243–256, 394–409;

Heinrich Scholz, "Die Religious philosophie des Herbert von Cherbury," *Studies zur Geschichte des neuven Protestantismus,* 5 (Giessen, 1914);

W. R. Sorley, *A History of British Philosophy to 1900* (Cambridge: Cambridge University Press, 1920), pp. 35–45;

Sorley, "The Philosophy of Herbert of Cherbury," *Mind,* 3 (1894): 491–508;

Wolfram Steinbeck, "Das Problem der Wahrheit und die Philosophie Herberts von Cherbury," *Blätter für deutsche Philosophie,* 7 (1934): 467–478.

Papers:

The largest collection of Edward, Lord Herbert of Cherbury's papers is in the National Library of Wales, Aberystwyth. Two versions of *De veritate* are in the British Library and in St. John's College, Cambridge. The two extant manuscripts for *The Life and Raigne of King Henry the Eighth* are at Jesus College and the Bodleian Library at Oxford. The manuscript for his anthology of lute music is in the Fitzwilliam Museum at Cambridge.

Thomas Hobbes

(5 April 1588 – 4 December 1679)

Susan P. Reilly
University of New Hampshire

See also the Hobbes entry in *DLB 151: British Prose Writers of the Early Seventeenth Century.*

BOOKS: *Ad Nobilissimum Dominum Guilielmum Comitem Devoniae, &c. De Mirabilibus Pecci, Carmen* (London, 1636?); translated as *De Mirabilius Pecci: Being the wonders of the peak in Darby-Shire, Commonly called the Devil's Arse of Peak. In English and Latine. The Latine Written by Thomas Hobbes of Malmesbury. The English by a Person of Quality* (London: Printed for William Crooke, 1678);

Elementorum Philosophiae Sectio Tertia De Cive, anonymous (Paris, 1642); revised as *Elementa Philosophica De Cive* (Amsterdam: Printed by Daniel Elzevir, 1647); translated by Hobbes as *Philosophicall Rudiments Concerning Government and Society. Or, A Dissertation Concerning Man in his severall habitudes and respects, as a Member of a Society, first Secular, and then Sacred. In Which is Demonstrated, Both what the Origine of Justice is, and wherein the Essence of Christian Religion doth consist. Together with the Nature, Limits, and Qualifications both of Regiment and Subjection.* (London: Printed by John Grismond for Richard Royston, 1651);

Humane Nature: or, The fundamental Elements of Policie. Being a Discoverie Of the Faculties, Acts, and Passions of the Soul of Man, from their original causes; According to such Philosophical Principles as are not commonly known or asserted (London: Printed by Thomas Newcomb for Francis Bowman, Oxford, 1650);

De Corpore Politico, or Elements of Law, moral & Politick. With discourses upon several heads; as of the law of nature. Oathes and covenants. Severall kind of government. With the changes of Revolutions of them (London: Printed for John Martin & John Ridley, 1650);

Leviathan, or, The Matter, Forme, & Power of a Common-Wealth Ecclesiasticall and Civill (London: Printed for Andrew Crooke, 1651); translated into Latin by Hobbes as *Leviathan, Sive de Materia, Forma, & Potestate Civilatis Ecclesiasticae et Civilis* (Amsterdam: Printed by John Blaeu, 1670);

*Thomas Hobbes; portrait by J. M. Wright, circa 1670
(National Portrait Gallery, London)*

Of Libertie and Necessitie: A Treatise, wherein all Controversie concerning Predestination, Election, Free-will, Grace, Merits, Reprobation, &c is fully decided and cleared, in Answer to a Treatise written by the Bishop of London-derry, on the same subject (London: Printed by William Bentley for Francis Eaglesfield, 1654);

Elementorum Philosophiae Sectio Prima de Corpore (London: Printed for Andrew Crooke, 1655); translated by Hobbes as *Elements of Philosophy, the First Section,*

Concerning Body. Written in Latine by Thomas Hobbes of Malmesbury. And now translated into English. To which are added Six Lessons to the Professors of Mathematicks of the Institution of Sr. Henry Savile, in the University of Oxford (London: Printed by Robert & William Leybourn for Andrew Crooke, 1656);

The Questions Concerning Liberty, Necessity, and Chance. Clearly Stated and Debated Between Dr. Bramhall Bishop of Derry, and Thomas Hobbes of Malmesbury. (London: Printed for Andrew Crooke, 1656);

Στιγμαι: *Αγεωμτίας, Αγροκιας, Αντιπολιτείας, Αμαθειας, or Markes of the Absurd Geometry Rural Language Scottish Church-Politicks and Barbarismes of John Wallis Professor of Geometry and Doctor of Divinity* (London: Printed for Andrew Crooke, 1657);

Elementorum Philosophiae Sectio Secunda De Homine (London: Printed by T. C. for Andrew Crooke, 1658);

Examinatio & Emendatio Mathematicae Hodiernæ. Qualis explicatur in libris Johannis Wallisii Geometriæ Professoris Saviliani in Academia Oxoniensi. Distributa in sex Dialogos. (London: Printed for Andrew Crooke, 1660);

Dialogus Physicus, sive De natura Aeris Conjectura sumpta ab Experimentis nuper Londini habitis in Collegio Greshamensi. Item De Duplicatione Cubi (London: Printed by J. B. for Andrew Crooke, 1661);

Problemata Physica: De Gravitate. Cap. I. De Æstibus Marinis. Cap. II. De Vacuo. Cap. III. De Calore & Luce. Cap. IV. De Duro & Molli. Cap. V. De Pluvia, Vento, aliisq; Coeli varietatibus. Cap. VI. De Motuum Speciebus. Cap. VII. Adjunctæ sunt etiam Propositiones duæ de Duplicatione Cubi, & Dimensione Circuli (London: Printed for Andrew Crooke, 1662); translated anonymously as *Seven Philosophical Problems, and Two Propositions of Geometry. By Thomas Hobbes of Malmesbury. With an Apology for Himself, and his Writings. Dedicated to the King, in the year 1662* (London: Printed for William Crooke, 1682);

Mr. Hobbes Considered in his Loyalty, Religion, Reputation, and Manners, by Way of Letter to Dr. Wallis (London: Andrew Crooke, 1662); republished as *Considerations upon the Reputation, Loyalty, Manners, & Religion, of Thomas Hobbes of Malmesbury. Written by himself, By way of Letter to a Learned Person* (London: Printed for William Crooke, 1680);

De Principiis & Ratiocinationae Geomentrarum. Ubi stenditur incertitudinem falsitatemque non minorem inesse scriptis eorum, quam scriptis Physicorum & Ethicorum (London: Pritned for Andrew Crooke, 1666);

Quadratum Circuli, Cubatio sphæræ, duplicatio cubi, una cum respoensione ad objectiones, geometriae profesoris saviliani Oxoniae editas anno 1669 (London: Printed for Andrew Crooke, 1669);

Three Papers Presented to the Royal Society Against Dr. Wallis. Together with Considerations on Dr. Wallis his Answer to them (London: Printed for the author, 1671);

Rosetum Geometricum. Sive Propositiones Aliquot Frustra antehac tentatæ. Cum Censura brevi Doctrinæ Walliaianæ de Motu (London: Printed by John Crooke Jr., for William Crooke, 1671); translated by Venterus Mandey as "A Garden of Geometrical Roses; Or Some Propositions Being hitherto Hid, are now made Known," in his *Mellificium Mensionis: or, The Marrow of Measuring. With some Choice Principles and Problems of Geometry conducing thereto. The whole Treatise being comprized in six Books* (London: Printed for the author, sold by Richard Chiswel, Benjamin Clark, and by the author, 1682), pp. 40–107;

Lux Mathematica: Excussa Collisionibus Johannis Wallisii Theol. Doctoris, Geometriæ in celeberrima Academia Oxoniensi Professoris Publici, et Thomæ Hobbesii Malmsburiensis (London: Printed by John Crooke Jr. for William Crooke, 1672);

Principia et Problemata Aliquot Geometrica Antè Desperata, Nunc breviter Explicata & Demonstrata (London: Printed by J. C. for William Crooke, 1674); translated by Mandey as "Some Principles and Problems in Geometry Thought formerly Desperate; Now Briefly Explained and Demonstrated," in his *Mellificium Mensionis* (1682), pp. 110–185;

Epistola Thomae Hobbes malmesburiensis ad dominum Antonium â Wood authorem Historiae & antiquitatum universitatis oxoniensis (London: William Crooke, 1674);

Decameron Physiologicum; or, Ten Dialogues of Natural Philosophy (London: Printed by John Crooke Jr., for William Crooke, 1678);

The History of the Civil Wars of England. From the Year 1640, to 1660, as T. H. (N.p., 1679);

Thomæ Hobbessii Malmesburiensis Vita. Authore Seipso (London, 1679); translated by Benjamin Farrington as "The Autobiography of Thomas Hobbes," in *The Rationalist Annual for the Year 1958* (London: Watts, 1957); translated by J. E. Parsons Jr. and Whitney Blair as "The Life of Thomas Hobbes of Malmesbury," *Interpretation*, 10 (January 1982): 1–7;

An Historical Narration Concerning Heresie, And the Punishment thereof (London: Printed for William Crooke, 1680);

The Life of Mr. Thomas Hobbes of Malmesbury. Written by himself In a Latine Poem. And now Translated into English, translated by Richard Blackbourne [?] (London: Printed for A. C., 1680); original Latin version published as *Thomae Hobbes Angli Malmesburiensis Philosophi Vita* (London: Printed for William Crooke, 1681);

The Art of Rhetoric, With a Discourse of The Laws of England (London: Printed for William Crooke, 1681);

Tracts of Thomas Hobb's [sic] *Containing I. His Life in Latine, part Written by Himself, Since his death finished by Dr. R.B. II. His Considerations upon his Reputation, Loyalty, Manners, and Religion. III. His Whole art of Rhetorick, in English IV. His Discourse by way of Dialogue, concerning the Common Laws of England. V. Ten Dialogues of Natural Philosophy, &c.* (London: William Crooke, 1681);

Tracts of Mr. Thomas Hobbs of Malmsbury. Containing I. Behemoth, the History of the Cause of the Civil Wars of England, from 1640. to 1660. printed from the author's own Copy: Never printed (but with a thousand faults) before. II. An Answer to Arch-Bishop Bramhall's Book, called the Catching of the Leviathan: *Never printed before. III. An Historical Narration of Heresie, and the Punishment thereof: Corrected by the true Copy. IV. Philosophical Problems, dedicated to the King in 1662. but never printed before* (London: Printed for William Crooke, 1682);

Historia Ecclesiastica Carmine Elegiaco Concinnata (London, 1688); translated anonymously as *A True Ecclesiastical History, from Moses, to the Time of Martin Luther* (London: E. Curll, 1772);

Thomas Hobbes: Three Discourses. A Critical Modern Edition of Newly Identified Works of the Young Hobbes, edited by Noel B. Reynolds and Arlene W. Saxonhouse (Chicago: University of Chicago Press, 1995)—comprises *Discourse upon the Beginning of Tacitus, Discourse of Rome,* and *Discourse of Laws.*

Editions: *Opera Philosophica, Quae Latiné scripsit, Omnia,* 2 volumes (Amsterdam: Printed by John Blaeu, 1668);

A Supplement to Mr. Hobbes His Works, Printed by Blaeu at Amsterdam, 1661. Being a third Volume (London: Printed by John Crooke Jr. for William Crooke, 1675);

Hobb's tripos, in Three Discourses: The First, Humane Nature, or the Fundamental Elements of Policy. Being a Discovery of the Faculties, Acts, and Passions of the Soul of Man, from their Original Causes, according to such Philosophical Principles as are not commonly known, or affected. The Second, De Corpore Politico. Or the Elements of Law, Moral and Politick, with Discourses upon several Heads, as of the Law of Nature, Oaths, and Covenants; several kinds of Governments, with the Changes and Revolutions of them. The Third, Of Liberty and Necessity, Wherein all Controversie, concerning Free-will, Grace, Merits, Reprobation, is fully decided and cleared. The Third Edition (London: Matt. Gilliflower and Henry Rogers, 1684);

The Moral and Political Works of Thomas Hobbes of Malmesbury. Never before collected together. To which is prefixed, The Author's Life, Extracted from That said to be written by Himself, as also from The Supplement *to the said*

Life *by Dr. Blackbourne; and further illustrated by the Editor, with Historical and Critical Remarks on his Writings and Opinions* (London, 1750);

The English Works of Thomas Hobbes of Malmesbury; Now First Collected and Edited, 11 volumes, edited by Sir William Molesworth (London: Bohn, 1839–1845);

Thomæ Hobbes Malmsburiensis Opera Philosophica Quæ Latine Scripsit Omnia in Unum Corpus Nunc Primum Collecta Studio et Labore Gulielmi Molesworth, 5 volumes, edited by Molesworth (London: Bohn, 1839–1845);

The Elements of Law Natural and Politic, edited by Ferdinand Tönnies (London: Simpkin, Marshall, 1889); edited by M. M. Goldsmith (New York: Barnes & Noble, 1969);

Behemoth or The Long Parliament, edited by Tönnies (London: Simpkin, Marshall, 1889); second edition, edited by Goldsmith (New York: Barnes & Noble, 1969);

Hobbes's Leviathan, introduction by W. G. Pogson Smith (Oxford: Clarendon Press, 1909);

Leviathan; or, The Matter, Forme and Power of a Commonwealth, Ecclesiasticall and Civil, edited by Michael Oakeshott (Oxford: Blackwell, 1946);

De Cive; or The Citizen, edited by Sterling P. Lamprecht (New York: Appleton-Century-Crofts, 1949);

Leviathan, edited by C. B. Macpherson (London: Pelican, 1968);

A Dialogue between a Philosopher and a Student of the Common Laws of England, edited by Joseph Cropsey (Chicago: University of Chicago Press, 1971);

Man and Citizen, edited by Bernard Gert (Garden City, N.Y.: Doubleday, 1972);

Critique du De Mundo de Thomas White, edited by Jean Jacquot and Harold Whitmore Jones (Paris: Vrin, 1973); translated by Jones as *Thomas White's De Mundo Examined* (London: Bradford University Press, 1976);

Hobbes's Thucydides, edited by Richard Schlatter (New Brunswick, N.J.: Rutgers University Press, 1975);

De Cive, The Latin Version, The Clarendon Edition of the Philosophical Works of Thomas Hobbes, volume 2, edited by Howard Warrender (Oxford: Clarendon Press, 1983);

De Cive, The English Version, The Clarendon Edition of the Philosophical Works of Thomas Hobbes, volume 3, edited by Warrender (Oxford: Clarendon Press, 1983);

The Rhetorics of Thomas Hobbes and Bernard Lamy, edited by John T. Harwood (Carbondale: Southern Illinois University Press, 1986);

Leviathan, edited by Richard Tuck (Cambridge: Cambridge University Press, 1991);

"1668 Appendix to Leviathan," translated, with an introduction and notes, by George Wright, *Interpretation*, 18 (1991): 323–414;

On the Citizen, edited and translated by Tuck and Michael Silverthorne (Cambridge & New York: Cambridge University Press, 1998).

OTHER: *Eight Bookes of the Peloponnesian Warre Written by Thucydides the Sonne of Olorus. Interpreted with Faith and Diligence Immediately out of the Greeke,* translated by Hobbes (London: Printed for Henry Seile, 1629);

A Briefe of the Art of Rhetorique. Containing in substance all that Aristotle hath written in his Three Bookes of that subject, Except onely what is not applicable to the English Tongue, translated anonymously by Hobbes (London: Printed by Thomas Cotes for Andrew Crooke, 1637);

"Objectiones Tertiæ," in *Meditationes de Prima Philosophia, in qva Dei Existentia, & animæ immortalitas demonstratur,* by René Descartes (Paris: Printed for Michael Soli, 1641); translated by William Molyneaux as "Objections Made against the Foregoing Meditations," in *Six Metaphysical Meditations; Wherein it is Proved That there is a God. And that Mans Mind is really distinct from his Body,* by Descartes, translated by Molyneaux (London: Printed by B. G. for Benjamin Tooke, 1680);

Preface to "Ballistica" and "Tractatus Opticus," in *Cogitata Physico Mathematica. In quibus tam naturæ quàm artis effectus admirandi certissimus demonstrationibus explicantur,* by Marin Mersenne, 3 volumes (Paris: Printed for Antony Bertier, 1644);

"The Answer of Mr. Hobbs to Sr. William D'Avenant's preface before Gondibert," in *A Discourse Upon Gondibert, An Heroick Poem, with an Answer to it by Mr. Hobbs,* by D'Avenant (Paris: Printed for Matthew Guillemot, 1650);

"To the Honourable *Edward Howard,* Esq.; on his intended Impression of his Poem of the British Princes," in *The British Princes: An Heroick Poem,* by Howard (London: Printed by T.N. for Henry Herringman, 1669);

The Travels of Ulysses; As they were Related by Himself in Homer's Ninth, Tenth, Eleventh & Twelfth Books of his Odysses to Alcinous King of Phæacia, translated by Hobbes (London: Printed by John Crooke Jr. for William Crooke, 1675);

Homer's Odysses. Translated by Thomas Hobbes of Malmsbury. With a Large Preface Concerning the Vertues of an Heroique. Written by the Translator (London: Printed by John Crooke Jr. for William Crooke, 1675);

Homer's Iliads in English. By Thomas Hobbes of Malmsbury. To Which May be Added Homer's Odysses Englished by the same Author (London: Printed by John Crooke Jr. for William Crooke, 1676);

"Considerations touching the faculty or Difficulty of Motions of a Horse on straight lines & Circular," in *A Catalogue of Letters and Other Historical Documents Exhibited in the Library at Welbeck,* compiled by Arthur S. Strong (London: Murray, 1903);

"Answer to Davenant's Preface to *Gondibert*" and "Preface to Homer," in *Critical Essays of the Seventeenth Century,* volume 2, edited by J. E. Spingarn (Oxford: Clarendon Press, 1908), pp. 54–76;

Fulgenzio Micanzio, O.S.M., "Lettere a William Cavendish (1615–1628) nelle versione inglese di Thomas Hobbes," edited by Roberto Ferrini, in *Scrinium historiale,* volume 15 (Rome: Insituto Storico O.S.M., 1987).

The most influential English philosopher before John Locke, Thomas Hobbes was a founder of modern political science. One of his greatest achievements lay in freeing morality and politics from subservience to theology. Hobbes's metaphysical system is a thoroughgoing mechanistic materialism that reduces all events, including thought, to the motion of physical particles. Owing to the importance he attaches to definitions, he has been considered a forerunner of modern linguistic philosophy. It has even been argued that Hobbes was the creator of English-language philosophy, and that his *Leviathan, or, The Matter, Forme, & Power of a Common-Wealth Ecclesiasticall and Civill* (1651) was the first great philosophical work in the language. Hobbes's writings include works on the sciences, human nature, mathematics, metaphysics, epistemology, vision and light, ethics, rhetoric, religion, and law. His dismissal of Christian terminology in his religious commentaries provoked a storm of abuse. An ardent Royalist, Hobbes defended secular monarchy in *Leviathan,* the anticlerical position of which made his situation difficult in Restoration England.

Hobbes was born in Westport parish, Malmesbury, Wiltshire, on Good Friday, 5 April 1588, to Thomas Hobbes, a country curate, and the daughter of a Brokenborough yeoman known only by her surname, Middleton (sometimes spelled Midleton). He was the second of two sons, and the family also included a daughter. His mother was apparently fond of repeating her belief that she gave birth to him prematurely because of her agitation at reports of the approach of the Spanish Armada; Hobbes said in his verse autobiography (translated, 1680; original Latin version, 1681) that as a result, he and fear were "born twins." The elder Hobbes was characterized by Hobbes's early biographer, John Aubrey, as "one of the ignorant 'Sir Johns' of Queen Elizabeth's time," a "Choleric man" who provided ill for his family and ultimately abandoned them.

Integer vitæ fcelerifque purus
Non eget Mauri jaculis nec areu,
Nec venenatis gravida fagittis
Fufce pharetra.
Sive per Syrtes iter æftuofas,
Sive facturus per inhofpifalem
Caucafium, vel quæ loca fabulofus
Lambit Hidafpis.

"Religion": an illustration for Philosophicall Rudiments
Concerning Government and Society *(1651),*
Hobbes's English translation of his De Cive,
published in 1642 and revised in 1647
(Library of Congress)

More recently his characterization as a man of "ignorance and clownery" who "disesteemed learning" has been reevaluated; A. P. Martinich says that the senior Hobbes had matriculated at Brasenose College, Oxford, in April 1587, "supposedly at the relatively superannuated age of forty."

At age four Hobbes was sent to school at Westport Church, and at age eight to Malmesbury school, which was kept by a Mr. Evans, the town minister. Later, under Richard Latimer at a private school in Westport, Hobbes mastered the curriculum of the sixteenth-century grammar school, which emphasized Latin and Greek. Aubrey says that he was "much addicted to music" and practiced on the bass viol. While still a pupil, he translated Euripides' *Medea* into Latin iambics.

At age fourteen Hobbes entered Magdalen Hall, Oxford University. Aubrey says that Hobbes "tooke gret delight to goe to the bookbinders' shops and lie gaping on mappes" and that he amused himself snaring jackdaws and reading travel books.

In 1603, while Hobbes was at Oxford, his father was convicted of slandering a fellow clergyman, discharged from his duties as curate, and excommunicated. Following a charge of assault on his accuser in the churchyard at Malmesbury the next year, he fled from the law and, according to Aubrey, "died in obscurity beyond London." After the elder Hobbes abandoned the family, his brother Francis, a glover in Malmesbury, provided for them.

Graduating with a B.A. in February 1608, Hobbes became tutor to the son of William Cavendish, Baron Hardwick and, from 1618, first earl of Devonshire, on the recommendation of Sir James Hussey, principal of Magdalen Hall. In addition to his duties as tutor to the son, also named William, he was to act as secretary, financial agent, and general adviser to the baron. This appointment began a lifelong connection with the house of Devonshire. Aubrey records that this patronage provided Hobbes with access to books, travel, leisure, and constant intercourse with men of letters and learning.

It has traditionally been thought that Hobbes accompanied the younger William Cavendish on a grand tour of the Continent beginning in 1610, but new evidence, cited by Martinich, suggests that they may not have embarked on the tour until 1614. On this trip they visited Italy and France. Hobbes learned to speak French and Italian and discovered the disfavor into which the Aristotelian thought proffered at Oxford had fallen. His translations of the letters of the Venetian friar Fulgenzio Micanzia, with whom his pupil corresponded after their return from Venice in 1615, caused Hobbes to develop an interest in the writings of Paolo Sarpi and to adopt a strong antipapal position.

Hobbes spent some years, probably between 1620 and 1625, working as a secretary to Francis Bacon, translating some of Bacon's essays into Latin and taking down his thoughts from dictation. There is disagreement as to the manner and degree of influence that Bacon exerted on Hobbes's thought. Hobbes resembles Bacon in the utilitarian importance he attaches to knowledge, but he does not share Bacon's enthusiasm for the inductive method. He regards science as deductive.

In 1629 Hobbes became tutor to Sir Gervase Clifton, with whom he traveled on a second Grand Tour to Paris, Switzerland, and possibly Venice. Hobbes's first published work—a translation of Thucydides' history of the Peloponnesian War—appeared in 1629. Thucydides was an opponent of democracy who approved of regal government, and Hobbes claims in his autobiography that he produced the translation to point out the dangers of democracy. Thucydides, he says, "taught me how stupid democracy is and by how much one man is wiser than an assembly."

It was probably on his tour with Clifton, in 1630, that Hobbes was introduced to Euclid's *Elements of Geometry* and began to study mathematics. Aubrey describes the incident in a famous passage:

> Hobbes was in a gentleman's house in which a copy of Euclid's *Elements* lay open on a desk. When he read proposition 47 [the Pythagorean theorem], he said, "By G———, this is impossible." So he read the demonstration of it, which referred him back to such a proposition; which proposition he read. *Et sic deinceps* [and thus one after another], that at last he was demonstratively convinced of that truth. This made him in love with geometry.

Hobbes's discovery of Euclidean geometry, along with the later influence of Galileo, helped to crystallize his idea that philosophy could be demonstrated deductively. He also studied geometry in order better to understand the modes of motion, and he began to develop his mechanical explanation of nature. A tract in the Harleian Manuscript collection at the British Library includes an early statement of his materialist theory of sensation and an attempt at working it through.

In 1630 Hobbes was called back from the Continent to tutor another William Cavendish, the third earl of Devonshire—the son of his first pupil. He devoted the next seven years to giving the boy lessons in rhetoric, logic, astronomy, and law. In the fall of 1634 Hobbes began his third trip to the Continent with the earl, visiting Italy and spending time in Paris. Around 1636, in Florence, he met Galileo, who was then under house arrest by the Inquisition. Through Galileo, Hobbes cultivated a relationship with Claudius Berigardus, professor of philosophy at Pisa. In Paris he made the acquaintance of the philosopher and mathematician René Descartes, the philosopher and scientist Pierre Gassendi, and Marin Mersenne, a Franciscan monk who was greatly interested in the new science. Gassendi's atomistic models influenced Hobbes's early physical and psychological theories. Both used mechanistic concepts in their ethical theories but for opposite purposes: Hobbes to argue for a deterministic universe in which free will does not exist, Gassendi to release humanity from natural necessity by allowing a person the free choice of moving in either of two directions.

Hobbes returned to England in 1636 and published a travel book in Latin verse: *Ad Nobilissimum Dominum Guilielmum Comitem Devoniae, &c. De Mirabilibus Pecci, Carmen* (translated as *De Mirabilius Pecci: Being the wonders of the peak in Darby-Shire, Commonly called the Devil's Arse of Peak. In English and Latine. The Latine Written by Thomas Hobbes of Malmesbury. The English by a Person of Quality,* 1678). It is an account of a short tour of the Peak District in Derbyshire that Hobbes took with the second earl of Devonshire in 1626. His *A Briefe of the Art of Rhetorique. Containing in substance all that Aristotle hath written in his Three Bookes of that subject, Except onely what is not applicable to the English Tongue* was published the following year.

After his return to England, Hobbes lived for the most part in Fetter Lane, London. There he continued his study of the classics and finished his *Elementorum Philosophiae Sectio Prima de Corpore* (1655; conventionally known as *De Corpore*) in Latin and in English. During this time he often conversed with William Harvey, discoverer of the human circulatory system; the jurist, historian, and antiquary John Selden, from whom he received a legacy; and John Vaughn, a Welsh lawyer and politician. He also made the acquaintance of the future poet laureate William D'Avenant, the Scottish poet Robert Ayton, and the philosopher, poet, and diplomat Edward Herbert, first Baron of Cherbury and elder brother of the poet George Herbert. Most important, he became acquainted with the Great Tew Circle, a group of young men who gathered at Great Tew, the Oxfordshire estate of Lucius Cary, Viscount Falkland, for intellectual discussions. Members of the Great Tew Circle included the playwright Ben Jonson; the poets Edmund Waller and Abraham Cowley; the statesmen Sidney Godolphin, Kenelm Digby, and Edward Hyde, later first Earl of Clarendon; and the theologian William Chillingworth. Many of the Great Tew Circle were members of the aristocracy and the clergy, and their interests were those of king and church. This bias may have been the enduring influence that Hobbes maintained from his visits to Great Tew. He was appointed a member of the Virginia Company and of the Somer Islands Company, which organized the settlement of Bermuda, and these positions brought him into further contact with politicians, writers, and lawyers.

Hobbes's "Elements of Law, Natural and Politic" was circulating in manuscript by 1640. According to Hobbes, the intent of the work was to justify absolutism in the light of first principles. He attempted to set out in mathematical fashion the rules of a political science, argued in favor of a monarchical government, and, under the impact of

Title page for the notorious work in which Hobbes shows that an absolute state is needed to prevent human life from being "solitary, poor, nasty, brutish, and short" (British Library)

lowed by other Royalists, who helped him gain the position of tutor in mathematics to the exiled Prince of Wales (later Charles II) in 1647.

Although he was deeply influenced by Cartesian thought, Hobbes disagreed with fundamental aspects of it. Like his French contemporaries Nicolas de Malebranche and Antoine Arnauld, he argued in print with Descartes and wrote a set of objections to Descartes's *Meditationes de Prima Philosophia, in qva Dei Existentia, & animæ immortalitas demonstratur* (1641; translated as *Six Metaphysical Meditations; Wherein it is Proved That there is a God. And that Mans Mind is really distinct from his Body*, 1680).

By 1642 civil war in England had begun in earnest, apparently persuading Hobbes to embark at once on the third part of his *Elementorum Philosophiae: De Cive*, a fuller statement of his new science of the state or "civil philosophy." The work was privately printed in 1642 and established his reputation. It elaborated more fully his notion that peace could only be obtained by the complete subordination of the church to the state. In 1647 he brought out a new edition of *De Cive* that included additional notes in answer to objections and a "Preface to the Reader." The edition was published by the French physician Samuel Sorbière at the Elzevir Press in Amsterdam. The English text appeared in 1651 as *Philosophical Rudiments Concerning Government and Society. Or, a Dissertation Concerning Man in his severall habitudes and respects, as a Member of a Society, first Secular, and then Sacred. Containing The Elements of Civill Politie in the Agreement with it hath both with Naturall and Divine Lawes.*

In 1646 Hobbes engaged in a debate on free will with John Bramhall, the refugee bishop of Derry, in the presence of William, Marquis of Newcastle. Hobbes allowed John Davys of Kidwelly to translate his reply into French; in 1654 Davies published the work in English, without Hobbes's consent, as *Of Libertie and Necessitie: A Treatise, wherein all Controversie concerning Predestination, Election, Free-will, Grace, Merits, Reprobation, &c is fully decided and cleared, in Answer to a Treatise written by the Bishop of London-derry, on the same subject,* and attached to it a prefatory letter denouncing all priests. An angry Bramhall published *A Defense of True Liberty* in 1655, to which Hobbes replied in *The Questions Concerning Liberty, Necessity, and Chance. Clearly Stated and Debated Between Dr. Bramhall Bishop of Derry, and Thomas Hobbes of Malmesbury* (1656). Bramhall wrote a further reply, *Castigations of Mr Hobbes,* in 1658. After a lapse of ten years Hobbes countered with "An Answer to a Book Published by Dr. Bramhall, Late Bishop of Derry, Called The Catching of the Leviathan." It was not published

the new philosophy, turned from humanist history to scientific theory—from historical examples to universal axioms. The content and doctrine of "Elements of Law" are similar to *De Cive* and *Leviathan* and anticipate their central concerns. "Elements of Law" was published in two versions in 1650 without Hobbes's permission: *Humane Nature: or, The fundamental Elements of Policie. Being a Discoverie Of the Faculties, Acts, and Passions of the Soul of Man, from their original causes; According to such Philosophical Principles as are not commonly known or asserted* and *De Corpore Politico, or Elements of Law, moral & Politick. With discourses upon several heads; as of the law of nature. Oathes and covenants. Severall kind of government. With the changes of Revolutions of them.* No complete edition of the work appeared in print until 1889, when Ferdinand Tönnies published it from the original manuscript.

When the Long Parliament assembled in 1640, Hobbes left England for France with the first group of Royalist émigrés and settled in Paris. He was fol-

until 1682, three years after Hobbes's death, when it appeared in *Tracts of Mr. Thomas Hobbs of Malmsbury.*

In 1650 Hobbes published a reply to D'Avenant's dedication of his heroic poem *Gondibert,* an uncompleted romantic epic of some 1,700 quatrains. *A Discourse upon Gondibert, an Heroick Poem Written by Sr. William Gondibert. With an Answer to it by Mr. Hobbes* expresses Hobbes's literary theory: poetry should "avert men from vice and incline them to virtuous and honourable actions." Hobbes holds that "Experience begets memory; Memory begets Judgment and Fancy; Judgment begets the strength and structure, and Fancy begets the ornaments of a Poem." His insistence on the priority of judgment over fancy did much to lay the foundations of the literary criticism of the last half of the seventeenth century.

In 1651 Hobbes's masterpiece of political philosophy, *Leviathan, or, The Matter, Forme, & Power of a Common-Wealth Ecclesiasticall and Civill,* was published in London. The title of the work refers to the sea monster in Psalms 74:14, Isaiah 27:1, and Job 41 and expresses Hobbes's concept of the power of the state. The work consists of four parts: part 1, "Of Man," offers a materialistic and mechanistic explanation of reality and of human senation, thought, emotion, and motivation: "every part of the Universe, is body, and that which is not Body, is no part of the Universe: And because the Universe is All, that which is no part of it is *Nothing;* and consequently *no where.*" The atheistic tendencies of such an ontology were quickly recognized by critics. Human beings are made up of small particles in motion; sensation is caused by "several motions of matter by which it presseth on our various organs diversely"; the motions are communicated to the substance inside the head. Senation is the basis of thought, which is merely "decaying sense." Human appetites and aversions are tiny internal motions in reaction to these external motions; they are always directed toward self-preservation. Accordingly, human beings are not, as Aristotle held, naturally social beings but are egoistic, greedy, and motivated above all by fear of a violent death. Although they are completely determined by physical laws, human beings are still free as long as their actions are not impeded by external objects.

In a transitional chapter, "Of Religion," between parts 1 and 2 Hobbes investigates the causes of religion and deals with superstition and other abuses of religion. Yet, he views religion as an essential component of the civil state.

Part 2 deals with the origins, function, and nature of government. The state of nature, or "natural condition of mankind," a hypothetical pregovernment situation in which people have "no common

power to keep them all in Awe," would be one of general war and insecurity and a low standard of living, a situation wherein human life would be "solitary, poor, nasty, brutish, and short." To escape this condition people would, in a flash of enlightened self-interest, establish a social contract or "covenant" in which they set up over themelves a ruler, "the sovereign," whose commands are law and whose power is absolute. This relationship having been established, "the Multitude so united in one Person, is called a Common-Wealth." To fulfill its function of keeping the peace the sovereign power must be indivisible; it cannot be divided, for example, between king and Parliament. Although the state is founded on the consent of the governed, that consent, once given, cannot be revoked: there is no right to revolution. The people, in the social contract, have authorized the sovereign to act in their name; thus, to revolt against the sovereign would be tantamount to revolting against themselves, which would be absurd. Furthermore, the subjects cannot claim a right to revolt on the basis that the sovereign has failed to keep his part of the social contract, because the sovereign is not a party to the contract: the contract is between the individuals in the state of nature, who become subjects or citizens by virtue of bestowing "the power of the sword" on the sovereign.

In part 3, "Of a Christian Commonwealth," Hobbes offers an analysis of scriptural composition. In part 4, "Of the Kingdom of Darkness," he shows that to prevent factionalism that might lead to civil war and, thus, to a return to the state of nature, the power of the church must be subordinate to that of the sovereign. *Leviathan* ends with a "Review and Conclusion," which holds that two things are required for sovereignty: a mighty power to protect people and their consent.

There was a wave of reaction against Hobbes's work. Sir Robert Filmer, while sympathetic to Hobbes's views on sovereignty, attacked his premises in the anonymously published *Observations Concerning the Originall of Government* (1652). More animadversions on *Leviathan* were offered by the Scot Alexander Rosse in 1653, by William Lucy in 1657, and by the Puritan Reverend George Lawson, who argued against Hobbes's utilitarian position the same year. Serious assaults on the work were waged by the Cambridge Platonists Henry More, who criticized Hobbes's materialism in his *Immortality of the Soul* (1659), and Ralph Cudworth, whose *The True Intellectual System of the Universe: The First Part; Wherein, All the Reason and Philosophy of Atheism Is Confuted; and Its Impossibility Demonstrated* (1678) is an elaborate examination of Hobbes's materialism. Throughout the

*Portrait of Hobbes by William Faithorne that appeared in the Latin
edition of his works published in Amsterdam in 1668
(Beinecke Library, Yale University)*

1660s and 1670s Hobbes was frequently attacked,
both from the pulpit and in print, for his supposed
atheism and denial of objective moral values. Hyde
was a prominent assailant of *Leviathan* in his *A Brief
View and Survey of the Dangerous and Pernicious Errors to
Church and State in Mr. Hobbes's Book Leviathan,* written
in 1670 and published in 1676.

There is much controversy concerning the alle-
gation that Hobbes was an atheist, however. Hobbes
himself objected to the charge in his *Problemata Physica*
(1662; translated as *Seven Philosophical Problems, and
Two Propositions of Geometry,* 1682): "There is nothing
in it against episcopacy. I cannot therefore imagine
what reason any episcopal men can have to speak of
me, as I hear some of them do, as of an atheist or
man of no religion, unless it be for making the
authority of the church depend wholly upon the
regal power."

Hobbes's appeal to self-interest was seen as
seditious in some quarters. The theologian Thomas
Tenison says in his *Creed of Mr. Hobbes Examined*
(1670) that since Hobbes identifies the law of nature
with the counsels of self-interest, "the Fundamentals
of . . . [his] Policy are hay, and apter to set all things
into blaze than to support government. . . . Woe to all
the Princes on earth, if this doctrine be true and
becometh popular; if the multitude believe this, the
Prince . . . can never be safe from the spears and
barbed irons which their ambitions and presumed
interest will provide."

In *Mr Hobbes' State of Nature Considered* (1672) the
Reverend John Eachard attacks Hobbes's view that
government is necessary because human beings are
wicked (actually, Hobbes expressly denied that
human nature is evil, saying in *Leviathan* that "The
Desires, and other Passions of man, are in themselves
no Sin. No more are the Actions, that proceed from
those Passions, till they know a Law that forbids
them: which till Lawes be made they cannot know:
nor can any Law be made, till they have agreed upon
the Person that shall make it"), and the lawyer John
Whitehall, in his *The Leviathan Found Out* (1679),
argues that Hobbes's book undermines both allegiance and property. John Dowel, in *The Leviathan
Heretical* (1683), charges that Hobbes accepted an
offer from Oliver Cromwell to defend the position of
the parliamentarian leaders against the crown. In his
two courses of Boyle lectures (1704–1705) Samuel
Clarke defends morality and free will against Hobbes.
The attacks and counterattacks may have contributed to the decision not to admit Hobbes as a member of the Royal Society of London after its founding
in 1660. Martinich suggests, however, that some
members of the society were keen to exclude him not
because they opposed his views but because those
views were too close to their own, knowledge of
which they were anxious to suppress.

Hobbes had aroused the hostility of the authorities in Roman Catholic France because of his antipa-
pist views; also, some of those around the Prince of
Wales thought that his denial of the divine right of
kings, and his claim that a subject only owed obedience to a sovereign as long as the sovereign was able
to provide protection, were attempts to legitimitize
Cromwell's rule. Feeling more endangered in France
than in England, therefore, Hobbes secretly fled back
home at the end of 1651. The following year he submitted to the Council of State of the Protectorate. He
returned to the Cavendish family in 1653 and spent
the rest of his life in their employ, although he continued to live in Fetter Lane so as to be close to the intellectual stimulation of London. During the next few
years he presented and connected his mature thoughts
on metaphysics, psychology, and political philosophy.

The major works of Hobbes's tripartite *Elementorum Philosophiae* (Elements of Philosophy) are *De Corpore, De Homine* (1658), and *De Cive* (1642), in which he intended to deal successively with matter, human nature, and society. *Elementorum Philosophiae* was never published as a whole, however, and the three parts appeared out of logical order: *De Corpore* is sequentially the first work in the set, though it was the second of the three to appear in print. *De Homine,* dealing with psychology, comes second but was published last. *De Cive,* which gives his political and religious theories, was published first, in 1642, though it is logically the third of the three parts.

De Corpore is an important document in the history of science, representing the shift from Aristotelian to modern scientific thought. It is divided into four parts: on logic; on the geometric proportions of motions; on magnitudes; and on physics, or the phenomena of nature. At the beginning of *De Corpore* Hobbes defines philosophy as the knowledge of effects or phenomena that is acquired through proper reasoning, which is, in turn, defined as computation, or the addition and subtraction of ideas or "phantasms." This knowledge can be achieved by two methods. The first, the analytic method, involves beginning with an effect and constructing hypotheses about its causes. The second method, the synthetic, entails commencing with a cause and explaining how it generates an effect. *De Homine* includes material that Hobbes covers more extensively elsewhere, and more than half of it is taken up with a discussion of optics. It is considered the least successful of the three books that comprise *Elementorum Philosophiae*. A translation of the last six chapters of *De Homine* was published in 1972, but, unlike the other two parts of the trilogy, the work has never been completely translated into English. *De Cive* was originally written and published in Latin, and it is customary to refer to the English translation by the Latin title, even though it appeared as *Philosophicall Rudiments Concerning Government and Society* in 1651. *De Cive* is divided into three parts, "Of Liberty" (*Libertas*), "Of Dominion" (*Imperium*), and "Of Religion" (*Religio*). "Of Liberty" sets out the theory Hobbes later employed in *Leviathan:* that human beings are not naturally social and that their cooperation needs to be guaranteed by covenants. "Of Dominion" discusses the causes and origin of government, the kinds of government, the nature and duties of sovereignty, the nature of civil law, and the causes of the dissolution of governments. "Of Religion" describes the relation between human and divine law and attempts to demonstrate that it is virtually impossible for a conflict between human and divine law to exist.

After the Restoration in 1660, Charles II granted his old tutor an annual pension. He could do nothing, however, to stop a bill in the House of Commons banning blasphemous books, among which *Leviathan* was listed. Hobbes was forbidden to publish any political or religious books, and those already in print were burned. In 1666, with some people believing that the London plague of 1665 and the Great Fire of 1666 were God's punishment for Hobbes's presence in the city, charges of heresy were brought against him in Parliament. Although nothing came of the allegations, Hobbes's investigation of the subject, as he prepared to defend himself, resulted in the posthumously published *An Historical Narration Concerning Heresie, And the Punishment thereof* (1680).

In 1674 Hobbes published his letter to the English antiquary Anthony à Wood, author of the *Historia et antiquitates universitatis Oxoniensis* (History and Antiquities of Oxford University, 1674). The epistle takes the form of a complaint to the king in answer to scurrilous passages that John Fell, dean of Christ Church, had attached to some autobiographical material Hobbes had entrusted to Wood for publication in his history of Oxford. Fell, who financed Wood's venture in part, excised without authorization several passages from Hobbes's vita and altered other parts of the narrative, damning *Leviathan* and intimating that *De Cive* was intended to stir up trouble. During this period Hobbes embarked on a translation of Homer in quatrains, publishing his rendition of the *Odyssey* in 1675 and of the *Iliad* the following year.

In 1675 Hobbes left London to live out the rest of his life between Hardwick and Chatsworth, the seats of the Devonshire family. Hobbes died at Hardwick on 4 December 1679. He is buried in the parish church of Hault Hucknall, beside the park of Hardwick Hall. A black marble slab bears the inscription "vers probus et fama eruditionis domi forisque bene cognitus" (an upright man well-known at home and abroad for his learning).

Behemoth, finished around 1668, is Hobbes's history of the English Civil Wars and the Interregnum. It was suppressed on the orders of Charles II, though a surreptitious edition appeared in 1679 under the title *The History of the Civil Wars of England. From the Year 1640, to 1660.* The first authorized edition was brought out by Hobbes's publisher, William Crooke, in 1682, three years after Hobbes's death, as part of *Tracts of Thomas Hobb's. Behemoth* consists of a series of dialogues between "A," who has lived through the wars, and "B," a younger person. In the first dialogue Hobbes establishes the legitimacy of the Stuart monarchy and attacks the Jesuits and

Hardwick Hall in Derbyshire, one of the homes of the Cavendish family, where Hobbes died in 1679

Roman Catholicism for their part in the Gunpowder Plot and for pre-Reformation abuses. The political dimensions of clerical celibacy, the confession of sins, the doctrine of transubstantiation, and the nature of heresy are detailed, after which the role of Presbyterianism in bringing on the conflict is elaborated. In the second dialogue Hobbes defends the three people closest to Charles I–Queen Henrietta Maria, Thomas Wentworth (Lord Stafford), and Archbishop William Laud–from the charge that they corrupted the king. The dialogue features a defense of the Anglican Church and an extended discussion of the improprieties of the Grand Remonstrance of 1641 and the Nineteen Propositions of 1642. The third and fourth dialogues comprise largely a narrative of the war through the time of Charles I's execution and a discussion of the Protectorate, respectively; according to Hobbes, they are based on James Heath's *A Briefe Chronicle of the Intestine War in the Three Kingdoms of England, Scotland and Ireland* (1663). *Behemoth* reinforces Hobbes's contention in *Leviathan* that only a strong ruler who has the absolute allegiance of the people can prevent civil war.

Hobbes was lampooned in seventeenth-century sermons, plays, and other literary works of the period. He is one of the three impostors, along with Baruch Spinoza and Edward, Lord Herbert of Cherbury, in Christian Kortholt's *De Tribus Impostoribus Magnus Liber* (1680). In the anonymous miscellany *Twelve Ingenious Characters* (1686) Hobbes is a dissolute town fop. The hypocritical debauchee carries a copy of Hobbes's work in his pocket in George Farquhar's farcical comedy *The Constant Couple,* produced in 1699. Francis Atterbury holds Hobbes up as a warning in a sermon on "the terrors of conscience," which was included in his *Sermons upon Several Occasions* (1734). In the Victorian period the Hobbesean assumption that self-interest is the prime motivation behind human conduct was absorbed by Jeremy Bentham into the utilitarian philosophy, which was reacted against by Thomas Carlyle, John Ruskin, and other Victorian prophet-sages. His work continues to influence political philosophy.

The most widely used versions of Hobbes's collected works are those prepared by Sir William Molesworth: the eleven-volume *English Works of Thomas Hobbes of Malmesbury* (1839–1845) and the five-volume *Thomæ Hobbes Malmsburiensis Opera Philosophica Quæ Latine Scripsit Omnia in Unum Corpus Nunc Primum Collecta* (1839–1845). These collections are incomplete and are now regarded as inaccurate, but nothing of comparable scope exists. Three previously unknown writings by the young Hobbes were discovered and published in 1995 as *Thomas Hobbes: Three Discourses.* Editions of individual works are being regularly brought to press–the 1998 Cambridge University Press edition *On the Citizen,* for example, is a new translation of *De Cive.* The Clarendon Press at Oxford has begun publishing a complete edition of the works, which is expected to be in progress for some years.

Letters:

The Correspondence of Thomas Hobbes, 2 volumes, edited by Noel Malcolm (New York & Oxford: Cambridge University Press, 1994).

Bibliographies:

Hugh MacDonald and Mary Hargreaves, *Thomas Hobbes: A Bibliography* (London: Bibliographical Society, 1952);

William Sacksteder, *Hobbes Studies (1879–1979): A Bibliography* (Bowling Green, Ohio: Bowling Green State Press, 1982);

Alfred Garcia, *Thomas Hobbes: Bibliographie Internationale de 1620 à 1986* (Caen, France: Centre de Philosophie Politique et Juridique, Université de Caen, 1986).

Biographies:

Richard Blackbourne, *Vitae Hobbianæ Auctarium,* in *Thomae Hobbes Angli Malmesburiensis Vita* (London: G. Crooke, 1681);

Andrew Clark, ed., *Aubrey's "Brief Lives," Chiefly of Contemporaries, Set Down by John Aubrey Between 1669 and 1696,* 2 volumes (Oxford: Clarendon Press, 1898);

Leslie Stephen, *Hobbes* (London: Macmillan, 1904);

John Laird, *Hobbes* (London: Benn / New York: Van Nostrand, 1934);

Richard Peters, *Hobbes* (Harmondsworth: Penguin, 1956; Westport, Conn.: Greenwood Press, 1979);

Arnold A. Rogow, *Thomas Hobbes: Radical in the Service of Reaction* (New York & London: Norton, 1986);

Richard Tuck, *Hobbes* (Oxford & New York: Oxford University Press, 1989);

Bruno Dix, *Lebensgefahrdung and Verpflichtung bei Hobbes* (Wurzburg, Germany: Konigshausen & Neumann, 1994);

A. P. Martinich, *Hobbes: A Biography* (Cambridge & New York: Cambridge University Press, 1999).

References:

John Bowl, *Hobbes and His Critics: A Study in Seventeenth-century Constitutionalism* (New York & London: Barnes & Noble, 1969);

Austin Clark, "Beliefs and Desires Incorporated," *Journal of Philosophy,* 91 (August 1994): 404–425;

C. A. J. Coady, "The Beautiful Axiom," *Philosophy,* 65 (January 1990): 4–17;

Maurice W. Cranston and Richard S. Peters, eds., *Hobbes and Rousseau: A Collection of Critical Essays* (Garden City, N.Y.: Anchor, 1972);

Renee J. Dalitz, "The Subjection of Women in the Contractual Society," in *Empirical Logic and Public Debate,* edited by Erik C. W. Krabbe (Amsterdam: Rodopi, 1993);

John Deigh, "Reason and Ethics in Hobbes's *Leviathan,*" *Journal of the History of Philosophy,* 34 (January 1996): 33–60;

Mary G. Dietz, ed., *Hobbes and Political Theory* (Lawrence: University of Kansas Press, 1990);

Daniel Flage, "Hume's Hobbism and His Anti-Hobbism," *Hume Studies,* 15 (Spring 1993): 51–59;

M. M. Goldsmith, *Hobbes's Science of Politics* (New York: Columbia University Press, 1966);

Leslie Friedman Goldstein, "Early European Feminism and American Women," in *Women's Rights and the Rights of Man,* edited by Andre Jean Arnaud (Aberdeen & Oxford: Aberdeen University Press, 1990);

Karen Green, "Christine de Pisan and Thomas Hobbes," *Philosophical Quarterly,* 44 (October 1994): 456–475;

Ian Harris and John Dunn, eds., *Hobbes* (Cheltenham, U.K. & Lyme, N.H.: Edward Elgar, 1997);

Charles H. Hinnant, *Thomas Hobbes* (Boston: Twayne, 1977);

Hinnant, *Thomas Hobbes: A Reference Guide* (Boston: Hall, 1980);

David C. Johnston, *Leviathan: Authoritative Text, Background, Interpretation* (New York & London: Norton, 1997);

Johnston, *The Rhetoric of Leviathan: Thomas Hobbes and the Politics of Cultural Transformation* (Princeton & Guilford: Princeton University Press, 1986);

A. P. Martinich, *A Hobbes Dictionary* (Oxford & Cambridge, Mass.: Blackwell, 1995);

Martinich, "On the Proper Interpretation of Hobbes's Philosophy," *Journal of the History of Philosophy,* 34 (April 1996): 273–283;

Audrey McKinney, "Hobbes and the State of Nature: Where Are the Women?" *Southwestern Journal of Philosophy,* 15 (Spring 1993): 51–56;

Jurgen Moltmann, "Covenant or Leviathan? Political Theory for Modern Times," translated by Nancy

Elizabeth Bedford, *Scottish Journal of Theology,* 47 (1994): 19–41;

Michael Oakeshott, *Hobbes on Civil Action* (Oxford: Blackwell, 1975; Berkeley: University of California Press, 1975);

Linda Levy Peck, "Hobbes on the Grand Tour: Paris, Venice, or London?" *Journal of the History of Ideas,* 57 (January 1996): 177–183;

G. A. J. Rogers, ed., *Critical Responses to Hobbes* (London: Routledge/Thoemmes, 1997);

Rogers, ed., *Leviathan: Contemporary Responses to the Political Theory of Thomas Hobbes* (Bristol: Thoemmes, 1995);

Rogers and Alan Ryan, eds., *Perspectives on Thomas Hobbes* (Oxford: Clarendon Press, 1988);

Rogers, J. M. Vienne, and Y. C. Zarka, eds., *The Cambridge Platonists in Philosophical Context: Politics, Metaphysics, and Religion* (Dordrecht & Boston: Kluwer, 1997);

Ralph Ross, Herbert W. Schneider, and Theodore Waldman, eds., *Thomas Hobbes in His Time* (Minneapolis: University of Minnesota Press, 1974);

William Sacksteder, "How Much of Hobbes Might Spinoza Have Read?" *Southwestern Journal of Philosophy,* 11 (Summer 1980): 25–40;

Quentin Skinner, *Reason and Rhetoric in the Philosophy of Hobbes* (Cambridge & New York: Cambridge University Press, 1996);

Tom Sorell, ed., *The Cambridge Companion to Hobbes* (Cambridge: Cambridge University Press, 1996);

Patricia Springborg, "Hobbes, Heresy, and the *Historia Ecclesiastica*," *Journal of the History of Ideas,* 55 (October 1994): 553–571;

Charles D. Tarlton, "'The Word for the Deed': Hobbes's Two Versions of *Leviathan*," *New Literary History,* 27 (Autumn 1996): 785–802;

Richard Tuck, *Philosophy and Government, 1572–1651* (Cambridge & New York: Cambridge University Press, 1993);

John W. N. Watkins, *Hobbes's System of Ideas: A Study in the Political Significance of Philosophical Theories* (London: Hutchinson, 1965);

Sheldon S. Wolin, *Hobbes and the Epic Tradition of Political Theory* (Los Angeles: University of California Press, 1970);

Frederick J. E. Woodbridge, ed., *The Philosophy of Hobbes* (Minneapolis: Wilson, 1903);

Michael Zuckert, "Hobbes, Locke, and the Problem of the Rule of Law," *Nomos,* 36 (1994): 63–79.

Papers:

The Bodleian Library, Oxford University, is a major repository of Thomas Hobbes's letters, documents, and first editions of his works. The MS Hardwick is at Chatsworth House. Collections of letters and papers are at Harvard University and at the Huntington Library, San Marino, California. Manuscript holdings are also collected at Hardwick Hall, the National Library of Wales, the British Library, the Royal Society of London, and Dr. Williams's Library in London.

David Hume

(7 May 1711 – 25 August 1776)

Peter S. Fosl
Transylvania University

BOOKS: *A Treatise of Human Nature: Being An Attempt to introduce the experimental Method of Reasoning into Moral Subjects,* 2 volumes, anonymous (London: John Noon, 1739);

A Treatise of Human Nature: Being An Attempt to introduce the experimental Method of Reasoning into Moral Subjects. With an Appendix. Wherein Some Passages of the Foregoing Volume Are Illustrated and Explained. Vol. III. Of Morals, anonymous (London: Thomas Longman, 1740);

An Abstract of a Book Lately Published; Entitled, a Treatise of Human Nature, etc. Wherein the Chief Argument of That Book is Farther Illustrated and Explained (London: Printed for C. Borbet [i.e., Corbet], 1740);

Essays, Moral and Political, 2 volumes, anonymous; volume 1 (Edinburgh: Printed by R. Fleming & A. Alison for Alexander Kincaid, 1741; revised, 1742); volume 2 (Edinburgh: Printed by R. Fleming & A. Alison for Alexander Kincaid, 1742); volumes 1 and 2 republished with *Three Essays, Moral and Political* (1748) as *Essays, Moral and Political,* third edition, corrected, with additions, 1 volume (London: Printed for A. Millar and for A. Kincaid, Edinburgh, 1748);

A Letter from a Gentleman to his Friend in Edinburgh: containing some Observations on a Specimen of the Principles Concerning Religion and Morality, said to be Maintain'd in a Book lately Publish'd, Intitled, A Treatise of Human Nature &c., anonymous (Edinburgh, 1745);

A True Account of the Behaviour and Conduct of Archibald Stewart, Esq.; late Lord Provost of Edinburgh. In a letter to a Friend, anonymous (London: Printed for M. Cooper, 1748);

Three Essays, Moral and Political: Never before Published (London: A. Millar; Edinburgh: A. Kincaid, 1748);

Philosophical Essays Concerning Human Understanding (London: Printed for A. Millar, 1748; revised edition, London: Printed for M. Cooper, 1751); republished as *An Enquiry Concerning Human Understanding* in *Essays and Treatises on Several Subjects* (London:

*David Hume; portrait by Allan Ramsay, 1766
(Scottish National Potrait Gallery)*

Printed for A. Millar and for A. Kincaid & A. Donaldson, Edinburgh, 1758);

An Enquiry concerning the Principles of Morals (London: Printed for A. Millar, 1751);

Political Discourses (Edinburgh: Printed by R. Fleming for A. Kincaid & A. Donaldson, 1752);

Scotticisms, anonymous (N.p., 1752?);

Essays and Treatises on Several Subjects, 4 volumes (London: Printed for A. Millar and for A. Kincaid & A. Donaldson, Edinburgh, 1753; revised, 1753–1756; revised again, 1 volume, 1758; revised again, 4 volumes, 1760; revised again, 2 volumes, 1764; revised again, London: Printed for A.

Millar and for A. Kincaid, J. Bell & A. Donaldson, Edinburgh, and sold by T. Cadell, 1768; revised again, 4 volumes, London: Printed for T. Cadell and A. Kincaid & A. Donaldson, Edinburgh, 1770; revised posthumous edition, 2 volumes, with author's last corrections, London: Printed for T. Cadell and A. Donaldson & W. Creech, Edinburgh, 1777);

The History of Great Britain, Vol. I, Containing the reigns of James I and Charles I (Edinburgh: Hamilton, Balfour & Neill, 1754; revised edition, London: A. Millar, 1759);

Four Dissertations (London: Printed for A. Millar, 1757);

The History of Great Britain, Vol. II, Containing the Commonwealth, and the Reigns of Charles II and James II (London: Printed for A. Millar, 1757; revised, 1759);

The history of England, under the house of Tudor: Comprehending the reigns of K. Henry VII. K. Henry VIII. K. Edward VI. Q. Mary, and Q. Elizabeth, 2 volumes (London: Printed for A. Millar, 1759);

The history of the proceedings in the case of Margaret, Commonly called Peg, only lawful sister to John Bull, esq., anonymous (London: W. Owen, 1760);

The history of England, from the invasion of Julius Caesar to the accession of Henry VII, 2 volumes (London: Printed for A. Millar, 1762);

The history of England, from the invasion of Julius Caesar to the Revolution in 1688 (6 volumes, London: Printed for A. Millar, 1762; revised, 8 volumes, 1763; posthumous edition with Hume's final revisions, London: Printed for T. Cadell, 1778);

Exposé succinct de la contestation qui s'est élevée entre M. Hume et M. Rousseau, avec les pièces justificatives, anonymous (Paris, 1766); translated as *A Concise and Genuine Account of the Dispute between Mr. Hume and Mr. Rousseau* (London: Printed for T. Becket & P. A. DeHondt, 1766);

The Life of David Hume, Esq. Written by Himself (London: W. Strahan & T. Cadell, 1777);

Two Essays (London, 1777);

Dialogues concerning Natural Religion (London: Printed for Robinson, 1779);

Essays on Suicide, and The Immortality of the Soul, Ascribed to the late David Hume, Esq. Never before published. With Remarks, intended as an Antidote to the Poison contained in these Performances, by the Editor. To Which is Added, Two Letters on Suicide, from Rosseau's [sic] Eloisa (London: Printed for M. Smith, 1783).

Editions and Collections: *The Philosophical Works of David Hume* (Edinburgh: Constable, 1825; Boston: Little, Brown, 1854);

David Hume: The Philosophical Works, 4 volumes, edited by Thomas Hill Green and Thomas Hodge Grose (London: Longmans, Green, Reader & Dyer, 1874–1875);

A Treatise of Human Nature, edited by L. A. Selby-Bigge (Oxford: Clarendon Press, 1888; second edition, with text revised and variant readings by Nidditch, 1978);

Enquiries concerning Human Understanding and concerning the Principles of Morals, edited, with an introduction, by Selby-Bigge (Oxford: Clarendon Press, 1894; third edition, revised by P. H. Nidditch, 1975);

Dialogues concerning Natural Religion, edited, with an introduction, by Norman Kemp Smith (Oxford: Clarendon Press, 1935);

History of England: from the Invasion of Julius Caesar to the Revolution of 1688, 6 volumes (Indianapolis: Liberty Classics, 1983–1985);

Essays: Moral, Political, and Literary, edited by Eugene F. Miller (Indianapolis: Liberty Classics, 1985);

The Natural History of Religion, edited by James Fieser (New York: Macmillan, 1992);

Enquiry concerning the Principles of Morals: A Critical Edition, edited by Tom L. Beauchamp (Oxford: Clarendon Press, 1998);

A Treatise of Human Nature, edited by David Fate Norton and Mary J. Norton, introduction by David Fate Norton (Oxford: Oxford University Press, 2000).

OTHER: *Petition of the Grave and Venerable Bellmen, or Sextons, of the Church of Scotland, To the Honourable House of Commons,* a skit (1751); accompanied by "A Letter to Member of Parliament" by the pseudonymous "Zorababel M'Gilchrist";

Introduction to *Essays and Observation, Physical and Literary, Read before a Society in Edinburgh and Published by Them,* edited by Hume and Alexander Monro (Edinburgh, 1754);

Anonymous letter concerning the *Epigoniad* by William Wilkie, *Critical Review,* 7 (April 1759): 323–334;

"Réflexions sur les doutes historique, par Mr. D. Hume," in *Mémoires littéraires de la grande bretagne pour l'an 1768,* edited by Edward Gibbon and George Deyverdun (London: T. Becket & P. A. DeHondt, 1768);

Christof Hermann von Manstein, *Memoirs of Russia, Historical, Political, and Military, from the Year MDCCXXVII to MDCCXLIV: A Period Comprehending Many Remarkable Events, in particular the wars of Russia with Turkey and Sweden, with a Supplement, Containing a Summary Account of the State of the Military, the Marine, the Commerce, &c. of that great Empire,* edited, with a preface, by Hume (London: Printed for T. Becket & P. A. DeHondt, 1770).

Called the "Great Infidel" by some and "*le bon David*" by others, David Hume was and has remained one of the most important British philosophers, essayists, and historians of the eighteenth century. Though Hume is known today in most circles for his contributions to philosophy, during his own lifetime he was renowned for his moral, political, and critical essays and for his *The history of England, from the invasion of Julius Caesar to the Revolution in 1688* (1762), the vehicle that principally carried his name into the nineteenth century. Hume himself believed his thinking to be important and revolutionary, writing about his first philosophical work, *A Treatise of Human Nature: Being An Attempt to introduce the experimental Method of Reasoning into Moral Subjects* (1739), that its principles are "so remote from the vulgar Sentiments on this Subject, that were they to take place, they wou'd produce almost a total Alteration in Philosophy."

Hume achieved the distinction of becoming the first major British writer to support himself independently of patronage or subscriptions, relying instead solely on the proceeds he reaped from book sales. If the philosophical implications of his thought were slowly received, they were nevertheless profound. Immanuel Kant, in whose work so much of subsequent continental philosophy is rooted, credited Hume with awakening him from his "dogmatic slumbers," that is, his adherence to speculative rationalism. Many of the central concepts and terms of criticism characterizing twentieth-century Anglo-American philosophy also find precedent in Hume. Hume's philosophical thought has been influential, especially after about 1925, in epistemology, philosophy of science, philosophy of religion, ethics, social-political philosophy, and aesthetics. The influence of Hume's political works has been more sustained over time, making its mark on not only British intellectuals but also founding figures of the United States, including Benjamin Franklin, Alexander Hamilton, and quite possibly James Madison. Hume's impact on eighteenth-century French social theorists was still more extensive. Yet, for all its influence and for all its indebtedness to contemporary and precedent intellectual strains in the eighteenth century, Hume's thought is also profoundly critical of the philosophical currents of his time. Indeed, in many ways the critical and skeptical dynamics of early modern culture reach their climax in Hume.

Hume was born David Home on 7 May (26 April, old style) 1711, to Joseph Home of Ninewells and Katherine Falconer, probably in their apartment on the south side of the Lawnmarket in Edinburgh, just east of the castle. Hume was the youngest of three children and the second son born to the couple, his siblings including Joseph, the oldest child, and Katherine. Hume's family had achieved moderate wealth and

Henry Home, Lord Kames, Hume's cousin and philosophical ally; portrait by David Martin (from J. Y. T. Greig, David Hume, 1931)

standing amid what would then have been called the middling ranks of eighteenth-century Scottish society. While Hume's adoption of a different spelling for his surname in his early twenties reflected a wish to have its Scottish pronunciation conform to English norms of spelling (and perhaps also Hume's desire to be recognized and accepted by English society), the new spelling is nevertheless consistent with that used by some of his ancestors, for example, his great-uncle Robert Hume of Hutton Hall.

Hume's family in Berwickshire can be traced as far back as 1138, though the estate around which his family centered itself, Ninewells, was established by Robert Hume's brother, George Home, much more recently, in the early sixteenth century. Hume's ancestral line was distinguished in politics and in the military. His paternal grandfather, John Home of Ninewells, was captain of the dragoon and, under banners carrying the family motto, *Jamais arrière* (Never behind), fought in Argyll for William and Mary against the viscount of Dundee. (Later the family took another motto: "True to the End.") Though at least nominally a Presbyterian, John Home was not a religious enthusiast, and he took part without pause in the prosecution and suppression of rebellious Scottish Covenanters during the late seventeenth century. Hume's more immediate predecessors, however, more often found their principal occupation in the law.

Hume's mother, Lady Katherine Home, née Falconer, was also stepsister to his father, a relationship not considered improper for marriage at the time. Her family hailed from the earls of Kintore, and her father, Sir David Falconer, who was perhaps Hume's namesake, had pursued a successful legal and political career. Dying in 1685, Sir David was buried in the Greyfriars cemetery in Edinburgh.

Joseph Home, Hume's father, lived a life of moderate distinction. Having attended the University of Edinburgh, he became an advocate in 1705 and the next year was made a burgess and a guild brother, *gratis,* by an act of the town council in Edinburgh. Hume, however, little knew this man, who died just five years after his marriage to Katherine and two years after Hume's birth. Lady Katherine never remarried. According to Hume's autobiography, *The Life of David Hume, Esq. Written by Himself* (1777), "My father, who passed for a man of parts, died when I was an infant, leaving me, with an elder brother and a sister, under the care of our mother, a woman of singular merit, who, though young and handsome, devoted herself entirely to the rearing and educating of her children."

The Homes of Ninewells were lowland Scots. Their estate was situated on the outskirts of the small village of Chirnside in Berwickshire, ten miles northwest of the town of Berwick-Upon-Tweed and the often-violated border with England. Hume's family was Whiggish in its sympathies, but on the side of moderate, "Political Whigs" rather than what Hume would have called "Religious Whigs." The Homes, then, were firmly anti-Jacobite (in other words, against the Pretender King James II and his heirs), supported the Revolution of 1688, the parliamentary union of Scotland with England in 1707, and the Hanoverian succession of 1714; but their support was animated by secular concerns rather than religious dogmatics.

Although Hume's mother was devout, the faith and practice of his family would have generally been temperate and resistant to the stridency characteristic of the more radical Presbyterians, or, as they were then often called, "high flyers." The Homes would have had nothing to do, for example, with the prosecution of witches, which continued in Scotland until well into the eighteenth century (the Anti-Witchcraft Act not having been repealed until 1728) or with the theocratic aspirations of the Kirk's general assembly. Rather, their tendencies were, relatively speaking, toward the secular, the moderate, the liberal, and the humane. Hume was to preserve something of this same sensibility throughout his life. He was, apparently, "religious when he was young," going so far as

to catalogue the vices set out in the *Whole Duty of Man* (1658), Richard Allestree's popular and influential book of religious didactics, to see how many of them he could detect within himself. Hume also, during those years, seems to have accepted John Knox's Calvinistic doctrines of original sin, the total depravity of human nature, predestination, and election. He was, however, never terribly passionate about such things and appears to have permanently lost his religious conviction (or at least his faith in Christianity) while attending or soon after leaving the university of Edinburgh. Later, as an adult, although Hume remained a consistent and severe critic of religious "enthusiasm" and superstition, regarding its effects to be among the most pernicious elements with which his society had to then struggle, he also maintained affable and even intimate relations with many of the liberal clergy of the Kirk. Like his views on religion, Hume's political philosophy was also simultaneously critical, moderate, and progressive. While he attacked established political norms and produced trenchant criticisms of Whiggish radicalism, the general thrust of Hume's political work was also in many ways supportive of the new political and commercial order unfolding around him.

Hume's early years seem to have been remarkably bookish. Writing in an important autobiographical letter of 1734, he remarked that "from my earliest Infancy, I found alwise a strong Inclination to Books & Letters." Forty-two years later, in his autobiography Hume describes himself as having been "seized very early with a passion for Literature which has been the ruling Passion of my Life, and the great Source of my Enjoyments." Most likely the young Hume would have been provided a private tutor, probably a young clergyman just out of college, in addition to receiving instruction from his mother and inspiration from his siblings, relatives, and pastor. Efforts would have been made to instruct at least the male children in languages, mathematics, and natural science (or, as it was then called, "natural philosophy"). Being a family of respectable means, many of whose male members typically pursued careers in the law, the household would have been provided with a fairly well-stocked library. Children in the family would have read didactic and religious material as well as, perhaps, fabulous, historical, and classical literature. Books in the library would have probably included works by William Shakespeare, John Dryden, John Milton, Alexander Pope, and assorted classical authors in Greek and, especially, Latin. Since the family would have been interested in fostering socially essential manners and insight in their aspiring sons, copies of Joseph Addison and Richard Steele's influential *Tatler* and *Spectator* periodicals would have also been on hand.

On 27 February 1723, at the age of eleven, "David Home" signed the University of Edinburgh's Matriculation Book under the page set aside for William Scott, professor of Greek. Hume's older brother, Joseph, matriculated under the same professor a few days later. Hume's age on entering the university would not have been terribly remarkable at the time, though perhaps he would have been a year or two younger than the average first-year university student.

Founded in 1582, the University of Edinburgh was located in 1723 on much the same site it is presently, though in Hume's time its situation placed the university at the southern extremity of the city, adjacent to the Potter Row Port in the ancient city wall. The elegant and sturdy eighteenth-century buildings of the New College of the university were unknown to Hume, having not been constructed until 1789, when Edinburgh embarked on a heady program of urban planning, renovation, and construction. Although certainly by his day it had acquired the reputation of being the most important university in Scotland, the physical plant of the university was poor.

Despite its appearance, the university Hume attended was remarkably vital and a different institution from the one that had educated his father twenty-six years earlier. The University of Edinburgh attended by Joseph Home in 1697 was run on a regent system whereby students matriculated under the tutelage of a single instructor and received all (or at least most) of their instruction from him. The leadership of the university, however, was even then exceedingly progressive in its pedagogical views and had been impressed by innovations instituted in the Netherlands at the universities of Leyden and Utrecht. Dutch thought and Dutch liberalism had been particularly influential among the law faculty in Edinburgh, where courses in jurisprudence devoted ample time to Dutch legal theorists such as Hugo Grotius.

In 1708, through the initiative of Principal William Carstares and other progressive figures, Edinburgh discarded its regency and adopted the new and innovative professorial system, under which students received instruction from different professors, each lecturing on his own specialty. An English traveler remarked in the year of Hume's matriculation that "In studying four Years at this College you commence Master of arts: The Scholars are not in Commons, and kept to strict Rules as in the College in *England,* nor wear Gowns; they lodge and diet in the Town, as at the College in *Holland,* and are required to attend their several Classes from eight in the Morning till twelve, and from two to four." As did the professors, Hume too probably took his lodgings in town, in his case at the family's "land," or apartment, in one of the towering, thin, and

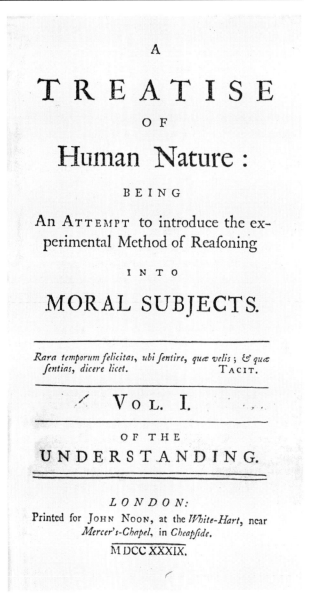

Title page for Hume's great work of epistemology and ethics, which was unappreciated in its time (courtesy of Special Collections, Thomas Cooper Library, University of South Carolina)

crowded tenement buildings of the High Street near the Edinburgh castle keep.

The curriculum offered to students in Hume's time was a four-year program of study. Students' first year was normally devoted to Latin under the direction of Professor of Humanity Laurence Dundas. The *bajan,* or second year, followed a course in Greek under Professor of Greek and Philosophy William Scot. The influence of the Dutch on Scot was particularly pronounced in an abridged edition of Grotius's ethical treatise, *De Jure Belli ac Pacis* (On the Law of War and Peace, 1625), which he edited. Through Scot, Hume may well have been exposed to this text and its ideas. Inasmuch as Hume matriculated under Scot, his three years of attendance likely followed the program of the second through fourth years, an indication that his Latin was already sufficiently competent or that he was receiving training in that language by some other means.

The *semi,* or third year, of the undergraduate program addressed rational and instrumental philosophy, which comprised topics in logic and metaphysics, including philosophy of mind, under the tutelage of Professor Colin Drummond. The fourth-year, or *magistrand,* class was devoted to natural philosophy, which at the time would have been emphatically Newtonian in its cast, under the direction of Professor Robert Stewart. Insofar as skepticism was a central topic of conversations occupying the scientific community of Edinburgh at the time, the fourth-year course would, however, not have been without some measure of anti-Newtonian criticism. Hume entered a subscription to Stewart's Physiological Library in 1724, and among the texts housed in the collection were several addressing skepticism in science, including Joseph Glanvill's important *Scepsis Scientifica or, Confest Ignorance, The Way to Science; in an Essay of the Vanity of Dogmatizing and Confident Opinion* (1665). Since Stewart had begun his academic career a Cartesian, only later converting to Newtonianism, he likely presented Hume not only with the doctrines of the popular Newtonianism but with its Cartesian antecedents as well.

In addition to these four regular courses, the university also offered its students a set of electives including Professor James Gregory's course in mathematics, William Law's course in pneumatical and ethical philosophy, and Professor of Universal History Charles Mackie's course in history. As Stewart required of his students one year of college mathematics, there is reason to believe Hume was exposed to the ideas of Gregory's rather avant-garde Newtonianism. Law's course would have addressed topics such as the immortality of the soul, the nature and attributes of God, natural theology, the origin and principles of government, as well as the ethical writings of authors such as Marcus Aurelius, Cicero, and Samuel von Puffendorf—topics that all later occupied the mature Hume. Mackie's course was remarkable in teaching not only military and political history but also literary and cultural history. Besides proper "courses," regular and frequent public-lecture series were also offered by the university.

A student paper by Hume that survives from this period, "An Historical Essay on Chivalry and modern Honour," may have been written for a class, possibly Mackie's or Law's, or perhaps it served as one of the papers that students were required, under Principal William Wishart, to present and defend in the great hall of the university library. The essay describes and comments on the corruption of classical notions of virtue attendant on the rise of Gothic chivalry. Although his view of history became more sophisticated over time and did so in such a way as to guard him against trans-historical judgments, Hume never fully abandoned the dismissive and critical view of the Middle Ages so common among Enlightenment figures and so powerfully cast by such historians as Edward Gibbon.

Hume's access to books would have come in part through the university library, the thirteen-thousand-volume collection of which, however, was not available for lending. Its reading room opened only two hours a day in winter, four in summer. More probably, Hume would have been exposed to books through friends, private libraries such as that of Professor Stewart's, and bookshops, especially the progressive, well-stocked establishment run by Allan Ramsay in the Luckenbooths. Ramsay's shop, like others in Edinburgh, provided a site for intellectuals to gather, to read, and to converse with one another about the latest periodicals and publications. Ramsay's establishment also supported readers by making it possible for patrons to rent books as well as buy them. Ramsay's son, also named Allan, became an accomplished portrait painter and man of letters as well as one of Hume's closest friends.

Another important source of texts for Hume would have certainly been the Library of the Faculty of Advocates. Established in 1689, the Advocates' Library had become by the eighteenth century the principal library of polite Edinburgh. With holdings approaching thirty thousand volumes, a collection far greater than that of the University Library, the Advocates' Library possessed another advantage that was perhaps more important to a young scholar—it extended lending privileges to its members, members who would have included Hume's friends and relatives.

There were still other avenues of intellectual life in Edinburgh open to Hume during his formative years. Outside of the university programs and the bookstores and libraries, students would have been able to engage intellectual pursuits through private tutors and independent clubs. Clubs and societies organized around intellectual interests began sprouting up in greater and greater numbers in Edinburgh during the eighteenth century. That these gatherings structured themselves according to notions of sociability was no accident but rather reflected a growing conviction that the progress of the intellect was bound up with the cultivation of conversation and manners. As with French notions of politesse, the objective of such cultivation was not simply the production of pleasant affectations, the acquisition of instruments necessary to navigate successfully institutions of power and commerce, or even the advancement of reason and knowledge. Such conventions aimed at nothing short of the restructuring of society itself together with the selves composing that society. In France conversation and society are famous for having flourished in aristocratic salons. In Scotland, by contrast, in the absence of a royal court and with intellectual life centered more around urban rather than aristocratic life, conversation and society developed amid clubs and societies that often held their meetings in taverns, oyster bars, coffeehouses, and restaurants. Indeed, Edinburgh's intelligentsia became affectionately known as the *eaterati*.

Hume himself later joined and founded several such organizations, including the Poker Club, the Select Society, and the Philosophical Society. The society most likely to have influenced the young student Hume would have been the Rankenian Club, whose members included many among the faculty at Edinburgh, such as Wishart, Mackie, and Colin Maclaurin. The society initiated a correspondence with the Irish philosopher, professor at Trinity College, and bishop of Cloyne, George Berkeley, who was so impressed with their inquiries that he later offered the members of the group positions at his projected college in Bermuda. The interests of the group were acutely progressive, and its membership was clearly committed to engaging much of the most avant-garde thought of the day.

Aside from Berkeley's *A Treatise concerning the Principles of Human Knowledge* (1710), intellectual matters in the air during this time would have included John Locke's *Essay concerning Human Understanding* (1689), Lord Shaftesbury's *Characteristiks of Men, Manners, Opinions, and Times* (1711), and Bernard Mandeville's *Fable of the Bees* (1705–1729). Samuel Clarke's Boyle Lectures of 1704 ("A Demonstration of the Being and Attributes of God") and 1705 ("A Discourse Concerning the Unchangeable Obligations of Natural Religion") had become central to English rationalistic attempts to prove, in the words of its charter, "the Christian Religion, against notorious Infidels, viz. Atheists, Theists, Pagans." The lectures fortified the aspiration of natural theology, both Christian and deistic, to develop reasoned arguments demonstrating theological claims. Against many such arguments, Hume later advanced devastating criticisms in his *Dialogues concerning Natural Religion,* published in 1779 but first written in the 1750s.

Joseph Butler, later Anglican bishop of Durham and clerk of Queen Caroline's closet, had led the secular and naturalistic response to Clarke in a series of letters published in 1713 as well as in his later *Fifteen Sermons Preached at the Rolls Chapel* (1726). Butler argued that philosophers must abandon the rationalistic study of "abstract relations" in ethics in favor of focusing on "matters of fact, namely, what the particular nature of man is, its several parts, their economy or constitution;

from whence it proceeds to determine what course of life it is which is correspondent to this whole nature." In 1725 Francis Hutcheson, who later attained the chair in moral philosophy at the University of Glasgow in 1730, advanced the naturalistic project enormously with his *Inquiry into the Original of Our Ideas of Beauty and Virtue* (1725), a text that, like Butler's, attempted to base ethical reasoning on a naturalistic rendering of humanity.

Hume remarked to James Boswell on his deathbed on "excelling his school fellows," and he was likely a successful student. In any case he probably left the university in 1725 after the destruction by fire of his family's land on the Lawnmarket. A tall and somewhat awkward boy, nicknamed "The Clod" by his schoolmates, Hume judged the quality of his education to be rather poor. His schooling, however, must not have been entirely without merit, for as he remarks in the advertisement to the authoritative edition of his *Essays and Treatises on Several Subjects* (1777), *A Treatise of Human Nature* was "projected before he left College."

After leaving the university Hume returned to Ninewells, where he embarked on an intense and prolonged period of study that lasted for the next eight years. As the second son in a family structured around traditions of primogeniture, Hume was compelled to seek a career of his own. Since the law had figured so strongly in his family's history, and since advocates formed such an important part of Edinburgh's intelligentsia, it was natural for Hume's interest to be turned in the direction of the law. Accordingly, legal studies occupied much of the first four years of this period. Hume attended the Court of Session to learn procedure and studied classical rhetoric in order to acquire the skills necessary to prepare a successful brief and address judicial officials. In this regard his cousin Henry Home, Lord Kames, may have guided him.

Kames, fifteen years Hume's senior and an advocate in 1726, pursued intellectual matters beyond the law and became an active participant in the Edinburgh club scene as well as a popular figure among aspiring students. Kames entered a brief correspondence with Clarke in 1723 concerning topics in metaphysics. He developed a more sustained epistolary relationship, however, with Andrew Baxter, skeptic and author of *An Enquiry into the Nature of the Human Soul* (1733). Kames's correspondence with Baxter principally addressed causation, a topic that became of central importance to Hume. (Kames defended an Aristotelian view while Baxter offered criticisms and defended Isaac Newton's concept of inertia.) Kames remained an intellectual presence in Hume's life and answered his skepticism with *Essays on the Principles of Morality and Natural Religion* (1751). In 1738 Hume reminisced about the "philosophical Evenings" spent with Kames, and in a letter of 13–

A
LETTER
FROM A
GENTLEMAN
TO
His FRIEND in *Edinburgh*:
CONTAINING
Some OBSERVATIONS
ON
A Specimen of the Principles concerning
RELIGION and MORALITY,
said to be maintain'd in a Book lately pu-
blish'd, intituled, *A Treatise of Human
Nature*, &c.

EDINBURGH,
Pinted in the Year M. DCC. XLV.

Title page for Hume's anonymous defense of his A Treatise of Human
Nature *against accusations of heterodoxy brought by opponents of his
candidacy for a teaching post at the University of Edinburgh
(Royal Society of Edinburgh)*

15 June 1745 he remarked on "the Regret that I shou'd
have so little Prospect of passing my Life with you,
whom I always regarded as the best Friend, in every
Respect, I ever possest."

In the end Hume found the law unsatisfying, and
he became engrossed in philosophical work. Later, in a
letter written to a physician in March or April 1734,
Hume recalled: "After much study and reflection, . . .
when I was about 18 Years of Age, there seem'd to be
open'd up to me a new Scene of Thought, which transported me beyond Measure, & made me, with an Ardor
natural to young men, throw up every other Pleasure of
Business to apply entirely to it. The Law, which was the
Business I design'd to follow, appear'd nauseous to me,
& I cou'd think of no other way of pushing my Fortune
in the World, but that of a Scholar & Philosopher. I was
infinitely happy in this course of Life." Sometime in the
spring of 1729 Hume abandoned his legal training and
immersed himself in a feverish study of literature and
philosophy. "My studious Disposition, my Sobriety,

and my Industry gave my Family a Notion that the Law
was a proper profession for me: But I found an unsur-
mountable Aversion to every thing but the pursuits of
Philosophy and general learning; and while they fan-
cyed I was pouring over Voet and Vinnius, Cicero and
Virgil were the Authors I was secretly devouring."
Hume found himself drawn to Virgil, the man of letters, rather than Cicero, the man of law and government, and the former's life became "more the Subject
of" his "Ambition." The trajectory of his intellectual life
at this time was not simply general learning and the
passive assimilation of the theoretical work of others,
however. He aspired to make a name for himself. While
society, conversation, literature, and commerce had
been generally embraced as instruments for constructing a new intellectual as well as social order, Hume set
himself to do things the hard way. His reading became
more and more focused, especially around issues of
skepticism, and he began compiling notes and memoranda to be used in the construction of a full-blown
philosophical system. His interest in issues of moral philosophy surely would have been piqued by the joint
publication of Hutcheson's seminal *Essay on the Nature
and Conduct of the Passions and Affections* and *Illustrations
Upon the Moral Sense* in 1728.

Apparently at this time, Hume's loss of faith in
religion and his skeptical doubts about the capacities of
reason and morals began to crystallize. His memoranda
indicate that he had been examining the arguments for
atheism compiled by the Cambridge Platonist Ralph
Cudworth in his *The True Intellectual System of the Universe:
The First Part; Wherein, All the Reason and Philosophy of Atheism is Confuted; and Its Impossibility Demonstrated* (1678).
Hume may have also read or at least learned the principal arguments of Cudworth's posthumously published
sequel, *A Treatise concerning Eternal and Immutable Morality*
(1731), a text whose announcements and reviews
Hume surely would have perused during this time. His
memoranda indicate he had been reading William
Law's *De Origine Mali* (1702). Pierre Bayle's *Dictionnaire
historique et critique* (Historical and Critical Dictionary,
1697) had rocked the intellectual world with its incisive
deployment of skeptical reasoning; memoranda and letters indicate that Hume had consulted this text and perhaps Bayle's *Œuvres diverses* (Various works, 1727–1731)
by 1732.

Indeed, like Newtonianism, skepticism was a pervasive topic of the time, and it would not have been
possible for a vigorous scholar who frequented an intellectual center as fertile and current as Edinburgh to
have remained isolated from it. The medical community was even imbued with the issue. Dr. George
Young's 1730–1731 lectures at the University of Edinburgh, for example, address the topic "Why Do We

Believe the Sun Will Rise?" and exhibit a lively interest in skepticism. Surprising similarities are to be found between Young's lectures and what became Hume's analysis of causation, probability, and practice.

Hume may have also been reading at this time directly from the principal ancient skeptical text of Pyrrhonian skepticism, Sextus Empiricus's *Outlines of Pyrrhonism* (second century A.D.). Hume was familiar with Pyrrhonism—or at least a caricature of Pyrrhonism—by the time he wrote *A Treatise of Human Nature*. Later, in *An Enquiry concerning the Principles of Morals* (1751), *An Enquiry Concerning Human Understanding* (1758), the *Essays and Treatises,* and "On the Populousness of Ancient Nations" (first published in *Political Discourses,* 1752) he quotes directly from this text as well as from Sextus's *Adversus Mathematicos* (Against the Professors), but the character of his references indicate he was using the then outdated 1651 edition of Peter and Jacob Chouet rather than the popular and well-known Johannes A. Fabricius edition of 1718, an oddity that suggests he was using the volume of a private collection. The Chouet text was held by neither the Advocates' nor the university libraries; they did, however, acquire many of the Greek, Latin, and vernacular translations. For example, an English translation of Sextus's *Outlines* could be found in Thomas Stanley's extremely popular *History of Philosophy* (1655–1661). Stanley's text was used as a sourcebook for undergraduates by Professor Charles Mackie during Hume's time at the University of Edinburgh, and both the Advocates' and the university libraries owned copies. Skepticism was also a common topic in the periodical and review literature of the day, and Hume would have encountered it there.

The fame of Michel de Montaigne's *Apologie pour Raimond Seybond* (Apology for Raimond Seybond, 1580) may well have brought Pyrrhonism to Hume's attention through its pages. A large footnote in Hume's essay "The Sceptic" (1742) suggests that he had, at least by the time that essay was written, acquired more than a passing familiarity with Montaigne's work. He may also have been familiar with Peter Ramus's *Dialectique* (1555) or the work of Montaigne's intellectual heir, Pierre Charron, whose *Les trois véritez* (The three truths, 1594) and *La sagesse* (Wisdom, 1601) were enormously popular, as were skeptical texts by François de La Mothe Le Vayer such as *Petit Traité sceptique sur cette façon de parler, n'avoir pas le sens commun* (A Short Skeptical Treatise on Speech Devoid of Common Sense, 1647) and *Discours pour montres que les doutes de la philosophie sceptique sont de grande usage dans les sciences* (Discourse to Show the Great Use of Skeptical Doubt for the Sciences, 1669).

Hume may have also been reading or at least become aware of the provocative work of Pierre-Daniel Huet at this time. In part 1 of *Dialogues concerning Natural Religion* he refers to the controversial and highly Pyrrhonian successor to Huet's *Alnetanae quaestiones de concordia rationis et fidei* (1690), *Traité philosophique de la foiblesse humain* (Philosophical Treatise on Human Weakness, 1723). A sensational work, since its author was a Roman Catholic bishop, the text was widely known and discussed. Huet's published works also include *Demonstratio Evangelica* (Demonstration of the Gospel, 1679), *Censura Philosophiae Cartesianae* (A Critique of Cartesian Philosophy, 1689), and *De imbecillitate mentis humanae* (On the Imbecility of the Human Mind, 1738).

Hume's profound immersion into the skeptical dimensions of contemporary literature eventually undermined what religious convictions he retained and produced pervasive doubts about the capacities of reason. In 1751 he wrote to his friend Gilbert Elliot of Minto that "tis not long ago that I burn'd an old Manuscript Book, wrote before I was twenty; which contain'd Page after Page, the gradual Progress of my Thoughts on that head. It begun with an anxious Search after Arguments, to confirm the Common Opinion: Doubts stole in, dissipated, return'd, again dissipated, return'd again; and it was a perpetual Struggle of a restless Imagination against Inclination, perhaps against Reason."

These years of struggle in late adolescence, however, seem to have been extremely productive. Not only had Hume worked out many of his thoughts on religious, epistemological, and moral skepticism; another letter to Elliot in 1751 also indicates that he had laid the groundwork for and "plan'd" *A Treatise of Human Nature* before he was twenty-one years old. The intensity of Hume's work, however, precipitated a period of physical and mental illness that impaired him for the next four years. As early as 1730 he began to complain of difficulties in eating and digestion, heart palpitations, anxiety, and depression. "I found that I was not able to follow out a Train of Thought, by one continued Stretch of View, but by repeated Interruptions & by refreshing my Eye from Time to Time upon other Objects," he observed in 1734. Hume consulted various physicians and submitted himself to a variety of treatments in order to restore his health, but to no lasting effect. In 1734, in an effort to repair his mind and body through engagement with more practical applications (and perhaps also to escape a paternity claim that was about to be lodged against him), Hume fled Scotland for first London and then Bristol. While in the capital he composed a long, autobiographical, and diagnostic letter that he intended to present to a prominent physician (perhaps John Arbuthnot or George Cheyne) but for some reason apparently never delivered it.

By mid March Hume had arrived in Bristol, the primary British port of the West Indian trade, where he took employment with a merchant, Michael Miller.

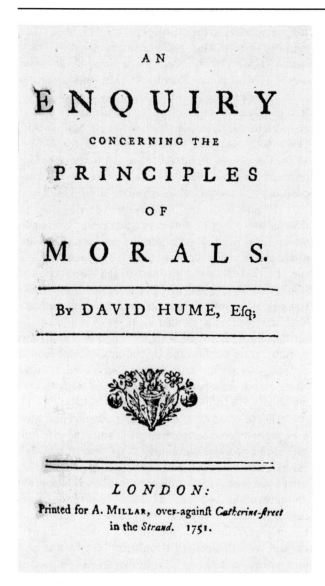

AN

ENQUIRY

CONCERNING THE

PRINCIPLES

OF

MORALS.

By DAVID HUME, Esq;

LONDON:

Printed for A. MILLAR, over-against Catherine-street
in the Strand. 1751.

Title page for Hume's reworking of book 3 of A Treatise of Human Nature, *in which he argues that morality has its source in human sympathy (courtesy of Special Collections, Thomas Cooper Library, University of South Carolina)*

The principal commodity with which Miller dealt was sugar. As, however, slaving would have been consistent with the normal practices of a sugar merchant of the time, it is likely that Miller—and thereby, at least indirectly, Hume—was involved in the slave trade. Hume's relations with his employer were difficult, and since his health had strengthened through his new mode of life, he resigned his post after just four months. As he records in his *Life:* "my Health being a little broken by my ardent Application, I was tempted or rather forced to make a very feeble Trial for entering into a more active Scene of Life. In 1734, I went to Bristol with some Recommendations to eminent Mer-

chants; but in a few Months found that Scene totally unsuitable to me."

By the midsummer of 1734 Hume had arrived in France, where he stayed for three years before returning to Britain in 1737. Among the philosophical works Hume had been reading over the preceding five years was that of François de Salignac de La Mothe Fénelon, author of *Traité de l'existence et des attributs de Dieu* (Treatise on the Existence and Attributes of God, 1713) and archbishop of Cambray. Fénelon was also a quietist and a well-known skeptical figure in Scotland. In the section of his memoranda he collects under the heading "Philosophy," Hume refers to Fénelon in connection with topics of necessity, metaphysics, and proofs of the existence of God. His connection to the archbishop, however, was more than intellectual, for it was one of Fénelon's most ardent disciples who welcomed him to Paris and with whom he stayed while there.

A Scottish expatriate and cousin of Hume's childhood friend Michael Ramsay of Mungale, the Chevalier Andrew Michael Ramsay was converted from Presbyterianism to Roman Catholicism by Fénelon and later became his biographer and literary inheritor. In 1724, through the influence of Fénelon, the chevalier had been tutor in Rome to the two sons of King James Edward the Pretender, Prince Charles (Bonnie Prince Charlie) and his brother, Henry.

While Hume was his guest, the chevalier was at work on his *Philosophical Principles of Natural and Revealed Religion, Unfolded in a Geometrical Order* (1748), a work exploring topics in the philosophy of religion and Pyrrhonism, which he undoubtedly discussed with Hume. Passages of this text related to Benedict de Spinoza seem especially similar to Hume's later expositions. Ramsay was also the author of the highly skeptical *Voyages de Cyrus* (Voyages of Cyrus, 1727), a work modeled on Fénelon's *Les aventures de Télémaque* (1699). *Voyages de Cyrus* circulated widely and was published in England in 1728 as well as in France during the period of Hume's intensive study. The text, therefore, would quite likely have been a topic of conversation with Hume's host. While lodging with Ramsay, Hume became interested in the recent miracles claimed to have occurred at the tomb of the Abbé Pâris. The alleged miracles had captured the imaginations of many in Britain as well as in France. Hume discussed the events with people and took notes both on the reports and on assessments of them published in the periodical literature.

Hume was and remained fond of Paris. His dealings with the chevalier and with the French intellectuals to whom he was introduced were warm and stimulating. The allowance he received from his family, however, was relatively small, apparently amounting to something less than £50 per annum. The sum was enough to endow a single male of the middling ranks with a rather humble standard of living, but it was insufficient to sustain Hume in the lifestyle to which he aspired to become accustomed, especially in a city as expensive and alluring as Paris. After a few months in the City of Light, then, Hume sought out a more affordable provincial center possessing a large population of intellectuals and well enough stocked library facilities to allow him to continue his studies without having to engage in paid employment.

Hume settled on Rheims, approximately one hundred miles northeast of Paris in the province of Champagne. The town was then home to nearly forty thousand citizens and the seat of a prominent university. Hume was provided with letters of introduction by the Chevalier Ramsay, and he soon began seeking access to various libraries. In Rheims he may well have become acquainted with Louis-Jean Lévesque de Pouilly, a correspondent of Henry Bolingbroke and a man of Scottish descent. Pouilly, whose thoughts on moral subjects were not far distant from Hume's, later published *Théorie des sentiments agréables* (Theory of pleasant feelings, 1736) an ethical treatise in the tradition of texts by Shaftesbury, Hutcheson, and the Abbé Jean-Baptiste Dubos's *Réflexions et critiques sur la poésie et la peinture* (Reflections and Critiques on Poetry and Painting, 1719).

In Rheims, Hume began composition of *A Treatise of Human Nature*. After about a year in that city, perhaps because of persistent financial frustrations, he left in 1735 for La Flèche in Anjou, nearly 150 miles southeast of Paris. Nestled in the rolling wine country of the Loire valley, La Flèche was then a sleepy town of about five thousand inhabitants. According to local lore, Hume lodged for the next two years at the manor house of Yvandeau on the slopes of Saint-Germain-du-Val.

La Flèche was an attractive spot for an intellectual and writer, not simply for its economy and its tranquillity but also because of its Jesuit college, where René Descartes had studied a century earlier. The college hummed with discussions of Cartesianism and its offspring, and it possessed an exceedingly well-endowed library, housing upward of 40,000 volumes when Louis the XV dissolved the institution in 1762. Hume was now determined to embark on "that Plan of Life, which I have steddily and successfuly pursued: I resolved to make a very rigid Frugality supply my Deficiency of Fortune, to maintain unimpaired my Independency, and to regard every object as contemptible, except to the Improvement of my Talents in Literature."

Hume would have been exposed to texts and conversations concerning Descartes's *Meditationes de Prima Philosophia* (1641; translated as *Meditations on First Philosophy: In Which the Existence of God and the Distinction between*

the Soul and the Body are Demonstrated), to which was attached assorted objections to the work from philosophers such as Thomas Hobbes, Antoine Arnauld, Marin Mersenne, and Pierre Gassendi, along with Descartes's replies to the objections. Hume may have also gained there knowledge of Nicolas de Malebranche's *De la recherche de la verité* (Search for the Truth, 1674–1675), a text that deeply informed his theory of mind.

Other texts addressing skepticism of interest to him in France would have included Mersenne's *La vérité des sciences contre les sceptiques ou Pyrrhoniens* (The Truth of Science against the Skeptics or Pyrrhonians, 1625); Arnauld and Pierre Nicole's so-called Port-Royal Logic, properly titled *La logique, ou l'art de penser: contenant, outres les reles communes, plusiers observations nouvelles, propre à former le jugement* (Logic, or The Art of Thinking: Containing, Outside the Ordinary Rules, Some New Observations, Necessary to Form Judgment, 1662); as well as the popular *Examen du Pyrrhonisme ancien et moderne* (Examination of Pyrrhonism Ancient and Modern, 1733) and *La logique ou système de réflexions qui peuvent contribuer à la netetté et l'entendue de nos conaissances* (Logic, or A System of Reflections that Can Contribute to the Clarity and the Understanding of Our Knowledge, 1712) by the Swiss philosopher Jean-Pierre Crousaz. A more popular and accessible work, *La logique* ran through several enlarged editions and appeared in English translation in 1724 as the two-volume *A New Treatise of The Art of Thinking, or a Complete System of Reflections Concerning the Conduct and Improvement of the Mind . . . Done into English.*

Spinoza's *Ethica* (1677) and *Renati Descartes Principiorum Philosophiae* (Rene Descarte's Philosophical Principles, 1663) would have also been available to Hume in France, as would have Gassendi's *Syntagma Philosophicum* (Philosophical Syntax) together with his Epicurean works (1647–1649). It is likely Hume also encountered the work of Gottfried von Leibniz at La Flèche, where he may have read Leibniz's *Traité sur les Perfections de Dieu* (1686; translated as *Discourse on Metaphysics,* 1953) and his *Essais de Théodicée sur la bonté de Dieu, la liberté de l'homme et l'origine du mal* (Essays of Theodicy on the Goodness of God, the Liberty of Man, and the Origin of Evil, 1710). Hume refers to Leibniz in the "Abstract" of *A Treatise of Human Nature.*

At La Flèche, Hume set himself to "prosecuting my Studies in a Country Retreat," and he completed there most of the remainder of his first and perhaps most magnificent work. By mid 1737 *A Treatise of Human Nature* was largely complete, and he returned to London to secure a publisher. After nearly a year of inquiries, he came to terms with John Noon at the White Hart near Mercer's Chapel in Cheapside, signing articles of agreement with him on 26 September 1738. Noon was a publisher of moderate standing, having issued encyclopedias, sermons, and attacks on Andrew Baxter, Joseph Butler, and William Wollaston. Hume was determined to publish without appeal to patronage or subscription. As an unknown author, however, he was forced to settle for terms of publication not entirely satisfactory to him. Noon would hold all rights to the first edition of *A Treatise of Human Nature* and would issue a run of one thousand copies, for which Hume was to receive £50 in return. On penalty of £50, Hume was prohibited from contracting for a second edition until either Noon had sold all of his copies of the first edition or Hume purchased them from him at the market price. Hume felt uncomfortably hamstrung by Noon's restriction on a second edition, and indeed, although he began preparing notes and corrections, a second edition was never published, Noon's first edition having never entirely sold out.

In the last week of January 1739, Noon published books 1 ("Of the Understanding") and 2 ("Of the Passions") of *A Treatise of Human Nature,* priced at twelve shillings. Hume was at that time still engaged in revising a third book, "Of Morals," which appeared in November 1740 through a different London publisher, Thomas Longman. In accordance with contemporary practice designed to shield authors from ad hominem attacks, political reprisals, and, indeed, shame in the face of failure, Hume published his text anonymously. Locke, Baxter, Hutcheson, Mandeville, and Wollaston had all done the same, although in many instances the authorship was obvious.

The version of *A Treatise of Human Nature* Hume finally released to the world was a somewhat different document than the one he had projected. He may have become concerned that the contents of *A Treatise of Human Nature* would be too provocative for his intended audience, as well as perhaps the state and ecclesiastical authorities. Hume may have also worried that portions of the text would offend Bishop Butler, whose good opinion he sought. Perhaps Hume was also worried that the epistemological and metaphysical subtleties of the text would be ignored in favor of a blunter and more popular attention to matters of religion. Such concerns would have been well founded in a young author whose first book surfaced amid the turbulence produced by the collected edition of Clarke's Boyle lectures, *A Defense of Natural and Revealed Religion,* published that same year (1739).

In a December 1737 letter to Kames, Hume describes being occupied with "castrating my work, that is, cutting off its nobler parts; that is, endeavouring it shall give as little offence as possible, before which, I could not pretend to put it into the Doctor's [i.e. Butler's] hands. This is a piece of cowardice, for which I

blame myself, though I believe none of my friends will blame me. But I was resolved not to be an enthusiast in philosophy, while I was blaming other enthusiasms." Hume enclosed "some *Reasonings concerning Miracles,*" which he "thought of publishing with the rest," but which he was afraid would "give too much offence, even as the world is disposed at present." The essay on miracles did not appear in print until 1748.

Hume's concerns about how to present *A Treatise of Human Nature* to the world also appear to have prevented him from composing an abridgment or summary of the sort commonly used in advertising a new work. The frustration he felt may well have motivated the cryptic motto he included on the title page of the treatise, a motto that seems to invite its audience to read between the lines for what Hume felt he could not state explicitly. He quotes from Tacitus: "*Rara temporum felicitas, ubi sentire, quæ velis; & quæ sentias, dicere licet*" (Seldom are people blessed with times in which they may think what they like, and say what they think). The epigram is similar to the title of the final chapter of Spinoza's *Tractatus Theologico-Politicus* (1670), chapter 20: "That in a Free State every man may Think what he Likes, and Say what he Thinks"; and the title of the treatise itself is similar to that of the second volume of Thomas Hobbes's *Elements of Law* (1650), titled *Human Nature,* which Hobbes often referred to simply as his "Treatise of Human Nature." These cues would alert Hume's readers to the secular and antireligious thrust of his work.

Hume famously bemoaned his disappointment with the reception of *A Treatise of Human Nature.* In *The Life of David Hume* he complained that "Never literary attempt was more unfortunate than my Treatise of Human Nature. It fell *dead-born from the press,* without reaching such distinction, as even to excite a murmur among the zealots." (Hume's remark quotes from Alexander Pope, who had written in one of his satirical epistles that "All, all but truth, drops dead-born from the press.") Hume's description of the reception of his work, however, is not entirely accurate. The *Neuen Zeitungen von gelehrten Sachen* published a critical, even hostile review on 28 May 1739 in Leipzig. Similar assessments appeared in the Dutch publication *Bibliothèque britannique, ou histoire des ouvrages des sçavans de la Grande-Bretagne* (1739) and the German *Göttingische Zeitungen* (1740). Favorable announcements were printed in the popular *Bibliothèque raisonnée des ouvrages des savans de l'Europe* (1739) in Amsterdam and the *Nouvelle bibliothèque, ou histoire littéraire des principaux éscrits qui se publient,* from The Hague. One year after its initial announcement, the *Bibliothèque raisonnée* (April–June 1740) published a forty-nine-page review of the treatise, and the *Nouvelle bibliothèque* published a review of forty-six pages. Criticisms of Hume's text properly situated it in the antirationalist tradition of Locke and Berkeley but complained about the obscurity, the inelegance, and even—failing to appreciate the skeptical characteristic of doing so—the first-person *"Egotisms"* of his prose. These assessments disappointed Hume, for whom matters of rhetoric were of great importance.

Philosophically speaking, however, although critics often got the details wrong, they generally recognized the skeptical implications of his text, especially surrounding matters of necessity and causation. The second account of Hume's text, published in the *Bibliothèque raisonnée,* castigates *A Treatise of Human Nature* for assuming a dogmatic tone while being Pyrrhonian in import. The reviewer aligns Hume's thoughts on causation with those of Sextus Empiricus in the *Outlines* and writes: "I fear that his paradoxes favour Pyrrhonism and lead to consequences that the author appears to disown. . . . There would be a hundred things to remark in our author, whether on the taste for Pyrrhonisms which reigns in his manner of philosophizing; whether on the inconsistency of so many of the singular propositions that he has been pleased to accumulate; whether finally on the pernicious consequences that could be drawn from his principles. What is most offensive is the confidence with which he delivers his paradoxes. Never has there been a Pyrrhonian more dogmatic."

The silence of prominent intellectuals in Britain, together with the critical assessments his text received, provoked Hume to prepare a defensive abstract of the treatise, which he initially intended to submit as an anonymous letter to the editor of the important English periodical *History of the Works of the Learned.* When, however, that journal published, in Hume's words, a "somewhat abusive" review of *A Treatise of Human Nature,* he instead published his abstract in London as a thirty-two-page pamphlet with the title *An Abstract of a Book Lately Published; Entitled, a Treatise of Human Nature, etc. Wherein the Chief Argument of That Book is Farther Illustrated and Explained* (1740). Later, his fury apparently having abated, Hume reissued the pamphlet with a less incendiary title.

Hume's focus in the abstract of *A Treatise of Human Nature* was, as it has been for many of his readers, on book 1. Hume emphasized his theories of causation, necessity, and perception, but most prominently featured are his contentions about what he called the "science of man." Hume advanced the startling notion that "all the sciences have a relation, greater or less, to human nature; and that however wide any of them may seem to run from it, they still return back by one passage or another. Even *Mathematics, Natural Philosophy, and Natural Religion,* are in some measure dependent on the science of MAN; since they lie under the cognizance of men, and are judged of by their powers and faculties."

Hume's bookplate

Contrary to Locke, then, for whom philosophy was understood as the underlaborer of natural science, Hume maintains that the science of humanity is logically prior to any other science.

Hume's gesture was, of course, not entirely new. Descartes's revolutionary inward turn, like those of subsequent systems developed by Malebranche and Berkeley, can be understood along similar lines. Indeed, even Martin Luther's insistence on personal religious experience can be seen as having preceded Hume's insight. Two features of Hume's thought, however, distinguish his work from that of his predecessors: his skepticism and his naturalism. Unlike Descartes, Malebranche, and Berkeley, Hume wished to root philosophy in human experience, without appeals to speculative, abstract reasoning and without reliance on metaphysical posits such as "spirit" or "God." In this way Hume understood himself to be following in and extending the naturalistic tradition of Newton, Shaftesbury, Mandeville, Hutcheson, and Butler, as well as the traditions of skepticism.

Hume similarly distinguished his thought from that of the ancients: "I found that the moral Philosophy transmitted to us by Antiquity, labor'd under the same Inconvenience that has been found in their natural Philosophy of being entirely Hypothetical, & depending more upon Invention than Experience. Every one consulted his Fancy in erecting Schemes of Virtue & of Happiness, without regarding human Nature, upon which every moral Conclusion must depend." His strategy aimed to limit and restrain thought to the world of experience common to all humanity. "When we see, that we have arrived at the utmost extent of human reason, we sit down contented; tho' we be perfectly satisfied in the main of our ignorance, and perceive that we can give no reason for our most general and most refined principles, beside our experience of their reality."

As did the naturalistic moralists and the Newtonian physicists before him, Hume wished to produce a secular and empirically grounded philosophy. This aspect of his thought accounts for the subtitle of *A Treatise of Human Nature:* "Being an Attempt to introduce the experimental Method of Reasoning into Moral Subjects." As a skeptic and a philosopher of humanity, however, Hume never lost sight of the fact that nature itself is only grasped through human life and experience, and it remained for him impossible to determine whether or not such experience is able to yield knowledge.

An indication of Hume's rigorous adherence to this position is indicated by the peculiar features of his theory of perception. Descartes and Malebranche had claimed that "ideas," including the constituents of perception, are innately implanted in the mind by their Creator. Berkeley, too, had rooted experience in the activity of God. Locke, following Gassendi and Galileo, had explained experience by appeal to powers in the natural, external world. Hume, in turn, like his predecessors, clung to the notion that experience is presented to a "mind" and that experiences are mental events; indeed, the figures he uses to describe the mechanics of perception are deeply indebted to Malebranche. He departs from other early modern thinkers, however, by attempting to bracket questions concerning the source and root of ideas and deal strictly with perceptions themselves.

Hume divides perceptions into two categories, "impressions" and "ideas." All ideas, whether sensuous or not, must for him be rooted in some fashion in impressions in order to have any meaning and legitimacy: "*All our simple ideas in their first appearance are deriv'd from simple impressions, which are correspondent to them, and which they exactly represent.*" The composition of these simpler elements is the product of the interaction of experience with various principles of human nature. Hume does qualify this position by maintaining the legitimacy of "relative ideas" concerning unobservable entities (for example, the force of gravity) as well as abstract ideas concerning historico-cultural dimensions of life (such as authority, marriage, and justice). Such ideas, however, must also be tethered to public experiences of common life.

Ideas are, for Hume, linked together through various "relations of ideas," principally the natural relations of "resemblance," "contiguity," and "cause and effect." In the delineation of these ordering principles, Hume sees himself as original. Writing in *An Abstract of a Book Lately Published* he remarks: "Thro' this whole book, there are great pretensions to new discoveries in philosophy; but if any thing can intitle the author to so glorious a name as that of an *inventor,* 'tis the use he makes of the principle of the association of ideas." Just as for Newton the motion of all material objects can be explained by appeal to three simple laws of nature, for Hume all mental phenomena are comprehended through a few basic relations of ideas. Just as for Newton all material objects are attracted to one another through the force of gravity, so for Hume all ideas are linked to others through the "gentle force" of the principles of association. Insofar as nature can only be experienced and understood through the mind, the importance of these principles is even more dramatic: "these are the only links that bind the parts of the universe together, or connect us with any other person or object exterior to ourselves. . . . they are really *to us* the cement of the universe." David Hartley further developed associationist psychology in his *Observations on Man, His Frame, His Duty, and His Expectations* (1749).

Hume's theory of impressions and ideas yields him tremendous critical power. He infuses thought and belief with radical contingency. If all complex ideas can be broken down into simpler ideas, then complex theories and dogmas can be deconstructed and reconstructed in various ways. Ideas are not self-ordering. Rather, they require the external and contingent direction of experience and the principles of association.

Rationalistic philosophy in physics, metaphysics, theology, and morals depends on the capacity of the mind either to intuit or rationally determine intrinsic relations among ideas. Simply by examining and reasoning with ideas themselves—and thereby appealing little, if at all, to experience—rationalists held that thinkers could determine scientific principles, the existence and nature of God, and various moral truths. By rendering, therefore, all relations of ideas exterior to them, Hume undercuts the basis of rationalism and with it the moral, theological, and scientific projects advanced by thinkers such as Descartes and Clarke. Outside of those sciences, such as mathematics, which appeal strictly to naturally founded relations of ideas, all of what goes by the name of knowledge is entirely empirical, or founded on experience. In a famous image Hume boldly asserts: "When we run over libraries, persuaded of these principles, what havoc must we make? If we take in our hand any volume; of divinity or school metaphysics, for instance; let us ask, *Does it contain any abstract reasoning concerning quantity or number?* No. *Does it contain any experimental reasoning concerning matter of fact and existence?* No. Commit it then to the flames: for it can contain nothing but sophistry and illusion."

One of the most important and best-known instances of Hume's critical philosophy is his theory of causation. For rationalists the idea of fire, for example, entails its causing one to feel heat. For Hume, by contrast, matters are quite different. Since one of the natural relations of ideas is causation, humanity is naturally disposed to experience the world in causal terms. Precisely which causes will produce which effects, however, can only, for Hume, be discovered through experience, not through conceptual analysis. Fire might conceivably just as well produce cold as heat. It might possibly produce flowers or turnips as well as smoke and ash. Indeed, for Hume, it is logically possible that events might occur without any cause, objects appearing ex nihilo, and nature itself might behave in entirely different ways tomorrow than it has today. Reason, Hume contends, cannot by itself inform one what the nature of the world is or what is likely to take place. Only the interaction of mind with the world and the resultant production of various "habits" or "customs" of thought yields belief in such things.

The "necessity" the human mind attributes to an effect following its cause—as well as the belief that things will behave in each successive occurrence as they have in the past—are not matters of demonstration or deduction; rather, they find their basis in the feelings generated in the mind by experience, feelings that are in turn projected upon the world. The mind ineluctably moves, through habit, from a present experience of what has in the past been found to be a cause to expect a subsequent effect. The necessity perceived within the motion of the mind becomes projected, for Hume, upon the event itself.

Hume does not suggest, however, that there are, in fact, no causes or that nature will not continue in its regular course. In 1754, responding to critic John Stewart, Hume emphasized that "I never asserted so absurd a Proposition *as that any thing might arise without a Cause; I* maintain'd, that our Certainty of the Falshood of that Proposition proceeded neither from Intuition or Dem-

onstration; but from another Source. *That Caesar existed, that there is such an Island as Sicily;* for these propositions, I affirm, we have no demonstrative or intuitive Proof. Woud you infer that I deny their Truth, or even their Certainty? There are many different kinds of Certainty; and some of them as satisfactory to the Mind, tho' perhaps not so regular as the demonstrative kind."

In a famous example Hume describes the interaction of two billiard balls:

> When I see a billiard ball moving towards another, my mind is immediately carry'd by habit to the usual effect, and anticipates my sight by conceiving the second ball in motion. There is nothing in these objects, abstractly considered, and independent of experience, which leads me to form any such conclusion: and even after I have had experience of many repeated effects of this kind, there is no argument, which determines me to suppose, that the effect will be conformable to past experience. The powers, by which bodies operate, are entirely unknown. We perceive only their sensible qualities: and what *reason* have we to think that the same powers will always be conjoined with the same sensible qualities? 'Tis not, therefore, reason which is the guide of life but custom. That alone determines the mind, in all instances, to suppose the future conformable with the past. However easy this step may seem, reason would never, to all eternity, be able to make it.

Hume's conception of the self comprises another important critique of the principal strains of early modern philosophy. The human self, as Hume renders it, is not a singular "I" or *cogito,* as Descartes and other central philosophical figures of the day had imagined: "But setting aside some metaphysicians . . . , I may venture to affirm of the rest of mankind, that they are nothing but a bundle or collection of different perceptions, which succeed each other with an inconceivable rapidity, and are in a perpetual flux and movement. Our eyes cannot turn in their sockets without varying our perceptions. Our thought is still more variable than our sight; and all our other senses and faculties contribute to this change; nor is there any single power of the soul, which remains unalterably the same, perhaps for one moment." In developing his bundle theory—a theory concerning which, it should be said, Hume was not himself entirely secure—Hume was the first major philosopher to abandon claims that there is a non-sensible substance, spirit, or soul beneath or in addition to the experienced perceptions of the mind.

The self is also, for Hume, diverse in another way. The customs and habits that are formed through human experience are not simply private affairs. Contrary to the model produced by Descartes of the solitary philosopher, determining truths about himself, the world, and God without any reference to his body,

DISSERTATION IV.

Of Suicide.

ONE confiderable advantage, that arifes from philofophy, confifts in the fovereign antidote, which it affords to fuperftition and falfe religion. All other remedies againft that peftilent diftemper are vain, or, at leaft, uncertain. Plain good-fenfe, and the practice of the world, which alone ferve moft purpofes of life, are here found ineffectual : Hiftory, as well as daily experience, ~~furnifhes~~ inftances of men, endowed with the ftrongeft capacity for bufinefs and affairs, who have all their lives crouched under flavery to the groffeft fuperftition. Even gaiety and fweetnefs of temper, which infufe a balm into every other wound, afford no remedy to fo virulent a poifon ; as we may particularly obferve of the fair fex, who, tho' commonly poffefs of thefe rich prefents of nature, feel many of their joys blafted by this importunate intruder. But when found philofophy has once gained poffeffion of the mind, fuperftition is effectually excluded ; and one may fafely affirm, that her

K 6 triumph

Page proof from an essay by Hume, with his corrections. Hume intended to include the essay in his Four Dissertations *(1757) but removed it under threat of prosecution. It was first published posthumously in 1783 (National Library of Scotland).*

the world, or society, the experiences into which people are immersed and through which they think are a social, cultural, and historical affair. Integrity and order are brought to the mind through the principles of association, but the mind is also structured through another external source—society. Humans, for Hume, are creatures of custom and habit to the core, but those customs and habits are determined by social history as well as by nature. Thoughts, feelings, desires, and beliefs are molded by social situations as well as by instincts. It is important to see, however, that Hume's acknowledgment of humanity being embedded in society and history in addition to his acknowledgment of the limits of reason not only affords him a new view of the human self; it also offers him a new model of philosophy, as well.

From its origins, much of philosophical thought has aspired to achieve some sort of transcendence. Whether from opinion to knowledge or from the secular to the divine, philosophy has generally attempted—usually through the putative capacities of reason—to escape what Hume calls the "gross, earthy mixture" of "common life." Plato aspired to knowing transcendent forms; Thomas Aquinas and Clarke struggled to understand the divine; Descartes wished to establish the sciences on an unshakable foundation, a *fundamentum inconcussum,* through the action of pure, disembodied reason. Hume, however, like the skeptics and the Epicureans with whom he associated himself, was a philosopher of finitude. Comparing his predecessors to Sisyphus and Tantalus, he maintained that philosophy must give up its vain quest to grasp objects beyond its reach and instead restrain itself to subjects regarding which its results will be "durable and useful." Ways of thinking that seek to transcend human finitude he identifies as "false" philosophy and religion.

"True philosophy," by contrast, is for Hume content not to seek transcendence or ultimate foundations. Indeed, properly construed, "philosophical decisions are nothing but the reflections of common life, methodized and corrected." In *An Enquiry concerning Human Understanding* Hume, personifying philosophy as female, characteristically writes: "Happy if she be thence sensible of her temerity, when she pries into these sublime mysteries; and leaving a scene so full of obscurities and perplexities, return, with suitable modesty, to her true and proper province, the examination of common life."

The third book of Hume's *A Treatise of Human Nature,* "Of Morals," was published on 5 November 1740. It attracted even less attention than the first two books. Although he maintained that book 3 can be read as an independent text, Hume's philosophy of common life connects this volume with its predecessors. Just as his theory of mind and reason is naturalistic and rooted

in common life, so too he constructs a naturalistic moral theory without appealing to the divine or to metaphysical guarantees. Hutcheson and Butler had preceded Hume in developing moral theories based upon an assessment of human nature, Hutcheson centering moral judgments on a natural "moral sense" and Butler appealing to what he described as the natural faculty of "conscience." Fearing the loss of moral objectivity, however, both these earlier thinkers appealed to God to justify the veracity of moral judgments made naturally by people.

Hume, by contrast, makes no such appeal, grounding his moral system instead only on humanity's animal capacity for "sympathy" and on the universalizing "moral sentiment" humans produce through a confluence of moral feeling and natural reason. Adam Smith followed out a similar line of thought in his *Theory of the Moral Sentiments* (1759). As with his theories of perception and causation, Hume's moral theory militates against Christian and rationalistic efforts, including those of Descartes and Locke, to deploy reason or revelation in the establishment of moral norms.

In an influential passage on the grounding of moral judgment, Hume distinguishes facts, which are the provenance of reason and perception, from values, which can only be established through internal feeling:

> Nor does this reasoning only prove, that morality consists not in any relations, that are the objects of science; but if examin'd will prove with equal certainty, that it consists not in any *Matter of fact,* which can be discover'd by the understanding. . . . So that when you pronounce any action or character to be vicious, you mean nothing, but that from the constitution of your nature you have a feeling or sentiment of blame from the contemplation of it. . . . I cannot forbear adding to these reasonings an observation, which may, perhaps, be found of some importance. In every system of morality, which I have hitherto met with, I have always remark'd, that the author proceeds for some time in the ordinary way of reasoning, and establishes the being of God, or makes observations concerning human affairs; when of a sudden I am surpriz'd to find, that instead of the usual copulations of propositions, *is,* and *is not,* I meet with no proposition that is not connected with an *ought,* or an *Ought not.* This change is imperceptible; but is, however, of the last consequence. For as this *ought,* or *ought not,* expresses some new relation or affirmation, 'tis necessary that it shou'd be observ'd and explain'd; and at the same time that a reason should be given, for what seems altogether inconceivable, how this new relation can be a deduction from others, which are entirely different from it.

Hume's moral theory also rejects the egoistic naturalism developed by Hobbes in the *Leviathan* (1651) and Mandeville in the *Fable of the Bees.* Maintaining that each individual is generally if not purely selfish, these earlier thinkers were taken to explain apparently altruistic and collectively beneficial actions according to the self-interest of the participants. Hume's strategy, like that of Hutcheson before him, was to accept the naturalistic, sentimental basis for morality developed by the egoists but to mitigate if not wholly undermine it by maintaining that the natural capacity for sympathy and moral sentiment–ignored by the egoists–extends human concern beyond the immediate self. Humans, then, are for Hume not so much selfish as partial. Such partiality, however, is variable and may be attenuated through the action of social customs and conventions so that, at its limit, sympathetic partiality may expand to include the whole of humanity (and perhaps even other animals). In such instances, concern for one's own feelings of pleasure and pain converges with universal regard for others.

What is "virtuous," then, is what is found pleasant or useful to the self and others, while "vicious" actions and characters are those found to be unpleasant and harmful. Some virtues people possess naturally, and–contrary to much of Christian morality–Hume holds that such qualities are to be esteemed. For Hume it is virtuous to be beautiful, cheerful, proud, and strong. Many virtues, however, are for Hume "artificial" and require the conventions and artifices of society for their existence. Justice is such a virtue. For Hume, what is just is not established independently by reason or revealed to humanity by God. Rather, in the face of human appetites and needs that expand and extend beyond the capacity of people to satisfy them, a society must develop "general rules" for the distribution of goods, services, and resources. Some sets of rules are found, by experience and only by experience, to yield greater human happiness than others.

Conventions of private property, among others, are legitimate because they have been found to secure effectively human happiness. Conventions of justice, accordingly, originate in people's selfish or at least partial efforts to secure their own benefit; but once established, they produce over time artificial sentiments that lead people to act for the benefit of the whole of humanity. In this sense Hume's moral philosophy may be said to prefigure later doctrines of utilitarianism, especially what has come to be known as rule utilitarianism. Hume's emphasis on the attributes of character and deliberation, on the other hand, connects his thought to traditions of virtue in ethics, in particular those of Cicero and Aristotle.

In 1739, probably accompanied by a gift of the first two books of *A Treatise of Human Nature,* Hume initiated what became a four-year correspondence with Hutcheson. Hume had returned to Scotland, and the two met in Glasgow during the winter of 1739. Each man seems to have responded warmly to the other, though Hutcheson criticized Hume's treatise for failing to promote virtue strongly enough. Hume dismissed Hutcheson's assessment, replying that he understood himself to be principally an "anatomist" rather than an advocate of virtue. The issue of the reception of his work among the learned, however, was an important one for Hume, and in his next literary project, his *Essays, Moral and Political* (1741–1742), he undertook to render his thoughts in a more pleasing and accessible form. In "Of Essay Writing" Hume dispenses with the portrayal of himself as a scientific anatomist and takes up another persona: "I cannot but consider myself as a Kind of Resident or Ambassador from the Dominions of Learning to those of Conversation; and shall think it my constant Duty to promote a good Correspondence betwixt these two States, which have so great a Dependence on each other."

Essays, Moral and Political was an immediate and popular success. The twenty-seven essays in the two volumes address a wide variety of topics in philosophy, literary and art criticism, politics, morality, and political economy and indicate Hume's thorough immersion in the common life of his culture. They reveal Hume's developing sentimental, naturalistic, and historicist theories on morals and aesthetics and exhibit his support for the new commercial order developing in Britain and the colonies at the time. A second, corrected edition of the first volume was quickly warranted and was published by midyear. Hume's essay on "A Character of Sir Robert Walpole" attracted perhaps the most immediate attention. Reprinted in many of the leading periodicals of the time–such as the *Gentleman's Magazine,* the *London Magazine,* and the *Scots Magazine*–the essay fell upon an eager public. The British House of Commons was then investigating evidence of corruption in the Westminster election, which had implicated Walpole and soon led to his fall. In contrast to the virulence of the political struggle in which it was situated, Hume's essay portrays Walpole in a moderate, even favorable light. Hume seems to have engaged the editors of the *Newcastle Journal* in an epistolary discussion of the essay. On Walpole's fall and the decline of public interest in the affair, he reduced the essay to a mere footnote in the 1748 edition of the *Essays;* in the 1777 edition it was excised completely.

In 1745 Hume failed to succeed John Pringle to the Chair of Ethics and Pneumatical Philosophy at the University of Edinburgh. His candidacy was

Manuscript page for Hume's The history of England, from the invasion of Julius Caesar
to the accession of Henry VII, *published in 1762 (Royal Society of Edinburgh)*

attacked by Principal William Wishart and by the body of clergy then called the Ministers of Edinburgh. Hume's candidacy was advanced by his cousin Henry Home and by the Reverend Robert Wallace, among whose sermons may be counted *Ignorance and Superstition a Source of Violence and Cruelty* (1746). Hume's writings, not least of all *A Treatise of Human Nature,* had earned him a reputation for atheism and skepticism, and the opposition to his appointment was furious. Concerning the protests, Hume wrote in a letter to Matthew Sharpe Hoddam dated 25 April 1745 "that such a popular Clamour has been raisd against me in Edinburgh, on account of Scepticism, Heterodoxy & other hard Names, which confound the ignorant, that my Friends find some Difficulty, in working out the Point of my Professorship, which once appear'd so easy." Surprisingly, however, Hume's candidacy was not only opposed by the clergy and by the populace; Hutcheson had also joined the opposition.

From April 1745 to April 1746 Hume served as tutor to the marquess of Annandale, whose manor house, Weldehall, stood near St. Albans in the hill country approximately twenty miles northwest of London. The marquess seems to have been mentally unstable, and Hume fell afoul of both him and the managers of his estate, producing a series of conflicts that culminated in Hume's resignation. If Hume's professional life was fraught with frustration during this time, however, his intellectual life flourished. While in the employ of the marquess he was able to make frequent trips to London and consult various libraries and intellectuals there. His efforts yielded several important works, including *Philosophical Essays Concerning Human Understanding* (published in 1748 and later titled *An Enquiry Concerning Human Understanding*) and *Three Essays, Moral and Political: Never before Published* (1748).

Philosophical Essays Concerning Human Understanding recast book 1 of *A Treatise of Human Nature* in a simpler, more direct, and more condensed form. Although the implications of his epistemological thought are as radical as ever, Hume portrays his work as "Academical" and anti-Pyrrhonian in its cast. The skeptics who had taken over Plato's Academy in ancient Athens—for example Arcesilaus of Pitane (who founded Second Academy circa 250 B.C.) and Carneades of Cyrene—had developed quasi-probabilistic criteria of truth in opposition to claims to epistemological certainty advanced by Stoics such as Cleanthes of Assus and Chrysippus of Soli. (Cleanthes and the Academic skeptic Philo of Larissa appear as voices in Hume's *Dialogues concerning Natural Religion.*)

Although their theories of probability were largely argumentative gambits, not their own positions, and although their views differed significantly from conceptions of probability developed by early modern thinkers, the ancient Academics came to be seen as more moderate and therefore less objectionable skeptics by readers of Hume's time. Much of this vision of the Academic skeptics can be attributed to Cicero's widely read *Academica,* a text that lays out many of the Academics' positions and arguments. In contrast, then, to "excessive" Pyrrhonism (of the sort, for example, engaged by Descartes), Hume characterizes his own brand of skepticism as one that restricts the application of doubt to those speculative ventures that stray beyond the limits of "daily practice and experience" as well as "custom" and "instinct"–in short, beyond "common life."

Hume's letters of the period indicate his dismay over the 1745 Jacobite uprising and invasion of England by the supporters of the Young Pretender, Prince Charles Edward Stuart. More than a year after the event he wrote, in a letter cited by Ernest Campbell Mossner in his 1954 biography of Hume, that "eight Millions of People" might "have been subdued and reduced to Slavery by five Thousand, the bravest, but still the most worthless amongst them." Hume intervened on behalf of his friend Archibald Stewart, Lord Provost of Edinburgh, who in the ensuing backlash of 1747 was prosecuted for surrendering the city too quickly to the Jacobites. In defense of Stewart, Hume wrote an anonymous pamphlet, *A True Account of the Behaviour and Conduct of Archibald Stewart, Esq.; late Lord Provost of Edinburgh. In a letter to a Friend,* (1748).

The oppressive and suspicious climate of the years following the revolt, however, affected Hume in a more direct fashion. His description of the content of his *Three Essays* in a letter of February 1748, shortly before its publication, distances the work from the prevailing political categories of the time: "One is against the original Contract, the System of the Whigs, another against passive Obedience, the System of the Tories; A third upon the Protestant Succession, where I suppose a Man to deliberate, before the Establishment of that Succession, which Family he shou'd adhere to, & to weigh the Advantages & Disadvantages of each." Out of fear of the response of Stuart opponents, "Of the Protestant Succession" was ultimately removed from the final copy, not to appear in print until 1752; it was replaced with another essay, "Of National Characters." In May 1746 Hume received and accepted an invitation from his relative, Lieutenant-General James St. Clair, to accompany him as secretary and then as judge advocate to his forces in a military campaign against the French in North America. The expedition, however, was diverted to France and attacked Lorient, an important center of the French East-India trade, on the coast of Brittany. The attack was a comic disaster, with the town sending out emissaries to negotiate its surrender only to find that the British had evacuated in retreat only hours before. Voltaire lambasted the British for their incompetence in his *Histoire de la Guerre de mil sept cent quarante & un* (History of the War of 1741, 1756). Hume described the event in an unpublished manuscript, "Descent on the Coast of Brittany"; he may have also been author of an answer to Voltaire appearing in the *Monthly Review* (April 1747). In 1747–1748 Hume accompanied St. Clair on another official adventure, a military embassy to Vienna and Turin.

The work Hume published during the period from 1748 to 1762 brought him great wealth and enormous fame among the worlds of British and French letters. Indeed, the 1750s marked the ascendancy of Scottish letters in general. After the publication of *Three Essays* and *Philosophical Essays concerning Human Understanding* in 1748, a reworking of book 3 of *A Treatise of Human Nature* titled *An Enquiry concerning the Principles of Morals* appeared in 1751; "of all my writings, historical, philosophical, or literary," Hume observed, it was "incomparably the best." In part 10 of the *Philosophical Essays,* Hume finally published his critical work "Of Miracles," a text that argues that belief in miracles cannot be rationally justified. As Hume expected, the text attracted a great deal of critical attention and provoked perhaps the greatest number of publications issued against his thought.

Indeed, during the 1750s assaults against Hume's work on religion, in the form of pamphlet literature, had reached a fever pitch, especially in Britain. Among the most widely read of such attacks was the Reverend John Leland's *View of the Principal Deistical Writers* (1755). The *Bibliothèque Raisonnée des ouvrages des savans de l'Europe* (April–May–June, 1740) called Hume one of "the most subtle advocates of unbelief." In 1766 Hume wrote to economist Anne Robert Jacques Turgot: "I cou'd cover the Floor of a large Room with the Books and Pamphlets wrote against me." Among the scholarly replies to Hume could be found publications by the Reverend Thomas Rutherforth of Cambridge University (*Credibility of Miracles defended against the Author of Philosophical Essays,* 1751), William Adams of Oxford (*Essay on Mr. Hume's Essay on Miracles,* 1751), John Douglas, later Bishop of Salisbury (*The Criterion: or, Miracles Examined,* 1752), and James Campbell, principal of Marischal College Aberdeen, who produced perhaps the most elaborate reply (*Dissertation on Miracles: Containing an Examination of the*

Principles advanced by David Hume, Esq; in an Essay on Miracles, 1762).

In 1752 Hume published *Political Discourses,* which he identifies in his autobiography as "the only work of mine that was successful on the first Publication." This text, perhaps more than any other, catapulted him into prominence. One of Hume's essays in *Political Discourses,* "Of the Populousness of Ancient Nations," enmeshed him in what was then an important controversy; indeed, in a letter to the Reverend Robert Wallace from 22 September 1751 Hume referred to it as "the most curious & important of all Questions of Erudition." Hume rejected the idea of cultural decline that had been dominant until the seventeenth century, but he also rejected the "modern" idea of progress that had gained favor in his own time. On the question of population he was the first thinker of rank to maintain, albeit cautiously, the greater populousness of the modern world over the ancient. Hume's principal though amiable opponent in the controversy was Wallace, whose *A Dissertation on the Numbers of Mankind in Antient and Modern Times* appeared in 1753.

In 1754 the first volume of Hume's powerful *History of England, The History of Great Britain, Vol. I, Containing the reigns of James I and Charles I,* was published; the last volume did not appear until 1762. By the mid 1750s Hume was also famous (or at least infamous) in Italy, so much so that in December 1761 his works were placed on the "Index" of forbidden texts maintained by the Roman Catholic Church. In 1748 the Baron de Montesquieu was so impressed with *Essays, Moral and Political* that he sent Hume a copy of his *Esprit des Loix,* in reply to which Hume returned a copy of the *Philosophical Essays.* In 1758 Edward Gibbon wrote of an exciting event: "I am . . . to meet . . . the great David Hume"; in 1773 Gibbon rejoined a friend in Edinburgh by writing that "You tell me of a long list of Dukes, lairds, and Chieftains of Renown to whom you are recommended; were I with you, I should prefer one David to them all."

In 1751, after the marriage of his brother, Hume moved from Ninewells to Edinburgh, taking residence with his sister on the south side of the Lawnmarket in "Riddle's Land," at the top of the Westbow. In 1753 the two removed to "Jack's Land" beyond the Netherbow in the Canongate, near the Tollbooth prison. Hume apparently kept a study in James's Court, however, on the Lawnmarket. He resided near the Canongate for the next nine years, during which time he composed and published much of the *History of England.*

In the latter months of 1751 Hume was dealt a difficult blow. The death of Thomas Craigie, who

Hume (left) with the Swiss-born French philosopher Jean-Jacques Rousseau. In 1765 Hume helped Rousseau escape from France, where he had been charged with treason (engraving by T. Holloway, circa 1766).

Archibald Campbell, third Duke of Argyll, formerly the earl of Islay, who was popularly known as the "King of Scotland." In the end the conservative and cautionary forces defeated Hume's candidacy and on 22 April 1752 installed Smith, who accordingly resigned to James Clow his prior position as chairman of logic.

Compensation for Hume's defeat in Glasgow, however, had already been secured in Edinburgh by his election to the post of librarian to the Faculty of Advocates on 28 January 1752, an appointment that gave him unrestricted access to the greatest library in Scotland and thereby immeasurably enhanced the resources available to him in the composition of the *History of England*. In the case of this appointment, the opposition to Hume was also vigorous and determined, being led by the lord president, Robert Dundas, and his son, dean of the faculty. In a letter to John Clephane dated 4 February 1752 Hume wrote: "The violent cry of Deism, atheism, and scepticism was raised against me; and 'twas represented that my election would be giving the sanction of the greatest and most learned body of men in this country to my profane and irreligious principles."

This time, however, popular opinion was mustered in support of Hume. Public demonstrations were organized, and the town became animated on the issue as it had on no other since the trial of Archibald Stewart. On Hume's victory, the elation of many overflowed into the streets; a torchlight parade was staged by the Edinburgh corporation of porters and messengers. In the same letter to Clephane he wrote: "The whole body of cadies brought flambeaux, and made illuminations to mark their pleasure at my success; and next morning I had the drums and town music at my door, to express their joy, as they said, of my being made a great man." Hume retained the office until January 1757, when he resigned the post and it was transferred to the philosopher and historian Adam Ferguson. Hume's tenure as librarian was not entirely serene, however, and after a dispute with the curators concerning the acquisition of controversial texts in 1754 he transferred his salary in the form of an annuity to the poet Thomas Blacklock, whom he continued to support after his resignation.

Displacing Catherine Macaulay's republican *History of England* (1763–1783) and Tobias Smollett's humane *Complete History of England* (1757–1758), Hume's *History of England* (1754–1762) became the chief text on the subject consulted by the literate Anglophonic world until well into the nineteenth century. So successful was it that the text became the best-selling history of any kind to be published in Britain before Gibbon's *The History of the Decline and*

had succeeded Hutcheson at the University of Glasgow as professor of moral philosophy in 1746, afforded Hume another opportunity to acquire an academic post. William Mure of Caldwell, Gilbert Elliot of Minto, professor of civil law Hercules Lindesay, and professor of anatomy William Cullen (who later became Hume's physician) supported his candidacy. Adam Smith, who had recently become acquainted with Hume and later became one of his closest friends, was, perhaps because of his concern over the public reaction, less than enthusiastic about supporting him. Indeed, the opposition was fierce, especially among the clergy, and seems to have in part been driven by the political machinations of

Fall of the Roman Empire (1776–1788). Hume's work is remarkable not only because of its enormous scope but also because of the new and critical historiography he developed. Whiggish histories, such as Macaulay's, advocated a progressive view of history, one in which human society had moved from a lower, primitive condition to a higher, more perfect one. For Whiggish historians, the trajectory of history could be charted from the infancy of liberty in the Magna Carta (1215) to the Glorious Revolution of 1688. Although in many ways, particularly in its view of the Middle Ages, Hume's text is consistent with such a view, he takes pains to understand historical events in terms of the participants' self-understandings and resists appealing to a transhistorical narrative to order his account. The result is an historiography more historicist and relatively more sympathetic to the decisions of historical figures than those of his contemporaries and predecessors.

The curious "Dialogue" (1751), appended to the *Enquiry concerning the Principles of Morals,* and Hume's essay "Of some Remarkable Customs" are consistent with this historiography in arguing for the relativity of morals and in portraying an attempt to understand ancient practices (which for those of Hume's time appeared as incestuous and parricidal) in terms of the norms employed by those who had engaged in them. Accordingly, Hume resisted judging Charles I and the Stuarts harshly, and his sympathetic restraint earned him a reputation for conservatism and condemnation from liberal leaders such as William Pitt the Elder.

Liberal criticism retarded the sales of Hume's *History of England,* at least at first, and in a sense such criticism is well founded. While it would be wrong to characterize Hume as a Jacobite or a monarchist, and while he supported an expanding commercial society, advocated the extension of liberty, and criticized the influence of religion on public affairs, he did not embrace the philosophical dynamics of liberal political theory. Book 3 of *A Treatise of Human Nature,* especially his sections on justice, as well as critical essays such as "Of the First Principles of Government" and "Of the Original Contract," aim to undermine liberal efforts to ground the legitimacy of government in an antecedent social contract. Not an adherent to the doctrine of intrinsic or God-given rights, Hume looked instead to custom, tradition, and the natural human capacities for pleasure, pain, and sympathy to legitimate the state, a position that excludes neither monarchical nor parliamentary rule.

Hume also found himself concerned about the enthusiastic excesses to which those committed to a metaphysically or rationalistically based liberalism were often inclined. Such concern, for example, led

Hume to condemn John Wilkes and those who fomented the Wilkes riots of 1762. The conservatism of Hume's political theory, then, is a form of philosophical skepticism. It holds that ultimately reason, theology, and metaphysics cannot and should not ground political institutions but that society must accept the finitude of the human condition and rely instead solely on historical practice and natural feeling. The Irish theorist Edmund Burke also attacked Wilkes in *Thoughts on the Cause of the Present Discontents* (1770), and in *Reflections on the Revolution in France* (1790) he criticized what he found to be the excesses that metaphysical liberalism had produced across the English Channel. In his regard for the importance of tradition and custom Burke produced a political theory that, though significantly more partisan, resembles Hume's in important ways. Burke and Hume had met in 1759. Hume had been impressed with Burke's *Philosophical Inquiry into the Origin of our Ideas of the Sublime and Beautiful* (1757). Burke seems to have regarded Hume as politically sympathetic, but he disapproved of his views on religion and grew increasingly distant and critical of him.

Aside from his publications, Hume's influence on Scottish letters was also felt through his participation in various scholarly societies. Late in 1751 he was elected to the position of joint secretary of the Philosophical Society of Edinburgh with Alexander Monro. In 1753 Hume was also elected to membership in the Literary Society of Glasgow, a group that had been established a year earlier. In 1754 Hume joined with Smith, Allan Ramsay, Kames, and his good friend Alexander Wedderburn in founding and serving as treasurer of the influential Select Society. The Philosophical Society, established in 1731 to collect and publish essays on medicine and surgery, had expanded in 1737 under the direction of Professor Colin Maclaurin to include arts, science, and letters more broadly conceived. In 1783, through the influence of William Robertson, the group was chartered as the Royal Society of Edinburgh. Under Hume's and Monro's editorship, the society published in 1754 *Essays and Observations, Physical and Literary, Read before a Society in Edinburgh and Published by Them.* In the process of producing this publication Hume brokered a dispute between Kames and Professor John Stewart on Newtonian physics. Hume's efforts through these societies is particularly significant in having helped religious moderates, such as his friends Robertson and Hugh Blair, supplant conservative elements of the Scottish Kirk.

In conservative churchmen, however, Hume found vigorous and hostile adversaries. The Reverend John Witherspoon—who became the only clerical signatory of the Declaration of Independence—had already attacked religious moderation together with Kames and Hume in his exceedingly popular *Ecclesiastical Characteristics* (1753). Witherspoon was joined in the assault by the Reverend George Anderson, in his *An Estimate of the Profit and Loss of Religion* (1753), and the Reverend John Bonar of Cockpen, in his *An Analysis of the Moral and Religious Sentiments contained in the Writings of Sopho, and David Hume, Esq.* (1755).

The General Assembly of the Church of Scotland considered formally prosecuting and excommunicating Hume and Kames in 1755 and 1756, an act of censure that would render social and professional life not impossible but decidedly more difficult for each man. Supporters of Hume, especially among the moderates, mounted a vigorous defense both in the press and before the General Assembly. The most impressive of these efforts were, perhaps, those of Wedderburn and Wallace, the former arguing that if Hume were in fact an atheist, a Christian body such as the Church of Scotland would have no jurisdiction over him: "Why are you to summon him before you more than any Jew or Mahometan who may happen to be travelling within your bounds? Your *liber,* as we lawyers call it, is *ex facie* inept, irrelevant, and null, for it begins by alleging that the defender denies and disbelieves Christianity, and then it seeks to proceed against him and to punish him as a Christian." The cases against first Kames and then Hume were ultimately dismissed.

In 1757 Hume published *Four Dissertations* with Andrew Millar in London. The original plan of the text was to include a now-lost essay on the metaphysical principles of geometry. Hume also considered including essays on suicide and the immortality of the soul but suppressed them both when, through the agency of the Reverend William Warburton, he was threatened with prosecution. *Four Dissertations* remains remarkable, however, for the presence of *The Natural History of Religion.* Although refusing to suppress it, Hume altered this text in the face of Warburton's threats. Its central thesis, nonetheless, remained intact: religious belief is the natural product of the human mind's confrontation with the natural world, and its progress from animism through polytheism through monotheism can be explained naturalistically. Furthermore, religious beliefs of various forms are liable to bear with them attending moral inclinations. Polytheism lends itself to superstition and moral variation but also to tolerance. Monotheism, although conceptually more sophisticated and more inclined to produce rigorous moral standards, is also given to intolerance. Hume, in *The Natural History of Religion,* not only carries on his social and moral critique of religion while naturalistically challenging the claims of religious dogma; he also uses naturalism to reconceive religion itself.

In October 1763 Hume assumed the position of private secretary to the British ambassador to France, the earl of Hertford. He held this position for a little more than two years, until January 1766, the last six months of which he also served as the ambassador's chargé d'affaires. On arrival in Paris and his presentation to the royal court at Fountainebleau, Hume, whose reputation had preceded him, was bathed in adulation. While in France he was a regular visitor to various salons, becoming personally close to the comtesse de Boufflers.

Hume's immersion in French intellectual life brought him into contact with many important French intellectuals. The *philosophe* Jean le Rond d'Alembert was among his favorites, and through him Hume became acquainted with the poet, critic, and dramatist Jean-François Marmontel. Georges-Louis Leclerc Comte de Buffon came to know Hume and presented him with a portion of his important *Histoire naturelle, génerale et particulière* (Natural History, General and Particular, 1749–1788). Hume also became familiar with figures such as Denis Diderot, editor and author of *L'encyclopédie* (1751–1776); Turgot; the novelist Charles Pinot Duclos; and the *philosophe* Claude-Adrien Helvétius, whose *De l'Esprit* (1758) Hume had refused to translate and whom Hume had declined to support for membership in the Royal Society in 1763. Hume had earlier engaged Paul Henri Thiry, Baron d'Holbach, in correspondence, and their friendship was resumed during his stay in France. Hume's affiliations with the French were generally pleasant for him, and he considered making permanent residence there. He found himself, however, at times disaffected among the *philosophes,* discovering his skeptical reserve to be as inconsistent with dogmatic atheism and deism as it had been with dogmatic Christianity.

In the latter part of 1765 Hume assisted Jean-Jacques Rousseau, author of *Du contrat social* (The Social Contract, 1762), in fleeing Switzerland and France, where he had been persecuted for sedition and impiety, for the protection of England. Traveling together, the two men embarked from Paris on 4 January 1766, reaching London on 13 January. Rousseau, however, who settled in Derbyshire, came to believe that Hume was in fact a conspirator with his enemies and by July had accused Hume of duplicity, breaking off all connection with him. News of the conflict spread among the intelligentsia on both sides of the Channel, ultimately provoking Hume to produce an account of the event, the pamphlet *Exposé suc-*

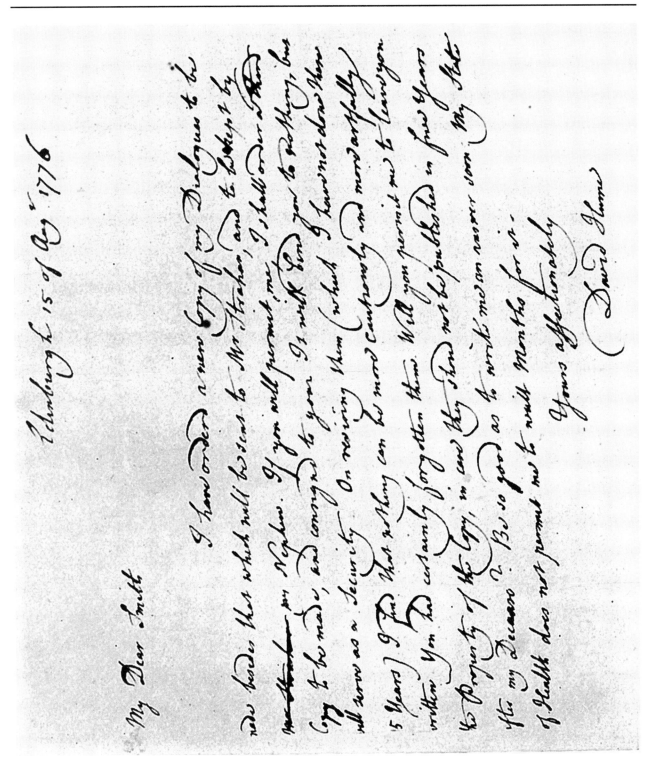

Hume's last letter to his friend Adam Smith, dated ten days before his death (Royal Society of Edinburgh)

cinct de la contestation qui s'est élevée entre M. Hume et M. Rousseau, avec les pièces justificatives (1766; translated as *A Concise and Genuine Account of the Dispute between Mr. Hume and Mr. Rousseau,* 1766), edited by D'Alembert and Jean-Baptiste Suard. Hume responded to Rousseau's accusations not with anger or resentment but considered them simply part of a sad and "miserable affair," and Rousseau returned to France in 1767.

In 1767 Hume took up residence in London, having assumed the post of undersecretary of state for the Northern Department of the British government. During this time he was able to circulate through venues of high society in the capital. Although his commission expired in January 1768, Hume remained in London until August 1769. Among the benefits of his connection to members of the government was his acquisition of permission from the Crown to inspect the papers of various government archives, access that assisted him in the continued writing and improvement of his *History of England.* Hume is thought to have authored at this time a letter to the editor of the *Gentleman's Magazine* (volume 39, 1769), accompanied by a translation of the prospectus to the Abbé Morellet's proposed *Dictionnaire de Commerce,* as well as an "Advertisement" for Baron Christof Hermann von Manstein's *Memoirs of Russia, Historical, Political, and Military, from the Year MDCCXXVII to MDCCXLIV.* Returning to Edinburgh in 1769, Hume took up residences in James's Court. In 1771 Hume completed construction on his last place of residence, a house on the southwest corner of St. Andrew's Square in the New Town, the corner of a lane that was soon dubbed "St. David's Street."

Criticism of Hume's thought in his later years centered around what became known as Scottish Common Sense Philosophy. Thomas Reid, professor of philosophy at King's College, University of Aberdeen, and a friendly acquaintance of Hume, had published the influential *Inquiry into the Human Mind, on the Principles of Common Sense* in 1764; Reid was followed by the poet James Oswald and philosopher Dugald Stewart, who wrote *Elements of the Philosophy of the Human Mind* (1792).

The more dramatic *An Essay on the Nature and Immutability of Truth; in opposition to Sophistry and Scepticism* (1770) brought common-sense criticism of Hume before the public's attention. Copies began to circulate of an unpublished pamphlet by Beattie, "Castle of Scepticism" (1767), which depicted Hume as the inhabitant of a forbidding castle who lured in the unsuspecting in order to subject them to various (skeptical) tortures. The work was enormously popular and ran through five editions by 1776. Hume never replied to Beattie directly, but in October 1775 he did take the extraordinary step of publishing an

"Advertisement" that he instructed his publisher to attach to the second volume of all future editions of *Essays and Treatises.* The advertisement was, he told his publisher Strahan, "a compleat Answer to Dr. Reid and to that bigotted and silly Fellow, Beattie." The advertisement is a curious addendum, for it disavows *A Treatise of Human Nature* as a "juvenile" work that he had sent "to the press too early." "Henceforth," writes Hume about the material in *Essays and Treatises,* including the *Enquiries,* "the Author desires, that the following Pieces may alone be regarded as containing his philosophical sentiments and principles."

Systematic philosophical inquiry of the sort Hume engaged was little known in the British colonies outside of a few private collections and important centers of learning such as Harvard College and the College of New Jersey (now Princeton University), where the former Edinburgher John Witherspoon–a conservative Presbyterian critic of Hume and religious moderation–had become president in 1768 and where Hume's thought almost certainly would have been addressed. On taking office Witherspoon condemned the excesses of Berkeley he found pervasive at the college, advocating in its place Scottish Common Sense philosophy, an alternative that also appealed to Thomas Jefferson.

Copies of Hume's *History of England* were rather common in the North American colonies. They were not, however, received uncritically. The history had acquired a reputation for being pro-Tory and was therefore widely condemned, often by prominent figures such as Jonathan Edwards and Jefferson. Writing to John Adams in 1816, Jefferson remarked that the *History of England* "has done more to sap the free principles of the English Constitution than the largest standing army." The severity of early American disapprobation for Hume's text was in 1771 so severe, in fact, that the colonial reprint publisher Robert Bell was unable to interest booksellers in an American edition. Despite the clamor against his texts, however, the frequency of reference to Hume's thought indicates that his work nevertheless managed to become widely read among political, literate Americans.

Among those devoted to Hume was Benjamin Franklin. The two men became acquainted with one another in 1757 when Franklin was in London. In 1760 and 1771 Franklin traveled to Edinburgh to visit Hume, and a 1760 letter from Franklin suggests that he had for some time been a consistent reader of Hume's work, at least his essays. Franklin wrote to Hume on 27 September 1760 that "I have lately read with great Pleasure, as I do every thing of yours, the excellent Essay on the *Jealousy of Commerce.*" Franklin sent Hume a paper on the lightning rod to be read before the Philosophical Society of Edinburgh, and, interestingly enough, Franklin made use of a rather Humean argument before the Philadelphia Convention of 1787 in maintaining that no high officers in any branch of government should receive a salary. Other colonial figures made use of Hume in advancing arguments on political issues, including whether to have a militia system or a standing army and whether governors or assemblies ought to be invested with the right to set crown officers' fees.

Alexander Hamilton, too, was acquainted with and influenced by Hume's work. The 1780 Committee on Finance in the Continental Congress studied Hume's economic essays, and in the 1787 Philadelphia Congress Hamilton appealed to Hume, perhaps speciously, in arguing against legally penalizing corrupt officeholders. Hume also apparently taught Hamilton that an expanding commercial order is consistent, even complementary, with a stable republic. In "Federalist No. 85," the last of *The Federalist Papers,* Publius (here Hamilton) quotes directly from Hume's important essay "Of the Rise and Progress of the Arts and Sciences." Hamilton writes of Hume: "The zeal for attempts to amend, prior to the establishment of the Constitution, must abate in every man who is ready to accede to the truth of the following observations of a writer equally solid an ingenious: 'To balance a large state or society [says he], whether monarchical or republican, on general laws, is a work of so great difficulty that no human genius, however comprehensive, is able, by the mere dint of reason and reflection, to effect it. The judgments of many must unite in the work; EXPERIENCE must guide their labor; TIME must bring it to perfection, and the FEELING of inconveniences must correct the mistakes which they *inevitably* fall into in their first trials and experiments.'"

James Madison's "Federalist No. 10," however, represents perhaps Hume's best-known point of influence on the new American state. Hume's 1752 essay "Idea of a Perfect Commonwealth" in the *Political Discourses* may well have provided the intellectual source and underpinning for Madison's vision. Revising the position developed by James Harrington in *Commonwealth of Oceana* (1656), Hume advanced the then-startling idea that a large, properly constituted republic could be established and made stable. Indeed, the very size of it, Hume asserted, would contribute to its stability by inhibiting the development of faction. This was a highly unusual notion, contrary to then-prevailing contentions supported by Montesquieu and most other political theorists of the time. Madison's defense of the new, relatively enormous

American republic in "Federalist No. 10" is astonishingly similar to Hume's account.

Other important colonial figures also apparently drew on Hume's work. Among the most prominent of these may be counted Samuel Adams, John Dickinson, Charles Lee, George Washington, John Randolph of Roanoke, Benjamin Rush, and Robert Carter of Nomini Hall. Those men whom Hume inspired, however, were not always members of the group of colonial figures who have retained widespread esteem. In producing pamphlets and apologetic literature, a number of proslavery authors also drew on Hume's work, specifically on the claims he advanced in a note appended to his essay "Of National Characters," about the inferiority of darker-skinned peoples.

Hume died at approximately four o'clock in the afternoon on 25 August 1776 in his home on St. Andrew's Square in Edinburgh. The apartment was situated on what was first popularly known as and then officially became "St. David's Street." His death was not sudden or unexpected, as he had been aware of himself wasting away through gastrointestinal disorders since 1772. In preparation for his death he drafted a will arranging for his burial on the south side of the Calton Hill Church Yard, overlooking the north side of the Old Town. He also arranged for a privately funded monument to be built over his grave, to be inscribed with only his name and the dates of his birth and death.

Hume made efforts to ensure the publication of manuscripts that had earlier been suppressed for reasons of prudence, as well as a short autobiography he produced in April 1776. Smith, to whom Hume had granted the right to make amendments, published *The Life of David Hume, Esq.: Written by Himself,* with William Strahan in 1777. *Two Essays,* on suicide and on the immortality of the soul, were released as an unauthorized publication the same year, receiving widespread and generally hostile attention for their heterodoxical positions on the subjects. Hume remained intellectually active until shortly before his demise, ordering and reading Smith's *The Wealth of Nations* (1776) and Gibbon's *The Decline and Fall of the Roman Empire* in the last months of his life. He apparently also took comfort in reading Lucian's *Dialogues of the Dead* as the end approached. He mused about arguments that others had produced in their attempts to convince Charon that their time had not yet come, but, he told Smith, he could not honestly advance any of them: "he had no house to finish, he had no daughter to provide for, he had no enemies upon whom he wished to revenge himself." According to Smith, Hume then remarked: "I have done every thing of consequence which I ever meant to do, and I could at no time expect to leave my relations and friends in a better situation than that in which I am now likely to leave them: I therefore have all reason to die contented."

In 1779, probably through the agency of Hume's nephew David, the *Dialogues concerning Natural Religion* was published. The text, on which Hume had been working since at least the early 1750s, followed the rhetorical format and often the argumentation of Cicero's *De Natura Deorum,* an allusion to which much of its audience would have been alert. Pitting a natural theologian (Cleanthes, who is aligned with Cicero's Balbus and whose name recalls the ancient leader of the Stoa) against a pious and enthusiastic believer (Demea, aligned with Cicero's Vellius) and a shrewdly rational skeptic (Philo, after Cotta from *De Natura Deorum* and Cicero's skeptical eclectic teacher, Philo of Alexandria), the text develops a series of trenchant lines of argument aimed at undermining the aspirations of what has been called "natural theology" or the attempt to employ natural reason in reflecting on the natural world in order to determined truths concerning the existence, nature, and commandments of God. Hume seems to have drawn arguments to undermine natural theology from Butler, Clarke, George Cheyne, and Colin Maclaurin in addition to Cicero and Sextus Empiricus.

Hume's exposition has seemed especially effective against the "argument from design," a line of reasoning pursued by natural theologians, which maintains that the order, beauty, complexity, and coherence of the natural world testify to the existence of an intelligent, purposeful, and supernatural designer. This argument gained significant currency after having been advanced by Newton in his *Philosophiae Naturalis Principia Mathematica* (1687). One of its most popular renditions appeared in Dutch scientist-theologian Bernard Nieuwentyt's *The Religious Philosophers* (1714; five English editions between 1718–1745). For many, *Dialogues concerning Natural Religion* has remained the definitive text for subverting the argument from design.

Hume's death had become an important, symbolic event for many, and crowds gathered to see whether or not the so-called Great Infidel would embrace Christianity on his deathbed. James Boswell, who had been corresponding with Hume since 1763, was particularly disturbed by his equanimity in the face of death, calling on him in 1775 and on 7 July 1776, shortly before he succumbed, to interview him about his convictions. The conversation apparently annoyed Hume and left Boswell deeply disturbed. Boswell recounts that he "said he never had entertained any belief in Religion since he began to read Locke and Clarke . . . He then said flatly that the Morality of every Religion was bad, and, I really thought, was not jocular when he said 'that when he heard a man was religious, he concluded he was a rascal, though he had known some instances of very good men being religious.' . . . I had a strong curiosity to be satisfied if he persisted in disbelieving a future state even when he had death before his eyes. I was persuaded from what he now said, and from his manner of saying it, that he did persist. I asked him if it was possible that there might be a future state. He answered It was possible that a piece of coal put upon the fire would not burn. . . . I asked him if the thought of Annihilation never gave him any uneasiness. He said not the least; no more than the thought that he had not been, as Lucretius observes."

Hume seems to have remained a skeptic until the end. In the immediate aftermath of his death and throughout the nineteenth century his influence seems to have been felt principally in matters of religion and history. Hume's naturalism too retained its vitality and influenced thinkers such as Charles Darwin and Thomas Henry Huxley. John Stuart Mill's inductive logical theory was greatly inspired by Hume. In the early twentieth century Hume's epistemology and philosophy of mind helped to determine the formation of positivism and advances in the philosophy of science. More recently, Hume's sociopolitical work has again attracted serious attention, and studies of his work have broadened from a relatively narrow focus on *A Treatise of Human Nature* and the *Enquiries* to interpretations of the Humean corpus as a whole. David Hume remains a central figure in college and university instruction in early modern philosophy.

Letters:

J. Y. T. Greig, ed., *The Letters of David Hume,* 2 volumes (Oxford: Clarendon Press, 1932);

Raymond Klibansky and Ernest C. Mossner, eds., *New Letters of David Hume* (Oxford: Clarendon Press, 1954).

Bibliographies:

Greig and Harold Beynon, *Calendar of Hume MSS in the Possession of the Royal Society of Edinburgh* (Edinburgh, 1932);

T. E. Jessop, *A Bibliography of David Hume and of Scottish Philosophy from Francis Hutcheson to Lord Balfour* (New York: Russell & Russell, 1966);

Roland Hall, *Fifty Years of Hume Scholarship: A Bibliographic Guide* (Edinburgh: Edinburgh University Press, 1978).

Biographies:

William Smellie, "The Life of David Hume, Esq." in *Literary and characteristical lives of John Gregory, Henry Home, lord Kames, David Hume, esq. and Adam Smith, L.L.D. To which are added A dissertation on public spirit, and three essays,* edited by Alexander Smellie (Edinburgh: Alex. Smellie, 1800);

John Hill Burton, *The Life and Correspondence of David Hume,* 2 volumes (Edinburgh: Tait, 1846);

J. Y. T. Greig, *David Hume* (London: Cape, 1931);

Ernest Campbell Mossner, *The Life of David Hume* (Edinburgh: Thomas Nelson, 1954).

References:

Páll Ardal, *Passion and Value in Hume's Treatise* (Edinburgh: Edinburgh University Press, 1966);

Tom Beauchamp and Alexander Rosenberg, *Hume and the Problem of Causation* (Oxford: Oxford University Press, 1981);

Laurence Bongie, *David Hume, Prophet of the Counter-Revolution* (Oxford: Clarendon Press, 1965);

Nicholas Capaldi, *David Hume the Newtonian Philosopher* (Boston: Twayne, 1975);

Ian C. Cunningham, "The Arrangement of the Royal Society of Edinburgh's David Hume Manuscripts," *Bibliotheck,* 15 (1988): 8–22;

"David Hume's 'An Historical Essay on Chivalry and modern Honour,'" *Modern Philology,* 45 (1947): 54–60;

Duncan Forbes, *Hume's Philosophical Politics* (Cambridge: Cambridge University Press, 1975);

J. C. A. Gaskin, *Hume's Philosophy of Religion* (London: Macmillan, 1978);

Hume Studies (1975–);

Peter Jones, *Hume's Sentiments, Their Ciceronian and French Context* (Edinburgh: Edinburgh University Press, 1982);

Donald W. Livingston, *Hume's Philosophy of Common Life* (Chicago: University of Chicago Press, 1984);

David Miller, *Philosophy and Ideology in Hume's Political Thought* (Oxford: Clarendon Press, 1981);

David Fate Norton, "Baron Hume's Bequest: The Hume Manuscripts and Their First Use," in *Year-book of the Royal Society of Edinburgh* (Edinburgh: 1987), pp. 26–43;

Norton, *David Hume, Common-Sense Moralist, Sceptical Metaphysician* (Princeton: Princeton University Press, 1982);

Terence Penelhum, *Hume* (New York: St. Martin's Press, 1975);

Nicholas Phillipson, *Hume* (London: Weidenfeld & Nicolson, 1989);

Donald T. Siebert, *The Moral Animus of David Hume* (Newark: University of Delaware Press, 1990);

Norman Kemp Smith, *The Philosophy of David Hume: A Critical Study of its Origins and Central Doctrines* (London & New York: Macmillan, 1941);

John P. Wright, *The Sceptical Realism of David Hume* (Manchester: Manchester University Press, 1983).

Papers:

The most significant holding of David Hume's papers is the Hume Manuscripts at the National Library of Scotland. Other manuscripts, journals, and official papers are held at the Huntington Library; the British Library; the British Museum; the Pierpont Morgan Library; the Keynes Library, King's College, Cambridge University; the Public Record Office, London; the William Andrews Clark Memorial Library; the City Chambers, Edinburgh; and the New Register House, Edinburgh.

Francis Hutcheson

(8 August 1694 – 8 August 1746)

Marie Martin
Clemson University

See also the Hutcheson entry in *DLB 31: American Colonial Writers, 1735–1781.*

BOOKS: *An Inquiry into the Original of our Ideas of Beauty and Virtue; In Two Treatises. In which the Principles of the late Earl of Shaftesbury are Explain'd and Defended, against the Author of the Fable of the Bees; and the Ideas of Moral Good and Evil are Establish'd, according to the Sentiments of the Antient Moralists. With an Attempt to Introduce a Mathematical Calculation in Subjects of Morality* (London: Printed by J. Darby, 1725; corrected and enlarged, 1726; fourth edition, corrected, London: Printed for D. Midwinter, A. Bettesworth & C. Hitch, J. & J. Pemberton, R. Ware, C. Rivington, F. Clay, A. Ward, J. & P. Knapton, T. Longman, R. Hett & J. Wood / Glasgow: R. Foulis, 1738);

An Essay on the Nature and Conduct of the Passions and Affections. With Illustrations on the Moral Sense (London: Printed by J. Darby & T. Browne, 1728; third edition, revised and enlarged, London: Printed for A. Ward, J. & P. Knapton, T. Longman, S. Birt, C. Hitch, L. Gilliver, T. Astley, S. Austen, and J. Rivington, 1742);

De naturali hominum Socialitate. Oratio Inauguralis (Glasgow: University Press, 1730);

Letters Between the late Mr. Gilbert Burnet and Mr. Hutchinson [sic], Concerning the True Foundations of Virtue and Moral Goodness . . . To Which Is Added, a Postscript, Wrote by Mr. Burnet Some Time Before His Death (London: Printed by W. Wilkins, 1735);

Considerations on Patronages. Addressed to the Gentlemen of Scotland (London: Printed for J. Roberts, 1735);

Philosophiae moralis institutio compendiaria, Ethices et Jurisprudentiae Naturalis elementa continens Lib. III (Glasgow: R. Foulis, 1742); translated as *A Short Introduction to Moral Philosophy, in Three Books; containing the Elements of Ethicks and the Law of Nature* (Glasgow: R. Foulis, 1747);

Francis Hutcheson; portrait by Allan Ramsay (University of Glasgow)

Metaphysicae Synopsis: ontologiam, et, pneumatologiam complectens (Glasgow: R. Foulis, 1742; revised and enlarged, 1744);

Reflections upon Laughter; and Remarks upon The fable of the Bees (Glasgow: Printed by R. Urie for Daniel Baxter, 1750);

A System of Moral Philosophy, in Three Books . . . Published from the Original Manuscript, by his son, Francis Hutcheson, M.D. To which is prefixed Some Account of the Life, Writings, and Character of the Author, by the Reverend William Leechman . . . , 2 volumes (Glasgow: Printed and sold by R. and A. Foulis / London: Sold by A. Millar and T. Longman, 1755);

Logicae Compendium. Praefixa est dissertatio de philosophiae origine, ejusque inventoribus aut excultoribus praecipuis (Glasgow: Robert & Andrew Foulis, 1756).

Editions and Collections: *Works,* 6 volumes (Glasgow: R. Foulis, 1769–1774);

Collected Works of Francis Hutcheson: Facsimile Editions, 7 volumes, edited by Bernard Fabian (Hildesheim: Georg Olms, 1969–1971);

Thomas Mautner, *Francis Hutcheson: Two Texts on Human Nature* (Cambridge: Cambridge University Press, 1993).

OTHER: *Meditations of Marcus Aurelius Antoninus. Newly translated from the Greek. With Notes, and an Account of his Life,* introduction, annotations, and translation of books 3–7 attributed to Hutcheson (Glasgow: R. Foulis, 1742).

Francis Hutcheson, leading figure in the Scottish Enlightenment, is too often considered a minor moral philosopher, of interest only for his influence on David Hume and Adam Smith. Yet, Hutcheson created the moral sense theory, and it was within that framework that Hume and Smith developed their own theories. He was a founder in a way that Hume and Smith were not. He was also one of the foremost moral philosophers of his day, and the influence of his moral thought ranged from Thomas Reid, who was first attracted to philosophy by reading Hutcheson, to the major political and theological thinkers in the American colonies. By the mid eighteenth century his works were taught at Harvard University, Yale University and the College of Pennsylvania. Hutcheson was an acute critic and original thinker, and within a sustained attack on the various forms of egoism and voluntarism prevalent among his predecessors and contemporaries he developed a form of moral naturalism rooted in the notion that human beings have irreducibly benevolent motives that are approved by a unique "moral sense."

Hutcheson was a third-generation Presbyterian minister, his grandfather having emigrated from Scotland to Ulster as part of the settlement in the late seventeenth century. Hutcheson, the second son of John Hutcheson's first marriage, was born on 8 August 1694 on his grandfather's estate in Drumalig, County Down, and shortly after settled with his family in Ballyrea, just outside Armargh, where his father was minister. At the age of eight years he returned to his grandfather's home to attend a local Dissenter's school, where he would have received a classical education. At the age of fourteen he was sent to a Dissenter's academy in Killyleagh, County Down. University education was not available to Presbyterians in Ireland, and such academies were established to provide higher learning. He appears to

have received an excellent background in classics and philosophy. Hutcheson was by all accounts a gifted scholar; his family decided to send him to the University of Glasgow to complete his studies. Already well advanced in his education when he entered in 1711, he completed his M.A. degree within a year and, after a year off, he entered the theological school in 1713, completing his studies four years later.

At the time Hutcheson matriculated, Glasgow was a provincial university more notable for religious orthodoxy than scholarship. Yet, there were notable exceptions. John Loudon, whose class on natural philosophy Hutcheson entered upon arriving, and Gershom Charmicheal, professor of moral philosophy, were both respected scholars, although both were proponents of the Reformed Scholasticism that informed the religious orthodoxy of Scottish Presbyterianism at the time. Two fundamental tenets of such scholasticism were the view that humans, having fallen, were utterly sinful or "depraved," and that, while all humans long for eternal happiness, only some are predestined, through divine grace, for salvation. In contrast John Simson, professor of divinity, and Alexander Dunlop, professor of Greek, both opposed the prevailing orthodoxy, advocating a more secularized learning and a more moderate theology. Simson expressed doubts about the naturally sinful state of man, emphasized the benevolence of God, and suggested the possibility of salvation for all who were virtuous—even heathens. Such views led in 1729 to Simson's suspension from teaching after conviction in the ecclesiastic courts on charges of heterodoxy. Dunlop, a kind and cultured man who became a lifelong friend of Hutcheson, was deeply committed to reviving interest in Greek and the classics. Hutcheson had already exhibited remarkable talent in classics and here developed the abiding love of classical learning evident throughout his philosophical works.

The first evidence of specifically philosophical leaning in Hutcheson's thought appeared in 1717, about the time he was finishing his theological study. He wrote a letter to Samuel Clarke criticizing Clarke's a priori method of argument concerning the existence of God. Clarke had delivered two series of Boyle lectures in 1704 and 1705. In the first he offered a demonstrative proof of the existence and attributes of God. In the second he developed a moral theory—a version of what is called moral rationalism—wherein moral good and evil are based on immutable and rationally discernable moral relations. Hutcheson's letter has not survived, nor is it known whether Clark replied. Years passed before Hutcheson took up the criticism of moral rationalism, first in his 1725 correspondence with Gilbert Burnet in the *London Journal* and next in his treatise *An*

Essay on the Nature and Conduct of the Passions and Affections. With Illustrations on the Moral Sense (1728).

After completing his studies Hutcheson returned to Ireland, where he was licensed as probationer in 1719. The conflict he had experienced at Glasgow between the orthodox and the moderates was a reflection of a wider conflict among Presbyterians during this period. Belfast was the center of a movement of those who refused to subscribe to the Westminster Confession. The nonsubscribers rejected the strict orthodoxy of traditional Calvinism in favor of the more moderate view. The Belfast ministers were supported by Presbyterian ministers in Dublin, and they invited Hutcheson to start a private dissenter's academy in Dublin. Such an undertaking was both ambitious and risky. To set up what was, in essence, a college for dissenters in Dublin, bastion of the established church, would require enormous tact and diplomacy, attributes that Hutcheson had in ample supply.

Indeed, he not only managed to avoid confrontation but soon became part of the "Molesworth Circle," a group of young men under the mentorship of Viscount Robert Molesworth. Molesworth was a retired merchant, former diplomat to the Danish Court, and prominent member of Dublin society. He had corresponded with Shaftesbury and espoused Shaftesbury's ideas, as did the members of his circle. He was also deeply concerned with reforming the Scottish universities. Also included in this circle were Edward Synge and James Arbuckle. Synge, an intimate of George Berkeley, later became a bishop of the Church of Ireland. Arbuckle had been in correspondence with Molesworth while a student at Glasgow and had already earned a literary reputation before joining the circle. Within this group Hutcheson published his first philosophical writings.

His first piece, "Reflections on our Common Systems of Morality," appeared in two installments of the *London Journal* in 1724 under the pen name "Philanthropos." It features a general preview of the themes that were later developed in his books: modern systems of morality are inconsistent with both piety and virtue. Virtue consists in love toward God and one's fellow creatures. The modern systems, which represent God as jealous, resentful, and vengeful, hurry over discussion of God's goodness so that they may "get into their favourite topicks of bribes and terrors, to compel men to love God and one another, in order to obtain the pleasures of heaven, and avoid eternal damnation." Surely such depictions are incapable of raising any genuine love toward God. Similarly, by representing men as being moved only by self-interest and by continually furnishing everyone "with a thousand observations about their wickedness and corruption," they are more apt to raise hatred or contempt toward fellow creatures than love. On the other hand, when God is seen as benevolent and merciful and fellow creatures are seen as possessing kind and tender instincts and affections, humans are naturally led to love both, which proves these qualities to be true principles of virtue and morality.

Hutcheson also criticizes the contracting of the moral sphere from the broad classical concern with how to live the best life to the narrow modern preoccupation with rights. Moderns "have very much left out of their systems, all enquiries into happiness, and speak only of the external advantages of peace and wealth. . . ." Likewise, there is little discussion of the duty to love others, a topic they "hurry over . . . till they come to the doctrine of rights, and proper injuries; and like the civilians, whose only business it is to teach how far refractory or knavish men should be compelled by force, they spend all their reasonings upon perfect or external rights."

These lines of argument are developed in detail in Hutcheson's first book, *An Inquiry into the Original of our Ideas of Beauty and Virtue; In Two Treatises. In which the Principles of the late Earl of Shaftesbury are Explain'd and Defended, against the Author of the Fable of the Bees; and the Ideas of Moral Good and Evil are Establish'd, according to the Sentiments of the Antient Moralists. With an Attempt to Introduce a Mathematical Calculation in Subjects of Morality,* published in January 1725. *An Inquiry into the Original of our Ideas of Beauty and Virtue* is actually two separate books, or "treatises" as Hutcheson called them, the first "Concerning Beauty, Order, Design" and the second "Concerning Moral Good and Evil." That Hutcheson would have introduced his philosophy with a theory of beauty is not surprising given the influence of Shaftesbury's ideas during this period. His likening moral beauty to aesthetic beauty is also Shaftesburian, although the analogy would have been familiar to him from classical thought as well. His thesis—that beauty consists in uniformity amid variety—is not original, nor did he claim it to be. In fact, when the reviewer in *Bibliotheque Angloise* (number 13, 1725) declared that the essence of Hutcheson's views were the same as the theory of Jean Pierre de Crousaz presented in *Traite du beau* (Treatise on beauty, 1715), Hutcheson sent an irritable reply to the editor claiming that, although he was not particularly influenced by Crousaz, he never intended to claim any originality.

More original is Hutcheson's notion of a sense of beauty or, borrowing Joseph Addison's term, an "internal" sense. This "superior sense" is reflexive, or secondary—it operates upon previous ideas. In this early work Hutcheson appears to allow that perceptions of the internal sense may arise either immediately from some previous sensations or impressions (in Nicolas de Malebranche's sense rather than Hume's) or from some previous conception. Thus, animals may have different senses of beauty whereby certain qualities that are indifferent to humans are "delightful" to them. Yet the human sense of beauty can also be aroused by the conception of abstract truths such as theorems that are apprehended as offering infinite particular truths or vast numbers of corollaries. Although the qualities or relations that arouse or produce the sensation of beauty exist in or among objects independent of the perception of them, the beauty is the effect on the perceiving mind. Hutcheson here first introduces an analogy that he later applies to the moral sense as well. The perceptions of the internal sense are like the perceptions of secondary qualities. By beauty "is not to be understood any Quality suppos'd to be in the Object . . . , without relation to any Mind which perceives it: For Beauty, like other Names of sensible Ideas, properly denotes the *Perception* of some Mind; so *Cold, Hot, Sweet, Bitter,* denote the Sensations in our Minds, to which perhaps there is no resemblance in the Objects, which excite these Ideas in us. . . . Were there no Mind with a *Sense* of Beauty to contemplate Objects, I see not how they could be call'd *beautiful.*"

As "Reflections on our Common Systems of Morality" reveals, Hutcheson's dissatisfaction with modern moral systems stemmed from what he perceived as a pernicious misrepresentation of both human and divine nature and the consequent shrunken and distorted conception of the moral realm. The moderns have turned away from the true aim of moral philosophy pursued by the ancients: discovery of the best life for human beings and instruction about how to live well. In the treatise "Concerning Moral Good and Evil" he presents his theory within the context of an extensive attack on the egoistic underpinnings of modern "selfish" systems.

Natural good is "the Pleasure in our sensible Perceptions of any kind." Objects that arouse this pleasure are called "immediate goods," while objects conducive to such goods are called "advantageous." Both are pursued from the motive of self-love. Modern systems mistakenly attempt to reduce moral good to some species of natural good. Such attempts can be divided into two sorts. First, there are those who, like Samuel Pufendorf, John Locke, and many orthodox theologians, claim that all moral qualities arise only in relation to a law imposed by a superior who is capable of enforcing them through the sanctions of rewards and punishments. Second, there are those who claim that moral good is not a mediate good or advantage but an immediate natural good. Virtue, whether in ourselves or others, is not pur-

AN
INQUIRY
INTO THE
ORIGINAL of our IDEAS
OF
BEAUTY and VIRTUE;
In Two TREATISES.
IN WHICH
The Principles of the late Earl of SHAFTESBURY are Explain'd and Defended, against the Author of the *Fable of the Bees:*
AND THE
Ideas of *Moral Good* and *Evil* are establish'd, according to the Sentiments of the Antient *Moralists.*
With an Attempt to introduce a *Mathematical Calculation* in Subjects of *Morality.*

Itaque eorum ipsorum quæ aspectu sentiuntur, nullum aliud animal pulchritudinem, venustatem, convenientiam partium sentit : Quam similitudinem natura ratioque ab oculis ad animum transferens, multo etiam magis pulchritudinem, constantiam, ordinem in consiliis, factisque conservandum putat : Quibus ex rebus conflatur & efficitur id quod quærimus honestum : Quod etiamsi nobilitatum non sit, tamen honestum sit : quodque etiamsi à nullo laudetur, naturâ est laudabile. Formam quidem ipsam & faciem honesti vides, quæ si oculis cerneretur, mirabiles amores excitaret sapientiæ.   *Cic. de Off. lib.* I. c. 4.

LONDON:
Printed by J. DARBY in *Bartholomew-Close,* for WILL. and JOHN SMITH on the *Blind Key* in *Dublin* ; and sold by W. and J. INNYS at the West-End of St. *Paul's* Church-yard, J. OSBORN and T. LONGMAN in *Pater-Noster-Row,* and S. CHANDLER in the *Poultry.* M. DCC. XXV.

Title page for Hutcheson's first work, which includes his scheme for a "moral calculus" that uses mathematical formulas to determine whether an act is right or wrong (British Library)

sued or approved for its advantages but for its immediate pleasure. Humans approve others' virtue and are motivated to virtue themselves to obtain this pleasure from a motive of self-interest. Hutcheson argues that such views misunderstand both the nature of moral approval and the nature of virtue.

Humans morally approve actions and characters from distant ages and places, and, indeed, even in fictional representation, which are in no way to their advantage or disadvantage. Imagining the advantages or disadvantages that would have been received had one been in the situation will not produce the required results because, were they totally self-interested, people would always imagine themselves on the "victorious" side and "admire and love the successful *Tyrant* or *Traitor.*" One can hardly expect the generality of humans to conduct the chain of reasoning (supposing there is such a chain) required to link any action in the distant past to their present advantage. For "must a man have the

Reflection of Cumberland or Puffendorf, to admire *Generosity, Faith, Humanity, Gratitude?*" Indeed, because of the design of a benevolent Providence it is true that whatever benefits any part of the system of rational beings must benefit the whole, of which some share will redound to each individual, but such reflections will only "recommend to us, from *Self-Interest,* those Actions, which at first View our *moral Sense* determines us to admire, without considering this *Interest.*"

Bernard Mandeville claims that leaders do not admire virtue but encourage it by praise because of its usefulness to the state. Traitors who betray their country to a rival state are as useful to that rival as the heroes who defend it, yet they are not judged alike virtuous. And, if all are self-interested, what could the praise of others mean except that they find one useful? But why would self-interested people sacrifice their own advantage for the "reward" of being considered useful to others? Moral approval is not grounded in any notion of personal advantage; it is the immediate perception of a moral sense. Mandeville argued that private vices unintentionally promote public benefits. Hutcheson stands Mandeville on his head by arguing that just as God gave people external senses to protect their bodies and a sense of beauty to love knowledge and know God, so they were given a moral sense to direct their actions "so that while we are only intending the *Good* of others, we undesignedly promote our own greatest *private good.*"

Just as moral approval is not based upon any prospect of personal advantage, neither can virtue be reduced to any form of self-interest. The morality of any action lies entirely in the motive or, in the case of characters, in the disposition of motives. All motivation lies in the affections, and the only immediately motivating affections are desire and aversion. Desire and aversion toward rational agents are called "love" (desire for the happiness of others) and "hatred" (desire for the misery of others). No motive of interest or prospect of advantage can raise love or hatred, however; otherwise, people could be bribed to love others entirely unknown to them or those they perceive as vicious and to hate those unknown or perceived as virtuous. But, though bribes and threats may make people attempt to ruin those they love or support those they hate, they can no more affect affections then the prospect of recovering one's health can make the required "nauseous potion" actually taste pleasant. If, then, virtue lies in the motivating affection, and the only motivating affections toward rational agents are forms of love and hatred, neither of which can be affected by any views of advantage, there must be some other basis to virtue than views of advantage.

The alternative route to reducing the motive of virtue to self-interest by claiming that virtue is sought for its immediate "concomitant" pleasure is also unsuccessful, because virtue is not always pleasant, and people do not choose their affections. "[W]e do not *love,* because it is *pleasant* to love; we do not *chuse* this State, because it is an *advantageous,* or *pleasant* State: This Passion necessarily arises from seeing its proper Object, a *morally good Character.*" Arguments claiming that people seek their children's good and avoid their misery because they are pleased with their children's pleasure and pained by their pain follow only on the supposition that parents first love their children.

Thus, neither the affection constituting virtue nor the approval of such affection are reducible to any motives of self-love. Virtue is a "*Determination of our Nature to study the Good of others,*" or benevolence, and the moral sense "determines us to *approve* the Actions which flow from *this Love* in our selves or others.*"

Such benevolence clearly extends in various degrees to all mankind, "where there is no *interfering* Interest, which from *Self-love* may obstruct it." People approve actions just insofar as they believe them to flow from benevolence and approve capacities and dispositions only insofar as they suppose them applicable to and designed for benevolent purposes. Usefulness is morally irrelevant, for no matter how useful, an action has no moral beauty if it is known to flow from no kind affection, and "an unsuccessful attempt of kindness, or promoting the publick good, shall appear as amiable as the most successful, if it flow'd from as strong benevolence."

Because the virtuous are motivated by love of others, or the desire of their happiness, they will naturally concern themselves with the issue of their actions and seek to promote the most happiness. Thus, their choice will be guided by the principle that "*that Action is best,* which procures the *greatest Happiness* for the *greatest Numbers. . . .*" In his early works Hutcheson introduces a complex and formalized calculus for "regulating our election." The formalization turned out to be the source of a good deal of criticism, even ridicule, and was dropped in the fourth edition, although the calculus sans mathematical formulations is left virtually intact. Weighed into the calculus are the moral importance or dignity of the person affected, which may compensate mere numbers, the agent's abilities, the difficulty of performing the action, and the degree of opposing, self-interested motives.

An important distinction is that this calculus is not a utilitarian calculus. The utilitarians argue that consequences determine the moral worth of actions, that what makes an action morally good or right is that it promotes the most happiness. Hutcheson flatly denies this premise. The only factor in determining the morality of actions is their motive. Consequences are only relevant in two respects: first, "a *strong Benevolence* will not fail to make us careful of informing our selves right, concerning the truest Methods of serving the Interests of Mankind" in calculating the likely effects of particular actions; second, "we do not see into each others Hearts," and can only judge motives by "external signs," most significantly, by actions. Therefore, the moral goodness, or virtue, of agents is generally judged by the amount of happiness produced by their actions, not, as utilitarians later claimed, because the morality of actions is determined by or derived from the natural good of the consequences. Rather, one looks to consequences as natural indications of the type and strength of an agent's motives. Such evaluations may, of course, be mistaken; moral judgments are fallible, just as any other empirical judgments.

Hutcheson claims that an important result of the calculus is that it makes certain important corollaries evident, the most important being that even the highest virtue is not the exclusive province of the elite: "no external Circumstances of Fortune, no involuntary Disadvantages, can exclude any Mortal from the *most heroick Virtue*." Thus, "not only the *Prince,* the *Statesman,* the *General,* are capable of *true Heroism,*" but also "an *honest Trader,* the *kind Friend,* the *faithful prudent Advisor,* the *charitable* and *hospitable Neighbour,*" pursuing the public good to the extent that their abilities and circumstances allow, are equally virtuous.

The diversity of moral principles observable in different nations and ages does not indicate the lack of a universal moral sense but results from different opinions, about either how to achieve happiness, the character of others, or the will and laws of the Deity. Mistakes about fact, ignorance of true causes, false associations of ideas, and superstition all provide ample sources for such differences. Hutcheson finds it remarkable that the absurd practices that have prevailed in the world should be taken as evidence that there is no such thing as a moral sense, yet all the stupid and ridiculous opinions that have led to these practices are not considered evidence that humans have no reason. The sense of virtue leads people accurately according to the opinions they form; and if these opinions are absurd it is no wonder that the practices should be so also. Most evils produced by human beings are not the result of viciousness but arise from a sense of virtue based on false opinions or confined or limited views of the object of virtue.

A major obstacle to virtue is the mistaken belief that it conflicts with self-interest or, conversely, that self-interest is a more effectual means to natural good or happiness than virtue. This belief appears to follow because the motive of self-love is the desire for private

happiness, while virtue, or benevolence, is the desire for the happiness of others. Hutcheson is not attempting to make the case that an enlightened view of the best long-term interest would lead one to virtue. If the motive is self-interest, whether short- or long-term, enlightened or foolish, it is not virtue. Virtue does not consist in what promotes self-interest. The one promotes the other only because of the design of a wise and benevolent Providence who has arranged it so.

Hutcheson's arguments for the superiority of mental pleasures over physical pleasures and moral pleasures over all others are largely classical, as were Shaftesbury's. Hutcheson points out two main mistakes often made in comparing different sorts of pleasures. First, people often attempt to judge from their own experience of the different pleasures where they are most apt to confound them. Instead, one should judge from the view of an impartial spectator and "examine the Sentiments, which Men universally form of the State of others, when they are no way immediately concern'd; for in these Sentiments *human Nature* is *calm* and *undistrub'd,* and shews it *true Face.*" People might be tempted to think themselves happy in a state of uninterrupted physical pleasure. But would they judge another "in a sufficiently happy State, tho his Mind was, without *Interruption,* wholly occupy'd with pleasant Sensations of *Smell, Taste, Touch, &c.* if at the same time all other Ideas were excluded? Should we not think the State *low, mean,* and *sordid,* if there were no *Society,* no *Love* or *Friendship,* no *good Offices?*"

The second mistake is making faulty comparisons between states: for example, between the state of someone who enjoys the pleasures of virtue but no physical pleasures and that of someone who enjoys all the physical pleasures and even some of the mental pleasures such as beauty, as well as many of the moral pleasures of the social virtues. The attraction of the physical pleasures always includes the notion of certain moral enjoyments of the society of others, some communication of pleasures in love and friendship, esteem and gratitude. A more accurate comparison would be between a state of physical pain, but including all the pleasures of virtue–love, compassion, esteem, friendship–and a state of physical pleasure experienced while friendless and loveless, alone with one's malice, vengefulness, and wrath.

Hutcheson ends *An Inquiry into the Original of our Ideas of Beauty and Virtue* with a discussion of how the notions of obligation, rights, and political authority arise from the moral sense. Contrary to the views of Pufendorf and Locke, obligation does not derive from the laws of a superior. There are two kinds of obligation, prudential and moral. Moral obligation is *"a Determination, without regard to our own Interest, to approve Actions, and to perform them; which Determination shall also make us displeas'd with our selves, and uneasy upon having acted contrary to it. . . ."* Such a determination to approve benevolent action and disapprove the opposite makes no reference to any laws or to any external advantages or disadvantages related to sanction. Prudential obligation is "*a Motive from Self-interest, sufficient to determine all those who duly consider it, and pursue their own Advantage wisely, to a certain Course of Actions. . . ."* Clearly one can be obligated in this sense without any reference to the law of a superior or its sanctions. The need for laws and sanctions is to counterbalance "apparent" motives of self-interest and the violent passions that can obscure or overcome the moral sense.

Hutcheson's notion of moral obligation is not at all clear. His stated intention is to derive the notion of obligation from the moral sense. The "determination to *approve* actions" is a function of the moral sense, but how this quality is related to the further determination to perform them is unclear. Actions require motives, and the only motivating affections are self-love or benevolence. There is veracity in the statement that perceptions of virtue are pleasurable and those of vice are painful. Hutcheson claims, however, that insofar as people are motivated to seek virtue as a means to this pleasure or to avoid this pain, they are obligated prudentially, not morally. Because the only moral motive is benevolence, Hutcheson leaves himself no means whereby moral approval or disapproval could be a motivation to virtue.

Hutcheson derives the notion of rights from the moral sense as follows: When "*a Faculty of doing, demanding, or possessing any thing, universally allow'd in certain Circumstances, would in the whole tend to the general Good,* we say that any Person in such Circumstances, has *a Right to do, possess, or demand that Thing.*" The moral sense approves any form of benevolence, but most approves extensive benevolence. The object of extensive benevolence is the public good, and whatever contributes to it must be approved by the moral sense. A right is proportioned to the degree of good it promotes. Perfect rights are those so necessary to public good that a universal violation of them would make human life intolerable. Such rights may be defended by force. In the state of nature the right to use force in pursuance of perfect rights founds the right to punish in order to oblige the violator to "repair the Damage, and give Security against such Offences for the future." Upon entering civil society this right is transferred to the magistrate. Perfect rights include the right to life, to the fruits of one's labors, to demand performance of contracts, and to direct one's own actions, either for the public good or innocent private good.

Imperfect rights are those that increase the positive good in society, but the violation of which would

not produce universal misery. Their violation would cause less evil than the use of force to compel their observance. These are the rights to humanity, kindness, charity, and good offices, which, if compelled, would strip them of all moral merit. Hutcheson also acknowledges a third class of "external" rights. These include cases in which the pursuance is actually detrimental to the public good in particular instances, but where allowing it would do less harm than denying it. Such are the rights of wealthy misers to recall loans from the poor but industrious or the right to demand the performance of covenants that are too burdensome. Because pursuing such rights would violate the imperfect rights of humanity and kindness, it would be immoral to do so. Yet, it would not be immoral to allow people to pursue them, because the motive would be the more extensive good of society.

There are two criteria for an alienable right: it must be possible to transfer it, and such transfer must serve some valuable purpose. The right to private judgments and sentiments fail the first criterion because no one can command themselves to think or feel what they please or what anyone else pleases. The right to worship as one sees fit fails the second criterion because it can serve no valuable purpose to make people worship in a manner they find objectionable. While no one can have a direct right over another's life, the right to life is alienable to the extent that one might risk death in promoting the public good and to serve such an end may subject oneself to the prudence of others in directing one's actions.

Most of what is useful to humans requires labor and industry; thus, some of the most important rights are founded in the necessity of effectively promoting industriousness. Because general benevolence is not a strong enough motive to induce the industry required, the additional motives of self-love and more particular affections of kinship, friendship, and gratitude are absolutely necessary to promote the good of the society. From this circumstance Hutcheson derives the rights of property, of disposing and transferring it according to one's own judgment, as well as the rights of commerce, contracts, and promises.

The great advantage of "unprejudic'd *Arbitrators*" and "prudent *Directors*" capable of instructing in the best way to promote and defend the public good—as well as having sufficient force to enforce their decrees—establishes the right to constitute civil government and transfer alienable rights to such governors in any way prudence suggests. "And so far as the People have subjected their *Rights,* so far the Governours have an *external Right* at least, to dispose of them . . . for attaining the Ends of their Institution; and no further." It follows that there can be no legitimate governmental authority except by the consent of the governed who voluntary transfer their alienable rights to governors.

Because all rights to govern are transferred upon the assumption that the power conferred will be used to serve the public good, this grant of civil power becomes void either when the governors openly profess any intention of destroying the state or "act in such a manner as will necessarily do it." All rights are founded on the public good, so there can be no right or limitation of right inconsistent with this good. It follows that in cases of extreme necessity it is legitimate to use powers beyond those granted, but only temporarily and not as a precedent. In such cases of flagrant necessity subjects may "justly resume the Powers ordinary lodg'd in their Governours, or may counteract them."

An Inquiry into the Original of our Ideas of Beauty and Virtue was an immediate success, as evidenced by the appearance of a second edition nine months after the first (although dated 1726, the second edition was actually published in October 1725) and by the addition of a dedication to Lord Carteret, later Lord Granville, lord-lieutenant of Ireland from 1724 until 1730. Carteret, impressed by the book, invited Hutcheson to court, where he became a regular visitor. During this time he married Mary Wilson of County Longford. His views on marriage expressed in later works indicate that his was a happy one.

Within the year following the publication of *An Inquiry into the Original of our Ideas of Beauty and Virtue* Hutcheson published a series of journal pieces. "The Reflections upon Laughter" appeared in three installments of the *Dublin Weekly Journal* in June 1725. In the same month the first two of three letters of a correspondence with Gilbert Burnet appeared in the *London Journal* (the last letter appeared in October). In February 1726 Hutcheson published "Remarks upon the Fable of the Bees," again in three installments in the *Dublin Weekly Journal*. The "The Reflections upon Laughter" and "Remarks upon the Fable of the Bees" were both attacks on specific egoistic positions. The former was a response to an essay in the *Spectator,* which argued for a Hobbesian interpretation of laughter. The latter was a criticism of Mandeville's infamous work, *The Fable of the Bees,* first published in 1705 as *The Grumbling Hive; Or Knaves Turn'd Honest.* While each includes additional criticisms of specific egoistic theses, the general attack on the perniciousness of such reductions is indicative of his arguments in *An Inquiry into the Original of our Ideas of Beauty and Virtue.*

In the correspondence with Burnet, on the other hand, Hutcheson first addresses a quite different sort of opponent—what is now called "moral rationalism." Perhaps the best-known proponent of

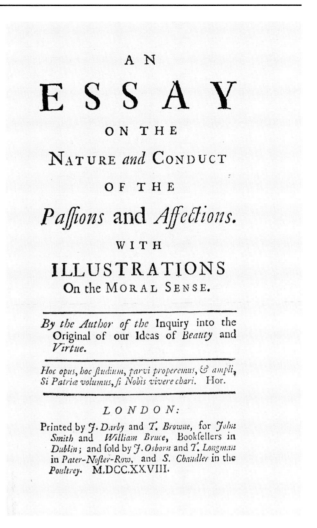

AN
ESSAY
ON THE
NATURE *and* CONDUCT
OF THE
Paſſions and *Affections.*
WITH
ILLUSTRATIONS
On the MORAL SENSE.

By the *Author of the* Inquiry into the Original of our Ideas of *Beauty* and *Virtue.*

Hoc opus, hoc ſtudium, parvi properemus, & ampli,
Si Patriæ volumus, ſi Nobis vivere chari. Hor.

LONDON:
Printed by *J. Darby* and *T. Browne,* for *John Smith* and *William Bruce,* Bookſellers in *Dublin*; and ſold by *J. Osborn* and *T. Longman* in *Pater-Noſter-Row,* and *S. Chandler* in the *Poultrey.* M.DCC.XXVIII.

Title page for Hutcheson's second published work, in which he contends that human beings have a sense for what is right and wrong that is similar to the five physical senses (British Library)

this position was Samuel Clarke, but John Balguy and William Wollaston were also representative. With moral rationalism the argument shifted from the nature of motivation to the nature of moral distinctions and how they are discerned. All held that moral distinctions are objective features discoverable in nature by reason. Clarke, for instance, claimed that moral distinctions were founded in certain abstract moral relations or eternal moral fitness. Wollaston claimed that such distinctions were founded on the signification of truth or falsehood in action. The issues raised in the Burnet correspondence are dealt with in greater depth in Hutcheson's second book, *An Essay on the Nature and Conduct of the Passions and Affections. With Illustrations on the Moral Sense,* published in 1728. Like *An Inquiry into the Original of our Ideas of Beauty and Virtue,* the latter work includes two distinct treatises. "An Essay on the Nature and Conduct of the Passions and Affection"s presents Hutcheson's account of the passions or affections, as well as two classical moralist topics: a comparison of higher and lower pleasures and a guide to managing desires to best achieve happiness. The second treatise, "Illustrations on the Moral Sense," is a criticism of various rationalist accounts of morality.

In "An Essay on the Nature and Conduct of the Passions and Affections" a sense is defined as "*every Determination of our Minds to receive Ideas independently on our Will, and to have Perceptions of Pleasure and Pain.*" Perceptions of the external senses arise immediately from "certain Motions raised in our Bodies" by external objects. Other perceptions, however, "arise only from some *previous Idea,* or *Assemblage,* or *Comparison of Ideas.*" Hutcheson makes no attempt to provide a complete or exhaustive account of the various senses, as "There seems to be some *Sense* or other suited to every sort of Objects which occurs to us." He confines his discussion to those senses most central to moral philosophy. The traditional division of external senses into five classes he describes as "ridiculously imperfect," and though he does not attempt to supply a new list of external senses, he does distinguish purely sensible ideas from ideas accompanying them such as those of number and duration. To the moral sense and sense of beauty he adds a public sense, whereby one is pleased with the happiness of others and pained by their misery, and a sense of honor, whereby one is pleased with the approbation, esteem, or praise of others and pained by the opposite. He suggests but does not insist on the existence of a sense of dignity, by which the "*Decency, Dignity, Suitableness to human Nature* in certain Actions and Circumstances" is perceived. The sense of dignity comes to play a more important role in later works.

Hutcheson's use of the term "sense" to describe these faculties of perceiving beauty and virtue, his description of the perceptions of these as "sensible ideas" or "sensations," and his comparison of them to secondary qualities, all appear to indicate that the mind is totally passive with respect to such perceptions. His discussion of the perception of beauty in *An Inquiry into the Original of our Ideas of Beauty and Virtue* also appears to allow that such perceptions can arise either directly from previous sensations or from previous ideas. In "An Essay on the Nature and Conduct of the Passions and Affections," however, he seems to suppose a necessary activity of the mind in all secondary perceptions. Objects or qualities must be brought before the mind and apprehended as things of certain kinds to produce the secondary perceptions. A plausible interpretation of Hutcheson's

thinking is that, unlike external sensation, secondary sensation requires prior mental activity and cognition. Once the mind apprehends an object as having certain qualities, though, a new passive sensation arises. This interpretation would rule out the possibility that perceptions of these senses could ever arise immediately from previous sensations.

The pleasurable and painful perceptions of the various senses produce desire, which Hutcheson divides into private (selfish) and public (benevolent). Any prospect of pleasurable or painful perception, or a means to such, produces either selfish or benevolent desires. Hutcheson again argues against any egoistic attempt to reduce public desires to private ones. Private and public desires, or affections, are also divided into calm and passionate. Passionate desires include "a *confused Sensation* either of Pleasure or Pain, occasioned or attended by some violent bodily Motions." As a result the mind is distracted, sometimes to the point that precludes "all *deliberate Reasoning* about our Conduct." Such passions are most often raised by the presence of particular objects to the senses. Calm affections arise upon reflection, from deliberative reasoning about objects or the means to them, without the distracting confused sensations that render affections passionate. Such affections may range from the particular to the general. For instance, a calm public affection may be directed toward a friend, toward a particular community, or toward a "more abstracted or general Community, such as a *Species* or System." This last possibility Hutcheson calls "universal calm benevolence."

Most people do not conduct their lives by any general calm affections but are moved by more particular passions and affections, whether private or public. Although the moral sense approves all kind affections considered in themselves, it also approves restraining or limiting the particular affections by calm universal benevolence. Just as the perfection of prudence would be to limit or restrict certain particular passions and affections by a calm general desire of the most extensive private good, so too the perfection of virtue would be to limit particular affections, whether private or public, by a calm general desire of the most extensive public good.

Hutcheson does not claim that human beings are necessarily determined to seek what they perceive as the greater good, whether for themselves or others. Particular selfish passions such as ambition, revenge, or anger may lead people to act contrary to what they know is their greater good, and particular benevolent passions such as compassion or natural affection may lead them to act contrary to what they know is the greater good of another. Calm desires are always proportioned to the amount of perceived good, however. Amounts of good are measured as a compound ratio of intensity and duration. "In computing the *Quantities* of Good or Evil, which we pursue or shun, either for our selves, or others, when the *Durations* are equal, the Moment is as the *Intenseness:* and when the *Intenseness* of Pleasure is the same, or equal, the Moment is as the *Duration.*"

Factored into the equation are the trouble, pain, or danger involved in acquiring or retaining any good, as well as the probability of acquiring or retaining it. The strength of calm public desires "is a Compound Ratio of the *Quantity of the Good itself, and the Number, Attachment, and Dignity of the Persons.*" By "attachment" Hutcheson means the strength or nearness of the tie to the person, and by "dignity" he means the person's moral excellence. Desire and aversion are the only genuine motives; they alone directly lead to action or volition through the apprehension of something as good or evil. People are also moved to action, however, by various nonrational natural propensities, instincts, or appetites. Unlike motives or rational desires, these other sources of action do not involve a prior apprehension of good and evil.

As in *An Inquiry into the Original of our Ideas of Beauty and Virtue,* Hutcheson argues that managing the passions is primarily a matter of forming true opinions of human and divine nature, avoiding false associations of ideas, avoiding partial views, and forming habits of reflection that will allow one to discern the true value of objects. Happiness consists in "the highest and most durable Gratifications of, either all our *Desires,* or, if all cannot be gratify'd at once, of those which tend to the greatest and most durable Pleasures. . . ." Although managing desire will contribute to happiness, or at least to the avoidance of much misery, there can be no unmixed happiness in life. Even virtue, the only source of pleasure that does not depend on external objects or events, will necessarily be the source of pains. Virtue is benevolence—the desire for the happiness of others; but the happiness of others cannot be ensured without the power of directing all events in the universe.

"An Essay on the Nature and Conduct of the Passions and Affections" offers a much-expanded comparison of types of pleasure, now including those of the public sense and sense of honor. It also uses the newly introduced standard of intensity and duration to measure quality of pleasure, and in doing so raises problems not found in *An Inquiry into the Original of our Ideas of Beauty and Virtue.* The comparisons of varieties of goodness in this work clearly supposes a difference in quality as well as quantity of pleasures. There is

"some *Excellency*" in moral qualities "which is superior to all other enjoyments." A mind occupied entirely by sensual pleasure is in a "low, mean, sordid" state. Some pleasures are "more *noble Pleasures*" than others. Hutcheson's appeal to the judgments of spectators to determine whether someone is truly living the best or happiest life makes sense within this context. In "An Essay on the Nature and Conduct of the Passions and Affections," however, he attempts to make the same case as *An Inquiry into the Original of our Ideas of Beauty and Virtue* using only intensity and duration as measures of pleasure. In this context many of the claims made about better pleasures are ungrounded. For instance, his claim that people are happier as adults with the pleasures of friendship, honor, and virtue than they were as children with their rattles, tops, and hobbyhorses is not at all evident if pleasure is measured entirely by quantity. Nor does the argument appealing to the judgment of spectators fit well in this context: while a spectator may judge the happiness of some state based on the amount of pleasure it gives, Hutcheson does not give them the ability to judge a state less happy because its pleasures are mean and sordid. In later works he came to see the problem in his *Essay* account and developed his notion of the sense of dignity to avoid it.

"Illustrations on the Moral Sense" begins by posing the two central questions of moral theory: what motives determine human election, or choice, and what qualities determine approbation? There are two equally intelligible and internally consistent views. Egoism claims that election is determined by prospects of private happiness or advantage and approbation is determined by perception of a tendency to promote private happiness. The moral sense view claims that election is determined by prospects of either private or public happiness and approbation is determined by apprehension of kind affections. Of these two theories only the second actually accords with the facts. Some have claimed that there is a third position, distinct from either of the two described. This supposed position claims that morality consists in "*Conformity to Reason,*" that "*Virtue* is acting according to the *absolute Fitness and Unfitness of Things,* or agreeably to the *Natures* or *Relations* of Things," and other similar views. Hutcheson argues that all versions of this third view either presuppose one of the first two positions or beg the central questions.

Hutcheson views reason as a strictly theoretical reason. Reason is the power of discovering true propositions. Reasonableness, then, must be conformity to true propositions, or conformity to truth. Given that there are as many truths about evil as there are about good, however, the conformity of one's actions to truth cannot be the distinguishing factor between virtue and vice. On the other hand, if conformity to reason means that the morality of action lies in the reason for action, one must examine the two kinds of reason for action: "exciting" reasons and "justifying" reasons. Exciting reasons are reasons for choosing an action; justifying reasons are reasons for approving an action. Hutcheson argues that all exciting reasons presuppose either private or public affections, and all justifying reasons presuppose a moral sense.

All action requires an intended or desired end, and ends can only be desired or intended either for oneself or others. Thus, no end can be desired previous to any affection. Hutcheson argues that the supposed distinction between reason and passion is spurious. Reason cannot excite any action previous to an intended end, and no end can be intended without some desire or affection. Can there be exciting reason previous to an end that moves a person to choose one end rather than another? Here, as in Aristotle, subordinate ends must be distinguished from ultimate ends. To suppose that an exciting reason is an ultimate end is to deny that it is actually ultimate.

What, asks Hutcheson, are the sorts of truths such authors suggest as exciting the election of, for example, the public good? Some claim that it is the end proposed by the Deity. But what exciting reason has one to conform to the will of the Deity? If it is because it will lead to one's happiness, then the exciting reason is self-love. If, as others claim, it is because the Deity is a benefactor, what is the exciting reason to conform to the will of a benefactor? Again, Hutcheson argues that there must be recourse to some affection. If the reason given is that the Divine ends are good, does one mean naturally good or morally good? If naturally good—conducive to pleasure—is this one's own pleasure or that of others? If one's own, then self-love is presupposed as the exciting reason; if others, public affections are presupposed. If one means the divine ends are morally good, then the equation is back where it started: What is moral goodness? Other suggested exciting reasons—for example, that the happiness of a system is greater than that of an individual, or that it is "best" that all be happy—are subject to the same arguments. They are exciting reasons only insofar as one presupposes either public or private affections.

If one considers the proffered reason as justifying reasons, reasons to approve actions, they do so only upon the supposition of a moral sense. What reason is there to approve conforming to God's will? As has been argued extensively, the fact that it is advantageous is not the source of moral approval. If

one claims that actions for the public good are morally approved because it is best that all be happy, is it morally best or naturally best? Those who argue that it is morally best have begged the question. If naturally best for oneself, then the reason for approval is not reasonableness but tendency to one's own advantage, which is not in fact the source of moral approval. If the action is naturally best for others, why should it be approved? Here, Hutcheson asserts, one must appeal to the moral sense.

Finally, the justifying reasons sometimes suggested are that it is one's duty to promote the public good, that one owes obedience to the Deity, and that the whole is to be preferred to the part. "But let these Words *Duty, Obligation, Owing,* and the meaning of that Gerund, *is to be preferred,* be explained; and we shall find our selves still at a Loss for *exciting Reasons* previous to *Affections,* or *justifying Reasons* without recourse to a *moral Sense.*" There are only two intelligible senses of obligation, prudential and moral. To say people are obligated to an action may mean "1. *That the Action is necessary to obtain Happiness to the Agent, or to avoid Misery:* Or, 2. *That every Spectator, or he himself upon Reflection, must approve his Action, and disapprove his omitting it, if he considers fully all its Circumstances.*" Prudential obligation presupposes selfish affections; moral obligation presupposes a moral sense. This definition of moral obligation differs from that of *An Inquiry into the Original of our Ideas of Beauty and Virtue,* which appears to make the moral sense itself both a determination to approve and a determination to perform actions. In this account, however, perceptions of the moral sense and the affections of the will are clearly distinct. Approval is not desire or aversion, and only desire and aversion can directly motivate action. Here all reference to moral obligation determining one to action is dropped. To say an action is morally obligatory is simply to say it is morally approved and its omission is morally disapproved.

Hutcheson goes on to criticize two specific versions of the view that morality consists in conformity to reason: Clarke's moral "fitness" view and Wollaston's "significancy of truth in action" view. The majority of the arguments are well known through Hume's repetition of them in book 3, section 1.1 of *A Treatise of Human Nature* (1739), although Hume substitutes his own theory of relations for Hutcheson's. The thrust of Hutcheson's arguments remains the same as his more general arguments: rationalist explications either presuppose affections and a moral sense or beg the question.

Three other points made in "Illustrations on the Moral Sense" are of particular historical significance. First, Hutcheson correctly notes that a consequence of his view is that the moral sense cannot itself be subject to moral approval or disapproval. Calling the moral sense virtuous or vicious is like calling the sense of taste "sweet," or the sense of sight "white" or "black." Both Hume and Adam Smith explicitly reject this view and, indeed, Hume boasts in the conclusion of book 3 of *A Treatise of Human Nature* that an advantage of his own theory is that it does not have this unhappy consequence.

Second, in response to the question of whether there could be a right or wrong state of the moral sense just as one may have a "*sickly Palate*" that affects our sense of taste or a "*vitiated Sight*" that misrepresents colors, Hutcheson extends and elaborates the analogy to secondary qualities that he first used in *An Inquiry into the Original of our Ideas of Beauty and Virtue*. Ideas of the moral sense are like perceptions of secondary qualities, which "are allowed to be only *Perceptions* in our Minds, and not Images of any like *external Quality*, as *Colours, Sounds, Tastes, Smells, Pleasure, Pain*." While such qualities might be altered by any disorder in the sense, "We do not denominate Objects from our *Perceptions during the Disorder,* but according to our *ordinary Perceptions,* or those of others in *good Health.* . . ." Likewise, "we denominate Objects from the Appearances they make to us in an *uniform Medium, when our Organs are in no disorder, and the Object is not very distant from them*." Hume adopts the same analogy and likewise uses it to show how standards of judgment are developed.

Third, according to Hutcheson, virtue lies entirely in the motive, never in the consequences of action. This assertion alone may explain Immanuel Kant's interest in him. Hutcheson's criticisms of certain rationalist accounts of moral merit foreshadow issues that later became central to Kant's moral philosophy. According to Hutcheson, "Some will not allow any *Merit* in *Actions* flowing from *kind Instincts: Merit,* say they, attends Actions to which we are excited by *Reason* alone, or to which we *freely* determine our selves. The Operation of *Instincts* or *Affections* is *necessary,* and not *voluntary.* . . ." Hutcheson's response is to reiterate the position he had argued previously—reason cannot excite to action without some end being proposed, and no end can be proposed without instincts and affections. Given that all motives presuppose affection, the only senses in which "freely determined" could be opposed to determined by affection would by either acting without any motive from arbitrary election or acting without any propellent desire of one action or end rather than another. Hutcheson asks his readers to consider whether they ever act in such a manner or whether they would morally approve such actions.

Hutcheson's reply clearly indicates that he rejected the view that to be free the will must not be determined by affections. Yet, he offers no analysis of what would constitute a free will. There is good reason why he might have thought it unnecessary to do so. The moral sense theory renders the question of whether motives are causally determined irrelevant. Free will was a particular concern to those who tied moral obligation to the laws of a superior. Reward and punishment require that agents be accountable for their actions, and agents can only be held accountable if they freely choose their actions. Hutcheson, however, denies that moral obligation arises from any laws of superiors. Rewards and punishments create only a prudential obligation, not a moral one. Those who insist that no person is punishable if it was not within that person's power "*to have abstained from the Action if he had willed it; perhaps are not mistaken.*" Because humans have many kind affections that naturally raise love and approval, and no natural affections that would raise malice, "it may be justly said to be in the *Power* of every one, by due attention, to prevent any *malicious Affections,* and to excite in himself *kind Affections* toward all."

An Essay on the Nature and Conduct of the Passions and Affections, like *An Inquiry into the Original of our Ideas of Beauty and Virtue,* was well received, and when Carmichael, professor of moral philosophy at Glasgow, died in 1729, Hutcheson was elected to replace him. Hutcheson lost both his father and a child in 1729, and he is likely to have viewed the prospect of a change in venue and a new set of responsibilities to occupy him as a relief. As an opponent of the prevailing orthodoxy at Glasgow he was clearly eager to help effect a change. His election was close—he won by one vote—and by no means reflected a new dominance of proponents of liberal learning over the stricter orthodox view. Throughout his career at Glasgow, Hutcheson was involved in political maneuvering to ensure the election of those holding the moderate view. The dominance of the new guard was not fully assured until shortly before his death.

After taking up his appointment in November 1730 he soon became involved in almost every aspect of college affairs, from such major chores as managing the finances to such minor ones as serving on a committee to determine the best way to order the seats in a fellow professor's classroom. One of his most important contributions was as a teacher. During the 1720s conflicts arose among the principal, regents, and students, leading to the appointment of a commission that in 1727 changed the college from a regent to a professorial system. Hutcheson has been credited with setting the standard of professorship.

A SHORT

INTRODUCTION

TO

MORAL PHILOSOPHY,

IN THREE BOOKS;

CONTAINING THE

ELEMENTS OF ETHICKS

AND THE

LAW OF NATURE.

BY FRANCIS HUTCHESON, LLD.
LATE PROFESSOR OF PHILOSOPHY IN
THE UNIVERSITY OF GLASGOW.

TRANSLATED FROM THE LATIN.

GLASGOW,
PRINTED AND SOLD BY ROBERT FOULIS.
PRINTER TO THE UNIVERSITY.
MDCCXLVII.

Title page for the English translation of the first of Hutcheson's philosophy textbooks, Philosophiae moralis institutio compendiaria, Ethices et Jurisprudentiae Naturalis elementa continens Lib. III, *which appeared in 1742*
(University of Münster)

Rather than adopt the traditional style of lecturing or dictating in Latin upon standard texts he lectured entirely in English. He was by all accounts an eloquent and passionate speaker and would stride about the classroom when lecturing, riveting the attention of students. His lectures were so popular that some students attended his class for many years after passing it. While he initially used the texts of others, including Pufendorf and Carmichael, he eventually devised his own course covering ethics, natural law, natural religion, and government. The subject matter of the course (which was taken by Smith) is included in *A System of Moral Philosophy, in Three Books . . . Published from the Original Manuscript, by his son, Francis Hutcheson, M.D. To which is prefixed Some Account of the*

Life, Writings, and Character of the Author, by the Reverend William Leechman . . . , which Hutcheson began about 1734. A draft was completed in 1737 and, as was his habit, he began to circulate it among friends for comments and criticisms. Some of these readers were slow in their replies, and in response to the eventual suggestions and criticisms as well as his own dissatisfaction with his "method, style, and some reasonings," he continued to revise the manuscript at least as late as 1741, when he despairingly wrote to a friend that he was now "adding confusedly to a confused book all valuable remarks in a farrago."

Hutcheson's problems with *A System of Moral Philosophy* are understandable. It is a monumental work, which—when eventually published in 1755, nine years after his death—comprised three books in two volumes numbering more than seven hundred pages. His college duties occupied him entirely during the term. In addition to his administrative and committee duties he lectured five days a week in his moral philosophy course. In cooperation with his old teacher and friend Dunlop he lectured three days a week on ancient ethics; he held private classes, and on Sundays he gave public lectures on Christianity. He was also a close mentor to students, especially Irish students who, being away from the watchful eyes of family and friends, often required a close reign. These duties left him only summers for his literary work and composing, and revising *A System of Moral Philosophy* was not the only project to occupy him during this period. A fourth edition of *An Inquiry into the Original of our Ideas of Beauty and Virtue* was published in 1738, and a third edition of *An Essay on the Nature and Conduct of the Passions and Affections* was published in 1742. Both editions were the last published in his lifetime and feature substantial revisions and additions. He also published *Meditations of Marcus Aurelius Antoninus. Newly translated from the Greek. With Notes, and an Account of his Life* in 1742. James Moor translated books 1 and 2 and Hutcheson, books 3 through 12. The introduction and annotations are also attributed to Hutcheson. Finally, in the same year he published *Philosophiae moralis institutio compendiaria, Ethices et Jurisprudentiae Naturalis elementa continens Lib. III* (translated as *A Short Introduction to Moral Philosophy, in Three Books; containing the Elements of Ethics and the Law of Nature,* 1747) and *Metaphysicae Synopsis: ontologiam, et, pneumatologiam complectens* (Metaphysical Synopsis: Encompassing Ontology and Pneumatology), the first two of three "Compends" meant to be used as textbooks, one on metaphysics and one on morals.

For all its infelicities of style, method, and "some reasonings" *A System of Moral Philosophy* remains an important expression of Hutcheson's mature thought.

Book 1 is divided into two parts, the first covering the faculties of the understanding and the will. The second part is concerned with the character best suited to happiness and also includes the fullest treatment of Hutcheson's philosophy of religion. While much of *A System of Moral Philosophy* remains the same as earlier works, there are important developments and related changes. In *A System of Moral Philosophy* he introduces into his account of human nature a "general determination of the soul to exercise all its active powers" and further develops the notion of a sense of dignity, which, combined with this determination, gives a sense of the dignity of some powers over others as well as determining their proper exercise. Finally, he extends the objects of the moral sense to include certain "moral dispositions," which, though not themselves benevolent affections, are to some degree naturally connected to them.

In *An Inquiry into the Original of our Ideas of Beauty and Virtue* Hutcheson accounted for our approval of natural talents and abilities by relating them to benevolence. They do not possess moral qualities but are morally approved of just insofar as they better enable people to do good to others. In *A System of Moral Philosophy* approval of them is not moral approval but a feeling of admiration, or "relish," arising from a sense of their dignity. This sense of dignity provides a standard of excellence for the exercise of each faculty as well as a value ranking of the faculties. Thus, human beings admire beauty, strength, and agility as perfected states and as containing more dignity than a strong stomach or delicate palate. Intellectual talents and capacities are held in even higher esteem as even more dignified and suitable to human nature. Finally, the sense of dignity indicates the "commanding nature" of the moral sense in regulating and controlling all other powers. On the other hand there are abilities and dispositions that are not any form of benevolent affection but are naturally connected to benevolence and inconsistent with high degrees of selfishness. These moral dispositions, such as fortitude, candor, sincerity, and veracity, are immediately approved by the moral sense and do not, as in his earlier view, depend upon the recognition of any connection with benevolent affections.

Both Hume in *A Treatise of Human Nature* and Joseph Butler in his dissertation "Of the Nature of Virtue" (1736) had claimed that the virtues of justice and veracity could not be derived from motives of benevolence. Here, while still maintaining that there is a natural connection between veracity and benevolence, Hutcheson allows that veracity is directly approved by the moral sense without any recognition of this connection. The virtue of justice he continues

to derive directly from motives of benevolence, clearly unconvinced by Hume's arguments refuting this claim in *A Treatise of Human Nature*. Hutcheson had already completed the draft of *A System of Moral Philosophy* by the time Hume sent him a copy of book 3 of *A Treatise of Human Nature* for comment in 1739. Although Hutcheson helped find Hume a publisher for book 3, and they continued to correspond for years, he did not alter his account of justice in *A System of Moral Philosophy,* and the account remains the same in his final work on moral philosophy, the textbook *Philosophiae Moralis Institutio Compendiaria,* composed during the time of the correspondence.

A System of Moral Philosophy also finds a new use for the sense of dignity in comparing pleasures. When comparing the same types of pleasures the value remains a function of intensity and duration. In comparing different kinds of pleasures, however, the value becomes a function of their dignity and durations. Hutcheson also introduced this change of formula into the third edition of *An Essay on the Nature and Conduct of the Passions and Affections,* published in 1742.

The Aristotelian elements in *A System of Moral Philosophy,* including the emphasis on the primacy of action over passion and the notion of excellence, or perfection in the proper exercise of the faculties, especially of those faculties distinctive to human nature, indicate the new direction Hutcheson's thought was taking. They do not combine smoothly with the moral sense theory, however. While perhaps possible that, had he more time for concentrated thought, he would have worked out a coherent way to combine such apparently disparate elements, he never did so. In *A System of Moral Philosophy* and *Philosophiae Moralis Institutio Compendiaria* there are two standards of value, the moral sense and the sense of dignity. Because the nature and functioning of the sense of dignity is never made clear, the relation between it and the moral sense remains obscure.

His discussion of religion in part 2 of *A System of Moral Philosophy* includes a design argument in which the order within parts argues intelligent design and the ordering of parts into an interconnected whole argues either a concerted intelligence of the parts or one supreme designing intelligence. Since there is no evidence of any self-ordering wisdom within the parts, it follows that there is a superior ruling Mind, which he argues must be eternal, immaterial, omnibenevolent, and unitary. Natural evil is a necessary consequence or attendant of greater natural and moral good. The highest enjoyments are those of the moral sense, and without pain there might still be pleasures of the public sense but there could be no benevolence, no desire to bring about happiness and

REFLECTIONS

UPON

LAUGHTER.

AND

REMARKS

UPON

The FABLE of the BEES.

BY

FRANCIS HUTCHESON, L.L.D.
Late Professor of Moral Philosophy in the
UNIVERSITY of Glasgow.

CAREFULLY CORRECTED.

GLASGOW:

Printed by R. URIE,
For DANIEL BAXTER, Bookseller.
MDCCL.

*Title page for Hutcheson's critique of philosophical opinions of the day,
particularly those in Bernard Mandeville's notorious satirical poem*
The Fable of the Bees, *published in 1714
(Houghton Library, Harvard University)*

prevent pain. Physical pleasure and pain are necessary for the preservation of the body, nor can one argue that less pain would have served the same purpose. Even the acutest pains do not always deter people from intemperance or give sufficient caution to the aged, never mind the young and rash. Finally, many evils are the necessary result of fixed natural laws without which there could be no action, no expectations that any particular motion will follow from one's will, or that any particular consequences will follow from any motion.

The mind or soul is recognized to be distinct from the body by the distinction in their qualities and the awareness that the perfection of the mind's qualities does not depend on the body's states. The belief in a future state is natural to humans and is con-

firmed by arguments proving the simplicity, unity, and immateriality of the objects of thought and affection. Further, although God has designed the moral order such that happiness is a natural consequent of virtue, they are not always entirely coincident in this life. People naturally desire that degrees of happiness should be consonant with degrees of virtue and justly expect that an all-knowing, all-powerful, and all-good God will compensate the worthy but unfortunate and give the "injurious and oppressive . . . cause to repent."

Book 2 features Hutcheson's natural jurisprudence, including a more detailed, in-depth discussion of natural rights and property than the accounts in *An Inquiry into the Original of our Ideas of Beauty and Virtue* and added discussions of the state of nature, obligations in the use of speech, and a section on commerce and the nature of coin. Other economic views are scattered among sections of book 2 and book 3.

Hutcheson continues to claim that the ultimate notion of rights is what tends to the public good, but here he emphasizes that the sense of a right (and corresponding obligation) does not require conceiving it as having this tendency. People immediately disapprove as cruel and selfish the interfering with anyone's innocent doing, possessing, or obtaining anything. There is also indication here that Hutcheson did not consider moral obligation to be identical with moral approval, even though in book 1 he explicitly states that to say an action is morally obligatory is simply to say that it is morally approved. His previous definitions of moral obligation claim not only that the action in question must be morally approved but also that the omission of it be morally disapproved. Here, in the context of his discussion of rights, his definition is entirely in terms of disapproval. One is morally obligated to an action "when he must find from the constitution of human nature that he and every attentive observer must disapprove the omission of it as morally evil." Surely, however, there are many benevolent actions that are approved as morally good, but the omission of them would not be condemned as morally evil. If so, then Hutcheson is committed to the view that moral obligation is not merely moral approval.

There is also a change in emphasis in his discussion of property. The account in *An Inquiry into the Original of our Ideas of Beauty and Virtue* justifies property and the attendant rights of exchange, commerce, and contracts, primarily in terms of the need to encourage industry. The account in *A System of Moral Philosophy* emphasizes the direct immorality of obstructing someone's innocent enjoyment of acquired goods as cruel and selfish. The further justification from the necessity of promoting industry, he now notes, would not hold in small societies in fruitful and mild regions. The account of property includes detailed examinations of the various means of acquiring and transferring property as well as the related rights of contracts and covenants. A particularly remarkable aspect of the account is the inclusion of a full section devoted to justifying conditions for the use of animals, conditions that become increasingly stringent as the extent of use increases. Hutcheson further attributes to animals the right not to be subjected to useless pain or misery.

Hutcheson avoids the need to appeal to such devices as the covenants or compacts used by Hugo Grotius and Pufendorf or Robert Filmer's invoking of the power granted to the mythical first parents of humanity by claiming that the goods of the earth are originally in "negative" as opposed to positive community. In negative community "things are not yet in property"; in positive community "not any individual, but a whole society have an undivided property." The origin of property lies in occupation of what was in negative community, with acquisition by prescription and accession following. The right to property as originally acquired includes three parts: a right to fullest use, a right to exclude others from any use, and a right of transfer to others.

Laws of nature are general rules, or precepts, formed "by reflecting upon our inward constitution, and by reasoning upon human affairs, concerning that conduct which our heart naturally must approve." These precepts are determined by what experience reveals tends to the good in all ordinary cases. If, in unusual cases, a different course of action is seen that would do more good, "we then have as good a law of nature . . . to recede from the ordinary rule in those rarer cases, as we have to follow it in ordinary cases." Thus, even the most important perfect rights can be contravened in certain circumstances. There is, then, no right to property so absolute that it could in no circumstances be overridden. By the same token, the importance of respecting property is so necessary to the good of society that only circumstances of great necessity would justify receding from the general rule.

In addition to private rights of individuals there are general rights of society or, conversely, duties of individuals to society or "mankind as a system." Like private rights or duties these may be perfect or imperfect. Perfect duties include refraining from suicide, supporting and educating children, refraining from indiscriminate propagation, sharing valuable inventions, and supporting oneself by labor and industry. Imperfect duties include cultivating one's abilities, sociability, diffusing the principles of piety and virtue, and practicing within one's capacities a profession or business that serves the public good.

Hutcheson thoroughly rejects the Hobbesian account of the state of nature. Such an account is not only founded on a false view of human nature but also includes two absurdities. It calls a state of war of all against all "natural," while at the same time arguing that human reason shows such a state to "be the most destructive imaginable; and that it is be shunned by every one as soon as he can." It also calls a state of absolute solitude natural when "in this condition neither could any of mankind come into being, or continue in it a few days without miraculous interposition." The state of nature or "natural liberty" is no fiction. It has existed, most likely continues to exist in primitive parts of the world, and always has existed between different nations. Natural affections, moral sense, and public sense, as well as many natural powers and instincts, all confirm that such a state is naturally social. Even supposing that in a solitary state one were provided with all necessities and means of sensual gratification and exempted from fears and dangers, there could be none of the social and moral pleasures necessary for human happiness.

Even though the state of nature is generally one of peace, controversies will inevitably arise, and self-interest can bias the judgment of even good people. When such controversies cannot be settled by the concerned parties the natural recourse is to disinterested arbiters, and everyone has a duty to be willing to serve in this capacity. In the state of natural liberty, however, when one or both parties refuse to submit to the arbiters, there remains the right to redress infringements of perfect rights by violence. The dangerous consequences of immoderate passions in the defense and prosecution of this right to violence most likely provided the first motive to contrive civil governments.

The discussion of civil polity in book 3 begins with an examination of three adventitious states that exist prior to any civil government but provide the ground for relationships that underlie civil polities: the relationships between husband and wife, parent and child, and master and servant. The family is the grounding social unit of all societies, and the "first relation in the order of nature is marriage." The nature of human instincts and affections as well as human reason informed by experience point out the rights and obligations of marriage. These instincts, affections, and judgments include the instinct to propagate, to acknowledge the helplessness of infants, and to accept the long, constant care required by child rearing; strong parental affection, which lightens the burden of this care; and the intimacy and bonds of affection that result from sexual relations. These factors indicate that sexual relations should be confined to marriage, that there should be strict fidelity in marriage, and that marriage should be a monogamous, equal partnership, entered into for life.

For the majority of human beings the support of both parents is necessary for child rearing. The obligation to confine sexual relations to marriage as well as to observe strict fidelity in marriage is equal for men and women. To ensure the parental affection necessary for enduring the onerous care of children, men must be assured of their offspring, and with no such assurance women are unjustly burdened with the entire support and education of offspring. Sexual relations are generally attended with special ties of love and affection, which enjoin that both men and women confine such relations to one partner in marriage. A woman who has engaged in such relations prior to marriage leaves her husband insecure that she will not continue to be subject to solicitations of past lovers, and the necessity of ascertaining the man's offspring obligates the woman to fidelity within marriage. A man is likewise obligated because the natural passions of the woman require a "friendly society, and unity of interest in the joint education of the common offspring," and it is the "plainest injustice and inequality" to suppose that "a man and his offspring should be the sole objects of the woman's affections . . . while his affections and cares are allowed to be divided among other women and their children." By allowing either infidelity or polygamy "one half of the species, which is equally entitled to all social and enjoyments and satisfactions with the other, is most injuriously deprived of many of the chief enjoyments of life."

A bond of friendship, love, and esteem is necessary for making the long joint venture of child rearing tolerable. One cannot enter a genuine friendship for a set term of years or upon conditions not in one's power. Thus, marriage, like all friendship, aims at perpetuity. This notion does not rule out divorce. To say that one cannot enter into genuine friendship for a specified length of time or until some particular goal is achieved does not entail that there can be no conditions that would make continuing in the friendship impossible. Any violation of the essential terms of marriage or events that make either party utterly incapable of the duties of such a relationship invalidate the bond. Adultery, desertion, implacable hatred, assaults, and perpetual madness are all legitimate grounds for divorce. Finally, there is no foundation in nature for "any proper jurisdiction or right of commanding" in marriage. The sentiments and affec-

tions show it to be an equal partnership or friendship, and not one "wherein one party stipulates to himself a right of governing in all domestick affairs, and the other promises subjection." Hutcheson argues that no strength or wisdom gives any human a right to rule, thus even if such superiority were granted to men—which Hutcheson does not—it would not justify subjecting the wife to the rule of the husband. Civil laws as "monstrous" as those that give husbands the power of life and death over wives, or even of corporeal punishment or of power over the "whole stock of the family, including the wife's portion" are "unjust and imprudent, as well as contrary to nature."

Just as natural affections and reflections on experience point out the rights and duties of marriage, so too they reveal the rights and duties of parents and children. The natural desire for posterity, the necessity of preserving children to maturity, parental affection, and the natural gratitude of children make God's intention manifest. Parental affection combined with the weakness of children suggest a permanent obligation of parents to preserve their children and seek their happiness. Because parental power is clearly intended for the good of the children, it cannot extend so far as to destroy or enslave them. Contrary to the view of Hobbes, children are not mere goods or chattels, nor is parental power, which is held equally between mother and father, based on mere procreation. Children "commence rational beings . . . with the same natural rights which their parents enjoy, as soon as they have reason to use them." Parental rights are based on the care and instruction, not the generation of children. Because a "child is a rational agent, with rights valid against the parents," any donations, legacies, or acquisitions of the child are the child's property. Parents may manage such goods, and in cases of necessity, justly use them for maintaining the child or the family. Parents who cannot support children have the right to give them up for adoption, or in cases of extreme necessity, to indenture them into any humane state for the term of years required for the child's support.

When conditions are such that some have no property or goods by which they can support themselves, and property holders need the labor of others and are willing to support them in exchange, the relationship of master and servant is introduced. As most healthy people laboring on their own are able to support a family and even provide some measure of amusement, it is evident that the labor of any person is of much more value than bare maintenance. Therefore, any just contract requires either wages or humane maintenance for the laborer's family. Whatever the term of the contract, the laborer retains all rights except the right to the specific labors transferred. Nor can the right to the worker's labors be transferred from one master to another unless expressly agreed upon in the contract. In the case of damages, injuries, or debts incurred, or in the punishment of criminals, the conditions of servitude may legitimately be more stringent and involuntary servitude permitted. As "No damage done or crime committed can change a rational creature into a piece of goods void of all right," however, even in such cases persons retain all rights except to their labor.

Unlike family relationships, the desire for political union does not arise directly from instincts and natural affections. All human beings love liberty, and to have one's actions subject to the will of another is always in itself disagreeable. Only the experience of the inconveniences of natural liberty create a desire for political society. The only natural method of constituting civil power is by consent, and no power of government is legitimate unless founded on consent. Because people only consent to civil authority when their experience shows that they may better promote their own good by doing so, the only end and purpose of civil power is to promote the good of society, and the legitimate extent and limits of all civil authority are determined by reference to this general good. No constitution of civil power can legitimately contravene any inalienable right or include a right to any useless or pernicious exercise of power. Subjects have a right to resist any usurpation of powers not granted, except in cases of extreme necessity, as well as to any abuses of power that would be dangerous to society. A people also has the right to change or reconstitute the plan of polity when experience reveals the original plan to be contrary to the good of society. Even when the plan and administration of it are, in fact, just, if the people form such an inveterate opinion to the contrary that they are in continual suspicion and fear, then, because public happiness is the sole legitimating end to civil power, the rulers cannot retain a right to power.

Hutcheson also acknowledges a right to secession of colonies, a point that later found great favor in the American colonies. If the plan of the mother country changes by force or by degrees from a gentle limited power to a harsh and absolute one or if oppressive laws are made with respect to the colonies, and the colonies can provide by themselves all the good ends of political union, then they are not bound to remain subject to the mother country. Such conditions, however, are not necessary to the moral legitimacy of secession. It is so inhumane and unnat-

Bronze medallion of Hutcheson by Antonio Selvi (Scottish National Portrait Gallery)

ural to require a society capable of all the good purposes of independent political union to remain subject to a distant government that "it is not easy to imagine there can be any foundation for it in justice or equity."

It is unknown whether Hutcheson abandoned all intention of revising and publishing *A System of Moral Philosophy* or whether he hoped at some point to return to it. It is a work clearly intended for scholarly readers, and his university duties as well as his involvement in the struggle for shifting control of the university left him little time for the intense concentration necessary for the task. During this time Hutcheson helped gain the appointment of William Leechman to the Chair of Divinity, provoking what Hutcheson described as the "furious indignation of our zealots." Leechman was elected in December 1743 and eventually, in 1761, became principal. Also during this time, Hutcheson opposed the appointment of Hume to the ethics professorship at Edinburgh, which became vacant in 1745. In his naive fashion Hume was shocked and hurt by Hutcheson's stand, even though he had years before written to Hutcheson that he did not think one's philosophical opinions were important except in the case of ministers or those involved in the instruction of the youth. Hutcheson was offered the position but refused it.

This circumstance ended the correspondence between them.

Rather than revise *A System of Moral Philosophy*, Hutcheson turned his attention to writing his three compends on morals, metaphysics, and logic. The *Philosophiae moralis institutio compendaria* was published in 1742 and translated into English as *A Short Introduction to Moral Philosophy, in Three Books* shortly after Hutcheson's death. It is a condensed version of *A System of Moral Philosophy*, presented in a style and tone suitable for students. The compend on metaphysics, *Metaphysicae Synopsis: ontologiam, et, pneumatologiam complectens*, was also published in 1742. The compend on Logic, *Logicae Compendium. Praefixa est dissertatio de philosophiae origine, ejusque inventoribus aut excultoribus praecipuis* (A Compend of Logic. With a Dissertation on the Origin of Philosophy and of its Principal Discoverers and Outstanding Practitioners Prefixed), was published posthumously in 1756. No translations of these have been published.

There is some disagreement among scholars about whether these works represent any change in Hutcheson's views. In *A Short Introduction to Moral Philosophy* his terminology is considerably altered, a type of pietistic tone quite unlike that of his other works is evident, and some views, such as those on the nature of rights, are apparently at odds with those expressed in other works. Whether any of these textbooks should be taken to represent his considered views, however, is best answered by his own recommendation in his preface to *A Short Introduction to Moral Philosophy*. "These elementary books are for your use who study at Universities, and not for the learned."

Francis Hutcheson wrote nothing further after the publication of the compends, although revised editions of the compends on morals and on metaphysics were published in 1744 and 1745, respectively. During the last year of his life he became involved in a final battle for shifting control of the university to the new guard. Both sides no doubt knew that this appointment would decide the balance of power and thus the direction of the university. In an April 1746 letter to his lifelong friend Thomas Drennen, Hutcheson described his work to promote his favored candidate as a "most intricate business, upon which the very soul of this College depends, and all may be ruined by

the want of one vote." The future of the university he had hoped for was ensured with the election of his candidate, James Moor, in June 1746. Six weeks later, while visiting Dublin, Hutcheson took ill and died on 8 August 1746. He was buried in St. Mary's Churchyard in Dublin.

Biography:

William Leechman, Preface to Hutcheson's *A System of Moral Philosophy* (Glasgow: R. & A. Foulis / London: A. Millar & T. Longman, 1755).

References:

William Blackstone, *Francis Hutcheson and Contemporary Ethical Theory* (Athens: University of Georgia Press, 1965);

Stephen Darwall, "Hutcheson: Moral Sentiment and Calm Desire," in his *The British Moralists and the Internal 'Ought': 1640–1740* (Cambridge: Cambridge University Press, 1995), pp. 207–243;

Knud Haakonssen, "Natural Law and Moral Realism: The Scottish Synthesis," in *Studies in the Philosophy of the Scottish Enlightenment,* edited by M. A. Stewart (Oxford: Clarendon Press, 1990), pp. 62–85;

Henning Jensen, *Motivation and Moral Sense in Francis Hutcheson's Ethical Theory* (The Hague: Nijhoff, 1971);

James Moore, "The Two Systems of Francis Hutcheson," in *Studies in the Philosophy of the Scottish Enlightenment,* pp. 37–59;

David Fate Norton, "Hutcheson's Moral Realism," *Journal of the History of Philosophy,* 23 (1985): 392–418;

Norton, "Hutcheson's Moral Sense Theory Reconsidered," *Dialogue,* 13 (1974): 3–23;

Bernard Peach, "Editor's Introduction" to Hutcheson's *Illustrations on the Moral Sense* (Cambridge, Mass.: Harvard University Press, 1971), pp. 3–100;

D. D. Raphael, *The Moral Sense* (London: Oxford University Press, 1947);

William Robert Scott, *Francis Hutcheson: His Life, Teaching and Position in the History of Philosophy* (Cambridge: Cambridge University Press, 1900);

Kenneth Winkler, "Hutcheson's Alleged Realism," *Journal of the History of Philosophy,* 23 (1985): 179–194.

John Locke

(29 August 1632 – 28 October 1704)

Justine J. Noel
Camosun College

See also the Locke entries in *DLB 31: American Colonial Writers, 1735–1781; DLB 101: British Prose Writers, 1660–1800, First Series;* and *DLB 213: Pre-Nineteenth Century British Book Collectors and Bibliographers.*

BOOKS: *Epistola de tolerantia, ad clarissimum virum T. A. R. P. T. O. L. A. scripta à P. A. P. O. I. L. A.,* anonymous (Gouda, Netherlands: Apud Justum ab Hoeve, 1689); translated by William Popple as *A Letter concerning Toleration: Humbly submitted, & c.,* anonymous (London: Printed for Awnsham Churchill, 1689);

Two Treatises of Government: In the Former, The False Principles and Foundation of Sir Robert Filmer, and His Followers, are Detected and Overthrown. The Latter is an Essay concerning the True Original, Extent, and end of Civil-Government, anonymous (London: Printed for Awnsham Churchill, 1690 [i.e., 1689]);

An Essay concerning Humane Understanding: In Four Books (London: Printed by Elizabeth Holt for Thomas Basset, 1690 [i.e., 1689]; revised and enlarged edition, London: Printed for Awnsham & John Churchill & Samuel Manship, 1694; revised and enlarged, 1700; revised and enlarged, 1706);

A Second Letter concerning Toleration, as Philanthropus (London: Printed for Awnsham & John Churchill, 1690);

Some Considerations of the Consequences of the Lowering of Interest, and Raising the Value of Money. In a Letter to a Member of Parliament, anonymous (London: Printed for Awnsham & John Churchill, 1692; revised, 1696);

A Third Letter for Toleration, to the Author of the "Third Letter concerning Toleration," as Philanthropus (London: Printed for Awnsham & John Churchill, 1692);

Some Thoughts concerning Education, anonymous (London: Printed for Awnsham & John Churchill, 1693; revised and enlarged, 1695; revised and enlarged, 1699; revised and enlarged, 1705);

Short Observations on a Printed Paper, Intituled, For Encouraging the Coining Silver Money in England, and after for

*John Locke; portrait by John Greenhill, 1672
(National Portrait Gallery, London)*

Keeping It Here, anonymous (London: Printed for Awnsham & John Churchill, 1695);

The Reasonableness of Christianity, As Delivered in the Scriptures, anonymous (London: Printed for Awnsham & John Churchill, 1695); enlarged as *The Reasonableness of Christianity, as delivered in the Scriptures. To which is added, A Vindication of the same, from Mr. Edwards's Exceptions* (London: Printed for Awnsham & John Churchill, 1696);

Further Considerations concerning Raising the Value of Money; Wherein Mr. Lowndes's Arguments for It in His Late Report concerning 'An Essay for the Amendment of the Silver Coins' Are Particularly Examined, anonymous

(London: Printed for Awnsham & John Churchill, 1695);

A Vindication of the Reasonableness of Christianity, &c. from Mr. Edwards's Reflections (London: Printed for Awnsham & John Churchill, 1695);

A Letter to Edward Ld Bishop of Worcester, concerning Some Passages Relating to Mr. Locke's Essay of Humane Understanding: In a Late Discourse of His Lordships, in Vindication of the Trinity (London: Printed by Henry Clark for Awnsham & John Churchill & Edward Castle, 1697);

A Second Vindication of the Reasonableness of Christianity, &c., as the author of *The Reasonableness of Christianity, &c.* (London: Printed for Awnsham & John Churchill, 1697);

Mr. Locke's Reply to the Right Reverend the Lord Bishop of Worcester's Answer to His Letter, concerning Some Passages Relating to Mr. Locke's Essay of Humane Understanding: In a Late Discourse of His Lordships, in Vindication of the Trinity (London: Printed by Henry Clark for Awnsham & John Churchill & Edward Castle, 1697);

Mr. Locke's Reply to the Right Reverend the Lord Bishop of Worcester's Answer to His Second Letter: Wherein, Besides Other Incident Matters, What His Lordship Has Said Concerning Certainty by Reason, Certainty by Ideas, and Certainty by Faith. The Resurrection of the Same Body. The Immateriality of the Soul. The Inconsistency of Mr. Locke's Notions with the Articles of the Christian Faith, and Their Tendency to Scepticism, Is Examined (London: Printed by Henry Clark for Awnsham & John Churchill & Edward Castle, 1699 [i.e., 1698]);

A Paraphrase and Notes on the Epistle of St. Paul to the Galatians (London: Printed for Awnsham & John Churchill, 1705);

A Paraphrase and Notes on the first Epistle of St. Paul to the Corinthians (London: Printed for Awnsham & John Churchill, 1706);

A Paraphrase and Notes on the second Epistle of St. Paul to the Corinthians (London: Printed for Awnsham & John Churchill, 1706);

Posthumous Works of Mr. John Locke: viz. I. Of the Conduct of the Understanding. II. An Examination of P. Malebranche's Opinion of Seeing All Things in God. III. A Discourse of Miracles. IV. Part of a Fourth Letter for Toleration. V. Memoirs relating to the Life of Anthony First Earl of Shaftesbury. To which is Added, VI. His New method of a Common-Place Book, written originally in French and Now Translated into English, edited by Peter King and Anthony Collins (London: Printed by W. B. for Awnsham & John Churchill, 1706);

A Paraphrase and Notes on the Epistle of St. Paul to the Romans (London: Printed for Awnsham & John Churchill, 1707);

A Paraphrase and Notes on the Epistle of St. Paul to the Ephesians (London: Printed for Awnsham & John Churchill, 1707);

A Paraphrase and Notes on the Epistles of St. Paul to the Galatians, I & II Corinthians, Romans, Ephesians. To Which is Prefix'd, An Essay for the Understanding of St. Paul's Epistles, by Consulting St. Paul Himself (London: Printed by J. H. for Awnsham & John Churchill, 1707);

Some Familiar Letters between Mr. Locke and Several of His Friends (London: Printed for Awnsham & John Churchill, 1708);

A Collection of Several Pieces of Mr. John Locke, Never Before Printed, or Not Extant in His Works. Published by the Author of the Life of the evermemorable Mr. John Hales, &c., edited by Pierre Desmaizeaux and Anthony Collins (London: Printed by James Bettenham for Richard Francklin, 1720);

Observations upon the Growth and Culture of Vines and Olives, the Production of Silk, the Preservation of Fruits; Written at the Request of the Earl of Shaftesbury: To whom it is inscribed (London: Printed for William Sandby by William Richardson & S. Clark, 1766);

The Physician's Art: An Attempt to Expand John Locke's Fragment "De arte medica," edited by Alexander George Gibson (Oxford: Clarendon Press, 1933);

Essays on the Law of Nature: The Latin Text, with a Translation, Introduction and Notes, Together with Transcripts of Locke's Shorthand in His Journal for 1676, edited and translated by Wolfgang von Leyden (Oxford: Clarendon Press, 1954);

The Library of John Locke, edited by John Harrison and Peter Laslett (Oxford: Published for the Oxford Bibliographical Society by the Oxford University Press, 1965);

John Locke: Two Tracts on Government, edited and translated, with introduction and notes, by Philip Abrams (Cambridge: Cambridge University Press, 1967).

Editions and Collections: *Several Papers Relating to Money, Interest and Trade, &c. Writ upon Several Occasions, and Published at Different Times* (London: Printed for Anshaw & John Churchill, 1696)—comprises *Some Considerations of the Consequences of the Lowering of Interest, and Raising the Value of Money, Short Observations on a Printed Paper, Intituled, For Encouraging the Coining Silver Money in England, and after for Keeping It Here,* and *Further considerations concerning Raising the Value of Money;*

The Works of John Locke, 10 volumes (London: Printed by Thomas Davison for Thomas Tegg & William

Sharpe, 1823; Aalen, Germany: Scientia Verlag, 1963);

Two Treatises of Government: A Critical Edition, edited, with an introduction, by Peter Laslett (Cambridge: Cambridge University Press, 1960; revised edition, Cambridge: Cambridge University Press, 1964; New York: New American Library / London: New English Library, 1965);

The Educational Writings of John Locke: A Critical Edition, edited by James L. Axtell (Cambridge: Cambridge University Press, 1968);

The Clarendon Edition of the Works of John Locke, edited by Peter H. Nidditch and others, 30 volumes projected (Oxford: Oxford University Press, 1975–   ).

OTHER: Robert Boyle, *The General History of the Air, Designed and Begun by the Honble. Robert Boyle Esq.,* edited by Locke (London: Printed for Awnsham & John Churchill, 1692);

Boyle, *Medicinal Experiments: or, A collection of choice and safe remedies, for the most part simple and easily prepared: useful in families, and very serviceble to country people,* volume 2, edited by Locke (London: Printed for Samuel Smith & B. Walford, 1693);

Æsop, *Æsop's Fables, in English & Latin, interlineary, for the benefit of those who do not having a master, would learn either of these tongues. With Sculptures,* edited by Locke (London: Printed for Awnsham & John Churchill, 1703).

SELECTED PERIODICAL PUBLICATION– UNCOLLECTED: "Locke's First Reply to John Norris," edited by Richard Acworth, *Locke Newsletter,* no. 2 (1971): 7–11.

John Locke is heralded as one of the most prominent British philosophers and men of letters. His most important philosophical work, *An Essay concerning Humane Understanding: In Four Books* (1689), had a profound influence on eighteenth-century thought and on the subsequent development of British empiricism. John Stuart Mill voiced what is still a widespread scholarly opinion when he pronounced Locke the "unquestioned founder of the analytic philosophy of mind." Locke's purpose in this work was to remove some of the "rubbish" standing in the way of knowledge, but he is widely viewed as achieving much more, for he laid the theoretical groundwork for new experimental methods in science. Locke's importance in the history of Western thought rests no less on his political work, *Two Treatises of Government: In the Former, The False Principles and Foundation of Sir Robert Filmer, and His Followers, are Detected and Overthrown. The Latter is an Essay concerning the True Original, Extent, and end of Civil-Government* (1689). The liberal

views expressed in *Two Treatises of Government* contributed to the intellectual origins of the American Revolution of 1776 and the French Revolution of 1789. His political theory underlies the capitalist parliamentary democracies of modern Western civilization. Locke was also a leading theoretician of religious toleration and his many writings on the subject moved later generations to a new spirit of tolerance. His greatest literary impact was on Laurence Sterne, who quotes him frequently in *The Life and Opinions of Tristram Shandy, Gentleman* (seven volumes, 1760–1767), and who was greatly impressed by Locke's theory of the random association of ideas. The scope of Locke's mind was truly remarkable, for he also published works on economics, education, medicine, and natural science. Locke was especially renowned for his common sense and practical nature, both of which are reflected in his writing and in the history of his life.

Locke was born at Wrington, a village in Somerset, England, on 29 August 1632. He grew up in a small manor, called Beluton, near the little market town of Pensford, not far from Bristol. His father, also named John Locke, was a country attorney of Puritan ancestry who later fought for the Parliamentary cause in the first English Civil War (1642–1646). Little is known about Locke's mother, Agnes Keene, as she died when he was a young man, but he spoke of her fondly as a "pious and affectionate woman." Locke was the eldest of three boys. His brother Peter died in infancy and his brother Thomas was born in 1637. For the first fourteen years of his life, Locke was educated with great rigor and discipline by his father, but as Locke matured, his father's strictness eased and the two grew closer.

Locke never married, but his correspondence reveals that he was romantically attached to several different women throughout his lifetime. Locke's best-known biographer, Maurice Cranston, describes Locke's women friends as "a formidable lot of dons' blue-stocking daughters." His longest-lasting relationship was with Damaris Cudworth, a beautiful and clever woman half his age, who was the daughter of the Cambridge Platonist and theologian Ralph Cudworth. Under the names "Philander" and "Philoclea" they wrote love letters and verses to each other beginning in 1681, but Cudworth was much more to Locke than a lover. She was an educated and witty woman, and Locke enjoyed her intellectual companionship through many conversations about philosophy, religion, and political affairs. There were, however, certain difficulties with the relationship, perhaps owing to ambivalence on both their parts as to whether or not they desired to be lovers or merely friends. In 1685 Cudworth married Sir Francis Masham, a widower with eight children. Locke and Cudworth, now Lady Masham, remained intimate

Page from a manuscript, thought to be in Locke's hand, for an early essay that formed the basis for his 1689 work
Epistola de tolerantia ad clarissimum virum *(Henry E. Huntington Library, San Marino, California)*

friends in spite of her marriage, and much of what is known about Locke's life and character has come through Lady Masham's eloquent writings.

Locke's formal education began in 1646 when he was admitted to Westminster School, then controlled by Parliament, though run by a Royalist headmaster, Richard Busby. For six years Locke endured the excessive emphasis on Greek and Latin at the school and the tedium of rote learning, a method that he later condemned in *Some Thoughts concerning Education* (1693). Locke's Victorian biographer, H. R. Fox Bourne, remarks that the curriculum of the school was so dull and grueling that "it is not strange that a good many Westminster boys should have become either pedants or dolts." One of Locke's most memorable days during his years at Westminster was probably the beheading of Charles I in Whitehall in January 1649. It seems unlikely that Locke actually witnessed the event, but given the proximity of the school to the execution site, it is possible that he was close enough to have heard the commotion. Locke lived through some of the most troubled times in English history–the bitter struggles between King Charles and Parliament, the rise to power of Presbyterians and Independents, and the rule of Oliver Cromwell. In his mature years he witnessed the Restoration of 1660, the reigns of Charles II and James II, the Glorious Revolution of 1688, and the constitutional settlement of William and Mary. At the time of Charles II's restoration Locke recalled, "I no sooner perceived myself in the world but I found myself in a storm which has lasted almost hitherto."

At Westminster, Locke was elected as king's scholar, enabling him to seek an election to a studentship (equivalent to a fellowship) at Christ Church, Oxford, where he was admitted in 1652. Locke received his B.A. in 1656, followed by an M.A. in 1658. He studied metaphysics, logic, rhetoric, Greek, and other classical languages. Locke's early years at Oxford were not altogether fruitful ones, and at times he regretted that his father had sent him there. He was dissatisfied with the scholastic teaching methods, particularly the public disputations in the schools, which he thought were "invented for wrangling and ostentation rather than to discover truth." Even philosophy he found "obscure" and full of "useless questions." Locke seems to have had little respect for his tutors, often choosing to remain in his room reading romances rather than attending lectures. When he did attend, he argued with the tutor and acted impudently by not taking any notes. Nevertheless, he went on to become a senior student of Christ Church in 1659, receiving lectureships and an appointment as Censor of Moral Philosophy in 1664.

Locke's father had intended him for the church, but Locke decided upon the profession of medicine

instead. By the late 1650s he had started taking detailed medical notes and conducting medical experiments. His medical studies were augmented by a course of reading in natural philosophy, in particular the anatomist William Harvey's *Exercitationes de Generatione Animalium* (Essays on the Generation of Animals, 1651), the work considered to be the foundation of modern embryology. During this time he also dabbled in chemistry and attended a class given by the German chemist Peter Stahl. In 1660 Locke met Robert Boyle and became acquainted with Boyle's new mechanical philosophy. The notes in Locke's commonplace books indicate that he was also reading René Descartes's *La Dioptrique* (Dioptics, 1637 or 1638), *Les Météores* (Meteors, 1637 or 1638), and *Principia Philosophiæ* (Principles of Philosophy, 1644), and at least some of Pierre Gassendi's Epicurean rejection of Descartes, *Syntagma Philosophicum* (Philosophical Treatise), first published in Gassendi's posthumous *Opera omnia* (Collected Works, 1658).

In 1665 Locke's medical studies were interrupted as he went away on a diplomatic mission, acting as secretary to Sir Walter Vane, ambassador to Frederick William, the elector of Brandenberg. The purpose of the mission was to convince the elector to become an ally of England against the Netherlands in the Second Anglo-Dutch War (1665–1667), or at least to ensure the neutrality of Brandenberg. The mission turned out to be futile, and Locke returned to Oxford after several months.

Once Locke was back in Oxford a chance event in 1666 determined the course of his entire career. Anthony Ashley Cooper, who was then Baron Ashley of Wimborne St. Giles, came to Oxford to drink some medicinal waters, which he expected his physician, David Thomas, to supply. Thomas was suddenly called out of town, so he passed the duty on to Locke, who was his partner in chemical experiments at the time. As a result of some muddle with the messenger whom Locke had employed to obtain the waters, when Ashley arrived the waters were not ready. Locke went himself to explain the embarrassment to Ashley. The subject of the waters was quickly forgotten and the two began conversing about other things. Each was greatly impressed with the other's social graces, and a strong friendship immediately developed. In 1667 Locke became physician to Ashley's household in London, where he resided for the next eight years. Locke is said to have saved Ashley's life by overseeing an operation to remove an abscess from his liver. Locke served his patron in many other capacities as well, such as political and financial adviser and tutor to Ashley's son.

While in London, Locke continued to read extensively in medicine. Shortly after his arrival he became acquainted with the distinguished physician Thomas

Sydenham. Locke was able to gain some clinical experience by accompanying Sydenham on his rounds. In collaboration with Sydenham, Locke wrote several essays on various medical topics, the most important being *De arte medica* (On the Art of Medicine), which was first published in an edition by Alexander George Gibson as *The Physician's Art* (1933). Scholars differ as to whether it was Locke or Sydenham who wrote the tract, but in keeping with Locke's general philosophy, the work advocates an empirical approach to medical practice over the corpuscularian principles advocated by Boyle.

In November 1668 Locke was elected a fellow of the prestigious Royal Society. Meetings were held twice a week, during which some of Locke's most eminent contemporaries gathered to discuss scientific experiments and philosophy. Although he served on the council at least once, he does not seem to have been an active member of the society. That same year Locke wrote the greater part of *Some Considerations of the Consequences of the Lowering of Interest, and Raising the Value of Money. In a Letter to a Member of Parliament,* though it was not published until 1692. In 1668 Locke also assisted Shaftesbury in drawing up a constitution for the new colony of Carolina, of which Shaftesbury was a principal proprietor. In the 1660s Locke seems to have read little philosophy. Mainly he seems to have been reading books about medicine, natural science, theology, and travel. As J. R. Milton observes, "In 1670 Locke was not yet a philosopher, as we would understand that term. He was however shortly to become one."

Around 1670 a famous meeting took place in Locke's chamber. In the "Epistle to the Reader" in *An Essay concerning Humane Understanding* Locke relates how he and five or six of his friends had met to discuss some "remote" subject. The discussion ran into unexpected difficulties, and Locke proposed that before they could continue "it was necessary to examine our own abilities and see what objects our understandings were or were not, fitted to deal with." This proposal became the central purpose of Locke's essay, which he states is "to enquire into the original, certainty, and extent of human knowledge, together with the grounds and degrees of belief, opinion and assent." He proposed to adopt what he referred to as an "historical, plain method" of inquiry, which he would use to investigate the ways in which human beings acquire knowledge and the kinds of things that human minds are capable of knowing.

In the years from 1672 to 1675 Locke was occupied with various administrative activities. When Ashley became the earl of Shaftesbury in 1672 and, that same year, lord chancellor, Locke became secretary of presentations, which post he held until Shaftesbury's dismissal in 1673. Locke then took up the post of secre-

tary of trade until 1675. The next four years were spent resting and traveling in France. Locke had suffered from asthma for years, and he had hoped that the escape from the smoke-filled air of London would improve his condition. He spent fifteen months at the health resort of Montpellier, where he had the opportunity to meet Pierre Regis, a well-known popularizer of Descartes's philosophy. The French government had forbidden the teaching of Cartesian philosophy at major universities, but Descartes's philosophy was still the center of attention in private circles. Lockes's interest in Cartesian philosophy was further stimulated by his discussions with Regis. In Lady Masham's words, "the first books, as Mr. Locke himself has told me, which gave him a relish of philosophical things were those of Descartes. He was rejoiced in reading these, because, though he often differed in opinion from this writer, he yet found that what he said was very intelligible." Descartes was a definite influence behind some of the departures in *An Essay concerning Humane Understanding* from the Scholasticism that Locke had learned at Oxford. Yet, Locke scholars disagree over the extent to which the metaphysics of the work is indebted to Descartes, for Locke was also extremely critical of Cartesianism.

As a favor to Shaftesbury, Locke went from Montpellier to Paris to act as tutor to Caleb Banks, the son of Shaftesbury's friend Sir John Banks. During his stay in Paris he had the opportunity to meet an influential follower of Gassendi, François Bernier. Locke and Bernier shared many interests, and through meetings with Bernier, Locke became better acquainted with Gassendi's criticisms of Descartes. In 1679 Locke returned to England to serve again as adviser to Shaftesbury. England was in a state of political crisis over the succession to the throne, with many, including Shaftesbury, opposed to the succession of Charles's brother and heir, James, Duke of York, on the grounds that he was Catholic. Shaftesbury had become the leader of the Parliamentary opposition to the Stuarts, attempting to replace James as heir with Charles's illegitimate son James Scott, Duke of Monmouth; when the attempt failed in 1681, Shaftesbury was arrested and tried for treason. Although he was acquitted, he fled for Holland, where he died in 1683. Fearing persecution on account of his close association with Shaftesbury, Locke also fled to Holland in 1683, remaining there until 1689.

While in Holland, Locke made many friends, including the theologian Philip van Limborch, the head of the Remonstrant College. In 1684 Locke discovered that Charles II had ordered John Fell, the dean of Christ Church, to deprive him of his studentship for behaving "factiously and undutifully to the Govern-

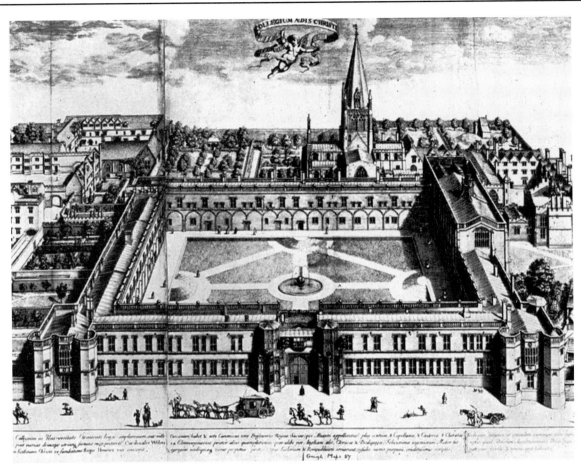

Locke's college, Christ Church, at Oxford University, as it appeared in 1676 (Bodleian Library, Oxford University)

ment." The next year the Dutch government was requested to hand Locke over on suspicion of being involved in the insurrection of Monmouth, who had attempted to overthrow the newly crowned James II in February 1685. Locke went into hiding under the assumed name of "Dr. van der Linder" until May 1685. James II was overthrown in the Glorious Revolution of 1688 and William of Orange, stadtholder of the Netherlands, was invited to assume the throne as King William II; when Princess Mary of Orange crossed the channel to be crowned Queen Mary II of England in February 1689, Locke accompanied the royal party.

During his exile in the Netherlands, Locke wrote extensively. He contributed an article, as well as reviews, to the *Bibliotheque universelle* (Universal Library) of Jean Le Clerc. These were his first published works. He wrote in Latin the *Epistola de tolerantia, ad clarissimum virum T. A. R. P. T. O. L. A. scripta à P. A. P. O. I. L. A.,* addressed to van Limborch, which was published anonymously in the Netherlands in April 1689 and published in London in October of that year in a translation by the Unitarian merchant William Popple

as *A Letter concerning Toleration: Humbly submitted, & c.,* a passionate and powerful defense of individual religious liberty. Locke also continued to work on *An Essay concerning Humane Understanding* and in 1688 the *Bibliotheque universelle* published an abstract of the work.

The English translation of *Epistola de Tolerantia* sold out quickly and a second edition appeared in a matter of months. Considerable controversy was aroused by the work. Jonas Proast, an Oxford clergyman, published a strong attack in 1690. Locke replied to Proast's anonymous pamphlet with *A Second Letter concerning Toleration,* which appeared later that same year, published under the pseudonym of Philanthropus. The second letter is fairly short, but Locke's reply to Proast's second anonymous attack, published in April 1691, was more than three hundred pages long; Locke's rebuttal (also published under the pseudonym of Philanthropus), *A Third Letter for Toleration, to the Author of the "Third Letter concerning Toleration,"* was published in June 1692.

Locke was furious when he discovered that van Limborch had divulged his authorship of *Epistola de Tol-*

erantia. Locke did not make a public admission of his authorship of this work until he wrote his will. Throughout his writing career Locke went to great lengths to guard his anonymity. He wrote in a secret code and sometimes used invisible ink. He kept secrets even from such close friends as James Tyrrell, behaving indignantly and evasively when Tyrrell questioned Locke about being the author of the *Two Treatises of Government.* Some of this secrecy was prudent, given that writers in Locke's time could face persecution for expressing unorthodox religious, political, and philosophical views. But some of Locke's passion for secrecy was somewhat neurotic, or perhaps, as Cranston cheekily suggests, manufactured "to add a much-needed touch of romance to Locke's relations with his woman friends."

Two Treatises of Government appeared anonymously in October 1689, though the title page bears the date 1690. The first treatise is a relentless criticism of Sir Robert Filmer's *Patriarcha, or, The Natural Power of Kings* (1680), which argues for the divine right of kings to rule independent of popular consent. Locke argued against Filmer's contention that the absolute power of the monarch was inherited from Adam. The second treatise provides a theory for the justification of government. As did Thomas Hobbes, Locke argued that government is necessary to avoid an undesirable state of nature, but he went beyond Hobbes in maintaining the right of each civil society to resist a ruler whose acts are not sanctioned by a majority of the representative assembly.

The date the work was composed and the order in which the treatises were written are unknown. There is some evidence that Locke may have written the second treatise first, sometime between 1679 and 1681. If so, the work was not intended to justify the Glorious Revolution of 1688, which is the purpose Locke provides to the reader in the preface. Rather, the purpose would have been to establish a theoretical foundation for the political aims of Shaftesbury and his followers in their struggle with Charles I. Some scholars have argued that Locke's real concern in the first treatise was not to demolish Filmer's flimsy position but rather to reply to the more powerful political teachings of Hobbes's *Leviathan, or, The Matter, Forme, & Power of a Common-Wealth Ecclesiasticall and Civill* (1651). As does Filmer, Hobbes argues that a monarch must have absolute power over the people. But unlike Filmer, Hobbes bases this contention on a theory of human nature, not divine right. For Hobbes, the only way to restrain people from exercising their natural greedy, savage, and power-seeking instincts is through an absolute monarchy that people obey through fear of coercion and punishment.

In the second treatise Locke follows Hobbes in arguing that government is needed to avoid an undesirable state of nature. A state of nature is not a state of war for Locke, as it is for Hobbes, rather the state of nature is one of peace, equality, goodwill, liberty, and preservation, whereas a state of war is one of "enmity, malice, violence and mutual destruction." In a state of nature, men and women are governed by the law of nature. Locke is unclear about the law of nature, but in his 1664 lecture notes, first published as *Essays on the Law of Nature* in 1954, he holds that natural law rests on the will of God and is discoverable by reason. Yet, Locke speaks of natural law as "writ in the hearts of all mankind," which suggests some kind of innateness. In a state of nature people are bound to preserve peace and liberty and to refrain from hurting one another. Since there is no government to ensure the preservation of natural rights, the execution of the law of nature is the responsibility of the people. Every individual has the right to punish transgressors of natural law. What is inconvenient about this arrangement is that there are no powers of enforcement guaranteeing rights. Moreover, people's biases often interfere with the fair enforcement and application of natural law. The solution for such inconveniences is civil government, where people give up their natural liberties and unite in a body politic that acts through the consent of the governed. The role of the state is to act as arbitrator, to protect life, liberty, and property, and to administer punishment. If a government begins to abuse rather than protect the natural rights of citizens, it may legitimately be overthrown.

One natural right that Locke emphasizes ought to be preserved and not abused by government is the individual's right to private property. The right of property belongs to any person, insofar as he was the first to discover, inherit, produce, or mix his labor with it. Locke qualifies this right by stating that one has a right only to what one produces or discovers insofar as one is not depriving another of the means of self-preservation. In other words, "the interests of the community as a whole must override the individual's right to private property." This socialist aspect of Locke's theory of property has been relatively ignored by political theorists.

Locke's most important work, *An Essay concerning Humane Understanding,* was published two months after *Two Treatises of Government* appeared—although the title page bears the publication date of 1690, it was actually published in December of 1689. The first book of *An Essay concerning Humane Understanding* begins with an attack on what was then an established opinion that human beings are born with knowledge of some truths, which supplies them with the foundations of knowledge. Locke argues that certain ideas have been thought of as being innate simply because people have no recol-

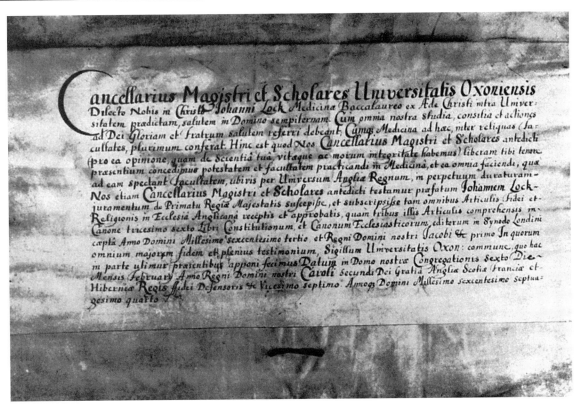

Locke's medical degree, which he received from Oxford University on 6 February 1675 (Bodleian Library, Oxford University)

lection of having first learned them. Moreover, he argues that God would not have provided humans with sense organs so fitted for acquiring knowledge if that knowledge were innate. Locke has a series of different arguments aimed against the appeal to innate origin as a guarantee of truth. Taken together, the arguments are constitutive of Locke's empiricist epistemology, which maintains that knowledge can be acquired only through experience. The mind at birth, according to him, is comparable to an "empty cabinet."

In book 2 Locke presents his argument that all ideas in the mind can be accounted for by experience. Ideas can be derived from two kinds of experience; either from "sensation" or "reflection." Ideas of sensation are derived from perceptions of physical objects or sensible qualities, and ideas of reflection are ideas derived from introspective activities such as doubting, believing, reasoning, and willing. Locke further distinguishes ideas into "simple" and "complex." Simple ideas (for example, brown, hot, sweet) are ideas that do not contain any other ideas and that the mind receives passively. Complex ideas (for example, golden mountain), on the other hand, are compounded of simple ideas and are produced by the power of the imagination to combine ideas. The power of the imagination to

combine simple ideas such as "gold" and "mountain" accounts for ideas that do not correspond to anything individuals have experienced previously.

The endless distinctions of this nature in *An Essay concerning Humane Understanding* are difficult to grasp, and Locke's critics are justified in pointing out that he never clearly or consistently defines the word "idea." The confusion over Locke's use of the word "idea" results from his extremely broad use of it. People have ideas in their minds, according to him, when they think and when they see, hear, smell, taste, or feel. In other words, Locke holds that only ideas are directly perceived, not physical objects themselves. This notion is central to Locke's epistemology and underlies a further crucial distinction in *An Essay concerning Humane Understanding* between "primary" and "secondary" qualities. Locke is not the inventor of this distinction, for it was drawn before him by Galileo, Descartes, and Boyle, but it was Locke's formulation of it that became the most well-known. Primary qualities are those qualities belonging to physical objects themselves, such as solidity, extension, figure, and mobility. Contrastingly, secondary qualities depend for their existence on the mind of the observer, for example, color, taste, sound, and smell. Locke's primary–secondary quality distinction was in

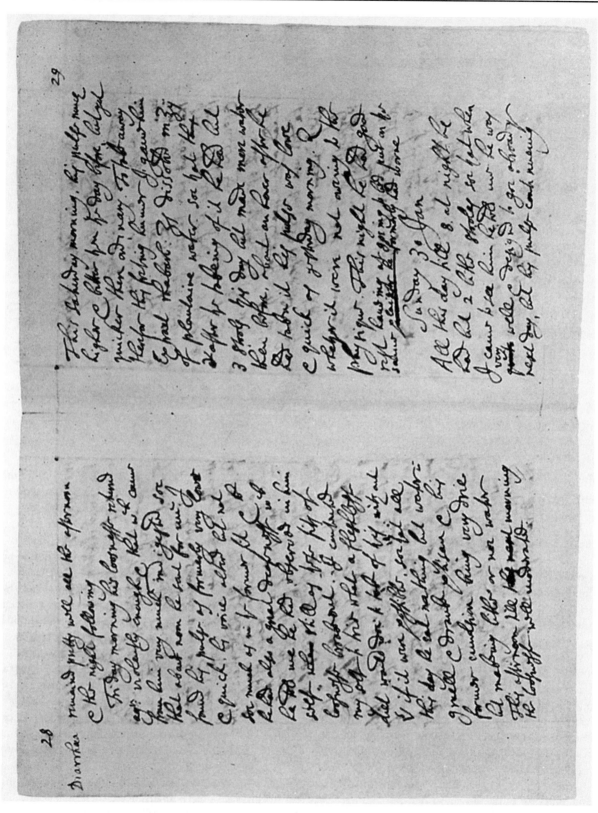

Pages from the journal that Locke began keeping during his stay in France from 1675 to 1679. The entries for 29 and 30 January 1678 describe the progress of a patient he treated for diarrhea (Bodleian Library).

keeping with the science of his day, which viewed the physical universe as colorless, tasteless, odorless, and silent. As Stephen Priest remarks in his *The British Empiricists: Hobbes to Ayer* (1990), "Interestingly, this has led to the view that what is mind-independent is more real than what is mind-dependent. We owe our opinion that matter is more real than mind to the seventeenth-century scientific revolution."

In book 3 of *An Essay concerning Humane Understanding* Locke discusses the "nature, use and signification" of language. Locke had intended to go from book 2 to a consideration of knowledge, but he became preoccupied with the close association between words and ideas. Locke commentators generally agree that the major fault of Locke's account of language is his insistence that words name ideas, but he is held by some to have made an important contribution nonetheless. Locke recognized the importance of language theories of the mind, as well as the usefulness of striving for clarity in the use of words as a means to avoiding theoretical confusion.

In the fourth and final book of *An Essay concerning Humane Understanding* Locke provides a positive account of knowledge. He defines knowledge as "nothing but the perception of the connection of and agreement, or disagreement and repugnancy of any of our ideas." Following Descartes, Locke distinguishes between intuitive, demonstrative, and sensitive knowledge. Intuitive knowledge is when the mind perceives an agreement or disagreement between ideas immediately, without the intervention of any other ideas. When knowledge is reached with the aid of other ideas, it is demonstrative. That which falls short of intuitive or demonstrative certainly is not knowledge, but mere faith or opinion. Sensitive knowledge is knowledge of what is actually present to one's senses at any given time. Locke contends that one's knowledge of one's own existence is intuitive: "we perceive it so plainly . . . that it neither needs nor is capable of any proof." David Hume attacked this view on the grounds that he had no perceptual experience of a self over and above his thoughts, sensations, and emotions. In large measure, Hume is thought to have succeeded in showing that intuitive knowledge of one's own existence cannot be reconciled with the Lockean doctrine of ideas. Nevertheless, Locke holds that intuitive knowledge is the basis for all knowledge. Each step in demonstration (for example, mathematics) where the mind perceives agreement or disagreement through other mediating ideas rests upon an intuition.

Locke maintains that one's knowledge extends only as far as does one's ideas themselves. Knowledge of any necessary connection between primary and secondary qualities is unattainable, and sensitive knowl-edge cannot extend to the real essence of physical objects. Locke does, however, offer some assurance when it comes to knowledge. For instance, he asserts that one can be certain that substance is present in all things or bodies, because the qualities one discerns must belong to something, even if one cannot discern that something. Bishop George Berkeley criticized Locke for "bantering the substance," but other critics brought the much more serious charge of atheism against him. Edward Stillingfleet, bishop of Worcester, claimed that Locke had promoted atheism by providing an impetus for the anti-Trinitarian movement. Clearly, the notion of substance is vital to religious doctrines of the Eucharist, the Incarnation, and the Trinity. Locke denied that he had done any such thing, and in two letters to Stillingfleet, published in 1697, he repeated the point he had made in *An Essay concerning Humane Understanding*: that one had to believe in substance, even though there is no actual proof of its existence. After 1696 Locke concentrated most of his writing on answering Stillingfleet's criticisms. Locke and Stillingfleet exchanged three lengthy letters and the controversy went on until the bishop's death in 1699. Locke did not wish to eliminate the doctrine of substance, for however extreme his latitudinarianism, he was still a Christian. He advised against accepting on faith anything "inconsistent with the clear and self-evident dictates of reason," but he did accept on faith certain propositions that could not be proved either through reason or empirical investigation.

Locke's example of a proposition based on faith is that the dead shall rise. There is no evidence for this belief, but in his view it can be accepted because it is not contrary to reason. The Catholic doctrine of transubstantiation, with its implicit proposition that the body of Christ is in more than one place at one time, on the other hand, is contrary to reason and therefore cannot be accepted. It should be noted that reason plays an important role in Locke's philosophy. Although he is often called the founder of modern empiricism, his rationalism must not be underestimated. He maintains, for example, that the existence of God can be established by rational proofs and that principles of morality are as demonstrable as those of geometry. Two main currents influenced the development of Locke's thought in this regard: the unformulated empiricism of Isaac Newton, Boyle, and other Royal Society members, and the systematic rationalism of Descartes. The empirical strain was the stronger of the two, however, and Locke's mission was to formulate empiricism in a new and significant way.

John Norris, an old friend of Lady Masham's, was the first to publish criticisms of *An Essay concerning Humane Understanding*, as an appendix to his *Christian*

L. 2

L. 2. C. 1

Of the Originall of our Ideas

1 Every man being conscious to himselfe yt he thinks
& yt wch his minde is imployd about whilst thinking
being ye Ideas yt are there, ti past doubt yt men have
in their minds severall Ideas such as are those
expressed by ye words whitenesse, hardnesse, sweet-
nesse, thinking motion, man, Elephant, army
drunkennesse & others, it is in ye first place then
to be enquird how he comes by them. I know it
is a received doctrine yt men have native Ideas
& originall characters stampd upon their minds
in their very first being. This opinion I have
at large examined already & I suppose wt I have
above sd will be much more easily admitted when
I have shewd (wch I think every ones experience will when he weighs it make out to him)
how all ye Ideas he has come into his minde
by degree & upon occasion.

2 Let us then suppose ye minde to be as we say
white ___ void of all characters all Ideas how
comes it to be furnished? whence comes it by yt
vast store wch ye busy & boundlesse phansy of men
comes to dress it selfe us in w an almost endlesse
variety wch furnish hoe ample an imployment
to ye reason & knowledge of mankind. And
to this I answer in one word Experience In

Page from a 1685 draft, possibly in the hand of a scribe, for Locke's 1689 work An Essay
concerning Humane Understanding *(Pierpont Morgan Library)*

Blessedness; or Discourses Upon the Beatitudes of our Lord and Saviour Jesus Christ (1690). Norris, an admirer of the French philosopher Nicolas Malebranche, was introduced to Locke through Lady Masham. Initially Locke and Norris were on friendly terms, but they had a falling-out when Locke came to suspect Norris of prying into his correspondence. Locke wrote a brief and angry reply to Norris's criticisms, titled "Locke's Answer to Mr. Norris's Reflection," dated 1692 and first published by Richard Acworth in the *Locke Newsletter* (1971). Approximately a year later, Locke wrote two more substantial pieces directed at Norris. Some of the new material found in the second edition of *An Essay concerning Humane Understanding* (1694) seems to be based on Locke's consideration of Norris and Malebranche's philosophy. By 1692 most educated people were familiar with Locke's essay and it was highly regarded by other prominent writers of his time. At about this time Locke began corresponding with William Molyneux of Dublin, who in his book *Dioptrica Nova: A Treatise of Dioptricks, in Two Parts* (1692) had praised Locke for delivering "profound truths." Molyneux, however, was also critical of parts of the essay, and many of the other changes in the second edition were a result of Locke's exchanges with Molyneux. In general, Locke was unreceptive to criticism of *An Essay concerning Humane Understanding*. Consequently, he disregarded some useful suggestions for revision from Molyneux and others.

Although the work had many supporters, many of the views expressed in it were criticized for undermining traditional Christianity. Locke's opposition to the search for true essences or forms, his theory of substance, his attack on innate ideas, and his emphasis on human ignorance with regard to spirits and the physical universe all offended the clergy. As a result, there was an order to ban *An Essay concerning Humane Understanding* in 1703, but it was never enforced. Locke worked on revising the work intermittently until his death, but he did not manage to eliminate its many inconsistencies, obscurities, and repetitive sections. Many fundamental philosophical questions raised in the work are never satisfactorily answered. Yet, Norman Kemp Smith is no doubt right to point out that its chief merit lies not so much in the answers Locke gives in it, but in the questions that he was the first to raise and which retain their central position in philosophy.

In July 1693 Locke published *Some Thoughts concerning Education,* the first work since *An Essay concerning Humane Understanding* to be published in his own name. The work is based on letters written by Locke from the Netherlands to his friend Edward Clarke advising him on the upbringing of his son. Some of his ideas about education were conventional, but others were revolutionary and added to the growing publicity surrounding

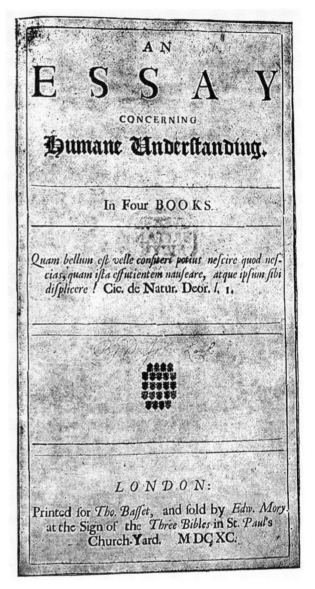

Title page for a variant issue of the first edition of the book in which Locke laid the basis for British Empiricism. The work is dated 1690 but was actually published in December of the previous year (Henry E. Huntington Library, San Marino, California).

his name. In response to "so many who profess themselves at a loss how to breed their children" Locke recommends that learning be governed by individual aptitudes rather than by rote and rod. Locke thought that games and humor should be used in teaching whenever possible. He emphasized virtue, practical wisdom, the development of character, and good health. The work was a transparent criticism of his own education at both Oxford and Westminster, which he had found so monotonous and ineffective. Several of Locke's recommendations for the upbringing of children may strike the modern reader as cruel and negli-

Locke in the final year of his life; portrait by Sir Godfrey Kneller (Royal Society of London)

gent. For example, he insists that even in winter children's feet should be washed daily in cold water. A child, he writes, should "have his shoes so thin that they might leak and let in water." Concerning diet, Locke says children's meals should be irregular so that their stomachs will not become accustomed to eating at particular times. Locke also recommends the avoidance of fruit as "a thing totally unwholesome for children." The idea behind much of his advice was to train the body to be vigorous and able to endure hardships if necessary. Locke took a stand against corporal punishment, although he did think that it was appropriate occasionally. He urges parents to use methods of approval and disapproval, or what he called "esteem and grace," instead. He further advises parents to do as his own father had done, and to first instil fear and awe in their children and as they grew up, to admit them into love and friendship. Most importantly, Locke stresses good manners, though he confessed that it might sound odd that a "bookish man" would maintain that "learning is the least part of good breeding." Locke perhaps underestimates the value of learning as itself a means of educating character, but parts of the work are so wise and commonsensical that it deserves its important place in the philosophy of education. It is worth noting that it has the historical importance of having

influenced Jean-Jacques Rousseau's *Emile; ou, De l'éducation* (Emile, or, On Education, 1762). Although Locke had no children of his own, his recommendations for the upbringing of children in *Thoughts concerning Education* were highly regarded by his contemporaries.

In Locke's last years he published *The Reasonableness of Christianity, As Delivered in the Scriptures,* which appeared anonymously in 1695. In this work Locke argued that the only thing essential to Christianity is the belief that Jesus Christ is the Messiah and that Scripture "was simply a collection of writings designed by God to instruct the illiterate bulk of mankind in the way of salvation." Locke repudiated the doctrine of original sin and insisted that Scripture be understood in the direct meaning of the terms it is delivered in. *The Reasonableness of Christianity* aroused a great deal of controversy among Locke's critics, the most prominent being the extreme Calvinist and clergyman John Edwards. In his book *Some Thoughts concerning the Several Causes and Occasions of Atheism, Especially in the Present Age* (1695) Edwards charged Locke's work with atheism. In 1695 Locke replied in *A Vindication of the Reasonableness of Christianity, &c. from Mr. Edwards's Reflections* that he had said nothing in his work that implied a rejection of any reasonable doctrine of Christianity. In 1697 he published *A Second Vindication of the Reasonableness of Christianity, &c.* in answer to Edwards's further attacks in *Socinianism Unmask'd* (1696).

In 1696 Locke accepted an appointment as a commissioner for trade. The Board of Trade and Plantations met at least three times a week, and Locke received £1,000 a year for his responsibilities. The work was exhausting, and Locke wrote to his friends expressing the desire to spend his last years in retirement. Although he tried to resign the following year for reasons of ill health, those in authority persuaded him to continue his duties and stay at Oates, the Masham estate in Essex to which he had retired in 1691, until his health improved. Locke accepted this proposal and sat on the board whenever his health permitted. In 1700 he resigned and avoided any further public employment.

The last four years of Locke's life were spent quietly at Oates, writing, resting, and horseback riding. One day a lump appeared on his back, which he thought responsible for the pain that had spread to his legs, and he was no longer able to ride. The leg pain became so debilitating that he became largely confined to his bed. On 28 October 1704, while Lady Masham was reading the Psalms to him, he died. Locke's death, said Lady Masham, was like his life, "truly pious, yet natural, easy and unaffected." Locke's burial took place in the churchyard of the parish church at High Laver, where his grave can still be seen. The epitaph on his tombstone tells people to turn to his writings to determine what sort of person he was. His writings reveal that he was a wise and sensible man, but from the writings of Lady Masham and others who knew him well, it is evident that he was also remarkably kind, charming, and modest. Lady Masham remembers that Locke was "naturally compassionate and exceedingly charitable to those in want," noting that his charity was always aimed toward "working, laborious, industrious people, and not to relieve idle beggars."

John Locke was one of the most learned men of his age, but it was characteristic that he never made a show of erudition. His mission to discover truth was placed far ahead of any desire for wealth or reputation. "That which makes my writings tolerable," he wrote, "is only this, that I never write for anything but truth and never publish anything to others which I am not fully persuaded of myself." "If," he says, "I have anything to boast of it is that I sincerely love and seek truth with indifference whom it pleases or displeases."

Letters:

Some Familiar Letters Between Mr. Locke, and Several of His Friends (London: Printed for Awnsham & John Churchill, 1708);

Original Letters of John Locke; Algernon Sydney; and Anthony, Lord Shaftesbury, author of the "Characteristics": With An Analytical Sketch of the Writings and Opinions of Locke and Other Metaphysicians, edited by Thomas Forster (London: Nichols, 1830);

Lettres Inédites de John Locke à ses amis Nicolas Thoynard, Philippe van Limborch et Edward Clarke, edited by Henri Ollion and T. J. de Boer (The Hague: Nijhoff, 1912);

The Correspondence of John Locke and Edward Clarke, edited by Benjamin Rand (London: Oxford University Press, 1927);

The Correspondence of John Locke, 8 volumes, edited by E. S. De Beer (Oxford: Clarendon Press, 1976–1989).

Bibliographies:

Halfdan Olaus Christophersen, *A Bibliographical Introduction to the Study of John Locke* (Oslo: Jacob Dybwad, 1930; New York: Burt Franklin, 1968);

Philip Long, *A Summary Catalogue of the Lovelace Collection of the Papers of John Locke in the Bodleian Library,* Oxford Bibliographical Society Publications, new series volume 8 (Oxford: Printed for the Society at the University Press, 1959);

Roland Hall and Roger Woolhouse, *80 Years of Locke Scholarship: A Bibliographical Guide* (Edinburgh: Edinburgh University Press, 1983);

John C. Attig, *The Works of John Locke: A Comprehensive Bibliography From the Seventeenth Century to the Present* (Westport, Conn.: Greenwood Press, 1985);

Jean S. Yolton and John W. Yolton, *John Locke: A Reference Guide* (Boston: G. K. Hall, 1985);

Jean S. Yolton, *John Locke: A Descriptive Bibliography* (Bristol, U.K. & Dulles, Va.: Thoemmes, 1998).

Biographies:

Jean Le Clerc, *The Life and Character of John Locke, Author of the Essay concerning Humane Understanding,* translated by T. F. P. (London: Printed for John Clark & sold by J. Nutts, 1706);

Peter King, *The Life of John Locke: With Extracts from His Correspondence, Journals, and Common-Place Books* (1 volume, London: Colburn, 1829; 2 volumes, revised edition, London: Colburn & Bentley, 1830);

H. R. Fox Bourne, *The Life of John Locke,* 2 volumes (London: Henry S. King, 1876; New York: Harper, 1876);

Alexander Campbell Fraser, *Locke* (Edinburgh & London: Blackwood, 1890; Philadelphia: Lippincott, 1890);

Maurice Cranston, *John Locke: A Biography* (London: Longmans, Green, 1957; New York: Macmillan, 1957; revised edition, Oxford & New York: Oxford University Press, 1985);

Kenneth Dewhurst, *John Locke, 1632–1704, Physician and Philosopher: A Medical Biography, with an Edition of the Medical Notes in His Journals* (London: Wellcome Historical Medical Library, 1963; New York: Garland, 1984).

References:

Richard Ithimar Aaron, *John Locke,* third edition (Oxford: Clarendon Press, 1971);

Peter Alexander, *Ideas, Qualities, and Corpuscles: Locke and Boyle on the External World* (Cambridge & New York: Cambridge University Press, 1985);

Richard Ashcraft, *Revolutionary Politics & Locke's Two Treatises of Government* (Princeton: Princeton University Press, 1986);

Ashcraft, ed., *John Locke: Critical Assessments,* 4 volumes (London & New York: Routledge, 1991);

Margaret Atherton, ed., *The Empiricists: Critical Essays on Locke, Berkeley, and Hume* (Lanham, Md. & Oxford: Rowman & Littlefield, 1999);

Jonathan Bennett, *Locke, Berkeley, Hume: Central Themes* (Oxford: Oxford University Press, 1971);

Vere Chappell, ed., *The Cambridge Companion to Locke* (Cambridge & New York: Cambridge University Press, 1994);

John Colman, *John Locke's Moral Philosophy* (Edinburgh: Edinburgh University Press, 1983);

John Dunn, *Locke* (Oxford & New York: Oxford University Press, 1984);

Dunn and Edward Harris, eds., *Locke,* 2 volumes, Great Political Thinkers, no. 9 (Cheltenham, U.K. & Lyme, N.H.: Elgar, 1997);

Gary Fuller, Robert Stecker, and John P. Wright, eds., *John Locke, An Essay Concerning Human Understanding in Focus* (London & New York: Routledge, 2000);

James Gibson, *Locke's Theory of Knowledge and its Historical Relations* (Cambridge: Cambridge University Press, 1917);

Ruth W. Grant, *John Locke's Liberalism* (Chicago & London: University of Chicago Press, 1987);

Richard W. F. Kroll, *The Material Word: Literate Culture in the Restoration and Early Eighteenth Century* (Baltimore: Johns Hopkins University Press, 1991);

Joseph M. Levine, *The Battle of the Books: History and Literature in the Augustan Age* (Ithaca, N.Y.: Cornell University Press, 1991);

J. L. Mackie, *Problems From Locke* (Oxford: Clarendon Press, 1976);

C. B. Martin and D. M. Armstrong, eds. *Locke and Berkeley: A Collection of Critical Essays* (London: Macmillan, 1968; Garden City, N.Y.: Anchor/Doubleday, 1968);

Kirstie Morna McClure, *Judging Rights: Lockean Politics and the Limits of Consent* (Ithaca, N.Y.: Cornell University Press, 1996);

C. R. Morris, *Locke, Berkeley, Hume* (Oxford: Clarendon Press, 1931);

Richard Henry Popkin, *The Third Force in Seventeenth Century Thought* (Leiden & New York: E. J. Brill, 1992);

Stephen Priest, *The British Empiricists: Hobbes to Ayer* (London: Penguin / New York: Viking Penguin, 1990);

G. A. J. Rogers, *Locke's Enlightenment: Aspects of the Origin, Nature and Impact of His Philosophy* (Hildesheim, Germany & New York: Olms, 1998);

Rogers, ed., *Locke's Philosophy: Content and Context* (Oxford: Clarendon Press / New York: Oxford University Press, 1994);

W. M. Spellman, *John Locke and the Problem of Depravity* (Oxford: Clarendon Press, 1988);

I. C. Tipton, ed., *Locke on Human Understanding: Selected Essays* (Oxford & New York: Oxford University Press, 1977);

James Tully, *An Approach to Political Philosophy: Locke in Contexts* (Cambridge & New York: Cambridge University Press, 1993);

Tully, *A Discourse on Property: John Locke and His Adversaries* (Cambridge: Cambridge University Press, 1980);

Karen Iversen Vaughn, *John Locke: Economist and Social Scientist* (Chicago: University of Chicago Press, 1980);

William Walker, *Locke, Literary Criticism, and Philosophy* (Cambridge & New York: Cambridge University Press, 1994);

Nicholas Wolterstorff, *John Locke and the Ethics of Belief* (Cambridge & New York: Cambridge University Press, 1996);

R. S. Woolhouse, *Locke* (Brighton, U.K.: Harvester, 1983; Minneapolis: University of Minnesota Press, 1983);

Woolhouse, *Locke's Philosophy of Science and Knowledge: A Consideration of Some Aspects of An Essay Concerning Human Understanding* (Oxford: Blackwell, 1971; New York: Barnes & Noble, 1971);

John W. Yolton, *A Locke Dictionary* (Oxford & Cambridge, Mass.: Blackwell, 1993);

Yolton, *Locke and French Materialism* (Oxford: Clarendon Press / New York: Oxford University Press, 1991);

Yolton, *Locke, an Introduction* (Oxford: Blackwell, 1985).

Papers:

The major collection of John Locke's manuscripts is the Lovelace Collection in the Bodleian Library, Oxford. Other important Locke manuscript holdings are in the British Library, London; the Pierpont Morgan Library, New York City; and the Huntington Library, San Marino, California.

Damaris Cudworth, Lady Masham

(18 January 1659 – 20 April 1708)

Kate Fletcher
University of Cambridge

BOOKS: *A Discourse Concerning the Love of God,* anonymous (London, 1696);

Occasional Thoughts in Reference to a Vertuous or Christian Life, anonymous (London: A. & J. Churchil, 1705).

As a learned lady in the late seventeenth century, Damaris Cudworth, Lady Masham imbued contemporary philosophical issues with personal significance and made them meaningful in the everyday life of a gentlewoman such as herself. Masham's two books, *A Discourse Concerning the Love of God* (1696) and *Occasional Thoughts in Reference to a Vertuous or Christian Life* (1705), deal with different aspects of practical morality. Each asserts the need for a rational grounding of Christian belief and the need for every individual to understand the basis of the virtuous ideals to which he or she was supposed to aspire, rather than to accept them on authority. Free choice between alternative philosophical ideas, which were instantiated in her own conduct and in her recommendations to others, was paramount for Masham.

Born 18 January 1659, Damaris Cudworth was the daughter of the leading Cambridge Platonist Ralph Cudworth and his wife, Damaris. In 1685 she married Sir Francis Masham, a country squire, and moved to Oates, his estate in Essex, where she lived until her death. Her only son, Francis Cudworth Masham, was born in 1686, but she also took on the nine children of her husband's previous marriage.

A Discourse Concerning the Love of God, published anonymously, is a sharp response to views put forward by John Norris and Mary Astell in their *Letters Concerning the Love of God, Between the Author of the Proposal to the Ladies, and J. Norris; Wherein His Late Discourse, Shewing That It Ought To Be Intire and Exclusive of All Other Loves, Is Further Cleared and Justified,* published in 1695. *Occasional Thoughts in Reference to a Vertuous or Christian Life,* also published anonymously, appealed to women to study intelligently the grounds of their religious belief.

Masham enjoyed an unusually rich intellectual background. She grew up in the Master's Lodge of Christ's College, Cambridge, was educated under the care of her father, and was early acquainted with the philosophical discussions of the Cambridge Platonists. Her subsequent success in combining intellectual pursuits with more recognized "feminine" virtues, however, elicited greater respect from those who came to know her. She was praised for her astute mind by Norris, with whom she was friends during the 1680s, by Dutch Arminians Jean Le Clerc and Philip van Limborch, whose acquaintance she made through her father, and by the German philosopher Gottfried Wilhelm Leibniz, with whom she conducted a philosophical correspondence from 1704 to 1705. Not the least of her eminent acquaintances was philosopher John Locke, with whom Masham conducted a close correspondence from about 1681, when she was twenty-two and he was forty-nine. Despite Locke's exile in Holland in the 1680s, the correspondence continued until 1690. Locke resided permanently at the house of Masham and her husband until his death in 1704.

Her letters to Locke, of which some forty survive, provided Masham with a welcome intellectual release from her unhappy situation—her constraint by the social conventions of the time, which disapproved of women wasting their time on study. She frequently complained of her frustration with domestic life and her isolation from intellectual company: "I am certainlie Plac'd n the Wretchedest neighborhood in the whole World and never had so Violent a Desire in my life as now to good Companie," she stated in a 17 January 1686 letter to Locke. In another letter she wrote to Locke on 14 November 1685, Masham expresses regret for the dulling effect that "Matrimonie and Familie Cares" were having on her: "the little Knowledge I once had, is now exchanged for Absolute Ignorance; I am taken off of All that I once did Know, and understand; . . . Household Affairs are the Opium of the Soul." The plaintiveness of some of Masham's letters was tempered by a general acceptance of her obligations and a refusal to submit totally to them.

Publicly, she complied with the conventions of the time. By these standards marriage was a divinely appointed state of subjection for women and an institution within which women were to exercise the qualities of patience and

Title page of Lady Masham's 1696 work, in which she argues that faith in God must be combined with reason based on earthly experience (British Library)

endurance necessary to prepare one for Heaven, rather than to seek happiness. Excessive learning by men was also denigrated since, as John Norris pointed out in his *Reflections upon the Conduct of Human Life* (1691), it "stands in Competition with Religion and the study of Vertue." He continues: "is here anything more Absurd and Impertinent in this, than in the present supposition, to have a Man who has so great a Concern upon his Hands as the Preparing for Eternity, all busie and taken up with Quadrants, and Telescopes, Furnaces, Syphons, and Air-Pumps?"

Privately, though, Masham subscribed to just such an impertinence, and admitted as much in a letter to Locke of 14 November 1685. She fancied that he would be amused at the "Fantastical Furniture" of her "Closet," things reflecting her intellectual interests alongside those objects related to household affairs. "Cowley and my Surfeit Waters Jumbled together; with Dr More and my Gally Potts of Mithridate and Dioscordium. My Receits and Account Books with Antoninus's his Meditations, and Des Cartes Principles; with my Globes, and my Spining Wheel." When Locke apparently jibed Masham about her domestic life, she threatened "I will set the Affronted Countrey Ladies too upon you, and They Shall Abuse you Ten times more than I can, for all your contempt of Theire Sublime Ideas of Goose Pye, and Bag Puding."

Masham probably suffered at the hands of the "Affronted Countrey Ladies" because of her unconventional pursuits. She spoke knowingly in her second book of the tribulations of one who might dare "to order the Course and Manner of her Life something differently from others of her Sex and condition": Her

> understanding of the Christian Religion would go near to render her suspected of heresy even by those who thought the best of her: Whilst her little Zeal for any Sect or Party would make the Clergy of all sorts give her out for a *Socinian,* or a *Deist:* And should but a very little Philosophy be added to her other Knowledge, even for an Atheist.

These grave warnings illustrate the centrality of religious debates in all walks of late-seventeenth-century life. The imprecision surrounding such appellations as "Deist" or "Atheist" increased, rather than decreased, popular suspicion of any form of unorthodoxy. The patriarchal institutions that Masham challenged may have been less concrete than those institutions involved with the repression of religious dissent—as she admitted, there were no laws or edicts forbidding women to read, although there were laws against religious nonconformism. However, she reminded, "The Law of Fashion, established by Repute and Disrepute, is to most People the powerfullest of all Laws."

Besides having to contend with criticism of her own conduct, Masham was familiar with—and a staunch defender against—accusations of Socinianism and atheism leveled at Locke and her father. In this period of massive social, religious, and political upheaval, allegations and counterallegations of violating Christian doctrine, through either words or conduct, reflected more than differences over tenets of faith. More fundamental political disputes over the basis of allegiance to the Crown and of religious authority were cloaked in philosophical discussion. Masham lent a special resonance to these disputes with respect to the social and intellectual role of women.

This resonance is most strikingly illustrated by the challenge that Masham presented to the patriarchal account of the legitimacy of government through descent from Adam. According to this account, the monarch inherited natural political power, divinely invested in "Adam's Race," and exercised this power over naturally subjected citizens, just as patriarchs naturally exercised unlimited and arbitrary power over their wives, children, slaves, and private property. This view, still popular in the 1680s, was professed not only by men but also by women such as the philosopher Mary Astell, who believed that a wife owed her husband the same obedience that a loyal subject owed his king. The only right a woman could exercise was to choose to whom she should subject herself, or not to marry at all, as was Astell's own choice.

Masham mocked this view. A poem sent to Locke in a letter from 13 March 1686 draws out parallel implications in the domestic and public spheres and epitomizes her witty intertwining of the different senses of philosophical terms. Although the poem was sent after her marriage, it was written around the beginning of 1685, "some months before ever I saw Sir F" (her husband), following a discussion she had with Locke. Making an analogy between the obligations of love or marriage and religion, the poem derides authoritarians—be they husbands, priests, or statesmen—who deny rationality to women, or to those "Whom Churchmen Call the Layetie." Thus women must love, and "the Vulgar" worship, as instructed by their superiors:

Our Duty it needs must Bee,
For What else were Created Wee?
The Text you'l find is very Plaine,
Eve was made only for the Man,
Then How can you your self deceive
And think you're not some Adam's Eve?
Or on the Man Look with a Frowne
Who only comes to Claime his owne?
And Begs but that You would Restore
The Ribb You Rob'd Him of before;
And though for th'Hall of Westminster,
The Man no Justice can have There,
Yet surely Sister it is Plaine
He ought to have his Ribb Againe.

Masham's idea of marriage was similar to Locke's idea of the origin of civil society in the form of a social contract. By this view, rational consent to the authority of government was actually a means of increasing individual liberty: in place of primitive anarchy, or "State of Nature," a system of justice, based on divine natural law, was instituted. As Locke maintained in his *Essay Concerning Humane Understanding. In Four Books* (1690): "where there is no law there is no freedom." Similarly, Masham believed that marriage could provide a structure within which a woman could freely pursue her own interests and strive to be virtuous.

Of her own forthcoming marriage, Masham advised Locke in a letter of 5 June 1685 that: "That Puzling Difficultie about Matrimonie might perhaps be soone Resolv'd; and Your Governess . . . might after a Long and Glorious Reigne Perchance Resigne Her Authoritie, and submit Her self Henceforwards to the more Humble Qualitie, and Condition, of a Subject." Although Masham described her sacri-

fice as a long overdue "Recantation," her marriage could also be viewed as "Stoical" acceptance of her lot, to be followed with a steadfast application to improving the lot of other women. She set about improving the lot of women not by advising women to avoid marriage and separate themselves from their tyrannical male oppressors, as did Astell. Instead she attacked traditional opinions and institutions that, by depriving women of rationality, were injurious to Christian morality, and she boldly claimed for women the independence and new public intellectual territory associated with the responsibility of educating their own children, recommending from personal experience the program described in Locke's *Some Thoughts Concerning Education* (1693).

A Discourse Concerning the Love of God addressed the contention of Astell and Norris that women should study only in order to fix their minds on the hereafter. On the contrary, Masham claimed that faith must be combined with reasoning derived from experience of earthly things—God's "creatures"—that "lead us to their invisible Author. And if we lov'd not the Creatures, it is not conceivable how we should love God." Derisively ascribing to Norris's lack of "inclination to this way of Living" his condemnation of all earthly pleasures as idolatrous, she inquired whether "Mr. N." would regard as sinful even the desire for warmth or food. Moreover, considered Masham, the implication of Norris's and Astell's *Letters Concerning the Love of God*—"that we are obliged to renounce the World and live in the Woods"— "Destroys the Duties and Obligations of Social Life," for which there "is nothing more evident than that Mankind is design'd." She goes on to argue that "one would certainly, by such a renunciation of all commerce with men, be likelier to grow Wild, than improve the great Virtue of Christianity, and Ornament of Humane Nature, Good Will, Charity, and the being Useful to others." Accordingly, Masham attacked those people who neglected to concern themselves with the everyday applications of theology, who considered the duties of social life—including "the Use of Reasoning, and internal Discourse"—"to be low matters, fit only to exercise the young Christian, not yet advanced to the spiritual state."

Masham shared the controversial conception of philosophy as a form of "public-spiritedness" with her father, Ralph Cudworth. That Cudworth approved of his daughter's involvement in the philosophical pursuit of "the good of the system" that he himself advocated is doubtful. Cudworth's highly gendered conception of philosophy is typical of the period. As his major work, *The True Intellectual System of the Universe: The First Part; Wherein, All the Reason and Philosophy of Atheism Is Confuted: And Its Impossibility Demonstrated* (1678), makes clear, the search for knowledge was construed as a most unfeminine activity: "to know and understand, as Anaxagoras of old determined, is . . . to "master" and "conquer" the thing known, and consequently not merely to suf-

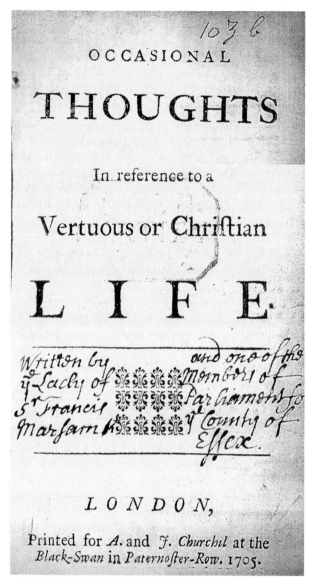

OCCASIONAL

THOUGHTS

In reference to a

Vertuous or Chriſtian

LIFE.

Written by and one of the
y Lady of Members of
S Francis Parliament for
Masham y County of
Eſſex.

LONDON,

Printed for *A.* and *J. Churchil* at the
Black-Swan in *Paternoſter-Row.* 1705.

Title page for Lady Masham's appeal to women to gain an appropriate
religious education (British Library)

Central both politically and philosophically to the worldview of Masham–and of Locke and the Cambridge Platonists–was belief in the individual's natural right to liberty of conscience. Religious conformity must be voluntary, inspired by God's love and driven by humanity's desire for salvation, not enforced. By this account, the rule of Catholicism exercised tyranny over the consciences of its subjects and was to be resisted. On the other hand, with the turbulence and disorder of the Civil War fresh in the popular memory, the need for a degree of consensus on the fundamental elements of Protestant theology was widely felt. Accordingly, the Broad Church toleration accorded to Protestant Dissenters stopped short of authorizing certain more extreme sects, such as the Ranters and Quakers, whose dogmatic assertions of divine "inspiration" were alleged as mere pretense, disguising self-interested attempts to subvert the established order.

Against Astell and Norris, Masham sharply pointed out that neglect of the role of rationality in religion exposed the individual to just such dangers: the "Popish" tyranny of authoritarian religious instruction stifled the "Natural Light" by which divine laws were recognizable, leaving one prey to the "tyranny in the head" of irrational spiritual fanaticism. Masham ascribed this condition, frequently attributed to the physiological inferiority of soft female minds, to ignorant credulity. Girls brought up "betwixt silly Fathers and ignorant Mothers," she argued in *Occasional Thoughts in Reference to a Vertuous or Christian Life,* become "blindly and conceitedly weded to the Principles and Opinions of their Spiritual Guides; who having the direction of their Consciences, rarely fail to have that also of their Affairs and Fortunes." Rather, she insisted:

> if Christianity be a Religion from God, and Women have Souls to be sav'd as well as Men; to know what this Religion consists in, and to understand the grounds on which it is to be receiv'd, can be no more than necessary Knowledge to a Woman, as well as to a Man: Which necessary Knowledge is sufficient to inable any one so far to answer the Opposers or Corrupters of Christianity, as to secure them from the danger of being impos'd upon by such Men's Argumentations.

On the other hand, Masham recognized that joining a religious sect could offer an avenue out of domestic misery. Many of the more radical sects appearing during this period practiced a greater egalitarianism than their orthodox counterparts, which made them a welcome spiritual refuge for women. In January 1685 Masham threatened to Locke that she might turn Quaker, although she was "not yet got into a Tammy Petticoat and Wastcoate, nor a Say Apron," the characteristic Quaker garb; of another group she suggested that if "there be any Happiness to be found in marriage it must Certainly be amongst them . . . who know no Interest Contrary to theire Inclination."

fer from it, or passively like under it." Indeed, privileged though Masham's education was, it is striking that such a great classicist as Ralph Cudworth should have neglected to teach her either Greek or Latin, the latter especially being a necessary accomplishment for any public figure at the time. Masham eventually followed Locke's recommendations of teaching herself enough of the language to suffice for the education of her son Francis. Of study generally, she reported to Locke having been "Diverted from It when I was Young, first by the commands of Others And Afterwards by that Weakness which Hapned in my Sight" in a 7 April 1688 letter. Nor were her studies a result of Locke's prompting; rather she claimed they were motivated by her own "Universal Love for All usefull Knowledge."

The nebulous but grave charge of falsely claiming religious inspiration was one against which Masham also defended the Cambridge Platonist John Smith, in her earliest recorded philosophical discussion with Locke. In his *Select Discourse* (1660) Smith had described a special, suprarational kind of understanding, achieved only by "The true Metaphysical and Contemplative man," which revealed divine truths to him. However, in *Essay on Human Understanding* draft extracts that Locke sent for Masham's perusal in February and April 1682, the mind is represented as a "tabula rasa": nothing could be in it that was not first in the senses. To Locke, Smith's assertion seemed "very little different from my Visionary's"—a false claimant to divine knowledge. Masham protested:

> I know not what you may call Vision nor how much you may attribute to the power of Reason, only as I understand them it seemes to mee that there may be something between these two things, there being (I think) such a Degree of Perfection to be attain'd to in this Life to which the Powers of meere Unassisted Reason will never Conduct a Man.

Probably the last—though not the least—of Masham's major philosophical engagements took place from 1704 to 1705 in her correspondence with Leibniz. Leibniz posited an entirely predetermined universe, a "little system of preestablished harmony," as he described it to her. Where Locke and the Cambridge Platonists portrayed matter as being "brute and stupid," Leibniz saw matter as possessing an essential, self-moving, sentient principle, so that it did not require God's continuing superintendence. In a reply of 8 August 1704, Masham expressed concern that Leibniz's hypothesis (as she defiantly insisted on regarding it) left no role for the operation of free will. Insisting that "freedome to act is necessarie to our being accountable for our actions," Masham set herself up as a defender of "English" liberty against the exaggerated rationalism of Leibniz's "Philosophy of Hanover." More significantly, perhaps, she rejected his theory on the grounds that the existence of innately sentient matter, as proposed by him, was inconceivable to her personally:

> wherever I have no Idea of a thing; or demonstration of the truth of any proposition, the truth of which is inconceivable by me, I . . . conclude, that I ought not to assent to what is asserted of either: since should I once do this I know not where I should stop; what should be called the boundaries of assent. Or why I might not believe alike one thing as another.

Thus, characteristically, Masham demonstrated her independence from her philosophical forebears by predicating the truth or falsity of Leibniz's assertions on her own ability or inability, as a rational individual, to conceive of them.

Masham died at Bath on 20 April 1708 and was buried in Bath Abbey. Sarah Hutton locates Masham's ambivalent philosophical allegiances in "Damaris Cudworth, Lady Masham: Between Platonism and Enlightenment" (1993). John A. Passmore, in *Ralph Cudworth; An Interpretation* (1951), treats Masham as a link in the transmission of supposed Cudworthian "influences" to Locke and his patron, the earl of Shaftesbury, who was also on friendly terms with Masham. Both of these approaches locate ideological similarities; however, they dislocate the philosophical debates from the political issues that drove them. Masham was neither a passive consumer nor just a transmitter of Cudworth's or Locke's ideas.

Letters:

Die Philosophischen Schriften von Gottfried Wilhelm Leibniz, 7 volumes, edited by C. I. Gerhardt (Darmstadt: Olms, 1965), III: 370;

Correspondence of John Locke, 8 volumes, edited by E. S. de Beer (Oxford: Clarendon Press, 1976–1979): II, III, and IV.

References:

Richard Acworth, *The Philosophy of John Norris of Bemerton (1657–1712)* (New York: Olms, 1979);

Rosalie Littell Colie, *Light and Enlightenment: A Study of the Cambridge Platonists and the Dutch Arminians* (Cambridge: Cambridge University Press, 1957);

Anne Conway, *The Principles of the Most Ancient and Modern Philosophy,* edited by Allison P. Coudert and Taylor Corse (New York: Cambridge University Press, 1996);

Maurice Cranston, *John Locke: A Biography* (London: Longmans, Green, 1957);

Sarah Hutton, "Damaris Cudworth, Lady Masham: Between Platonism and Enlightenment," *British Journal for the History of Philosophy,* 1 (1993);

Nicholas Jolley, *Leibniz and Locke: A Study of the New Essays on Human Understanding* (Oxford: Clarendon Press, 1984);

John A. Passmore, *Ralph Cudworth; An Interpretation* (London: Cambridge University Press, 1951);

John Redwood, *Reason, Ridicule and Religion: The Age of Enlightenment in England* (London: Thames & Hudson, 1976);

Ada Wallas, *Before the Bluestockings* (London: Allen & Unwin, 1929).

Papers:

The major collection of Damaris Cudworth, Lady Masham's correspondence, forty letters to John Locke, are part of the Locke papers at the Bodleian Library, Oxford University. There are also two letters written by Cudworth in King's College Modern Archive Centre, Cambridge University.

Henry More

(October 1614 – 1 September 1687)

Sarah Hutton
University of Hertfordshire

See also the More entry in *DLB 126: Seventeenth-Century British Nondramatic Poets, Second Series.*

BOOKS: *Psychodia Platonica: or, A Platonicall song of the soul, consisting of foure severall poems: viz. Psychozoia. Psychathanasia. Antipsychopannuchia. Antimonopsychia. Hereto is added a paraphrasticall interpretation of the answer of Apollo consulted by Amelius, about Plotinus soul departed this life* (Cambridge: Printed by Roger Daniel, 1643);

Democritus Platonissans: or, An Essay upon the Infinity of Worlds out of Platonick Principles. Hereunto is annexed Cupids conflict together with The philosophers devotion: And a particular interpretation appertaining to the three last books of the Song of the soul (Cambridge: Printed by Roger Daniel, 1646);

Philosophical Poems (Cambridge: Printed by Roger Daniel, 1647);

Observations upon Anthroposophia Theomagica, and anima magica abscondita, as Alazonomastix Philalethes (London, 1650);

The Second Lash of Alazonomastix: containing a solid and serious reply to a very uncivill answer to certain observations upon Anthroposophia Theomagica and Anima Magica Abscondita Abscondita, as Alazonomastix Philalethes (London: Printed by James Flesher, 1651);

An Antidote against Atheisme: or, An Appeal to the Natural Faculties of the Minde of Man, whether there be not a God (London: Printed by Roger Daniel, 1653);

Conjectura Cabbalistica: or, A Conjectural Essay of Interpreting the Minde of Moses According to a Threefold Cabbala: viz., Literal, Philosophical, Mystical, or, Divinely Moral (London: Printed by James Flesher for William Morden, 1653; enlarged, 1662);

Enthusiasmus Triumphatus; or, A Discourse on the Nature, Causes, Kinds and Cure, of Enthusiasme, as Philophilus Parresiastes (London: Printed by James Flesher for W. Morden, 1656);

The Immortality of the Soul, so farre forth as it is Demonstrable from the Knowledge of Nature and the Light of Reason

HENRY MORE, *D.D.*
Obijt Sept. 1. 1687 Ætatis 72 Annorum, Mensium 10, Dierum 20.

Engraving by David Loggan

(London: Printed by James Flesher for William Morden, 1659);

An Explanation of the Grand Mystery of Godliness; or, A True and Faithfull Representation of the Everlasting Gospel of our Lord and Saviour Jesus Christ, the onely begotten Son of God and sovereign over men and angels (London:

Printed by James Flesher for William Morden, 1660);

A Collection of Several Philosophical Writings of Dr. Henry More: As Namely, his Antidote against atheism. Appendix to the Said Antidote. Enthusiasmus triumphatus. Letters to Des-Cartes, &c. Immortality of the Soul. Conjectura cabbalistica (London: Printed by James Flesher for William Morden, 1662);

A Modest Enquiry into the Mystery of Iniquity, the First Part, Containing a Careful and Impartial Delineation of the True Idea of Antichristianism in the Real and Genuine Members Thereof . . . Synopsis prophetica: or, The Second Part of the Enquiry into the Mystery of Iniquity: Containing a Compendious Prospect into Those Prophecies of the Holy Scripture, wherein the Reign of Antichrist . . . Is Prefigured . . . The Apology of . . . H. More . . . Wherein Is Contained as Well a more General Account of the Manner and Scope of His Writings, as a Particular Explication of Several Passages in his Grand Mystery of Godliness . . . (London: Printed by James Flesher for William Morden, 1664);

Epistola H. Mori ad V.C. quæ apologiam complectitur pro Cartesia, quæque, introductionis loco esse poterit ad universam philosophiam Cartesianam (London, 1664);

Enchiridion Ethicum: Praecipua Moralis Philosophiae Rudimenta Complectens, Illustrata Utplurimum Veterum Monumentis, & ad Probitatem Vitae Perpetuò Accommodata (London: Printed by James Flesher for William Morden, 1667); translated by Edward Southwell as *An Account of Virtue: or, Dr. Henry More's Abridgment of Morals, put into English* (London: Printed for Benjamin Tooke, 1690);

Divine Dialogues, Containing Sundry Disquisitions and Instructions Concerning the Attributes and Providence of God. The First Three Dialogues, Treating the Attributes of God . . . , as Franciscus Evistor Palaeopolitanus (London: Printed by James Flesher, 1668);

An Exposition of the Seven Epistles to the Seven Churches; Together with a Brief Discourse of Idolatry; with Application to the Church in Rome (London: Printed by James Flesher, 1669);

Enchiridion metaphysicum; sive, De rebus incorporeis succincta & luculenta dissertatio. Pars prima: de exsistentia & natura rerum incorporearum in genere. In qua quamplurima mundi phænomena ad leges Cartesii mechanicas obiter expenduntur illiúsque philosophiæ & aliorum omnino omnium qui mundana phænomena in causas purè mechanicas solvi posse supponunt vanitas falsitasque detegitur (London: Printed by James Flesher for William Morden, 1671);

A Brief Reply to a Late Answer to Dr Henry More his Antidote against Idolatry. Shewing that there is nothing in the said answer that does any ways weaken his proofs of idolatry against the Church of Rome, and therefore all are bound to take heed how they enter into, or continue in the communion of that Church as they tender their own salvation (London: J. Redmayne for Walter Kettilby, 1672);

Remarks upon Two Late Ingenious Discourses; the One, an Essay Touching the Gravitation and Non-gravitation of fluid Bodies; the Other, Touching the Torricellian Experiment: so far forth as they may concern any passages in his Enchiridion Metaphysicum (London, 1676);

Apocalypse Apocalypseos, or, The Revelation of St John the Divine Unveiled: Containing a Brief but Perspicuous and Continued Exposition, from Chapter to Chapter, of the Whole Book of the Apocalypse (London: Printed by John Maycock for J. Martyn & W. Kettilby, 1680);

Tetractys anti-astrologica, or, The four chapters in the Explanation of the Grand Mystery of Godliness, which Contain a Brief but Solid Confutation of Judiciary Astrology, with Annotations upon Each Chapter: wherein the Wondrous Weaknesses of John Butler, B.D. his Answer called A vindication of astrology, &c. Are Laid Open to the View of Every Intelligent Reader (London: Printed by John Maycock for Walter Kettilby, 1681);

A Plain and Continued Exposition of the Several Prophecies or Divine Visions of the Prophet Daniel: Which Have or May Concern the People of God, Whether Jew or Christian: Whereunto Is Annexed a Threefold Appendage Touching Three Main Points, the First Relating to Daniel, the Other Two to the Apocalypse (London: Printed by Miles Flesher for Walter Kettilby, 1681);

An Answer to Several Remarks upon Dr Henry More his Expositions of the Apocalypse and Daniel, as also upon his Apology (London: Printed by Miles Flesher for Walter Kettilby, 1684);

Paralipomena Prophetica: Containing Several Supplements and Defences of Dr Henry More his Expositions of the Prophet Daniel and the Apocalypse, whereby the Impregnable Firmness and Solidity of the Said Expositions Is Further Evidenced to the World. Whereunto Is also Added Phililicrines upon R.B. his Notes on the Revelation of S. John (London: Printed for Walter Kettilby, 1685);

An Illustration of Those Two Abstruse Books in Holy Scripture, The Book of Daniel and the Revelation of S. John, by Continued, Brief, but Clear Notes, from Chapter to Chapter, and from Verse to Verse: with very usefull and apposite arguments prefixt to each chapter (London: Printed by Miles Flesher for Walter Kettilby, 1685);

Discourses on Several Texts of Scripture, edited, with a preface, by John Worthington (London: J. R. for Brabazon Aylmer, 1692);

Letters on several subjects, by the late pious Dr. Henry More. With several other letters. To which is added by the publisher, two letters, one to the Reverend Dr. Sherlock, Dean of St. Paul's; and the other to the Reverend Mr. Bentley. With other discourses. Publish'd by the Reverend E. Elys

(London: Printed by W. Onely for John Evering-ham, 1694);

Two Letters Concerning Self-Love, written to a late learned Author: with another to William Penn, Esq; about Baptism and the Lord's-Supper (London: J. Downing, 1708); republished as *An Essay on Disinterested Love; in a letter to Bishop Stillingfleet* (Glasgow, 1756); republished as *A Letter to William Penn, Esq., Concerning Baptism and the Lord's Supper, and Some Usages of the Quakers* (Philadelphia: Potter, 1810);

The Theological Works of the Most Pious and Learned Henry More, D.D.: According to the Author's Improvements in His Latin Edition (London: Printed by J. Downing, 1708);

The Complete Poems of Henry More (1614–1687): For the First Time Collected and Edited: with Memorial-Introduction, Notes and Illustrations, Glossarial Index, and Portrait, &c, edited by Alexander B. Grosart (Edinburgh: T. & A. Constable, 1878);

Philosophical Poems of Henry More Comprising Psychozoia and Minor Poems, edited by Geoffrey Bullough (Manchester: Manchester University Press, 1931).

Edition: *H. Mori Cantabrigiensis opera omnia,* 3 volumes (London: J. Maycock for J. Martyn & W. Kettilby, 1675–1679)–comprises volume 1, *Opera theologica;* volume 2, *Opera philosophica;* volume 3, *Scriptorum philosophicorum.*

OTHER: Joseph Glanvill, *Sadducismus triumphatus: or, A Full and Plain Evidence Concerning Witches and Apparitions,* edited by More (London: Printed for J. Collins & S. Lownds, 1681);

Glanvill and George Rust, *Two Choice and Useful Treatises: the one Lux Orientalis; or an Enquiry into the Opinions of the Eastern Sages Concerning the Praeexistence of Souls. Being a Key to Unlock the Grand Mysteries of Providence. In Relation to Mans Sin and Misery. The Other, A Discourse of Truth by the late Reverend Dr. Rust, Lord Bishop of Dromore in Ireland. With Annotations on them both,* edited by More (London: Printed for James Collins & Sam. Lowndes, 1682).

Henry More was one of the most important members of the seventeenth-century group of philosopher-theologians known as the Cambridge Platonists. The denomination "Platonist" was coined by nineteenth-century historians on account of the fact that the group drew significantly on the corpus of Platonic philosophy. The label, however, detracts from the fact that they had considerable importance as a third alternative to the outdated Aristotelianism of schools of the time and the uncompromising modernity of Thomas Hobbes. Central to their philosophy was a metaphysics of spirit, which they pro-

posed as a corrective supplement to contemporary natural philosophy. In moral philosophy they emphasized practical ethics founded on absolute and self-existing moral principles coterminous with Christian values. They were, moreover, the first English thinkers to employ consistently the vernacular as the language of philosophy.

Henry More published considerably more than his Cambridge Platonist colleagues, and he had a large readership: according to his publisher, Richard Chiswell, his publications "ruled all the booksellers in London." Moreover, he published on a wide variety of philosophical and religious themes and employed a diversity of genres from poetry to bible commentary, from dialogues to austere academic treatises. His writing style, too, is rich in texture, enlivened by neologisms, some of which have passed into standard usage (for example, *Cartesianism* and *bungle*). He had some reputation as a poet. In his day he was regarded one of the leading philosophers of his time. In divinity his relatively tolerant position was inspirational to the broad church movement, since nicknamed latitudinarianism.

Henry More was the youngest of the seven sons of Alexander More, a gentleman from Lincolnshire established at Grantham, where he served as alderman (in 1594) and mayor (in 1617). Henry's mother was Anne, daughter of William Lacy. More was born in Grantham, where he was baptized on 11 October 1614. He attended Grantham Grammar School until the age of fourteen, when his uncle, Gabriel More, recognizing his precocity, persuaded his parents to send him to Eton College. In 1631 he enrolled at Christ's College, Cambridge, where his tutor was Robert Gell, and whence he graduated with a B.A. in 1636 and an M.A. in 1639.

In 1641 More was elected fellow of Christ's College in place of Gell. Also in 1641 he was ordained, and his uncle, Gabriel More, presented him with the advowson of Ingoldsby near Grantham. Although he lived through the Civil War and its aftermath, More led a life remarkably untroubled by the political upheavals of his time. He survived the earl of Manchester's purge of Cambridge dons in 1644 by taking the Solemn League and Covenant (though he later denied that he had). The only time that his career was put in jeopardy was at the Restoration of Charles II, but he managed to survive attempts to eject him from Cambridge, probably because he had the backing of Edward, Viscount Conway and of the future lord chancellor, Heneage Finch. More remained a fellow of Christ's College for the rest of his life, declining preferment. He resided for the most part in Cambridge, making visits to London, to Grantham, and to the Conways' residence at Ragley Hall, Warwickshire. He also traveled abroad on a few occasions–at least twice to the Netherlands, and also to Paris in 1656, whither he accompanied Anne, Viscountess Conway, when she went there in the hopes of being cured of the debilitating headaches from which she suffered. In the "Epistle Dedicatory" of his *The Immortality of the Soul, so farre forth as it is Demonstrable from the Knowledge of Nature and the Light of Reason* (1659) he recalls with affection this visit to Paris, "when I had the honour and the pleasure of reading *Des-Cartes* his *Passions* with your Lordship in the Garden of *Luxenburg* to pass away the time." More died on 1 September 1687 after a short illness and was buried in Christ's College chapel.

The chief respect in which the upheavals of the time left their mark on him was in confirming his moderate stance, and his tolerant position in respect of religious belief. He reacted early to the strict Calvinism of his upbringing. As quoted by Richard Ward in his *The Life of the Learned and Pious Dr. Henry More* (2000), he recorded his boyhood horror at the Calvinist doctrine of predestination, as well as the "deep Aversion in my Temper to his Opinion, and so firm and unshaken a Perswasion of the Divine Justice and Goodness." This anti-Calvinism sustained the religious moderation that earned him recognition as "father" of the latitudinarians.

More did not marry. Most of his friends were drawn from the male academic environment in which he lived and worked. They included, as one might expect, fellows of Christ's College, such as William Outram, George Rust (Bishop of Dromore), and Henry Hallywell. Many of his friends were like-minded thinkers and figures closely connected with the Cambridge Platonists, notably Ralph Cudworth and John Worthington. The younger generation of More's acquaintance included John Ray, John Sharp (future archbishop of York), Edmund Elys, Joseph Glanvill, John Norris, and his biographer, Ward. Among the friends with whom he formed a close attachment was John Finch, whom he met between 1647 and 1650, while Finch was studying at the Christ's College. Finch spent the rest of his life in the company of another Christ's graduate of More's acquaintance, Thomas Baines, who accompanied him on his travels and his embassy to the Ottoman Empire. Another close friend was Finch's sister Anne (later Lady Conway). Initially, Finch put More in contact with his sister in order that he might give her instruction in philosophy. One result was a friendship and intellectual companionship that lasted until Conway died in 1679. Another result of More's tutoring was that Conway was able to develop her interest in philosophy far beyond the expectations of a woman of her time. She subsequently became a philosopher in her own right, one of the few women to do so in the seventeenth century. Another particularly close friend was John Davies, who is described by Ward as his "passionate friend and lover." More also was acquainted with Jeremy Taylor, of whom Lord Conway was chief patron. Among his younger friends he had a reputation for sanctity—William Outram called him "The Holiest Person upon the Face of the Earth." His religious irenicism, profound

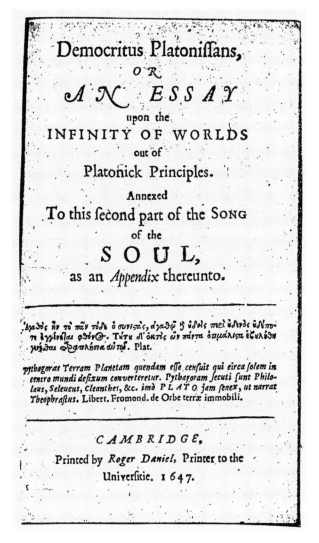

Title page for More's collection, which features a poetic essay influenced by the scientific innovations of Galileo and Nicolaus Copernicus and the philosophy of René Descartes (Houghton Library, Harvard University)

piety, and gentle disposition earned him the sobriquet "the Angel of Christ's." Two examples of his dependability as a friend are his unfailing support for Anne Conway through the tribulations and isolation of illness and the assistance he gave to Worthington, who faced destitution following ejection from Cambridge in 1660 and failure thereafter to secure a permanent living. More bestowed on Worthington his living at Grantham in 1666.

More's career was outwardly uneventful: Ward quotes him as saying "That he had liv'd a sort of Harmless and Childish Life in the World." In the dedication to Lord Conway from *The Immortality of the Soul* More depicts himself as a lover of solitude, recalling "that pleasant retirement I enjoyed at *Ragley* during my abode with you there—the solemness of the Place, those shady Walks, those Hills & Woods, wherein often having lost sight of the rest of the world, and the World of me, I found out in that hidden solitude the choicest Theories in the following Discourse." The picture of contemplative retirement, however, belies the engaged activism that characterizes his intellectual life and the high regard in which he came to be held by his contemporaries; for More was a man of ideas, deeply engaged with new developments in contemporary thought, and a staunch spokesman for moderation in religious affairs. His writings are the best evidence of these qualities. The prefaces to his major works, and especially to his collected writings (*A Collection of Several Philosophical Writings of Dr. Henry More: As Namely, his Antidote against atheism. Appendix to the Said Antidote. Enthusiasmus triumphatus. Letters to Des-Cartes, &c. Immortality of the Soul. Conjectura cabbalistica,* 1662, and *H. Mori Cantabrigiensis opera omnia,* 1675–1679), show his skill in presenting and re-presenting himself to his public.

After taking his degree he read widely among "the *Platonick* writers, *Marsilius Ficinus, Plotinus* himself, *Mercurius Trismegistus;* and the *Mystical Divines,*" according to Ward. Among the last, More admits a special affection for "that little golden book," the fourteenth-century *Theologia germanica* attributed to Johannes de Francfordia. He claimed that reading these authors helped to rescue him from a skeptical crisis. Thereafter he redirected his philosophical energies toward the Platonist metaphysics that underpins his thought. The first fruits of his Platonism were the allegorical poems that he composed between 1639 and 1640. The first of these poems was published in 1643 with the title *Psychodia Platonica: or, A Platonicall song of the soul, consisting of foure severall poems: viz. Psychozoia. Psychathanasia. Antipsychopannuchia. Antimonopsychia. Hereto is added a paraphrasticall interpretation of the answer of Apollo consulted by Amelius, about Plotinus soul departed this life;* it was republished with the further poems in the collection *Philosophical Poems* (1647). Greatly influenced by Edmund Spenser, these poems are philosophical allegories on themes that remain central to his later writings: the existence, preexistence, and immortality of the soul and the operations of spirit in the works of nature. The poems established More's credentials as a Platonist deeply read in the philosophy of Plotinus: for example, the first in the series, "Psychozoia," on the life of the soul, gives a "Platonicall description of Universall life." The collection also shows his interest in contemporary thought, notably the new science of Galileo and Nicolaus Copernicus and the new philosophy of René Descartes. This interest is most explicitly acknowledged in the title poem in his *Democritus Platonissans: or, An Essay upon the Infinity of Worlds out of Platonick Principles. Hereunto is annexed Cupids conflict together with The philosophers devotion: And a particular interpretation appertaining to the three last books of the Song of the soul* (1646), in which More gives an imagi-

native account of the infinity of the universe. More was, in fact, one of the first Englishmen to take up Cartesianism. His interest was such that, encouraged by Samuel Hartlib, he entered into correspondence with Descartes in 1648. He recommended that Cartesianism be taught as part of the curriculum of English universities. Subsequently, More revised his initial enthusiasm for Cartesianism on theological grounds, but this reappraisal appears to have occurred gradually. His *Epistola H. Mori ad V.C. quæ apologiam complectitur pro Cartesia, quæque, introductionis loco esse poterit ad universam philosophiam Cartesianam* (1664) is a more cautious appraisal of Descartes. His reservations did not give way to refutation until the publication of his *Enchiridion metaphysicum; sive, De rebus incorporeis succincta & luculenta dissertatio. Pars prima: de exsistentia & natura rerum incorporearum in genere. In qua quamplurima mundi phænomena ad leges Cartesii mechanicas obiter expenduntur illiúsque philosophiæ & aliorum omnino omnium qui mundana phænomena in causas purè mechanicas solvi posse supponunt vanitas falsitasque detegitur* in 1671.

In 1650 More became embroiled in controversy with the alchemist Thomas Vaughan. He appears to have been motivated to attack Vaughan (who wrote under the name Eugenius Philalethes) by a desire to distance his own philosophical Platonism from the mystical Paracelsianism of Vaughan. More adopted the nom de plume Alazonomastix Philalethes for the controversy, which rapidly degenerated into mutual lampooning, in which Vaughan proved himself a match for his opponent. More was probably happy to retire from the fray. He did not think his contribution was worthy of inclusion in his collected writings. He offered his last words on the subject in *Mastix his Letter to a Private Friend Concerning his Reply* (1656), written for John Finch, a fact that suggests that Finch may have played a part in More's decision to attack Vaughan.

In 1653 More published the first of his serious apologetic works, *An Antidote against Atheisme: or, An Appeal to the Natural Faculties of the Minde of Man, whether there be not a God,* dedicated to Lady Conway. In it More sets out to demonstrate the existence of God by using arguments that he believed any rational person had to accept. These arguments are based on deduction from self-evident axioms and on conclusions drawn from natural phenomena. More's Platonism is evident in the work that followed: his *Conjectura Cabbalistica: or, A Conjectural Essay of Interpreting the Minde of Moses According to a Threefold Cabbala: viz., Literal, Philosophical, Mystical, or, Divinely Moral,* which was written at the behest of Lady Conway, was dedicated to Ralph Cudworth and published in 1653. *Conjectura Cabbalistica* expounds philosophical and moral teachings that More claims to be hidden in the book of Genesis. More's professed aim is to demonstrate the compatibility of philosophy and religion, showing that the Bible was the fountainhead of philosophy as well as religion. The core elements of this *pia philosophia* bear striking resemblance to More's own position: an atomistic natural philosophy integrated with a Platonic metaphysics. More continued to develop the philosophical commentary to this work in subsequent editions, adding a lengthy "Defence of the Philosophick Cabbala," which was followed in 1662 by "Appendix to the Defence of the Philosophick Cabbala."

More's next publication after *Conjectura Cabbalistica* was his *Enthusiasmus Triumphatus; or, A Discourse on the Nature, Causes, Kinds and Cure, of Enthusiasme* (1656), which deals with the opposite phenomenon to atheism, namely theism so overzealous that it results in bogus claims to divine inspiration. For this "misconceit of being inspired" More employs the contemporary term "enthusiasm." In a survey of varieties of prophetic experience, he analyzes the phenomenon, explaining it as a largely physiological disorder. The book reflects the confusion generated by the proliferation of sects during the Interregnum and the difficulties their rival claims posed for sincere believers. More was, on the whole, dismissive of the new sects and their leaders. An exception was the German mystic and so-called Teutonic philosopher Jacob Boehme, in whom he had showed an interest in the 1640s and whose writings he subjected to separate analysis for the benefit of Lady Conway and her companion Elizabeth Foxcroft. More's "Philosophia teutonica censura" (published in *H. Mori Cantabrigiensis opera omnia* in 1679) concludes that Boehme was a sincerely pious man but mistaken in his views.

More's most important philosophical work was his *The Immortality of the Soul*, which resumes the apologetic themes of *An Antidote against Atheisme* with a fuller exposition of More's philosophy of spirit. In order to demonstrate the immortality of the soul More first sets out to demonstrate the existence of incorporeal substance, aiming his argument at materialists who deny that incorporeal substance is conceivable. The chief opponent he has in mind is Hobbes. The work exemplifies More's apologetic method, "to beat the atheist at his own weapon." In it he attempts to develop a mode of rational demonstration that, he believed, any rational materialist would be bound to accept: deduction from self-evident axioms, sense perception, and natural phenomena. The self-evidence of the axioms he sets out is open to question. More convincing is his establishing common ground with his putative opponent by conceding skepticism about the human capacity to truly know material substance. He then proceeds to define spirit in terms obverse to those in which a materialist defines material substance. Where matter is defined as extended, divisible, but impenetrable, More defines spirit as extended, indivisible, and penetrable. Where matter is essentially inert, spirit is essentially active. He denies that thought or motion can be explained in terms of the properties of matter. In order to explain the operations of the physical world he puts forward his

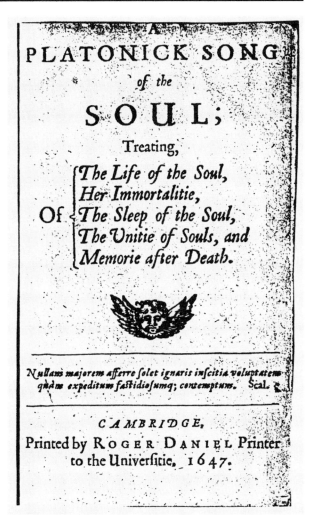

Internal title page for the first part of More's Philosophicall Poems. A Platonick Song of the Soul *was originally published in 1643 as* Psychodia Platonica: or, A Platonicall song of the soul *and was More's first book (Houghton Library, Harvard University).*

hypothesis of the "spirit of nature." This hypothesis, also known as the "hylarchic principle," is one on which he places increasing emphasis in later writings.

More's most important statement of his theological position is his *An Explanation of the Grand Mystery of Godliness; or, A True and Faithfull Representation of the Everlasting Gospel of our Lord and Saviour Jesus Christ, the onely begotten Son of God and sovereign over men and angels*, which was published in 1660. Written in the period immediately preceding the return of the monarchy, this work anticipates the restoration of the Church of England and may be interpreted as a bid to influence any future ecclesiastical settlement as well as to justify the position of the moderates who had found an accommodation with the previous regime. The book clearly exhibits More's theological latitudinarianism and his understanding of the relationship between reason and faith. In it he proposes a minimum set of essential doctrines as a conciliatory basis for ecclesiastical comprehension. More himself welcomed the restored church. Nevertheless, he was attacked by doctrinaire Anglican traditionalists, chief among whom were Joseph Beaumont and Herbert Thorndike. The heterodox character of some of his religious beliefs (such as his revival of the early Christian father Origen's doctrine of the preexistence of the soul) added grist to his opponents' mill. In 1664 he defended himself in his *The Apology of Henry More*—published in *A Modest Enquiry into the Mystery of Iniquity, the First Part, Containing a Careful and Impartial Delineation of the True Idea of Antichristianism in the Real and Genuine Members Thereof*—which constitutes a careful statement of his understanding of the role and importance of reason in divinity. He never succeeded, however, in placing himself above suspicion in the eyes of High Church Anglicans. His Platonism and Origenism continued to be regarded as heterodox, notably by Samuel Parker, future bishop of Oxford, who attacks both in his *Free and Impartial Censure of the Platonick Philosophy* and his *Account of the Divine Dominion and Goodness,* both published in 1666.

After the Restoration, More consolidated his reputation as a philosopher by publishing his writings as *A Collection of Several Philosophical Writings* in 1662. This edition adds appendices and *scholia* in which he develops and defends his ideas. He followed the collection with two works aimed at a more popular audience: his manual of ethics, *Enchiridion Ethicum: Praecipua Moralis Philosophiae Rudimenta Complectens, Illustrata Utplurimum Veterum Monumentis, & ad Probitatem Vitae Perpetuò Accommodata* (1667), and a set of dialogues that summarize his philosophico-theological position, *Divine Dialogues, Containing Sundry Disquisitions and Instructions Concerning the Attributes and Providence of God. The First Three Dialogues, Treating the Attributes of God . . .* (1668), which appeared under the pseudonym Franciscus Evistor Palaeopolitanus. It has been suggested that interlocutors of these five dialogues were More's own friends—Baines as "a young witty, and well moralized materialist," Hylobares; Finch as "a zealous but airy-minded Platonist and Cartesian," Cuphophron; Lord Conway, "the pious and loyal politican" Philopolis; Worthington as Evistor, a "man of criticism, philologie and history"; Cudworth as Philotheus; and More himself as the profound Bathynous. Both the *Enchiridion ethicum* and *Divine Dialogues* proved to be popular. They were followed in 1671 by a more systematic work of academic philosophy written in Latin, his *Enchiridion metaphysicum*. In many ways the *Enchiridion metaphysicum* is a systematic restatement of the ideas and doctrines set out in earlier works. In it More propounds his theory that the operative causal agent in the natural world is an incorporeal spirit that he calls the "Spirit of Nature" or "Principium Hylarchicum" and elaborates on the idea of infinite space adumbrated in earlier writings. He also pre-

sents a sustained critique of Cartesian natural philosophy, radically revising his earlier enthusiasm for Descartes. Much of the treatise deals with phenomena, such as the tides and the sympathetic vibration of springs, that cannot be accounted for by Descartes's natural philosophy, which sought to explain the movement of all bodies by motion transferred by impact, without an immaterial agency of any kind. By this time More had dubbed Descartes a "nullibist," literally a "nowhere-ist," on account of the fact that although he claims that souls exist he is unable to explain their whereabouts. The *Enchiridion metaphysicum* was, however, the occasion of controversy: Robert Boyle objected to More's attempt to appropriate his own experiments to support his concept of the "Spirit of Nature," an explanatory hypothesis to which Boyle did not subscribe. Boyle took the unusual step of expressing his censure publicly in *Tracts . . . containing New Experiments touching the Relation betwixt Flame and Fire* (1672). The work was also attacked by Sir Matthew Hale in *Difficiles nugae* (1675), which includes a critique of the Spirit of Nature hypothesis.

Between 1670 to 1679 More was occupied with the translation of his works into Latin. His three-volume *H. Mori Cantabrigiensis opera omnia* was financed by a legacy from a young admirer, John Cockshute, and was published in 1675–1679. This collection adds lengthy *scholia* that expand points and answer criticisms of works already published. It also includes a few items not published elsewhere, among them two critiques of the philosophy of Benedict de Spinoza: his "Demonstratio duarum propositionum," which attacks Spinoza's *Ethica* (1676), and "Ad V.C. epistola altera," aimed at Spinoza's *Tractatus theologico-politicus* (1670). More regarded Spinoza as a materialist and atheist. It may have been the example of Spinoza that persuaded More to finally reject Cartesianism, since he regarded Spinoza's philosophy as a compound of the worst errors of Hobbes and Descartes.

More's *Opera omnia* also shows that his intellectual endeavors were not confined to philosophy: the first volume, *Opera theologica* (1675), is devoted to his studies of biblical prophecy. From the 1660s onward, taking over the mantle of his learned forebear at Christ's, Joseph Mede, he had devoted increasing attention to the interpretation of prophecy. His *Synopsis Propheticon* (1664) continues themes opened in *An Explanation of the Grand Mystery of Godliness,* and he continued to publish on such themes for the rest of his life, in *An Exposition of the Seven Epistles to the Seven Churches; Together with a Brief Discourse of Idolatry; with Application to the Church in Rome* (1669); *Apocalypse Apocalypseos, or, The Revelation of St John the Divine Unveiled: Containing a Brief but Perspicuous and Continued Exposition, from Chapter to Chapter, of the Whole Book of the Apocalypse* (1680); *A Plain and Continued Exposition of the Several Prophecies or Divine Visions of the Prophet Daniel: Which*

1653 letter from More to Anne Conway, his friend and intellectual ally (British Library)

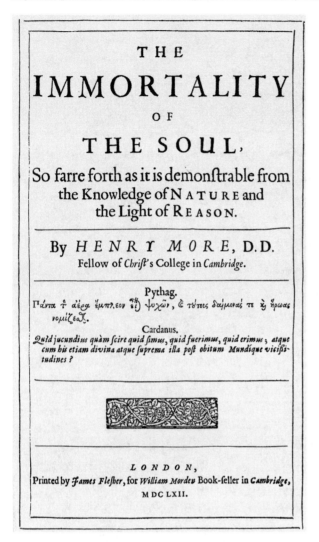

THE

IMMORTALITY

OF

THE SOUL,

So farre forth as it is demonſtrable from
the Knowledge of NATURE and
the Light of REASON.

By *HENRY MORE*, D.D.
Fellow of *Chriſt's* College in *Cambridge.*

Pythag.
Γάντα τ᾽ ἀέρα ἔμπλεον ͖} ψυχῶν, ὃ τύτοις δαίμονάς τε χ ἥρωας
νομίζεαχ.

Cardanus.
*Quid jucundius quàm ſcire quid ſimus, quid fuerimus, quid erimus, atque
cum his etiam divina atque ſuprema illa poſt obitum Mundique viciſſi-
tudines ?*

LONDON,
Printed by *James Fleſher,* for *William Morden* Book-ſeller in *Cambridge,*
M DC LXII.

Special title page in A Collection of Several Philosophical Writings
of Dr. Henry More *(1662) for More's most important philosophical
work, a defense of the existence of an incorporeal soul against the
materialism of Thomas Hobbes that was originally published
in 1659 (Beinecke Library, Yale University)*

*Have or May Concern the People of God, Whether Jew or Chris-
tian: Whereunto Is Annexed a Threefold Appendage Touching
Three Main Points, the First Relating to Daniel, the Other Two to
the Apocalypse* (1681); and *Paralipomena Prophetica: Containing
Several Supplements and Defences of Dr Henry More his Expositions
of the Prophet Daniel and the Apocalypse, whereby the Impregnable
Firmness and Solidity of the Said Expositions Is Further Evidenced to
the World. Whereunto Is also Added Phililicrines upon R.B. his Notes
on the Revelation of S. John* (1685). These works bespeak a
genuine belief in millenarianism and also a desire to defend
the orthodoxy of millenarianism within the Protestant inheritance of Anglican theology. More appears to have wished
to distance himself and other Anglican millenarians from
the extremism of political radicals, whom he represents as
subversive fanatics. His studies of biblical prophecy received

stimulus and encouragement from Anne Conway, and it
was an interest he shared with his younger contemporary
from Grantham, Isaac Newton.

Another line of inquiry that occupied More in his
later years was his exploration of esoteric thought, in particular the Cabala. His interest in cabalism was, like his
interest in prophecy, shared by Conway, and is already
evident in his *Conjectura cabbalistica.* At that time he had little direct acquaintance with cabalistic writings, and his
view of the Cabala was largely conceptual, as an esoteric
repository of ancient wisdom. His interest received fresh
impetus in the 1670s from his encounter with cabalistic
writings mediated to him by Francis Mercury van Helmont, friend of the German cabalistic scholar Christian
Knorr von Rosenroth, who at that time was engaged in
preparing his *Kabbala denudata,* a collection of cabalistic
writings translated into Latin, of which the first volume
was published in 1677.

At around the same time that More began corresponding with Knorr, he entered into dialogue with the
leading Quakers (including Robert Barclay, George
Keith, and William Penn). He did so at the behest of
Conway, who was becoming increasingly interested in
Quakerism. More had rejected the Quakers as "enthusiasts" in his *Enthusiasmus triumphatus.* First-hand acquaintance softened his attitude toward them, especially
Keith, whom he regarded as "absolutely the best
Quaker of them all." He never warmed to George Fox,
however, of whom he is reported as saying that "in conversing with him, he felt himself, as it were, turn'd to
brass." In the late 1670s he argued strenuously against
their beliefs as unorthodox.

In 1681 More edited Joseph Glanvill's *Sadducismus
triumphatus: or, A Full and Plain Evidence Concerning Witches
and Apparitions,* a compilation of sightings of ghosts and
instances of witchcraft. In Glanvill's compilation More
found a comprehensive version of the kind of evidence
that he had himself adduced in both *An Antidote against
Atheisme* and *The Immortality of the Soul* to demonstrate the
reality of supernatural phenomena. To underline the
connection with this theistic agenda More added to
Glanvill's book chapters 27 and 28 from his *Enchiridion
metaphysicum* with the title "The easie, True and Genuine
Notion of a Spirit." His inclusion in the same book of a
reply to a letter from the nonconformist leader Richard
Baxter resulted in a controversy with Baxter about the
immortality of the soul and interpretations of the Apocalypse. Baxter responded to More's "Answer to a Letter
of a Learned Psychopyrist" with his own, "Of the
Nature of Spirits," which he printed in his *Of the Immortality of Man's Soul* (1682).

From a modern perspective More's studies of
prophecy and the Cabala and his belief in witchcraft
appear incompatible with his philosophical interests and

status as a fellow of the Royal Society (he was elected in 1664). Although his concept of infinite space makes him a precursor of Newton, historians have found it hard to reconcile this position with, for example, his interest in esoteric learning. More is therefore a difficult figure to classify. He was not untypical of his time, however, in holding such interests to be both compatible and rational. What is unusual about More's investigations of witchcraft is his attempt to apply the principles of "experimentalism" to the paranormal, by collecting and collating evidence according to the principles of observational science.

The Latin translation of his works made More's philosophy available to a non-Anglophone audience overseas. He thus came to the notice of Leibniz and of Pierre Daniel Huet, for example. His reputation at home continued into the next century. His philosophical legacy is evident, in different ways, in the work of Conway, Norris, and Ray. His theological legacy is to be traced in the latitudianrian movement. Among his later admirers, John Wesley included some of his sermons in his *Christian Library*.

Letters:

Conway Letters: The Correspondence of Anne, Viscountess Conway, Henry More, and Their Friends, 1642–1684, Collected from Manuscript Sources, edited by Marjorie Hope Nicolson (New Haven: Yale University Press, 1930; revised, with an introduction and new material by Sarah Hutton, Oxford: Clarendon Press, 1992);

G. Lewis, *Descartes. Correspondence avec Morus et Arnauld* (Paris, 1953).

Bibliography:

R. Crocker, "A Bibliography of Henry More," in *Henry More, 1614–1687. Tercentenary Studies,* edited by Sarah Hutton (Dordrecht: Kluwer, 1990).

Biographies:

Alexander B. Grosart, "Memorial Introduction," in *The Complete Poems of Henry More* (Blackburn, 1876);

Robert Crocker, "Henry More, a Biographical Essay," in *Henry More, 1614–1687. Tercentenary Studies,* edited by Sarah Hutton (Dordrecht: Kluwer, 1990);

Richard Ward, *The Life of the Learned and Pious Dr. Henry More,* edited by Hutton, Crocker, and R. Hall (Dordrecht: Kluwer, 2000).

References:

Jan van den Berg, *Menassah ben Israel, Henry More and Johannes Hoornbeck on the Pre-existence of the Soul* (Leiden: E. J. Brill, 1989);

Brian Copenhaver, "Jewish Theologies of Space in the Scientific Revolution: Henry More, Joseph Raphson, Isaac Newton and their Predecessors," *Annals of Science,* 37 (1980): 489–548;

Allison Coudert, "A Cambridge Platonist's Kabbalist *Nightmare,*" *Journal of the History of Ideas,* 36 (1975): 633–652;

Alan Gabbey, "Philosophia cartesiana triumphata: Henry More, 1646–1671," in *Problems of Cartesianism,* edited by Thomas M. Lennon, John M. Nicholas, and John W. Davis (Kingston, Ont.: McGill-Queen's University Press, 1982);

R. A. Greene, "Henry More and Robert Boyle on the Spirit of Nature," *Journal of the History of Ideas,* 23 (1962): 451–474;

Rupert Hall, *Henry More–Magic, Religion, and Experiment* (Oxford & Cambridge, Mass.: Blackwell, 1990);

Sarah Hutton, "Henry More and the Book of Revelation," *Studies in Church History,* 10 (1995);

Hutton, "More, Newton and the Language of Biblical Prophecy," in *The Books of Nature and Scripture: Recent Essays on Natural Philosophy, Theology, and Biblical Criticism in the Netherlands of Spinoza's Time and the British Isles of Newton's Time,* edited by James E. Force and Richard H. Popkin (Dordrecht & Boston: Kluwer, 1994), pp. 39–54;

Hutton, ed., *Henry More, 1614–1687. Tercentenary Studies* (Dordrecht & Boston: Kluwer, 1990);

Alexandre Koyré, *From the Closed World to the Infinite Universe* (Baltimore: Johns Hopkins University Press, 1957);

Samuel Mintz, *The Hunting of Leviathan: Seventeenth-Century Reactions to the Materialism and Moral Philosophy of Thomas Hobbes* (Cambridge: Cambridge University Press, 1962);

Marjorie Nicolson, "Christ's College and the Latitude-Men," *Modern Philology,* 27 (1929): 35–53;

J. E. Power, "Henry More and Isaac Newton on Absolute Space," *Journal of the History of Ideas,* 31 (1970): 289–296;

Charles Webster, "Henry More and Descartes, Some New Sources," *British Journal for the History of Science,* 4 (1969): 359–377.

Papers:

No original manuscripts of Henry More's writings survive, although there are several holdings of More's correspondence. The most important collection is in the British Library Additional Manuscripts, most of which have been published in *Conway Letters.* Other letters are held at Christ's College, Cambridge; Sheffield University Library (Hartlib Papers); the Bodleian Library, Oxford; Amsterdam University Library; the library of Friends House, London; the Huntington Library; Nottingham University Library; and Dr. Williams's Library, London.

Sir Isaac Newton

(25 December 1642 – 20 March 1727)

Susan P. Reilly
University of New Hampshire

BOOKS: *Philosophiæ Naturalis Principia Mathematica* (London: Printed by Joseph Streater for the Royal Society, 1687; revised edition, edited by Roger Cotes, Cambridge: C. Crownfield, 1713; revised again, edited by Henry Pemberton, London: Printed by William Bowyer for Will. & Joh. Innys, 1726); translated by Andrew Motte as *The Mathematical Principles of Natural Philosophy. To which are added, The Laws of the Moon's Motion, according to Gravity. By John Machin*, 2 volumes (London: Printed for Benjamin Motte, 1729);

Opticks: or, A Treatise of the Reflexions, Refractions, Inflexions and Colours of Light. Also Two Treatises of the Species and Magnitude of Curvilinear Figures (London: Printed for Samuel Smith & Benjamin Walford, 1704; enlarged edition, London: Printed by W. Bowyer for W. Innys, 1717; enlarged again, London: Printed for W. & J. Innys, 1718; revised, 1721; revised again, 1730);

Arithmetica Universalis: sive De Compositione et Resolutione Arithmetica Liber. Cui accessit Halleiana Aequationum Radices Arithmetice inveniendi methodus. In Usum juventutis Academiae, by Newton and Edmund Halley, edited by William Whiston (Cambridge: Printed by the University Press for Benjamin Tooke, 1707); translated by Joseph Raphson as *Universal Arithmetick: or, a Treatise of Arithmetical Composition and Resolution, to which is added, Dr. Halley's method of finding the roots of the Æquations arithmetically*, edited by Samuel Cunn (London: Printed for J. Senex, W. Taylor, T. Warner & J. Osborn, 1720); revised edition of the original Latin version, with chapter by Halley omitted (London: Printed for Benjamin & Samuel Tooke, 1722);

Analysis Per Quantitatum Series, Fluxiones, ac Differentias: Cum Enumeratione Linearum Tertii Ordinis, edited by William Jones (London: Printed by Pearson, 1711);

Abrégé de la chronologie de M. le chevalier Isaac Newton, fait par lui-même, & traduit sur le manuscrit Anglois, translated by Nicolas Fréret (Paris: Guillaume Cavelier fils, 1725); translated anonymously as *Sir Isaac*

Isaac Newton; portrait by Sir Godfrey Kneller, 1689 (courtesy of Lord Portsmouth and the Trustees of the Portsmouth Estates)

Newton's Chronology, Abridged by Himself. To which are Added, Some Observations on the Chronology of Sir Isaac Newton. Done from the French, by a Gentleman (London: Printed for J. Peele, 1728); original English version revised as *The Chronology of Ancient Kingdoms Amended. To which is Prefix'd, A Short Chronicle from the Memory of Things in Europe, to the Conquest of Persia by Alexander the Great* (London: Printed for J. Tonson, J. Osborn & T. Longman, 1728);

Optical Lectures Read in the Publick Schools of the University of Cambridge, Anno Domini 1669. By the Late Sir Isaac Newton, Then Lucasian Professor of the Mathematicks. Never Before Printed. Translated into English out of the Original Latin (London: Printed for Francis Fayram, 1728);

Observations upon the Prophecies of Daniel, and the Apocalypse of St. John (London: Printed by J. Darby & T. Browne and sold by J. Roberts, J. Tonson, W. Innys & R. Manby, J. Osborn & T. Longman, J. Noon, T. Hatchett, S. Harding, J. Stagg, J. Parker & J. Brindley, 1733);

The Method of Fluxions and Infinite Series; with its Application to the Geometry of Curve-Lines. By the Inventor Sir Isaac Newton, Kᵗ Late President of the Royal Society. Translated from the Author's Latin original not yet made publick. To which is subjoin'd, A Perpetual Comment upon the whole Work, consisting of Annotations, Illustrations, and Supplements, In order to make this Treatise A compleat Institution for the use of Learners, edited and translated by John Colson (London: Printed by Henry Woodfall, sold by John Nourse, 1736);

A True Copy of a Paper Found, in the Hand Writing of Sir Isaac Newton, among the Papers of the Late Dr Halley, Containing a Description of an Instrument for Observing the Moon's Distance from the Fixt Stars at Sea (London: Printed for T. Woodward & C. Davis, 1742);

Opuscula Mathematica Philosophica et Philogica. Collegit partimque Latin vertit ac recensuit Joh. Castillioneus . . . Accessit commentariolus de Vita Auctoris, 3 volumes (Lausanne & Geneva: Printed for Marc-Michael Bousqeut, 1744);

Two Treatises of the Quadrature of Curves and Analysis by Equations of an Infinite Number of Terms Explained; containing the treatises themselves, translated, with commentary, by John Stewart (London: James Bettenham, 1745);

Two Letters of Sir Isaac Newton to Mr. Le Clerc, Late Divinity Professor of the Remonstrants of Holland. The Former Containing a Disertation upon the Reading of the Greek Text, I John, v. 7. The Latter upon That of I Timothy, iii. 16 (London: Printed for J. Payne, 1754);

Isaaci Newtoni opera quae exstant omnia, 5 volumes, edited by Samuel Horsley (London: Printed by John Nichols, 1779–1785);

Sir Isaac Newton's Enumeration of Lines of the Third Order, Generation of Curves by Shadows, Organic Description of Curves, and Construction of Equations by Curves, translated, with notes, by C. R. M. Talbot (London: Bohn, 1860);

Unpublished Scientific Papers of Isaac Newton: A Selection from the Portsmouth Collection in the University Library, Cambridge, edited and translated by A. R. Hall and M. B. Hall (Cambridge: Cambridge University Press, 1962);

Isaac Newton's Papers and Letters on Natural Philosophy and Related Documents, edited by Hall, Bernard Cohen, and Robert E. Scholfield (Cambridge, Mass.: Harvard University Press, 1978);

Certain Philosophical Questions: Newton's Trinity Notebook, Cambridge, edited by J. E. MacGuire and Martin Tamny (Cambridge: Cambridge University Press, 1983).

Editions: *Sir Isaac Newton's Principia reprinted for Sir William Thomson, LL.D., late Fellow of St. Peters College, Cambridge, and Hugh Blackburn, M.A., late Fellow of Trinity College, Cambridge; Professors of Natural Philosophy and Mathematics in the University of Glasgow* (Glasgow: James Maclehose, 1871);

Sir Isaac Newton's Daniel and the Apocalypse: With an Introductory Study of the Nature and Cause of Unbelief, of Miracles and Prophecy, edited by Sir William Whitla (London: Murray, 1922);

Sir Isaac Newton's Mathematical Principles of Philosophy and His System of the World, Translated into English by Andrew Motte in 1729: the Translations Revised, and Supplied with an Historical and Explanatory Appendix, edited by Russell Tracy Crawford and Florian Cajori (Berkeley: University of California Press, 1934);

Opticks; or, a Treatise of the Reflections, Refractions, Reflections, & Colours of Light (New York: Dover, 1952);

Newton's Philosophy of Nature, edited, with notes, by H. S. Thayer (New York: Hafner, 1953);

Mathematical Works, 2 volumes, edited by Derek T. Whiteside (New York: Johnson, 1964, 1967);

Philosophiæ Naturalis Principia Mathematica: The Third Edition (1726), with Variant Readings, 2 volumes, edited by I. Bernard Cohen and Alexandre Koyré (Cambridge, Mass.: Harvard University Press, 1972);

The Optical Papers of Isaac Newton, edited by Alan E. Shapiro (Cambridge & New York: Cambridge University Press, 1984).

OTHER: "De Natura Acidorum," "Enumeratio Linearum Tertii Ordinis," and "Tractatus de Quadratura Curvarum," in *Lexicon Technicum; or, An Universal Dictionary of Arts and Sciences: Explaining not only the terms of arts, but the arts themselves,* edited by John Harris, volume 2 (London: Dan. Brown, Tim Goodwin, and others, 1710);

"Three Reports by Sir Isaac Newton, as Master of the Mint, dated 3 March 1711–12; 23 June 1712; 21 Set 1717," in *A Short Essay on Coin,* by Bryan Robinson (Dublin, 1737);

"Dissertation upon the Sacred Cubit of the Jews and the Cubits of the several nations; in which, from the dimensions of the greatest Egyptian Pyramid, as taken by Mr. Greaves, the antient Cubit of Memphis is determined," translated by John Greaves, in *Miscellaneous Works of Mr. John Greaves, Professor of Astronomy in the University of Oxford,* volume 2, edited by Thomas Birch (London: Printed by J.

Hughs for J. Brindley & C. Corbett, 1737), pp. 405–433;

"Representations of Sir Isaac Newton on the Subject of Money. 1712–17," in *A Select Collection of Scarce and Valuable Tracts on Money, from the Originals of Vaughan, Cotton, Petty, Lowndes, Newton, Prior, Harris, and Others,* edited by John Ramsey McCulloch (London: Printed for the Political Economy Club, 1856), pp. 267–279;

"Monetary Reports (1701–2) signed by Sir Isaac Newton," in *The Silver Pound and England's Monetary Policy since the Restoration: Together with the History of the Guinea,* by S. Dana Horton (London: Macmillan, 1887), pp. 261–271.

SELECTED PERIODICAL PUBLICATIONS–
UNCOLLECTED: "Remarks upon the Observations made upon a Chronological Index of Sir Isaac Newton, translated into French by the Observator, and publish'd at Paris," anonymous, *Philosophical Transactions of the Royal Society,* 33 (1725): 315–321;

"A Letter from Sir Isaac Newton to a person of distinction who had desired his Opinion of the learned Bishop Lloyd's Hypothesis concerning the Form of the Most Ancient Year; from a Manuscript," *Gentleman's Magazine,* 35 (1755): 3–5.

Sir Isaac Newton, mathematician and natural philosopher, has been called the greatest English scientist and the father of modern empirical science. He invented the method of fluxions, which forms the basis of modern calculus; discovered the composition of light; formulated the law of universal gravitation, which he presented to the world in his major work, *Philosophiæ Naturalis Principia Mathematica* (better known as the *Principia,* 1687); formalized Galilean mechanics; and made notable contributions to the theory of light and the science of thermometry. Like Albert Einstein, he revealed the microcosm and the macrocosm together, reducing a welter of phenomena to a single formula: Newton's equation for the law of gravity, $F=Gm_1m_2/r^2$, is considered the historical equivalent of Einstein's equation for the equivalence of energy and mass, $E=mc^2$.

Newton's mechanistic worldview replaced the long-held cosmology of Aristotle, and his influence on post-Enlightenment thinking across several disciplines is incalculable. His work profoundly influenced seventeenth- and eighteenth-century philosophers. Much of the philosophy of John Locke, the first of the great British Empiricists, can be seen as the working out of the philosophical implications of Newtonian mechanics; the publication of Locke's *An Essay concerning Humane*

Newton's birthplace; sketch by Newton's biographer William Stukeley, 1721 (Royal Society of London)

Understanding (1689) followed closely on that of the *Principia,* which brought about the previously unthought-of alliance between geometrical reasoning and experimental method through which significant scientific progress could be made. Astronomical discoveries and calculations achieved by Newton set the trend in physics and cosmology that dominated the next two centuries. Newton's theological works, left unfinished at his death, have recently received new scholarly and critical attention.

Newton was born on 25 December 1642 in the manor house at Woolsthorpe, a hamlet of the parish of Colsterworth about six miles south of Grantham, Lincolnshire, and was baptized on 1 January 1643. Michael White describes the town in his *Isaac Newton: The Last Sorcerer* (1997) as "little more than a collection of small farms and humble country dwellings" clustered around the estate. Newton was the "only and posthumous child," as his early biographer William Stukeley put it, of the illiterate but propertied Isaac Newton, who had died at the age of thirty-six in October. His mother, Hannah Ayscough, from Market-Overton in Rutlandshire, was a member of the lower gentry. She had married the elder Newton in April 1642. On 27 January 1645 she married Barnabas Smith, rector of North Witham, by whom she had three children. Newton was left at Woolsthorpe in the care of his grandparents,

James and Margery Ayscough, and modern biographers have suggested that this abandonment by his mother set the course of his life as a "neurotic," "obsessive," "lonely, difficult and driven man" who was bleak, self-seeking, arrogant, deceitful, and fond of flattery. He was tutored at home and then sent to small day schools at Skillington and Stoke. In private jottings from this time he admits to having threatened to burn down the house at Woolsthorpe with his mother and stepfather in it.

In 1654 Newton was sent to King's School, run by Henry Stokes in the market town of Grantham. The school was some seven miles from his grandparents' home, so Newton boarded with the town apothecary, a man named Clark (his first name is unknown). According to townspeople interviewed by Stukeley, Newton's interest in alchemy dated from this time. Surviving notebooks reveal the young boarder transcribing prescriptions and cures, along with methods of paint production and of cutting glass with chemicals. During his stay with the Clarks, Newton emerged as a mechanical genius, constructing kites, sundials, and "water-clocks." A windmill that had recently been built near Grantham was the inspiration for a miniature replica powered by a mouse. Newton invented the trick of taking a paper lantern with a candle in it and tying it to the tail of a kite, which gave the appearance of a comet when flown at night and formed the basis for the episode of Sydrophel and his comet in canto 3 of Samuel Butler's *Hudibras* (1663–1678). Newton later demonstrated that the behavior of comets was not erratic but obeyed the law of gravitation, and that their orbits were subject to exact calculation.

The standard education of the time consisted of Greek, Latin, Scripture, and Euclidean mathematics; in addition, a writing master was employed by the school to give lessons in composition. By his own account, Newton was indifferent to his studies. To compensate for the dullness of his schoolwork he read widely outside the curriculum, first in books handed down to him by his stepfather and later in volumes in the library of St. Wulfram's Church in Grantham. Among his diversions were verse writing and portrait drawing.

Newton's stepfather died in 1656, and his mother returned to Woolsthorpe. She called Newton home from school to take part in the management of the family farm, but he was frequently negligent and was known to send his manservant to do business in his place. He found it congenial to sit reading in the fields or to go on market days in search of what Stukeley characterizes as books on "physic, botany, anatomy, philosophy, mathematics, astronomy, and the like" in Clark's garret. His mother viewed his bookishness as foolery, but his old schoolmaster Stokes, who was then rector of Colsterworth, implored her to return him to his schooling. According to some reports Newton's uncle, William Ayscough, rector of Burton Coggles, Lincolnshire, offered the same advice. She finally agreed, and Newton returned to Grantham to prepare to enter the University of Cambridge.

On 5 June 1661 Newton matriculated at Trinity College, Cambridge, as a sizar (a student who pays his way at the university by doing odd jobs and waiting on his tutor) under Benjamin Pulleyne, who later became regius professor of Greek. There is, however, evidence to suggest that Newton was sizar to Humphrey Babington, brother-in-law of the Grantham apothecary Clark and fellow of Trinity College. Newton and Babington remained in contact throughout Newton's early years at Cambridge. Because of the interruption in his schooling, Newton was two years older than the average student of his year, which may have been to his advantage academically. His first roommate was Francis Wilford; eighteen months after his arrival, however, Newton began rooming with John Wickins, the son of the master of Manchester Grammar School. Their rooms, according to at least one account, became a live-in laboratory, crowded with furnaces and bottles of chemicals.

The curriculum at Cambridge had been set by the Elizabethan Statues of 1571. First-year studies consisted of rhetoric, classical history, geography, art, Scripture, and literature; by the end of their first year students were expected to be fluent in Latin, Greek, and Hebrew. At twenty-one Newton came into contact with Isaac Barrow, Lucasian Professor of Mathematics, who recognized his abilities, encouraged his mathematical studies, and directed his attention to optics. Newton made some observations on halos in 1664, which he later described in his *Opticks: or, A Treatise of the Reflexions, Refractions, Inflexions and Colours of Light. Also Two Treatises of the Species and Magnitude of Curvilinear Figures* (1704). On 28 April of that year he was elected a scholar of Trinity College.

An account of Newton's Cambridge expenditures from a notebook in the Conduitt collection of materials bequeathed to Newton's niece and her husband shows that he purchased the mathematician Frans van Schooten's *Miscellanies* and William Oughtred's *Clavis mathematicae* (1631) and borrowed the works of John Wallis. He visited the beer house, played cards for money, and when he went home for vacations brought presents for his mother; his half brother, Benjamin; and his half sisters, Mary ("Marie" in some accounts) and Hannah. He applied himself to René Descartes's *Geometry* in van Schooten's second Latin edition (1661) and Wallis's *Arithmetica Infinitorum* (1655) and attended Barrow's mathematical lectures. He received a B.A. in April 1665.

In the summer of 1665 Newton was forced to leave Cambridge because of an outbreak of the plague. He returned to the family home at Woolsthorpe; according to his own account, it was at Woolsthorpe in the autumn of 1665 that the idea of universal gravitation occurred to him. The story that the hypothesis was inspired by the fall of an apple was first told by Voltaire, who claimed to have heard it from Newton's niece. Shortly before his death Newton described his speculations to Stukeley:

> Why should that apple always descend perpendicularly to the ground, thought he to himself. Why should it not go sideways or upwards, but constantly to the earths centre? Assuredly, the reason is, that the earth draws it. There must be a drawing power in matter: and the sum of the drawing power in the matter of the earth must be in the earths centre, not in any side of the earth. Therefore dos this apple fall perpendicularly, or towards the center. If matter thus draws matter, it must be in proportion of its quantity. Therefore the apple draws the earth, as well as the earth draws the apple. That there is a power, like that we here call gravity, which extends its self thro' the universe.

Henry Pemberton reports in his preface to *A View of Sir Isaac Newton's Philosophy* (1728) that Newton speculated that since gravity is not found to be diminished at the highest points on the earth, and, therefore, the remotest distances from the center of the earth, it appeared reasonable to conclude that this power must extend much farther than was usually thought. This conclusion was the beginning of his speculations on the place of gravity in maintaining the orbits of the Moon and planets. It has been suggested that Newton fabricated the story of watching the apple fall himself, and that without his long and earnest immersion in alchemy the idea of this "drawing power" would have been inconceivable to him. Long before Newton, however, people had thought that objects fell because of the pull of the earth. The important advance in Newton's work is the use of experimentation and observation.

The period 1665–1666 was a fruitful one in Newton's intellectual development. In a manuscript written circa 1716 Newton says that in 1665 he found the method for approximating series and the rule for reducing the power of a binomial to such a series. In May he found the method of tangents of Gregory and Slusius, and in November he discovered the direct method of fluxions—the elements of the infinitesimal calculus. In January of the next year he developed his theory of colors, and in May 1666 he found an entrance into the inverse method of fluxions—the elements of the integral calculus. That year he began to

The reflecting telescope that Newton built and presented to the Royal Society of London in 1671 (Royal Society of London)

think of gravity as "extending to the orb of the moon."

Early in 1667 Newton returned to Cambridge and was soon elected a minor fellow of Trinity College. The next year he became a major fellow and received his M.A. That year he entered "Of Reflections" in his "Waste Book," a partially filled notebook in which his stepfather had recorded his thoughts on a variety of theological subjects; it had been passed down to Newton on his stepfather's death, along with some 250 books. Through experiments on sunlight passed through a prism, he concluded that rays of light that differ in color also differ in refractivity—a discovery that suggested that the indistinctness of the image formed by the object lens of a refracting telescope was caused by the differently colored rays of light being brought to focus at different distances. He concluded that it was impossible to produce a distinct image with such a telescope and was led to construct a reflecting telescope. He built his first telescope in 1668, casting and grinding the mirror from an alloy of his own formulation, polishing it, and making the tube, the mount, and the fittings. With it he saw the satellites of Jupiter. He sent his second telescope to the Royal Society of London in December 1671, and it was discussed at society meetings early in the following year. His device was a significant technical achievement of unsurpassed quality and power for the time; but for all the overzealous claims of the Royal Society, he never pretended to be the first to design a reflecting telescope. James Gregory's concept, if not the practical design, had been in circulation for more than a century. The form devised by Newton reached perfection in the hands of William Herschel and William Parsons, third Earl of Rosse.

In the fall of 1669 Barrow resigned the Lucasian chair at Cambridge, and Newton was elected to succeed him. Earlier that year Newton had sent the manuscript for his *Analysis Per Quantitatum Series, Fluxiones, ac Differentias: Cum Enumeratione Linearum Tertii Ordinis* (1711) to the collector and publisher John Collins, and Newton traveled to London in November to meet him. In January 1670 he delivered the first of his lectures on optics. In January 1672 he was elected a fellow of the Royal Society. The following month he sent to Henry Oldenburg, secretary of the society, a letter that included his paper "Theory of Light and Colours." Robert Hooke, the curator of experiments for the society, was assigned to analyze Newton's paper and write a report on it. Hooke had already been critical of Newton in regard to the telescope: he claimed to have invented a similar device earlier and had declared as much at a meeting of the Royal Society. Newton's theory was at odds with Hooke's own long-held ideas about the nature of light, and he gave the work only a superficial perusal, admitting later that he had spent just three hours analyzing the complex paper. His report to the society was dismissive and condescending. Infuriated, Newton wrote a response that was perceived as insulting and caused Hooke to mount a further attack. Newton had the support of Christiaan Huygens, who commended greater respect than Hooke in the scientific community. Soon, however, other critics began to comment on Newton's theory of light. A Jesuit priest and professor of rhetoric in Paris, Ignace-Gaston Pardies, rejected Newton's hypothesis. Newton at first dismissed Pardies as an amateur, but when the attacks continued he responded in writing, and after several exchanges Pardies finally accepted the theory. Hooke, however, was not as easily persuaded, and in April 1672 he complained to Oldenburg about what he viewed as Newton's superior attitude. Oldenburg's reproach provoked Newton's outrage: he declared that he would hold back papers that he had planned to send and refused to allow the publication of others. Ultimately, Hooke was officially chastised and instructed to conduct a complete reappraisal of Newton's original paper.

In a series of lectures between the fall of 1672 and early 1673 Newton's former supporter Huygens turned against him, arguing that Newton's theory of colors was insufficiently proved and was merely a hypothesis. In reaction, Newton sent a letter of resignation to the Royal Society; but Oldenburg smoothed the matter over, and Newton stayed on as fellow.

In December 1675 Newton read two papers to the society. "Hypothesis explaining the Properties of Light" explains how reflection, refraction, and diffusion of light are all caused by the "corpuscles" of light being made to change speed and direction as they pass through different media. Newton makes it clear that colors are not produced by these effects, reiterating that white light is composed of many different colors. The second paper, "Discourse of Observations," describes experiments by which Newton attempted to prove his hypothesis. His efforts sparked a new battle with Hooke, who claimed that Newton had not only taken inspiration from his *Micrographia* (1664) but also had used it to demonstrate an opposing theory of light. The controversy was formally settled by an exchange of exaggeratedly polite letters between the two men; in his letter of 5 February 1676 Newton made the famous self-deprecating comment that if he had seen further than others, it was because he was standing on the shoulders of giants—including, by implication, Hooke. Nevertheless, Newton, who was pathologically sensitive to any sort of criticism, carried a grudge against Hooke that lasted until the latter's death in 1703.

Between 1673 and 1675 the German philosopher and mathematician Gottfried Wilhelm Leibniz had mirrored Newton's own development of a decade earlier and had produced a version of the calculus. In 1673 he had begun a correspondence with Collins, who had encouraged his work and sent him the latest ideas circulating within the Royal Society, including those of Newton. Convinced that Leibniz was about to publish his findings, Collins, along with Oldenburg, tried to persuade Newton to publish first. Though they persisted for years, the most they could obtain from Newton was a promise to correspond with Leibniz, which he began to do in 1676. After Leibniz published his paper on the calculus in 1684, Newton accused him of theft. The verdict of history is that the methods were invented independently and that although Newton was the first inventor, a greater debt is owed to Leibniz for the superior facility and completeness of his method. Although the two great rivals achieved individually the mathematical breakthroughs each claimed as his own, Newton never acknowledged Leibniz's contribution and never forgave what he saw as a criminal attempt to intrude into his exclusive domain.

In August 1684 the astronomer Edmond Halley visited Cambridge to ask whether Newton could prove that an inverse-square relationship governed planetary motions; others, including Hooke, had tried and failed to do so. Newton answered that he had solved the problem years before but could not find the proof among his papers, and he promised to send it to Halley. Three months later he sent Halley a nine-page paper, "De motu corporum in gyrum" (On the Motions of Bodies in Orbit), in which he proved the inverse-square hypothesis. Halley urged him to expand the paper into a book. Newton presented the manuscript to the Royal Society on 28 April 1686; it was published by the society in midsummer 1687 as *Philosophiæ Naturalis Principia Mathematica*. The money for the publication was advanced by Halley; the society had exhausted its funds on the publication of a history of fish.

Newton's greatest work is divided into three books: "De motu corporum: Liber primus," "De motu corporum: Liber secundus," dealing with the motion of bodies in resisting media," and "De systemate mundi" (The System of the World). The first book is a treatise on mechanics in which nearly everything is a pioneering discovery. One of Newton's greatest achievements was to explain the motion of the heavenly bodies on the basis of the laws of motion and universal gravitation. The notion that the same laws governed the movement of earthly and heavenly bodies went against the ideas of those who preceded him, including Hooke, Halley, and Christopher Wren. Because of its presentation of the law of gravity and of Newton's rules for reasoning from physical events, the *Principia* signified the beginning of a new era in scientific investigation.

The *Principia* begins with a statement of the three laws of motion, with due acknowledgment to Galileo for anticipating the first two: every body continues in its state of rest or uniform motion in a straight line unless it is compelled to change that state by a force impressed upon it; the change of motion of the body is proportional to the force impressed and is in the direction of the straight line in which the force is impressed; and–Newton's completely original contribution–for every action there is an equal and opposite reaction. The Sun attracts all of the planets, and they attract the Sun and each other; and the earth and the Moon attract each other. Each spherical body behaves as if its mass were concentrated at a point at its center. The elliptical orbits of the planets are caused by the massiveness of the Sun compared to the planets and the distance of the planets from each other; the inward-pulling or *centripetal* (a word coined by Newton) force exerted by the Sun and planets on each

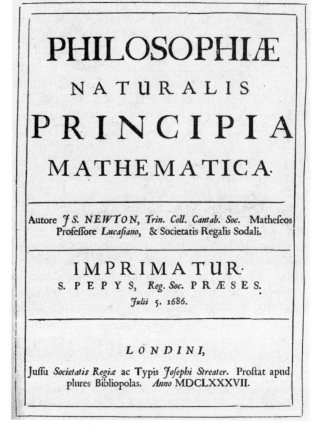

Title page for Newton's work that revolutionized modern science (Royal Society of London)

other is balanced by the outward-pulling or *centrifugal* (a word coined by Huygens and borrowed by Newton) force of the planets endeavoring to move in a straight line outward from the Sun.

In the first book all motions are considered as taking place in empty space, with no resistance to the movement. In the second book Newton deals with motions in fluids that offer resistance. He shows that Descartes's theory that the planets move in great vortices of fluid is inconsistent with their actual motion; therefore, the space between the planets is empty. Perhaps the most important aspect of this book is Newton's mathematical treatment of wave motion.

In the third book Newton announces that from the same principles he will demonstrate the structure of "the system of the world"; he proceeds to do so with such thoroughness that for the next two hundred years work in the field by the most able minds consisted largely of extensions and improvements of his theories. In proposition VII he states the law of universal gravitation: every particle of matter, however large or small, attracts every other with a force directly proportional to their masses and inversely proportional to the square of the distance between them. He

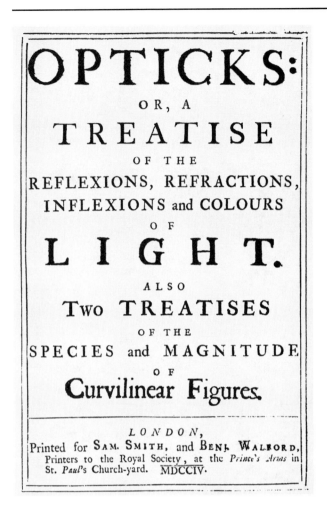

OPTICKS:
OR, A
TREATISE
OF THE
REFLEXIONS, REFRACTIONS,
INFLEXIONS and COLOURS
OF
LIGHT.
ALSO
Two TREATISES
OF THE
SPECIES and MAGNITUDE
OF
Curvilinear Figures.

LONDON,
Printed for SAM. SMITH, and BENJ. WALFORD,
Printers to the Royal Society, at the Prince's Arms in
St. Paul's Church-yard. MDCCIV.

Title page for the work in which Newton presents his proof that sunlight is composed of various colors (Royal Society of London)

thereby unifies the earthbound mechanics of Galileo with Johannes Kepler's laws of planetary motion, which had previously been viewed as having no relationship to everyday earthly existence. Extending the results of book 1, he deals with the motions of the satellites of Jupiter, Saturn, and Earth in terms of his gravitational theory. Breaking completely new ground, he shows how to find the masses of the Sun and the other planets from the mass of the earth, for which he calculates a value close to that which was found later using more advanced methods. He calculates the precessions of the equinoxes resulting from the conical movement of the earth's axis and argues that the earth is flattened at the poles and bulges at the equator, which produces a slight twisting force. Using the results of the first book he works out the major irregularities of the motion of the Moon produced by the pull of the Sun and does the same for other satellites. He shows that comets are part of the solar system and move under the influence of the Sun's

attraction, and that, consequently, their orbits can be calculated.

The book sold readily and brought Newton great fame. Journals in Paris and Leipzig carried long and favorable reviews. The learned world recognized it at once as a work of great power and genius. Yet, the *Principia* was difficult to understand, and fifty years or more had to pass before Newton's work was generally accepted and taught. The Scottish Universities of St. Andrews and Edinburgh were probably the first to teach Newtonian science.

Copies of the first edition of the *Principia* were rare and commanded a high price. Newton's friend Richard Bentley urged him to bring out a second edition, which appeared in 1713 with a preface by the editor, Roger Cotes. The second edition includes new information about the resistance of fluids and the motions of the heavenly bodies, in particular those of the Moon and comets, as well as some new experiments on the motion of liquids. The importance of the *Principia* was more widely recognized, and editions appeared in Amsterdam in 1714 and 1723. In the latter year printing of a third edition began in England. Newton chose Pemberton to help with revisions and see the work through to press. The third edition, the last one in Newton's lifetime, appeared in 1726. An English translation appeared in 1729, two years after Newton's death, and has often been reprinted in Britain and the United States. A French translation came thirty years later, a German translation in 1872, and in the twentieth century the book was published in Italian, Russian, and Swedish.

In February 1687 the Catholic king James II tried to force Cambridge to admit a Benedictine monk, Alban Francis, to the degree of master of arts without requiring him to take the oath of supremacy (an oath to uphold the Church of England). The move was regarded as the first step in a plan by the king to Catholicize the university, and Newton was a member of a delegation elected by the university senate that appeared before the Ecclesiastical Commission in London in April to oppose Francis's admission. In May the judge in the case, Lord George Jeffreys, decided in favor of the university. As a result of his participation in the case, in January 1689 Newton was elected as a Whig to represent Cambridge University in the Convention Parliament that was called to establish a legal foundation for the Glorious Revolution of 1688, in which James had been driven into exile and replaced by the Protestant William of Orange from Holland. Newton made many new acquaintances in London, including Locke, with whom he formed a firm friendship, and Samuel Pepys, who introduced him to various people of importance. He also entered into an

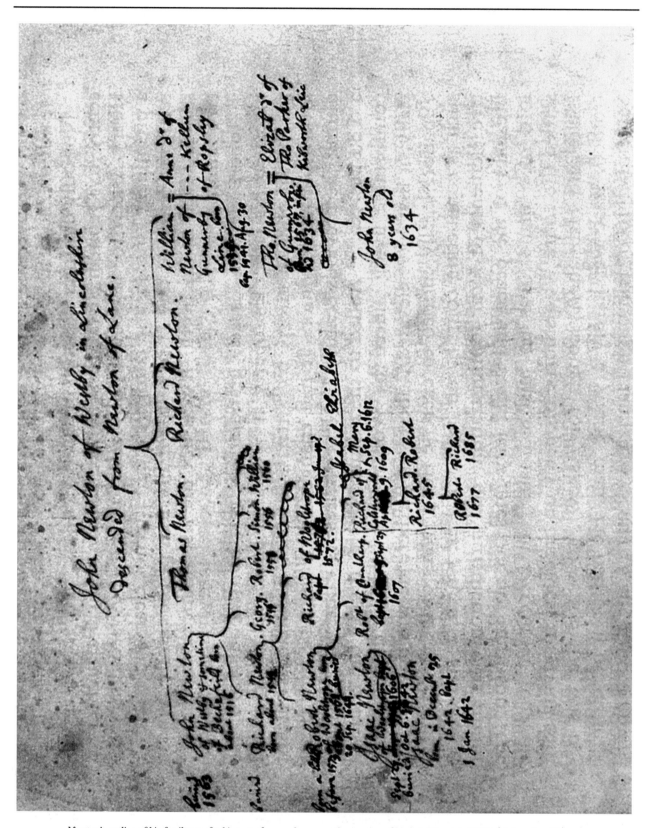

Newton's outline of his family tree for his coat of arms, drawn on the occasion of his knighthood in 1705 (University of Texas)

John Flamsteed, the royal astronomer, who engaged in a lengthy dispute with Newton over Flamsteed's observations of irregularities in the orbit of the moon; portrait by Thomas Gibson, circa 1712 (Royal Society of London)

intensely close friendship with the Swiss mathematician Nicholas Fatio de Duillier, and a flurry of letters passed between the two. White implies that the relationship may have been sexual in nature. The parliament was dissolved after thirteen months, and Newton returned to Cambridge.

Newton corresponded with Locke in July 1692 on Robert Boyle's alchemistic method for "multiplying gold." In 1693 the relationship with Fatio de Duillier was broken off, and, whether as a cause or a consequence of the breakup, Newton suffered an apparent nervous breakdown. It has been suggested that mercury poisoning was the cause of Newton's malady, and P. E. Spargo and C. A. Pounds, in "Newton's 'Derangement of the Intellect': New Light on an Old Problem" (1979), support this theory by analyzing surviving samples of Newton's hair (they also found high concentrations of lead). In *Never at Rest: A Biography of Sir Isaac Newton* (1980) Richard S. Westfall objects to the hypothesis, arguing that Newton failed to display the characteristic symptoms of tremor and loss of teeth and that, though the effects of mercury poisoning are long-term and sometimes even permanent, he made a full recovery within a matter of a few months. In his *Life of Sir Isaac Newton* (1833) Jean Baptiste Biot speculated that the breakdown of the 1790s accounted for the lack of productivity in the last forty years of Newton's life, a contention supported by Westfall.

John Flamsteed, the royal astronomer, had provided astronomical facts and figures, especially on comets, which had formed the basis of some calculations in the *Principia*. Flamsteed had been critical of the *Principia* and had felt slighted by Newton's lack of acknowledgment of his data, and the two scientists had become estranged. By September 1694, however, the two were again corresponding, this time over irregularities in the movement of the Moon. Flamsteed communicated all the information that was asked of him, but Newton's criticism of the data and his more and more frequent demands strained their association. Newton offered the astronomer money for his data;

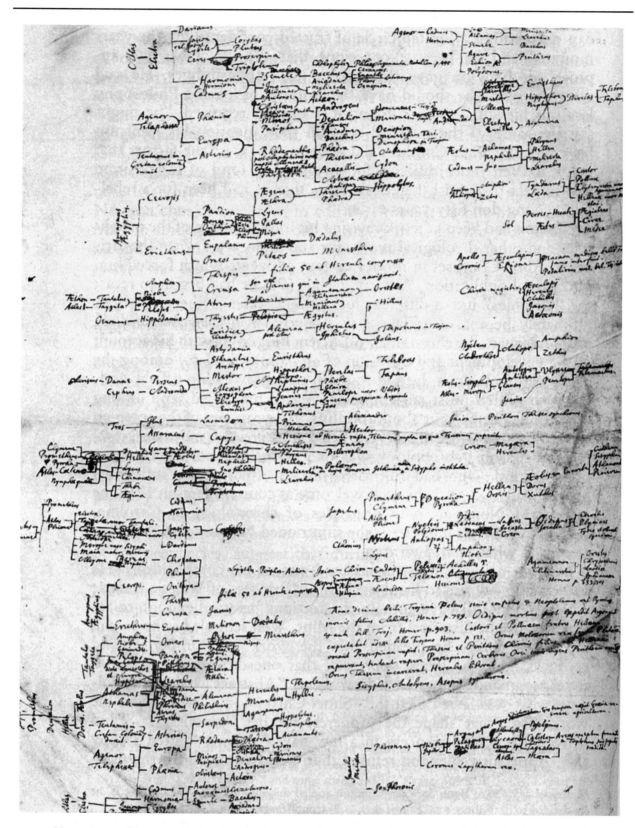

Manuscript page for a system of ancient chronology prepared by Newton, probably between 1710 and 1715 (New College, Oxford)

Death mask of Newton by Louis François Roubiliac
(Trinity College, Cambridge)

Flamsteed was insulted, and their relationship again cooled.

In 1696 Newton was made warden of the mint through the efforts of his friend, the politician Charles Montague. The Tower of London had been the home of the mint since 1300, and Newton's duties required him to take up residence in London. After a short stay in quarters next to the mint room, he moved to 88 Jermyn Street. As he had never married, his niece Catherine Barton came to keep house. The post of warden was generally regarded as little more than a sinecure, but Newton brought to the job an energy and enthusiasm that matched his efforts in his scientific pursuits. Recoinage was desperately needed, as many of the coins in circulation had been minted in Elizabethan times and were an easy target for clippers and counterfeiters. The process of recoinage had been set in motion before Newton's appointment, but little thought had been given to the details of this monumental task. During Newton's tenure a new system of milled coinage was minted and put into circulation. Newton also took an active role in tracking down and prosecuting counterfeiters, sending some of them,

including a picturesque scofflaw named William Chaloner, to the gallows. Between June 1698 and Christmas 1699 he conducted some two hundred cross-examinations of witnesses, informers, and suspects, and in a single week in February 1699 attended seven sessions and had ten prisoners in Newgate Prison awaiting hanging. He was promoted to master of the mint in 1699. In 1700 he moved to 87 Jermyn Street, next door to his first home.

On 30 November 1703 Newton was elected president of the Royal Society, agreeing to accept the position only because his rival Hooke had died earlier that year. He took great interest in the affairs of the society and was annually reelected to the office for the next twenty-five years. In 1704 he published *Opticks: or, A Treatise of the Reflexions, Refractions, Inflexions, and Colours of Light,* which includes two mathematical treatises on curves written long before. The science of optics had made some progress before Newton's time, most recently by Galileo and Kepler. The prevailing hypothesis on the nature of light, however, was that of Descartes, who believed that it was a "pressure" transmitted through a transparent medium called the ether. Newton conducted a set of experiments with prisms that showed sunlight to be composed of various colors, the differences among which were determined by differing degrees of refraction. He concluded that light was made up of corpuscles, or particles. Light could not be a pressure, he wrote in his notebook, "for we should see in the night a[s] well or better than in the day[;] we should se[e] a bright light above us becaus[e] we are pressed downewards . . . there could be no refraction since the same matter cannot presse 2 ways. . . . the Sun could not be quite eclipsed[,] the Moone & planetts would shine like sunns." On 16 April 1705 Newton was knighted by Queen Anne at Trinity College for his work on optics.

All of the work described in the *Opticks* was done before Newton came to London. He notes in the preface that part of it was written in 1675, much of the rest was added about twelve years later, and the last part of the book was "put together out of scattered papers." To the second edition, which came out in 1717, he made some remarkable additions that he set down as "Queries" at the end of the book. Among the ideas in the queries are the suggestions that the forces that hold atoms together may be electrical and that it may be through these forces that matter acts on light.

Meanwhile, to gain access to Flamsteed's lunar data for a projected new edition of the *Principia,* Newton sought a commission from Prince George of Denmark, Queen Anne's consort, to publish Flamsteed's *Historia Coelestis Britannica* (British History of the Heavens); the prince agreed, and Flamsteed could do little but comply. The project was begun in 1705 and proved a disaster from the start. Newton's first move was to use his authority as president of the Royal Society to set up an editorial board that excluded Flamsteed. He then persuaded Prince George to limit the investment in the project to about £850, thereby ensuring that Flamsteed's expansive ideas concerning the scope of the work would be curtailed and that Newton would have access to the data more quickly. The printing of the volume moved at a glacial pace, but an unauthorized version of the work was finally brought out in 1712. The second edition of the *Principia*, which drew on calculations printed in *Historia Coelestis Britannica*, was published the following year.

During the remaining years of his life Newton made no great scientific discoveries, nor did he devote any large part of his thought to scientific problems. His *Arithmetica Universalis: sive De Compositione et Resolutione Arithmetica Liber. Cui accessit Halleiana Aequationum Radices Arithmetice inveniendi methodus. In Usum juventutis Academiae* was published in 1707; it was translated in 1720 as *Universal Arithmetick: or, a Treatise of Arithmetical Composition and Resolution, to which is added, Dr. Halley's method of finding the roots of the Æquations arithmetically.* His papers "De Natura Acidorum," "Enumeratio Linearum Tertii Ordinis," and "Tractatus de Quadratura Curvarum" were published in 1710 in a technical encyclopedia, *Lexicon Technicum; or, an Universal Dictionary of Arts and Sciences: explaining not only the terms of arts, but the arts themselves,* edited by John Harris and others. *Analysis Per Quantitatum Series, Fluxiones, ac Differentias,* the mathematical treatise so important for the calculus, was first published in 1711. It is characteristic of Newton that work he had done as a young man should be appearing in print, with his rather grudging consent, for the first time in his old age.

In the fall of 1709 Newton moved briefly to Chelsea. From September 1710 until 1725 he resided in a large brick house, to which he added an observatory, at 35 St. Martin's Street, south of Leicester Fields (now Leicester Square).

In a letter to Caroline, Princess of Wales, in 1715 Leibniz criticized the religious views of the English. King George I heard of the attack and expressed a wish that Newton reply. In a conversation with the princess he mentioned a system of chronology—an attempt to determine the dates of ancient events from astrological considerations—that he had composed in Cambridge, and shortly afterward he gave her a copy. The Abbé Antonio Conti, under a strict promise of secrecy, was allowed to make a copy of it. On his return to France, Conti violated his promise and gave the work to Nicolas Fréret, who wrote a refutation and published it together with Newton's

Roubiliac's statue of Newton in the chapel of Trinity College, Cambridge

work, without Newton's permission, in 1725. Fréret had determined that Newton's dating was wrong by centuries, and Newton began to prepare a revised version for the press but died before completing it. The book was published in 1728 as *The Chronology of Ancient Kingdoms Amended. To which is Prefix'd, A Short Chronicle from the Memory of Things in Europe, to the Conquest of Persia by Alexander the Great.*

Newton had begun writing on theological issues at an early age, and he remained keenly interested in religion throughout his life. Soon after he had written the *Principia,* he had carried on a correspondence with Locke on the prophecies of Daniel and other theological matters. In 1690 he had sent Locke a manuscript, "An Historical Account of Two Notable Corruptions of Scripture," so that Locke could take it to Holland to be translated into French and published. Locke's trip had been postponed, and Locke had sent the manu-

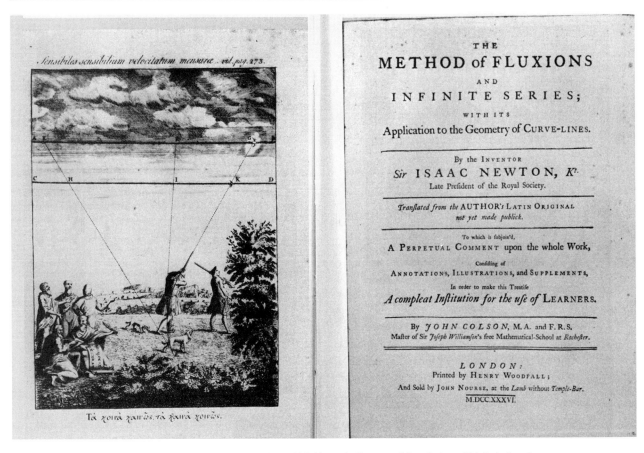

Sensibiles sensibilium velocitatum mensura. vid.pag.273.

Tà xοινà xαιρὸς, τà xαινà xοιρὸς.

Frontispiece and title page for the posthumous work in which Newton's discovery of the calculus, which he had made seventy years previously, was first published (Royal Society of London)

script to Jean Le Clerc, a leader of the Dutch Remonstrants, an Arminian sect (that is, they denied the doctrine of predestination), who undertook to carry out the translation and publication of the work. Newton changed his mind, however, and Le Clerc left the manuscript in the library of the Remonstrants. It was published in an incomplete form in 1754 as *Two Letters of Sir Isaac Newton to Mr. Le Clerc, Late Divinity Professor of the Remonstrants of Holland. The Former Containing a Disertation upon the Reading of the Greek Text, I John, v. 7. The Latter upon That of I Timothy, iii. 16* (1754) and under the original title, and in a more complete and accurate form, in Samuel Horsley's edition of Newton's works (1779–1785). Newton's *Observations upon the Prophecies of Daniel, and the Apocalypse of St. John* (1733) also appeared in print after his death.

Although Newton agreed with the deist view that God's existence could be seen in the operations of nature, his insistence on the vital role played by divine prophecy in religion conflicts with deist doctrine. Newton subscribed to Arianism, the denial of the Trinitarian nature of God. Such beliefs were considered heretical, and if Newton's views had been made

public, they might have ruined his career. He thought that the Cambridge Platonist Henry More had proved the immortality of the soul and maintained a role for the Creator in the governance of the universe: according to More, matter is guided by spirit and manipulated by God entirely at his discretion. The *Principia* tries to avoid the troublesome questions posed by the notions of attraction and of action at a distance: Newton had both philosophical and theological reasons for insisting that matter is inherently passive; yet, the *Principia* seems to show that matter can exert force. Newton tried repeatedly to find his way through this tangle but never succeeded.

Newton's interest in alchemy has long been downplayed by scholars, but it was no secret to his contemporaries. He discussed and corresponded with Boyle and Locke, for example, on alchemical issues. Newton's work in mechanics can, in fact, be seen as forming a brief parenthesis in his life's work of synthesizing the alchemy of his day. Drawing on material from Newton's library, which was ignored until it was purchased by John Maynard Keynes in 1936, White depicts him not as the pure scientist of lore but as a practicing alchemist who dabbled in the occult and possibly even the black arts, while expending vast amounts of time in the study of Scripture. Keynes himself compared Newton to Faustus in his relentless search for the secrets of God and nature.

At eighty-three Newton began to suffer from inflammation of the lungs and was persuaded to leave the smoke of London for the fresh air of the village of Kensington. In 1727 he went into London to preside at a meeting of the Royal Society. He returned home ill and never recovered. According to Joseph Spence's *Anecdotes, Observations, and Characters of Books and Men Collected from the Conversations of Mr. Pope, and Other Eminent Persons of His Time* (1820), Newton said shortly before his death on 20 March 1727: "I do not know what I may appear to others, but to myself I seem to have been only like a boy playing on the seashore . . . whilst the great ocean of truth lay all undiscovered before me."

Sir Isaac Newton was buried with highest honors in Westminster Abbey, where a monument was erected to him in 1731. William Calder Marshall's bust of Newton, eroded by the weather, stands near the Newton Gate at the southwest corner of Leicester Square Gardens. The most significant monument to Newton is his home at Woolsthorpe. It became the property of the National Trust in 1943 and is open to the public during part of the year. The sundials he constructed as a boy are no longer there, but some geometrical carvings in the stonework of a window in the north bedroom, presumably by Newton, were discovered in 1947. On a tablet in the room in which Newton was born is inscribed the celebrated couplet by Alexander Pope:

Nature and Nature's laws lay hid in night:
God said "Let Newton be," and all was light.

Letters:

Four Letters from Sir Isaac Newton to Dr. Bentley, containing some Arguments in Proof of a Deity (N.p., 1756);

Thirteen Letters from Sir Isaac Newton, representative in Parliament of the University of Cambridge, to John Covel, D.D., Vice-chancellor. From Original MSS. in the Library of Dawson Turnet, Esq., Yarmouth (Norwich: Charles Muskett, 1848);

Correspondence of Sir Isaac Newton and Professor Cotes, Including Letters of Other Eminent Men, Now First Published from the Originals in the Library of Trinity College, Cambridge; together with an Appendix, Containing other Unpublished Letters and Papers by Newton; with Notes, and a Variety of Details Illustrative of his History, edited by J. A. Edleston (London: John W. Parker / Cambridge: John Deighton, 1850);

Sir Isaac Newton and England's Prohibitive Tariff upon Silver Money. An Open Letter to Prof. W. Stanley Jevons, edited by S. Dana Horton (Cincinnati: R. Clarke, 1881);

The Correspondence of Sir Isaac Newton, 1661–1713, 7 volumes, edited by Herbert Westren Turnbull, J. F. Scott, and A. R. Halls (Cambridge: Cambridge University Press, 1959–1978);

Rupert A. Hall, "Further Newton Correspondence," *Notes and Records of the Royal Society,* 37 (1982): 7–34.

Bibliographies:

George J. Gray, ed., *A Bibliography of the Works of Sir Isaac Newton, Together with a List of Books Illustrating his Life and Works* (Cambridge: Bowes & Bowes, 1888; revised and enlarged, 1907);

H. Zeitlinger, "A Newtonian Bibliography," in *Isaac Newton (1642–1727),* edited by W. J. Greenstreet (London: Bell, 1927), pp. 148–190;

Peter Wallis and Ruth Wallis, *Newton and Newtoniana, 1672–1975: A Bibliography* (Folkestone, U.K.: Dawson, 1977);

Isaac Newton: A Catalogue of Rare Books and One Manuscript (London: Dawson Rare Books, 1978).

Biographies:

Bernard Le Bouvier de Fontenelle, *The Life of Sir Isaac Newton: With an Account of His Writings* (London: Printed for James Woodman & David Lyon, 1728);

Sir David Brewster, *The Life of Sir Isaac Newton* (New York: Harper, 1831);

Jean Baptiste Biot, *Life of Sir Isaac Newton,* translated by Howard Crawford Elphinstone (London: Society for the Diffusion of Useful Knowledge, 1833);

Selig Brodetsky, *Sir Isaac Newton: A Brief Account of His Life and Work* (London: Methuen, 1927);

Richard de Villamil, *Newton: The Man* (London: Knox, 1931);

L. T. More, *Isaac Newton: A Biography* (New York: Scribners, 1934);

William Stukeley, *Memoirs of Sir Isaac Newton's Life, 1752; Being Some Account of his Family and Chiefly the Junior Part of his Life,* edited by A. Hastings White (London: Taylor & Francis, 1936);

J. W. N. Sullivan, *Isaac Newton, 1642–1727* (London: Macmillan, 1938);

Edward Neville da Costa Andrade, *Isaac Newton* (London: Parrish, 1950);

Andrade, *Sir Isaac Newton* (London: Collins, 1954; Garden City, N.Y.: Doubleday, 1958);

Herbert Douglas Anthony, *Sir Isaac Newton* (London & New York: Abelard-Schuman, 1960);

John David North, *Isaac Newton* (London: Oxford University Press, 1967);

Colin A. Ronan, *Isaac Newton: An Illustrated Life of Sir Isaac Newton, 1642–1727,* adapted by Peter Limm (Princes Risborough, U.K.: Shire, 1976);

James Seymour English, *". . . And All Was Light": The Life and Work of Sir Isaac Newton* (Lincoln, U.K.: Lincolnshire Library Service, 1977);

Frank E. Manuel, *A Portrait of Isaac Newton* (London: Muller, 1980);

Richard S. Westfall, *Never at Rest: A Biography of Sir Isaac Newton* (Cambridge & New York: Cambridge University Press, 1980);

A. Rupert Hall, *Isaac Newton: Adventurer in Thought* (Oxford: Blackwell, 1992);

Michael White, *Isaac Newton: The Last Sorcerer* (London: Fourth Estate / Reading, Mass.: Addison-Wesley, 1997).

References:

Eric J. Aiton, "The Contributions of Newton, Bernoulli, and Euler to the Theory of Tides," *Annals of Science,* 11 (1955): 206–223;

Richard T. W. Arthur, "Newton's Fluxions and Equably Flowing Time," *Studies in History and Philosophy of Science,* 26 (June 1995): 323–351;

Anthony Blunt, "Blake's 'Ancient of Days': The Symbolism of the Compasses," *Journal of the Warburg and Courtauld Institutes,* 2 (1938–1939): 53–63;

Marie Boas and Rupert A. Hall, "Newton's Chemical Experiments," *Archives internationales d'historie des sciences,* 11 (1958): 113–152;

Edward Booth, "Kant's Critique of Newton," *Kantstudien,* 87 (1996): 149–165;

V. I. Boss, *Newton and Russia: The Early Influence, 1698–1796* (Cambridge, Mass.: Harvard University Press, 1972);

Gale E. Christianson, *In the Presence of the Creator: Isaac Newton and His Times* (New York: Free Press / London: Collier Macmillan, 1984);

Bernard I. Cohen, *Franklin and Newton: An Enquiry into Speculative Newtonian Experimental Science, and Franklin's Work in Electricity as an Example Thereof* (Philadelphia: American Philosophical Society, 1956);

T. G. Cowling, *Isaac Newton and Astrology* (Leeds: Liverpool University Press, 1977);

Betty Jo Teeter Dobbs, *The Foundation of Newton's Alchemy, or, "The Hunting of the Greene Lyon"* (Cambridge: Cambridge University Press, 1975);

Dobbs, *The Janus Faces of Genius: The Role of Alchemy in Newton's Thought* (Cambridge & New York: Cambridge University Press, 1991);

James E. Faulconer, "Newton, Science, and Causation," *Journal of Mind and Behavior,* 16 (Winter 1995): 77–86;

John Fauvel and others, eds., *Let Newton Be! A New Perspective on His Life and Works* (Oxford: Oxford University Press, 1988);

Vincenzo Ferrone, *The Intellectual Roots of the Italian Enlightenment: Newtonian Science, Religion, and Politics in the Early Eighteenth Century,* translated by Sue Brotherton (Atlantic Highlands, N.J.: Humanities Press, 1995);

James E. Force and Richard H. Popkin, *Essays on the Context, Nature, and Influence of Isaac Newton's Theology* (Dordrecht, Netherlands & Boston: Kluwer, 1990);

Rupert A. Hall, *Isaac Newton: Eighteenth-Century Perspectives* (New York: Oxford University Press, 1998);

John Harrison, *The Library of Isaac Newton* (Cambridge: Cambridge University Press, 1978);

Robert H. Hurlbutt, *Hume, Newton, and the Design Argument,* revised edition (Lincoln & London: University of Nebraska Press, 1985);

Margaret C. Jacob, *The Newtonians and the English Revolution, 1689–1720* (Ithaca, N.Y.: Cornell University Press, 1976);

L. W. Johnson and M. L. Wolbarsht, "Mercury Poisoning: A Probable Cause of Isaac Newton's Physical and Mental Ills," *Notes and Records of the Royal Society,* 34 (1979): 1–9;

John Maynard Keynes, "Newton the Man," in *Newton Tercentenary Celebrations: At the Anniversary Meeting of the Royal Society, 30 November 1942* (Cambridge: Cambridge University Press, 1943), pp. 27–34;

Thomas H. Leahey, "Waiting for Newton," *Journal of Mind and Behavior,* 16 (Winter 1995): 9–19;

E. F. MacPike, *Hevelius, Flamsteed, and Halley: Three Contemporary Astronomers and Their Mutual Relations* (London: Taylor & Francis, 1937);

Frank E. Manuel, *Isaac Newton, Historian* (Cambridge, Mass.: Harvard University Press, 1963);

Manuel, *The Religion of Isaac Newton: The Fremantle Lectures, 1973* (Oxford: Clarendon Press, 1974);

Ernan McMullin, *Newton on Matter and Activity* (Notre Dame, Ind.: University of Notre Dame Press, 1978);

Robert K. Merton, *On the Shoulders of Giants: A Shandean Postscript* (New York: Free Press, 1965);

John D. Norton, "The Force of Newtonian Cosmology: Acceleration Is Relative," *Philosophy of Science,* 62 (December 1995): 511–522;

Henry Pemberton, *A View of Sir Isaac Newton's Philosophy* (London: Printed by S. Palmer, 1728);

Michael John Petry, ed., *Hegel and Newtonianism* (Dordrecht, Netherlands & London: Kluwer, 1993);

G. A. J. Rogers, "Locke, Newton, and the Cambridge Platonists on Innate Ideas," *Journal of the History of Ideas,* 40 (April–June 1979): 191–205;

A. I. Sabra, *Theories of Light from Descartes to Newton* (London: Oldbourne, 1967);

Paul Salstrom, "Vico, Newton, and Leibnitz: The Frustration of the Goals of Three Contemporaries," *Journal of the West Virginia Philosophical Society,* 16 (Spring 1979): 17–18;

Alan E. Shapiro, *Fits, Passions, and Paroxysms: Physics, Method, and Chemistry and Newton's Theories of Colored Bodies and Fits of Easy Reflection* (Cambridge & New York: Cambridge University Press, 1993);

P. E. Spargo and C. A. Pounds, "Newton's 'Derangement of Intellect': New Light on an Old Problem," *Notes and Records of the Royal Society of London,* 43 (July 1979): 11–32;

Joseph Spence, *Anecdotes, Observations, and Characters of Books and Men Collected from the Conversations of Mr. Pope, and Other Eminent Persons of His Time,* edited by Edmond Malone (London: Murray, 1820);

Gordon L. Stiles, "The 'Genius' of Einstein versus a Simple Problem Reflecting Newtonian Laws of Motion," *Explorations in Knowledge,* 11 (1994): 1–11;

H. W. Turnbull, *The Mathematical Discoveries of Isaac Newton* (London: Blackie, 1945);

Edmund Turnor, *Collections for the History of the Town and Soke of Grantham, containing authentic Memoirs of Sir Isaac Newton, now first published from the original MSS.*

in the possession of the Earl of Portsmouth (London: Bulwer, 1806);

Voltaire, *Elements de la Philosophie de Newton,* translated and edited by Robert L. Walters and William Henry Barber (Oxford: Voltaire Foundation, Taylor Institution, 1992);

Richard S. Westfall, *Force in Newton's Physics* (London: MacDonald, 1971);

Westfall, "Newton and the Hermetic Tradition," in *Science, Medicine, and Society,* volume 2, edited by A. G. Debus (New York: Science History Publications, 1972), pp. 183–198;

Westfall and I. Bernard Cohen, eds., *Newton: Texts, Backgrounds, Commentaries* (New York: Norton, 1995).

Papers:

Sir Isaac Newton materials are in collections around the world. John Maynard Keynes preserved much of this material for the library of King's College, Cambridge. More than one thousand folios are kept in the Bodleian Library, Oxford, including the Chemical Notebook from the period 1667–1668. The Pierpont Morgan Library, New York, has the "Notebook of Sir Isaac Newton." The Trinity Notebook and most of what remains of Newton's libraries are at the Trinity College Library, Cambridge. University Library, Cambridge, holds the Portsmouth Collection. The Alchemical Notebook and other important manuscripts and papers are at the Jewish National and University Library, Jerusalem.

John Norris

(2 January 1657 – ?3 February 1712)

Melvyn New
University of Florida

BOOKS: Ἀποδοκιμασίας ἀποδοκιμασία, *sive, Tractatus adversus reprobationis absolutæ decretum. Novâ methodo et succinctissimo compendio adornatus et in duos libros digestus* (London: Sold by James Norris, 1683);

An Idea of Happiness, in a Letter to a Friend: Enquiring Wherein the Greatest Happiness Attainable by Man in this Life Does Consist (London: Printed for James Norris, 1683);

A Murnival of Knaves; or, Whiggism Plainly Display'd, and (if not grown shameless) Burlesqu't Out of Countenance, as Philanax (London: Printed for James Norris, 1683);

Poems and Discourses Occasionally Written (London: Printed by John Harefinch for James Norris, 1684); enlarged as *A Collection of Miscellanies: Consisting of Poems, Essays, Discourses, and Letters, Occasionally Written* (Oxford: Printed at the Theater for John Crosley, 1687; revised edition, London: Printed for John Crosley & Samuel Manship, 1692; revised edition, London: Printed for Samuel Manship & sold by Percivall Gilbourne, 1699; revised edition, London: Printed for Samuel Manship, 1704; revised, 1706; revised, 1710);

A *Sermon Preach'd before the University of Oxford at St. Peters Church in the East on Mid-Lent Sunday, March 29, 1685* (Oxford: Printed by Leonard Lichfield for Thomas Fickus, 1685);

The Theory and Regulation of Love. A Moral Essay, in Two Parts; To Which Are Added, Letters Philosophical and Moral, Between the Author and Dʳ Henry More (Oxford: Printed at the Theatre for Henry Clements, 1688);

Reason and Religion: Or, The Grounds and Measures of Devotion, Consider'd from the Nature of God, and the Nature of Man, in Several Contemplations. With Exercises of Devotion Applied to Every Contemplation (London: Printed for Samuel Manship, 1689);

Reflections Upon the Conduct of Human Life, With Reference to the Study of Learning and Knowledge. In a Letter to the Excellent Lady, the Lady Masham. To Which Is Annex'd, a Visitation Sermon (London: Printed for Samuel Manship, 1690; enlarged, 1691);

Christian Blessedness; or Discourses Upon the Beatitudes of our Lord and Saviour Jesus Christ; to which are added, Reflections upon a Late Essay Concerning Human Understanding (London: Printed for Samuel Manship, 1690); enlarged as *Christian Blessedness; or Discourses Upon the Beatitudes of our Lord and Saviour Jesus Christ; to which are added, Reflections upon a Late Essay Concerning Human Understanding: With a Reply to the Remarques made upon them by the Athenian Society* (London: Printed for Samuel Manship, 1692); republished as *Practical Discourses upon the Beatitudes of our Lord and Saviour Jesus Christ; to which are added, Reflections upon a late Essay concerning Human Understanding: With a Reply to the Remarques made upon them by the Athenian Society* (London: Printed for Samuel Manship, 1694);

The Charge of Schism Continued: Being a Justification of the Author of Christian Blessedness for his Charging the Separatists with Schism, notwithstanding the Toleration. In a Letter to a City-Friend (London: Printed for Samuel Manship, 1691; revised, 1703);

Practical Discourses Upon Several Divine Subjects: Volume Two (London: Printed for Samuel Manship, 1691);

The Grossness of the Quaker's Principle of the Light Within: With Their Inconsistency in Explaining It. Discours'd in a Letter to a Friend (London: Printed for Samuel Manship, 1692);

Two Treatises Concerning the Divine Light: The First, Being an Answer to a Letter of a Learned Quaker, Which He Is Pleased to Call, A Just Reprehension to John Norris for His Unjust Reflections on the Quakers, in His Book Entituled, Reflections upon the Conduct of Human Life, &c. The Second, Being a Discourse Concerning the Grossness of the Quakers Notion of the Light Within, with Their Confusion and Inconsistency in Explaining it (London: Printed for Samuel Manship, 1692);

Practical Discourses Upon Several Divine Subjects: Volume Three (London: Printed for Samuel Manship, 1693);

Spiritual Counsel, or, The Father's Advice to His Children (London: Printed for S. Manship, 1694);

Letters Concerning the Love of God, Between the Author of the Proposal to the Ladies and Mr. John Norris. Wherein his late Discourse, shewing That it ought to be intire and exclusive of all other Loves, is further cleared and justified, by Norris and Mary Astell (London: Printed for Samuel Manship, 1695; revised and enlarged edition, London: Printed for Samuel Manship & Richard Wilkin, 1705);

An Account of Reason and Faith: in Relation to the Mysteries of Christianity (London: Printed for Samuel Manship, 1697);

Practical Discourses Upon Several Divine Subjects: Volume Four (London: Printed for Samuel Manship, 1698);

An Essay Towards the Theory of the Ideal or Intelligible World. Design'd for Two Parts. The First Considering It Absolutely in It Self, and the Second in Relation to Human Understanding, 2 volumes (London: Printed for Samuel Manship & William Hawes, 1701, 1704);

Of Religious Discourse in Common Conversation: In Three Parts (London: Printed for Samuel Manship, 1701);

A Practical Treatise Concerning Humility. Design'd for the Furtherance and Improvement of that Great Christian Vertue Both in the Minds and Lives of Men (London: Printed for Samuel Manship, 1707);

A Philosophical Discourse Concerning the Natural Immortality of the Soul: Wherein the Great Question of the Soul's Immortality Is Endeavour'd to be Rightly Stated and fully Clear'd. Occasion'd by Mr. Dodwell's late Epistolary Discourse. In Two Parts (London: Printed for Samuel Manship, 1708);

A Letter to Mr. Dodwell Concerning the Immortality of the Soul of Man: In Answer to One from Him Relating to the Same Matter, Being a Farther Pursuance of the Philosophical Discourse (London: Printed for Samuel Manship, 1709);

A Treatise Concerning Christian Prudence, or, The Principles of Practical Wisdom: Fitted to Use of Human Life, and Design'd for the Better Regulation of It (London: Printed for Samuel Manship, 1710).

Editions and Collections: *Treatises Upon Several Subjects: Formerly Printed Singly, Now Collected into One Volume* (London: Printed for Samuel Manship, 1697); republished as *Treatises Upon Several Subjects: viz. Reason and Religion, or The Grounds and Measures of Devotion, Reflections upon the Conduct of Human Life, The Charge of Schism Continued, Two Treatises Concerning Divine Light, Spiritual Counsel, or, the Fathers Advice to His Children* (London: Printed for Samuel Manship & John Jones, 1698);

Reflections upon the Conduct of Human Life: With Reference to Learning and Knowledge. Extracted from Mr. Norris, edited by John Wesley (London: London: Printed by William Strahan & sold by Thomas Harris & at the Foundery, near Upper-Moor-Fields, 1741);

A Treatise on Christian Prudence: Extracted from Mr. Norris, edited by Wesley (London: Printed by William Strahan & sold by Thomas Harris, by Thomas Trye & at the Foundery, near Upper-Moor-Fields, 1742);

The Poems of John Norris, of Bemerton: For the First Time Collected and Edited after the Original Texts, edited, with an introduction and notes, by Alexander B. Grosart, Miscellanies of the Fuller Worthies' Library, volume 3 (Blackburn, U.K.: Privately printed, 1871);

Cursory Reflections upon a Book Call'd, An Essay Concerning Human Understanding (1690), edited, with an introduction, by Gilbert D. McEwen, Augustan Reprint Society Publications, no. 93 (Los Angeles: University of California, William Andrews Clark Memorial Library, 1961);

An Essay Towards the Theory of the Ideal or Intelligible World (Hildesheim & New York: Olms, 1974);

Christian Blessedness, 1690 (New York & London: Garland, 1978);

A Collection of Miscellanies, 1687 (New York & London: Garland, 1978);

An Essay Towards the Theory of the Ideal or Intelligible World, 1701–1704, 2 volumes (New York & London: Garland, 1978);

Treatises Upon Several Subjects, 1698 (New York & London: Garland, 1978);

Where's My Memorial: The Religious, Philosophical and Metaphysical Poetry of John Norris of Bemerton, edited by Peter D. E. White (Sidmouth, U.K., P. D. E. White, 1991);

Philosophical and Theological Writings: John Norris, 8 volumes, edited, with an introduction, by Richard Acworth (Bristol: Thoemmes, 2001).

OTHER: Hierocles of Alexandria, *Hierocles upon the Golden Verses of the Pythagoreans. Translated immediately out of the Greek into English*, translated by Norris (London: Printed by Miles Flesher for Thomas Fickus, 1682);

Robert Waring, *Effigies amoris in English; or, The Picture of Love Unveil'd*, translated by Norris, as Phil-icon-erus (London: Printed by Margaret White for James Good, 1682);

John Norris the Elder, *A Discourse concerning the Pretended Religious Assembling in private Conventicles: Wherein the Unlawfullness and Unreasonableness of It Is Fully Evinced by Several Arguments*, edited by Norris (London: Printed for James Norris, 1685);

Xenophon, *Κύρου Παιδεία: or, The Institution and Life of Cyrus the Great. Written by that Famous Philosopher and General, Xenophon of Athens. And from the Original Greek Made English*, translated by Norris and Francis Digby (London: Printed for Matthew Gilliflower & James Norris, 1685.

The only claim to philosophical fame John Norris of Bemerton seems to have is that he was the first English respondent to John Locke's *An Essay concerning Humane Understanding* (1690). To some extent, this lack of reputation is a result of Norris's subordination of his own philosophical thinking to that of the French empirical idealist Nicolas Malebranche (1638–1715). Norris's *An Essay Towards the Theory of the Ideal or Intelligible World* (1701, 1704) is, in fact, so dominated by extensive quotations from Malebranche (and from St. Augustine and St. Thomas Aquinas) that whatever is original in Norris's thinking is all but lost. And to some extent, Norris's eclipse is the result of having chosen the wrong side: the triumph of Locke over René Descartes in eighteenth-century Britain was almost total, and, indeed, one could argue that the very notion of "French philosophy" has hardly yet fully recovered its status across the channel. Locke's *An Essay concerning Humane Understanding* went through more than twenty editions by the end of the century; Norris's *An Essay Towards the Theory of the Ideal or Intelligible World* was not republished until the twentieth century. Indeed, when philosophical idealism was revived in the latter half of the eighteenth century, the revivers found its sources in German rather than French mysticism and, excepting Samuel Taylor Coleridge, in the writings of the classical Neoplatonists rather than among those of the Cambridge Platonists, of whom Norris is usually considered the last representative.

Yet, it is possible to make a case for reading Norris's works in the twenty-first century: first, because many of his writings remained popular for decades after his death and appear to have influenced such significant figures as the philosophers Arthur Collier and George Berkeley, the poets James Thomson and Isaac Watts, the theologians William Law and John Wesley, and the novelists Samuel Richardson and Laurence Sterne; and second, because contemporary philosophy is now marked by the reemergence of ethics as "first philosophy," a priority with which Norris would have agreed: *"we cannot do better Service to Religion, than by resolving the Practical Duties of it* [ethics] *into Principles of Philosophy, or make a better use of Philosophick Notions, than to employ them in the Service, and for the interest of Religion,"* he writes in the dedicatory epistle to *Practical Discourses Upon Several Divine Subjects: Volume Three* (1693).

John Norris was born in Collingbourne-Kingston, Wiltshire, on 2 January 1657, the third surviving child of John and Elizabeth Norris. When Charles II was restored to the throne three years later, Norris's father was ousted from his position as vicar of the parish. That the elder Norris was not, however, a devoted Commonwealth man is indicated by his being awarded shortly afterward the vicarage of Aldbourne in the same Salisbury diocese, where he resided until his death in 1682. The son entered Winchester College in 1670 and Exeter College, Oxford in 1676. After receiving the bachelor of arts degree in 1680, he stayed on at Oxford as a fellow of All Souls, spending almost the entire decade in study and writing, though he

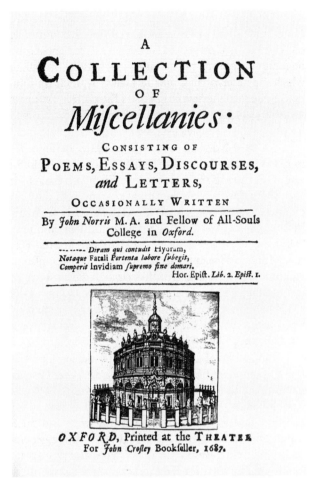

A

COLLECTION

OF

Miscellanies:

CONSISTING OF

POEMS, ESSAYS, DISCOURSES,

and LETTERS,

OCCASIONALLY WRITTEN

By *John Norris* M.A. and Fellow of All-Souls College in *Oxford.*

------ *Diram qui contudit* Hydram,
Notaque Fatali Portenta labore subegit,
Comperit Invidiam *supremo fine domari.*
Hor. Epist. *Lib.* 2. *Epist.* 1.

OXFORD, Printed at the THEATER
For *John Crosley* Bookseller, 1687.

Title page for John Norris's most popular work, an enlarged version of his 1684 collection Poems and Discourses Occasionally Written *(Beinecke Library, Yale University)*

took time out in 1684 to receive ordination in the Church of England.

His publications during this period include *The Theory and Regulation of Love. A Moral Essay, in Two Parts; To Which Are Added, Letters Philosophical and Moral, Between the Author and Dr Henry More* (1688), which includes his 1685–1686 correspondence with the poet and philosopher of religion Henry More, and *Reason and Religion: Or, The Grounds and Measures of Devotion, Consider'd from the Nature of God, and the Nature of Man, in Several Contemplations. With Exercises of Devotion Applied to Every Contemplation* (1689). His most popular work, however, was *A Collection of Miscellanies: Consisting of Poems, Essays, Discourses, and Letters, Occasionally Written* (1687), an amplified version of his *Poems and Discourses Occasionally Written* (1684), which includes the poetry on which his slight but secure reputation as a late metaphysical poet is established, as well as essays on a wide range of subjects, from the "Demonstration of God" to the "Advantages of Thinking," from "Contemplation and

Love" to the "True Notion of Plato's Ideas and Platonic Love." One could make a strong argument that almost all of Norris's later philosophical themes, with their strong tinge of Platonism, are adumbrated in this collection, which the anonymous editor of *Letters Written by Eminent Persons in the Seventeenth and Eighteenth Centuries* went through at least nine editions by 1730 and which noted was "still read and applauded."

In 1689 Norris surrendered his fellowship in order to marry and accepted a position as rector of Newton St. Loe in Somerset. He and his wife, Elizabeth, had three sons and a daughter. In the spring of 1692, with the help of Locke and mutual friends, including Lady Damaris Masham, he was awarded the benefice of Bemerton near Salisbury, where he remained until his death in early February 1712. His life in Bemerton was one of contemplation and writing; he considered his clerical duties a chore because they consumed time he preferred to devote to the retirement necessary—in his view—for the proper study of life, whether considered as philosophy or theology, or a combination of the two.

Norris was abundantly prolific, producing four volumes of sermons: *Christian Blessedness; or Discourses Upon the Beatitudes of our Lord and Saviour Jesus Christ* (1690) was republished as *Practical Discourses upon the Beatitudes of our Lord and Saviour Jesus Christ* (1691); this work and three subsequent volumes (1691, 1693, 1698) with the general title of *Practical Discourses Upon Several Divine Subjects* are commonly referred to as *Practical Discourses*. Norris's response to Locke, *Cursory Reflections upon a book Call'd, An Essay Concerning Human Understanding*, was published bound with the first volume of *Practical Discourses*, though it had separate pagination and a separate title page. Another sermon was published with a popular discourse on education, *Reflections Upon the Conduct of Human Life, With Reference to the Study of Learning and Knowledge. In a Letter to the Excellent Lady, the Lady Masham. To Which Is Annex'd, a Visitation Sermon* (1690; enlarged, 1691). An exchange with Mary Astell, one of several educated women with whom he regularly corresponded, was published as *Letters Concerning the Love of God Between the Author of the Proposal to the Ladies and Mr. John Norris. Wherein his late Discourse, shewing That it ought to be intire and exclusive of all other Loves, is further Cleared and Justified* (1695). A second edition, with revisions by both Astell and Norris, was published in 1705. *An Account of Reason and Faith in Relation to the Mysteries of Christianity* (1697) constitutes Norris's contribution to the public debate about the credibility of the mysteries of Christianity that had been prompted by John Toland's publication of *Christianity not Mysterious* (1696). Norris also published another collection of miscellaneous essays, *Treatises Upon Several Subjects: Formerly Printed Singly, Now Collected into One Volume* (1697), which comprises several previously published tracts, including *Spiritual Counsel, or, The Father's Advice to His Children* (1694), bound together with a cancel title page; and, in 1701, volume 1 of his philosophical magnum opus, *An Essay Towards the Theory of the Ideal or Intelligible World;* volume 2 appeared in 1704.

Subsequent writings include two volumes of a projected series on the Christian virtues, *A Practical Treatise Concerning Humility. Design'd for the Furtherance and Improvement of that Great Christian Vertue* (1707) and *A Treatise Concerning Christian Prudence, or, The Principles of Practical Wisdom: Fitted to Use of Human Life, and Design'd for the Better Regulation of It* (1710). Norris also ventured into the "pamphlet war" about the mortality or immortality of the soul, weighing in with the judicious *A Philosophical Discourse Concerning the Natural Immortality of the Soul: Wherein the Great Question of the Soul's Immortality Is Endeavour'd to be Rightly Stated and fully Clear'd. Occasion'd by Mr. Dodwell's late Epistolary Discourse. In Two Parts* (1708). When Henry Dodwell, who had been vociferously attacked by such writers as Samuel Clarke for advancing the theory that the soul was naturally mortal, publically thanked Norris for the courteous tone of his objections, Norris replied with *A Letter to Mr. Dodwell Concerning the Immortality of the Soul of Man: In Answer to One from Him Relating to the Same Matter, Being a Farther Pursuance of the Philosophical Discourse* (1709).

Almost everything Norris wrote achieved more popularity than did *An Essay Towards the Theory of the Ideal or Intelligible World*. Given an intellectual community that equated philosophical idealism with Cartesian abstraction and religious enthusiasm, it is perhaps unsurprising that Norris's contemporary reputation as a philosopher is probably best represented by the title of Thomas D'Urfey's parodic *An Essay Towards the Theory of the Intelligible World: Intuitively Considered. Designed for Forty-Nine Parts. Part III. Consisting of a Preface, a Postscript, and a Little Something Between. Enriched with a Faithful Account of His Ideal Voyage, and Illustrated with Poems by Several Hands, as Likewise with Other Strange Things Not Insufferably Clever, Nor Furiously to the Purpose* (1705).

The essential difference between Locke and Norris was not epistemological but theological. Locke believed a path to truth could be opened by separating religious belief from philosophical investigation; it is not a coincidence that many arguments of *An Essay concerning Humane Understanding* attempt to distinguish between operations of faith and reason, between enthusiasm and the Holy Spirit. Norris, on the contrary, from the beginning to the end of his career argued that epistemology was theology, that the notion of God gave validity to every other thought, that the necessary and eternal truths (ideas) that make thought possible were in God and could be known only in Him. Hence, Norris's most serious objection to Locke's work was its seeming reduction of ideas to material substances, for this reduction would reduce the idea of God to an object of sense. In that both writers reject innate ideas, the difference in their thought comes down to Locke's confession that it was incomprehensible to him how sense impressions became ideas ("This I can resolve only into the good pleasure of God, whose ways are past finding out," he writes in his 1693 "Examination of P. Malebranche's Opinion of Seeing All Things in God"), and Norris's assertion in *Cursory Reflections upon a book, Call'd An Essay Concerning Human Understanding,* echoing Malebranche, that "we see all things in God": "I account for the Mode of *Human Understanding* . . . by the Presentialness of the Divine λόγος [Logos] or Ideal World to our Souls, wherein we see and perceive all things." Locke, to be sure, found this concept equally incomprehensible, but Norris's argument in "Cursory Reflections" is ontologically coherent: "God himself cannot *make* an Idea of himself: For such an Idea, what-ever it be, must be a Creature; and can a Creature represent God! . . . There is but one possible Idea of God, and that is his *Son,* the Divine λόγος [Logos]. . . . 'Tis he that is the Idea of God, and of the whole Creation, that both *is,* and *represents* all things." Behind Malebranche's and Norris's thought one finds Descartes's meditation on infinity as the necessary ground from which cogito emerges, by no means an irrelevant philosophical idea in the twenty-first century. And as did Descartes, Norris understands God's infinite Mind in relation to the finite and flawed mind of the human being. A strong thread of Cartesian skepticism runs throughout Norris's Platonic Christianity, leaving ample room for revelation and mystery to function where reason necessarily fails. Norris's urge to see philosophy as the handmaiden of theology tends to suggest that *An Essay Towards the Theory of the Ideal or Intelligible World* is an inadequate entry into his thought, even though it consists heavily of extracts from other theologian-philosophers, such as Aquinas, the Spanish Jesuit Francisco Suarez, Malebranche, and Augustine.

Indeed, Norris's excessive borrowing suggests the limitations of this work, and thus the reader may more profitably turn to the first "discourse" in Norris's third volume of *Practical Discourses* for a better understanding of his thoughtful extension of Scholastic and Neoplatonic thought, as Christian enterprises, into the new world created by the writings of Francis Bacon, Thomas Hobbes, Descartes, and Locke. Several other "discourses" would serve almost as well, the important point being that Norris's philosophy ought not be considered apart from his theology; in this respect, he might be said to have more in common with Søren Kierkegaard than with Immanuel Kant, certainly more in common with Jacob Boehme than with Bishop George Berkeley, who was far more successful than Norris in separating philosophical inquiry from clerical discourse.

"A Discourse concerning the Measure of Divine Love, with the Natural and Moral Grounds upon which it Stands" takes for its text one of Norris's favorite biblical

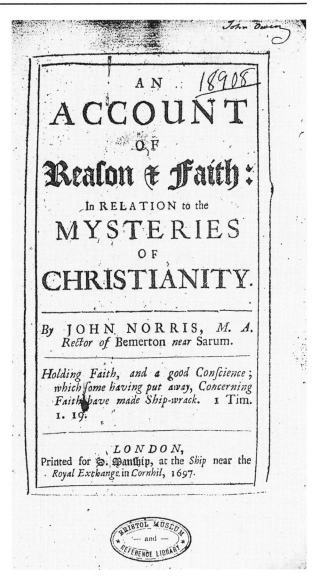

Title page for Norris's reply to John Toland's Christianity Not Mysterious, *published in 1690 (Bristol Public Library)*

passages, Matt. 22:37: "Thou shalt love the Lord thy God with all thy heart, and with all thy soul, and with all thy mind." The injunction seems so obvious that Norris begins by questioning its usefulness:

> why . . . should there be need of any Command to a *Rational* Soul to love *God?* Does not an intelligible Good bear the same proportion to a reasonable Nature, as a sensible Good does to Sense . . . ? Yes certainly, and infinitely more: For these things, tho they are the *proper* Goods of their respective Powers, yet they are not wholly commensurate. . . . God is not only the proper Good of the Soul (as Light is of the Eye) but is withal a Good so transcendently excellent as to be able to fill the whole Capacity of its intellectual Powers. . . . nay, were our Capacity infinite, he would be sufficient to fill it.

In this opening paragraph it is already difficult to separate theology from philosophy, for example, in the dualism inherent in dividing sense from intellect, or in the rational thrust toward commensurability in analogy, or, a third example, in the transcendental countermove, by which God and the Good (the moral character of God) are accessible through the Infinite, defined as the source of all necessary, unchanging, eternal essences, an infinity characterized by an indeterminateness that is not inadequacy but the fullness and perfection of God's mind.

When Norris rejects the usual reading of his text as a command merely to love God before or above the things of this world, he suggests its error is the result of faulty philosophical thinking, whereby it is deemed that "sensible Objects contain in themselves somewhat answerable to what we feel by their Occasion . . . That the Bodies that surround us do really act in and upon us, not only by making impression upon our *Bodies,* and striking upon our Organs of *Sense,* but also by raising and exciting those Sensations our Spirits are conscious of, so as to be the true efficient Causes of our *Pleasure* and our *Pain*." His own argument is different: the text commands that the reader love only God, and no created being; this proposition requires "a Train of Argument and Consequence to make it appear reasonable, and must be proved in a way of Science and Demonstration."

To justify his explication, then, Norris looks for "a proper Ground for it in *Philosophy,*" beginning with God as the "Author or Cause of our Love," defined as the human tendency toward the Good: "this Motion of the Soul is a necessary Adherent to our Beings, such as we were never without, and such as we can never put off." Humans have no power to stop this desire for the Good, an impotence that argues it is an appetite arising not from within them but from God: "Who else could fix such a strong *Spring* in our Souls, and actuate our Beings with such a mighty Energy?" Love, Norris argues, is to the moral and intellectual world what motion is to the natural; but in that love comes from God, he has the sole and complete right to it.

In this argument the reader should recognize the Platonic merging of God and "the Good," so that any suggestion that human "love of the creature" is what God has allowed is to suggest an "effect" unworthy of its "cause." Rather, God is both the "Author" and the "Natural End and Term" of human desire for "the Good," since "he moves us to Good no otherwise, than by moving us towards himself." Once again, Norris's language is a mixture of the old theology and the new science: "We must conclude, that God is the true great *Magnet* of our Souls; that he continually draws and moves them, not from, but to himself, as being both *their,* and his *own* great End." Sin, then, is any motion against this "great Bias of our Natures" toward the Good.

Norris's Christianity requires that he acknowledge this "Bias" rarely directs us, but interestingly, he suggests as a predominant cause a lapse of philosophical reason: human beings lazily believe that their pleasures come from sensible objects, and even though some modern thinkers (Descartes, Locke) now realize that bodies do not have in themselves "something answerable to the Sensations which we feel in the use of them," they still argue that these objects do cause sensations "*Eminently* and *Potentially,* though not *Formally*." Only Malebranche argues differently, and in the middle of his sermonic discourse Norris names his philosophical guide, he who was able to see that "the *Concomitancy* of one thing with another" is not the same as arguing "*Causal Dependance*." His example has become a commonplace of idealistic argumentation: "When you approach the Fire you feel Heat, and when you prick your Hand with a Needle you feel Pain; but as you *do* not therefore fancy any such thing as Pain to be in the Needle, so neither *ought* you to suppose any such thing as Heat to be in the Fire."

Norris acknowledges that the "Reformers of Philosophy" no longer are foolish enough to suggest that bodies have sensations answerable to their own, having "reason'd upon clear and distinct Ideas," but they continue to argue that Bodies do "*cause* and *produce* Sensations in us." His own argument, based on his view that "there is nothing in Bodies but *Motion* and *Figure,*" finds that neither quality is able to produce "a Sensation, a Sentiment of the Mind, a *Thought*": "Is there any Proportion . . . between an Affection of a Body, and a Sentiment of the Soul?" Norris separates completely the motion that is always toward the Good from sensations that may be either pleasure or pain: "That Motion of the Fire which occasions Pleasure, differs only in Degree from that which occasions Pain. Whence it is evident, that these Causes are not in themselves equivalent to their Effects, nor have any Natural Relation to them, but are indifferent to either, as being disproportionate to both." Norris's reliance on the "Order both of *Science* and of *Nature*" makes it impossible for him to conceive of a world in which "any thing may produce any thing, and any thing may follow from any thing." The insistence on proportionality signals here not only the presence of both Newtonian physics and Platonic harmony but also his strong disagreement with the Cartesian notion that God's will determines truth; for Norris, truth exists necessarily and eternally as aspects of the divine intelligibility: truth and God are always one and the same.

If matter cannot produce sensation or thought, how does one explain the feelings that seem to result from the proximity of fire? According to Norris's analysis, what the fire may do to the body is distinct from the sensation felt by the soul: "the Sensation which I feel is not in my Body, but in my Soul, and consequently is not of the Fire's producing, but must be ascribed to some other Cause." Nor will he accept any explanation that depends on the close connection of body with soul because they are two distinct substances. Indeed, in a move that distinguishes his Christian morality from the secular, sentimental morality that began to replace it as the century progressed, Norris denies that there is any natural connection between body and body, soul and soul: "does the pain or grief which another Soul indures . . . affect mine? Is *another's* Pain *mine?*" He goes on to note that one can, in a moral sense, "interest" oneself in another's pain, but then the pain that is "felt" by the soul is one's own.

Although body and soul have no natural connection, they can be connected by a positive law, a law that requires a sensation be produced by the soul on every occasion when fire acts on the body. This law is Malebranche's "Occasionalism," and it proves useful for Norris's argument that positive law is nothing more or less than the will of God: "so then according to this account 'tis *God* that is the true Efficient Cause of that Sensation, either of Pleasure or Pain which we feel at the impression of the Fire." The sensationalist's way of thinking, whereby the fire affects the soul by the mediation of the body, is crossed out by chiasmus: "'tis God that acts upon the Soul by the *Mediation* of the *Fire*." What is perhaps most important for Norris in this sequence is the careless thinking he discovers in the sensationalists, who take the most obvious road, while he, by transcending this "Prejudice of Sense," by a much deeper thought, reaches the truth. Malebranche's famous dictum that "attention is the natural prayer of the soul" dominates all Norris's thinking. To will the direction of all one's intellectual resources to the problem at hand, as guided by the beauty of holiness (grace), is the utmost ethical response possible in a fallen world; sin is, to the contrary, the failure to think through the nature of the world to its origin in the mind of God.

Norris insists again and again on a theocentric universe in which only God can cause feelings or sentiments: "So then 'tis not the Sun that enlightens us, but God by the Sun. . . . The whole matter of the Creation though in continual Motion, is yet as to us, that is, to our Spirits, an idle, dead, unactive thing." Such an argument may well be contrary to common sense, Norris admits, but "if ever Philosophy were a Hand-Maid to Divinity, it is now, as furnishing us with a certain Ground for the most sublime and noble Conclusion in the World, the full, perfect and intire Love of God, which now appears to be . . . demonstrable in a clear and distinct Order of Reasoning." His logic is soritic: one is to love nothing but what is lovable; nothing is lovable but what is good; nothing is good but what gives one pleasure; nothing causes pleasure in one but God; therefore, one is to love nothing but God.

In the remainder of the discourse Norris refines but never wavers from his essential position. Thus, while he admits that "creatures" can be good, having been created

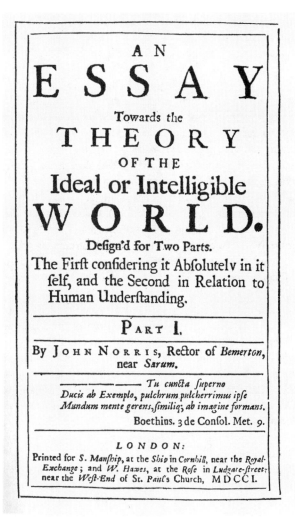

Title page for the first volume of Norris's philosophical magnum opus, in which he claims that human knowledge is dependent on the assistance of God (Beinecke Library, Yale University)

by God who "can make nothing but what is so," they nevertheless cannot be humanity's good, because they are unable to "affect us with so much as one pleasing Sentiment, . . . one real degree of Happiness." But above all, he demonstrates how his philosophy is coincident with one scriptural verse after another, citing Mark 10:18, "Why callest thou me good? *there is* none good but one, *that is,* God"; Ps. 4:7, "Thou hast put gladness in my heart"; and Matt. 6:24, "No man can serve two masters. . . . " To similar effect, he cites 1 John 2:15, James 4:4, and Gal. 6:14, all of which reject any "love of the World." In doing so, Norris would appear to be rebuking the stirrings of any new "Protestant ethic": "there can be no such thing as loving the World with *Moderation*," he argues, "since we ought not to love it at all."

When Richardson wanted his character Anna Howe to send some money privately to her friend, the oppressed eponymous heroine of *Clarissa; or, The History of a Young Lady: Comprehending the Most Important Concerns of Private Life* (seven volumes, 1747–1748), he had her slip the notes into a copy of "Norris's *Miscellanies*"; when Thomson wanted to write about happiness, he borrowed from the same work; and when Sterne wanted to discuss the relationship of body and soul, or the nature of Heaven, he incorporated verbatim passages from Norris's *Practical Discourses* into his *The Life and Opinions of Tristram Shandy, Gentleman* (nine volumes, 1759–1767) and *A Sentimental Journey through France and Italy, by Mr. Yorick* (two volumes, 1768). The modern reader may perhaps find it difficult fully to understand why the popularity of the last Cambridge Platonist endured well into the mid eighteenth century, but John Norris seems to have captured certain profound ambiguities of his age better than many of his philosophical contemporaries. Thus, while they were busily separating philosophy from theology, he was, in every essay and book he wrote, arguing for a new unity: "you may see what noble Divinity may be dug up out of the Mines of Philosophy, and how necessary it is to have a right System of Nature in order to the thorough Comprehension of *Christian Morality*, which has its Bottom and Foundation in the Nature of things, and is accordingly as capable of Demonstration as any Theorem in that Science, whose Character is *Evidence* and *Certainty*."

References:

Richard Acworth, "Malebranche and his Heirs," *Journal of the History of Ideas,* 38 (1977): 673–676;

Acworth, *The Philosophy of John Norris of Bemerton 1657–1712* (Hildesheim & New York: Olms, 1979);

John C. English, "John Wesley's Indebtedness to John Norris," *Church History,* 60 (1991): 55–69;

Patrick Grant, *Images and Ideas in Literature of the English Renaissance* (Amherst: University of Massachusetts Press, 1979);

John Hoyles, *The Waning of the Renaissance, 1640–1740: Studies in the Thought and Poetry of Henry More, John Norris and Isaac Watts* (The Hague: Martinus Nijhoff, 1971);

Charlotte Johnston, "Locke's *Examination of Malebranche* and John Norris," *Journal of the History of Ideas,* 19 (1958): 551–558;

Aharon Lichtenstein, *Henry More: The Rational Theology of a Cambridge Platonist* (Cambridge, Mass.: Harvard University Press, 1962);

Flora Isabel MacKinnon, *The Philosophy of John Norris of Bemerton,* Psychological Review Publications: The Philosophical Monographs, volume 1, no. 2 (Baltimore: The Review Publishing Company, 1910);

Charles J. McCracken, *Malebranche and British Philosophy* (Oxford: Clarendon Press / New York: Oxford University Press, 1983);

John H. Muirhead, *The Platonic Tradition in Anglo-Saxon Philosophy: Studies in the History of Idealism in England and America* (London: Allen & Unwin / New York: Macmillan, 1931);

Melvyn New, "The Odd Couple: Laurence Sterne and John Norris of Bemerton," *Philological Quarterly,* 75 (1996): 361–390;

Frederick James Powicke, *A Dissertation on John Norris of Bemerton* (London: George Philip, 1893);

John K. Ryan, "John Norris: A Seventeenth-Century English Thomist," *New Scholasticism,* 14 (1940): 109–145;

Garry Sherbert, *Menippean Satire and the Poetics of Wit: Ideologies of Self-Consciousness in Dunton, D'Urfey, and Sterne* (New York: Peter Lang, 1996);

Derek Taylor, "Clarissa Harlowe, Mary Astell, and Elizabeth Carter: John Norris of Bemerton's Female Descendants,'" *Eighteenth-Century Fiction,* 12 (1999): 19–38.

William Paley

(July 1743 – 25 May 1805)

Frederick Ferré
University of Georgia

BOOKS: *A Defence of the Considerations on the Propriety of Requiring a Subscription to Articles of Faith, in Reply to a Late Answer from the Clarendon Press,* as "A Friend of Religious Liberty" (London: Printed for J. Wilkie, 1774);

Caution Recommended on the Use and Application of Scripture Language (London: Printed for R. Faulder, 1777; Cambridge, Mass.: Printed by J. Archdeacon for T. & J. Merrill, 1777);

Advice Addressed to the Young Clergy of the Diocese of Carlisle, in a Sermon Preached at a General Ordination, Holden at Rose-Castle, on Sunday July 29th, 1781 (London: Printed & sold by R. Faulder & T. Merril, Cambridge, 1781);

A Distinction of Orders in the Church Defended upon Principles of Public Utility: in a Sermon Preached in the Castle-Chapel, Dublin, at the Consecration of John Law, D.D. Lord Bishop of Clonfert and Kilmacduagh, September 21, 1782 (London: Printed for R. Faulder, 1782);

The Principles of Moral and Political Philosophy (London: Printed for R. Faulder, 1785; Philadelphia: Printed for Thomas Dobson, 1788);

Horae Paulinae; or, The Truth of the Scripture History of St. Paul Evinced, by a Comparison of the Epistles Which Bear His Name with the Acts of the Apostles, and with One Another (London: Printed by J. Davis for R. Faulder, 1790; Cambridge, Mass.: Printed & sold by W. Hilliard, 1806);

The Use and Propriety of Local and Occasional Preaching: A Charge Delivered to the Diocese of Carlisle, in the Year 1790 (London: R. Faulder, 1790);

Reasons for Contentment; Addressed to the Labouring Part of the British Public (Carlisle, U.K., 1792);

A View of the Evidences of Christianity (3 volumes, London: Printed for R. Faulder, 1794; 1 volume, Boston: Printed by Manning & Loring for S. Hall and others, 1795; Philadelphia: Thomas Dobson, 1795);

Dangers Incidental to the Clerical Character: Stated, in a Sermon, Preached Before the University of Cambridge, at Great St. Mary's Church, on Sunday July 5th, Being

William Paley (from The Works of William Paley, D.D., Archbishop of Carlisle, *1850)*

Commencement Sunday (London: Printed for R. Faulder, 1795);

A Sermon, Preached at the Assizes at Durham July 29th, 1795 (London: Printed for R. Faulder, 1795);

A Short Memoir of the Life of Edmund Law, D.D. Bishop of Carlisle. . . . Extracted from Hutchinson's 'History of Cumberland' (London: Printed by Davis, Taylor & Wilks, 1800);

Natural Theology; or, Evidences of the Existence and Attributes of the Deity, Collected from the Appearances of Nature (London: Printed for R. Faulder by Wilks & Taylor, 1802; Philadelphia: Printed for John Morgan by H. Maxwell, 1802);

Sermons, on Several Subjects (London: Longman, Hurst, Rees & Orme, 1808; Philadelphia: Printed by Fry & Kammerer for Hopkins & Earle, 1808);

Sermons and Tracts (London: R. Faulder, 1808).

Editions and Collections: *The Works of William Paley; with a Life by Alexander Chalmers,* 5 volumes (London: Printed for F. C. & J. Rivington, 1819);

The Works of William Paley, D.D., with a Biographical Sketch of the Author, by the Rev. D. S. Wayland, 2 volumes (Derby: H. Mozley, 1825);

The Complete Works of William Paley. With Extracts from His Correspondence: and a Life of the Author by the Rev. Robert Lynam, 4 volumes (London: Printed by J. F. Dove for G. Cowie, 1825);

The Works of William Paley, D.D., edited by Edmund Paley, 7 volumes (London: C. & J. Rivington, 1825);

The Works of William Paley, D.D., Archdeacon of Carlisle; Comprising the Additional Volume of Sermons First Published in 1825. With a Memoir of His Life, 6 volumes (Cambridge: Hilliard & Brown, 1830);

The Works of William Paley, D.D., Archbishop of Carlisle (Philadelphia: Crissy & Markley, 1850);

Natural Theology: Selections, edited, with an introduction, by Frederick Ferré (Indianapolis & New York: Bobbs-Merrill, 1963).

OTHER: "Observations on the Character and Example of Christ, and an Appendix on the Morality of the Gospel," in *Reflections on the Life and Character of Christ,* by Edmund Law (London: R. Faulder, 1776);

The Clergyman's Companion, in Visiting the Sick, compiled by Paley (London: Printed for R. Faulder, 1805; Philadelphia: M. Carey, 1818);

The Young Christian Instructed in Reading and in the Principles of Religion. Compiled for the use of the Sunday Schools in Carlisle, compiled by Paley (Carlisle, 1790; Andover, Mass.: Published by Mark Newman, 1819).

William Paley was born in Peterborough, Northamptonshire, England, in July 1743 and baptized in the cathedral there 30 August 1743. He was the only son of William and Elizabeth Clapham Paley, who subsequently had three daughters. Paley's father had been educated at Christ's College, Cambridge, and at the time of his son's birth he was a minor canon of the cathedral church at Peterborough. Two years later, the elder William Paley was appointed headmaster of the Giggleswick Free Grammar School in the Yorkshire parish where the Paley family had held a small estate for several generations.

Young William Paley was educated at the Giggleswick school, where he was known not only for his considerable scholastic aptitude but also for his physical awkwardness. By the time he was fifteen, he had risen to the top of the school, and in November 1758 the elder Paley took his son to Cambridge, where he applied and was accepted for admission to Christ's College the following autumn. He fell off his horse seven times on this trip, and later enjoyed making fun of his horsemanship: "I was lighter then than I am now, and my falls were not likely to be serious; –My father, on hearing a thump, would turn his head half aside, and say, 'Take care of thy money, lad.'"

Paley entered Christ's College in October 1759, and in December he received two scholarships, one from an endowment devoted to the support of students from the Giggleswick school and the other from Christ's College. Though he liked to sleep late and frequent after-dinner coffeehouses, Paley was a good student. When he took his bachelor's degree in January 1763, he emerged senior wrangler (that is, first among the best debaters in the college).

On leaving Cambridge, Paley accepted a position as second assistant tutor at the Greenwich Academy, teaching Latin to youths anticipating careers in the army or navy. He maintained his connections with Cambridge, submitting a Latin dissertation in defense of Epicurean ethics to an annual competition for Latin prose in 1765 and winning first prize despite a controversy caused because the notes he attached were in English rather than Latin. At about the same time, he was ordained deacon and became curate to the vicar of Greenwich, John Hinchliffe. Paley continued in this role even after resigning in protest from the Greenwich Academy over what he considered to be the unfair distribution of gift funds sent by parents for the assistants.

In June 1766 Paley was elected a fellow of Christ's College and returned to Cambridge. He acquired his master's degree in 1767 and the same year was ordained a priest in a ceremony held on 21 December at St. James Chapel, London. In 1768 he was hired as a junior tutor at Christ's Church, where he divided duties and began an important lifelong friendship with John Law, son of the distinguished Dr. Edmund Law, who in 1768 became bishop of Carlisle. Paley taught metaphysics, morals, and Greek New Testament, while John Law covered mathematics and "natural philosophy" (the sciences). The residence at Cambridge University was a happy one, with Paley's and Law's lectures drawing much renown to Christ's College. Paley was particularly admired for his lectures on John Locke, Samuel Clarke, and Joseph Butler and for a set of lectures on ethics. He was organized and clear, finding ways to avoid bogging down in the doctrinal disputes that were rife at the time.

In January 1774 Bishop Edmund Law published an anonymous pamphlet, *Considerations on the Propriety of Requiring a Subscription to Articles of Faith,* a moderate expression of concern about imposing new requirements in religious matters. It was strongly attacked by another anonymous pamphlet, *An Answer to the Considerations,* published in May 1774 by Dr. Thomas Randolph, president of Corpus Christi College, Oxford. In June came a third contribution to the pamphlet war, *A Defence of the Considerations on the Propriety of Requiring a Subscription to Articles of Faith, in Reply to a Late Answer from the Clarendon Press,* whose dialectical skills and sharpness of argument were widely admired. The author was Paley, who had signed himself "A Friend of Religious Liberty" but whose characteristic style was hard to conceal. The pamphlet earned him powerful enemies as well as the lasting gratitude of Bishop Law and his son.

In 1774 Bishop Law gave his son ecclesiastical appointments in Carlisle and elsewhere, and the following year the bishop gave Paley a similar appointment to the rectory of Musgrove in Westmoreland. Later in the same year Paley met and became engaged to Jane Hewitt of Carlisle. In May 1776 he resigned from Christ's College, and on 6 June he and Hewitt were married in Carlisle by their friend John Law.

In December 1776 Paley was given an additional appointment, the vicarage at Dalston, and the following September he was given the still-more-valuable vicarage of Appleby and resigned from Musgrove. The Paleys began dividing their residential year between Dalston and Appleby, spending six months at each parish for the next five years.

During that period Paley produced various minor works. One was "Observations on the Character and Example of Christ, and an Appendix on the Morality of the Gospel," which was published as an addendum to the 1776 edition of Bishop Law's *Reflections on the Life and Character of Christ.* This addendum is interesting primarily because it shows that Paley had not yet worked out his own theory of ethics, which he published in his first full-length book nine years later. Another minor work, based on a visitation sermon preached at Carlisle in July 1777, is *Caution Recommended on the Use and Application of Scripture Language,* which warns against carelessly taking biblical expressions or concepts out of their historical context—a stricture that anticipates one of the fundamental principles underlying modern biblical criticism. A third minor work of this period was a manual, *The Clergyman's Companion, in Visiting the Sick* (1777), which was

initially published anonymously in Carlisle and went through five subsequent London editions before Paley's name appeared on the title page. The manual is a practical and unoriginal compilation of bedside prayers, scriptural passages, and methods to use in talking to sick people and their families.

A new and important phase in Paley's career began in August 1782, when he was installed archdeacon of Carlisle. The position was a sinecure, requiring little or no attention, and it brought with it a prebendal house in Carlisle and a good income. Paley resigned from Appleby and thenceforth divided his residential year between Carlisle and Dalston, becoming chancellor at Carlisle in 1785. Paley's first publication after becoming archdeacon was a version of a sermon he preached in Dublin at the consecration of his friend John Law as Bishop of Clonfert and Kilmacduagh in Ireland. This sermon, *A Distinction of Orders in the Church Defended upon Principles of Public Utility: in a Sermon Preached in the Castle-Chapel, Dublin, at the Consecration of John Law, D.D. Lord Bishop of Clonfert and Kilmacduagh, September 21, 1782,* shows that by this time Paley had arrived at the essential elements of his ethical theories, which became known as Utilitarian.

During 1783 and 1784–free from many distractions or duties and reminded by his friends of his earlier successes as lecturer in moral philosophy at Cambridge–Paley wrote one of the most popular and significant ethics books of his era, *The Principles of Moral and Political Philosophy* (1785). It went through seventeen London editions by 1809, eleven American editions by 1825, and reappeared in many abridged editions, versions with commentary, and even a catechetical form, produced at Cambridge University in 1824. On its appearance the book was immediately adopted as a standard text at Cambridge. Its popularity stimulated the philosopher Jeremy Bentham, who is often considered the founder of Utilitarianism, to publish his own *Introduction to the Principles of Morals and Legislation* in 1789.

The enthusiastic reception given Paley's *The Principles of Moral and Political Philosophy* owed much to the clear organization, lucid style, and down-to-earth examples through which Paley conveyed his unapologetic adoption of human happiness as the fundamental good. The applicability of Paley's ethical system to daily life and its synthesis of commonsense ethical reflections with Christian theological doctrine also contributed to its popularity. Paley wrote in his preface about his experience at Cambridge, in which (like every good teacher) he found it necessary to make problems gripping to his students before he could interest them in solutions. He carried over this lesson into his book. For example, he wrote provocatively

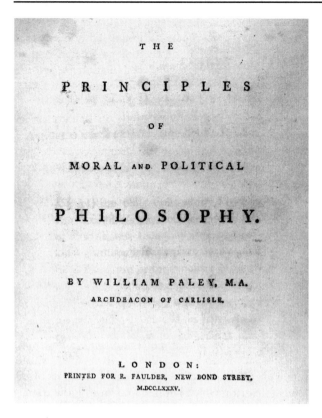

THE

PRINCIPLES

OF

MORAL AND POLITICAL

PHILOSOPHY.

BY WILLIAM PALEY, M.A.
ARCHDEACON OF CARLISLE.

LONDON:
PRINTED FOR R. FAULDER, NEW BOND STREET.
M.DCC.LXXXV.

*Title page for the work in which Paley asserts that happiness
is the fundamental human good (courtesy of
The Lilly Library, Indiana University)*

about private property, illustrating ownership by a flock of pigeons meekly hoarding grain for the benefit of one of their number, perhaps the weakest and worst, and pecking mindlessly at any bold "robber" pigeon who might try to take any away. This particular example outraged many wealthy property holders; even his friend John Law warned him that it might cost him a bishop's miter (which Paley never did attain); and forever after Paley was humorously known as "Pigeon Paley." Yet, the pigeon story vividly illustrates the pedagogical problem: why should an absurd institution be preserved and defended by rational people? Paley's answer was couched in terms of general utility (or happiness); to prove his point he argued at length that, despite first appearances, the institution of private property is supportive of human happiness in the long run and on the whole.

Paley's version of Utilitarianism became known as Rule Utilitarianism. He defended the sacrifice of short-term particular happiness for the sake of maintaining rules of conduct that are demonstrably conducive to long-term, general happiness. Furthermore, it is Theological Rule Utilitarianism, because he defined *virtue* as "the doing good to mankind, in obe-

dience to the will of God, and for the sake of everlasting happiness." In the end, he believed, there was no conflict between the human motive of seeking happiness and the divine will that people should be happy. As he put it, the "good of mankind" is the subject of virtue, the "will of God" is the rule of virtue, and "everlasting happiness is the motive of virtue." With these principles, Paley was able to deal with the whole range of moral questions that exercised his age–from slavery to suicide and dueling to divorce–in a humane and commonsense way that attracted an immense response.

The book was initially offered for £300 to Faulder's of Bond Street, London, which had earlier published some of Paley's sermons, but Robert Faulder would not budge beyond paying £250. Another London publisher, on Paternoster Row, heard about the manuscript and communicated to Paley, through a Carlisle bookseller, a readiness to offer £1,000. When Paley heard this news, he wrote immediately to Bishop John Law, who was in London at the time handling the negotiations for the book. "Never did I suffer so much anxious fear," Paley later told his close companion, G. W. Meadley, "as on this occasion, lest my friend should have concluded the bargain with Mr. Faulder, before my letter could reach him." The letter reached Law in time, and Faulder capitulated, paying the elated Paley £1,000 for the right to publish what turned out to be one of the best-sellers of its era.

Paley responded to Bishop Edmund Law's death (which occurred in 1787) by writing a short memoir of Bishop Law, which was included in William Hutchinson's *History of the County of Cumberland* (1794) and in the third edition of *Encyclopaedia Britannica* (1788–1797) before it was separately published in 1800. In 1788 Paley began to write against the slave trade, putting into political action the principles he had enunciated in his book. These writings have not been preserved. By the time of the first great slavery debate in the House of Commons in 1789, Paley had become a major spokesman for the antislavery movement in Great Britain.

During this time Paley was also at work in his next full-length book. Published in 1790, *Horae Paulinae; or, The Truth of the Scripture History of St. Paul Evinced, by a Comparison of the Epistles Which Bear His Name with the Acts of the Apostles, and with One Another* was the least successful of his four major publications. The book is perhaps the most original of Paley's works, an attempt to show by internal evidence the historical reliability of the Pauline epistles as compared with the Acts of the Apostles. The writing is characteristically clear, the arguments are well laid out, and the topic was of considerable contemporary interest at a time when attacks on the historical truth of Scripture were widespread. Yet, public taste is notoriously unpredictable, and despite its merits, Paley's book did not catch on with the British reading public. It did have scholarly influence, particularly on the Continent, through a 1797 German translation.

In May 1791 Paley's wife of fifteen years died after a long illness. Never a robust woman, Jane Paley had given her husband four sons and four daughters. One year later, in May 1792, Paley was presented a new vicarage, Addingham, near Great Salkeld, and in the following year still another, Stanwix, near Carlisle. During the interval between the death of his wife and his move from Dalston to Stanwix in 1793, Paley entered into various controversies. First came his "Speech on the Abolition of the Slave Trade, Delivered at a Meeting of the Inhabitants of Carlisle, on Thursday, Feb. 9th, 1792." According to newspaper accounts of this speech, Paley refuted, with much force, the various arguments given by slave traders in defense of their activities. After the speech the assembly unanimously adopted a set of ten resolutions urging abolition of the slave trade, which were presented to the House of Commons on 27 February 1792. By this time the French Revolution had created tumult in Britain, stimulating loud voices of reaction and reform. Paley's response was moderate and reasonable. In Carlisle he published a short tract, *Reasons for Contentment; Addressed to the Labouring Part of the British Public* (1792), in which he relied on his principles of utility and his debater's skills in an attempt to persuade his intended audience that they should be happy in their condition. For example, near the end of the essay he argues that working people should not envy the rich who never work because the indolent classes cannot know the special pleasures of resting from hard labor. Also in this vein and in the same year, Paley republished the chapter defending the utility of the British Constitution from his *Principles of Moral and Political Philosophy*. To counter the passions of the times, he pointed out in his advertisement for this excerpt, it is salubrious to reflect on what has been thought in tranquility.

Another controversy involving Paley was carried out with considerable good humor. In the February 1792 issue of *The Gentleman's Magazine* the Reverend Mr. J. Robertson, author of a well-known spelling book, accused Paley of having committed plagiarism by inserting portions of the speller in his *The Young Christian Instructed in Reading and in the Principles of Religion* (1790). Replying in the May 1792 issue of the same magazine, Paley noted that he was only the "compiler," not the author, of *The Young Christian* and admitted that he took some lists of one-syllable

words from Robertson's speller. Pointing out that he had put together his book only for the Sunday schools of Carlisle and that it had brought no commercial benefit to himself or others, Paley argued that there was no real competition between his work and Robertson's and offered to give all rights for *The Young Christian* to Robertson, if he should want anything so inelegant. Paley concluded by offering an apology to Robertson and expressing his "regret, that there should be one column in *The Gentleman's Magazine* which hath no employment more worth of it than to convey to the public, what the public have no concern in, a beggarly dispute about a few pages of a spelling book, by the stealing of which, (for so let it be called), neither the plagiarist hath gained, nor the proprietor lost, a fraction of a farthing."

In May 1793 Paley, nearing fifty, moved to his new residence at Stanwix, where he devoted himself to the preparation of his third major book, *A View of the Evidences of Christianity,* which appeared early in 1794. The book is in three parts: part 1 lays out direct historical evidence, particularly stressing the responses of the early disciples to the miraculous events they had witnessed and the absence of similar miracle stories in other religions. Part 2 presents auxiliary considerations in support of the truth of Christianity, such as prophecy, the morality of the Gospel, the originality of Christ's character, and the coherence of biblical narratives with independent accounts. Part 3 deals in debate style with the refutation of popular objections, such as the discrepancies between the four Gospels, erroneous opinions held by the apostles, or supposed negative effects of Christianity. The book is a major effort of organization and exposition that demonstrates once again Paley's excellent skills as a tactician and expositor, but it is not original. The first two parts are largely reworked from Nathaniel Lardner's massive *The Credibility of the Gospel History* (1741–1762), often called a foundation stone of modern biblical critical research, and the work as a whole is also heavily dependent on Bishop John Douglas's *Letter on the Criterion of Miracles* (1754).

In an age of revolutionists and freethinkers such as Thomas Paine, Paley's impressive defense of the truth of Christianity was warmly welcomed by the leadership of the established Church. For the first time Paley's case was taken up by patrons outside the Carlisle region. Honors and preferments came rapidly. In August 1794 Bishop Beilby Porteus of London appointed him prebendary of St. Pancras in the St. Paul's Cathedral, a post requiring neither duties nor residence in London. In January 1795 Bishop John Pretyman of Lincoln installed Paley as subdean of Lincoln Cathedral, an appointment that required

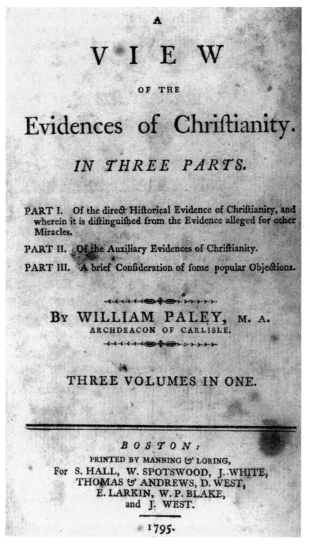

A

VIEW

OF THE

Evidences of Chriftianity.

IN THREE PARTS.

PART I. Of the direct Hiftorical Evidence of Chriftianity, and wherein it is diftinguifhed from the Evidence alleged for other Miracles.

PART II. Of the Auxiliary Evidences of Chriftianity.

PART III. A brief Confideration of fome popular Objections.

By WILLIAM PALEY, M. A.
ARCHDEACON OF CARLISLE.

THREE VOLUMES IN ONE.

BOSTON:
PRINTED BY MANNING & LORING,
For S. HALL, W. SPOTSWOOD, J. WHITE,
THOMAS & ANDREWS, D. WEST,
E. LARKIN, W. P. BLAKE,
and J. WEST.

1795.

Title page for Paley's defense of the truth of Christianity on the basis of historical accounts and internal biblical criticism (courtesy of The Lilly Library, Indiana University)

residence for only the first three months of each year. In March 1795 Bishop Shute Barrington of Durham caused him to be inducted to the wealthy rectory at Bishop-Wearmouth. Deeply gratified, Paley resigned from the positions at Carlisle that required his residence in those environs and moved to Bishop-Wearmouth, where he lived–except for three-month absences to satisfy the residency requirements in Lincoln–for the rest of his life.

In 1795 Paley also achieved his doctor of divinity degree from Cambridge. The only requirements for a man at Paley's career level who had earned a B.A. were sermons in Latin and in English. Paley's Latin sermon occasioned mirth because of his accent, but his English sermon, *Dangers Incidental to the Clerical Character: Stated., in a Sermon, Preached Before the Univer-*

sity of Cambridge, at Great St. Mary's Church, on Sunday July 5th, Being Commencement Sunday (1795), delivered several months later, was well received and later published. In it he warned his fellow clergy against the insensibility that comes from frequent repetition of sacred things and from approaching the religious life as a job rather than a constant source of inspiration.

In December 1795 Paley married a Miss Dobinson of Carlisle, whom he had known for several years. In Bishop-Wearmouth, Paley became a local magistrate, and despite a tendency to irascibility in that role he was a popular figure there and in Lincoln.

In 1800 Paley suffered the onset of kidney disease, with attacks so severe that it was impossible for him to carry out his pastoral duties. Often in pain and aware of his mortality, Paley began to write his last and best-known book, *Natural Theology; or, Evidences of the Existence and Attributes of the Deity, Collected from the Appearances of Nature* (1802).

Paley's goal was to prove the existence, and defend the character, of God on the basis of evidence from ordinary experience of nature. He did not try to offer an abstract mathematical demonstration but rather a proof as secure and reasonable as commonsense and science could accept as adequate. The main principle behind the proof is causal analogy: that is, since like effects come from like causes, whenever effects are found to be similar it is rational to infer similar causes behind them. Once one observes that designed objects, artifacts produced by purpose and intelligence, have certain distinctive characteristics, one is entitled to infer that any objects with those characteristics are also the products of design.

Paley's best-known example invokes the image of a watch. If one finds a rock on a heath, that is nothing to wonder about. But if one stumbles on a watch there, one can and should infer that it has been produced by intelligence. It is made of parts that work together for the production of a useful effect, and if the parts were differently organized, that effect could not have been reached. These qualities are the characteristic marks of design. Therefore, when one finds such marks richly displayed in natural objects, one can rightly infer that they too have been designed by intelligence. If the telescope is undoubtedly a designed object—because it is made up of finely shaped transparent lenses held together by an opaque framework, is put together in just such a way that results in a useful image, and is capable of being focused—so also must the living eye originate from intelligent design, since the eye has the same characteristics as the telescope to an even more impressive degree.

Paley's *Natural Theology* is filled with hundreds of examples of such natural contrivances as the human frame, fish, birds, insects and heavenly bodies, but he insisted that all these instances are logically redundant. The argument from one clear example, like the eye, he asserted, should be enough to convince any rational person of the existence of an intelligent designer behind nature. He acknowledged that such an empirical approach to God cannot defend the deity's omnipotence, omniscience, or omnipresence because evidence from human experience is always limited and partial. But such words may be retained in faithful speech as "superlatives," he argued, by means of which one can offer praise beyond what one can logically determine.

In his final substantive chapter, "Of the Goodness of the Deity," Paley considered how the supremely great intelligence, reasonably inferred from the evidence of nature, can also be shown to be good. In that chapter he used all his well-practiced skills to show that the world is made for happiness, not just for the human race but for all sentient beings. This assertion required, of course, that he account for poisonous insects and reptiles as being, fundamentally, for the best, and it also required that he defend God's goodness in the face of painful illnesses like his own. Paley wrote that one major evidence of the goodness of God is the joy and relief that comes to a sick person from the remission of pain. That is, pain

> may be violent and frequent; but it is seldom both violent and long continued; and its pauses and intermissions become positive pleasures. It has the power of shedding a satisfaction over intervals of ease, which, I believe, few enjoyments exceed. A man resting from a fit of the stone, or gout, is, for the time, in possession of feelings which undisturbed health cannot impart.

After three more years of suffering with courage and cheerfulness, Paley died on 25 May 1805 and was buried next to his first wife in an aisle of the Carlisle Cathedral on 4 June 1805.

Like *The Principles of Moral and Political Philosophy* and *A View of the Evidences of Christianity*, *Natural Theology* was adopted as a standard text at Cambridge and elsewhere. In 1831, when he was a student at Cambridge, Charles Darwin was required to read these three books, and Paley's works were required reading elsewhere as well. In the United States, for example, Dickinson College in Carlisle, Pennsylvania, required a special examination on *Natural Theology* for all graduating students well into the mid nineteenth century.

Yet, the work of Darwin and other scientists of his generation eventually took their toll on Paley's first argument in *Natural Theology*. His tacit assumption was that natural organisms were fairly recently created "as is," with all their various organs and structures. Darwin changed the temporal framework of creation to vast periods of geological time, during which vast changes occurred in organs and structures as creatures evolved. By giving an alternative causal account for Paley's "marks of design," Darwin undercut the argument Paley had formulated.

Paley's *Natural Theology* is not remembered for its originality. Even his famous example of the watch on the heath was anticipated by the Dutch theologian Bernard Nieuwentyt, and in general his comparison of the universe with clockwork had been already been used widely. Nor is the book valued for its convincing power. The Darwinian revolution has changed the framework of discussion, even for contemporary defenders of some modified version of the argument for divine design. Paley's *Natural Theology* is instead honored as the most earnest and complete statement ever made of the argument for God's design in its classical form.

William Paley was the epitome of the moderate, cheerful, confident Christian philosopher of the eighteenth century. He used to say that his four books made up a system. The first, *The Principles of Moral and Political Philosophy,* rests ethics on the promise of eternal happiness and needs the support, in *Horae Paulinae,* of St. Paul's testimony to life after death. This structure, in turn, needs the defense, in *A View of the Evidences of Christianity,* that the early Christian witnesses to the miracles of the Gospels were telling the truth. Finally, the whole structure rests on the proofs in *Natural Theology* that it is reasonable to believe in a God who is intelligent and good. For Paley, the fabric of his religious beliefs, his ethical and political convictions, and his scientific knowledge hung seamlessly together. He was no zealot; he saw no need to defend the literal truth of scripture or to worry that the apostles occasionally made factual mistakes. Likewise, he was no keen reformer; he thought it best not to tamper with the British Constitution, not because it was already perfect but because changing things would likely cause more things to go wrong and create more unhappiness in the end. He was skilled in exposition, keen in debate, honored in his time, comfortable in his station, and untroubled in his beliefs. He was a man of his age whose life and writings highlight vividly how different the present age has become.

Biographies:

George Wilson Meadley, *Memoirs of William Paley, D.D.* (Sunderland: Printed for the author by J. Graham and sold by Cradock & Joy, London, and J. Deighton, Cambridge, 1809; enlarged and corrected edition, Edinburgh: Printed by George Ramsay for Archibald Constable, Edinburgh; Cradock & Joy, London; and J. Deighton, Cambridge, 1810);

Alexander Chalmers, *Life of William Paley,* volume 1 of *The Works of William Paley; with a Life by Alexander Chalmers,* 5 volumes (London: Printed for F. C. & J. Rivington, 1819);

Robert Lynam, biographical sketch of Paley, in *The Complete Works of William Paley. With Extracts from His Correspondence: and a Life of the Author by the Rev. Robert Lynam,* 4 volumes (London: Printed by J. F. Dove for G. Cowie, 1825);

Edmund Paley, *The Life of Dr. Paley,* volume 1 of *The Works of William Paley, D.D.,* edited by Edmund Paley, 7 volumes (London: C. & J. Rivington, 1825);

D. S. Wayland, Biography of Paley, in *The Works of William Paley, D.D., with a Biographical Sketch of the Author, by the Rev. D. S. Wayland,* 2 volumes (Derby: H. Mozley, 1825);

Henry Digby Beste, Memoir of Paley, in his *Personal and Literary Memorials* (London: Coburn, 1829).

References:

Ernest Barker, "Paley and His Political Philosophy," in his *Traditions of Civility: Eight Essays* (Cambridge: Cambridge University Press, 1948);

M. L. Clarke, *Paley: Evidences for the Man* (London: SPCK, 1974; Toronto: University of Toronto Press, 1974);

D. L. LeMahieu, *The Mind of William Paley* (Lincoln & London: University of Nebraska Press, 1976).

Papers:

William Paley's papers may be found at the British Library; the University Library, Cambridge; the Boston Public Library; the Edinburgh University Library; the National Library of Scotland; the Bodleian Library, Oxford; the Giggleswick School, Yorkshire; and King's College, Cambridge.

Joseph Priestley

(13 March 1733 – 6 February 1804)

Alan Tapper
Edith Cowan University

BOOKS: *The Rudiments of English Grammar; Adapted to the Use of Schools. With Observations on Style* (London: Printed for R. Griffiths, 1761);

The Scripture Doctrine of Remission which Showeth that the Death of Christ Is No Proper Sacrifice nor Satisfaction for Sin: But that Pardon Is Dispensed Solely on Account of Repentance or A personal Reformation of the Sinner (London: Printed for C. Henderson & R. Griffiths & P.A. De Hondt, 1761);

A Course of Lectures on the Theory of Language, and Universal Grammar (Warrington: Printed by William Eyres, 1762);

No Man Liveth to Himself. A Sermon Preached Before an Assembly of Protestant Dissenting-Ministers, of the Counties of Lancaster and Chester, Met at Manchester, May 16, 1764, to Carry into Execution a Scheme for the Relief of Their Widows and Children (Warrington: Printed by William Eyres, 1764);

A Description of a Chart of Biography: with a Catalogue of All the Names Inserted in It, and the Dates Annexed to Them, second edition (Warrington: Printed by William Eyres for the author & sold by himself & by John Bowles, London, 1765);

An Essay on a Course of Liberal Education for Civil and Active Life. With Plans of Lectures on I. The Study of History and General Policy. II. The History of England. III. The Constitution and Laws of England. To Which Are Added, Remarks on a Code of Education, Proposed by Dr. Brown, in a Late Treatise, Intitled, Thoughts on Civil Liberty, &c. (London: Printed for C. Henderson, T. Becket & P. A. de Hondt, and Joseph Johnson & Davenport, 1765);

A Syllabus of a Course of Lectures on the Study of History (Warrington: Printed by William Eyres, 1765);

A Catechism for Children and Young Persons (London, 1767); abridged as *Extracts from Dr. Priestley's Catechism for Children and Young Persons* (Salem, Mass.: Printed by Samuel Hall, 1785);

The History and Present State of Electricity, with Original Experiments (London: Printed for James Dodsley, Joseph Johnson & B. Davenport, and Thomas

Joseph Priestley; painting by Rembrandt Peale, 1794 (New-York Historical Society)

Cadell, 1767; corrected and enlarged, 1769; corrected and enlarged again, 2 volumes, London: Printed for C. Bathurst & T. Lowndes, J. Rivington & Joseph Johnson & T. Becket & Thomas Cadell, 1775);

An Essay on the First Principles of Government; and on the Nature of Political, Civil, and Religious Liberty (London: Printed for James Dodsley, Thomas Cadell, and Joseph Johnson, 1768; corrected and enlarged edition, London: Printed for Joseph Johnson, 1771);

A Familiar Introduction to the Study of Electricity (London: Printed for James Dodsley, Thomas Cadell, and Joseph Johnson, 1768);

Considerations on Church-authority; Occasioned by Dr. Balguy's Sermon, on That Subject; Preached at Lambeth Chapel, and Published by Order of the Archbishop (London: Printed for Joseph Johnson & J. Payne, 1769);

Considerations on Differences of Opinion among Christians: with a Letter to the Reverend Mr. Venn, in Answer to His Free and Full Examination of the Address to Protestant Dissenters, on the Subject of the Lord's Supper (London: Printed for Joseph Johnson & J. Payne, 1769);

A Free Address to Protestant Dissenters, as Such, as A Dissenter (London: Printed for G. Pearch, 1769; enlarged edition, London: Printed for Joseph Johnson, 1771);

A Free Address to Protestant Dissenters, on the Subject of the Lord's Supper (London: Printed for Joseph Johnson, 1769);

The Present State of Liberty in Great Britain and her Colonies, as an Englishman (London: Printed for Joseph Johnson & J. Payne, 1769);

Remarks on Some Paragraphs in the Fourth Volume of Dr. Blackstone's Commentaries on the Laws of England, Relating to the Dissenters (London: Printed for Joseph Johnson & J. Payne, 1769; Philadelphia: Printed by Robert Bell, 1772);

A Serious Address to Masters of Families, with Forms of Family-Prayer (London: Printed for Joseph Johnson & J. Payne, 1769);

A View of the Principles and Conduct of the Protestant Dissenters, with Respect to the Civil and Ecclesiastical Constitution of England (London: Printed for Joseph Johnson & J. Payne, 1769);

Additions to the Address to Protestant Dissenters, on the Subject of the Lord's Supper, with Some Corrections on it ; and A Letter to the Author of the Protestant Dissenter's Answer to It (London: Printed for Joseph Johnson, 1770; Boston: Printed by Thomas & John Fleet, 1774);

An Answer to Dr. Blackstone's Reply to Remarks on the Fourth Volume of Commentaries on the Laws of England (Dublin: Printed by James Williams, 1770; Philadelphia: Printed by Robert Bell, 1772);

An Appeal to the Serious and Candid Professors of Christianity. On the Following Subjects, viz. I. The Use of Reason in Matters of Religion. II. The Power of Man to Do the Will of God. III. Original Sin. IV. Election and Reprobation. V. The Divinity of Christ. And, VI. Atonement for Sin by the Death of Christ, anonymous (Leeds, 1770; Philadelphia: Printed & sold by Robert Bell, 1784);

A Description of a New Chart of History, Containing a View of the Principal Revolutions of Empire, That Have Taken Place in the World, second edition (London: Printed for Joseph Johnson, 1770; New Haven, Conn.: Printed by T. & S. Green for Amos Doolittle, 1792);

A Familiar Introduction to the Theory and Practice of Perspective (London: Printed for Joseph Johnson & J. Payne, 1770);

A Free Address to Protestant Dissenters, on the Subject of Church Discipline; With a Preliminary Discourse, Concerning the Spirit of Christianity, and the Corruption of it by False Notions of Religion (London: Printed for Joseph Johnson, 1770);

Letters to the Author of Remarks on Several Late Publications Relative to the Dissenters, in a Letter to Dr. Priestley (London: Printed for Joseph Johnson, 1770);

Letters and Queries Addressed to the Anonymous Answerer of An Appeal to the Serious and Candid Professors of Christianity; to the Rev. Mr. Tho. Morgan, and to Mr. Cornelius Caley (Leeds: Sold by J. Binns, 1771);

Directions for Impregnating Water with Fixed Air; in Order to Communicate to it the Peculiar Spirit and Virtues of Pyrmont Water, and Other Mineral Waters of a Similar Nature (London: Printed for Joseph Johnson, 1772);

A Familiar Illustration of Certain Passages of Scripture: Relating to the Power of Man to Do the Will of God, Original Sin, Election and Reprobation, the Divinity of Christ, and Atonement for Sin by the Death of Christ, as A Lover of the Gospel (London: Printed for Joseph Johnson, 1772); as Priestley (Philadelphia: Printed by Thomas Dobson, 1794);

The History and Present State of Discoveries Relating to Vision, Light and Colours (London: Printed for Joseph Johnson, 1772);

Institutes of Natural and Revealed Religion. Vol. I. Containing the Elements of Natural Religion; To Which Is Prefixed, An Essay on the Best Method of Communicating Religious Knowledge to the Members of Christian Societies (London: Printed for Joseph Johnson, 1772);

Observations on Different Kinds of Air (London: Printed by W. Bowyer & J. Nichols, 1772); revised as volume 1 of *Experiments and Observations on Different Kinds of Air* (2 volumes, London: Printed for Joseph Johnson, 1774, 1775; enlarged, 3 volumes, 1777–1781);

An Address to Protestant Dissenters, on the Subject of Giving the Lord's Supper to Children (London: Printed for Joseph Johnson, 1773);

Institutes of Natural and Revealed Religion. Vol. II. Containing the Evidences of the Jewish and Christian Revelations (London: Printed for Joseph Johnson, 1773);

A Letter of Advice to Those Dissenters Who Conduct the Application to Parliament for Relief from Certain Penal Laws. With Various Observations Relating to Similar Subjects, as The Author of the *Free Address to Protestant Dissenters, as Such* (London: Printed for Joseph Johnson, 1773);

A Sermon, Preached Before the Congregation of Protestant Dissenters at Mill-Hill-Chapel in Leeds, May 16, 1773. By Joseph Priestley, LLD. F.R.S., on Occasion of His

Resigning His Pastoral Office among Them (London: Printed for Joseph Johnson, 1773);

An Address to Protestant Dissenters of All Denominations: on the Approaching Election of Members of Parliament, with Respect to the State of Public Liberty in General, and of American Affairs in Particular (London: Printed for Joseph Johnson, 1774; Philadelphia: Printed & sold by James Humphreys Jr., 1774);

An Examination of Dr. Reid's Inquiry into the Human Mind on the Principles of Common Sense, Dr. Beattie's Essay on the Nature and Immutability of Truth, and Dr. Oswald's Appeal to Common Sense on Behalf of Religion (London: Printed for Joseph Johnson, 1774);

Institutes of Natural and Revealed Religion. Vol. III. Containing a View of the Doctrine of Revelation (London: Printed for Joseph Johnson, 1774);

A Letter to a Layman, on the Subject of the Rev. Mr. Lindsey's Proposal for a Reformed English Church, upon the Plan of the Late Dr. Samuel Clarke (London: Printed for J. Wilkie, 1774);

Considerations for the Use of Young Men and the Parents of Young Men (London: Printed for Joseph Johnson, 1775);

Philosophical Empiricism: Containing Remarks on a Charge of Plagiarism Respecting Dr. H———s, Interspersed with Various Observations Relating to Different Kinds of Air (London: Printed for Joseph Johnson, 1775);

Observations on Respiration, and the Use of the Blood . . . Read at the Royal Society, Jan. 25, 1776 (London, 1776);

A Course of Lectures on Oratory and Criticism (London: Printed for Joseph Johnson, 1777);

Disquisitions relating to Matter and Spirit. To which is added the History of the Philosophical Doctrine concerning the Origin of the Soul, and the Nature of Matter; with its Influence on Christianity, especially with respect to the doctrine of the Pre-existence of Christ (1 volume, London: Printed for Joseph Johnson, 1777; second edition, improved and enlarged, 2 volumes, Birmingham: Printed by Pearson & Rollason for Joseph Johnson, 1782);

The Doctrine of Philosophical Necessity Illustrated; Being an Appendix to the Disquisitions relating to Matter and Spirit. To which is added an Answer to the Letters on Materialism, and on Hartley's Theory of Mind (London: Printed for Joseph Johnson, 1777); enlarged as *The Doctrine of Philosophical Necessity Illustrated; Being an Appendix to the Disquisitions relating to Matter and Spirit. To which is added, An Answer to Several Persons Who Have Controverted the Principles of It* (Birmingham: Printed by Pearson & Rollason for Joseph Johnson, London, 1782);

A Free Discussion of the Doctrines of Materialism and Philosophical Necessity, in a Correspondence between Dr. Price and Dr. Priestley. To which are added, by Dr. Priestley, an Introduction explaining the Nature of the Controversy, and Letters to Several Writers who have Animadverted on His Disquisitions Relating to Matter and Spirit, or his Treatise on Necessity (London: Printed for Joseph Johnson & Thomas Cadell, 1778);

Miscellaneous Observations Relating to Education. More Especially, as it Respects the Conduct of the Mind. To Which Is Added, an Essay on a Course of Liberal Education for Civil and Active Life (Bath: Printed by R. Cruttwell for Joseph Johnson, London, 1778; New London, Conn.: Printed by J. Springer for T. C. Green, S. Green & J. Trumbull, Norwich, 1796);

The Doctrine of Divine Influence on the Human Mind: Considered, in a Sermon, Published at the Request of Many Persons Who Have Occasionally Heard it (Bath: Printed by R. Cruttwell and sold by Joseph Johnson, London, 1779; Northumberland, Pa.: Printed by John Binns, 1804);

A Letter to the Rev. Mr. John Palmer, in Defence of the Illustrations of Philosophical Necessity (Bath: Printed by R. Cruttwell & sold by Joseph Johnson, London, 1779);

Experiments and Observations Relating to Various Branches of Natural Philosophy with a Continuation of the Observations on Air, 3 volumes (London: Printed for Joseph Johnson, 1779–1786);

A Harmony of the Evangelists in English; With Critical Dissertations, an Occasional Paraphrase, and Notes for the Use of the Unlearned (London: Printed for Joseph Johnson, 1780);

A Letter to Jacob Bryant, Esq. In Defence of Philosophical Necessity (London: Printed by H. Baldwin for Joseph Johnson, 1780);

Letters to a Philosophical Unbeliever, Part I. Containing an Examination of the Principal Objections to the Doctrines of Natural Religion, and especially those contained in the Writings of Mr. Hume (Bath: Printed by R. Cruttwell and sold by Joseph Johnson, London, 1780);

A Second Letter to the Rev. Mr. John Palmer, in Defence of the Doctrine of Philosophical Necessity (London: Printed by H. Baldwin for Joseph Johnson, 1780);

Two Letters to Dr Newcome, Bishop of Waterford, on the Duration of Our Saviour's Ministry (Birmingham: Printed by Pearson & Rollason for Joseph Johnson, London, 1780);

A Sermon, Preached December the 31st, 1780 at the New Meeting in Birmingham, on Undertaking the Pastoral Office in That Place (Birmingham: Printed by Pearson & Rollason for Joseph Johnson, London, 1781);

A Scripture Catechism, Consisting of a Series of Questions: with References to the Scriptures Instead of Answers (London: Printed for Joseph Johnson, 1781);

A Third Letter to Dr Newcome, Bishop of Waterford, on the Duration of Our Saviour's Ministry (Birmingham:

Printed by Piercy & Jones for Joseph Johnson, London, 1781);

Additional Letters to a Philosophical Unbeliever, in Answer to Mr. William Hammon (Birmingham: Printed by Pearson & Rollason for Joseph Johnson, London, 1782);

An History of the Corruptions of Christianity, 2 volumes (Birmingham: Printed by Piercy & Jones for Joseph Johnson, London, 1782; Boston: Printed by William Spotswood, 1797);

The Proper Constitution of a Christian Church, Considered in a Sermon, Preached at the New Meeting in Birmingham, November 3, 1782. To Which Is Prefixed, a Prefatory Discourse, Relating to the Present State of Those Who Are Called Rational Dissenters (Birmingham: Printed by Pearson & Rollason, 1782);

Two Discourses; I. On Habitual Devotion; II. On the Duty of Not Living to Ourselves: Both Preached to Assemblies of Protestant Dissenting Ministers, and Published at Their Request (Birmingham: Printed by Piercy & Jones for Joseph Johnson, London, 1782);

A General View of the Arguments for the Unity of God: and Against the Divinity and Pre-existence of Christ, from Reason, from the Scriptures, and from History (Birmingham: Printed by Piercy & Jones for Joseph Johnson, London, 1783; Philadelphia: Printed & sold by Robert Bell, 1784);

A Reply to the Animadversions on the History of the Corruptions of Christianity, in the Monthly Review for June, 1783: with Additional Observations Relating to the Doctrine of the Primitive Church, Concerning the Person of Christ (Birmingham: Printed by Piercy & Jones for Joseph Johnson, London, 1783); republished in *Defences of the History of the Corruptions of Christianity* (London: Printed for Joseph Johnson, 1792?);

Letters to Dr. Horsley, in Answer to His Animadversions on the History of the Corruptions of Christianity. With Additional Evidence That the Primitive Christian Church Was Unitarian (Birmingham: Printed by Pearson & Rollason for Joseph Johnson, London, 1783); republished in *Defences of the History of the Corruptions of Christianity* (London: Printed for Joseph Johnson, 1792?);

Letters to Dr. Horsley, Part II.: Containing Farther Evidence That the Primitive Christian Church Was Unitarian (Birmingham: Printed by Pearson & Rollason for Joseph Johnson, London, 1784); republished in *Defences of the History of the Corruptions of Christianity* (London: Printed for Joseph Johnson, 1792?);

Remarks on the Monthly Review of the Letters to Dr. Horsley; in Which the Rev. Mr. Samuel Badcock, the Writer of That Review, Is Called upon to Defend What He Has Advanced in it (Birmingham: Printed by Pearson & Rollason for Joseph Johnson, London, 1784);

republished in *Defences of the History of the Corruptions of Christianity* (London: Printed for Joseph Johnson, 1792?);

The Importance and Extent of Free Inquiry in Matters of Religion: A Sermon, Preached Before the Congregations of the Old and New Meeting of Protestant Dissenters at Birmingham. November 5, 1785. To Which Are Added, Reflections on the Present State of Free Inquiry in this Country (Birmingham: Printed by M. Swinney for Joseph Johnson, London, 1785);

An History of Early Opinions Concerning Jesus Christ, Compiled from Original Writers; Proving That the Christian Church Was at First Unitarian (Birmingham: Printed for the author by Pearson & Rollason and sold by Joseph Johnson, London, 1786);

Letters to Dr. Horsley, Part III.: Containing an Answer to His Remarks on Letters, Part II. To Which Are Added Strictures on Mr. Howe's Ninth Number of Observations on Books Ancient and Modern (Birmingham: Printed by Pearson & Rollason for Joseph Johnson, London, 1786); republished in *Defences of the History of the Corruptions of Christianity* (London: Printed for Joseph Johnson, 1792?);

Letters to the Jews; Inviting Them to an Amicable Discussion of the Evidences of Christianity (Birmingham: Printed by Pearson & Rollason and sold by Joseph Johnson, London, 1786); republished in *Letters from Dr. Priestley to the Jews; Inviting Them to an Amicable Discussion of the Evidences of Christianity* (New York: Printed by J. Harrison for Benjamin Gomes, 1794);

An Account of a Society, for Encouraging the Industrious Poor: with a Table for Their Use. To Which Are Prefixed, Some Considerations on the State of the Poor in General (Birmingham: Printed by Pearson & Rollason, 1787);

Discourses on Various Subjects, Including Several on Particular Occasions (Birmingham: Printed for the author by Pearson & Rollason & sold by Joseph Johnson, London, 1787);

A Letter to the Right Honourable William Pitt, First Lord of the Treasury, and Chancellor of the Exchequer; on the Subjects of Toleration and Church Establishments; Occasioned by His Speech Against the Repeal of the Test and Corporation Acts, on Wednesday the 28th of March, 1787 (London: Printed for Joseph Johnson & James Debrett, 1787; corrected and enlarged, 1787);

Letters to a Philosophical Unbeliever. Part II.: Containing a State of the Evidence of Revealed Religion, with Animadversions on the Two Last Chapters of the First Volume of Mr. Gibbon's History of the Decline and Fall of the Roman Empire (Birmingham: Printed by Pearson & Rollason for Joseph Johnson, London, 1787);

Letters to Dr. Horne, Dean of Canterbury: to the Young Men, Who Are in a Course of Education for the Christian Min-

istry, at the Universities of Oxford and Cambridge; to Dr. Price; and to Mr. Parkhurst; on the Subject of the Person of Christ (Birmingham: Printed for the author by Pearson & Rollason and sold by Joseph Johnson, London, 1787);

Letters to the Jews. Part II. Occasioned by Mr. David Levi's Reply to the Former Letters (Birmingham: Printed for the author by Pearson & Rollason and sold by Joseph Johnson, London, 1787); republished in Letters from Dr. Priestley to the Jews; Inviting Them to an Amicable Discussion of the Evidences of Christianity (New York: Printed by J. Harrison for Benjamin Gomes, 1794);

Defences of Unitarianism for the Year 1786. Containing Letters to Dr. Horne, Dean of Canterbury; to the Young Men, Who Are in a Course of Education for the Christian Ministry at the Universities of Oxford and Cambridge; to the Rev. Dr. Price; and to the Rev. Mr. Parkhurst; on the Subject of the Person of Christ, 3 volumes (Birmingham: Printed for the author by Pearson & Rollason and sold by Joseph Johnson, London, 1788);

Defences of Unitarianism for the Year 1787. Containing Letters to the Rev. Dr. Geddes, to the Rev. Dr. Price, Part I, and to the Candidates for Orders in the Two Universities; Part II, Relating to Mr. Howes's Appendix to His Fourth Volume of Observations on Books, A Letter by an Undergraduate of Oxford, Dr. Croft's Bampton Lectures, and Several Other Publications (Birmingham: Printed for the author by Pearson & Rollason & sold by Joseph Johnson, London, 1788);

Lectures on History, and General Policy to Which Is Prefixed, An Essay on a Course of Liberal Education for Civil and Active Life, 2 volumes (Birmingham: Printed by Pearson & Rollason for Joseph Johnson, London, 1788; Philadelphia: Printed for P. Byrne, 1803);

A Sermon on the Subject of the Slave Trade: Delivered to a Society of Protestant Dissenters, at the New Meeting, in Birmingham; and Published at Their Request (Birmingham: Printed for the author by Pearson & Rollason and sold by Joseph Johnson, London, 1788);

The Conduct to Be Observed by Dissenters in Order to Procure the Repeal of the Corporation and Test Acts, Recommended in a Sermon Preached Before the Congregations of the Old and New Meetings at Birmingham, November 5, 1789 (Birmingham: Printed by J. Thompson & sold by Joseph Johnson, London, 1789);

Defences of Unitarianism for the Years 1788 & 1789. Containing Letters to Dr. Horsley, Lord Bishop of St. David's, to the Rev. Mr. Barnard, the Rev. Dr. Knowles, and the Rev. Mr. Hawkins (Birmingham: Printed by J. Thompson for Joseph Johnson, London, 1790);

Dr. Priestley's Letters to the Candidates for Orders in Both Universities on Subscription to Articles of Religion, with an Address to Conforming Arians, &c. (Cambridge: Sold by J. & J. Merrill & J. Bowtell, Cambridge, D. Prince, Oxford & Joseph Johnson, London, 1790);

Familiar Letters, Addressed to the Inhabitants of the Town of Birmingham, in Refutation of Several Charges, Advanced Against the Dissenters, by the Rev. Mr Madan, Rector of St. Philip's, in His Sermon, Entitled 'The Principal Claims of the Dissenters Considered.' Preached at St. Philip's Church, on Sunday February 14, 1790 (Birmingham: Printed by F. Thompson & sold by Joseph Johnson, London, 1790);

A General History of the Christian Church to the Fall of the Western Empire (2 volumes, Birmingham: Printed by Thomas Pearson and sold by Joseph Johnson, London, 1790; 4 volumes, Northumberland, Pa.: Printed for the author by Andrew Kennedy, 1803);

Letter to the Rev. Edward Burn, of St. Mary's Chapel, Birmingham, in Answer to His on the Infallibility of the Apostolic Testimony, Concerning the Person of Christ (Birmingham: Printed by J. Thompson & sold by Joseph Johnson, London, 1790);

Reflections on Death. A Sermon, on Occasion of the Death of the Rev. Robert Robinson, of Cambridge, Delivered at the New Meeting in Birmingham, June 13, 1790 (Birmingham: Printed by J. Belcher & sold by Joseph Johnson, London, 1790);

A View of Revealed Religion; A Sermon, Preached at the Ordination of the Rev. William Field of Warwick, July 12, 1790 (Birmingham: Printed by J. Thompson & sold by Joseph Johnson, London, 1790);

An Appeal to the Public, on the Subject of the Riots in Birmingham. To Which Is Added, Strictures on a Pamphlet, Intitled "Thoughts on the Late Riot at Birmingham" (Birmingham: Printed by J. Thompson and sold by Joseph Johnson, London, 1791);

A Discourse on Occasion of the Death of Dr. Price: Delivered at Hackney, on Sunday, May 1, 1791 (London: Printed for Joseph Johnson, 1791);

The Duty of Forgiveness of Injuries: A Discourse Intended to Be Delivered Soon after the Riots in Birmingham (Birmingham: Printed by J. Thompson for Joseph Johnson, London, 1791);

The Evidence of the Resurrection of Jesus Considered: in a Discourse First Delivered in the Assembly-room, at Buxton, on Sunday, September 19, 1790. To Which Is Added, An Address to the Jews (Birmingham: Printed by J. Thompson for Joseph Johnson, London, 1791);

Letters to the Members of the New Jerusalem Church, Formed by Baron Swedenborg (Birmingham: Printed by J. Thompson & sold by Joseph Johnson, London, 1791);

Letters to the Right Honourable Edmund Burke: Occasioned by His Reflections on the Revolution in France, &c. (Birmingham: Printed by Thomas Pearson & sold by

Joseph Johnson, London, 1791; New York: Printed by Hugh Gaine, 1791);

A Particular Attention to the Instruction of the Young Recommended, in a Discourse, Delivered at the Gravel-pit Meeting, in Hackney, December 4, 1791, Entering the Office of Pastor to the Congregation of Protestant Dissenters, Assembling in That Place (London: Printed for Joseph Johnson, 1791);

The Proper Objects of Education in the Present State of the World: Represented in a Discourse, Delivered on Wednesday, the 27th of April, 1791, at the Meeting-house in the Old-Jewry, London, to the Supporters of New College at Hackney (London: Printed for Joseph Johnson, 1791);

Letters to a Young Man: Occasioned by Mr. Wakefield's Essay on Public Worship; to Which Is Added, a Reply to Mr. Evanson's Objections to the Observance of the Lord's Day (London: Printed for Joseph Johnson, 1792);

Letters to a Young Man, Part II. Occasioned by Mr. Evanson's Treatise on the Dissonance of the Four Generally Received Evangelists (London: Printed for Joseph Johnson, 1793);

Experiments on the Generation of Air from Water; to Which Are Prefixed, Experiments Relating to the Decomposition of Dephlogisticated and Inflammable Air (London: Printed for Joseph Johnson, 1793);

Letters to the Philosophers and Politicians of France, on the Subject of Religion (London: Printed for Joseph Johnson, 1793; Boston: Printed & sold by Samuel Hall, 1793);

A Sermon Preached at the Gravel Pit Meeting, in Hackney, April 19th, 1793, Being the Day Appointed for a General Fast (London: Printed for Joseph Johnson, 1793);

An Answer to Mr. Paine's Age of Reason, Being a Continuation of Letters to the Philosophers and Politicians of France, on the Subject of Religion; and of the Letters to a Philosophical Unbeliever (Northumberland, Pa., 1794; London: Printed for Joseph Johnson, 1795);

A Continuation of the Letters to the Philosophers and Politicians of France, on the Subject of Religion; And of The Letters of a Philosophical Unbeliever; In Answer to Mr. Paine's Age of Reason (Northumberland, Pa.: Printed by Andrew Kennedy, 1794);

Discourses on the Evidences of Revealed Religion (London: Printed for Joseph Johnson, 1794; Boston: Printed & sold by William Spotswood, 1795);

Heads of Lectures on a Course of Experimental Philosophy: Particularly Including Chemistry, Delivered at the New College in Hackney (London: Printed for Joseph Johnson, 1794);

The Present State of Europe Compared with Antient Prophecies: a Sermon, Preached at the Gravel Pit Meeting in Hackney, February 28, 1794: Being the Day Appointed for a General Fast . . . with a Preface Containing the Reasons for the

Author's Leaving England (London: Printed for Joseph Johnson, 1794); republished in *Two Sermons Viz. I. The Present State of Europe Compared with Antient Prophecies; Preached on the Fast-day in 1794; with a Preface, Containing the Reasons for the Author's Leaving England. II. The Use of Christianity, Especially in Difficult Times; Being the Author's Farewell Discourse* (Philadelphia: Printed by Thomas Dobson, 1794);

The Use of Christianity, Especially in Difficult Times: a Sermon, Delivered at the Gravel Pit Meeting in Hackney, March 30, 1794. . . . Being the Author's Farewell Discourse to His Congregation (London: Printed for Joseph Johnson, 1794); republished in *Two Sermons Viz. I. The Present State of Europe Compared with Antient Prophecies; Preached on the Fast-day in 1794; with a Preface, Containing the Reasons for the Author's Leaving England. II. The Use of Christianity, Especially in Difficult Times; Being the Author's Farewell Discourse* (1794);

Observations on the Increase of Infidelity. First Prefixed to the American Edition of Letters to the Philosophers and Politicians of France on the Subject of Religion, but Now Much Enlarged (Northumberland, Pa.: Printed by Andrew Kennedy, 1795; London: Printed for Joseph Johnson, 1796);

Considerations on the Doctrine of Phlogiston, and the Decomposition of Water (Philadelphia: Printed by Thomas Dobson, 1796);

Discourses Relating to the Evidences of Revealed Religion: Delivered in the Church of the Universalists at Philadelphia, 1796 (Philadelphia: Printed by Thomas Dobson, 1796); republished as *Discourses Relating to the Evidences of Revealed Religion. Vol. II, Being the First Delivered at Philadelphia in 1796* (London: Printed for Joseph Johnson, 1796);

Unitarianism explained and defended in a discourse delivered in the Church of the Universalists at Philadelphia, 1796 (Philadelphia: Printed by John Thompson, 1796; London: Printed for Joseph Johnson, 1796);

The Case of Poor Emigrants Recommended: in a Discourse, Delivered at the University Hall in Philadelphia, on Sunday, February 19, 1797 (Philadelphia: Printed by Joseph Gales & sold by W. Y. Birch & the booksellers in Philadelphia, New York and Baltimore, 1797);

An Address to the Unitarian Congregation at Philadelphia, Delivered on Sunday, March 5, 1797 (Philadelphia: Printed by Joseph Gales, 1797);

Letters to Mr. Volney: Occasioned by a Work of His Entitled Ruins, and by His Letter to the Author (Philadelphia: Printed by Thomas Dobson, 1797);

Observations on the Doctrine of Phlogiston and the Decomposition of Water. Part the Second (Philadelphia: Printed by Thomas Dobson, 1797);

An Outline of the Evidences of Revealed Religion (Philadelphia: Printed by T. Dobson, 1797; London: Printed for the British and Foreign Unitarian Association, 1833);

Discourses Relating to the Evidences of Revealed Religion: Delivered in Philadelphia 1796; and Published at the Request of Many of the Hearers Vol. II (Philadelphia: Printed by Thomas Dobson, 1797); republished as *Discourses Relating to the Evidences of Revealed Religion. Vol. III, Being the Second Delivered at Philadelphia in 1797* (London: Printed for Joseph Johnson, 1799);

A Comparison of the Institutions of Moses with Those of the Hindoos and Other Ancient Nations: With Remarks on Mr. Dupuis's Origin of All Religions, the Laws and Institutions of Moses Methodized, and an Address to the Jews on the Present State of the World and the Prophecies Relating to it (Northumberland, Pa.: Printed for the author by Andrew Kennedy, 1799);

The Doctrine of Phlogiston Established, and That of the Composition of Water Refuted (Northumberland, Pa.: Printed for the author by Andrew Kennedy, 1800);

Sermons, by Priestley and Richard Price (London: Printed by J. Davis, 1800);

An Inquiry into the Knowledge of the Antient Hebrews Concerning a Future State (London: Printed for Joseph Johnson, 1801);

Letters to the Inhabitants of Northumberland and its Neighbourhood on Subjects Interesting to the Author and to Them: To Which Is Added a Letter to a Friend in Paris, Relating to Mr. Liancourt's Travels in the North American States (Philadelphia: Printed by John Bioren for John Conrad, 1801);

A General History of the Christian Church, from the Fall of the Western Empire to the Present Time, 4 volumes (Northumberland, Pa.: Printed for the author by Andrew Kennedy, 1802);

A Letter to an Antipædobaptist (Northumberland, Pa.: Printed by Andrew Kennedy, 1802);

A Letter to the Reverend John Blair Linn, A.M: A Pastor of the First Presbyterian Congregation in the City of Philadelphia, in Defence of the Pamphlet, Entitled, Socrates and Jesus Compared (Northumberland, Pa.: Printed by Andrew Kennedy for P. Byrne, Philadelphia, 1803);

A Second Letter to the Revd. John Blair Linn, D.D., Pastor of the First Presbyterian Congregation in the City of Philadelphia: A Reply to His Defence of the Doctrines of the Divinity of Christ and Atonement (Northumberland, Pa.: Printed by Andrew Kennedy for P. Byrne, Philadelphia, 1803);

Notes on All the Books of Scripture, for Use of the Pulpit and Private Families, 4 volumes (Northumberland, Pa.: Printed for the author by Andrew Kennedy, 1803-1804);

The Originality and Superior Excellence of the Mosaic Institutions Demonstrated (Northumberland, Pa.: Printed by Andrew Kennedy for P. Byrne, Philadelphia, 1803);

Socrates and Jesus Compared (London: Printed for Joseph Johnson, 1803);

The Doctrine of Heathen Philosophy: Compared with Those of Revelation (Northumberland, Pa.: Printed by John Binns, 1804);

Index to the Bible in Which the Various Subjects Which Occur in the Scriptures Are Alphabetically Arranged, with Accurate References to All the Books of the Old and New Testaments (Philadelphia, 1804; London: Printed for Joseph Johnson, 1805);

Discourses on Various Subjects: Intended to Have Been Delivered in Philadelphia; To Which Are Added, Some Others, Selected from the Same Author (Northumberland, Pa.: Printed by John Binns, 1805);

Four Discourses: Intended to Have Been Delivered in Philadelphia (Northumberland, Pa.: Printed by John Binns, 1806);

Memoirs of Dr. Joseph Priestley, to the Year 1795, Written by Himself: with a Continuation, to the Time of His Decease, by His Son, Joseph Priestley and Observations on His Writings, by Thomas Cooper, President Judge of the 4th District of Pennsylvania, and the Rev. William Christie (Northumberland, Pa.: Printed by John Binns, 1806; London: Printed for Joseph Johnson, 1806);

The Theological and Miscellaneous Works of Joseph Priestley, LL.D. F.R.S. &c., 25 volumes, edited by John Towill Rutt (London: Printed by George Smallfield, Hackney, 1817-1831).

Editions: *Priestley's Writings on Philosophy, Science and Politics,* edited by John A. Passmore (New York: Collier, 1965);

Autobiography of Joseph Priestley, edited by Jack Lindsey (Bath: Adams & Dart, 1970);

Political Writings, edited by Peter N. Miller (Cambridge: Cambridge University Press, 1993).

OTHER: *Hartley's Theory of the Human Mind, on the Principle of the Association of Ideas; With Essays Relating to the Subject of It,* edited, with an introduction, by Priestley (London: Printed for Joseph Johnson, 1775).

PERIODICAL   PUBLICATION–UNCOLLECTED: "Observations and Experiments relating to Equivocal, or Spontaneous Generation," *Transactions of the American Philosophical Society,* 6 (1809): 119-129.

Joseph Priestley's range of intellectual interests was great, even by the standards of the eighteenth cen-

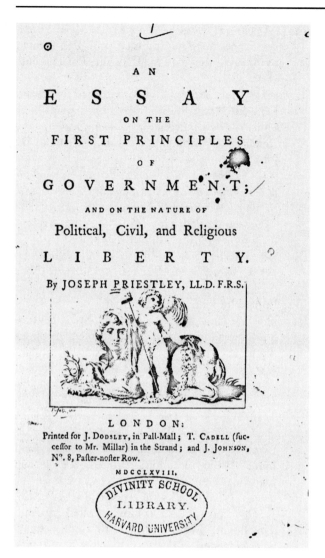

AN

ESSAY

ON THE

FIRST PRINCIPLES

OF

GOVERNMENT;

AND ON THE NATURE OF

Political, Civil, and Religious

LIBERTY.

By JOSEPH PRIESTLEY, LL.D. F.R.S.

LONDON:

Printed for J. DODSLEY, in Pall-Mall; T. CADELL (fuc-
ceffor to Mr. Millar) in the Strand; and J. JOHNSON,
Nº. 8, Pafter-nofter Row.

MDCCLXVIII.

*Title page for Priestley's first philosophical work, a defense of individual
freedom against state power*

penetrating criticisms. His attempt to combine theism, materialism, and determinism is audacious and original. He tried to show that such a system does not lapse into pantheism.

As a political thinker he distinguished usefully between civil and political liberty and argued the case for extensive civil liberties. His liberalism is closely bound up with his account of historical progress. He was perhaps the most thorough British exponent of a Providentialist account of progress. His ultimate aim was to combine Enlightenment principles with a modernized Christian theism.

Three notable philosophers of Priestley's generation held him in some regard. One, Richard Price, was his lifelong friend, despite their different moral and metaphysical outlooks. Reid, by contrast, had no liking for Priestley, but he was much occupied by Priestley's doctrines, and his writings are often directed against him. More surprisingly, Priestley is complimented in Immanuel Kant's *Critique of Pure Reason* (1781) with the remark that he "knew how to combine his paradoxical teaching with the interests of religion." The paradox, Kant says, is that of a man who, though "a pious and zealous teacher of religion," has striven to "pull down two such pillars of religion as the freedom and immortality of the soul (the hope of a future life is for him only the expectation of the miracle of a future resurrection)." Priestley, in Kant's judgment, "was concerned for the interests of reason, which must suffer when we seek to exempt certain objects from the laws of material nature, the only laws which we can know and determine with exactitude." Furthermore, Priestley's political writings had the dubious distinction of provoking the wrath of Edmund Burke. At the time of the American Revolution, Burke and Priestley were philosophical allies; by the 1790s they had parted company, arguing opposite positions on the French Revolution, both with considerable force.

Priestley was born not far from Leeds in 13 March 1733. The family was Yorkshire Calvinist, or Independent. His father was a cloth-dresser. His mother died when Joseph was still young, and he went to live with a childless aunt, Sarah Keighley, also staunchly Calvinist, whose home was nevertheless a center for Dissenting ministers of all persuasions. As a young, largely self-taught philosopher, Priestley's heroes were John Locke, Sir Isaac Newton, and David Hartley. He was educated at Daventry Academy, where, he said, "the students were about equally divided upon every question of much importance, such as liberty and necessity, the sleep of the soul, and all the articles of theological orthodoxy and heresy; in consequence of which, all these topics were the subject of continual discussion." He was a quick student of history, languages, and the

tury. He was a Dissenting minister, and his chief concerns were theological. His scientific work, for which he is now best known, occupied much of his remaining time. In addition he wrote extensively on history, education, rhetoric, and politics. In his day Priestley was also a philosopher of some importance. He argued the case for materialism perhaps more cogently than did any British thinker before recent times. He presented determinism vigorously, with a focus on the central issue of the nature of causation. He speculated interestingly, following Jesuit scientist Roger Joseph Boscovich, on the nature of matter. He defended scientific realism against Thomas Reid's Common Sense realism and against (as he saw it) David Hume's phenomenalism. He articulated, against Hume, a working scientist's account of causation, induction, and scientific progress. He defended the argument from design against Hume's

sciences, but his deepest early lessons concerned the value of tolerance and open argument.

The strict Calvinism of Priestley's circle taught that it was necessary to experience a "new birth" if salvation is to be obtained. Priestly found to his dismay that he lacked any such experience, but he continued to consider himself a good Christian, which caused a rift with his aunt, his family, and his local parish. He continued throughout life to cast off doctrines others thought essential to Christianity, while yet retaining a deep attachment to the faith as he saw it. Unorthodoxy and controversy were his vocations; after an Arminian and an Arian period, he became eventually the chief exponent of Unitarianism in Britain. A deep intellectual and personal belief in divine Providence sustained him throughout; there is no sign that he was simply an intellectual in incomplete transit to deism, pantheism, or agnosticism.

After six difficult years as an unknown Dissenting clergyman and schoolteacher, in 1761 Priestley was offered the position of tutor in languages and literature at Warrington Academy. In the 1760s Warrington was lively and prosperous, earning the title of the "Athens" of northern England. There he lectured on modern history, rhetoric, literary criticism, and aesthetics. He first made his name as an author with three works: a textbook on English grammar, *The Rudiments of English Grammar; Adapted to the Use of Schools. With Observations on Style* (1761); a study of the theory of language; and an essay on the aims and practice of education. At Warrington he found time to start a new career as an historian of science, beginning with *The History and Present State of Electricity, with Original Experiments* (1767), a well-received history of discoveries in electricity, for which he conducted many experiments of his own. The project led him to membership in the Royal Society and to a friendship with Benjamin Franklin that lasted until Franklin's death. It also set him on the path toward his brilliant experimental career.

Success as a lecturer and promise as a scientist did not satisfy Priestley's deeper desire to be a Dissenting minister. In 1767 he accepted an invitation to a chapel at Mill Hill, Leeds. In this period he wrote his most substantial political work, *An Essay on the First Principles of Government; and on the Nature of Political, Civil, and Religious Liberty* (1768), which is also his first philosophical essay. It is a defense of civil liberty, including the religious liberty of Dissenters, against John Brown's proposal for a system of uniform state education devoted to producing a more law-abiding citizenry. Against this "Spartanism" Priestley was a convinced "Athenian," and he mustered many of the arguments in favor of social and intellectual diversity later used by John Stuart Mill in *On Liberty* (1859). Some have thought that *An Essay on the First Prin-*

ciples of Government prefigures utilitarianism, because Jeremy Bentham recollected finding in it the phrase "the greatest happiness of the greatest number." The phrase is not in Priestley's text, though. He does say that "the good and happiness of the members" of society, "that is, the majority of the members of any state, is the great standard by which every thing relating to that state must finally be determined."

The importance of *An Essay on the First Principles of Government* lies mainly in its restatement of a Lockean political philosophy of natural rights and in its clear distinction between political and civil liberty. Political liberty is "the power which the members of the state reserve to themselves, of arriving at the public offices, or, at least, of having votes in the nomination of those who fill them." Civil liberty is "that power over their own actions, which the members of the state reserve to themselves, and which their officers must not infringe." To leave one's "natural" condition and enter the state of society is to sacrifice part of one's civil liberty. The consent of the governed is "the only true and proper foundation of all governments subsisting in the world," and any people has the right to remove a government that is deemed oppressive. There are no natural political rights, however. Political rights vary in place and time. No one form of government–from absolute monarchy to radical democracy–is naturally better than any other. Good government is not a matter of form but of the moderation of the rulers, of uniform laws, and of respect for civil liberties. Priestley regards the civil sphere as far more important than politics to a people's happiness, for it is in the civil sphere that truth is discovered, material progress is cultivated, and genuine religion is practiced. His later radicalism arose not from any marked philosophical change but from coming to think the British government immoderate and intrusive.

In 1773 Priestley was employed as the librarian and companion of William Petty, Lord Shelburne, with much free time to pursue his scientific and other writings. During this period he entered into the metaphysical disputes of his day. He began conventionally enough, setting out the case for "natural religion" in his three-volume theological primer, *Institutes of Natural and Revealed Religion* (1772–1774). Priestley's theism is based on the argument from design. He sees nature as everywhere exhibiting order, and yet as not in any way self-ordering, since nothing seen in nature shows order arising naturally. The order must come from "outside," and since it resembles human productions it must derive from intelligence, indeed, a supreme intelligence. He reinforces this position with an appeal to the cosmological argument. Nothing in *Institutes of Natural and Revealed Religion* suggests the controversies that soon followed.

AN

EXAMINATION

OF

Dr. REID's *Inquiry into the Human Mind*
on the Principles of Common Sense,

Dr. BEATTIE's *Essay on the Nature and*
Immutability of Truth,

AND

Dr. OSWALD's *Appeal to Common Sense*
in Behalf of Religion.

By JOSEPH PRIESTLEY, LL. D. F. R. S.

As some men have imagined innate ideas, because they had forgot
how they came by them; so others have set up almost as many
distinct instincts as there are acquired principles of acting.

Preliminary Dissertation to Law's translation of King's
Origin of Evil.

L O N D O N:
PRINTED FOR J. JOHNSON, N°. 72, ST. PAUL'S CHURCH-YARD.
M.DCC.LXXIV.

Title page for Priestley's attack on Scottish "Common Sense" realism, in
which he argues that ideas can represent objects without resembling them
(Sterling Memorial Library, Yale University)

Priestley's most remarkable philosophical work is his defense of materialism, which he wrote while with Shelburne. English philosophy had long been dominated by dualism. The few extant versions of materialism had almost no influence on Priestley's version. He admired Hobbes but did not borrow from him. He discussed materialism with Paul-Henri Dietrich, Baron d'Holbach, on a visit to Paris in 1774–d'Holbach's *Système de la Nature* (The System of Nature) had appeared in 1770–but the beginnings of his own version predate that visit; and his later defenses of the doctrine bear little resemblance to d'Holbach's. The French materialists of the 1770s were using materialism to attack Christianity; Priestley's intentions were to defend Christianity by making its metaphysical framework more intelligible, even if doing so entailed denial of free will and the soul.

Priestley's materialism rests on three main arguments, each of which bears interesting scientific connections. He first arrived at the doctrine in the course of defining the Lockean theory of ideas–the theory that

perceptions are mediated by sensations–against Reid's Common Sense attack on that theory in his *An Inquiry into the Human Mind* (1764). Reid believed that Berkeley and Hume had destroyed the claim that ideas represent reality by showing that sensations do not in fact resemble the qualities of external objects. From these assumptions Berkeley and Hume had concluded that there is no access to external reality, while Reid concluded that, since reality is indeed apprehended, that apprehension occurs without the aid of the philosophers' fictitious ideas. Priestley's response, in his *An Examination of Dr. Reid's Inquiry into the Human Mind on the Principles of Common Sense, Dr. Beattie's Essay on the Nature and Immutability of Truth, and Dr. Oswald's Appeal to Common Sense on Behalf of Religion* (1774), was to reject the assumption that sensations or ideas must resemble their objects in order to represent them. For him ideas are not images, and the theory of ideas is not a theory of pictures in the brain. His theory, rather, requires only that objects and ideas stand to each other as cause to effect.

Reid's main contention had been that representation requires resemblance, but he also had been inclined to attack the claim that objects can cause ideas. Mind and matter, he says in *An Inquiry into the Human Mind,* are so different that "we can find no handle by which one may lay hold of the other." He takes this lack of association to show that perception is a process causally independent of its objects. Priestley seized upon this argument as showing Reid to be an occasionalist, or unwitting idealist. In making this argument he is accepting Reid's suggestion that totally dissimilar substances cannot interact. He takes as given, however, that objects do produce ideas. From this contention follows that ideas and objects must be of the same substance. He rejects Berkeley's idealism because it supposes that every act of perception is produced by a divine intervention, which he regards as not consonant with the simplicity usually displayed in God's actions. Following this logic, Priestley had no alternative but to declare himself a materialist.

Underlying this debate is an issue about causal relations. Priestley's view contrasts with that of his near-contemporary Hume, whom Priestley regarded as insufficiently acquainted with real science to have any useful opinions on the philosophy of science. Priestley agreed with Hume that causal relations indicate regularities between events, but he denied that they are merely regularities. Causally related events are not for him thus "loose and separate": they are bound together by the productive agency of some mechanism. His rejection of interactionist dualism stems from its admitted inability to supply such a mechanism for interaction.

The second source of Priestley's materialism is to be found in his theory of matter, which he made a central theme of his *Disquisitions relating to Matter and Spirit. To which is added the History of the Philosophical Doctrine concerning the Origin of the Soul, and the Nature of Matter; with its Influence on Christianity, especially with respect to the doctrine of the Pre-existence of Christ* (1777). Newtonian dualists such as Price, Reid, and Andrew Baxter had urged that matter and mind are irreconcilable because one is intrinsically passive and the other intrinsically active. Priestley thought that talk of matter as a "dead and torpid substance" betrayed the influence of ancient Gnosticism, a religion that regarded matter as evil. According to the Newtonians, the apparent activity of matter is to be wholly ascribed to the action of immaterial forces. Priestley asks, however, if matter is wholly powerless, then what use is it, and why suppose it to exist at all? He follows John Michell–a fellow scientist-clergyman–in likening the Newtonian theory of matter and force to a structure of material bricks and immaterial mortar in which the mortar is doing all the work. Priestley and Michell were themselves indebted to Boscovich, whom they had both met.

Closer scrutiny reveals some differences between Boscovich and Priestley. Priestley wholly accepted Boscovich's insistence on the powerfulness of matter. Boscovich had reached this conclusion by arguing that the Newtonian account of mechanical impulse required finite velocities to be lost and gained in a single instant of time, thus violating the Leibnizian law of continuity. This argument is never mentioned by Priestley. For him mechanical impulse may or may not be theoretically intelligible; his objection is that the Newtonians have not shown that it actually occurs. Rather, the phenomena show clear instances of forces acting at a distance and exhibit nothing that cannot be readily explained by forces. In his view the first of Newton's "Rules of Reasoning in Philosophy" in the *Philosophiæ Naturalis Principia Mathematica* (1687)–that "we are to admit no more causes of things than such as are both true and sufficient to explain appearances"–requires arguing that matter consists of "powers of attraction and repulsion" and doing without the hypothesis of solid, impenetrable atoms.

For Priestley the great theoretical weakness of the atomic theory is that it cannot account for the internal cohesion of the atom. He is attracted to Boscovich's theory of the microstructure of matter as infinite powers of repulsion located at dimensionless point-particles, but he treats that theory as no more than a valuable speculation. The theory is consistent with all data, but it lacks confirmation from experience or analogy. By contrast, the more general theory of matter as "powers of attraction and repulsion" does command assent, for simplicity and analogy count in its favor.

Priestley diagnoses the Newtonian notion of the passivity of matter as arising from what might be termed the "billiard table illusion." That billiard balls do not move without first being struck does not show that they are not powerful agents, for the table is level and thus neutralizes the natural tendency of the balls to move downward. The fact that bodies are sometimes in equilibrium shows only that sometimes their natural powers balance each other out, not that they have no natural powers. Priestley concludes that if matter can have these natural powers, there is no reason in principle why they might not have others, such as the power of consciousness.

Priestley's third and main argument for materialism is a methodological one. He argues in the *Disquisitions relating to Matter and Spirit* that in postulating a soul dualists are making the same mistake that the Newtonians make in postulating solid matter: both argue for an entity whose existence is not directly evident and for which there is no indirect evidence that cannot be otherwise accounted for. Both thus fall foul of Newton's "universally received" rules of reasoning. Following Hartley, he takes it that, as far as can be told, states of mind are universally correlated with states of the brain, a proposition that none of his critics contested. In *A Free Discussion of the Doctrines of Materialism and Philosophical Necessity, in a Correspondence between Dr. Price and Dr. Priestley. To which are added, by Dr. Priestley, an Introduction explaining the Nature of the Controversy, and Letters to Several Writers who have Animadverted on His Disquisitions Relating to Matter and Spirit, or his Treatise on Necessity* (1778). Price argues that Priestley's move from correlations between body and mind to an identity theory is a fallacious one. Priestley replies that of course not all universal correlations are cases of identity–his claim is only a theoretical entity such as the soul must not be postulated when the phenomena can be attributed to a known entity such as the brain.

Priestley had professed rigorous adherence to Newton's rules and required that his reasoning "be tried by this and by no other test." Reid was the only critic to take up this challenge. Priestley thought the rules discriminated between acceptable and unacceptable hypotheses; Reid thought they proscribed hypotheses altogether. According to Reid, the clause in the first rule requiring causes to be "true" rules out any cause that is "barely conjectured to exist without proof." Priestley is more liberal: for him a hypothetical cause can be regarded as "true" if it is modeled on a real existent. Reid typically employs the "sufficiency" criterion to exhibit the "insufficiency" of some hypothesis against those who would oversimplify the complexity of nature. Priestley typically contrasts "sufficient" with "superfluous" against those who would overpopulate ontology.

Eyewitness sketch of the destruction of Priestley's house and laboratory by a mob during the Birmingham Riots of 14 July 1791

The crux of the disagreement is in their attitudes to analogy. Newton's second rule asserts that "to the same effects we must, as far as possible, assign the same causes." Reid adopts a strict interpretation of "same" and thus empties the rule of analogical content. Priestley reads "sameness" as equivalent to "likeness"; for him, science transcends the observable, on the basis of analogical inference from the observable. For Reid, part of Newton's greatness was that he refused to pronounce on the nature of gravity, and in that sense he discovered only the law of gravity, not its cause. In contrast, Priestley's science does deal with the nature of things and not just with the laws of their superficial phenomena. For him, the human ontology is expanded by analogy.

The application of Reid's principles to the mind is somewhat unclear. He has to treat the immateriality of the mind as axiomatic. Priestley's principles apply more straightforwardly. He allows that mental phenomena are in some respects sui generis, and that they cannot thus be wholly explained by analogies; but he denies that these features are any better explained by dualism. He analogizes that humans do not know exactly how the brain thinks, but then they also do not know how magnets work. In both cases power

should be ascribed to its apparent source and not to any hypothetical agent. Had the brain been demonstrably incapable of performing the role required of it, then the method of analogy described by Newton's second rule could be used to enlarge the scheme of causes. As it seems "sufficient" and is undoubtedly "true," however, the first rule requires reducing the ontology. Not to follow this rule is tantamount to supposing that "every particular substance to which any powers or properties are ascribed may have a separate soul also." The first rule requires simplicity, but it does not entail reductionism. The brain's powers reside in its structure or organization. Nature, in Priestley's view, is a multilevel set of systems, in which different powers belong to different levels of organization. Simplicity does not reduce everything to physics.

Priestley's determinism rests on one main argument, forcefully expounded in his *The Doctrine of Philosophical Necessity Illustrated* (1777). The work was presented as an "appendix" to his materialism and suggests that materialism and determinism are mutually supporting, although he argues for determinism on independent grounds. Hume had been wrong, Priestley contends, to take the mechanism out of causation, but he was right to insist that causal relations are regular. They hold not essentially between single pairs of events but between kinds of pairs of events. Causal relations are universal, lawlike relations. This account of causation is, he argues, incompatible with libertarianism. If in the same circumstances a person could on one occasion do X and on another occasion do Y, then it cannot be those circumstances that caused him to do either. But neither could his will be said to cause either action. Any self-determining power, "bearing an equal relation to any two different decisions, cannot be said to be the cause with respect to them both." This dilemma has only two solutions. Perhaps neither the circumstances nor human will produces the action, in which case the action is "an effect without a cause" and the libertarian must give up the doctrine that every event has a cause; or it must be that such undetermined actions are impossible, and libertarianism itself must be abandoned.

Priestley's main critics, Price and Reid, took up opposing lines of attack. In *A Free Discussion of the Doctrines of Materialism and Philosophical Necessity* Price contends that causation is not a unitary concept and that a different kind of causation operates in the human sphere from that which reigns in nature. Natural causes are lawlike; human causes are not. For him, motives are both the final causes and the occasions of human action, but they are not coercive: humans are the agents, not them. Against this argument Priestley contends that the conception of causation is not shaped by the kinds of substances to which it applies: the concept must be one and the same in all cases, whether human or natural. He claims that the will can no more be said to determine actions than the motion of the air can be said to determine the direction of the wind. It is understood that the motion of the air does not cause any particular wind simply by understanding the concept of causation. He concludes that Price's ontological considerations do not divide the concept into two different kinds of causation.

Unlike Price, Reid accepted that Priestley's conception of causation does lead to determinism, and in his *Essays on the Active Powers of Man* (1788) he directs his attack against that conception (though with little mention of Priestley). He argues that all real causation is free conscious agency, whether human or divine, and that natural causes are only the superficial appearances of regularity occasioned by the hidden operation of conscious agents. He attacks Priestley's conception mainly on the grounds that it cannot account for accidental generalizations, such as the alternating succession of night and day. If all regular relations are causal relations, then night and day must be causally related. Priestley regards regularities as part of the causal relation and also as evidence of causation. Regularities

point to the existence of a mechanism that is in turn the explanation of the regularity. Science advances from the regularities to the mechanism by experimentally analyzing the "proximate cause." He gives as an example his own discovery of why frequently breathed air is fatal to animal life: experiment shows that in being breathed the composition of the air is changed. This explanation is only a partial one, but it can in principle be extended toward a complete account of the matter. It is not clear whether or how on his view it would be possible to investigate a regularity and discover no intervening proximate mechanism, so it must be said that he offered no criterion for detecting universal accidental generalizations.

In 1780 Priestley left Shelburne, in part because his philosophical controversies were beginning to embarrass his patron. He returned to his clerical career, in charge of Birmingham's prosperous "New Meeting," where he was also surrounded by a flourishing scientific and industrial culture in which he felt at home. Both friends and foes, however, tried to persuade him that philosophy was not his forte. In a sense he did modify his course at this time; little more was said about materialism thereafter. His next work, *Letters to a Philosophical Unbeliever, Part I. Containing an Examination of the Principal Objections to the Doctrines of Natural Religion, and especially those contained in the Writings of Mr. Hume* (1780), took up again the defense of the argument from design, against that most vigorous critique of the argument, Hume's *Dialogues concerning Natural Religion,* published posthumously in 1779.

Dialogues concerning Natural Religion attacks the design argument in a variety of ways. One of Hume's contentions is that the origins of life and order are necessarily unknowable because the history of the universe is a single, unique event, and no part of the universe can be used as a model by which to explain the whole. More generally, the "slow and deliberate" steps of science can never enable humans to reach cosmic conclusions. Priestley thinks that analogical reasoning, following Newton's second rule, is strong enough to bridge these difficulties. He admits that a genuine singularity would be inexplicable but denies that the Creation is an entirely singular event. God, he says, "is to be placed in the general class of intelligent and designing agents, though infinitely superior to all others of that kind." By Priestley's account of Newton's rules, however, analogy only has a constructive role when the known resources of science have been exhausted. If materialism is sufficient to account for consciousness, why is not naturalism sufficient to do the same for the order of nature? Hume had argued that nature features many principles of order and cites as examples "instinct," "vegetation," and "generation." He sets up

Priestley's house in Northumberland, Pennsylvania, where he lived after emigrating from England in 1794 (photograph by Karl G. Rath)

the principles of life in opposition to the design theorist's model of reason as the basic source of order. "The world," says Philo (Hume's skeptical spokesman), "plainly resembles more an animal or a vegetable than it does a watch or knitting-loom": "A continual circulation of matter in it produces no disorder: a continual waste in every part is incessantly repaired: the closest sympathy is perceived throughout the entire system: and each part or member, in performing its proper offices, operates both to its own preservation and to that of the whole."

In Priestley's view, however, these features of life—its orderliness and mutual adjustment—demand some sort of external explanation. Hume had foreseen this kind of reply, which he suggested begs the question: both reason and life are equally principles of order in nature, and it is arbitrary to give one priority over the other. Priestley makes two suggestions as to why life cannot be "sufficient" for the task Hume requires of it. In the first place, even if life is supposed to have been eternal, this supposition will not explain how the various species came to be so well adapted to their physical environments. Secondly, he claims that even the power

of reproduction is only superficially a process in which life brings order out of disorder. Reproduction is itself possible only because of the intricate mechanisms plants and animals possess for their own procreation. He denies then that plants and animals bestow order and organization on their offspring, and he ascribes that ordering power to their reproductive apparatus. In thus distinguishing between the power of life as such and the power of reproduction, he is trying to show that it is not he but Hume who begs the question.

Priestley had not only to defend his theism against Hume—he also had to defend it, as it were, against himself. Price, and later Samuel Taylor Coleridge, contended that materialism and determinism are in some sense inconsistent with belief in a transcendent deity, and they tend toward the pantheism of Benedict de Spinoza. Priestley's materialism was based not only on methodology but also on the problem of interaction and the theory of matter. The theological counterpart of the problem of mind-body interaction is the problem of "how an immaterial being, not existing in space, can create, or act upon matter," a difficulty so great that he concludes humans must regard God as being in some sense a material being. He observes that this solution leads to a further difficulty, for theorists are being required to suppose that nature is somehow filled by an infinite material substance. Here Priestley turns for help to the Boscovichian hypothesis: on the theory of forces and powers, solidity and impenetrability are not essential to matter, and the interpenetration of substances becomes a possibility. God, then, is quite literally a being in whom "we live, and move, and have our being," to quote one of Priestley's favorite biblical passages, Acts 17:28.

This position might be called a monism of attributes—everything is material, even, in some sense, God. Some of Priestley's critics and commentators, from Coleridge onward, have ascribed to him a monism of substance; somehow his quite strenuous opposition to this version of monism has gone unremarked. His opposition to pantheism could hardly be more explicit: "for the same reason that the maker of the table . . . must be different from the table. It is equally manifest that the maker of myself, of the world, and of the universe . . . must be a being different from myself, the world, or the universe; which is sufficient answer to the reasoning of Spinoza, who, making the universe itself to be God, did, in fact, deny that there was any God." The analogy central to the argument from design entails the ontological distinction between maker and made. Spinoza rejected the design argument because he rejected final causes, which he took to be incompatible with determinism, and because he thought the design theory involved God employing means to achieve ends, which he took to be an impossible mode of operation for a perfect being. Priestley, on the other hand, saw no difficulty in reconciling final causes with determinism or in God employing means to ends, so long as in all cases the causal relations are regular.

Priestley also thought that pantheism could be refuted without recourse to the argument from design. This premise can be seen in his *Additional Letters to a Philosophical Unbeliever, in Answer to Mr. William Hammon* (1782), written in reply to Matthew Turner (writing under the name "Hammon"), who had given chemistry lectures at Warrington Academy when Priestley was there. Turner espoused a pantheism in which God is identical with the "forces of nature." Priestley objects that this hypothesis of an intelligent, self-designing universe is "contrary to any analogy in nature." He recognizes that Turner's intelligent material universe bears some resemblance to his own conception of a thinking brain; but, he says, the analogy is not a good one, for the universe lacks the homogeneity found in the brain. This rejoinder is surprising, for it is precisely the contention of the argument from

design that the universe is not disjointed but is in fact a harmonious and simple structure.

Priestley also considers the question of whether, if human intelligence resides in a brain, God too, though distinct from the universe, must "have in him something resembling the structure of the brain." He rejects this suggestion, contending that "The divine mind . . . may be intelligent, in common with the mind of man, and yet not have the visible and tangible properties, or any thing of the consistence of the brain."

> Many things have common properties that are very dissimilar in other respects. If we had known nothing elastic beside steel, we might have concluded that nothing was elastic but steel, or something equally solid and hard; and yet we find elasticity to belong to so rare a substance as air. . . .

Priestley's claim is that analogies are sometimes misleading. Analogy does suggest that elastic objects are somehow steel-like, and the analogy of materialism does likewise suggest that God has a brain. Even so, his main objection to pantheism still stands; that is, the argument that the analogy of human creativity suggests God is to the world as maker to made.

Late in life Priestley encountered an evolutionary rival to his theism from Erasmus Darwin (Charles Darwin's grandfather), in the 1801 third edition of his *Zoonomia* (1794–1797). Darwin resembled Hume in that he thought of the biological order as having been generated by a primordial living principle. He postulated what he called "molecules with formative aptitudes" as the chief agents in reproduction and the driving force in the generation of new life-forms. Priestley's last scientific experiments were directed against the doctrine of spontaneous generation that he thought Darwin's evolutionary hypothesis entailed. (The results were published after his death in the *Transactions of the American Philosophical Society* in 1809.) Darwin, he thought, had attributed to his "particles" just the same sort of impossible spontaneity that the libertarian assigns to free will; he had given no account of how these particles are supposed to work. He denied that what Darwin called the "lower" forms of life are essentially simpler forms: on his view all species are highly complex, and all their complexities are finely adjusted to their environment.

Priestley's general position, then, is that naturalism fails to make sense of biology. Hume ascribed to life itself powers that belong only to the level of life's components; Darwin invented a mechanically impossible entity to bridge the gulf between the nonliving and the living. Since both these moves fail, mankind is forced to postulate an intelligent Creator, following the analogy of human creativity. In the case of the mind,

Priestley's grave, with the tombstone erected in 1971 by the Northumberland Cemetery Association directly in front of the original stone (photograph by Ralph E. Laird, Bucknell University)

Newton's rules favor a reduced ontology; in the case of nature, an expansion.

For a time Priestley's contemporaries were either greatly repelled or attracted by his combination of politics, religion, and philosophy. Burke's *Reflections of the Revolution in France* of 1790, which attacked Priestley and Price with considerable vehemence, and the Birmingham Riots of 1791–in which a mob championing "Church and King" destroyed Priestley's home and his library–are both monuments of the hostility he inspired in some. A cartoon of the day, labeled "Dr Phlogiston, the Priestley politician or the political priest," depicts him as an enraged firebrand standing on a tract called "Bible explained away," waving a "Political sermon" and with his "Essays on Matter and Spirit" protruding from one pocket. This antagonism led to his immigration to the United States in 1794, where he was for a short time feted as a democratic hero but soon afterward was attacked as a French Revolutionary sympathizer.

Yet, to the young English radicals of 1790 Priestley was a hero: this admiration appears in figures as diverse as Coleridge, William Wordsworth, Charles Lamb, William Hazlitt, William Godwin, Mary Wollstonecraft, Bentham, and James Mill. As Leslie Stephen observed in his *History of Thought in the Eighteenth Century* (1876), this enthusiasm was "swept away by stronger currents." In a world starting to become divided between English Christian conservatism and French radical atheism, Priestley's ambition had been to put the most "advanced" Enlightenment ideas into the service of a rationalized though heterodox Christianity, under the guidance of the basic principles of scientific method. In this project he had little success. Some of his admirers moved toward Romantic philosophy and Christian orthodoxy, others toward atheism and empiricism. By the turn of the century Priestley's influence had dwindled to the narrow stream of rational Unitarians. He died on 6 February 1804 at his home in Northumberland, Pennsylvania.

Since his death Priestley's philosophical reputation has been marginal, for two reasons. His combination of materialism, determination, and theism has appeared paradoxical to subsequent scholars. Stephen described it as "an unnatural alliance" and declared that his methods of thought "would, if consistently applied, destroy the last citadel of supernaturalism." Further, his remarkable versatility has aroused suspicion. As Stephen put it, he "possessed one of those restless intellects which are incapable of confining themselves to any single task, and, unfortunately, incapable in consequence of sounding the depths of any philosophical system."

Joseph Priestley's life was one of perpetual disputation. He always regarded controversy as a service to truth, and it was his custom to answer every objection his critics could propose. When his arguments led him to seemingly paradoxical conclusions, he held to the arguments rather than reject the premises from which he started. In "The Late Dr. Priestley" (1829) Hazlitt said that Priestley "was certainly the best controversialist of his day, and one of the best in the language"; and, he added, "in boldness of inquiry, quickness and elasticity of mind, and ease in making himself understood, he had no superior."

Letters:

A Scientific Autobiography of Joseph Priestley, 1733–1804: Selected Scientific Correspondence, edited by Robert E. Schofield (Cambridge, Mass.: MIT Press, 1966).

Bibliography:

Ronald E. Crook, *A Bibliography of Joseph Priestley, 1733–1804* (London: Library Association, 1966).

Biographies:

F. W. Gibbs, *Joseph Priestley: Adventurer in Science and Champion of Truth* (London: Thomas Nelson, 1965);

Robert E. Schofield, *The Enlightenment of Joseph Priestley: A Study of His Life and Work from 1733 to 1773* (University Park: University of Pennsylvania Press, 1997).

References:

R. G. A. Anderson and Christopher Lawrence, eds., *Science, Medicine and Dissent: Joseph Priestley (1733–1804): Papers Celebrating the 250th Anniversary of the Birth of Joseph Priestley Together with a Catalogue of an Exhibition Held at the Royal Society and the Wellcome Institute for the History of Medicine* (London: Wellcome Trust/Science Museum, 1987);

Margaret Canovan, "Two Concepts of Liberty–Eighteenth-Century Style," *Price-Priestley Newsletter*, 2 (1978): 27–41;

Martin Fitzpatrick, "Toleration and Truth," *Enlightenment and Dissent*, 1 (1982): 3–32;

Jack Fruchtman Jr., *The Apocalyptic Politics of Richard Price and Joseph Priestley: A Study in Late Eighteenth-Century English Republican Millennialism* (Philadelphia: American Philosophical Society, 1983);

Knud Haakonssen, ed., *Enlightenment and Religion: Rational Dissent in Eighteenth-Century Britain* (Cambridge: Cambridge University Press, 1996);

P. M. Heimann, "Voluntarism and Immanence: Conceptions of Nature in Eighteenth-Century Thought," *Journal of the History of Ideas*, 39 (1978): 271–283;

Lester Kieft and Bennett R. Willevord Jr., eds., *Joseph Priestley: Scientist, Theologian, and Metaphysician: A Symposium Celebrating the Two Hundredth Anniversary of the Discovery of Oxygen by Joseph Priestley in 1774* (Lewisburg, Pa.: Bucknell University Press, 1980);

Anthony H. Lincoln, *Some Political and Social Ideas of English Dissent, 1763–1800* (New York: Octagon, 1971);

J. G. McEvoy and J. E. McGuire, "God and Nature: Priestley's Way of Rational Dissent," *Historical Studies in the Physical Sciences*, 6 (1975): 325–404;

Robert E. Schofield, "Joseph Priestley: Theology, Physics and Metaphysics," *Enlightenment and Dissent*, 3 (1983): 69–82;

A. Truman Schwartz and John G. McEvoy, eds., *Motion Toward Perfection: The Achievement of Joseph Priestley* (Boston: Skinner House, 1990);

Alan Tapper, "The Beginnings of Priestley's Materialism," *Enlightenment and Dissent*, 1 (1982): 73–82;

John Yolton, *Thinking Matter: Materialism in Eighteenth-Century Britain* (Minneapolis: University of Minnesota Press, 1983).

Papers:

Many of Joseph Priestley's nonscientific papers and letters were destroyed in the Birmingham Riots. Collections are in the Dr. Williams Library, London; Dickinson College, Pennsylvania; the American Philosophical Society Library, Pennsylvania; and the Royal Society, London. See also the careful "Select Bibliography" in Robert E. Schofield, *The Enlightenment of Joseph Priestley. A Study of His Life and Work from 1733 to 1773* (University Park: University of Pennsylvania Press, 1997).

Thomas Reid

(26 April 1710 – 7 October 1796)

Peter J. Diamond
New York University

See also the Reid entry in *DLB 31: American Colonial Writers, 1735–1781.*

BOOKS: *An Inquiry into the Human Mind, on the Principles of Common Sense* (Edinburgh: Printed for A. Millar, London, and A. Kincaid & J. Bell, Edinburgh, 1764);

Essays on the Intellectual Powers of Man (Edinburgh: Printed for John Bell, Parliament-Square and G. G. J. & J. Robison, London, 1785); republished in *Essays on the Intellectual and Active Powers of Man,* 2 volumes (Philadelphia: Printed by William Young, 1793);

Essays on the Active Powers of Man (Edinburgh: Printed for John Bell, Parliament-Square and G. G. J. & J. Robison, London, 1788); republished in *Essays on the Intellectual and Active Powers of Man,* 2 volumes (Philadelphia: Printed by William Young, 1793);

Analysis of Aristotle's Logic, with Remarks (Edinburgh: Printed for William Creech, 1806);

Philosophical Orations of Thomas Reid, Delivered at Graduation Ceremonies in King's College, Aberdeen, 1753, 1756, 1759, 1762, edited, with an introduction, by W. R. Humphries (Aberdeen: Aberdeen University Press, 1937); new edition, translated by Shirley D. Sullivan, edited, with an introduction and bibliography, by D. D. Todd (Carbondale & Edwardsville: Southern Illinois University Press, 1989);

Thomas Reid's Lectures on the Fine Arts, edited, with notes, by Peter Kivy (The Hague: Martinus Nijhoff, 1973);

Thomas Reid's Lectures on Natural Theology (1780), edited, with an introduction, by Elmer H. Duncan (Washington, D.C.: University Press of America, 1983);

Practical Ethics: Being Lectures and Papers on Natural Religion, Self-Government, Natural Jurisprudence, and the Law of Nations, edited, with an introduction and a commentary, by Knud Haakonssen (Princeton: Princeton University Press, 1990);

Thomas Reid *(from Dagobert D. Runes,* A Pictorial History of Philosophy *[New York: Philosophical Library, 1959])*

Thomas Reid on the Animate Creation: Papers Relating to Life Sciences, edited, with an introduction, by Paul Wood (University Park: Pennsylvania State University Press, 1996).

Editions: *Works of Thomas Reid: With an Account of His Life and Writings,* 4 volumes, edited by Dugald Stewart (Charlestown, Mass.: Etheridge, 1813–1815);

Philosophical Works, 2 volumes, notes and supplementary dissertations by Sir William Hamilton, introduction by Harry M. Bracken (Hildesheim: Olms, 1967);

An Inquiry into the Human Mind, edited, with an introduction, by Timothy Duggan (Chicago: University of Chicago Press, 1970);

Thomas Reid's Inquiry and Essays, edited by Ronald E. Beanblossom and Keith Lehrer (Indianapolis: Hackett, 1983);

An Inquiry into the Human Mind: on the Principles of Common Sense, edited by Derek R. Brookes (University Park: The Pennsylvania State University Press, 1997).

OTHER: "Statistical Account of the University of Glasgow," in *Statistical Account of Scotland: Drawn Up from the Communications of the Ministers of the Different Parishes,* 21 volumes, edited by Sir John Sinclair (Edinburgh: William Creech, 1791–1799), XXI: Appendix: 1–50;

"Observations on the Danger of Political Innovation, from a discourse delivered on the 28th November 1794, before the Literary Society in Glasgow College, by Dr. Reid, and published by his consent," in *Sketch of the Character of the Late Thomas Reid* (Glasgow: Reprinted in the Courier Office, from the Glasgow Courier, for J. McNayr & Co., 1796), pp. 9–16;

"Thomas Reid's *Cura Prima* on Common Sense," edited by David Fate Norton, in *Claude Buffier and Thomas Reid: Two Common-Sense Philosophers,* Louise Marcil-Lacoste (Kingston, Ont. & Montreal: McGill-Queen's University Press, 1982), pp. 179–208.

SELECTED PERIODICAL PUBLICATIONS–UNCOLLECTED: "An Essay on Quantity; Occasioned by reading a treatise, in which simple and compound ratios are applied to virtue and merit," *Philosophical Transactions of the Royal Society,* 45 (1748): 505–520;

"A Sketch of Dr Smith's Theory of Morals," in "Thomas Reid on Adam Smith's Theory of Morals," by J. C. Stewart-Robertson and David Fate Norton in *Journal of the History of Ideas,* 45 (1984): 309–321;

"Of Power," in "An Essay by Thomas Reid on the Conception of Power," edited by John Haldane, in *Philosophical Quarterly,* 51 (2001): 1–12.

Thomas Reid's painstaking inquiries into the nature and extent of human knowledge represent a turning point in the history of philosophy. His *An Inquiry into the Human Mind, on the Principles of Common Sense* (1764) established his reputation for overthrowing the view that the world is mediated through "ideas," which had been entertained by philosophers from René Descartes to David Hume, and which he considered a source of modern skepticism. His alternative conception of mental activity, according to which ordinary beliefs about the world arise from "principles of common sense," was a decisive contribution to mental science conceived along the lines of Isaac New-

ton's natural philosophy. Reid's ideas were soon adopted by writers more alarmed than he by the skeptical values of the Enlightenment. As a result of the attention accorded their more popular writings, Reid became known as the founder of the Scottish school of common-sense philosophy. Although most of his published writings concern epistemology and morals, he was in fact a polymath. He was known by his contemporaries as a first-rate mathematician, and he conducted research in electricity, optics, astronomy, natural history, and chemistry at various times during his career. Neglected for much of the last century, his writings have recently attracted the attention of philosophers of mind and action, science, aesthetics, morals, and politics, as well as historians of the Scottish Enlightenment.

Reid was born on 26 April 1710 in Strachan, a parish in Kincardineshire in the Northeast of Scotland, where his father was the minister. Both of his parents, Lewis Reid and Margaret Gregory, had learned and accomplished forebears. One of his distant cousins among the Reids was the Greek and Latin secretary for James VI (later James I of Great Britain); another was physician to Charles I. The Gregorys were more recently distinguished as mathematicians and scientists. A granduncle, James Gregory, was professor of mathematics at St. Andrews University and then at Edinburgh University and invented the reflecting telescope; three of his uncles were mathematics professors at Scottish universities, one of whom went on to become Savilian Professor of Astronomy at Oxford.

Little is known of Reid's early years. Both parents were staunchly Whig and Presbyterian. They sent Reid to the parish school in Kincardine and then to the Aberdeen Grammar School. He enrolled at Marischal College, Aberdeen, in October 1722, when he was twelve-and-a-half years old. Though he later reported that his education there was slight and superficial, he was introduced to the latest and most important currents in the natural and moral sciences while a Marischal student. His teacher was George Turnbull, one of several bright young intellectuals who were then helping to transform the college into one of the leading centers of Newtonianism in Scotland. Although Turnbull has been largely forgotten, he went on to become a prolific writer who believed that the nature and purpose of human existence could be ascertained by applying the experimental or inductive methods of natural philosophy to the study of the powers of the human mind. Turnbull's scientistic claims were extravagant, and Reid likely came to recognize them as such. The idea that practical moral principles should be based on the empirical study of the powers of the human mind took hold of Reid's attention, however, and remained an ideal he pursued throughout his life.

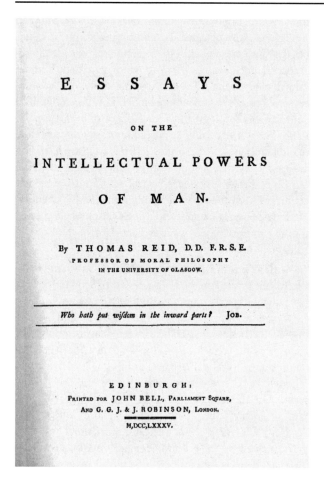

Title page for Reid's collection of some of his lectures at Glasgow University and talks before the Glasgow College Literary Society (Ximenes rare-book catalogue)

Reid received his M.A. in April 1726 and began his studies for the ministry at Marischal the following October. The surviving evidence of this period suggests that he took the time to cultivate his interest in mathematics and in the methodological reform of the moral sciences. He worked through Newton's *Principia Mathematica* (1687) with John Stewart, a former classmate under Turnbull and at that point the Liddel Professor of Mathematics at Marischal, and he thought deeply about the notion of quantity, the subject of an essay he published in 1748 in the *Philosophical Transactions of the Royal Society*. As to his theological training, he was able to avoid the narrow, dogmatic Presbyterianism prevailing elsewhere in Scotland in favor of a more rational and tolerant approach to Christian principles. In this respect his religious education and outlook resembled those of the Edinburgh "Moderates"—such as Hugh Blair, John Home, William Robertson, Adam Ferguson, and Alexander Carlyle—who began to shape the religious culture of Scotland at midcentury. Unlike the Moderates, however, Reid rarely took an active interest in ecclesiastical politics. His inclinations

were philosophical rather than political, though it would be a mistake to infer that he was unworldly or that he took little interest in moral pedagogy. On the contrary, he was taught to believe that good philosophy should be based upon and tested against ordinary experience and that its value depends upon its usefulness in teaching men and women to be morally and civically virtuous.

Reid completed his theological studies in 1731 and was admitted to the ministry of the Church of Scotland. For a time he was clerk to the presbytery of Kincardine O'Neil and an occasional preacher, and in 1733 he was appointed librarian of Marischal College, a position endowed in 1624 by his ancestor and namesake. The librarianship enabled him to continue his study of mathematics, natural philosophy, and the philosophy of mind (what the Scots called "pneumatology"). For a brief period in 1736 and again in 1737 he was a member of a local philosophical club that discussed topics in Newtonian philosophy, theories of human nature, and the debate over freedom of the will from a scientist standpoint. Reid interrupted his studies to spend most of 1736 touring England with Stewart, where their family connections enabled them to stop in London, Oxford, and Cambridge. There is a story to the effect that while in Cambridge, Reid inadvertently offended some of the members of the university by explaining "off-hand" what the incomprehensible mathematical symbols on Newton's sundial at Trinity College meant. In 1737 he was presented to the rural parish of New Machar by King's College, Aberdeen. As was often the case in Scotland at this time, the settlement did not go smoothly. The right of the college to settle the parish was disputed by its parishioners, who had objected to the (apparently illicit) behavior of the previously intruded minister and asserted their right to elect their own minister. Their passions were also inflamed by the sermonizing of a leading member of the Evangelical or Popular Party in the Kirk, John Bisset, who denounced the aristocratic interference of the college in parish affairs. In consequence Reid was physically assaulted at his ordination and had to be protected, with drawn sword, when he gave his first sermon.

What little is known of Reid's pastorate suggests that he gained his parishioners' loyalty and affection with his gentle and unassuming manner and his devotion to their spiritual and material needs. It is unlikely that he won them over from the pulpit. In contrast to the "blunt, bold, unrestrained manner and diction" of John Bisset (who had been the minister at New Machar ten years before), Reid's style, according to John Ramsay of Ochtertyre, "was far from being popular or alluring, being clear, plain mathematical reasoning little indebted to voice or action." His habit of preaching the sermons of the latitudinarians Samuel Clarke, Archbishop John Tillotson, and the Dissenter John Evans suggests that he was trying to enlighten his congregation by introducing them to the sensible, restrained religious instruction favored by polite society. The "fermfolk" of New Machar likely did not appreciate Reid's efforts—Clarke's sermons, especially, may have struck them as somewhat overintellectualized fare—but not because of his "uncommon modesty and diffidence" or because he "neglected the practice of composition" in his divinity education, as some of his early critics have alleged. It is far more likely that Reid was experimenting with a style of pulpit oratory designed to cultivate a sociable and irenic Christianity. By preaching the sermons of latitudinarians and Dissenters, Reid was attempting to bridge whatever doctrinal differences may have existed among his parishioners and to strengthen their faith by appealing to scientific knowledge of an orderly and providential creation. A quarter of a century later, Reid discussed in his lectures on eloquence at Glasgow University the difficult task of enlightening one's audience while avoiding overrefinement or affectation. In August 1740 he married his London cousin, Elizabeth Reid, whose work with the sick and poor of the parish was remembered long after she and her husband left New Machar. In an anonymous piece titled *Sketch of the Character of the Late Thomas Reid, D.D.,* Reid himself was said to have been "uncommonly active in establishing the Infirmary at Aberdeen."

Reid's philosophical interests ranged widely in the fourteen years he spent at New Machar. Reid was reported to be an avid gardener and botanist, and his surviving manuscripts from this period deal with topics in the philosophy of mind, moral philosophy, mathematics, mechanics, and astronomy. In November 1748 he read a paper titled "An Essay on Quantity; Occasioned by reading a treatise, in which simple and compound ratios are applied to virtue and merit" before the Royal Society, which published it in its *Philosophical Transactions* for that year. The treatise under review was Francis Hutcheson's *Inquiry into the Original of our Ideas of Beauty and Virtue* (1725), in which he not only sought to buttress his moral reasoning by expressing certain axioms as mathematical proportions, but he also implied that "demonstrative conclusions" would flow from the application of this method. Although Hutcheson had removed this material from the fourth edition of 1738, Reid was apparently anxious to turn his reflections on the philosophical foundations of mathematics to account by criticizing what amounted to a misconceived piece of scientism on Hutcheson's part. "An Essay on Quantity" also includes a discussion of the *vis viva* dispute between Newtonians and Leibnitzians concerning the measurement of forces.

In late 1751 Reid was prevailed upon by King's College, Aberdeen—and his wife—to give up the living of New Machar, despite his desire to remain there until he completed some literary projects, and become a regent in

philosophy. The appointment soon enabled him to take part in the reform of the arts curriculum, as both Aberdeen universities (first Marischal and then King's) were beginning to consider how they might replace their formally scholastic teaching methods with ones that took full account of the now apparent relationship between the natural and the moral sciences. Both colleges revised the order of teaching so that mathematics and natural philosophy preceded pneumatology and moral philosophy, but only Marischal abandoned regenting in favor of the professorial system. It was said that Reid led King's College to remain the last Scottish university to employ the regenting system, in which students were taught Greek for a year and then conducted through all facets of the three-year philosophy course by a single teacher, or regent. This format allowed regents to emphasize the connections between natural and moral philosophy and (as Reid and other members of the college argued) enabled them to supervise closely the intellectual and moral development of their young students.

A general indication of the content of Reid's lectures and of his own intellectual development while a King's College regent is provided in the public graduation orations he delivered, in Latin, at the end of each of his regencies in 1753 (after completing the last two years of the late Alexander Rait's course), 1756, 1759, and 1762. Although they were not composed for publication, they are far more than summaries of his philosophy course. They are attempts to clear the ground for a properly scientific study of human nature, based upon an examination of the principles and powers of the human mind. As such, they forecast the program of research Reid pursued to the end of his life. The first two orations bear a strong imprint of Francis Bacon's influence insofar as they propose laws of philosophy capable of guiding philosophers in their search for the fundamental principles of "life and morals." He believed that such laws would, if adopted, bring much-needed methodological unity to the multitude of fractious philosophical sects that were unable to recognize the self-evident principles of common sense. Reid's proposed canons of inquiry are far more allusive than concrete, but they do make plain his belief that the pursuit of human perfection involves reasoning from common sense principles, and that Thomas Hobbes, "who maintains . . . that there is no natural distinction between what is base and what is honorable," and Hume, "who asserts . . . that no trust should be placed in the senses," had manifestly lost sight of what is "clear and obvious to the multitude." Reid had not yet elaborated any common sense principles, nor had he explained how authentic principles could be distinguished from spurious ones. He appears to have been more concerned at this stage with analyzing why things had gone wrong than with demonstrating how they might be put right.

In January 1758 Reid helped to found the Aberdeen Philosophical Society, or "Wise Club," as it came to be called, which was organized along lines that paralleled the metaphilosophical and methodological maxims that he had sketched in his second oration. As the first secretary of the society Reid had a hand in specifying its perspective and sphere of interest, which were to be strictly philosophical. The society refused to be diverted by grammatical, historical, or philological topics, confining itself instead to the discussion of every principle of science that may be deduced by just and lawful induction from the phenomena either of the human mind or of the material world; all observations and experiments that may furnish materials for such inductions; the examination of false schemes of philosophy and false methods of philosophizing; and the subserviency of philosophy to arts, the principles they borrow from it, and the means of carrying them to their perfection.

Although their focus was relatively narrow, the society debated social, political, economic, religious, and philosophical questions of local and national interest and read formal discourses in the natural and moral sciences. The discourses often served as drafts of some of the most important philosophical works published in Scotland during the second half of the eighteenth century, including Reid's *An Inquiry into the Human Mind,* James Beattie's *Essay on the Nature and Immutability of Truth* (1770), Alexander Gerard's *Essay on Genius* (1774), and George Campbell's *Philosophy of Rhetoric* (1776). Reid was one of the more active members of the society during his tenure in Aberdeen. He proposed nine questions over a broad array of topics, including pneumatology, moral philosophy, economics, education, population, and botany. Of the nine discourses he composed, seven considered sense perceptions and formed the basis of *An Inquiry into the Human Mind.* The remaining two were his "Observations on the transit of Venus" and "Euclid's definitions and axioms." He remained secretary of the Wise Club until December 1760 and then served as president until January 1762.

Reid was a member of another "improving" society founded in 1758, the Gordon's Mill Farming Club—a cooperative effort on the part of Aberdeenshire's scientists, moralists, farmers, and landowners to advance the prosperity of the rural Northeast. Although Reid was far less active in this club than in the Philosophical Society, the former periodically drew on his knowledge of gardening, botany, and mechanics. In 1760 he provided the Farming Club with "A Short System of Bookkeeping for the Farmer," an essay that was published in *The Scottish Educational Journal* (14 August 1937, 21 May 1937), which was intended to rationalize all aspects of farming life.

By mid 1758 Reid had begun to elaborate what, in retrospect, may be termed a dual approach to the project of putting the science of human nature on a law-governed, and hence progressive, footing. One part of this project was essentially negative, for it consisted of undermining what he considered the chief obstacle to progress in pneumatology and all the moral sciences—the "theory of ideas." In a series of presentations before the Philosophical Society between 1758 and 1763, and again in his third and fourth graduation orations, Reid argued that modern philosophers—principally Descartes, Nicholas Malebranche, John Locke, George Berkeley, and Hume—had adopted the theory of ideas in order to explain the workings of the human mind in terms of the mechanical operation of physical objects. Such objects (in other words, simple ideas) were said to impinge upon the mind in the form of sense impressions, which in turn were combined to form complex ideas of things and events. Accordingly, what is immediately thought about is always some impression or idea representing a real object, never the object itself. Reid concluded that this theory is utterly without foundation, for there is no empirical evidence that the actions of the mind are anything like those of the body; indeed, common sense suggests that mental and physical phenomena are quite unlike one another. The fact that philosophers were prepared to think otherwise was a deplorable example of the sort of conjectural reasoning made possible by the lawless condition of philosophy. Reid did not merely reject the theory of ideas out of hand, however. He also demonstrated that many conceptions and beliefs cannot be understood in terms of impressions and ideas. Most importantly, he argued that the theory "plunges everything into the abyss of skepticism," as Hume had demonstrated in his *A Treatise of Human Nature* (1739–1740). For as soon as "the chain that links ideas and things has been broken" (as when one has reason to distrust one's senses or memory), then all that remains are the ideas in the mind. A person has no means of knowing that the real world even exists.

The Philosophical Society spent a considerable portion of its time debating Hume's philosophy, with several of its members convinced that Humean skepticism posed a threat to the practice of religion and morals. Reid was more concerned with the effect of skepticism on the philosophy of mind, however. He feared that Hume's efforts would undermine the possibility of a universal science of human nature by preventing a Baconian conjunction of labors among philosophers, whose productive efforts require that they reason from a standpoint of commonly agreed-upon principles. Morals, on the other hand, were plainly a matter of common sense and hence not readily influenced by theories, skeptical or otherwise. Reid did not say that skepticism had no relation to practical morality, however. He believed that the task of moral education was to describe "most favorably the internal feelings of an upright man who is struck by the love of virtue." From this standpoint he regarded philosophical skepticism as useless.

The other part of Reid's project was positive, consisting of an attempt to discover the laws of nature governing the faculties of the mind. In seven of his formal presentations to the Philosophical Society he pursued an inductive and empirical review of the five senses and of perception, attempting to discover the most primary and elementary principles of the phenomena of the mind, principles that everyone agrees with because they belong to the original constitution of human nature. In general terms Reid argued that the mind is not a passive recipient of ideas but an active entity, comprising the perceptual properties (sensation, conception, and belief) that make people aware of the external world. That is, sensations create conceptions and beliefs concerning the external world by certain innate suggestions. Sensations act as natural signs (the signification of which is not learned by experience), which suggest external objects as the things signified. No one can explain why sensation should compel belief, but such is the nature of mental operations. They are simple and original acts of mind that can be accounted for only in terms of the laws governing their operation.

By late 1763 Reid had completed the revisions to his Philosophical Society discourses, which were published the following year as *An Inquiry into the Human Mind, on the Principles of Common Sense*. It was an ambitious and at times a highly polemical response to Humean skepticism, premised on the beliefs that scientific knowledge of the laws governing human nature is in fact possible, provided the methodological strictures of Bacon and Newton were followed; and that such knowledge would enable men to control and hence to improve their temporal circumstances. Perhaps the most significant difference between *An Inquiry into the Human Mind* and the discourses from which it was drawn is the declamatory rhetoric of the former work. In *An Inquiry into the Human Mind* Reid ridicules Humean skeptics in order to provoke his readers into realizing that such beliefs are absurd when considered from the standpoint of ordinary social existence. "If they should carry their closet belief into the world," he argued, "the rest of mankind would consider them as diseased, and send them to an infirmary. . . . for this philosophy is like a hobby-horse, which a man in bad health may ride in his closet, without hurting his reputation; but if he should take him abroad with him to church, or to the exchange, or to the play house, his heir would immediately call a jury, and seize his estate."

Reid's point was that philosophy should be based upon common sense principles, "which we are under a necessity to take for granted in the common concerns of life, without being able to give a reason for them." Indeed, it does not make sense to justify the principles governing

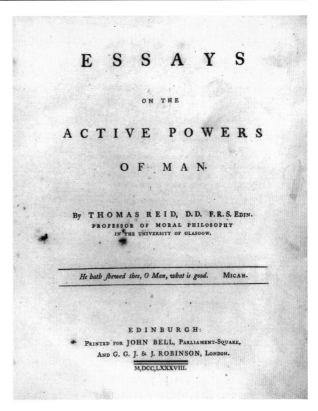

Title page for the work in which Reid deals with human action, freedom of the will, and moral obligation (courtesy of The Lilly Library, Indiana University)

human faculties, for the justification assumes the thing to be proven, that these faculties are trustworthy and not fallacious. The problem arises when people allow themselves to be reasoned away from the principles of common sense, as when, in solitary and speculative moments, they are convinced by "metaphysical" arguments such as Hume's. Reid warned that in such cases, "piety, patriotism, friendship, parental affection, and private virtue, would appear as ridiculous as knight-errantry."

There are two problems with this line of attack. First, his warning of the possible practical and moral dangers of skepticism is not wholly consistent with his belief that it cannot withstand the light of day. For he argued that it is only necessary that those afflicted by skeptical beliefs return to society, where common sense will recover its authority. Reid's reductio ad absurdum and ad hominem arguments were meant to encourage this goal. Second, such ridicule could easily lead his readers to conclude that the appeal to common sense was nothing more than an appeal to popular opinion, which, as he conceded, might be the result of an erroneous interpretation of the signs by which nature makes herself known. What is perhaps more troubling is that Reid's persuasive techniques could detract from the empirical and inductive mental anatomy, which, as he argued, is requisite to a proper interpretation of the first principles of the mind.

The publication of *An Inquiry into the Human Mind* quickly transformed Reid's provincial reputation as an uncommonly intelligent regent in philosophy (Marischal College made him an honorary doctor of divinity in 1762) into that of an internationally respected philosopher of common sense. On the whole *An Inquiry into the Human Mind* was favorably reviewed, though far more of its readers applauded its opposition to skepticism and its appeal to common sense principles than took the trouble to grapple with its demanding anatomy of the mind. Though it may not have been read carefully, it was nevertheless popular, for it went through four editions during Reid's lifetime.

One man who did study Reid's arguments carefully was Hume, to whom Reid sent the manuscript (in two installments) prior to its publication. Their brief correspondence offers a fascinating glimpse of their intellectual relationship and of the extent to which, despite their differences, they understood themselves to be pursuing similar objectives. On the negative side, it is most unlikely that Hume was troubled by Reid's arguments against the theory of ideas, about which he was relatively silent. Hume could afford to say little in his own defense because (whatever its limitations) the theory of ideas was not the linchpin of his science of human nature, as Reid supposed. Hume regarded that theory as merely the best available exposition of the principle that there is nothing in the mind unless it perceives or senses something; but he knew it was a hypothesis that might be found to be false. Moreover, Hume's project (as most scholars now believe) was not merely a negative extension of the empirical principles of Locke and Berkeley. Its positive doctrines about the passions, morals, and government found in books 2 and 3 of *A Treatise of Human Nature* went unnoticed in *An Inquiry into the Human Mind.*

Hume's principal objection was to Reid's appeal to common sense, which he perceived as leading to a dogmatic form of innatism, according to which humans are led by their nature to form unrevisable beliefs about the world that are supernaturally guaranteed. Hume, of course, was quite unwilling to rest his philosophical conclusions on the providential design of the universe, but that impression was exactly what the moralizing rhetoric of *An Inquiry into the Human Mind* created: that common sense principles are derived from God. Reid struggled to combine the roles of philosopher and practical moralist, a task Hume deemed impossible. Indeed, he took exception to "one particular Insinuation" in Reid's draft of *An Inquiry into the Human Mind,* adding, "I wish the Parsons wou'd confine themselves to their old Occupation of worrying one another; & leave Philosophers to argue with Temper, Moderation & good Manners." Hume had good reason to

be nettled at Reid's mode of expression, but in fact Reid—unlike several of Aberdeen's prominent clerics (to whom Hume may also have been referring)—avoided responding to Hume on religious grounds.

On the positive side, Hume and Reid recognized that they were both committed to the methodological reform of the moral sciences along Baconian lines, beginning with the classification and description of mental operations. Reid's attack on Hume's theory of ideas has tended to obscure their broad agreement, but as Reid told Hume, "I shall always avow my self your Disciple in Metaphysicks." He meant that his understanding of the origin, certainty, and extent of human knowledge had been shaped by Hume. More specifically, Reid acknowledged that what Hume had argued about the efficient causes of natural phenomena was right: science can explain nothing of the manner in which causes produce their effects. It can tell nothing of the origin or nature of matter, the origin of notions of existence, of judgment, of universal conceptions, or of first principles. All that can be known are the general laws according to which change takes place. Hume treated this idea as a sobering but useful doctrine that helps clarify the nature and value of empirical science; Reid agreed, but he also found that its greatest value lay in maintaining God's providential presence in nature as the first and foremost agent of all change.

In May 1764 Reid was elected to the prestigious Glasgow chair of moral philosophy, three of whose former occupants—Gershom Carmichael, Francis Hutcheson, and Adam Smith—were philosophers of international reputation. Reid was not the only candidate for the position, but he had powerful allies in James Ogilvy, Lord Deskford, and Henry Home, Kames, both of whom were leading promoters of improvement in Scotland. For the next sixteen years Reid was immersed in the academic and administrative affairs of Glasgow University. As at Aberdeen, he soon became an active member of the faculty, serving on a variety of committees, as quaestor of the library, and twice as the representative for the university to the General Assembly of the Church of Scotland. When Edmund Burke was elected rector in 1784–1785, he appointed Reid vice rector. Although Reid was devoted to the collegiate ideal, much of his time and energy was consumed by rancorous faculty infighting over administrative control of the university that plagued Glasgow throughout his tenure. Reid's involvement in these disputes was inevitable, and he complained bitterly to his Aberdeen friends that "there is no part of my time more disagreeably spent" than in these endless squabbles.

As professor of moral philosophy, Reid conducted two courses: a "public" class, which covered pneumatology, ethics, and politics, and a "private" class for advanced students, in which he explored the practical ramifications of his philosophical principles, treating "the culture of the human mind," the connection between mind and body, the fine arts, and, especially, eloquence. Both of these courses differed markedly from those of his predecessors. From the time of Carmichael the public course consisted of natural theology and jurisprudence, though Hutcheson and Smith paid somewhat less attention to theology and more to politics. Reid concentrated on pneumatology, however, believing it to be the foundation of the moral sciences. His pneumatology lectures began with an anatomy of the human mind "because its powers & faculties, are the Engines we must use in every disquisition, and because the principles of those branches of Philosophy which relate to Mind such as Natural Theology, Morals, Jurisprudence, & Politicks must be drawn from the constitution of the human Mind." After dealing with the intellectual and active powers of the mind, Reid lectured on the nature of the soul and the existence and nature of God. His ethics lectures were divided into two sections: speculative and practical. In the former he dealt with theories of morals from ancient times to the present; in the latter he organized the course according to the modern, juridical system of duties to God, to oneself, and to others. Reid's politics lectures were also divided into two parts: the first having to do with the forms of government and the second with "police," or the means of promoting the well-being and prosperity of a state. Reid's private class similarly broke with tradition. Whereas Hutcheson treated the ancient moralists and Smith taught rhetoric and belles-lettres, Reid again adopted an empirical, anti-speculative approach to the principles of the mind as a necessary preliminary to the treatment of practical moral subjects.

When taken together, Reid's Glasgow lectures indicate that he intended to elaborate a comprehensive science of human nature, the aim of which was to determine how persons could best use what talents and abilities God had given them to understand themselves (and others) and so to live virtuously in an emerging commercial society. Reid's posthumous reputation has not, until recently, reflected this intention, however, largely because he published only those portions of his Glasgow lectures pertaining to the intellectual and active powers of the mind. Reid may have believed that these topics were the only ones about which he had something new to say; certainly he was unwilling to have anyone consider his work as a comprehensive or systematic treatment of the powers of the mind or of human nature in general. Be that as it may, student notes of Reid's fine arts and natural theology lectures were published, in 1973 and 1983 respectively, but neither offers more than a partial view of his thinking at particular times. His considered theory of aesthetics was published as the essay "Of Taste" in his *Essays on the Intellectual Powers of Man* (1785). His natural theology lectures rely

heavily on the arguments of Clarke and Joseph Butler demonstrating the being and attributes of God and were written with the practical purpose of nurturing his students' devotion to Christian principles. Student notes of his lectures of 1779 and 1780 refer to Hume's posthumously published *Dialogues Concerning Natural Religion* (1779) and warn that Hume's rejection of the chief argument for a divine existence, the argument from design, "strikes at the root of all Religion" and "cuts all of the sinews of virtuous conduct, robs it of all its splendor & rests it on a very weak & slippery foundation." Reid believed that Hume's rejection of that argument, calling into question the premise that an intelligent cause may be inferred from marks of wisdom in the effects, was incorrect. The truth of the premise is not learned from experience or from reasoning; rather, it is a necessary principle of common sense whose truth is self-evident. Evidently, Reid considered his common-sense defense of the argument from design worth publishing, for he included a revised version of it, omitting any mention of the threat to virtue posed by Hume's theory, in *Essays on the Intellectual Powers of Man.*

Reid's Glasgow lectures on practical ethics, which Knud Haakonssen published in 1990 as *Practical Ethics: Being Lectures and Papers on Natural Religion, Self-Government, Natural Jurisprudence, and the Law of Nations,* are far more substantial than those on fine arts or natural theology. They indicate that Reid's approach to practical ethics changed as a result of his Glasgow profession. His Aberdeen lectures on that subject had been humanist in orientation: he held that the pursuit of human perfection requires that individuals learn to govern themselves by understanding and cultivating their intellectual and moral powers. Such an approach tended to be preoccupied with problems of moral pedagogy, which Reid and the other members of the Aberdeen Philosophical Society discussed with great frequency. Reid modeled his account of the principles of practical morality on Xenophon's moral and material economy of the household. This approach emphasized the necessary dependence of the individual upon others and the need for a social life that begins with the family and culminates in the community, whose educational institutions seek to nurture the moral and civic virtues upon which its existence depends. The development from individual to community is regarded as a natural phenomenon, so there cannot be any true opposition between the best interest of the community and that of the person. It was an approach well suited to the relatively isolated, rural society to which Reid belonged. At Glasgow, however, he began to discuss practical ethics within a juridical framework of duties, which he reckoned was better suited to the demands of Christian casuistry than was the virtue ethics of the ancients. Although he shared with the latter view a fundamental concern with human nature and the means of its improvement, he came to realize that

1

All the Objects of Human Knowledge, may be divided into two Kinds - those of Body and those of Mind - The Arts and Sciences may likewise be divided into two great Branches, concerning Things material & immaterial:. Theology. Pneumatology. Logic &c. derive their first Principles from the Philosophy of the Mind - They are adressd to it. and are intended to produce some Effect upon it — Astronomy Medicine; Chymistry. Physics Botany &c. and all the arts of human Life, derive their first Principles from the Philosophy of Body. and are intended to produce some Effect upon it —

But there is a third Branch, under which are

First page of the manuscript for Reid's Lectures on the Fine Arts, *which was not published until 1973 (Edinburgh University Library)*

an ethics grounded in human nature alone is morally indeterminate. Even the cardinal virtues of prudence, temperance, fortitude, and justice are not properly moral but merely prudential ends, unless they are considered as duties imposed by divine law. In other words, Reid recognized that in a large, commercial society such as Glasgow, in which the pursuit of wealth threatened to corrupt both personal and public morals, the practice of virtue was best treated as a Christian duty. Reid arranged his system of practical ethics as a taxonomy of corresponding rights and duties that ideally structure the moral world. His basic idea is that whenever humans act in society they assume an office or a set of obligations, which are pointed out by the common good and the law of nature and are matched by corresponding rights. Reid knew that a system of rights tends to produce unacceptably individualistic outcomes, but he also recognized that "men may attend more willingly to their rights, which put them in mind of their dignity, than to their duties, which suggest their dependence." Reid avoided this dilemma by maintaining that rights are legitimate only when they do not interfere with the common good but as far as possible contribute to it. He chose not to discuss the radical political implications of this position before his students, but he did explore the topic with his colleagues.

Reid's membership in the Glasgow College Literary Society enabled him to discuss economic and political questions of the day as well as to present philosophical discourses that he eventually revised and published, as he had done in Aberdeen. On questions of economic policy he consistently favored removing impediments to commercial expansion, though not at the expense of the poor. In each of his extant addresses (on the corn laws, on interest rates, and on coinage) Reid assumed that the pursuit of wealth was not just a manifestation of man's rationality but was instrumental to its practice. Yet, he expressed different sentiments respecting moneymaking and the possession of property in a 1794 discourse, "Some Thoughts on the Utopian System," in which he pointed his political reflections beyond the pursuit of a common good defined in terms of the order and peaceableness of society, to an imaginary state in which the common good was realized in the perfection of human nature. This state involved the abolition of private property in favor of communal ownership, a system of public honors for virtuous conduct, and an educational program dedicated to the formation of character. Reid had no desire to have his speculations put into practice; though he was a liberal Whig who sympathized with the French Revolution, he also feared sudden or violent change. His utopian speculations were, like most of his writings, intended to heighten awareness of the nature and limits of human perfectibility. Most of Reid's discourses before the Literary Society treat philosophical subjects, including the intellectual powers of the

mind, the concept of active power, the will, and the principles of action. Only a few of these discourses have survived, but he clearly began to refine his appeal to common sense and its principles on the assumption that "it would contribute greatly to the stability and to the improvement of human knowledge, if the first principles upon which the various branches of it are grounded were pointed out and ascertained." He delivered several discourses on Joseph Priestley's materialism. Priestley had publicly denounced Reid and two other antiskeptics, Beattie and James Oswald, because their appeal to common sense seemed to threaten rational religion and the Dissenting cause. Reid did not respond publicly to Priestley's attack, but he did criticize the latter's philosophical assumptions. Reid particularly wished to counter the necessitarian (or determinist) ramifications of the theory of ideas by establishing the common-sense principle that man has power over his will. He recognized that unless people are free to act on what they have learned, then the idea of an improvement-oriented science of human nature loses its purpose.

Reid's teaching duties and his involvement in college affairs left little time to publish. He did pen "A Brief Account of Aristotle's Logic, with Remarks" for Lord Kames to include in his *Sketches on the History of Man* (1774). Reid no doubt welcomed the opportunity to collaborate with Kames, who had become a close friend, to offer an analytic account of why syllogistic reasoning was abandoned as an instrument of scientific reasoning in favor of induction, and to rehearse a favorite theme: that progress in the moral sciences awaits unanimity among philosophers regarding the foundational principles of common sense.

In 1780 Reid retired from teaching and began to revise his lectures and some of his Literary Society discourses for publication. The first of two volumes, *Essays on the Intellectual Powers of Man,* appeared five years later. The book covers some of the same ground as *An Inquiry into the Human Mind:* the refutation of the ideal system; the account of perception, as distinct from sensation, according to which some sign immediately gives rise to a conception of the object perceived and a belief in its existence; and the appeal to common sense—though these themes were now given extended treatment as part of a comprehensive and highly self-conscious analysis of the powers of the mind. References to common sense had long exercised a pivotal role in Reid's thinking, as he sought to ground philosophy in principles "that snatch up assent from the very constitution of human nature." *Essays on the Intellectual Powers of Man* offers his first systematic account of this notoriously ambiguous notion, which (as he recognized) ordinarily refers to so wide a range of abilities as to "fill up all the interval between idiocy on one hand and uncommon discernment and penetration on the other."

The term consequently possesses enormous rhetorical value (for no one, by definition, can plausibly contradict the edicts of common sense), which he was not unwilling to exploit when attacking Hume, but its lack of clarity and distinctness meant that it was of little philosophical value. Reid sought to remedy this problem in *Essays on the Intellectual Powers of Man* by defining common sense as the power to judge truth and falsity in light of a self-evident first principle, without reasoning. No sooner are such principles understood than they are believed. "The judgment follows the apprehension of them necessarily, and both are equally the work of nature, and the result of our original powers." By depicting the judgments of common sense as intuitive and irresistible he was attempting to parry Hume's skeptical claim that such principles cannot be accounted for by reason. To Reid's credit, that attempt was not a dogmatic appeal to public opinion. For while he maintained that there are marks by which one can distinguish genuine from false principles (they are irresistible, garner universal consent, and arise before experience could account for them), he also acknowledged that such marks are not foolproof. They may help identify a first principle, but they are not proof that a particular belief is true. Indeed, the beliefs of common sense are justified only until shown to be false. Reid concluded his account by dividing first principles into two categories: those that are necessary and immutable and whose contrary is impossible (for example, those pertaining to grammar, logic, mathematics, taste, morals, and mathematics) and those that are contingent and mutable and depend upon some effect of will and power (in other words, those informing people of the truth of their convictions arising from their natural faculties).

Essays on the Intellectual Powers of Man was followed three years later by *Essays on the Active Powers of Man* (1788), in which Reid treats the nature of human action, the freedom of the will, and the nature of moral obligation. It is, like almost all of his published writing, abstract and demanding, and seemingly far removed from the world of practical affairs; but its thesis is simple and straightforward: that the most important fact of human nature relative to the perfection of humans as rational beings is the power of self-government. Reid argues that every person of sound mind is a moral agent, that he possesses "a power over the determinations of his own will." Only on these terms can one make sense of the fact that one is an accountable being, capable of improving oneself and others. The problem Reid faced was explaining how one can have free will in a law-governed universe, in which all events, even acts of will, are caused. Necessitarians maintained that the two positions are incompatible, on grounds that acts of will are caused by earlier events and circumstances. Reid rejected their claim, however, because it conflicts with common-sense beliefs about freedom and moral responsibility. Reid's solution to the problem was to argue that free acts of will are not caused by any prior events; rather, they are caused by the agent's power to determine whether or not to perform an action. His elaboration of this argument, including his account of the role of motives in influencing the will, remains one of the most insightful and compelling treatments of moral freedom ever written. Reid's theory of action and morals was partly a response to Hume's claim that reason is incapable of determining human ends. Reid was convinced that Hume's attempt to show that reason must do the bidding of the passions failed to take account of the extent to which the pursuit of virtue depends upon the ability "to observe the connections of things, and the consequences of our actions." In arguing that reason directs people toward "our good upon the whole" and "what appears to be our duty," Reid sought to valorize those actions that cannot be reduced to self-interest and upon which the common good depends.

Essays on the Intellectual Powers of Man and *Essays on the Active Powers of Man* were well received by the established periodicals, with the former receiving the warmer reception of the two volumes. The volumes were never as popular with the literate public as *An Inquiry into the Human Mind,* but their widespread use as university textbooks, particularly in the United States, gave them a far deeper and more lasting influence. After the publication of *Essays on the Active Powers of Man,* Reid continued to devote himself to social and political causes, the latter chiefly associated with the French Revolution. He also remained philosophically active. In 1794, at the request of principal and faculty at the University of Glasgow, he wrote "A Statistical Account of the University of Glasgow," a pedagogically self-conscious description of the structure and practices of the university. It was published posthumously, as an appendix to Sir John Sinclair's authoritative *Statistical Account of Scotland: Drawn Up from the Communications of the Ministers of the Different Parishes* (1791–1799). By the 1790s Reid's infirmities prevented him from attending the meetings of the Literary Society regularly, though he continued to present discourses: on Euclid's *Elements,* on the utopian system of government, and, within a year of his death, on the muscular motions of the body. This last discourse was the result of Reid's attempt to anatomize his own experience of the physical effects of aging. He died on 7 October 1796 after a brief illness.

Reid's reputation as the founder of the Scottish philosophy of common sense was cemented in the 1770s, when *An Inquiry into the Human Mind* and the highly popular works of his followers Beattie and Oswald were collectively receiving critical scrutiny in Britain and on the Continent. After his death Reid's philosophy (as interpreted by one of his students, Dugald Stewart) dominated university curricula in France, Scotland, and particularly the United States well into the 1860s. Thereafter its influence declined, though Reid's writings have continued to influence individual thinkers to the present day.

Letters:

"Correspondence of Dr. Reid," in *The Works of Thomas Reid, D. D., now fully collected, with selections from his unpublished letters,* edited by Sir William Hamilton (Edinburgh: Maclachlan & Stewart, 1846), pp. 39–92;

"Unpublished Letters of Thomas Reid to Lord Kames, 1762–1782," edited by Ian Ross, *Texas Studies in Literature and Language,* 7 (Spring 1965): 17–65.

Bibliographies:

Nina Mikhalevsky, "Bibliography," in *Thomas Reid: Critical Interpretations,* edited by Stephen F. Barker and Tom L. Beauchamp (Philadelphia: University City Science Center, 1976), pp. 133–140;

Richard A. Legum, "An Updated Bibliography of Works on the Philosophy of Thomas Reid," *Monist,* 61 (April 1978): 340–344.

Biographies:

Dugald Stewart, *Account of the Life and Writings of Thomas Reid, D. D. F. R. S. Edin. Late Professor of Moral Philosophy in the University of Glasgow* (Edinburgh: A. Neill, 1802);

John Ramsay of Ochtertyre, *Scotland and Scotsmen in the Eighteenth Century,* 2 volumes, edited by Alexander Allardyce (Edinburgh & London: Blackwood, 1888);

A. Campbell Fraser, *Thomas Reid* (Edinburgh: Oliphant, Anderson & Ferrier, 1898);

Paul Wood, "Thomas Reid, Natural Philosopher," dissertation, University of Leeds, 1984.

References:

Stephen F. Barker and Tom L. Beauchamp, eds., *Thomas Reid: Critical Interpretations* (Philadelphia: University City Science Center, 1976);

Melvin Dalgarno and Eric Matthews, eds., *The Philosophy of Thomas Reid* (Dordrecht & Boston: Kluwer, 1989);

Norman Daniels, *Thomas Reid's "Inquiry": The Geometry of Visibles and the Case for Realism* (Stanford: Stanford University Press, 1989);

George E. Davie, *The Scottish Enlightenment* (London: Historical Association, 1981), p. 18;

Peter J. Diamond, *Common Sense and Improvement: Thomas Reid as Social Theorist* (Frankfurt am Main: Peter Lang, 1998);

Roger D. Gallie, *Thomas Reid and "the Way of Ideas"* (Dordrecht & Boston: Kluwer, 1989);

S. A. Grave, *The Scottish Philosophy of Common Sense* (Oxford: Clarendon Press, 1960);

Laurens Lauden, "Thomas Reid and the Newtonian Turn of British Methodological Thought," in *The Methodological Heritage of Newton,* edited by Robert E. Butts and John W. Davis (Toronto: University of Toronto Press, 1970), pp. 103–131;

Keith Lehrer, *Thomas Reid* (London & New York: Routledge, 1989);

Erich Lobkowicz, *Common Sense und Skeptizismus: Studien zur Philosophie von Thomas Reid und David Hume* (Weinheim: Acta Humaniora, VCH, 1986);

Louise Marcil-Lacoste, *Claude Buffier and Thomas Reid: Two Common-Sense Philosophers* (Kingston, Ont. & Montreal: McGill-Queen's University Press, 1982);

Marcil-Lacoste, "Dieu, Garant de Véracité, ou Reid Critique de Descartes," *Dialogue,* 14 (December 1975): 584–606;

"The Philosophy of Thomas Reid," *Monist,* 61 (April 1978): 167–344;

D. D. Raphael, *The Moral Sense* (London: Oxford University Press, 1947);

William L. Rowe, *Thomas Reid on Freedom and Morality* (Ithaca, N.Y.: Cornell University Press, 1991);

"Thomas Reid and His Contemporaries," *Monist,* 70 (October 1987): 383–526;

Nicholas Wolterstorff, *Thomas Reid and the Story of Epistemology* (Cambridge: Cambridge University Press, 2001);

P. B. Wood, "Hume, Reid, and the Science of the Mind," in *Hume and Hume's Connexions,* edited by M. A. Stewart and John P. Wright (University Park: Pennsylvania State University Press, 1995), pp. 119–139.

Papers:

The largest and most important collections of Thomas Reid's manuscripts are held by Aberdeen University Library, which includes the Birkwood Collection, Reid's papers to the Aberdeen Philosophical Society, and isolated letters. Additional letters and student notes of Reid's lectures exist at the university libraries in Glasgow and Edinburgh. There is also an extensive set of a student's lecture notes from Reid's 1779–1780 class at the Mitchell Library, Glasgow. Glasgow University Archives also has letters and papers relating to Reid's handling of college business. Isolated letters and papers exist at the National Library of Scotland and at the Scottish Record Office, Edinburgh.

Adam Smith

(circa 5 June 1723 – 17 July 1790)

Kurt Norlin
Claremont Graduate University

See also the Smith entry in *DLB 104: British Prose Writers, 1660–1800.*

BOOKS: *The Theory of Moral Sentiments* (London: Printed for A. Millar and A. Kincaid & J. Bell, Edinburgh, 1759; revised, 1761); revised and enlarged as *The Theory of Moral Sentiments. To which is added A Dissertation on the Origin of Languages* (London: Printed for A. Miller and A. Kincaid & A. Bell, Edinburgh; and sold by T. Cadell, 1767); republished as *The Theory of Moral Sentiments; or, An Essay towards an Analysis of the Principles by which Men naturally judge concerning the Conduct and Character, first of their Neighbours, and afterwards of themselves* (London: Printed for W. Strahan, J. & F. Rivington, W. Johnston, T. Longman, and T. Cadell, and for W. Creech, Edinburgh, 1774; revised, 1781; enlarged and corrected edition, 2 volumes, London: Printed for A. Strahan and A. Cadell; and W. Creech and J. Bell, Edinburgh, 1790; first American editions, Philadelphia: Anthony Finley, 1817; Boston: Wells & Lilly, 1817);

An Inquiry into the Nature and Causes of the Wealth of Nations, 2 volumes (London: W. Strahan & T. Cadell, 1776; revised, 1778); revised and corrected edition, 3 volumes (1784); first American edition (Philadelphia: Dobson, 1789);

Essays on Philosophical Subjects . . . To Which is prefixed An Account of the Life and Writings of the Author by Dugald Stewart, edited by Joseph Black and James Hutton (London: T. Cadell, Jun. & W. Davies and W. Creech, Edinburgh, 1795);

Lectures on Jurisprudence, edited by Edwin Cannan (Oxford, U.K.: Clarendon Press, 1896);

Lectures on Rhetoric and Belles Lettres, Delivered in the University of Glasgow by Adam Smith, Reported by a Student in 1762–63, edited by John M. Lothian (London & New York: Thomas Nelson, 1963);

Editions: *The Works of Adam Smith. With an Account of his Life and Writings by Dugald Stewart,* 5 volumes (Lon-

Adam Smith; medallion by James Tassie, 1787 (Scottish National Portrait Gallery)

don: T. Cadell & W. Davies and W. Creech, Edinburgh, 1811–1812);

The Glasgow Edition of the Works and Correspondence of Adam Smith, 7 volumes (Oxford: Clarendon Press, 1976–1987);

Lectures on Jurisprudence, edited by Ronald L. Meek, David D. Raphael, and Peter G. Stein (Oxford: Clarendon Press, 1978).

OTHER: Review of Samuel Johnson's *A Dictionary of the English Language, Edinburgh Review,* 1 (1755): 61–73;

Letter to the editors, *Edinburgh Review,* 2 (1756): 63–79;

"Considerations concerning the first formation of languages, and the different genius of original and compounded languages," *Philological Miscellany,* 1 (1761): 440–479;

"Letter from Adam Smith, LL.D. to William Strahan, Esq.," *Scots Magazine,* 31 (1777): 5–7;

"Smith's Thoughts on the State of the Contest with America," edited by G. H. Guttridge, in *American Historical Review,* 38 (1933): 714–720.

Today Adam Smith is known mainly as an economic theorist, author of *An Inquiry into the Nature and Causes of the Wealth of Nations* (1776), and virtual patron saint of the free market. In his own time, however, Smith first gained fame for his treatise on ethics, *The Theory of Moral Sentiments* (1759), in which he develops a psychologically oriented account of moral judgment, similar to David Hume's account but more elaborate in its treatment of the phenomenon called *sympathy,* the emotional response of one person to another person's situation. Smith's views on this subject are often cited respectfully by social psychologists and have, in recent years, again attracted the attention of philosophers.

Smith grew up in Kirkcaldy, a mid-sized industrial town on Scotland's east coast, near Edinburgh. Agriculture in the surrounding Fife countryside was gradually picking up following the union of Scotland and England in 1707, but local coal and salt manufacture had begun to feel the effects of increased competition from elsewhere. Smith's father, also named Adam, was a man of finance and public affairs, appointed in 1714 as comptroller of customs at Kirkcaldy. He was a widower with an eleven-year-old son before he wed Margaret Douglas in November 1720. Robust health did not run through the men in this branch of the Smith family. After two years of marriage the elder Adam Smith died at only forty-three years of age, of an unknown illness. Adam junior was born some six months later, presumably within a few days of his recorded baptism on 5 June 1723. His mother was a self-reliant woman from a landed Scottish family. Like her husband, she was devoutly Presbyterian but genuinely respectful of, and interested in, secular culture. Recognizing her son's gift for scholarship, she saw to it that he had every available educational advantage. He returned her devotion in full measure and continued in close relationship with her until she died, in 1784, only six years before he did. He never married. Both he and his half brother, Hugh Smith, inherited their father's weak constitution, which in Adam's case provided a basis in fact for a

lifelong inclination toward hypochondria and psychosomatic illness. Hugh died in 1750.

After attending Kirkcaldy's highly regarded grammar school, where the other pupils treated their bookish, sickly, but good-natured classmate with affection, Smith went to Glasgow University in 1737. Entering the university at age fourteen was then not unusual, and Glasgow was apparently a relatively safe and wholesome place for a young person to live (in contrast to Edinburgh). Smith's favorite subjects during this time were mathematics and natural philosophy, that is, natural science. The modern physics that produced Isaac Newton's *Philosophiæ Naturalis Principia Mathematica* (1687) had been readily embraced at Glasgow, partly because the modestly endowed university, dependent on student tuitions for income, was forced to keep abreast of developments in the various disciplines. Smith maintained an interest in scientific theory and experiment all his life. The professional domain of Smith's favorite teacher at Glasgow, however, was moral philosophy. Frances Hutcheson was a liberal Presbyterian with a favorable, anti-Calvinist view of human nature and, like Smith's parents, an admiration for the greats of pagan antiquity, particularly Cicero and the other Stoics. Moral philosophy then being understood more broadly than today, the popular Hutcheson gave lectures (in English rather than the customary Latin) not only on ethics but also on aesthetics, economics, law, and political science.

Hutcheson's views on ethics were set in the context of a controversy begun some eight or nine decades earlier by Thomas Hobbes. One of the first thinkers to connect philosophical ethics to the emerging new physics, Hobbes asserted that all value in the world was subjective—a perception-dependent attribute of things, on a par with color or taste, rather than a perception-independent attribute, like shape or size. Hobbes also declared—or at least was taken to have declared—that people are naturally selfish and that all their actions are aimed at self-preservation. This doctrine was widely rejected by later British moralists in a debate that lasted the better part of two centuries and revolved mostly around questions of moral epistemology, with implications for moral metaphysics. Some critics of Hobbes insisted that moral judgment is an operation of reason, producing knowledge of a perception-independent reality, and that this knowledge can motivate people entirely apart from considerations of personal interest. Other critics, however, saw sentiment rather than reason as the engine of moral judgment. They agreed with Hobbes about value's subjectivity while differing with him over people's alleged selfishness. To this latter group belonged

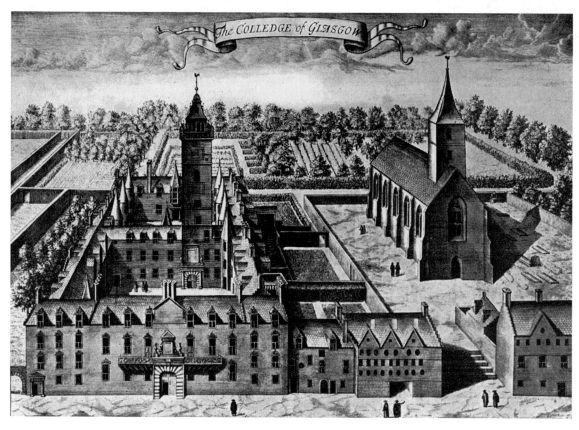

Glasgow University, where Smith studied and later taught; print by Slezer, circa 1693 (Mitchell Library, Glasgow)

Hutcheson. Hutcheson took from Anthony Ashley Cooper, third Earl of Shaftesbury, the idea of a moral sense but jettisoned the Aristotelian elements in Shaftesbury's doctrine. He maintained that people have an inborn faculty that approves of benevolence and thereby motivates solicitude for others. Although virtue and vice exist only in the eyes of moral perceivers, kindness is seen as a virtue quite apart from any benefit it produces for the perceiver.

In 1740 Smith, who had distinguished himself as a promising student but earned no degree from Glasgow, went to Balliol College, Oxford on a scholarship intended for prospective clergy in the Church of England. Finding the instruction at his new school old-fashioned in content and negligently conducted, however (Oxford possessed a large endowment), Smith was forced to study more or less on his own, to great intellectual profit but at some cost to his health. During this time Smith wrote, or at least began, his essay on "The History of Astronomy," later included in *Essays on Philosophical Subjects* (1795). The view of scientific inquiry he there propounds is, like the theory

of morality he develops later, psychological in its focus. He describes science as a quest for aesthetic satisfaction, in which physical theory is used to smooth over disconcerting gaps and irregularities in the imaginative tracing of the flow of natural events. The Humean flavor of these speculations, and in certain places the very phrasing, gives some credence to an anecdote about the heads of Balliol catching young Smith surreptitiously reading Hume's infamous *A Treatise of Human Nature* (1739–1740). Smith's "The History of Astronomy" preaches the value of economy: the most satisfactory scientific theory is the one that smooths over the most problems using the fewest principles. Newtonian astronomy, which derives the complex motions of the planets and their moons from a single principle, namely the inverse square law of gravitation, is the model of sound philosophical science.

After six years at Balliol, Smith left in disgust. He probably never seriously meant to take to the pulpit, but in any event Oxford had given him little besides a facility with standard, southern English, which men of letters throughout Britain preferred to the Scottish variety. It was common in those days for young men to step from the university into a traveling tutorship in the service of young noblemen. Failing to gain such employment, however, Smith returned to Kirkcaldy to live again with his mother and continued his private studies over the next two years. He probably did further work on "The History of Astronomy," and apparently he also corresponded with other, more established men of learning. A small group of them, including Henry Home (later Lord Kames), were sufficiently impressed to sponsor Smith in a lectureship at the University of Edinburgh. Between 1748 and 1751 Smith taught rhetoric, literature, and law with great success. Student notes from later versions of the lectures, given at Glasgow, survived and were published long after Smith's death as *Lectures on Jurisprudence* (1896) and *Lectures on Rhetoric and Belles Lettres, Delivered in the University of Glasgow by Adam Smith, Reported by a Student in 1762–63* (1963). Probably while lecturing at Edinburgh, Smith made personal acquaintance with Hume, twelve years older than he and trying, unsuccessfully, to gain an appointment at the same institution. That the two men became over time the best of friends testifies to Hume's generous disposition.

In 1751 Smith's growing reputation earned him an election to the chair of logic at his alma mater, Glasgow University. Shortly thereafter, Smith took over the chair of moral philosophy when Hutcheson's successor resigned for health reasons. Smith's students esteemed him for his engaging lectures and marveled at his absentmindedness. He habitually talked to himself and, when addressing others, was so unmindful of his surroundings that he once fell into a tanning pit. Even so, he proved adept not only at teaching but also at administration, holding several posts involving the supervision of the university's financial business and the maintenance and improvement of its facilities.

The lectures Smith prepared in moral philosophy became the basis for his first major published work, *The Theory of Moral Sentiments*. The book found favor with the "Mob of Literati," as Hume teasingly wrote in a letter to Smith, and the initial printing of perhaps five hundred copies sold out quickly, as Smith apparently learned through a letter from Hume, whose own published efforts over the years had received a much less enthusiastic reception. *The Theory of Moral Sentiments* went through six editions during Smith's lifetime, some of them involving extensive revisions. With translations into French and German, it was widely read on the Continent. Smith himself always regarded it as the best of all his works.

In the last part of *The Theory of Moral Sentiments* Smith begins a survey of different systems of moral philosophy by identifying two key questions:

> First, wherein does virtue consist? Or what is the tone of temper, and tenour of conduct, which constitutes the excellent and praise-worthy character, the character which is the natural object of esteem, honour, and approbation? And, secondly, by what power or faculty in the mind is it, that this character, whatever it be, is recommended to us? Or in other words, how and by what means does it come to pass, that the mind prefers one tenour of conduct to another, denominates the one right and the other wrong; considers the one as the object of approbation, honour, and reward, and the other of blame, censure, and punishment?

The first question is the practical, normative one: what is the proper way to be and to act? The second question is about moral epistemology: how are right and wrong known? Although Smith discusses answers to the first question, and at one point seems to imply that it is the more important of the two, most of *The Theory of Moral Sentiments* is actually devoted to the epistemological question. This emphasis is reflected in the title of the 1774 republication of the work: *The Theory of Moral Sentiments; or, An Essay towards an Analysis of the Principles by which Men naturally judge concerning the Conduct and Character, first of their Neighbours, and afterwards of themselves.* Smith sees three possibilities for what he calls "the principle of approbation": self-love, as Hobbes would have it; reason, as Ralph Cudworth contends; and sentiment, as Hutcheson counters.

Smith agrees with Hutcheson, Hume, and Kames in arguing that moral judgment is ultimately a matter of feeling. Hutcheson, however, refused to give any account of how the moral sentiments arise, taking the view that they follow directly as a response to the contemplation of an agent's motives, unmediated by any further act of reason or the imagination. Smith objects that the idea of a faculty whose only known function is moral perception is contrary to the "economy of Nature," the principle that Nature produces many effects from a single cause. In other words, Smith would prefer to explain the moral sentiments in terms of psychological phenomena already known—as his essay on astronomy says is the proper procedure. Hume has the same wish. For both men, sympathy is the key to explaining where the moral sentiments come from. Hume's account is fairly simple: when contemplating a person or a person's actions, the spectator sympathizes with everyone the person comes in contact with, being vicariously affected in the same manner as the people the actor comes into

THE

THEORY

OF

MORAL SENTIMENTS.

By ADAM SMITH,
Professor of Moral Philosophy in the
University of Glasgow.

LONDON:
Printed for A. Millar, in the Strand;
And A. Kincaid and J. Bell, in Edinburgh.
M DCC LIX.

Title page for the ethical treatise that made Smith famous (Special Collections, University of California, Riverside)

contact with are actually affected. If the overall effect of the person's behavior on others is pleasant, the observer feels pleasure on the contemplation; but if the effect is unpleasant, the observer feels displeasure. This pleasure or displeasure constitutes the moral sentiment of approval or disapproval.

Smith agrees with Hume that the moral sentiments spring from the sympathetic experience corresponding to someone else's situation. But whereas for Hume the sympathy is with anyone *affected* by the person whose actions are being judged, in Smith's scheme the sympathy is with the *agent,* the one doing the acting. In judging an agent, Smith theorizes, the spectator imagines him- or herself in the agent's circumstances. After the spectator experiences a reaction, the spectator then compares this reaction with the one the spectator observes in the agent. If the spectator finds a similarity, he or she feels pleasure at the correspondence, and this second-order feeling is the sentiment of approval; if the spectator finds disparity, the spectator feels displeasure, and this second-order feeling is the sentiment of disapproval. One reason Smith prefers his model is that it naturally explains, among other things, why moral judgment is directed at human agents rather than being just one species of judgments of utility generally. Hume's handling of moral judgment, as Smith points out, puts the judgment of virtue on a par with the judgment of the utility of a chest of drawers, since sympathy with the user of a well-made piece of furniture works just like sympathy with the associates of a kindly, even-tempered person. In Smith's account, by contrast, moral judgment involves sympathy with the one judged and thus is distinctively directed at conscious agents. Smith allows that although perception of utility reinforces moral approval, it is not the source.

Any moral theory based on feeling faces a difficulty, however: if moral judgments are mere expressions of the possibly idiosyncratic feelings the judge happens to have on a given occasion, then any moral judgment would seem to be as correct as any other. Hutcheson, Hume and Smith all address this problem by understanding moral judgments as expressions of feelings arising under standardized conditions. Smith, in particular, lays great stress on full knowledge and impartiality: the judge's sympathy must be informed by full knowledge of the agent's circumstances and must be free of influence from any personal connection the agent has to the agent's actions. The sympathy must be, in Smith's phrase, that of an "impartial spectator."

Once the device of an impartial spectator is in place, however, a new question arises for Smith. Some of the most important moral judgments, after all, are the ones people make about themselves. An adequate explanation of moral judgments in terms of approval and disapproval has to give an account of the self-directed versions of those sentiments. Yet, if moral judgment is an expression of the feelings of an impartial spectator who sympathizes with the agent in question, how do agents manage to judge their own actions? Do they somehow sympathize with themselves? Smith's way of dealing with this issue is to take his sympathy-based theory, developed to explain how spectators judge the actions of agents, and to reverse the direction in which sympathy operates: when agents judge their own actions, they sympathize with an impartial spectator, imagining how their actions would appear to a person who was well-informed but had no special stake in the results.

Then the agents examine their own feelings about their situation and again have a second-order response: similarity of reaction leads to approval–self-approval, this time–while dissimilarity leads to self-disapproval.

This bidirectional account of moral judgment, with sympathy flowing from spectator to agent and from agent to spectator, has two notable ramifications. First, it goes hand in hand with, and perhaps rationalizes, a curious mix in Smith's interests: on the one hand his fascination with the varieties of sympathetic emotional experience, especially as these arise through watching stage drama or reading literature or historical narrative, and on the other hand his attraction to Stoicism, which enjoins self-control and equanimity in the face of trouble. The first half of this odd combination comes to the fore when Smith concentrates on the experience of the spectator, who by sympathy is transported from his or her native, neutral situation (which typically lacks any features likely to stir up strong emotion) to that of a person in the middle of some specific and often emotion-charged situation. (In drama and literature, situations are of course often deliberately charged.) The Stoic side of Smith's thinking looms large when he reflects on the fact that spectators do not enter fully into the situations of those they observe, and that anyone who wants to gain the approval of the spectator (or, what comes to the same thing, his or her own self-approval) must respond to his or her own situation only with that restrained level of emotion that another, imagining his or her situation, can share. The moral point of view is reached from the one direction by a scaling up of feeling and from the other direction by a scaling down. It is Smith's attention to both directions of emotional travel that allows some critics to describe him as a writer of great sensitivity, while other critics see abundant evidence of the Stoic influence on Smith's thought.

The second major ramification of Smith's bidirectional use of sympathy is to fix the moral point of view as a meeting point midway between the impartial spectator and the person being judged. Thus the phrase "impartial spectator" is, in isolation, somewhat misleading: through sympathy, the initially neutral spectator becomes, to some degree, the agent's partisan. In other words, the moral standard implicit in Smith's theory of moral judgment requires of agents not a complete silencing of selfish considerations but only a toning down. And in fact, too much toning down is positively bad. Thus Smith declares, for instance, that the spectator disapproves of agents who are insufficiently resentful of injuries done to them. Although Smith finds Stoicism appealing, he

cautions more than once that it requires people to regard their own interests with an apathy so complete as to create a shortfall in emotion relative to what the sympathetic impartial spectator would feel on their behalf. So whereas Hume's model of moral judgment, a model based on equal sympathy with everyone affected by the action in question, tends in a utilitarian direction, Smith's model gives, relatively speaking, more weight to the agent's egocentric concerns. On the other hand, Smith describes God, the director of nature, as being determined to maintain in nature the greatest possible quantity of happiness. Part of the ordering of nature is people's tendency to act out of a balance of self-centered and other-centered concerns, guided by the approvals and disapprovals of the sympathetic impartial spectator. Since Smith believes that this tendency works for the greatest overall good, he does display a utilitarian bent in his ethical thought.

Difference of detail between Smith and Hume aside, Smith's major contribution to moral philosophy is a conception of moral objectivity that is far more substantial than Hume's. Smith's image of a sympathetic impartial spectator is far more detailed than Hume's notion of a common, or general, point of view in *A Treatise of Human Nature* and also *An Enquiry concerning the Principles of Morals* (1751). In fact, the impartial spectator is so substantial as to develop not just one identity but two: not only the personification of neutral human observers but also something experienced by moral agents as a felt internal presence, the "man within the breast." It has been suggested that Smith anticipates elements of Sigmund Freud's theory of the superego in regarding conscience as the internalized voice of other people.

The Theory of Moral Sentiments has several weaknesses, however. Although orderly in its overall structure, it is sometimes more ambitious than purposeful in the range of topics it tackles and is filled with illustrations that are often entertaining, and sometimes moving, but not always necessary or even helpful. Page after page is taken up with ruminations on suicide, on the legendary physical courage of the natives in North America, and on the common man's interest in the lifestyles of the rich and famous, to name just a few of the subjects examined. Another occasional shortcoming of the treatise is the facile use of sympathy to explain phenomena when, the reader may suspect, the opposite phenomena would have been just as readily explained–which leads to the suspicion that Smith's psychological model lacks predictive import. The most serious fault in *The Theory of Moral Sentiments,* however, is a failure to keep in coherence all the ingredients in the picture of the impartial spectator. Smith holds the spectator up as the embodiment of the moral point of view, and at one point he flatly declares that the feelings of the well-informed, sympathetic impartial spectator are the very measure of vice and virtue. This conflict of elements in his portrait of the impartial spectator is a serious defect.

Even apart from internal difficulties, *The Theory of Moral Sentiments* represented a theoretical stance that had already peaked and was beginning gradually to fall from favor. Immanuel Kant, though he read and admired *The Theory of Moral Sentiments* in his precritical period, later rejected sentiment as being a merely contingent foundation for morality, not the necessary foundation morality demanded and practical reason supplied. Later nineteenth-century philosophers increasingly adopted a reason-based position more or less by default. *The Theory of Moral Sentiments* remained until the 1830s one of the most discussed works on ethics (second only to Hume's *A Treatise of Human Nature,* which had eventually found its audience), but thereafter its popularity fell off.

A century later, however, interest in Smith revived. Roderick Firth, in "Ethical Absolutism and the Ideal Observer" (1952), gave a spectator-based analysis of moral propositions and cited Smith as his chief predecessor. Because the focus of recent moral philosophy is less on conceptual analysis and more on empirical psychology, there is little ongoing study of the impartial spectator as a construct, but much interest in sympathy as a key element in human social interaction. Scholars writing on sympathy and its role in interpersonal relationships often acknowledge a debt to Smith and his work in *The Theory of Moral Sentiments,* and build on his and Hume's observations. Controlled studies, which demonstrate the existence of not just one but several distinct kinds of sympathetic experience, validate much of what both Smith and Hume said on the basis of anecdotal evidence.

The popularity of his treatise made Smith a natural candidate for the sort of assignment he had failed to secure earlier. In late 1763 he accepted an offer to accompany the eighteen-year-old duke of Buccleuch on the grand European tour then customary for wealthy young men seeking polish and worldly experience. Smith had his doubts about the value of such an excursion for the pupil, but he himself gained a great deal from the two-year trip. Smith and the duke spent much of their time in the south of France, in and around Toulouse, learning to speak French at least well enough to be understood and to make the occasional favorable impression on the French ladies. Although not a handsome man, Smith could charm with his enthusiastic, even passionate opinions in conversation.

More important, Smith had a chance to observe the politics and economy of France and to meet some of that country's intellectuals, including the Physiocrats, who held that the economy of a country was analogous to the human body, in which capital is the life-giving "blood" circulating through the body politic. Although Smith thought the Physiocrats underestimated the importance of specialized industrial manufacture and concentrated too much on agriculture, he agreed with them that a nation's wealth consisted not in a government-held stock of goods, such as gold, but in the cooperative union of a strong labor force and enterprising industrialists. These ideas Smith began to set down on paper while in Toulouse. When the tour ended tragically with the death of the duke's younger brother, Smith returned to Kirkcaldy. Supported by an annuity from Buccleuch for most of the next decade, Smith produced his best-known work, *An Inquiry into the Nature and Causes of the Wealth of Nations.* The first-edition printing of five hundred copies rapidly sold out. The work went on to become an even greater success than *The Theory of Moral Sentiments,* securing Smith's place in the first rank of social theorists.

The Wealth of Nations, as the work is conventionally known, sets forth a theory of what makes nations prosperous. Smith argues that a government wishing its nation to grow strong through industry should give the financial barons and the workers free rein to act in accordance with their own private interests. Encyclopedic in scope and in its use of examples, *The Wealth of Nations* is nearly three times as long as *The Theory of Moral Sentiments.* Most of the work is of far less philosophical interest than *The Theory of Moral Sentiments,* but the central role *The Wealth of Nations* assigns to self-interest is often noted. On first sight, the emphasis on sympathy in the former book and on self-interest in the latter may look like an inconsistency. However, the moral psychology in *The Theory of Moral Sentiments* not only acknowledges human self-interest but makes ample room for it as ethically permissible and even sees it as part of a generally beneficial scheme. What Smith implicitly condemns in *The Theory of Moral Sentiments* is behavior motivated solely by self-interest.

Furthermore, sympathy is not for Smith the same thing as benevolence. In *The Theory of Moral Sentiments* he distinguishes between benevolence and justice and connects both virtues to sympathy. The difference between the two virtues relates to the greater importance of justice in maintaining social stability. A society made up of people cooperating

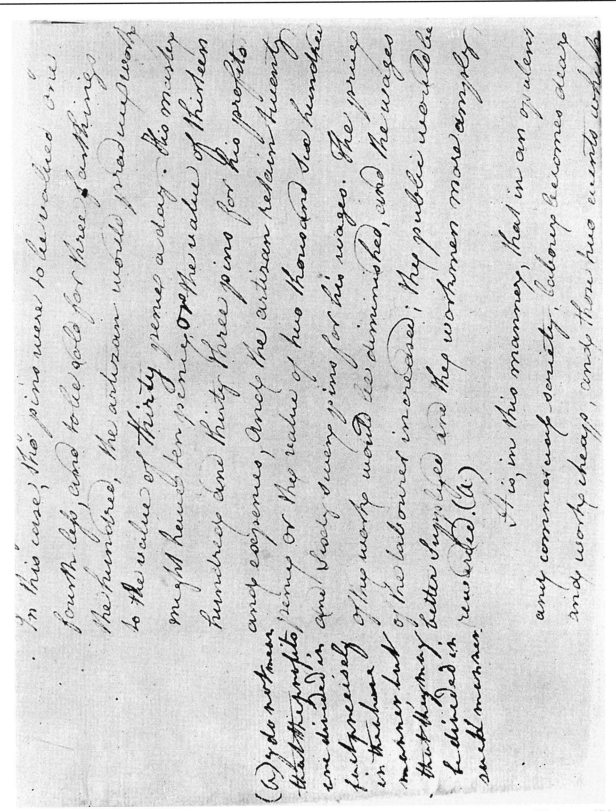

Page from an early draft for Smith's great work of economic theory, An Inquiry into the Nature and Causes of the Wealth of Nations, *published in 1776 (Dalkeith House, Charter Room, Charles Townshend MSS)*

with one another purely for personal gain, and without benevolence, in "a mercenary exchange of good offices," would survive, Smith believes, though it would be less happy or agreeable than one characterized by benevolence. By contrast, a society whose members were always ready to do one another injustice, in the form of bodily injury and broken promises, could not last even a short while. For this reason, Nature's god has associated a stronger psychological sanction with justice than with benevolence. In both cases, though, the sanction operates through sympathy with the impartial spectator. Benevolence, which even in *The Theory of Moral Sentiments* is downplayed as a factor in human motivation, is only part of the province of sympathy. Thus, when in *The Wealth of Nations* Smith famously declares that "it is not from the benevolence of the butcher, the brewer, or the baker, that we expect our dinner, but from their regard to their own interest," the setting aside of benevolence as an economically significant force does not entail the setting aside of sympathy. Quite the contrary: sympathy with the impartial spectator, as motivator of the practice of justice of, is essential to the maintenance of an orderly social scheme in which people can conduct transactions without fear of being robbed or cheated. Although sympathy is not mentioned in *The Wealth of Nations,* it operates in the background.

The extent to which Smith is sensitive to the moral dimension and risks of the free market in *The Wealth of Nations* is illustrated by the influence Smith had on Karl Marx, apostle of a ideology mostly antithetical to his economic vision. Marx greatly admired *The Wealth of Nations.* Critics have suggested that he found common ground with Smith in the latter's warnings about the potential for workers, and for the public at large, to be exploited and deceived by those, such as the investor class, whose interests do not always coincide with those of the communal whole.

Smith's pleasure at the success of *The Wealth of Nations* was mixed with melancholy when Hume succumbed, later in the same year, to an intestinal disorder (most likely cancer). Smith had agreed to act as his friend's literary executor. But despite Hume's express wishes, Smith resisted participating in the posthumous publication of Hume's *Dialogues concerning Natural Religion* (1779). The reasons for Smith's reluctance are unclear. Perhaps, as Ian Ross speculates in his authoritative *The Life of Adam Smith* (1995), the deist Smith found the arguments against natural theology in the *Dialogues concerning Natural Religion* unsettling, and perhaps he was also unwilling to draw another round of public ire similar to the one he had set off with "Letter from Adam Smith, LL.D.

to William Strahan, Esq." (1777), his eulogy of Hume. The letter scandalized many readers with its extravagant praise of Hume.

After 1776, Smith intended to publish two more major works, one in literary theory and one in political science; he had begun work on the first of these works when he was persuaded, partly through the influence of his former pupil, the duke of Buccleuch, to put his bureaucratic talents to use as a commissioner of customs in Edinburgh. Thus it came about that Smith spent the last years of his life in his father's profession. Having championed the loosening of government regulation of trade so that commercial agents might more freely pursue their private gain, he now collected taxes on imported tea and ordered the burning of smuggled contraband, while quietly giving away much of his substantial income to acquaintances in need. Smith did put some of his economic principles into practice, by pushing through a lowering or removal of certain import taxes. One industry especially hard-hit by this action was Kirkcaldy's coal production, already struggling.

The customs work, though not burdensome, was enough to distract Smith from his scholarly projects, which were never completed. Sometime after his move back to Edinburgh, Smith began to suffer from a real and increasingly severe ailment of the stomach or intestines. By 1790 he was gravely ill. Maintaining in his final ordeal the same calmness his friend Hume had displayed, he died on the night of 17 July 1790, in the company of a few close friends. Most of his papers, apparently including all notes from his lectures at Edinburgh and Glasgow, had been burned at his insistence some days earlier. "The History of Astronomy" and several other essays, however, were by his instruction published posthumously as *Essays on Philosophical Subjects.*

Biography:

Ian Simpson Ross, *The Life of Adam Smith* (Oxford: Clarendon Press, 1995; New York: Oxford University Press, 1995).

References:

Vivienne Brown, *Adam Smith's Discourse: Canonicity, Commerce, and Conscience* (London & New York: Routledge, 1994);

Roderick Firth, "Ethical Absolutism and the Ideal Observer," *Philosophy and Phenomenological Research* 12 (1952): 317–345;

Samuel Fleischacker, *A Third Concept of Liberty: Judgment and Freedom in Kant and Adam Smith* (Princeton: Princeton University Press, 1999);

Michael Fry, ed., *Adam Smith's Legacy: His Place in the Development of Modern Economics* (London & New York: Routledge, 1992);

Charles L. Griswold Jr., *Adam Smith and the Virtues of Enlightenment* (New York & Cambridge: Cambridge University Press, 1999);

Knud Haakonssen, ed., *Adam Smith* (Aldershot Hants, U.K. & Brookfield, Vt.: Ashgate, 1998);

Haakonssen and Andrew S. Skinner, comps., *Index to the Works of Adam Smith* (New York & Oxford: Oxford University Press, 2001);

Gilbert Harman, "Moral Agent and Impartial Spectator," in *Explaining Value and Other Essays in Moral Philosophy* (Oxford: Clarendon Press, 2000; New York: Oxford University Press, 2000);

Peter Jones and Skinner, *Adam Smith Reviewed* (Edinburgh: Edinburgh University Press, 1992);

Cheng-Chun Lai, ed., *Adam Smith Across Nations: Translations and Receptions of the Wealth of Nations* (New York & Oxford: Oxford University Press, 2000);

Robin Paul Malloy and Jerry Evensky, eds., *Adam Smith and the Philosophy of Law and Economics* (Dordrecht & Boston: Kluwer, 1994);

Hiroshi Mizuta, ed., *Adam Smith: Critical Responses,* 6 volumes (New York: Routledge, 2000);

Mizuta, ed., *Adam Smith's Library: A Catalogue* (Oxford: Oxford University Press, 1999; New York: Oxford University Press, 2000);

Mizuta and Chuhei Sugiyama, eds., *Adam Smith: International Perspectives* (New York: St. Martin's Press, 1993);

Jerry Z. Muller, *Adam Smith in His Time and Ours: Designing the Decent Society* (Princeton: Princeton University Press, 1995);

Martha C. Nussbaum, "Steerforth's Arm: Love and the Moral Point of View," in *Love's Knowledge: Essays on Philosophy and Literature* (New York & Oxford: Oxford University Press, 1990), pp. 335–364;

Jan Peil, *Adam Smith and Economic Science: A Methodological Reinterpretation* (Northampton, Mass. & Cheltenham, U.K.: Elgar, 1999);

John Reeder, ed., *On Moral Sentiments: Contemporary Responses to Adam Smith,* Key Issues series, no. 18 (Bristol, U.K.: Thoemmes Press, 1997);

Ian Simpson Ross, ed., *On the Wealth of Nations: Contemporary Responses to Adam Smith,* Key Issues series, no. 19 (Bristol, U.K. & Dulles, Va.: Thoemmes Press, 1998);

Skinner, *A System of Social Science: Papers Relating to Adam Smith,* second edition (Oxford: Clarendon Press, 1996);

Keith Tribe and Mizuta, eds., *Critical Bibliography of Adam Smith* (London & Burlington, Vt.: Pickering & Chatto, 2002);

Gloria Vivenza, *Adam Smith and the Classics: The Classical Heritage in Adam Smith's Thought* (Oxford: Oxford University Press, 2001);

Patricia Werhane, *Adam Smith and His Legacy for Modern Capitalism* (New York: Oxford University Press, 1991);

John C. Wood, ed., *Adam Smith: Critical Assessments* (4 volumes, London: Croom Helm, 1984; 3 volumes, New York: Routledge, 1994);

Jeffrey T. Young, *Economics as a Moral Science: The Political Economy of Adam Smith* (Cheltenham, U.K. & Lyme, N.H.: Elgar, 1997).

Papers:

Glasgow University Library holds the largest and most important collection of manuscripts related to Adam Smith. Several dozen other worldwide locations of original documents are listed in the bibliography of Ian Simpson Ross's *The Life of Adam Smith.* Most of the books that made up Smith's personal library are now split between the Edinburgh University Library and the Faculty of Economics Library at the University of Tokyo Graduate School of Economics.

John Smith

(1618 – 7 August 1652)

Jay G. Williams
Hamilton College

BOOK: *Select Discourses: Treating 1. Of the true Way or Method of attaining to Divine Knowledge. 2. Of Superstition. 3. Of Atheism. 4. Of the Immortality of the Soul. 5. Of the Existence and Nature of God. 6. Of Prophecy. 7. Of the Difference between the Legal and the Evangelical Righteousness, the Old and the New Covenant, &c. 8. Of the Shortness and Vanity of a Pharisaick Righteousness. 9. Of the Excellency and Nobleness of True Religion. 10. Of a Christians Conflicts with, and Conquests over, Satan. By John Smith, late Fellow of Queen's College in Cambridge. As also a Sermon preached by Simon Patrick (then Fellow of the same College) at the Author's Funeral: With a brief account of his Life and Death,* edited, with an introduction, by John Worthington (London: Printed by James Flesher for William Morden, Cambridge, 1660; revised edition, Cambridge: Printed by John Hayes for William Morden, 1673).

Editions: *Select Discourses: To Which Is Prefixed a Brief Memoir of the Author,* abridged by John King (London: Hatchard, 1820);

Select Discourses: To Which Is Added a Sermon, Preached at the Author's Funeral, by Symon Patrick, Containing a Brief Account of His Life and Death (London: Rivingtons & Cochran, 1821);

Select Discourses: To Which Is Added a Sermon, Preached at the Author's Funeral, by Symon Patrick, Containing A Brief Account of the Author's Life and Death, edited by Henry Griffith Williams (Cambridge: Cambridge University Press, 1859);

The Natural Truth of Christianity: Selections from the "Select Discourses" of John Smith, M.A., edited by W. M. Metcalfe, introduction by Matthew Arnold (London: Alexander Gardner, 1882);

"A Discourse Concerning the True Way or Method of Attaining to Divine Knowledge," "A Discourse Demonstrating the Immortality of the Soul," "A Discourse Concerning the Existence and Nature of God," and "The Excellency and Nobleness of True Religion," in *The Cambridge Platonists: Being Selections from the Writings of Benjamin Whichcote, John Smith and Nathanael Culverwel,* edited by Ernest

Trafford Campagnac (Oxford: Clarendon Press, 1901), pp. 77–209;

Select Discourses (New York & London: Garland, 1978);

Select Discourses (1660): John Smith, the Cambridge Platonist, introduction by C. A. Patrides, Scholars' Facsimiles & Reprints, volume 335 (Delmar, N.Y.: Scholars' Facsimiles & Reprints, 1979).

John Smith was one of the most important second-generation Cambridge Platonists to teach at that university during the Interregnum period. It is unfortunate that he died at an early age, for his one, posthumously published work reveals a keen discerning intellect.

Little is known about his life. Smith was born in 1618 near Oundle in Northhamptonshire. In the funeral sermon that Simon Patrick preached for Smith he remarks that Smith's parents were elderly and had long been childless before his birth. In April 1636 he entered as a pensioner at Emmanuel College, Cambridge, where he studied under the tutorship of Benjamin Whichcote, who not only directed his studies but also apparently supported him financially. Although Emmanuel was the leading Puritan college at the time, Smith was encouraged by Whichcote to develop a non-authoritarian, philosophical theology. After proceeding B.A. in 1640 and M.A. in 1644 Smith was approved by the Westminster Assembly of Divines (the consultative body on ecclesiastical matters convened by Parliament in 1643) to be appointed a fellow at Queen's College, the same year his mentor, Whichcote, was appointed provost of King's College by Parliament. At Queen's College Smith lectured on mathematics and developed a reputation as one of the outstanding Cambridge Platonists, advancing to the position of dean and catechist of his college. His career, however, was cut short when he died of consumption on 7 August 1652. His funeral sermon was preached by his friend Patrick, who later became bishop of Ely, and Smith was buried in the chapel of his college. His papers were given by his executor, Samuel Cradock, a fellow of Emmanuel College who became rector of North Cadbury in Somersetshire, to John Worthington, a fellow Cambridge Platonist. Worthington edited some of Smith's papers, which were printed in London and published in Cambridge under the title *Select Discourses* in 1660, with an introduction and the text of the funeral sermon. The second edition of this work was published, with corrections, in Cambridge in 1673; this edition was republished in Edinburgh, as the so-called third edition, in 1756. Subsequent editions appeared in 1821 and 1859. Two abridged versions, edited by John King and W. M. Metcalfe, respectively, were published in 1820 and 1882. In 1901 Ernest Trafford Campagnac published *The Cambridge Platonists*, which includes significant selections from the work. Modern facsimile editions of the first edition were published by Garland Publishing in 1978 and Scholars' Facsimiles and Reprints in 1979.

Smith obviously learned much from his tutor, for on almost every page of his *Select Discourses* the influence of Whichcote's charitable and undoctrinaire religious attitude is evident. Smith, however, reveals much more directly the influence of Neoplatonic literature, to which he refers repeatedly. One of the central motifs that dominates the various discourses is found in the first pages of the initial discourse, "A Discourse Concerning the true Way or Method of Attaining to Divine Knowledge." Divine things, says Smith, are to be understood by spiritual sensation rather than verbal description or mere speculation. The essence of religion cannot be understood through words or ideas alone, but through the divine life. "To seek our Divinity meerly in Books and Writings," he says, "is *to seek the living among the dead*. . . . that which enables us to know and understand aright in the things of God, must be a living principle of Holiness within us."

Therefore, Smith consistently refuses to prove the articles of faith that he considers basic. He believes that such doctrines as the existence of God and the immortality of the soul are natural to humanity. At the same time, Smith does not believe that all seemingly universally held notions can be accepted as the laws and maxims of nature, for he realizes that error and superstition are widespread. Nevertheless, he affirms that a belief in the existence of God and in the immortality of the soul are universal. To intuit these essential doctrines one need only purge oneself of bodily lust and self-will. The task of natural theology is not to prove that they are true, but only to show that the arguments offered against them are false.

Smith's arguments in defense of the immortality of the soul are directed primarily against those who wish to reduce all reality to bodies in motion. His major points are the predictable and obvious ones: first, it is impossible to explain sensation and thought through reference to inert matter, for inert matter, by definition, cannot think. Materialists cannot explain humans' conscious apprehension of the fact that they are thinking. Second, there is within human beings a source for self-motion that is inexplicable if the "billiard ball" conception of cause is accepted. Third, it is impossible to explain the presence of mathematical notions in the mind if one believes that all knowledge is derivable from sense experience. Fourth, materialists adopt the wrong epistemological starting point, for in reality the soul is more knowable than the body. Because Smith believes that an individual's knowledge of him- or herself is the most certain knowledge of all, he bases his knowledge of God's attributes upon it. In the fifth discourse, "Of the Existence and Nature of God," Smith says, "*the Best way to know God is by an attentive reflexion upon our own Souls*." To be sure, "the whole fabrick of this visible Universe be whispering out notions of a Deity"; however, "it must be *something within* that must instruct us in all these Mysteries"–humans can only know God through his handiwork after they have first known him within themselves.

One knows, for instance, that one can reason but that one is not the source of that reason. Human reason is not the light of the universe, but is, to use Whichcote's favorite expression, the "candle of the Lord," which has power and usefulness only because God has made other minds and the universe to be somehow commensurate with it. An introspective understanding of one's own reason, then, makes one aware of human dependence upon the reason of God. The same can be said for human power and will. All humans have power within themselves; they can act and exercise their free will. But it is also obvious that human power is not absolute. Human beings cannot create themselves. While humans are potent, God is omnipotent.

Smith also derives the attributes of eternity, omnipresence, and freedom in the same way. Above all, he says, one can know God as "*Almighty Love*" by examining human love. Nevertheless, he also perceives that there is a difference between our love and God's. Human love is never satisfied; it ebbs and flows, always seeking something beyond itself. God's love, however, is perfect, unchangeable, eternal, and self-satisfying. Human love (that is, Eros) is the basis for religion. Humans have an appetite for infinity, a passionate impulse that drives them to God. They are impelled by an inner desire to be religious.

Smith does not mean, of course, that religion is irrational. On the contrary, God is the direct source of all true reason. True religion clarifies and quickens reason; it does not destroy it. Still, God cannot be comprehended through reason alone. Corresponding to the idea of God, which is rationally apprehensible, there is the inherent human love for God that gives theological

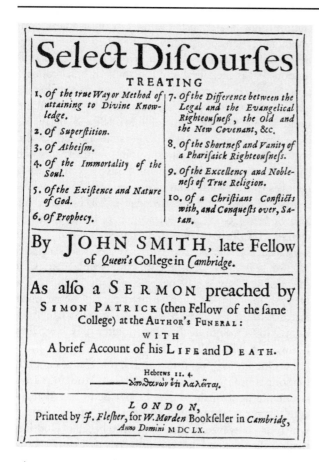

Title page for John Smith's sole book, a posthumously published collection
of lectures and sermons in which he attempts to reconcile Neoplatonist
concepts with Christian doctrine (Beinecke Library, Yale University)

concepts meaning and importance. The true end of
humanity, then, is the knowledge and love of God,
what in chapter 5 of his "Of the Existence and Nature
of God" Smith calls "that *Omnipresent Life* that penetrates
and runs through all things, containing and holding all
fast together within himself."

Smith's dependence upon the Neoplatonists for
this understanding of religion is both obvious and
definitive. He qualifies this Platonism, however, by
introducing some specifically Christian ideas that
would not have been acceptable to a philosopher such
as Plotinus. Although the true end of humanity is to be
found in God, says Smith, humans can never know
God without revelation. Philosophy was originally
divine, but has degenerated because of human sinful-
ness. As did St. Augustine, Smith believes that humanity has been corrupted by self-will and pride so that
instead of loving God, humans seek fulfillment in sensual pleasure, in concupiscence. The passions, though
essentially good, have been turned from God to unworthy ends and thus lead humans astray.

Nor is this sinful condition something that
humans can remove through the exercise of free will. In

the seventh discourse, "Of the Difference between the
Legal and the Evangelical Righteousness, the Old and
the New Covenant, &c.," Smith observes that St. Paul
attacked the "Judaizers" for basing their religion upon
two ideas. First, they believed that humans have perfect
free will and sufficient power to attain for themselves
true virtue and goodness. Second, they believed that
"the Law delivered to them [the Jews] upon Mount
Sinai was a sufficient Dispensation from God" for true
righteousness. Smith does not completely deny free
will, for he argues from human awareness of free will to
a knowledge of God's more perfect will; yet, he agrees
with Paul that the will is corrupt and thus is insufficient
for the attainment of true righteousness.

In "A Discourse demonstrating the Immortality
of the Soul" Smith defines the relation between humanity's inherent, though misdirected, love from God and
revealed religion:

> The Nature of God and our own Immortal Souls both shew us
> what our Religion should be, and also the necessity of
> it, and the Doctrine of *Free grace in Christ,* the sweet and
> comfortable means of attaining to that perfection and
> Blessedness which the other Belief teaches us to aime
> at.

Thus, God completes through grace what is known to
humans through reason and spiritual sensation.

One of the ideas that Smith attacks repeatedly
throughout his discourses is that religion is only a belief
in what God has "objectively" done for humanity. In
chapter 4 of "A Discourse of Legal Righteousness, and
of the Righteousness of Faith, &c.," for example, Smith
declares that the gospel is not merely a history to be
believed, but "a mighty *Efflux* and Emanation of *life and
spirit,* freely issuing forth from an Omnipotent source of
Grace and Love." This force transforms human
beings—"*It is whereby God comes to dwell in us, and we in
him.*"

Smith believes firmly in justification by faith; but
faith, for him, is an influx of divine power that reforms
and restores the soul rather than simply an empty pardon for sin. This conception of grace as power implies
for him a perfectionist view of the Christian life. Smith
does discuss, in "A Christians Conflicts and Conquests," the continual warfare that a Christian must
wage against the power of Satan within. He realizes that
the struggle with the old Adam is not easily won. Nevertheless, he affirms that success and victory over the
devil is certain and that the peace of true religion will
eventually be established. This perfectionism envisioned by Smith is not, however, a new form of legal-
ism. In fact, he proclaims that the more one advances in
quelling the power of the devil, the less one needs the

law. Religion, says Smith, should consist in love for, and friendship with God and not in irrational obedience and slavish fear. Grace not only clarifies the law written upon the heart; it empowers humans to will that the law be fulfilled without fear or rancor. The law, revelation, and the gospel are conceived to be purely and wholly theonomous.

Although Smith admits that humans are completely dependent upon God for salvation, he does not emphasize the doctrines of predestination and election. One cannot save oneself, but one can purify oneself enough through free will so that God's grace, which is shed abroad through Jesus Christ, can become operative. Unsurprisingly, when John Wesley was compiling a "Christian Library" in 1749, he saw fit to include large excerpts from Smith's discourses. Conversely, it is also not surprising that, because Smith was not wholly explicit about this matter, the Puritans should have appointed him to an important position at Queens' College. Despite his popularity at Puritan-controlled Cambridge, however, Smith was essentially, if not wholly, a Neoplatonist. His vision of the culmination of the religious life is reminiscent of the writings of Neoplatonists in almost every age. After the mists of doubt and fear of death have been removed, he says in "A Discourse Concerning the Existence and Nature of God," the soul

> may then fly upwards from one heaven to another, till it be beyond all orbe of Finite Being, swallowed up in the boundless Abyss of Divinity . . . beyond all that which darker thoughts are wont to represent under the Idea of *Essence.*

Whichcote's most illustrious pupil was undoubtedly John Smith, who, though he died at an early age, bequeathed to posterity one of the most readable and most lauded set of discourses written by any member of the Cambridge Platonist movement. In his introduction to *Select Discourses,* Worthington writes of "some other pieces of this Author's (both English and Latin) which may make another considerable Volume, especially if some other papers of his (in other hands) can be retriev'd." Despite Worthington's promise to "endeavour that not the least Fragment of his may be conceal'd," Smith's "other pieces" were never published and are presumably no longer extant. His *Select Discourses,* however, constitute an impressive achievement in themselves.

References:

Robert L. Armstrong, "Cambridge Platonists and Locke on Innate Ideas," *Journal of the History of Ideas,* 30 (April–June 1969): 187–202;

John Herman Randall, *The Career of Philosophy: From the Middle Ages to the Enlightenment* (New York: Columbia University Press, 1962), pp. 471–494;

John K. Ryan, "John Smith (1616–1652): Platonist and Mystic," *New Scholasticism,* 20 (January 1946): 1–25;

J. E. Saveson, "Descartes Influence on John Smith, Cambridge Platonist," *Journal of the History of Ideas,* 20 (1959): 258–263;

John Tulloch, *The Cambridge Platonists,* volume 2 of his *Rational Theology and Christian Philosophy in the Seventeenth Century,* 2 volumes (Edinburgh: Blackwood, 1872).

John Toland

(30 November 1670 – 11 March 1722)

Stephen H. Daniel
Texas A&M University

BOOKS: *Two Essays Sent in a Letter from Oxford to a Nobleman in London,* as L. P. (London: R. Baldwin, 1695);

Christianity Not Mysterious: or, a Treatise shewing, that there is nothing in the Gospel contrary to reason, nor above it: and that no Christian doctrine can properly be call'd a mystery (London, 1696; revised edition, London: Samuel Buckley, 1696);

An Apology for Mr. Toland: In a Letter from Himself to a Member of the House of Commons in Ireland, Written the Day Before his Book was Resolv'd to be Burnt by the Committee of Religion: To Which is Prefix'd a Narrative Containing the Occasion of the Said Letter (London, 1697);

A Defence of Mr. Toland in a Letter to Himself (London: E. Whitlock, 1697);

A Letter to a Member of Parliament, Shewing, that a restraint On the Press is inconsistent with the Protestant Religion, and dangerous to the Liberties of the Nation (London: Printed by John Darby, 1698);

The Militia Reform'd, or, An Easy Scheme of Furnishing England with a Constant Land-force: Capable to Prevent or Subdue any Forein Power, and to Maintain Perpetual Quiet at Home, without Endangering the Publick Liberty (London: Printed by John Darby, 1698);

Amyntor, or a defence of Milton's life: containing, I. A catalogue of above fourscore books (as Gospels, Acts, Epistles, Revelations, &c.) attributed in the primitive times to Jesus Christ, his apostles, &c. With several important remarks and observations relating to the canon of scripture; II. A compleat history of the book intituled Icon Basilike, proving Dr. Gauden, and not King Charles the First, to be the author of it; III. Reasons for abolishing the observation of the 30th of January (London: Booksellers of London & Westminster, 1699);

Clito: A Poem on the Force of Eloquence, as Adeisidaemon (London: Booksellers of London & Westminster, 1700);

Anglia Libera: or the Limitations and Succession of the Crown of England explain'd and asserted; as grounded on His Majesty's Speech; the procedings in Parlament; the desires of the people (London: Bernard Lintott, 1701);

John Toland (from Urban Gottlob Thorschmid, Versuch einer Vollständige Englandische Freydenker-Bibliothek, *volume 3 [Cassel: Hemmerde, 1766]; Sterling Memorial Library, Yale University)*

The Art of Governing by Partys: particularly in religion, in politics, in Parlament, on the bench, and in the ministry: with the ill effects of Partys on the People in general, the King in particular, and all our Foren Affairs, as well as on our

Credit and Trade, in Peace or War, &c (London: Bernard Lintott, 1701);

Propositions for Uniting the Two East India Companies: In a Letter to a Man of Quality, who Desir'd the Opinion of a Gentleman not Concerned in Either Company (London: Bernard Lintott, 1701);

I. Reasons for Addressing His Majesty to invite into England their Highnesses, the Electress Dowager and the Electoral Prince of Hanover: and likewise, II. Reasons for Attaining and Abjuring the Pretended Prince of Wales, and all other pretending any Claim, Right, or Title from the Late King James and Queen Mary: with Arguments for Making a Vigorous War against France (London: Printed and sold by John Nutt, 1702);

Vindicius Liberius: or M. Toland's Defence of Himself Against the Late Lower House of Convocation, and Others: Wherein (besides his Letters to the prolocutor) Certain Passages of the Book, intitul'd Christianity not Mysterious, are explain'd, and others corrected: with a full and clear account of the authors principles relating to church and state: and a justification of the Whigs and commonwealthsmen, against the misrepresentations of all their opposers (London: Bernard Lintott, 1702);

Letters to Serena: Containing, I. The origin and force of prejudices. II. The history of the soul's immortality among the heathens. III. The origin of idolatry, and reasons of heathenism . . . (London: Bernard Lintott, 1704);

An Account of the Courts of Prussia and Hanover; sent to a Minister of State in Holland (London: Printed by John Darby, 1705);

The Memorial of the State of England: in vindication of the Queen, the church, and the administration: design'd to rectify the mutual mistakes of Protestants and to unite their affections in defence of our religion and liberty (London: Booksellers of London & Westminster, 1705);

Socinianism truly Stated (London, 1705);

Some Plain Observations Recommended to the Consideration of every Honest English-Man (London, 1705);

The Declaration Lately Publish'd, In Favour of his Protestant Subjects, by the Elector Palatine (London: A. Baldwin, 1707);

Adeisidaemon, sive Titus Livius a superstitione vindicatus: In qua dissertatione probatur, Livium historicum in sacris, prodigiis, & ostentis Romanorum enarrandis, haudquaquam fuisse credulum aut superstitiosum; ipsamque superstitionem non minùs reipublicae (si non magis) exitiosam esse, quam purum putum atheismum (The Hague: Thomas Johnson, 1709);

The Jacobitism, Perjury, and Popery of High-Church Priests (London: Printed for J. Baker, 1710);

The Judgment of K. James the First, and King Charles the First, Against Non-Resistance: Discover'd by their own Letters, and now Offer'd to the Consideration of Dr.

Sacheverell and his Party (London: Printed by J. Baker, 1710);

Mr. Toland's Reflections on Dr. Sacheverelle's Sermon (London: J. Baker, 1710);

The Description of Epsom, with the humors and politicks of the place: in a letter to Eudoxa . . . There is added a Translation of Four Letters our of Pliny, as Britto-Batavus (London: A. Baldwin, 1711);

High-Church Display'd: Being a Compleat History of the Affair of Dr. Sacheverel, in its Origin, Progress, and Consequences: In Several Letters to an English Gentleman at the Court of Hanover (London, 1711);

Cicero Illustratus, Dissertatio Philologico-critica: sive consilium de toto edendo Cicerone (London: Printed by John Humphreys, 1712);

Her Majesty's Reasons for Creating the Electoral Prince of Hanover a Peer of this Realm: or, The Preamble to his patent as Duke of Cambridge (London: A. Baldwin, 1712);

An Appeal to Honest People Against Wicked Priests; or, The very heathen laity's declarations for civil obedience and liberty of conscience, contrary to the rebellious and persecuting principles of some of the old Christian clergy; with an application to the corrupt parts of the priests of this present time, publish'd on occasion of Dr. Sacheverrell's last sermon, as Hierophilus (London: Printed for Mrs. Smith, 1713);

Dunkirk or Dover; or, The Queen's honour, the nation's safety, the liberties of Europe, and the peace of the world, all at stake till that fort and port be totally demolish'd by the French (London: A. Baldwin, 1713);

The Art of Restoring; or, The piety and probity of General Monk in bringing about the last restoration: evidenc'd from his own authentic letters: with a just account of Sir Roger, who runs the parallel as far as he can; in a letter to a minister of state, at the court of Vienna (London: J. Roberts, 1714);

The Grand Mystery Laid Open: Namely, by dividing of the Protestants to weaken the Hanover succession, and by defeating the succession to extirpate the Protestant religion. To which is added, The sacredness of Parliamentary securities: against those, who wou'd indirectly this year, or more directly the next (if they live so long) attack the publick funds (London: J. Roberts, 1714);

Reasons for Naturalizing the Jews in Great Britain and Ireland: on the Same Foot with All Other Nations: Containing also a Defence of the Jews against All Vulgar Prejudices in all Countries (London: Printed for J. Roberts, 1714);

The State Anatomy of Great Britain; Containing a particular account of its several interests and parties, their bent and genius; and what each of them, with all the rest of Europe, may hope or fear from the reign and family of King George; being a memorial sent by an intimate friend to a foreign minister, lately nominated to come for the Court of

England, as Patricola (London: Printed for John Phillips, 1717);

The Second Part of the State Anatomy of Great Britain; Containing a short vindication of the former part, against the misrepresentations of the ignorant or the malicious, especially relating to our ministers of state and to foreigners; with some reflections on the design'd clamor against the army, and on the Suedish conspiracy. Also, letters to His Grace, the late Archbishop of Canterbury, and to the dissenting ministers of all denominations, in the year 1705–6, about a general toleration, with some of their answers to the author: who now offers to publick consideration, what was then transacted for private satisfaction; together with a letter from Their High-Mightinesses the States-General of the United Provinces, on the same subject, as Patricola (London: Printed for John Phillips, 1717);

The Destiny of Rome: or, the probability of the speedy and final destruction of the pope. Concluded partly, from natural reasons, and political observations; and partly, on occasion of the famous prophesy of St. Malachy, Archbishop of Armagh, in the XIIth century . . . In a letter to a divine of the Church of England, from a divine of the Church of the First-born, as X. Z. (London: Printed and sold by J. Roberts & A. Dodd, 1718);

Nazarenus, or, Jewish, Gentile, and Mahometan Christianity. Containing the History of the Antient Gospel of Barnabas, and the modern Gospel of the Mahometans, attributed to the same apostle, this last Gospel being now first made known among Christians: also, The Original Plan of Christianity occasionally explain'd in the history of the Nazarens, wherby diverse controversies about this divine (but highly perverted) institution may be happily terminated. With the Relation of an Irish Manuscript of the Four Gospels, as likewise a summary of the antient Irish Christianity, and the reality of the Keldees (an order of lay-religious) against the two last bishops of Worcester (London: J. Brown, 1718);

Pantheisticon; sive Formula Celebrandae Sodalitas Socraticae, in tres particulas divisa, quae pantheistarum, sive sodalium, continent I, Mores et axiomata: II, Numen et philosophiam: III, Libertatem, et non fallentem legem, neque fallendam, as Janus Junius Eoganensius (London, 1720); translated anonymously as *Pantheisticon: or, The form of celebrating the Socratic-Society . . . To which is prefix'd a discourse upon the ancient modern societies of the learned, as also upon the infinite and eternal universe. And subjoined, a short dissertation, upon a two-fold philosophy of the Pantheists, that is to be followed; together with an idea of the best and most accomplished man* (London: Sam Peterson, 1751);

Reasons most humbly offer'd to the Honble House of Commons: Why the bill sent down to them from the most Honble House of Lords entitul'd, An Act for better Securing the Dependency of the Kingdom of Ireland upon the Crown of Great-Britain, Shou'd not Pass into a Law (London: Printed for R. Franklin, 1720);

A Short Essay upon Lying (London: A. Moore, 1720);

Tetradymus. Containing I. Hodegus; or, The pillar of cloud and fire, that guided the Israelites in the wilderness, not miraculous: but, as faithfully related in Exodus, a thing equally practis'd by other nations, and in those places not onely useful but necessary. II. Clidophorus; or, Of the exoteric and esoteric philosophy, that is, of the external and internal doctrine of the antients: the one open and public, accommodated to popular prejudices and the establish'd religions; the other private and secret, wherin, to the few capable and discrete, was taught the real truth stript of all disguises. III. Hypatia; or, The history of a most beautiful, most virtuous, most learned, and every way accomplish'd lady; who was torn to pieces by the clergy of Alexandria, to gratify the pride, emulation, and cruelty of their Archbishop Cyril. IV. Mangoneutes: being a defense of Nazarenus, address'd to the Right Reverend John, lord bishop of London; against his lordship's chaplain Dr. Mangey, his dedicator Mr. Patterson, and . . . the Reverend Dr. Brett (London: J. Brotherton & W. Meadows, 1720);

A New Edition of Toland's History of the Druids: With an Abstract of His Life and Writings; and a Copious Appendix, Containing Notes Critical, Philological, and Explanatory, edited by Robert Huddleston (Montrose: Printed by James Watt for P. Hill, 1814).

Collection: *A Collection of Several Pieces of Mr. Toland: Now first Publish'd from his Original Manuscripts: with some Memoirs of His Life and Writings*, 2 volumes, edited by Pierre Desmaizeaux (London: J. Peele, 1726).

OTHER: Bernardo Davanzati-Bostici, *A Discourse upon Coins*, translated, with a preface, by Toland (London: Awnsham & John Churchill, 1696);

Jean LeClerc, *A Treatise on the Causes of Incredulity: Wherein Are Examin'd the General Motives and Occasions which Dispose Unbelievers to Reject the Christian Religion: with Two Letters, containing a Direct Proof of the truth of Christianity*, translated, with a preface, by Toland (London: Awnsham & John Churchill, 1697);

Anonymous, *A Lady's Religion*, prefatory epistle by Toland as Adeisidaemon (London: T. Warren, 1697);

"The Life of John Milton," in *A Complete Collection of the Historical, Political, and Miscellaneous Works of John Milton: With som Papers never before Publish'd: in Three Volumes: to which is Prefix'd the Life of the Author, containing Besides the History of his Works, Several Extraordinary Characters of Men and Books, Sects, Parties, and Opinions*, 3 volumes (Amsterdam, 1698);

Memoirs of Lieutenant General Ludlow, The Third and Last Part, edited, with a preface, by Toland (London: John Darby, 1699);

"The Life of James Harrington," in *"The Oceana" of James Harrington, and his other works,* edited by Toland (London: Booksellers of London & Westminster, 1700);

Pierre de Boissat, *The Fables of Aesop: With the moral reflections of Monsieur Baudoin,* translated, with a preface, by Toland (London: Printed for Thomas Leigh & Daniel Midwinter, 1704);

The Ordinances, Statutes, and Privileges of the Royal Academy, Erected by his Majesty the King of Prussia, translated by Toland (London: John Darby, 1705);

Matthew Cardinal Schiner, *A Phillipick Oration to Incite the English against the French,* translated by Toland (London: Egbert Sanger & John Chantry, 1707);

Sophie Charlotte of Prussia, *A Letter Against Popery,* dedicatory letter by Toland, as J. Londat (London: A. Baldwin, 1712);

Quintus Tullius Cicero, *The Art of Canvassing at Elections,* translated, with a preface, by Toland (London: J. Roberts, 1714);

A Collection of Letters Written by His Excellency General George Monk, edited, with an introduction, by Toland (London: J. Roberts, 1714);

Letters from the Right Honourable The Late Earl of Shaftesbury to Robert Molesworth, edited, with an introduction by Toland, as Z. Z. (London: J. Peele, 1721).

SELECTED PERIODICAL PUBLICATIONS–UNCOLLECTED: Letter from Toland to Jean LeClerc on Daniel Williams's *Gospel Truth Stated and Vindicated, Bibliothéque universelle et historique,* 23 (1692): 504–509;

"Lettre de Mr. Toland, sur le *Spaccio della bestia triomphante," Nova Bibliotheca Lubecencis,* 5 (1754): 158–162.

As the major deistic thinker of the decades before and after 1700, John Toland linked biblical criticism, metaphysical speculation, and political pamphleteering in ways that intrigued, enraged, and embarrassed a generation of writers. John Locke, Daniel Defoe, Jonathan Swift, and Gottfried Wilhelm Leibniz felt compelled to respond to his critiques of religious belief. His discussions of John Milton, sectarian toleration, the Protestant Succession, and the status of the Jews and the Irish in Great Britain made him a significant spokesman for Whig causes. His work on Giordano Bruno, the Druids, and exoteric philosophy introduced a distinctive perspective into philosophic exchanges of the period.

Probably the bastard son of an Irish cleric and his concubine, John Toland was born in Londonderry, Ire-

land, on 30 November 1670. He was christened in the Roman Catholic Church as "Janus Junius" (which he later employed as a pseudonym), but as a schoolboy he was given the name John to stop his classmates from making fun of him when the roll was called. At sixteen he rejected Catholicism ("the insupportable Yoke of the most Pompous and Tyrannical *Policy* that ever enslav'd Mankind under the name or shew of *Religion*") and became associated with Protestant dissenters. In 1687 he enrolled in the College of Glasgow and received an M.A. degree from the University of Edinburgh in 1690. Through the support of Presbyterians in London, he was able to study at the University of Leyden with Friedrich Spanheim the Younger, from whom he learned exegetical techniques of biblical criticism developed by Baruch Spinoza, Pierre Bayle, and Richard Simon. In his "The Life of John Milton" (1698) and *Amyntor, or a defence of Milton's life: containing, I. A catalogue of above fourscore books (as Gospels, Acts, Epistles, Revelations, &c.) attributed in the primitive times to Jesus Christ, his apostles, &c. With several important remarks and observations relating to the canon of scripture; II. A compleat history of the book intituled Icon Basilike, proving Dr. Gauden, and not King Charles the First, to be the author of it; III. Reasons for abolishing the observation of the 30th of January* (1699), Toland challenged the scriptural canon and other ancient texts based on his training in original Greek and Hebrew sources.

At the Rotterdam house of the English merchant Benjamin Furly, Toland met the Dutch Remonstrant theologians Philip van Limborch and Jean LeClerc, through whom he was introduced to Locke as a "freespirited ingenious man" and an "excellent and not unlearned young man . . . frank, gentlemanly, and not at all of a servile character." Late in 1693 Toland settled in Oxford to work at the Bodleian Library on an Irish dictionary and a dissertation proving that Ireland had once been a colony of the Gauls. In conservative Oxford his coffeehouse polemics quickly gained him a reputation as "a man of fine parts, great learning, and little religion." Locke's *Reasonableness of Christianity* (1695) seems to have been written at least partially in response to points raised by Toland.

Toland was twenty-five years old when he published anonymously his most famous work, *Christianity Not Mysterious: or, a Treatise shewing, that there is nothing in the Gospel contrary to reason, nor above it: and that no Christian doctrine can properly be call'd a mystery* (1696). His doctrine that no tenets of true Christianity could be contrary to or above human reason–because if they were unintelligible to reason, they could not be objects even of faith–immediately drew him into the thick of debates on rational religion. Before the end of the year a second edition appeared, this time naming Toland as the author. Soon afterward, he traveled to Ireland, only to hear his book attacked from the pulpit and condemned by the Irish Parliament. To avoid being arrested he fled the country and spent the next five years

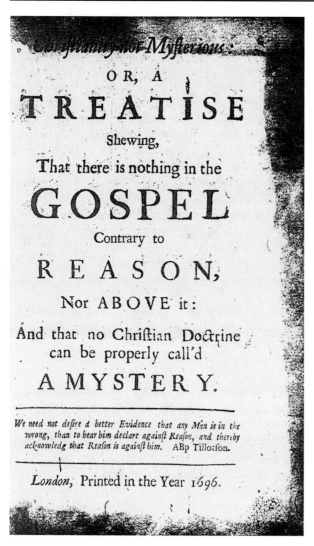

Title page for Toland's best-known work, in which he argues that religious truths must be intelligible by human reason (Lamont Library, Harvard University)

defending his "juvenile thoughts" (as he called them) before finally deciding not to endorse further printings of the work.

Toland's learning and his free-spirited method of inquiry attracted the attention of patrons such as Anthony Ashley Cooper, third Earl of Shaftesbury, and Robert Harley, first Earl of Oxford. With Shaftesbury he shared an interest in antiquity, philosophy, religion, and opposition to superstition. He also strongly supported the traditional Whig ideals of toleration of dissenting religious sects and the Protestant Succession of William and Mary. In *The Militia Reform'd, or, An Easy Scheme of Furnishing England with a Constant Land-force: Capable to Prevent or Subdue any Forein Power, and to Maintain Perpetual Quiet at Home, without Endangering the Publick Liberty* (1698) he supported the effort of Harley's Country Party coalition of Jacobite Tories and

republican Whigs to prevent William's standing army from coming into England. Commissioned to write biographies of John Milton (1699) and James Harrington (1700), Toland soon became a foremost Whig writer. His justification of the Protestant Succession, *Anglia Libera: or the Limitations and Succession of the Crown of England explain'd and asserted; as grounded on His Majesty's Speech; the procedings in Parliament; the desires of the people* (1701), prompted Harley to request that Toland be selected as a secretary to the embassy of Hanover under Charles Girard, second Earl of Macclesfield. Toland had the honor to present the Act of Settlement and a copy of his book to the Electress Sophia, who in turn introduced him to the court in Berlin and to her daughter, Sophie Charlotte, queen of Prussia. Amused by his wit and attracted by his good looks, the queen liked to walk and converse with Toland for hours at a time.

In Berlin, in many discussions in the presence of the queen, Toland and Leibniz began a philosophical exchange that lasted for several years. Although Leibniz expressed doubts about Toland's manners, he respected the young man's intellect and even wrote a brief reply to *Christianity Not Mysterious* (which Toland received with great pleasure). Toland's suggestions that Leibniz pay special attention to the works of Bruno were generally ignored, but his promotion of the Italian thinker gained Toland notoriety for his knowledge of rare books and manuscripts containing heterodox doctrines.

From 1701 to 1707 Toland traveled to Hanover at least three times. On each trip, while passing through Holland, he met individuals with whom he later corresponded. On one occasion Toland met Bayle, who later incorporated some of Toland's remarks into his *Dictionnaire Historique et Critique* (1697). On another occasion Toland met Baron von Hohendorf, chief lieutenant to Prince Eugene of Savoy, commander of the armies of the Austrian Hapsburgs. After this meeting Toland was commissioned by Hohendorf to increase Prince Eugene's library of rare and clandestine works. Especially in this context, Toland's interest in Bruno had widespread influence in clandestine circles.

In 1702 Toland returned to England from his second visit to Hanover and Berlin and began work on his *Letters to Serena: Containing, I. The origin and force of prejudices. II. The history of the soul's immortality among the heathens. III. The origin of idolatry, and reasons of heathenism . . .* (1704), in which he examines prejudice and superstition and argues that motion is essential to matter, rejecting both Spinoza's ahistorical account of motion and Isaac Newton's reliance on divine agency. Followers of Newton (notably Samuel Clarke) were quick to recognize that Toland's attack on Newtonian physics had been motivated by his political objections to the belief that individuals need to be inspired and organized by external (monarchical, clerical, or spiritual) sources.

When Harley became secretary of state in 1704, Toland expected to receive a more stable income than that provided by his occasional pieces. Harley continued to rely on Toland merely as a source of information about intrigues on the Continent and as a propagandist, however. While returning from his third trip to Hanover, Toland learned that Harley had been forced out of office; so with little prospect for fortune in England, he remained in Holland. For the next two years he looked into how primitive Christianity could be retrieved from centuries of institutionalized superstition. Some of this work he published in *Adeisidaemon, sive Titus Livius a superstitione vindicatus: In qua dissertatione probatur, Livium historicum in sacris, prodigiis, & ostentis Romanorum enarrandis, haudquaquam fuisse credulum aut superstitiosum; ipsamque superstitionem non minùs reipublicae (si non magis) exitiosam esse, quam purum putum atheismum* (1709) and dedicated to his friend and fellow freethinker, Anthony Collins. Fuller development of his biblical and textual research into ancient gospels, a purported Irish manuscript of the four Gospels, and a summary of ancient Irish Christianity appeared later in *Nazarenus, or, Jewish, Gentile, and Mahometan Christianity. Containing the History of the Antient Gospel of Barnabas, and the modern Gospel of the Mahometans, attributed to the same apostle, this last Gospel being now first made known among Christians: also, The Original Plan of Christianity occasionally explain'd in the history of the Nazarens, wherby diverse controversies about this divine (but highly perverted) institution may be happily terminated. With the Relation of an Irish Manuscript of the Four Gospels, as likewise a summary of the antient Irish Christianity, and the reality of the Keldees (an order of lay-religious) against the two last bishops of Worcester* (1718).

After Harley's return to power in the Tory government of 1710, Toland believed that he was primarily committed to the Protestant Succession and the regency of Queen Anne. So Toland returned to England early in 1711 in hopes of obtaining a position through Harley's assistance. When Harley was almost killed in an assassination attempt in March 1711, however, enemies of Toland spread a rumor that the would-be assassin was one of his correspondents—a rumor Toland denied to no avail.

For the next two years Toland's lifelong interests in religious toleration and civil liberty became the focus of his writings. When those principles seemed to have been thoroughly ignored in the negotiation by the government of a commercial treaty with France in the Peace of Utrecht (1713), Toland declared his final break with Harley in his bitter work *The Art of Restoring; or, The piety and probity of General Monk in bringing about the last restoration: evidenc'd from his own authentic letters: with a just account of Sir Roger, who runs the parallel as far as he can; in a letter to a minister of state, at the court of Vienna* (1714). Because Toland had been a close friend and dependent of Harley, his explicit attack con-

LETTERS
TO
SERENA:

CONTAINING,

I. The Origin and Force of Prejudices.

II. The History of the Soul's Immortality among the Heathens.

III. The Origin of Idolatry, and Reasons of Heathenism.

As also,

IV. A Letter to a Gentleman in Holland, showing SPINOSA's System of Philosophy to be without any Principle or Foundation.

V. *Motion essential to Matter*; in Answer to some Remarks by a Noble Friend on the *Confutation of* SPINOSA.

To all which is Prefix'd,

VI. A Preface; being a Letter to a Gentleman in London, sent together with the foregoing Dissertations, and declaring the several Occasions of writing them.

By Mr. TOLAND.

Opinionum Commenta delet Dies,
Naturæ Judicia confirmat.   *Cic. de Nat. Deor. l. 2.*

LONDON;

Printed for *Bernard Lintot* at the Middle-Temple Gate in Fleet-street. M.DCC.IV.

Title page for Toland's collection of essays on various philosophical topics (courtesy of The Lilly Library, Indiana University)

firmed the suspicions of many Englishmen that Harley (now Lord Oxford) no longer supported the ideals of the Protestant Succession. Toland's book went through ten printings in less than a year, providing him with the financial independence he needed to compose his equally popular treatise on Whig political theory, *The State Anatomy of Great Britain; Containing a particular account of its several interests and parties, their bent and genius; and what each of them, with all the rest of Europe, may hope or fear from the reign and family of King George; being a memorial sent by an intimate friend to a foreign minister, lately nominated to come for the Court of England* (1717).

In 1718 Toland published the results of his earlier work on biblical criticism and turned his attention to a projected monumental study on the Druids. He was fascinated by the secretive activities of the ancient Irish, and in his *Tetradymus. Containing I. Hodegus; or, The pillar of cloud and fire, that guided the Israelites in the wilderness, not miraculous: but, as faithfully related in Exodus, a thing equally practis'd by other nations, and in those places not onely useful but necessary. II. Clid-*

ophorus; or, Of the exoteric and esoteric philosophy, that is, of the external and internal doctrine of the antients: the one open and public, accommodated to popular prejudices and the establish'd religions; the other private and secret, wherin, to the few capable and discrete, was taught the real truth stript of all disguises. III. Hypatia; or, The history of a most beautiful, most virtuous, most learned, and every way accomplish'd lady; who was torn to pieces by the clergy of Alexandria, to gratify the pride, emulation, and cruelty of their Archbishop Cyril. IV. Mangoneutes: being a defense of Nazarenus, address'd to the Right Reverend John, lord bishop of London; against his lordship's chaplain Dr. Mangey, his dedicator Mr. Patterson, and . . . the Reverend Dr. Brett (1720) and *Pantheisticon; sive Formula Celebrandae Sodalitas Socraticae, in tres particulas divisa, quae pantheistarum, sive sodalium, continent I, Mores et axiomata: II, Numen et philosophiam: III, Libertatem, et non fallentem legem, neque fallendam* (1720; translated as *Pantheisticon: or, The form of celebrating the Socratic-Society . . . To which is prefix'd a discourse upon the ancient modern societies of the learned, as also upon the infinite and eternal universe. And subjoined, a short dissertation, upon a two-fold philosophy of the Pantheists, that is to be followed; together with an idea of the best and most accomplished man*) he examines how the distinction between esoteric and exoteric doctrines function in religion and philosophy. His interest in the topic had appeared as early as in *Letters to Serena,* and he had coined the term "pantheist" in his *Socinianism Truly Stated* (1705) to describe individuals who tolerate promiscuous communication. In his *Origines Judaicae* (1709), published as part of *Adeisidaemon,* he associates pantheists with Spinozists because their methodological toleration required that they limit philosophical discussion to what can be observed, bodies in motion. If life itself is nothing more than such motion, he concludes, then the adoption of a pantheistic attitude toward the universe and God should provide a tranquil temperament and peace of mind.

Toland lost what little property he had in the financial collapse of the South Sea Company in 1720. The following year his health began to decline, aggravated by the polluted air of London. Although he moved out of the city to Putney, his condition did not improve appreciably. He died, on 11 March 1722, in such extreme poverty that no grave marker was placed at the spot where he was buried in Putney churchyard. It is said that when asked, immediately before he died, whether he wanted anything, he replied he wanted only death. After bidding those around him farewell, he simply said that he was going to sleep—expressing an attitude of his that Voltaire greatly admired.

After his death the most noticeable impact of John Toland's philosophy appears in the French Enlightenment. Denis Diderot and Paul Henri Thiry, Baron D'Holbach, in particular retrieve his doctrine of the essential activity of matter. Though Toland's promotion of clandestine writings does not seem to have had a direct influence in the development of freemasonry, it did indicate how the dissemination of pantheism, like other religious beliefs, required the support of social practices. His suggestion that polemics, toleration, and scholarship can be united as a basis for metaphysics became a model for the Enlightenment critique of religious excess.

Letters:

State Papers and Correspondence Illustrative of the Social and Political State of Europe from the Revolution to the Accession of the House of Hanover, edited by John M. Kemble (London: Parker, 1857);

F. H. Heinemann, "John Toland and the Age of Reason," *Archive für Philosophie,* 4 (1950): 35–66;

Die Philosophischen Schriften von Gottfried Wilhelm Leibniz, volumes 3 and 6, edited by C. I. Gerhardt (Hildesheim: Georg Olms, 1960);

Giancarlo Carabelli, "John Toland e G. W. Leibniz: Otto Lettere," *Rivista critica de storia della filos fia,* 29 (1974): 412–431.

Bibliographies:

Giancarlo Carabelli, *Tolandiana: materiali bibliogra fici per lo studio dell'o pera e della fortuna di John Toland* (Florence: Nuova Italia, 1975);

Carabelli, *Tolandiana . . . Errata, addenda e indici* (Ferrara: Universita de Ferrara, 1978).

References:

Paolo Casini, "Toland e l'attività della materia," *Rivista critica di storia della filoso fia,* 22 (1974): 24–53;

Stephen H. Daniel, *John Toland: His Methods, Manners, and Mind* (Kindston, Ont.: McGill-Queen's University Press, 1984);

Robert Rees Evans, *Pantheisticon: The Career of John Toland* (New York: Peter Lang, 1991);

Chiara Giuntini, *Panteismo e ideologia repubblicana: John Toland (1670–1722)* (Bologna: Il Mulino, 1979);

F. H. Heinemann, "John Toland and the Age of Enlightenment," *Review of English Studies,* 20 (1994): 125–146;

Margaret C. Jacob, *The Newtonians and the English Revolution, 1689–1720* (Ithaca, N.Y.: Cornell University Press, 1976);

J. G. Simms, "John Toland (1670–1722), a Donegal Heretic," *Irish Historical Studies,* 16 (1969): 304–320;

Robert E. Sullivan, *John Toland and the Deist Controversy: A Study in Adaptations* (Cambridge: Harvard University Press, 1982).

Papers:

Manuscript material by and about John Toland is located in the British Library; the Bodleian Library, Oxford; Lambeth Palace Library; the Public Record Office, London; and the National Austrian Library, Vienna.

Catharine Trotter
(16 August 1679 – 11 May 1749)

Catherine M. Rodriguez
University of South Florida

See also the Trotter entry in *DLB 84: Restoration and Eighteenth-Century Dramatists.*

BOOKS: *Agnes de Castro: A Tragedy as it is acted at the Theatre Royal by His Majesty's servant written by a young lady* (London: Printed for H. Rhodes, R. Parker, 1696);

Fatal Friendship: A Tragedy, as it is acted at the New-Theatre in Little-Lincolns-Inn-Fields (London: Printed for Francis Saunders, 1698);

The Unhappy Penitent: A Tragedy. As it is acted, at the Theatre Royal in Drury Lane, by His Majesty's Servants (London: Printed for William Turner and John Nutt, 1701);

Love at a Loss: or, Most Votes Carry It: A Comedy. As it is now acted at the Theatre Royal in Drury-Lane, by His Majesty's Servants (London: Printed for William Turner, 1701);

A Defence of Mr. Lock's Essay of Human Understanding: Wherein Its Principles with Reference to Morality, Reveal'd Religion, and the Immortality of the Soul, are Consider'd and Justify'd. In Answer to Some Remarks on that Essay, anonymous (London: Printed for William Turner and John Nutt, 1702);

The Revolution of Sweden: A Tragedy. As it is acted at the Queens Theatre in the Hay-Market (London: Printed for James Knapton & George Strahan, 1706);

A Discourse Concerning A Guide in Controversies; in Two Letters: Written to one of the Church of Rome, By a Person Lately Converted from That Communion (London: Printed for A. & C. Churchill, 1707);

A Letter to Dr. Holdsworth: Occasioned by His Sermon Preached Before the University of Oxford, on Easter Monday Concerning the Resurrection of the Same Body (London: B. Motte, 1726);

Remarks Upon Some Writers in the Controversy Concerning the Foundation of Moral Virtue and Moral Obligation. With Some Thoughts Concerning Necessary Existence; the Reality and Infinity of Space; the Extension and Place of Spirits; and on Dr. Watt's Notion of Substance (London, 1743);

*Catharine Trotter after her marriage to Patrick Cockburn in 1708
(Folger Shakespeare Library)*

Remarks Upon the Principles and Reasonings of Dr. Rutherford's Essay on the Nature and Obligations of Virtue: In Vindication of the Contrary Principles and Reasonings, Inforced in the Writings of the Late Dr. Samuel Clarke (London: Printed for J. & P. Knapton, 1747);

The Works of Mrs. Catharine Cockburn, Theological, Moral, Dramatic, and Poetical. Several of them now first pub-

357

lished, 2 volumes, edited by Thomas Birch (London: Printed for J. & P. Knapton, 1751).

Editions: *Olinda's Adventures; or The Amours of a Young Lady,* introduction by Robert Day Adams (Los Angeles: William Andrews Clark Memorial Library, 1969);

The Plays of Mary Pix and Catharine Trotter, volume 2, edited by Edna L. Steeves (New York: Garland, 1982).

OTHER: *Olinda's Adventures: Or the Amours of a Young Lady,* anonymous, in *Letters of Love and Gallantry and Several Other Subjects. All Written by Ladies* (London: Printed for Sam. Briscoe, 1693).

PLAY PRODUCTIONS: *Agnes de Castro,* London, Drury Lane, December 1695;

Fatal Friendship, London, Lincoln Inn Fields, May 1698;

Love at a Loss: Or Most Votes Carry It, London, Theater Royal, 23 November 1700;

The Unhappy Penitent, London, Drury Lane, 4 February 1701;

The Revolution of Sweden, London, Queen's Theater, 11 February 1706.

Catharine Trotter began her public writing career at the age of fourteen with her short epistolary novel, *Olinda's Adventures: Or the Amours of a Young Lady* (1693). She proceeded to write across several genres, including poetry, drama, and philosophy. Trotter had her first dramatic work, a tragedy, *Agnes De Castro* (1695), produced in London when she was just sixteen years old. She followed this success with four additional plays in the next thirteen years. Her first and most recognized philosophical tract, *A Defence of Mr. Lock's Essay of Human Understanding: Wherein Its Principles with Reference to Morality, Reveal'd Religion, and the Immortality of the Soul, are Consider'd and Justify'd. In Answer to Some Remarks on that Essay* (1702), received considerable attention for its perspicuous comprehension of John Locke's work. After her final play was produced in 1706, Trotter devoted the remainder of her writing career primarily to philosophical endeavors. Trotter's pen brought her into a friendship with William Congreve and drew letters of commendation from such notable men of her day as Bevil Higgons, George Farquhar, and Locke. As a result of the awakened interest in previously overlooked female authors, Trotter's plays began receiving a surge of critical attention in the 1970s that continues through the present. The Augustan Reprint Society's 1969 edition of *Olinda's Adventures* initially drew little attention; however, more-recent studies of the development of the novel as a genre in conjunction with the movement to recognize the contributions of women writers have gained a small place for Trotter in the history of the novel. Known primarily as a defender of Locke and Samuel Clarke in philosophical circles, Trotter has received only slight recognition for her prose treatise. This neglect may be attributed to her subject matter; focusing primarily on religious and moral issues, the ideas expressed in these treatises have lost currency over time. Although Trotter's primary subject matter lacks relevancy, her consistent theme of intellectual freedom and equality for women secures her place in history.

According to her biographer Thomas Birch, Catharine Trotter was born in London on 16 August 1679 to David Trotter, a Scottish gentleman and commander of the Royal Navy under Charles II, and Sarah Trotter (née Ballendon), near kin to Lord Ballendon and several other "illustrious" Scottish families of the time—including the Drummond and Maitland families. When Catharine was five years old, her father died at sea of the plague along with the other chief officers aboard his ship. The remaining crewmen defrauded Captain Trotter's widow and children of the effects that he carried at sea, and the goldsmith to whom he had entrusted the greater part of his money on land went bankrupt soon after the captain's death. In memory of his faithful servant, Charles II granted Sarah Trotter a widow's pension that expired with the king's death in 1685 and was not restored until the accession of Anne to the throne in 1702. One can only assume that in the meantime she raised her family in genteel poverty and was forced to seek support from her relatives of the Scottish nobility.

As a child, Catharine showed early signs of genius, surprising on occasion friends and family with extemporaneous verses. She learned and mastered French on her own but had assistance in her studies of Latin grammar and logic. She composed her own abstract of logic, which she drew upon later in her *Defence of Mr. Lock's Essay of Human Understanding.* Such precocity, combined with her family's dire financial circumstances, perhaps accounts for Trotter, at the age of fourteen, beginning to pursue correspondence with prominent literary figures and attempting to have her own work published. In 1693 she composed verses that she sent to Higgons on the occasion of his recovery from smallpox.

That same year Samuel Briscoe published *Olinda's Adventures* in his epistolary miscellany, *Letters of Love and Gallantry and Several Other Subjects. All Written by Ladies. Olinda's Adventures* consists of eight letters written by the fictional heroine, Olinda. Seven of them are addressed to her male confidant—Cleander, a platonic friend—upon whose request she describes her many amorous encounters. Olinda, an eighteen-year-old woman, lives in impoverished circumstances with her widowed mother, who is anxious to see Olinda married and well provided for. Olinda has some close calls but manages to avoid the altar throughout her adventures. Preferring her independence, she has no interest in a future with any of her suitors, except Cloridon, who happens to be married. The novel has an open ending, with the eighth and final letter, to Cloridon, concluding: "I will endeavour to forget you; don't Write to me, if you love me well enough to forbear it: And if you can cease to love me, without hating me; for I don't find I have force enough to bear so great a misfortune. . . ." Robert Day Adams, in his introduction to the 1969 edition of the novel, suggests that with its ending, control of style, and subplot, *Olinda's Adventures* anticipates the English domestic and realistic novel.

The publication history of *Olinda's Adventures* indicates that it may have reached a surprising number of readers. In 1718 Briscoe assembled another collection, *Familiar Letters of Love and Gallantry and Several Occasions,* in which he again included the novel. The title page of the 1724 edition of this collection numbers it as the sixth. In addition, *Olinda's Adventures* enjoyed another distinction for British literature prior to the 1700s; it appeared in 1695 in a French translation under the title *Les Amours d'une belle Angloise: ou la vie et les avantures de la jeune Olinde: Ecrites par Elle mesme en forme de lettres a un Chevalier de ses amis.*

Olinda's Adventures stands out as a bit of an anomaly in Trotter's canon; her other works gained a reputation for their didacticism and advocation of morality. Trotter herself was frequently praised for her beauty in her youth and her irreproachable morals throughout her life. Although Mary Delariviere Manley's autobiographical novel *The Adventures of Rivella* (1714), casts Trotter as a promiscuous young lady, the portrayal was considered false and scandalous. Margarette R. Connor notes, however, that in a letter to George Burnet in 1707, the year prior to her marriage, Trotter writes of having recently visited a daughter-in-law and of having become a grandmother. Connor suggests the possibility that Trotter lied about her date of birth. If her traditionally accepted birth date is accurate, then Trotter may have become a mother in her early teens. No other mention is made of this unknown child and investigation into his existence remains to be conducted. Verification of this child would provide impetus for further biographical and psychoanalytical interpretation of Trotter's work as love, money, and contractual relations stand out as prominent themes in her novel and her first four dramas. Trotter began her career as a dramatist in 1695 with the production of *Agnes de Castro* in the Theater Royal. It met with some success and was published the following year. Based on Aphra Behn's English translation of a French novel, *Agnes de Castro* portrays the Prince of Portugal enmeshed in a love triangle. The Prince, in love with his wife's devoted servant, Agnes, conceals his passion. The Princess, although she discovers her husband's illicit passion, continues in her love for both Agnes and the Prince. This harmony enrages Elvira, the Prince's sister, whose interference produces a series of mistaken identities and murders. Trotter appealed to the earl of Dorset and Middlesex for his support of *Agnes de Castro,* which he graciously provided. Trotter addresses her dedication to him, in which she writes: "This little Off-spring of my early Muse was first Submitted to Your Lordship's Judgement, whether it should be Stifled in the Birth, or Preserv'd to try its Fortune in the World; and . . . 'tis from Your Sentence it has ventur'd thus far."

This production garnered much attention as Trotter was the first woman to write for the London stage since the death of Behn in 1689. She does not appear to have been hindered by the belief that neither the theater nor any public intellectual activity were proper professions for a woman. She was soon followed on the stage by other women writers, including Mary Pix and Manley. These three were later satirized in the anonymous play *The Female Wits: Or the Triumvirate of Poets at Rehearsal,* which opened at Drury Lane in September 1696. This play censures Trotter as a dramatist worthy of little merit and one pretentious to learning. Trotter continued undeterred from her writing, however. In 1697 she began her correspondence with Congreve, who looked favorably upon and encouraged her literary achievements.

Her next drama, *Fatal Friendship,* another tragedy, was performed at Lincoln Inn Fields in May 1698 and published the same year. *Fatal Friendship* depicts the misfortunes of Gramont and his friend Castalio; Gramont, secretly already married, finds himself pressured into a bigamous marriage to Castalio's beloved, Lamira. After a series of entanglements the play concludes with Gramont accidentally wounding Castalio and stabbing himself just before the arrival of a messenger who bears tidings of a royal pardon for all. Trotter wrote *Fatal Friendship* with the explicit intent to reform the stage. In her dedication of the play she states that "its end is the most noble, to discourage vice, and recommend a firm unshaken virtue." Dedicating *Fatal Friendship* to Princess Anne, Trotter makes an appeal for patronage: "when a Woman appears in the world under any distinguishing character, she must expect to be the mark of ill nature; but most one, who seems desirous to recommend herself by what the other sex think their peculiar prerogative." *Fatal Friendship* met with "great applause" at the theater and is still considered her most successful play. It drew letters of commendation from Higgons and Farquhar among others. Although *Fatal Friendship* was praised by its contemporary audience for its moralizing and didacticism, many critics now suggest that Trotter's plays and her career as a dramatist were marred by these same qualities.

In 1700 Trotter comprised one of the nine anonymous female authors of *The Nine Muses,* a folio of verses lamenting the death of the poet laureate, John Dryden. That same year her only comedy, *Love at a Loss: Or Most Votes Carry It,* opened at the Theatre Royal. According to her dedication of this play, it was originally intended as a

Fatal Friendfhip.

A

TRAGEDY.

As it is Acted at the

NEW-THEATRE

IN

Little-Lincolns-Inn-Fields.

LONDON,

Printed for *Francis Saunders* at the *Blue-Anchor* in the
Lower-Walk of the *New-Exchange*, 1698.

*Title page for the published version of Trotter's most popular play, which
she wrote to encourage the moral reform of English drama (Henry E.
Huntington Library, San Marino, California)*

subplot for one of her tragedies; alone, it became a highly moralized comedy. Each of the three heroines nearly loses her man as a result of her own folly. Throughout, the lovers solve their problems using good sense, and in the end, each points to a moral. The following year, Trotter's fourth play, *The Unhappy Penitent* (1701), premiered on the London stage. This tragedy, another highly moralized play, focuses on the marriage of Charles VIII of France. Although long contracted to Margarite of Flanders, he delays because he desires to marry Ann of Brittanie. In the meantime Margarite considers herself free from the contract and secretly marries the duke of Lorrain. Ann's moralizing and the interference of the duke of Brittanie, who also hopes to marry Margarite, result in slander and confusion. In the end Margarite makes a grand renunciation and joins a convent. *The Unhappy Penitent* presents its audience with a love triangle similar to that of *Fatal Friendship*. Both plays conclude with similar priggish moralizing in a "haste makes waste" vein. Although now considered dull, *The Unhappy Penitent* met with some approval from its contemporary audience.

At the age of twenty-two Trotter left London to spend some time with her patron, Lady Piers. She then settled in Salisbury, Wiltshire, with her sister, who was married to Dr. Inglis. There she became acquainted with Bishop Gilbert Burnet, developed a close friendship with his wife, and began her philosophical writing. In 1702 Trotter published her first philosophical essay, *A Defence of Mr. Lock's Essay of Human Understanding*, in which she defends Locke's work primarily against accusations that it provides for theistic voluntarism. She articulates her main objective: "to vindicate [*The Essay*] from a defect in the foundation of certainty, in those things, which are of greatest concern to us: which I doubt not to do; it being clear to me, that whatever we can know at all, must be discoverable by Mr. Locke's principles; for I cannot find any other way to knowledge. . . ." Trotter's friends George Burnet of Kemney and the wife of Bishop Burnet, were privy to the secret of Trotter's authorship of this work and recommended its anonymous publication, believing that her youth and sex would count against her work. This work drew much attention for its perspicacity; its readers were amazed that a woman could have such an acute comprehension of Locke's essay. Locke himself was so impressed that he endeavored to discover its anonymous author, and upon discovery, he sent Trotter some books as a present, along with a letter expressing his appreciation and praising the "strength and clearness of [her] reasoning."

In February 1706 Trotter's last dramatic work, *The Revolution of Sweden*, opened at the Queen's Theater, Heymarket, but closed after the sixth day. After conducting a critical study of the works of Dryden, William Shakespeare, Thomas Otway, and Nathaniel Lee, Trotter concluded that the subject of lovers' misfortune is ill suited for tragedy; therefore, she chose patriotism as the major passion in *The Revolution of Sweden*. This historical play depicts Gustavus's emancipation of Sweden from the Danes and his election as king. Concomitantly, it commingles the adventures of two married couples with military exploits. One heroine, Christina, disguises herself as a young man, fights for the Swedes, and soliloquizes on female courage, while the other heroine, Constantia, argues theology with the archbishop while she is in captivity. Congreve pointed out the weakness of the play in a letter to Trotter written after he had read an early draft of it; while he found the general design noble, he thought it would gain more audience appeal if the heroines engaged in some *belle passion*. Although *The Revolution of Sweden* was unsuccessful as a play, it does succeed in making an early feminist statement. In addition to portraying female characters who are both physically and intellectually capable, Trotter addresses the English view of women's intellectual ability in her dedication of the play to Lady Godolphin:

Encouraging indulgence to the Endeavours of our Sex . . . might incite some greater Geniuses among us to exert themselves, and change our Emulation of a Neighbouring Nation's Fopperies, to the commendable Ambition of Rivalling them in their illustrious Women; Numbers we know among them, have made considerable Progress in the most difficult Sciences, several have gain'd the Prizes of Poesie from their Academies, and some have been chosen Members of their Societies. This without doubt is not from any Superiority of their Genius to ours; But from the much greater Encouragement they receive, by the Publick Esteem, and the Honors that are done to them . . . .

Here, Trotter refers to the reception of female intellectuals in France, where the Academie of Francaise awarded the Prix de Poesie to Catherine Durand in 1701. After *The Revolution of Sweden* Trotter left dramatic writing and devoted the remainder of her career almost entirely to philosophical and moral issues.

Although raised Anglican, Trotter converted to Catholicism at a young age and continued in the Roman Catholic Church until 1707. Trotter's own spiritual conflict gave impetus to her second philosophical pamphlet, *A Discourse Concerning A Guide in Controversies; in Two Letters: Written to one of the Church of Rome, By a Person Lately Converted from That Communion* (1707), in which she discusses the problem of denominational Christianity. Trotter's primary contention with the Roman Catholic Church centers around the belief in the infallibility of the church to underpin the authority of Christianity and the Scriptures. By the time she published these letters Trotter was intent on marrying a clergyman and was pursued, according to her letters, by George Burnet, a Mr. Fenn, Patrick Cockburn, and "some others."

Trotter chose Cockburn and married him in 1708. For the next eighteen years she set aside her pen while she attended to household duties and the needs of a growing family. Of this time she wrote in a 1738 letter to Alexander Pope, "in 1708 I bid adieu to the muses and so wholly gave myself to the cares of a family, and the education of my children, that I scarce knew, whether there was any such a thing as books, plays, or poems stirring in Great Britain." The Cockburns and their four children lived most of this time in reduced circumstances, for Patrick Cockburn refused to take the oath of abjuration. Once reconciling himself to taking the oath in 1726, he accepted a position as minister to the Episcopalian congregation at Aberdeen in Scotland, which afforded him and his family a more comfortable living.

In 1724, after reading a sermon by Winch Holdsworth in which he professes to "examine and answer the cavils, false reasonings and false interpretations of scripture, of Mr. Locke and others, against the resurrection of the same body," Trotter picked up her pen once again and wrote a letter to Holdsworth, in which she defends both herself and Locke. After sending this letter to Holdsworth proved of no avail in swaying his opinion, she published it as *A Letter to Dr. Holdsworth: Occasioned by His Sermon Preached Before the University of Oxford, on Easter Monday Concerning the Resurrection of the Same Body* in 1726. Holdsworth immediately responded with the publication of *A Defence of the Doctrine of the Resurrection of the Same Body* (1727). In her reply, "A Vindication of Locke's Christian Principles," Trotter explains that her reason for taking issue with Holdsworth had less to do with the question of the resurrection of the same body than with her concern that Holdsworth spuriously adds to the doctrine of faith by insisting on the resurrection of the same body as an essential tenet of the faith. This second defense of Locke remained unpublished until it appeared posthumously in Birch's 1751 collection of Trotter's works.

While residing at Aberdeen, Trotter planned to revise her dramatic works but only completed the revision of her comedy, *Love at a Loss,* which was never republished. She continued writing despite ill health and declining age. In 1732 she wrote "Verses Occasioned by the Busts in the Queen's Hermitage" (1737). Although Trotter originally intended to present this poem to the queen, no evidence exists to suggest that she ever received it; the verses were published in the *Gentlemen's Magazine* in May 1737. In the winter of 1739 Trotter began writing *Remarks Upon Some Writers in the Controversy Concerning the Foundation of Moral Virtue and Moral Obligation. With Some Thoughts Concerning Necessary Existence; the Reality and Infinity of Space; the Extension and Place of Spirits; and on Dr. Watt's Notion of Substance* (1743). In this work she purposes to defend Samuel Clarke's account of the foundation of moral virtue and obligation through considering a series of objectors that includes Edmund Law and William Warburton. Although the *Dictionary of National Biography* faults Trotter for not perceiving the inconsistency between Clarke's and Locke's ethical theories, Martha Brandt Bolton, in "Some Aspects of the Philosophical Work of Catharine Trotter" (1993), suggests that Trotter finds common ground with Clarke as both acknowledge the "moral relevance of God's will without yielding ground to voluntarism." Furthermore, Trotter employs this theory in her 1702 defense of Locke. Brandt calls attention to Trotter's consistent theme in *Remarks Upon Some Writers,* an argument that might otherwise seem diffuse: Although Trotter agrees with her opponents on grounding morality in religion, she rebuts their arguments on points that in some way ground morality in self interest, "the pursuit of divine or natural benefits for oneself." John Sharp, the archdeacon of Northumberland, read *Remarks Upon Some Writers* in manuscript and encouraged its publication. Trotter found no publisher until 1743, however, when it appeared in the August issue of *The History of the Works of the Learned.* Trotter continues the same argument in her final work, *Remarks Upon the Principles and Reasonings of Dr. Ruther-*

ford's *Essay on the Nature and Obligations of Virtue: In Vindication of the Contrary Principles and Reasonings, Inforced in the Writings of the Late Dr. Samuel Clarke* (1747), published with a preface by Bishop Warburton. Rutherford maintains that human beings have no natural motive or inclination for beneficent actions and that the prospect for reward motivates the practice of virtue, while Trotter continues to argue that the foundation of moral actions lies in the nature of God and the nature of man.

Trotter's last two works were well received and cause for much admiration. Two years after publishing her remarks on Rutherford's essay, Trotter died on 11 May 1749, just four months after the death of her husband. Prior to her death her friends urged her to assemble and publish the collection that eventually appeared as *The Works of Mrs. Catharine Cockburn, Theological, Moral, Dramatic, and Poetical. Several of them now first published* (1751). She died before finishing this project, so Birch undertook the completion of it. At the time of her death Trotter was known primarily for her moral and philosophical writing, which possibly explains the absence of her novel and all but one of her plays in Birch's collection. That Trotter took issue with inconsequential men of her day accounts in part for the current obscurity of her philosophical work. Although important to her contemporaneous audience, her subject matter lacks relevancy today.

In his 1916 address to the Royal Society of Literature, Edmund Gosse said that Catharine Trotter's later writings on philosophy and religion are so dull that the mere thought of them "brings tears into one's eyes." The fact that she wrote at all, however, and with clarity and genius in her reasoning equal to that of any man of her time, earns Trotter a place in the history of philosophy. She overcame the obstacles of living most of her life in genteel poverty, having only limited access to education, and becoming an object of public derision. In her "Verses Occasioned by the Busts in the Queen's Hermitage," Trotter articulates the plight of female authors in the eighteenth century:

> . . . those restraints, which have our sex confin'd,
> By partial custom, check the soaring mind:
> Learning deny'd us, we at random tread
> Unbeaten paths, that late to knowledge lead;
> By secret steps break through the obstructed way,
> Nor dare acquirements gain'd by stealth display.
> If some advent'rous genius rare arise.
> Who on exalted themes her talent tries,
> She fears to give the work, tho' prais'd, a name,
> And flies not more from infamy than fame.

Writing against all odds, Catharine Trotter took every opportunity to champion the cause of intellectual freedom for women throughout her fifty-six-year career.

Biographies:

Thomas Birch, "The Life of Mrs. Catharine Cockburn," in *The Works of Mrs. Catharine Cockburn, Theological, Moral, Dramatic, and Poetical. Several of them now first published*, 2 volumes (London: Printed for J. & P. Knapton, 1751);

Margarette R. Connor, "Catharine Trotter: An Unknown Child?" *ANQ: A Quarterly Journal of Short Articles, Notes, and Reviews*, 8 (1995): 11–14.

References:

Robert Day Adams, Introduction to *Olinda's Adventures: or, The Amours of a Young Lady*, by Trotter (Los Angeles: William Clark Memorial Library, 1969);

Adams, "Muses in the Mud: The Female Wits Anthropologically Considered," *Women's Studies*, 7 (1980): 61–74;

Martha Brandt Bolton, "Some Aspects of the Philosophical Work of Catharine Trotter," *Journal of the History of Philosophy*, 31 (1993): 565–588;

Constance Clark, "Catharine Trotter," in her *Three Augustan Women Playwrights* (New York: Peter Lang, 1986), pp. 35–95;

Nancy Cotton, "The Female Wits: Catharine Trotter, Delariviere Manley, Mary Pix," in her *Women Playwrights in England: c. 1363–1750* (Lewisburg, Pa.: Bucknell University Press / London: Associated University Presses, 1980), pp. 81–121;

Edmund Gosse, "Catharine Trotter: The Precursor of the Bluestockings," in *Transactions of the Royal Society of Literature of the United Kingdom*, volume 34 (London: Adlard, 1916), pp. 87–118;

Fidelis Morgan, *The Female Wits: Women Playwrights on the London Stage, 1660–1720* (London: Virago, 1981);

Myra Reynolds, *The Learned Lady in England, 1650–1760* (Boston: Houghton Mifflin, 1920);

Edna Steeves, "Dipped in Ink: Catharine Trotter's *Olinda's Adventures*," in *Selected Essays on Scottish Language and Literature: A Festschrift in Honor of Allen H. MacLaine*, edited by Steven R. McKenna (New York: Mellen, 1992), pp. 125–132;

Jane Williams, "The Poetess, A.D. 1725–1750: Catharine Cockburn," in *The Literary Women of England: Including a Biographical Epitome of All the Most Eminent to the Year 1700; and Sketches of the Poetesses to the Year 1850; with Extracts from Their Works, and Critical Remarks*, edited by Williams (London: Sanders, Ottley, 1861), pp. 170–188.

Benjamin Whichcote

(11 March 1609? – May 1683)

Jay G. Williams
Hamilton College

BOOKS: *Φεοφορουμένα Δόγματα or, Some Select Notions of that learned and reverend Divine of the Church of England, Benj. Whitchcot, D.D., lately deceased. Faithfully collected from him by a pupil and particular friend of his, and published pro bono publico per & pro philanthropo,* (London: Printed & sold by Israel Harrison, 1685);

Select Sermons of Dr. Whichcot, edited by Lord Shaftesbury (London: Printed for Awnshum & John Churchill, 1698);

Several Discourses by the Reverend and Learned Benjamin Whichcote, edited by John Jeffrey, 4 volumes (London: Printed for James Knapton, 1702–1707);

The True Notion of Peace in the Kingdom or Church of Christ, stated by the late Eminent and Learned Dr. Whitchcot, in a Sermon preach'd by him upon the malignity of Popery, edited by Jeffrey (London: Printed for James Knapton, 1717);

Select Sermons of Dr. Whichcot, edited by William Wishart (Edinburgh: Printed by T. W. & T. Ruddimans for G. Hamilton & J. Balfour, 1742);

The Works of the Learned Benjamin Whichcote, D.D. Rector of St. Lawrence Jewry, London, 4 volumes (Aberdeen: Printed by J. Chalmers for Alexander Thomson, 1751);

Moral and Religious Aphorisms: collected from the manuscript Papers of the Reverend and Learned Doctor Whichcote, and published in MDCCII by Dr. Jeffrey. Now re-published with very large additions from the Transcripts of the latter. by Samuel Satter. D.D. . . . to which are added Eight Letters, which passed between Dr. Whichcote, provost of King's College, and Dr. Tuckney, master of Emmanuel College, in Cambridge: On several very interesting subjects (London: Printed for J. Payne, 1753).

Benjamin Whichcote is best known as the founder of the school of Cambridge Platonists, which flourished during the Interregnum and Restoration periods. Besides Whichcote, the movement included John Smith, Nathaniel Culverwel, John Worthington, Henry More, and Ralph Cudworth. Among these colleagues, More and Cudworth

Benjamin Whichcote (Emmanuel College, Cambridge University)

were the most prolific. By contrast, Whichcote published little during his lifetime and is best remembered through transcriptions of his sermons, which were made by auditors and published posthumously.

Whichcote's exact birthday is under dispute, but John Tillotson, who preached his funeral oration, gives 11 March 1609 as his natal day, and that choice seems probable. He was born to an "ancient and honorable family," the sixth son of Christopher and Elizabeth Fox Whichcote of Stoke-on-Tern Shropshire. Virtually nothing is known about his early life, but his matriculation at Emmanuel

College, Cambridge in 1626 would seem to indicate a strong penchant toward Puritanism on his part or on the part of his family, for Emmanuel was perhaps the most Puritan of the Cambridge colleges at that time. Indeed, his tutors Anthony Tuckney and then Thomas Hill eventually became Westminster divines and, as it were, models of what seventeenth-century Puritanism stood for.

In 1651 Tuckney wrote to Whichcote, questioning his rationalistic theological position. Indeed, that set of correspondence, edited by Samuel Salter and published in 1753, reveals clearly the dimensions of the tension between the Puritan position and that of the men of latitude that Whichcote came to represent.

That Whichcote should emphasize reason in his theology is not surprising, for many leading Puritans of the time, including John Preston, the master of Emmanuel, did the same. The whole educational system at Cambridge emphasized Aristotle far more than John Calvin, and, if the Puritans tended to stress new directions in logic like that taken by Peter Ramus, the result was, nonetheless, a highly scholastic education full of subtle logical distinctions and a metaphysical systematization. What distinguished Whichcote was not his use of reason in theology but his attempt to generate a whole theological methodology on the basis of Prov. 20:27, which he translates as "the reason of man is the candle of the Lord."

Whichcote received his B.A. in 1629 and his M.A. in 1633. He was immediately elected a fellow of his college and began taking pupils. In this capacity as a neophyte teacher Whichcote began to influence a new generation of Cambridge students and ultimately the history of English intellectual thought. Apparently this influence was because of his broad-minded tolerance and sweet temper more so than to a carefully developed philosophical position. Little is known, in fact, about either his philosophy or his teaching methods or the content of his curriculum. He was, according to Gilbert Burnet, a man of "rare temper" who emphasized liberty of conscience. He disliked intensely the "dry and systematical" education still in vogue at Cambridge and encouraged his students to explore Plato, Cicero, and Plotinus, perhaps largely as an antidote to the scholasticism that the university still had not shaken off.

There is little evidence, however, that he espoused anything like a systematic Platonic or Neo-platonic position, nor is there any particular evidence of influence from the Italian Neoplatonists such as Marsilo Ficino and Pico della Mirandola, as Professor Ernst Cassirer has suggested in his *The Platonic Renaissance in England* (1953). Whichcote remained to the end a Christian preacher and exegete who sought to correct the excesses of the extremists by an appeal to reason in theology and life. His method of teaching and his theological stance clearly became attractive to many, for he gathered about him a variety of students and colleagues who perpetuated his vision of a broad-minded,

all-inclusive theology that was meant to unite rather than divide the Church of England.

In 1636 Whichcote was ordained both deacon and priest and soon thereafter was appointed to the Sunday afternoon lectureship at Trinity Church, Cambridge. This position was an extraordinarily prestigious one that had been held in the past by such outstanding Puritan preachers as Richard Sibbes, John Preston, and Thomas Goodwin. Clearly Whichcote's appointment indicates that he was still considered a member of the Puritan "Spiritual Brotherhood." As the divines sat at Westminster laboring to reform the Church of England and, therefore, English life according to the theology of the Calvinists, one of their own was setting forth a more irenic, rational, and latitudinarian theology at the intellectual fountainhead of the Puritan tradition. Moreover, despite the caveats of men such as Tuckney, he retained that prestigious platform for almost twenty years.

In 1640 Whichcote proceeded B.D. Because of a rule that limited the tenure of a fellow to twelve years, however, he was not able to continue teaching at the university. While retaining his lectureship at Trinity Church, he also became, probably in absentia, minister of the North Cadbury Church in Somersetshire.

At the same time, freed from the rules of celibacy that bound university fellows, he married Rebecca Cradok, the widow of Matthew Cradok, a wealthy merchant and former governor of the Massachusetts Bay Company. Thus, Whichcote augmented his own apparently ample resources with a considerable fortune. Perhaps this financial independence preserved Whichcote from the ignominies that often accompanied the conflict of the 1640s.

In 1644 Whichcote was invited to return to Cambridge as provost of King's College. The position was an attractive one, but there were reasons for hesitation, for he was called to replace the great scholar and teacher Samuel Collins, who was being ejected over the objections of his colleagues after thirty years of service. Moreover, Whichcote himself did not quite qualify for the post because he had never studied at King's. Nevertheless, he eventually accepted the offer with the understanding that Collins would receive half of the provost's salary as long as he lived. In March 1645, therefore, Whichcote returned to Cambridge.

Despite a great deal of political pressure he was able to persevere, working to protect his fellows from political reprisals. In 1649 he received a D.D. degree and in 1651 was elected vice chancellor of the university. In the meantime, at the height of Puritan power, his fellow "Platonists" also prospered. Ralph Cudworth became master of Clare Hall in 1644 and of Christ's College in 1654. John Smith was appointed a fellow of Queen's in 1644, while John Worthington became dean of Jesus College in 1644.

In 1651 Tuckney, responding to a commencement address of Whichcote, called into question his former student's basic theological position. In his responses Whichcote reveals the ways in which he both continued and forsook the Puritan/Calvinist view of theology. Whichcote, in particular, believed that not everything can be proved by an appeal to Scripture, because Scripture itself is ambiguous. Instead, he asserts that the Church ought to emphasize only those doctrines that are clear in Scripture and employ reason to prepare for the work of the Holy Spirit. Throughout, Whichcote reveals little emphasis upon any sort of specific Platonic position. As in his sermons, he expresses himself as a liberal Christian but not as a philosopher of any particular school.

In 1651 and 1652 the so-called Platonic school received severe blows. Smith and Culverwel, two of its younger and more articulate members, died. They left behind them works to be published posthumously, but their contribution to the movement was complete. Only Whichcote, Worthington, More, and Cudworth were left. More and Cudworth continued to publish during the Restoration period, but their essential ideas had already been established during the Interregnum. When Cudworth finally published in 1678 his magnum opus, *The True Intellectual System of the Universe,* it was already considered passé. Thus, Cambridge Platonism should be thought of as primarily a movement of the Interregnum period more than of the Restoration.

The return of the king in 1660 meant a great uprooting for Whichcote. Charles II, favoring a royal chaplain, ejected Whichcote, who had supported the Crown, from his position at King's and seated James Fleetwood in his place. Although the college, in general, resisted the change, there was little that could be done. Whichcote's appointment had been irregular; he should not, according to the charter, have been appointed in the first place.

Whichcote left Cambridge, however, not for obscurity but to become a well-known preacher at St. Anne's Blackfriars in London. At the same time, King's College rewarded him with a sinecure living at Milton, about five miles from Cambridge. When St. Anne's burned in the fire of London, Whichcote retired to Milton, but his retreat to a country parish was only momentary. In 1668 he was again called to London, this time to preach at St. Lawrence Jewry, a new church designed by Sir Christopher Wren. During this period he became known to such leading intellectuals as Tillotson and John Locke, both of whom admired him greatly.

One of the last references to Whichcote comes from the famous diarist John Evelyn, who in 1682 apparently heard (or failed to hear) Whichcote preach to St. Lawrence's. He described him as old and feeble and virtually inaudible. About a year later Whichcote traveled to Cambridge to visit his old friend and colleague Cudworth.

According to a contemporary account, while there he caught cold, fell into a distemper, and within a few days died, in May. He was buried at St. Lawrence Jewry. His funeral oration was given by Tillotson, and many facts about Whichcote's life have been gleaned from his account. In that eulogy Tillotson emphasizes not so much his finely developed theology as his exemplary life and personality. Clearly his impact upon the world was of a man who remained throughout his life broad-minded, even-tempered, and reasonable. Those qualities, as much as any specific ideas, helped to make him one of the fathers of the English Enlightenment.

Insofar as one can piece together Whichcote's theological position from his posthumous sermons, he appears as a classic Protestant liberal. Like most Protestants he accepts the Bible as the basis for all theology, but Whichcote maintains that in Scripture (particularly in Prov. 20:27 and Rom. 1:20) there is an emphasis upon the importance of reason. Reason, as he uses it, is not so much to prove God's existence as it is to discern the principles of morality. Reason, he says, depends upon God as its source and guarantor; God gives humans confidence that they can know the world. Therefore, to attempt to prove God is to involve oneself in circular reasoning. Reason can, however, discern the truth of things and hence basic moral principles. Whichcote thus reverts to the scholastic notion of *synderesis,* the source of the infallible natural recognition of moral principles. If the Hebrew Scriptures are revelation, they are a revelation of God through *synderesis* and hence teach no more about morality than any person can know naturally.

God, for Whichcote, is the incontingent and eternal fountain of being from which all things flow, the unity of Wisdom, Goodness, and Power. Human beings flowing from the fount are naturally good as well. The soul is meant to control the body, but the body as an expression of God's creation is good and useful. Whichcote is not a dualist, nor does he regard the body as an impediment or tomb. He does acknowledge that there is something wrong with humanity that has thrown human life out of tune, but he tends to attribute that to finitude. Therefore, he implies that through Christ's forgiveness and empowerment humans can approach as close to perfection as their finite condition will allow.

Christ is seen not merely as a vehicle of divine forgiveness but primarily as a pattern for the Christian life. Although Whichcote often acknowledges the work of the Holy Spirit in repentance and the necessity of grace for the good life, he also intimates that the good life is within the power of humans to live. He may argue with Tuckney in defense of his orthodoxy but his words often make him sound Pelagian, that is, a follower of Pelagius, a fifth-century proponent of human free will.

Whichcote believes that ultimately what is most important are not doctrines or words but the good life. In his conception of the good life, he reveals the strong influence of Aristotle, for he emphasizes the proper functioning of soul and body. The aim of human life is happiness, and happiness is found when the soul controls the body according to the rational principles discovered through reason and held up in the life of Jesus. Theology and ritual are important insofar as they prompt and further Christian living.

When theology and ritual become ends in themselves, however, dogmatism replaces compassion and vindictiveness replaces a sense of justice. Throughout his sermons Whichcote displays a breadth of compassion and understanding and a willingness to "sit lightly upon" controversial theological doctrines. Never the technical thinker, he clearly is most interested in exhorting his listeners to live the good life. Whatever notions he develops are simply instruments for that end.

Whichcote is far from Deism, for he remained a good churchman to the end, sometimes reinterpreting but seldom discarding the central beliefs of Christendom. Nevertheless, his broad-minded approach to theology distinguishes him from both his scholastic predecessors and his Puritan contemporaries and makes him at least a father if not a representative of the English enlightenment.

Letters:

Eight Letters of Anthony Tuckney and Benjamin Whichcote, edited by Samuel Salter (London: J. Payne, 1753).

References:

A. W. Argyle, "The Cambridge Platonists," *Hibbert Journal,* 53 (1954–1955): 225–261;

Robert L. Armstrong, "Cambridge Platonists and Locke on Innate Ideas," *Journal of History of Ideas,* 30 (April–June 1969): 187–202;

Eugene Munger Austin, "The Ethics of the Cambridge Platonists," Ph.D. thesis, University of Pennsylvania, 1935;

Jerold G. Braver, "Puritan Mysticism and the Development of Liberalism," *Church History,* 19 (September 1950): 151–170;

Ernest Trafford Campagnac, *The Cambridge Platonists* (Oxford: Clarendon Press, 1901), pp. 1–75;

Rosalie L. Colie, *Light and Enlightenment: A Study of the Cambridge Platonists and the Dutch Arminians* (Cambridge: Cambridge University Press, 1957), pp. 1–162;

G. R. Cragg, *The Cambridge Platonists* (New York: Oxford University Press, 1968), pp. 1–49, 61–74, 408–436;

Cragg, *From Puritanism to the Age of Reason* (Cambridge: Cambridge University Press, 1950);

Paul Miles Davenport, *Moral Divinity with a Tincture of Christ: An Interpretation of the Theology of Benjamin Whichcote* (Nijmegen, Holland: Peters Tissen, 1972);

John J. Deboer, *The Theory of Knowledge of the Cambridge Platonists* (Madras, India: Methodist Publishing House, 1931), pp. 1–160;

Robert A. Greene, "Whichcote, the Candle of the Lord, and Synderesis," *Journal of the History of Ideas,* 52 (October–December 1991): 617–644;

Greene, "Whichcote, Wilkins, 'Ingenuity,' and the Reasonableness of Christianity," *Journal of the History of Ideas,* 42 (April–June 1981): 227–252;

William Inge, *The Platonic Tradition in English Religious Thought* (New York: Longman, Green, 1926), pp. 38–69;

Simon Patrick, "A Brief Account of the New Sect of Latitude-Men," *The Phenix,* 2 volumes (London: J. Morphew, 1708), II: 499–518;

C. A. Patrides, *The Cambridge Platonists* (Cambridge, Mass.: Harvard University Press, 1969), pp. 1–89;

G. P. H. Pawson, *The Cambridge Platonists and Their Place in Religious Thought* (London: Society for Promoting Christian Knowledge, 1930);

Frederick J. Powicke, *The Cambridge Platonists* (Cambridge, Mass.: Harvard University Press, 1926), pp. 1–86;

John Herman Randall Jr., *The Career of Philosophy from the Middle Ages to the Enlightenment* (New York: Columbia University Press, 1962), pp. 471–494;

James Deotis Roberts, *From Puritanism to Platonism in Seventeenth Century England* (The Hague: Nyhoff, 1968), pp. 1–300;

G. A. J. Rogers, "Locke, Newton, and the Cambridge Platonists on Innate Ideas," *Journal of the History of Ideas,* 40 (April–June 1979): 191–205;

John Tulloch, *Rational Theory and Christian Philosophy in the Seventeenth Century,* 2 volumes (Edinburgh: Blackwood, 1872) II: 1–16;

Jay G. William, *The Life and Thought of Benjamin Whichcote* (Ann Arbor, Mich.: University Microfilms, 1964).

Papers:

The Public Record Office, London, has in its Shaftesbury Papers two manuscript volumes of Benjamin Whichcote's sermons. The British Library holds the "Letter from Benjamin Whichcote, D.D. afterwards Provost of King's College, Cambridge to A. Wheelock, relating to the question of the election of Sir N. Spelman as Burgess for Cambridge University."

Mary Wollstonecraft

(27 April 1759 – 10 September 1797)

Fiona A. Montgomery
Edge Hill College of Higher Education

See also the Wollstonecraft entries in *DLB 104: British Prose Writers, 1660–1800; DLB 39: British Novelists, 1660–1800;* and *DLB 158: British Reform Writers, 1789–1832.*

BOOKS: *Thoughts on the Education of Daughters; with Reflections on Female Conduct, in the More Important Duties of Life* (London: Printed for Joseph Johnson, 1787);

Mary, A Fiction (London: Printed for Joseph Johnson, 1788);

Original Stories from Real Life; With Conversations, Calculated to Regulate the Affections, and Form the Mind to Truth and Goodness (London: Printed for Joseph Johnson, 1788; revised, 1791);

The Female Reader; Miscellaneous Pieces in Prose and Verse; Selected from the Best Writers and Disposed under Proper Heads; For the Improvement of Young Women, as Mr. Cresswick, teacher of Elocution (London, 1789);

A Vindication of the Rights of Men, in a Letter to the Right Honourable Edmund Burke, anonymous (London: Printed for Joseph Johnson, 1790; revised, 1790);

A Vindication of the Rights of Woman: With Strictures on Political and Moral Subjects (London: Printed for Joseph Johnson, 1792; Boston: Printed by Peter Edes for Thomas & Andrews, 1792; Philadelphia: Printed and sold by William Gibbons, 1792);

An Historical and Moral View of the Origins and Progress of the French Revolution; and the Effect It Has Produced in Europe (London: Joseph Johnson, 1794); republished as *An Historical and Moral View of the French Revolution, and the Effect It Has Produced in Europe* (London: Printed for Joseph Johnson, 1794; Philadelphia: Printed by Thomas Dobson, 1795);

Letters Written during a Short Residence in Sweden, Norway, and Denmark (London: Printed for Joseph Johnson, 1796; Wilmington, Del.: Printed for and sold by J. Wilson & J. Johnson, 1796);

Posthumous Works of the Author of A Vindication of the Rights of Woman, 4 volumes, edited by William Godwin (London: Printed for Joseph Johnson and G. G. & J. Robinson, 1798);

*Mary Wollstonecraft; portrait by John Opie, circa 1791
(Tate Gallery, London)*

Maria; or, The Wrongs of Woman: A Posthumous Fragment (Philadelphia: Printed by James Carey, 1799).

Editions and Collections: *A Vindication of the Rights of Woman,* edited by Carol H. Poston (New York: Norton, 1975; second edition, expanded, 1988);

Letters Written During a Short Residence in Sweden, Norway, and Denmark, edited by Poston (Lincoln & London: University of Nebraska Press, 1976);

Mary and The Wrongs of Woman, edited by Gary Kelly (London: Oxford University Press, 1976);

A Wollstonecraft Anthology, edited by Janet Todd (Bloomington: Indiana University Press, 1977);

A Critical Edition of Mary Wollstonecraft's A Vindication of the Rights of Woman: With Strictures on Political and Moral Subjects, edited by Ulrich H. Hardt (Troy, N.Y.: Whitston, 1982);

A Short Residence in Sweden, Norway, and Denmark, by Wollstonecraft and William Godwin, *Memoirs of the Author of the Rights of Woman,* edited by Richard Holmes (Harmondsworth, U.K.: Penguin, 1987);

The Collected Works of Mary Wollstonecraft, 7 volumes, edited by Marilyn Butler, Janet M. Todd, and Emma Rees-Mogg (London: Pickering & Chatto, 1989);

Mary, Maria, and Matilda, edited by Todd (London: Pickering & Chatto, 1991);

A Vindication of the Rights of Men; with, A Vindication of the Rights of Woman, and Hints, edited by Sylvana Tomaselli (Cambridge & New York: Cambridge University Press, 1995).

TRANSLATIONS: Jacques Necker, *Of the Importance of Religious Opinions, Translated from the French of Mr. Necker* (London: Printed for J. Johnson, 1788);

Maria Geertruida van de Werken de Cambon, *Young Grandison: A Series of Letters from Young Persons to Their Friends. Translated from the Dutch of Madame de Cambon, with Alterations and Improvements,* 2 volumes (London: Printed for J. Johnson, 1790);

Christian Gotthilf Salzmann, *Elements of Morality, for the Use of Children; With an Introductory Address to Parents. Translated from the German of the Rev. C. G. Salzmann,* 3 volumes (London: Printed for J. Johnson, 1790–1791; 1 volume, Providence, R.I.: Printed by Carter & Wilkinson, 1795).

Mary Wollstonecraft is the most famous feminist of the eighteenth century. Her writings provided an inspiration for later feminist movements and became particularly popular with second-wave feminism in the 1960s. She earned her own living as a paid companion, teacher, and writer, and as a translator for the radical publisher Joseph Johnson. She spent two years in France observing the revolution, had a child out of wedlock, and attempted suicide twice. She later married the political anarchist William Godwin and died in childbirth.

Her best-known work is *A Vindication of the Rights of Woman: With Strictures on Political and Moral Subjects,* published in 1792. She believed in education as a means of liberating women, and she denied the sexual double standard. Reason was not the prerogative of men alone. By the end of her life she was championing the natural rights of all victims of a patriarchal society, which classified people according to their gender, class, and age. Wollstonecraft used her own experience as the founda-

tion of much of her writings. Thus remembering the effect of primogeniture on her own family, she highlighted the devastating consequences it could have on women, questioned the positioning of men ahead of women in families, and pointed out the inequalities in education that forced many women into positions of subservience and dependence. Wollstonecraft wanted women to be equal to men both within society and within personal relationships. Although she is remembered chiefly for her feminism, her philosophy is not simply restricted to women's issues since she championed radical theories in education.

Mary Wollstonecraft was born in London on 27 April 1757. She was the second child of seven of John Edward Wollstonecraft and Elizabeth Dickson. Wollstonecraft's early experiences did much to determine her later ideas. Her elder brother, Edward ("Ned"), was the family favorite, which Wollstonecraft bitterly resented. Her childhood was beset by financial worries and emotional insecurities. Her father, who ruled the family in a despotic fashion, was no businessman and, despite trying his hand at various farming enterprises, succeeded only in squandering all his inheritance. These ventures necessitated the family's moving frequently in the period from 1759 to 1768, including to Epping and Barking. Wollstonecraft's mother suffered from domestic violence and was obviously downtrodden, a fact not lost on Wollstonecraft, who despised her for her submissiveness.

In 1768 another move was made, this time to a farm in Yorkshire. Wollstonecraft always resented the fact that her claims to an education came far down her parents' list of priorities. She attended a day school and became friendly with Jane Arden. During this time she also began to develop intellectually. Another financial crisis compelled the family to move back to Hoxton in North London in 1774, and the next year Wollstonecraft met Frances Blood ("Fanny"), who became her closest friend. In 1776 the family briefly moved back to Wales, returning to London in 1777. Wollstonecraft now found the situation at home intolerable, and as a way out she took one of the few positions open to a middle-class woman, that of lady's companion. She stayed with her employer, Mrs. Dawson, for two years in Bath, Windsor, and Southampton but found the entire experience unedifying. Her mother, meanwhile, was growing weaker, and Wollstonecraft was called home to nurse her. In 1782 her mother died; her father remarried; her sister Eliza married Meredith Bishop; and Wollstonecraft moved in with her friend Fanny Blood. The Bloods were even more impoverished, and Wollstonecraft saw at first hand the types of occupation—for example, needlework—that they had to endure to try to make ends meet.

Eliza was suffering from postpartum depression, and at her husband's request Wollstonecraft went to nurse her in the winter of 1783. This circumstance was the occasion of the first major scandal in Wollstonecraft's life. In defiance of all social conventions she took Eliza away from the marital home, leaving her child with its father. The baby died the following August.

On the death of her mother and the breakup of her family, Wollstonecraft took it upon herself to look after her father and her younger siblings. To do so, along with her sisters, Everina and Eliza, and Fanny Blood she set up a school in Newington Green, London. Newington Green at this time was a hotbed of Dissent, with many well-known radicals, such as Richard Price, preaching on the necessity of parliamentary reform and the need to cultivate reason. Dissenters rejected the state church in their long struggle for liberty and equality. Wollstonecraft was particularly impressed with the strength of the Dissenting women. These encounters had an influence on Wollstonecraft's intellectual development, giving her a chance to consider her experiences of domestic tyranny, both at home and while working for Dawson. As a result, she realized that she was not alone in working for personal independence, but that she was part of a larger political struggle.

Initially the school prospered, but problems were growing. Fanny was in love with Hugh Skeys, but he was not in a hurry to marry her. She was also stricken with tuberculosis. In 1784 she married Skeys and went to Portugal to live with him. She soon became pregnant. Wollstonecraft, fearing for Fanny's life, abandoned her school to be at the birth. She arrived as Fanny died and thereafter wore a ring of her hair on her finger.

Returning to England in 1786, Wollstonecraft found that her school was now failing and she was heavily in debt. As a stopgap she turned to writing and produced her first work. *Thoughts on the Education of Daughters; with Reflections on Female Conduct, in the More Important Duties of Life* was published in 1787 by Johnson, the most famous publisher in England, who played an important part in her life. *Thoughts on the Education of Daughters* took six weeks to write. It was designed to show the dire effects of an education based on accomplishments rather than intellectual rigor on middle-class girls who were "left without a fortune" and clearly reflected her experiences as a companion and teacher.

Education is the means by which women could achieve reason, equality, and virtue. Breast-feeding is important so that children would grow up with a strong constitution to enable them to develop their studies. Wollstonecraft believes that universal benevolence is the

Publisher Joseph Johnson, whose support of Wollstonecraft played an important role in her literary career; engraving after a portrait by Moses Haughton (British Museum)

first virtue, but parents must ensure that their children are able to deal with the inevitable problems of life. Resignation is not an option. Interestingly, at this stage Wollstonecraft still sees a woman's role as primarily that of a wife and mother.

Wollstonecraft received ten guineas (£10.50) for *Thoughts on the Education of Daughters* and used the money not for herself but to send the Bloods to Ireland. She was, however, still without employment and so turned to working as a governess, again one of the few positions open to a middle-class woman. She was appointed as governess to Lord and Lady Kingsborough, two of the richest aristocrats in Ireland, at Mitchelstown, County Cork. While she got on well with her charges, she did not approve at all of Lady Kingsborough, feeling that she treated her animals better than her children. This dislike was mutual, and in 1787, while the family was at Bristol, she was dismissed. For a penniless, young middle-class woman, employment opportunities were limited: serving as a lady's companion or governess, running a school– Wollstonecraft had tried them all with varying degrees of success. As a lady's companion and governess she had found the element of subservience particularly irksome and demeaning.

While at the Kingsboroughs', Wollstonecraft had produced her first novel, *Mary, A Fiction* (1788). *Mary* is a fictional account of her own childhood and relationship with Fanny Blood. In the book she was determined to produce what she called a "new breed" of thinking heroines. As she said in the preface, "In delineating the heroine of this fiction, the author attempts to develop a character from those generally portrayed. This woman is neither a Clarissa, a Lady Gregory, or a Sophie. . . . The author will not copy but will rather show how those chosen few wish to speak for themselves and not to be an echo—even of the sweetest sounds—or the reflection of the most sublime beams. The paradise they ramble in must be of their own creating." It ends with her reflection that "there is neither marrying, nor giving in marriage" for women. Though a sentimental novel, in its descriptions of abject poverty and moral degeneration it foreshadows some of Wollstonecraft's later themes. It was published by Johnson in 1788 and confirmed Wollstonecraft's determination to earn her living as a writer. Johnson gave her work as a translator; among the works she translated for him were Jacques Necker's *Of the Importance of Religious Opinions* (1788) from the French and Christian Gotthilf Salzmann's *Elements of Morality, for the Use of Children* (1791) from the German.

Johnson set up a new journal, the *Analytical Review,* which provided Wollstonecraft with a steady stream of income. In her work for the *Analytical Review* she reviewed a wide range of literature, including poetry, travel, biographies, natural history, and educational work. In this way she was brought into contact with the works of Madame Anne-Louise-Germaine de Staël, Emanuel Swedenborg, Jean-Jacques Rousseau, Lord Kames, and other acclaimed writers of the period and thus widened her own personal education. Furthermore, at Johnson's house, itself a hub of liberal thought, she also met many of the leading intellectuals of the period: the radical Tom Paine, the German-Swiss painter and commentator Henry Fuseli, the radical and poet William Blake, the novelist Thomas Holcroft, and the political and social theorist William Godwin. This group believed in the possibility of moral progress through the use of reason, which would overcome privilege and prejudice. Passion needed to be controlled through reason, education, and disciplined habits.

In 1788 Johnson published Wollstonecraft's third work and the second on education: *Original Stories from Real Life; With Conversations, Calculated to Regulate the Affections, and Form the Mind to Truth and Goodness.* In *Original Stories from Real Life* she tells of rapacious landlords, suicide, and poverty—not the usual fare for children. The governess Mrs. Mason teaches her charges through a series of anecdotes designed to strengthen moral fiber and encourage understanding and analytical thinking. Unless children could reason, they would be unable to distinguish truth from fiction. They should also learn how to exercise love, truth, and virtue and to respect all of God's creation.

Wollstonecraft believed that coeducation would enable women to become rational wives and mothers instead of the vain, frivolous childlike beings she felt them to be. She considered mothers to be the best educators, and educated mothers would obviously ensure that the next generation of daughters would not perpetrate the cycle of ignorance. She also produced an anthology in 1789, *The Female Reader; Miscellaneous Pieces in Prose and Verse; Selected from the Best Writers and Disposed under Proper Heads; For the Improvement of Young Women,* designed for the improvement of young readers. Her selection included material on religion and history, excerpts encouraging the virtues (especially modesty), dialogues to improve speech, and antislavery passages.

In 1789 revolution broke out in France. The Revolution was generally welcomed in England even by conservatives such as Prime Minister William Pitt the Younger, on the grounds that at last the French were merely catching up with the equivalent of the 1688 Glorious Revolution in England—that is, a constitutional change without recourse to violence and bloodshed. Price preached a sermon, "Discourse on the Love of Our Country," at the Revolution Society, which had been founded in 1788 to commemorate the centenary of the Whig Revolution. This sermon, a plea for religious equality and democracy, was published along with a congratulatory address to the French National Assembly. Price reiterated the principles of the society: the right to liberty of conscience in religion, the right to resist power when abused, and the right "to choose our own governors; to cashier them for misconduct; and to frame a government for ourselves." Edmund Burke published in November 1790 his *Reflections on the Revolution in France,* thereby initiating a debate on the nature of the Revolution in France. The French had overthrown absolutism and were determined to rebuild society on first principles. Burke championed the French queen and savaged the new order. He wished to defend the existing social system not just in France but also in England and appealed to the importance of custom, habit, and tradition in politics. He also made a venomous attack on Price.

Wollstonecraft, enraged by the views Burke expresses in *Reflections on the Revolution in France,* wrote a stinging reply—*A Vindication of the Rights of Men, in a Letter to the Right Honourable Edmund Burke,* published anonymously in 1790. In *A Vindication of the Rights of Men* she denounces the existing state of society, arguing for greater equality for humanity and for the removal of the traditional injustices of property and rank; she also abuses Burke for what she sees as his shallow emotionalism. In particular she attacks his support of aristocracy and class distinctions, seeing inheritance as the instrument of social oppression since it left both rich and poor without incentive. She contrasts Burke's treatment of Marie Antoinette with his lack of interest in the "distress of so many industrious mothers." Upper-class women are considered as only half human. Their entire life is devoted to pleasing men, which undermines their power of understanding, making them, in Wollstonecraft's eyes, weak and contemptible. Instead of pursuing physical beauty, women should cultivate moral virtue. This position became the message of *A Vindication of the Rights of Woman*. A second edition of *A Vindication of the Rights of Men* was published in January 1791, this time bearing its author's name. When it was realized that the author was a woman, the response was outrage. Wollstonecraft was pilloried by conservative opinion.

Wollstonecraft then turned to the most glaring social injustice–that of the lack of rights of women. Her next work was a challenge to the domestic tyranny of men. *A Vindication of the Rights of Woman* is addressed to the women of the middle class "because they appear to be in the most natural state," uncorrupted by the luxury of wealth and not ground down by drudgery as are the poor. Wollstonecraft wishes to emphasize the importance of rational will in place of sentimental feelings, which reinforce female submissiveness. The chief obstacle to women gaining equality was domestic tyranny, which denied women their political rights, an education, and careers. Wollstonecraft argues that femininity was a *construct,* that is, women are born equal but are taught to be subordinate, weak, and featherbrained by masculine assumptions of what constitutes "feminine" behavior. Because women have nothing with which to occupy their minds, they become interested only in trifles. It is important therefore to understand the roots of oppression. These lie in men's assumption that women by their nature are mentally inferior. Total equality between the sexes is needed, for which women require economic independence. Women's financial dependence on men in marriage is akin to legal prostitution. The need for education therefore is at the forefront of Wollstonecraft's thesis.

Much of *A Vindication of the Rights of Woman* deals with her views on education. It did not therefore simply assert the moral autonomy of women; it also made a political statement. She argues that there are no "sexual virtues," by which she means virtues belonging exclusively to one sex. Thus, courage, modesty, and chastity could apply to either. In line with her earlier works and that of some of her contemporaries she takes the view that education and male expectations of women have degraded them. She argues that women never really

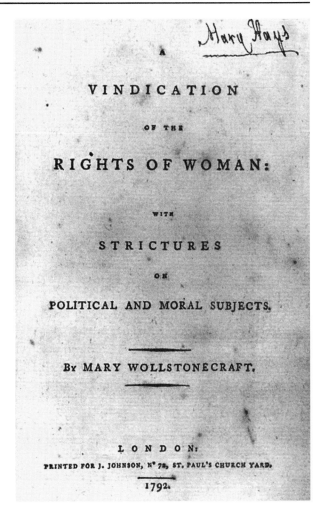

Title page for Wollstonecraft's best-known work, in which she argues that women are born equal to men and taught to be subordinate to them (from Diane Jacobs, Her Own Woman: The Life of Mary Wollstonecraft, *2001)*

become full adults, but because "femaleness" is instilled into them from an early age, they are always liable to be carried away by their emotions.

Education is needed to teach children how to think: to analyze and to generalize. Children should not be repressed, but as future responsible citizens they should be encouraged. There should be coeducation of boys and girls of all social classes up to the age of nine. After nine, working-class boys and girls should be separated in the afternoons to receive training for their future work, while those in the upper classes could continue together. *A Vindication of the Rights of Woman* was dedicated to Abbé Charles-Maurice de Talleyrand-Périgord in the hope that it would be used to influence French legislation on education. Until society was differently constituted, however, developments in education would be long coming.

A Vindication of the Rights of Woman also calls for an end to the double standards of morality and makes a claim for women's rights to independent work and civil and political life. Looking to the possibility of a "revolution in female manners" that would help to transform the political and moral order for all, not just workers, she advocates political representation for all women and even a limited political role for women "of a superior cast." As she points out, it would be unrealistic for women to complain about being disenfranchised when so many men equally do not have the vote despite having to pay taxes. In the meantime, women need activity. If they were properly educated, women's options would not be limited to marriage, menial jobs, or prostitution. They should have the right to work in trades and the professions; women should not be dependent on their husbands' incomes. Despite this mention of prostitution, Wollstonecraft has no scheme for relieving the poor. Using a radical republican analysis, she enjoins women to be good citizens and mothers as part of their duty to themselves. *A Vindication of the Rights of Woman* was surprisingly well received by reviewers. Written in only a few weeks, it included many typographical errors; a corrected second edition was issued before the year was out.

While Wollstonecraft's career as a writer was now taking off, her personal life was still in turmoil. She had formed an attachment to Fuseli, who was already married. To both Fuseli's and his wife's amazement she suggested a social ménage à trois, which they had no hesitation in declining. Whether impelled by this rejection or simply as a result of her long-standing interest in France, Wollstonecraft decided in December 1792 to visit France to view the Revolution herself. She intended to go for six weeks but stayed for two years. By this stage France was at war with most of Europe. The Revolution, as evidenced by the September Massacres and the imprisonment of Louis XVI, was moving from its reformist to its revolutionary phase. She witnessed Louis XVI on the way to his trial. Within a few weeks Louis had been beheaded and France was at war with England. She was drawn to the Girondins, in particular to Madame Roland. She did not become involved with the women of the poor or the militant feminists. She was still an intellectual snob at this stage. In the summer of 1793 the Jacobins took power, and many Girondins, including some of Wollstonecraft's friends, were guillotined.

Wollstonecraft initially found the Revolution disappointing, then extremely upsetting. The Reign of Terror made her question ideas of human perfectibility. She was distressed at the sight of the guillotine spattered with blood. In a letter to Johnson ("Letter on the Present Character of the French Nation," not published until after her death), she chronicled her disappointment at seeing folly and prejudice instead of virtue. She sympathizes with Louis XVI on a personal level and questions whether the French will be able to improve their situation

after all. This emotional response was the type for which she had criticized Burke. By the time she came to write *An Historical and Moral View of the Origins and Progress of the French Revolution; and the Effect It Has Produced in Europe* (1794), however, she had moderated her response and warned readers not to judge with emotion but to use reason. *An Historical and Moral View* was intended to be the initial volume of a series, but the series was never finished. Thus, it covers only the early months of the Revolution in 1789, but it is informed by her knowledge of later events. The facts of this history were taken from French government records and English periodicals such as the *New Annual Register* (which took a British Liberal standpoint). It embraces the debates and actions of the National Assembly, the work of Necker, the actions of Comte de Mirabeau and the Marquis de Lafayette, the storming of the Bastille on 14 July, and the people's march to Versailles on 5 October.

An Historical and Moral View aims to show that the barbarities of the Revolution resulted not from inherent weakness in rationalist philosophy, but from the fact that the French had been degraded by the previous existing despotic, feudal government. Thus since the temporary failure of the Revolution was occasioned by French, and not human, depravity, the rest of humanity could still hope for government by reason. Furthermore, if viewed from the longer perspective of French history, it was successful, since all the present chaos will eventually result in a freer environment for all and in turn occasion an improvement in their character. Thus social progress would ensue.

An Historical and Moral View also includes Wollstonecraft's own personal opinions, which serves to explain her concentrated attack on commerce (her recalcitrant lover, Gilbert Imlay, was involved in commerce). Commerce degrades both masters and men. While *An Historical and Moral View* continues the philosophical position of *A Vindication of the Rights of Men* and *A Vindication of the Rights of Woman,* surprisingly it says little about the role of women in the Revolution. Indeed, she is highly critical of the working-class women who marched on Versailles, describing them as "market women, and the lowest refuse of the streets . . . not to be confounded with the honest multitude who took the Bastille." Published in 1794, the book had a favorable reception, and a second edition came out in 1795. By this time, however, England had experienced the Treason Trials of 1794, and the mood of the country had swung to the right. A wave of reaction followed, during which radicalism went underground.

Among the French sympathizers in Paris, Wollstonecraft met Imlay, an American speculator. She fell deeply in love with him and, defying convention, lived with him, abandoning her ambition to become an independent woman: as she wrote to Imlay, "Let me indulge the thought that I have thrown out some tendrils to cling to the elm by which I wish to be supported." Wollstonecraft became pregnant, and Imlay left Paris for Le Havre. After some time she went to Le Havre herself, and her daughter, whom she called Fanny after Fanny Blood, was born. In accordance with her principles, she breast-fed Fanny. Such happiness was to be short-lived. Imlay had no intention of being tied down and constantly was involved with other women. In early 1795 she traveled to London, but Imlay still refused to commit to her. Her reaction was to attempt suicide using laudanum.

Imlay's response was to beg her to help him save his failing business. Imlay was involved in smuggling goods out of blockaded France, but his Norwegian partner had stolen the ship. His solution was to send Wollstonecraft, along with their infant daughter, to Norway as his legal representative; it was a hazardous challenge, but she was more than successful in the endeavor. While in Scandinavia she wrote constantly to Imlay, and these letters were published as *Letters Written during a Short Residence in Sweden, Norway, and Denmark* in 1796. The book was considered by many to be her best work; Godwin wrote: "If ever there was a book calculated to make a man in love with its author, this appears to me to be the book." The narrative was written in the form of a personal journal monologue and, as well as providing a description of the countries and peoples, offers political commentary and philosophical observations as well as anguish over her relationship with Imlay. She is shrewd, romantic, and observant, critical of bad male behavior and the menial tasks performed by women. Wherever she went she examined the condition of women—mothers, daughters, wives, servants, old women, and girls. She also comments on penal reform and attacks capital punishment, lawyers, commerce, and meaningless ceremony. Public executions serve no useful purpose; they simply become a form of amusement. She was appalled by the poverty she found. She also provides a scathing critique of the spread of capitalism. This work was popular, partly because there was little written in the first person on Scandinavia in English at this time.

Returning to England without having saved Imlay's business, she was hopeful of a complete reconciliation. Instead, she found Imlay living with a young actress. Unable to cope, she wrote a letter asking Imlay to look after Fanny and made another attempt at suicide, this time by trying to drown in the River Thames. She was spotted by two boatmen and carried to safety. She determined not to attempt suicide again but continued to have feelings for Imlay till the end of spring 1796, when she bade him "eternal farewell."

Anarchist philosopher William Godwin, whom Wollstonecraft married in 1797 even though both had criticized the institution of marriage in their writings; portrait by John Opie (National Portrait Gallery, London)

Resuming her friendships with Johnson's circle, Wollstonecraft found herself drawn to the political philosopher Godwin. Godwin was well known as a political anarchist. His *Enquiry concerning Political Justice and its Influence on Morals and Happiness* (1793) denounces sentimentalism; men were not the slaves of passion or the environment. Hope lay in the use of reason. He believed in the perfectibility of human beings and in total freedom from all forms of oppression, including marriage. Godwin encouraged Wollstonecraft to continue to write.

A sequel to *A Vindication of the Rights of Woman* took shape in the form of a novel: *Maria; or, The Wrongs of Woman*, designed to expose the injustices suffered by women under the English legal system. Again relying heavily on Wollstonecraft's own experiences, the text is a powerful critique of a society ruled by men. Her aim is "the desire of exhibiting the misery and oppression, peculiar to women, that arise out of the partial laws and customs of society." The political and personal are one. The heroine is called Maria, and her lover has more than a passing resemblance to Imlay. Maria shares many of the characteristics of Wollstonecraft's earlier heroine, Mary, and of many other fictional heroines in eighteenth-century fiction. In Jemima, the former prostitute, how-

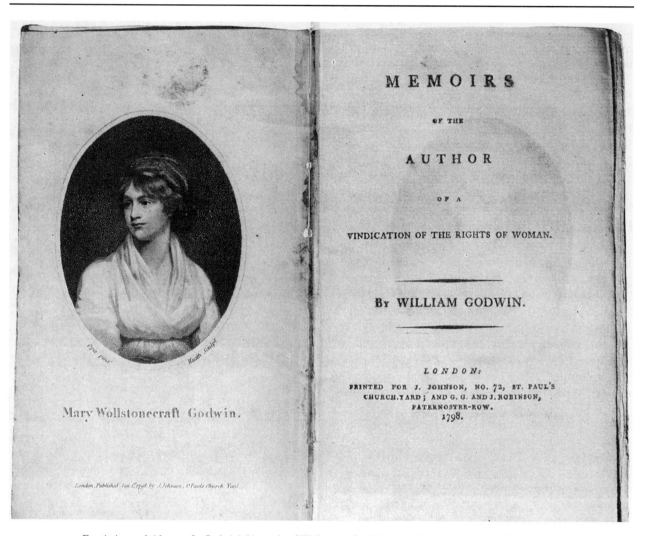

Frontispiece and title page for Godwin's biography of Wollstonecraft, which created a scandal because of its frankness
(from Claire Tomalin, The Life and Death of Mary Wollstonecraft, *1974)*

ever, Wollstonecraft breaks new ground by presenting the first fully sympathetic portrait of a working-class woman in English literature. Jemima is thoroughly exploited: an illegitimate orphan, she is later raped, becomes pregnant, aborts her child, turns to beggary and prostitution, thieves, is imprisoned, and ends up in the workhouse. From there she takes the position of a keeper in the workhouse in which Maria is later imprisoned.

Wollstonecraft demonstrates that the poor are not happy with their lot and that the supposed reward in the next life is not adequate recompense for their exploitation in this one. Nor is charity a sufficient solution. She points out that the sexual oppression of women cuts across class boundaries and emphasizes the importance of education as a means for women to escape degradation and exploitation. Marriage makes women property. While Wollstonecraft had written *A Vindication of the Rights of Men* in less than a month and *A Vindication of the Rights of Woman* in six weeks, she found it difficult to finish

Maria, and after a year working on it she had completed only a third.

Wollstonecraft and Godwin became lovers, and in December, Wollstonecraft was pregnant. Both had written strongly against marriage as an institution. Nevertheless they were aware of all the opprobrium heaped on illegitimate children, as had happened to Fanny, and on 29 March 1797, much to the amusement of their friends, the two arch-opponents of marriage tied the knot. To enable them to devote time to their writing careers, they kept their separate houses in the same street. The marriage, however, was happy. A daughter, Mary, was born on 30 August 1797, but the placenta did not fully come away. On 10 September 1797 Wollstonecraft died of puerperal fever, leaving Godwin distraught.

He was determined to publicize Wollstonecraft's life and works to the world. In 1798 he published *Posthumous Works of the Author of A Vindication of the Rights of Woman,* which included the unfinished *Maria,* her letters to Imlay, and his memoirs. His account of her life was totally honest, chronicling her love affair with Imlay, the birth of her illegitimate child, her suicide attempts, and her financial problems. Such revelations were seen as totally scandalous and in the reaction to the French Revolution and the Revolutionary Wars proved a gift to conservative polemicists, who ridiculed both Godwin and Wollstonecraft. Wollstonecraft was depicted as a whore, and her feminist ideas were seen as inciting women to sexual impropriety. A similar reaction took place in the United States. The effect of this negative image was to push feminism back for at least a generation and meant that her works quickly became unread. It was not until the late nineteenth century, with the renewed agitation for women's rights, that any sustained interest was paid to her. The second wave of feminism in the 1960s led to a fairer reassessment and a revival of interest in her work. Wollstonecraft's daughter Fanny committed suicide in 1816 and Mary Godwin later married the poet Percy Bysshe Shelley and achieved fame as the author of *Frankenstein* (1818).

Letters:

Godwin & Mary: Letters of William Godwin and Mary Wollstonecraft, edited by Ralph M. Wardle (Lawrence: University of Kansas Press, 1966);

Collected Letters of Mary Wollstonecraft, edited by Wardle (Ithaca, N.Y.: Cornell University Press, 1979).

Biographies:

William Godwin, *Memoirs of the Author of A Vindication of the Rights of Woman* (London: Printed for J. Johnson by G. G. & J. Robinson, 1798);

Ralph M. Wardle, *Mary Wollstonecraft: A Critical Biography* (Lawrence: University of Kansas Press, 1951);

Margaret George, *One Woman's "Situation"; A Study of Mary Wollstonecraft* (Urbana, Chicago & London: University of Illinois Press, 1970);

Emily Sunstein, *A Different Face: The Life of Mary Wollstonecraft* (Boston: Little, Brown, 1970);

Eleanor Flexner, *Mary Wollstonecraft* (New York: Coward, McCann & Geoghegan, 1972);

Claire Tomalin, *The Life and Death of Mary Wollstonecraft* (London: Weidenfeld & Nicolson, 1974; revised edition, Harmondsworth, U.K. & New York: Penguin, 1992);

Janet Todd, *Mary Wollstonecraft: A Revolutionary Life* (London: Weidenfeld & Nicolson, 2000);

Diane Jacobs, *Her Own Woman: The Life of Mary Wollstonecraft* (New York: Simon & Schuster, 2001).

References:

Miriam Brody, "Mary Wollstonecraft: Sexuality and Women's Rights," in *Feminist Theorists: Three Centuries of Women's Intellectual Traditions,* edited by Dale Spender (London: Women's Press, 1983), pp. 40–59;

Maria J. Falco, *Feminist Interpretations of Mary Wollstonecraft* (University Park: Pennsylvania State University Press, 1996);

Maura Ferguson and Janet Todd, *Mary Wollstonecraft* (Boston: Twayne, 1984);

Tom Furniss, "Gender and Revolution: Edmund Burke and Mary Wollstonecraft," in *Revolution in Writing: British Literary Responses to the French Revolution,* edited by Kelvin Everest (Milton Keynes, U.K. & Philadelphia: Open University Press, 1991), pp. 65–100;

Harriet D. Jump, *Mary Wollstonecraft, Writer* (New York: Harvester Wheatsheaf, 1994);

Gary Kelly, *Revolutionary Feminism: The Mind and Career of Mary Wollstonecraft* (Basingstoke, U.K.: Macmillan, 1996);

Jennifer Lorch, *Mary Wollstonecraft: The Making of a Radical Feminist* (New York & Oxford: Berg, 1990);

Edna Nixon, *Mary Wollstonecraft: Her Life and Times* (London: Dent, 1971);

Barbara Taylor, "Mary Wollstonecraft and the Wild Wish of Feminism," *History Workshop Journal,* 33 (1992): 179–219;

Eileen Janes Yeo, *Mary Wollstonecraft and 200 Years of Feminisms* (London & New York: Rivers Oram, 1997).

Checklist of Further Readings

Adams, Robert Day. "Muses in the Mud: The Female Wits Anthropologically Considered," *Women's Studies,* 7, no. 3 (1980): 61–74.

Adamson, Robert. *The Development of Modern Philosophy: With Other Lectures and Essays,* edited by W. R. Sorley, 2 volumes. Edinburgh: Blackwood, 1903.

Argyle, A. W. "The Cambridge Platonists," *Hibbert Journal,* 53 (1954–1955): 225–261.

Atherton, Margaret. "Cartesian Reason and Gendered Reason," in *A Mind of One's Own: Feminist Essays on Reason and Objectivity,* edited by Louise M. Antony and Charlotte Witt. Boulder, Colo. & Oxford: Westview Press, 1993, pp. 19–34.

Atherton, ed. *The Empiricists: Critical Essays on Locke, Berkeley, and Hume.* Lanham, Md.: Rowman & Littlefield, 1999.

Ayer, Alfred Jules, and Raymond Winch, eds. *British Empirical Philosophers: Locke, Berkeley, Hume, Reid, and J. S. Mill.* London: Routledge & Kegan Paul, 1952.

Ayers, Michael, and Daniel Garber, eds. *The Cambridge History of Seventeenth-Century Philosophy,* 2 volumes. Cambridge: Cambridge University Press, 1998.

Becker, Carl L. *The Heavenly City of the Eighteenth-Century Philosophers.* New Haven: Yale University Press, 1932.

Berman, David. *A History of Atheism in Britain: From Hobbes to Russell.* London & New York: Croom Helm, 1988.

Braver, Jerold G. "Puritan Mysticism and the Development of Liberalism," *Church History,* 19 (September 1950): 151–170.

Broadie, Alexander. *The Tradition of Scottish Philosophy: A New Perspective on the Enlightenment.* Edinburgh: Polygon, 1990.

Brown, Stuart, ed. *British Philosophy and the Age of Enlightenment.* Routledge History of Philosophy, volume 5. London & New York: Routledge, 1996.

Brown, ed. *Philosophers of the Enlightenment.* Royal Institute of Philosophy Lectures, volume 12. Brighton: Harvester, 1979.

Campbell, Roy Hutcheson, and A. H. Skinner, eds. *The Origins and Nature of the Scottish Enlightenment.* Edinburgh: Donald, 1982.

Canovan, Margaret. "Two Concepts of Liberty—Eighteenth-Century Style," *Price-Priestley Newsletter,* 2 (1978): 27–41.

Carré, Meyrick Heath. *Phases of Thought in England.* Oxford: Clarendon Press, 1949.

Cassirer, Ernst. *The Philosophy of the Enlightenment,* translated by Fritz C. A. Koelln and James P. Pettegrove. Princeton: Princeton University Press, 1951.

Cassirer. *The Platonic Renaissance in England,* translated by Pettegrove. Austin: University of Texas Press, 1953.

Chappell, Vere Claiborne, ed. *Essays on Early Modern Philosophers: From Descartes and Hobbes to Newton and Leibniz,* 12 volumes. Hamden, Conn.: Garland, 1991–1992.

Colie, Rosalie Littell. *Light and Enlightenment: A Study of the Cambridge Platonists and the Dutch Arminians.* Cambridge: Cambridge University Press, 1957.

Copleston, Frederick. *A History of Philosophy,* 9 volumes. London: Burns & Oates, 1946–1975.

Cragg, Gerald R. *The Cambridge Platonists.* New York: Oxford University Press, 1968.

Cragg. *From Puritanism to the Age of Reason.* Cambridge: Cambridge University Press, 1950.

Daniels, Normal. *Thomas Reid's "Inquiry": The Geometry of Visibles and the Case for Realism,* with a new afterword. Stanford: Stanford University Press, 1989.

Darwall, Stephen L. *British Moralists and the Internal "Ought," 1640–1740.* Cambridge & New York: Cambridge University Press, 1995.

Davie, George E. *The Scottish Enlightenment and Other Essays.* Edinburgh: Polygon, 1991.

Desmond, Adrian. *The Politics of Evolution: Morphology, Medicine, and Reform in Radical London.* Chicago: University of Chicago Press, 1989.

Ferrier, James Frederick. *Scottish Philosophy: The Old and the New: A Statement.* Edinburgh: Sutherland & Knox, 1856.

Ferrone, Vincenzo. *The Intellectual Roots of the Italian Enlightenment: Newtonian Science, Religion, and Politics in the Early Eighteenth Century,* translated by Sue Brotherton. Atlantic Highlands, N.J.: Humanities Press, 1995.

Flynn, Philip. *Enlightened Scotland: A Study and Selection of Scottish Philosophical Prose from the Eighteenth and Early Nineteenth Centuries.* Edinburgh: Scottish Academic Press, 1992.

Fox, Christopher, and others, eds. *Inventing Human Science: Eighteenth-Century Domains.* Berkeley: University of California Press, 1995.

Garland, Martha McMackin. *Cambridge Before Darwin: The Ideal of a Liberal Education 1800–1860.* Cambridge: Cambridge University Press, 1980.

Gay, Peter. *The Enlightenment: An Interpretation,* 2 volumes. New York: Knopf, 1966–1969.

Gillespie, Charles Coulston, ed. *Dictionary of Scientific Biography,* 16 volumes. New York: Scribners, 1970–1980.

Graham, William. *English Political Philosophy from Hobbes to Maine.* London: E. Arnold, 1899.

Grant, Edward. *Much Ado About Nothing: Theories of Space and Vacuum from the Middle Ages to the Scientific Revolution.* Cambridge & New York: Cambridge University Press, 1981.

Grant, Patrick. *Images and Ideas in Literature of the English Renaissance.* Amherst: University of Massachusetts Press, 1979.

Grave, S. A. *The Scottish Philosophy of Common Sense.* Oxford: Clarendon Press, 1960.

Haakonssen, Knud. *Natural Law and Moral Philosophy: From Grotius to the Scottish Enlightenment.* Cambridge & New York: Cambridge University Press, 1996.

Haakonssen, ed. *Enlightenment and Religion. Rational Dissent in Eighteenth-Century Britain.* Cambridge: Cambridge University Press, 1996.

Halévy, Elie. *The Growth of Philosophical Radicalism,* translated by Mary Morris. London: Faber & Gwyer, 1928.

Hazard, Paul. *The European Mind, 1680–1715,* translated by J. Lewis May. London: Hollis & Carter, 1953.

Hazard. *European Thought in the Eighteenth Century: From Montesquieu to Lessing,* translated by May. London: Hollis & Carter, 1954.

Heimann, P. M. "Voluntarism and Immanence: Conceptions of Nature in Eighteenth-Century Thought," *Journal of the History of Ideas,* 39 (1978): 271–283.

Hobby, Elaine. *Virtue of Necessity: English Women's Writing, 1649–88.* Ann Arbor: University of Michigan Press, 1989.

Hope, Vincent, ed. *Philosophers of the Scottish Enlightenment.* Edinburgh: Edinburgh University Press, 1984.

Inge, William. *The Platonic Tradition in English Religious Thought.* New York: Longmans, Green, 1926.

Jacob, Margaret C. *The Newtonians and the English Revolution 1689–1720.* Hassocks, U.K.: Harvester / Ithaca, N.Y.: Cornell University Press, 1976.

Jones, Peter, ed. *Philosophy and Science in the Scottish Enlightenment.* Edinburgh: Donald, 1988.

Jones, Richard Foster, and others. *The Seventeenth Century: Studies in the History of English Thought and Literature from Bacon to Pope.* Stanford: Stanford University Press, 1951.

Koyré, Alexandre. *From the Closed World to the Infinite Universe.* Baltimore: Johns Hopkins University Press, 1957.

Kroll, Richard. *The Material World: Literate Culture in the Restoration and Early Eighteenth Century.* Baltimore: Baltimore University Press, 1991.

Kroll, Richard Ashcraft, and Perez Zagorin. *Philosophy, Science, and Religion in England, 1640–1700.* Cambridge & New York: Cambridge University Press, 1992.

Lange, Friedrich Albert. *The History of Materialism,* translated by Ernest Chester Thomas. New York: Arno, 1974.

Laski, Harold J. *Political Thought in England from Locke to Bentham.* New York: Holt, 1920.

Levine, Joseph. *The Battle of the Books: History and Literature in the Augustine Age.* Ithaca, N.Y.: Cornell University Press, 1991.

Lieberman, David. *The Province of Legislation Determined: Legal Theory in Eighteenth-Century Britain.* Cambridge: Cambridge University Press, 1989.

Lincoln, Anthony H. *Some Political and Social Ideas of English Dissent, 1763–1800.* New York: Octagon, 1971.

MacCarthy, B. G. *The Female Pen: Women Writers and Novelists 1621–1818,* second edition. New York: New York University Press, 1994.

MacCracken, Charles J. *Malebranche and British Philosophy.* Oxford: Clarendon Press, 1983.

Mackintosh, James. *Dissertation on the Progress of Ethical Philosophy: Chiefly during the Seventeenth and Eighteenth Centuries.* Edinburgh: Adam & Charles Black, 1836.

Masson, David. *Recent British Philosophy: A Review, with Criticisms; Including Some Comments on Mr. Mill's Answer to Sir William Hamilton.* London & Cambridge: Macmillan, 1865.

McCosh, James. *The Scottish Philosophy: Biographical, Expository, Critical: from Hutcheson to Hamilton.* London: Macmillan / New York: R. Carter, 1875.

Mendelson, Sara Heller. *The Mental World of Stuart Women: Three Studies.* Amherst: University of Massachusetts Press, 1987.

Metz, Rudolf. *A Hundred Years of British Philosophy,* edited by J. R. Muirhead, translated by J. W. Harvey, T. E. Jessop, and Henry Sturt. London: Allen & Unwin / New York: Macmillan, 1938.

Meyer, Gerald Dennis. *The Scientific Lady in England 1650–1760: An Account of Her Rise, with Emphasis on the Major Roles of the Telescope and Microscope.* Berkeley & Los Angeles: University of California Press, 1955.

Mintz, Samuel. *The Hunting of Leviathan: Seventeenth-century Reactions to the Materialism and Moral Philosophy of Thomas Hobbes.* Cambridge: Cambridge University Press, 1962.

Morell, John Daniel. *On the Philosophical Tendencies of the Age: Being Four Lectures Delivered at Edinburgh and Glasgow in January 1848.* Bristol: Thoemmes, 1990.

Morrell, Jack, and Arnold Thackray. *Gentlemen of Science: Early Years of the British Association for the Advancement of Science.* Oxford: Clarendon Press, 1981.

Morris, George Sylvester. *British Thought and Thinkers: Introductory Studies, Critical, Biographical and Philosophical.* Chicago: S. C. Griggs, 1880.

Muirhead, John H. *The Platonic Tradition in Anglo-Saxon Philosophy.* New York: Macmillan, 1931.

Olson, Richard. *Scottish Philosophy and British Physics, 1750–1880.* Princeton: Princeton University Press, 1975.

Patrides, C. A. *The Cambridge Platonists.* Cambridge, Mass.: Harvard University Press, 1969.

Paul, Leslie Allen. *The English Philosophers.* London: Faber & Faber, 1953.

Perry, Ruth. "Radical Doubt and the Liberation of Women," *Eighteenth-Century Studies,* 18 (Summer 1985): 472–493.

Pocock, J. G. A. *Virtue, Commerce, and History: Essays on Political Thought and History, Chiefly in the Eighteenth Century.* Cambridge: Cambridge University Press, 1985.

Pocock, ed. *The Varieties of British Political Thought, 1500–1800.* Cambridge & New York: Cambridge University Press, 1993.

Popkin, Richard H. *The History of Scepticism from Erasmus to Descartes,* revised edition. New York: Harper & Row, 1964.

Popkin. *The Third Force in Seventeenth Century Thought.* Leiden: E. J. Brill, 1992.

Powicke, Frederick James. *The Cambridge Platonists.* London: Dent, 1926.

Randall, John Herman. *The Career of Philosophy,* 2 volumes. New York: Columbia University Press, 1962.

Raphael, D. D. *The Moral Sense.* London: Oxford University Press, 1947.

Redwood, John. *Reason, Ridicule and Religion.* London: Thames & Hudson, 1976.

Reynolds, Myra. *The Learned Lady in England, 1650–1760.* Boston: Houghton Mifflin, 1920.

Roberts, James Deotis. *From Puritanism to Platonism in Seventeenth Century England.* The Hague: Nyhoff, 1968.

Robertson, John M. *The Dynamics of Religion: An Essay in English Culture History,* second edition, revised with additions. London: Watts, 1926.

Robinson, Daniel Sommer, ed. *The Story of Scottish Philosophy, a Compendium of Selections from the Writings of Nine Pre-eminent Scottish Philosophers, with Biobibliographical Essays.* New York: Exposition Press, 1961.

Rockwood, R. O., ed. *Carl Becker's Heavenly City Revisited.* Ithaca, N.Y.: Cornell University Press, 1958.

Rogers, J. M. Vienne, and Y. C. Zarka, eds. *The Cambridge Platonists in Philosophical Context: Politics, Metaphysics, and Religion.* Dordrecht & Boston: Kluwer, 1997.

Rothblatt, Sheldon. *The Revolution of the Dons: Cambridge and Society in Victorian England.* Cambridge: Cambridge University Press, 1968.

Rowe, William L. *The Cosmological Argument.* Princeton: Princeton University Press, 1975.

Russell, Bertrand. *A History of Western Philosophy.* New York: Simon & Schuster, 1945.

Schiebinger, Londa. *The Mind Has No Sex?: Women in the Origins of Modern Science.* Cambridge, Mass.: Harvard University Press, 1989.

Schmitt, C. B., Quentin Skinner, Eckhard Kessler, and Jill Kraye, eds. *The Cambridge History of Renaissance Philosophy.* Cambridge & New York: Cambridge University Press, 1998.

Seth, Andrew. *Scottish Philosophy: A Comparison of the Scottish and German Answers to Hume.* Edinburgh: Blackwood, 1885.

Seth, James. *English Philosophers and Schools of Philosophy.* London: Dent, 1912.

Sidgwick, Henry. *Outlines of the History of Ethics for English Readers.* London & New York: Macmillan, 1886.

Smith, Hilda L. *Reason's Disciples: Seventeenth-Century English Feminists.* Urbana: University of Illinois Press, 1982.

Sorley, William Ritchie. "The Beginnings of English Philosophy," in *The Cambridge History of English Literature,* volume 4, edited by A. W. Ward and A. R. Waller. Cambridge: Cambridge University Press, 1907–1927.

Sorley. *A History of British Philosophy to 1900.* Cambridge: Cambridge University Press, 1920; reprinted, 1965.

Stephen, Leslie. *History of English Thought in the Eighteenth Century,* revised edition, 2 volumes. New York: Harcourt, Brace & World, 1962.

Stephen. *Selected Writings in British Intellectual History,* edited by Noel Annan. Chicago: University of Chicago Press, 1979.

Stephen, and Sidney Lee, eds. *Dictionary of National Biography,* 66 volumes. London: Smith, Elder, 1885–1901.

Stewart, Michael Alexander, ed. *Studies in the Philosophy of the Scottish Enlightenment.* Oxford: Clarendon Press, 1990.

Sutton, John. *Philosophy and Memory Traces.* Cambridge: Cambridge University Press, 1998.

Torrey, Norman L. *Voltaire and the English Deists.* New Haven: Yale University Press, 1930.

Tuck, Richard. *Philosophy and Government, 1572–1651.* Cambridge & New York: Cambridge University Press, 1993.

Tulloch, John. *Rational Theory and Christian Philosophy in England in the Seventeenth Century,* 2 volumes. Edinburgh: Blackwood, 1872.

Van Leeuwen, Henry G. *The Problem of Certainty in English Thought, 1630–1690.* The Hague: Martinus Nijhoff, 1970.

Waithe, Mary Ellen, ed. *A History of Women Philosophers,* volume 3. Dordrecht: Kluwer, 1991.

Webster, Charles. *The Great Instauration: Science, Medicine and Reform, 1626–1660.* London: Duckworth, 1975.

Wiles, Maurice. *Archetypal Heresy: Arianism through the Centuries.* Oxford: Clarendon Press / New York: Oxford University Press, 1996.

Willey, Basil. *The Eighteenth Century Background: Studies on the Idea of Nature in the Thought of the Period.* London: Chatto & Windus, 1940.

Willey. *The English Moralists.* London: Chatto & Windus, 1964.

Willey. *The Seventeenth Century Background: Studies in the Thought of the Age in Relation to Poetry and Religion.* London: Chatto & Windus, 1934.

Windelband, Wilhelm. *A History of Philosophy,* translated by James H. Tufts. New York & London: Macmillan, 1893.

Yolton, John W. *Thinking Matter: Materialism in Eighteenth-Century Britain.* Oxford: Blackwell / Minneapolis: University of Minnesota Press, 1983.

Yolton, John Valdimir Price, and John Stephens, eds. *The Dictionary of Eighteenth-Century British Philosophers.* Bristol: Thommes Press, 1999.

Yolton, ed. *Philosophy, Religion, and Science in the Seventeenth and Eighteenth Centuries.* Rochester, N.Y.: University of Rochester Press, 1990.

Contributors

R. D. Bedford . . . . *University of New England, New South Wales*

Erin Lang Bonin . . . . *University of North Carolina at Chapel Hill*

Jacqueline Broad . . . .*Monash University*

William E. Burns. . . . . *Howard University*

Stephen H. Daniel . . . . *Texas A&M University*

Rosalind Davies. . . . .*University College London*

Peter J. Diamond . . . .*New York University*

Anthony J. Draper . . . .*University College London*

James Dybikowski . . . .*University of British Columbia*

Frederick Ferré . . . . *University of Georgia*

Kate Fletcher . . . . *University of Cambridge*

Peter S. Fosl. . . . . *Transylvania University*

James A. Harris . . . . *Balliol College, University of Oxford*

Terry G. Harris. . . . . *Louisiana State University at Shreveport*

Sarah Hutton. . . . . *Middlesex University*

Marie Martin. . . . .*Clemson University*

Fiona A. Montgomery. . . . . *Edge Hill College of Higher Education*

Melvyn New . . . . *University of Florida*

Justine J. Noel . . . . *Camosun College*

Kurt Norlin . . . . *Claremont Graduate University*

Susan P. Reilly. . . . . *University of New Hampshire*

Catherine M. Rodriguez . . . . *University of South Florida*

Patricia Sheridan . . . . *University of Western Ontario*

Susan Spencer . . . . *University of Central Oklahoma*

Alan Tapper . . . . *Edith Cowan University*

Keith E. Welsh . . . .*Webster University*

James Whitlark . . . . *Texas Tech University*

Jay G. Williams . . . .*Hamilton College*

Cumulative Index

Dictionary of Literary Biography, Volumes 1-252
Dictionary of Literary Biography Yearbook, 1980-2000
Dictionary of Literary Biography Documentary Series, Volumes 1-19
Concise Dictionary of American Literary Biography, Volumes 1-7
Concise Dictionary of British Literary Biography, Volumes 1-8
Concise Dictionary of World Literary Biography, Volumes 1-4

Cumulative Index

DLB before number: *Dictionary of Literary Biography,* Volumes 1-252
Y before number: *Dictionary of Literary Biography Yearbook,* 1980-2000
DS before number: *Dictionary of Literary Biography Documentary Series,* Volumes 1-19
CDALB before number: *Concise Dictionary of American Literary Biography,* Volumes 1-7
CDBLB before number: *Concise Dictionary of British Literary Biography,* Volumes 1-8
CDWLB before number: *Concise Dictionary of World Literary Biography,* Volumes 1-4

C

L

Q

R

ISBN 0-7876-4669-5